The Great Ideas

"Election Day in Philadelphia," by John Lewis Krimmel (1815).

"It should be evident upon reflection that the people . . . are ultimately in control of the operations of the general government." (See p. 58.)

The Great Ideas Today

1987

Encyclopædia Britannica, Inc.

CHICAGO
AUCKLAND • GENEVA • LONDON • MANILA • PARIS • ROME • SEOUL • SYDNEY • TOKYO • TORONTO

AY
59
.G7
1987

Library of Congress Number: 61-65561
International Standard Book Number: 0-85229-470-0
International Standard Serial Number: 0072-7288
Printed in the U.S.A.

A NOTE ON REFERENCE STYLE

In the following pages, passages in *Great Books of the Western World* are referred to by the initials '*GBWW*,' followed by volume, page number, and page section. Thus, '*GBWW*, Vol. 39, p. 210b' refers to page 210 in Adam Smith's *The Wealth of Nations*, which is Volume 39 in *Great Books of the Western World*. The small letter 'b' indicates the page section. In books printed in single column, 'a' and 'b' refer to the upper and lower halves of the page. In books printed in double column, 'a' and 'b' refer to the upper and lower halves of the left column, 'c' and 'd' to the upper and lower halves of the right column. For example, 'Vol. 53, p. 210b' refers to the lower half of page 210, since Volume 53, James's *Principles of Psychology*, is printed in single column. On the other hand, 'Vol. 7, p. 210b' refers to the lower left quarter of the page, since Volume 7, Plato's *Dialogues*, is printed in double column.

Gateway to the Great Books is referred to by the initials '*GGB*,' followed by volume and page number. Thus, '*GGB*, Vol. 10, pp. 39–57' refers to pages 39 through 57 of Volume 10 of *Gateway to the Great Books*, which is James's essay, "The Will to Believe."

The Great Ideas Today is referred to by the initials '*GIT*,' followed by the year and page number. Thus '*GIT* 1968, p. 210' refers to page 210 of the 1968 edition of *The Great Ideas Today*.

Contents

Preface

This, as everyone knows, is the Bicentennial Year for the United States, and the only difficulty about saying so is that, as distinct from the last bicentennial the country celebrated, it is not so evident now just what the statement really means. Then, in 1976, it was clear that a certain event was the cause of the festivities. The event was Independence—not the fact, but the famous Declaration, which has come to be more important than the fact, or at any rate than the acceptance of the fact indicated by the Treaty of Paris, signed between the United States (as already they called themselves) and Great Britain in 1783. Now, in 1987, it might again be clear that what is being celebrated is a document, namely the Constitution of the United States, were it not that this itself was no event at all, was nothing until 1788, when enough states had ratified it for it to be considered the supreme Law of the Land (in its own terms)—and had it been, even then, anything more than a promise of the day in March 1789, when the government thus ordained was at last established. There is some ambiguity, in other words, to the notion of a bicentennial of the United States, as compared with that of the Declaration of Independence, which we have to acknowledge. It is the difference between an end and a beginning, and so considered it is not perhaps surprising that, as with other beginnings, we are uncertain as to what the crucial moment was.

Important things can nevertheless be said about the document itself and the degree to which it reflected the thought and circumstances of the times. Thus, in this issue of *The Great Ideas Today*, George Anastaplo observes that the self-proclaimed source of the Constitution, "We the People," assumes that in 1787 there already existed such an entity with many facets that required many powers in order to provide for its common needs, as it needed a variety of restraints and sanctions to ensure that the powers did not do it in. Readers may be surprised to discover the many ways in which "the people" appear in, or are taken for granted by, the Constitution.

Similarly, Marcus Cunliffe notes that the office of the President, while never before defined by any government in quite the way the Constitution undertook to do, had nevertheless its sources in the Colonial experience—which did not prevent it from becoming a political issue that the early presidents, notably Jefferson, used for their own ends, as other holders of the office, not to mention candidates for it, have done since.

The American nation, which indirectly is the focus of these two essays, is the subject as well of Lester C. Thurow's discussion of the economy that has come to exist in the United States since the end of the Second World War—and not only in the United States, of course, for there is no longer any such thing as the "American economy" apart from the world economy that America once dominated, but in which it now plays, and can hope to play, only a part. Professor Thurow's account of these matters will be familiar to those who know *The Zero-Sum Society* and *The Zero-Sum Solution,* books he has written previously, and of which the essay published here is in some respects a concise update.

It may seem subversive of these articles that we present also this year a discussion, in the portion of the volume devoted to "Reconsiderations of Great Books and Ideas," of Marx's *Capital.* And, as far as that goes, the timing is to some extent coincidental, a contributor who could do a good job on the subject, and wished to undertake it, having only lately been found. But the combination of *Capital* and the Constitution is in another sense quite proper. As the eighteenth-century Founders saw in the crisis to which privilege had brought the Western world the need for republican institutions, so Marx later perceived that another critical division of society—that between the rich and the poor—had occurred as well, and this pointed, he believed, to a socialist society. That such a solution now is taken in our part of the world as contradictory of the republican vision of the Founders is a recognition of what strike us as historical realities, but this should not obscure the fact that the greater portion of the human race is struggling with common problems and trying to meet the same needs. All of which, and much more, is suggested by Thomas K. Simpson in the essay on *Capital* with which he has provided us in this issue of *The Great Ideas Today.*

On a quite different tack, the signal feature of this volume is the publication of essays we have long sought to have on Great Books of the East. The contributor capable of accomplishing such a task proved to be William Theodore de Bary, who is not only distinguished as a student of Chinese thought but has established a program of studies in Great Books of the East at Columbia University, where he teaches. Professor de Bary agreed to produce the essay we had in mind on condition that he be permitted to find other writers who would add short accounts of particular Eastern books to what he himself had to say on the subject generally. This we were happy to allow, and the result is the collection of writings we publish here, among which his own contribution serves as a kind of introduction and indicates the very different problems that arise before we can even begin to think about something like Great Books of the East, as compared with those that must be faced with Western writings. But the several parts of the essay as a whole give some sense of the literatures with which they deal, even as they show the difficulties that lie in the way of providing any more comprehensive view of so many different cultures.

We publish also this year another essay by our consulting editor, Otto Bird, on one of the authors in the *Great Books of the Western World*, this time Thomas Aquinas. The *Summa Theologica*, that crowning expression of medieval thought, is discussed in an article which shows how readers can grasp the structure of the work and find their way through it without having to acquire either the Latin or the learning it exemplifies, both of which can be found, however, in Mr. Bird himself, who is among other things a fine medievalist. How worthwhile it might be to do this will be seen when it is recalled that the *Summa* is devoted to the proposition that the truth of this world and of eternal things is in both cases available to the intellect—that, indeed, truth itself is finally one—and that this rejection of duality has made all the difference in the development of the Western mind.

The length of these various articles and essays, taken together, has limited the number of "Additions to the Great Books Library" we could provide this year to two, both of which are, however, appropriate to material that appears elsewhere in the volume. One of the works reprinted is Thomas Paine's *The Rights of Man*, a book written in defense not of the American Revolution but of the French one, and which Paine undertook by way of a reply to Edmund Burke's *Reflections* on that upheaval. It reminds us that America was born in revolutionary times, and that the most significant event of those times was the one that occurred in France, beginning in 1789.

Our other reprint is a play, *Śakuntalā and the Ring of Recollection*, translated from the Sanskrit of Kālidāsa, commonly considered the greatest writer in that language, if not, indeed, the greatest writer that India has produced. As translated here by Barbara Stoler Miller (who contributes an essay on the play elsewhere in the volume), it is an absorbing and even touching work to read—not by any means incomprehensible to those of us whose education has been Western, yet indicative of a different culture in which we must take great interest as having known what, after all, seem only to be human things about the human heart.

PART ONE

Current Developments
in the
Arts and Sciences

The American Economy

Lester C. Thurow

Well known among American economists of our day, Lester C. Thurow likes to call himself an "economics educator," and in his many writings and frequent speaking engagements he has endeavored to clarify and illuminate economics for the lay public, providing informed commentary on public policy issues and the state of the economics profession. Among his books is *The Zero-Sum Solution* (1985), which indicates what will have to be done if the United States is again to be competitive in the world economy. He is the author also of *Poverty and Discrimination* (1969), for which he received the Wells prize for the best book written by a young economist; *The Impact of Taxes on the American Economy* (1971); and *Dangerous Currents: The State of Economics* (1983). In addition, he is coauthor, with Robert Heilbroner, of standard texts which have run to many editions on both macro- and micro-economics.

Mr. Thurow, who was a member of the Council of Economic Advisers in the administration of President Lyndon Johnson (1964–68), has taught at Harvard, from which he received a doctorate in 1968, and at MIT, where he is now Gordon Y Billard Professor of Economics and Management and Dean of the Sloan School of Management. A frequent contributor to the *New York Times,* he writes often for the *Los Angeles Times* as well, was for several years a columnist and contributing editor for *Newsweek,* and often appears on televised public affairs programs.

Looking backward into the 1950s, we see an American economy with effortless superiority producing a per capita gross national product (GNP) much larger than that of any other country in the world. Looking at 1986, we see equality: with the dollar purchasing approximately 160 Japanese yen and 2 West German Deutsche Marks, the GNPs of the United States, West Germany, and Japan are all narrowly clumped together, producing around $15,000 to $17,000 per person. Looking forward, what do we see—a return to effortless superiority, a continued equality, or a further slippage into a position of inferiority?

The answer to that question is not a matter of predicting economic motion as one would predict heavenly motion, but a matter of what Americans are or are not willing to do over the next twenty-five years. For the first time in a long time the world economy is full of real, technologically equal, competitors for Americans. Those who successfully compete are those who can change with the times, who can give up formerly useful standard operating procedures and replace them with new ways. Americans are being tested, and are going to be tested further between now and the turn of the century, to determine whether they are as flexible and creative as they like to think that they are.

While returning to the effortless economic superiority of the 1950s is probably impossible (it was produced to a great extent by the destruction of most of the rest of the industrial world in World War II), there are no technical reasons why the United States cannot continue to be a world economic leader. But that is a position that must be earned the old-fashioned way by proving that we are as smart and as able to work productively as anyone else in the world.

How America got to where it is

To look forward, it is necessary to look backward. If we do not understand the path the American economy took to get to its present position, we cannot understand the forces that will determine where it is going.

For reasons that to this day remain mysterious to economic historians, the Industrial Revolution began earlier in Great Britain than it did anywhere else in the world. This early start allowed Great Britain to open up a nineteenth-century economic lead on America. Britain was the preeminent industrial economic power. Starting at about the time of the Civil War, however, America put on a burst of industrial steam. From 1860 to 1900 industrial production grew at an annual rate of 4.9%, rising almost sevenfold over that period of time. By 1900 the United States had caught up with Great Britain and could once again make a claim to economic parity with the best in the world.

America continued to grow rapidly between 1900 and 1929 (industrial production rose at a 4.6% annual rate), but Germany had also closed its gap with Great Britain, and the period of time before the Great Depression is best seen as a period where Great Britain, Germany, and the United States were economic equals. Each country had industrial areas where it was clearly the world's economic leader: the Germans, chemical engineering; the British, shipbuilding; the Americans, steelmaking. America probably had a slightly higher standard of living than either of the other two, but it did not in any fundamental sense outclass the competition.

In 1929 disaster struck. With the collapse of, first, the stock market, and then the banking system, the American real per capita GNP fell 44% (67% if one does not correct for the decline in the price level). Unemployment rose from 3.2% in 1929 to 24.9% in 1933, and in 1939 it was still above 17% with little evidence of any recovery in sight.

In the United Kingdom the Great Depression was very mild. Its 1986 unemployment level exceeds the peak level reached in the Great Depression. This was just as sharp in Germany as it was in the United States, but Germany's recovery was much faster. As a result, in the late 1930s any economic advantage that the United States had enjoyed over Great Britain and Germany in the 1920s had been lost, or perhaps more than lost.

What would have happened to the American economy if World War II had not intervened to bring an end to the Great Depression remains a subject of historical speculation. World War II did intervene, and it led to a very different role for the American economy. This came to hold a position of dominance that it had never held before. The human, physical, and infrastructure capital of all of America's economic competitors had been destroyed. Germany and Japan were occupied. America's allies either retreated into positions of economic isolation behind the iron curtain or, like Britain and France, were substantially damaged and perhaps exhausted from their war efforts. Even more important, America had gained some of Europe's best scientists. Einstein and Fermi were gifts to the American economy that were hard to duplicate.

The period from 1945 to 1965 was a period of effortless American economic superiority. America's per capita GNP was twice that of any of its competitors and eight times that of the Japanese. The United States

"America continued to grow rapidly between 1900 and 1929. . . ." Scenes
like that depicted in "Construction Steel Workers," painted in 1924 by
Reginald Marsh, typified the economic spirit of the times.

could do things and afford things that the rest of the world could not.

America competed, not with lower costs of production, but with better technology. The Boeing 707 flew; the British Comet did not. Yet there was one ominous feature in the American hegemony. Even in this period of economic dominance, American firms were not export-orientated. Foreign markets were secondary markets, and Americans preferred to serve them with offshore foreign production. They would buy a foreign firm or establish an overseas subsidiary to manufacture for foreign markets, rather than directly export from the United States. Since there was no problem in exporting enough products to pay for the imports that the United States needed (there were enough unique products that could not be produced abroad to meet those limited goals), Americans did not learn to export when it would have been easy to export.

If one looks at the history of international trade, one sees a United States that used to be only lightly involved. In 1929 the United States imported or exported about 5% of its GNP. Trade was but a small tail on a very big economic dog. Surprisingly, this was still true in 1949, and true even as late as 1969. Only about 5% of the GNP was involved. America was a big player in the world economy because of the great size of America's GNP relative to that of the rest of the world, but the world economy was not a big player in the American economy.

This relationship was about to change, however. Between 1969 and 1986 imports rose to 11% of the GNP and exports rose to 9% of the GNP. If one looks at manufactured goods, as much as 25% of America's consumption may now be coming from abroad. Where the world was once a minor player in the American economy, it has become a major player. It is not too much to say that the American economy has died and has been replaced by a world economy. There is no American economy any longer; there is only a world economy.

Unless you believed that Americans are smarter than those in the rest of the industrial world, that Americans work harder than those in the rest of the industrial world, or that Americans are better organized than those in the rest of the industrial world, it was inevitable that sooner or later the rest of the industrial world was going to close the economic and technological gap between itself and the United States. Since in fact Americans are not smarter, do not work harder, and are not better organized, the only question was one of timing. "If" was not a question. "When" was the only matter in doubt.

Between 1965 and 1985 the technological gap between the United States and its major international competitors essentially closed. That is what those equal per capita GNPs denote. One can argue about the exact real standards of living from one country to another, since they depend to some extent on past accumulated wealth and variables such as space per person, but when it comes to technological competence in those industries where exports and imports occur, the level of technology abroad is as high as it is in the United States. Indeed, further falls in the value of the dollar will be necessary for the United States to balance its international trading accounts, so one can even argue that technology in exporting industries favors Japan or Germany.

When we talk about economic technology, we are not talking about the theoretical knowledge that wins one a Nobel Prize. We are talking about mastering the best technology for producing the cheapest products. It is perfectly possible for a country to win more than its share of Nobel Prizes yet still fall behind technologically when it comes to economic production. If one does not make video recorders, as the United States does not, it does not matter whether one understands how video recorders work, or if one is in fact the country where video recorders were invented, which the United States is. Countries that have mastered the technology and dominate production are the world's economic leaders, regardless of the level of technical expertise in the United States.

By 1986 the United States had once again become an equal among equals, as in the 1930s. It was no longer superior, it was not yet inferior. In some technologies it led, in other technologies it lagged; on average, it was average. Average countries compete based on their ability to be the world's lowest cost producer of different goods and services. If America was the lowest cost producer of something, that was produced in America. If America was not the lowest cost producer, that was not produced in America.

In 1986 the United States trade deficit stood at $170 billion. Americans bought $170 billion more things from foreigners than foreigners bought from Americans. While the country has before had trade deficits of a few billion dollars, it has never had deficits of that magnitude. Since it takes one million full-time year-round workers to produce $42 billion worth of goods in American manufacturing, a $170 billion trade deficit essentially means that four million people are not working in manufacturing who would be working in manufacturing if the United States were balancing its exports and imports. Many of those millions of people are not unemployed but are employed at much lower paying service jobs, so that curing the trade deficit would not raise employment by four million, but the number of quality, high-paying, jobs would rise substantially if the trade deficit were eliminated. The aim of any economy is not a job, but a good job.

In the early 1980s, a slow rate of growth of the money supply coupled with a large budget deficit produced American interest rates four times as high as those in West Germany and Japan. These interest rates not surprisingly attracted foreign capital, but to move German money, say, into the United States, one must sell marks and buy dollars. This lowers the value of the mark and raises the value of the dollar. With a high-valued dollar, American products became expensive in foreign markets and foreign products became cheap in American markets. A large trade deficit quickly followed as a consequence.

More fundamental was a slow rate of growth of productivity. Where productivity had grown at about 3.3% per year from 1948 through 1965, it grew at only about 0.8% per year from 1978 through 1985. In the rest of the industrial world productivity was meanwhile growing in the 3–5% per year range. As a consequence, the real costs of producing goods and services were falling faster in the rest of the world than they were in the United States, and the United States was gradually becoming noncompetitive in world markets.

America's balance of payments could always be balanced by lowering the value of the dollar. At 200 yen to the dollar, a Japanese wage of 1,600 yen per hour translates into $8 per hour, at 160 yen to the dollar it translates into $10 per hour, and at 100 yen to the dollar it translates into $16 per hour. At some value of the yen Japanese wages become so high that high-cost Japanese labor cannot compete with low-cost American labor. But the goal of the United States is not just to balance its international accounts; it is to balance those accounts and simultaneously to pay wages as high as those that are being paid in the most developed industrial nations. To do this, it needs a much higher productivity growth rate.

A black hole in the world economy

While analysts have long talked about trade deficits and surpluses, it is important to understand that today's American trade deficit (or the rest of the world's trade surplus) is something qualitatively different from anything discussed in the past. As the deficits or surpluses have become larger and larger, they have qualitatively changed in terms of their future impacts on the world's economies.

If the United States had balanced its balance of payments with either more exports or less imports it would have had four million additional workers in manufacturing and the rest of the world would have had four million fewer workers in manufacturing. Based on bilateral trade patterns, one-third of those lost jobs would be in Japan, one-third would be in Europe and Canada, and one-third would be elsewhere in the world.

The American trade deficit and the buildup in its international debts has essentially reached a point where it is to economics what a black hole is to astronomy. As one gets into a black hole it gets harder and harder to get out. Once in a black hole, the entire structure and behavior of matter changes. So too with an economic black hole. The longer the American trade deficit lasts, the larger will be the ultimate changes that will have to be made in the trading structure of the economies of the world, and the harder it will be to avoid a crisis within the economic alliances of the industrial democracies.

Both the United States and the rest of the world have essentially become drug addicts, but they are addicted to different drugs. The American drug is foreign loans. Foreign lending is providing almost $200 billion, or about one-third of America's investable funds. To go without those funds would mean a substantial reduction in the American standard of living. By importing more than they export, Americans now enjoy a consumption standard of living that is more than 4% above their production standard of living. If foreign lending were to stop, they would lose that 4% addition to their standard of living. They would also have to run a trade surplus to pay interest on their outstanding foreign debts. Every $40 billion in annual interest payments would generate another 1% reduction in their standard of living. While a 5 or 6% reduction in the American standard of living might not sound like much, it would be a reduction four or five times as large as that caused by the United States' largest post-World War II recession.

The foreign drug is the American market. Whole industries have been built abroad to service that market. Their output is so large that it could not possibly be diverted to the home or other markets. As has been mentioned, at American levels of productivity about four million foreign workers are dependent on the American market. At generally lower foreign levels of productivity the actual number is larger, and this number does not count the indirect jobs that would be lost because export workers would have less income and would spend less on other domestic products, thereby causing other workers to lose their jobs.

In the United States jobs would go up, but living standards and wages would go down when its trade deficit disappears. In the rest of the world jobs would go down, but living standards and wages would go up for those who managed to remain employed when their countries' export surpluses disappeared.

And disappear they will. The current patterns of world trade simply are not viable in the long run. To say so is not to make a forecast but to express a truism of economic arithmetic. The world economy faces two certainties and one uncertainty.

First, no country can forever run a large trade deficit. To finance deficits, countries must borrow and go into debt. No country can forever accumulate larger and larger debts. Yet this is exactly what a deficit country must do, since it must borrow to finance both its continuing trade deficits and to make interest payments on previously accumulated debts. No lender will forever lend, and no lender has infinite sums of money to lend. As a result the lending will at some point stop.

To pay interest on its loans, a country must run a trade surplus to accumulate the funds necessary to make those interest payments. There is no other way to get the necessary funds. Sooner or later international debtors have to run trade surpluses. To be paid interest on their loans, international creditors must run trade deficits. Unless a creditor does that, borrowers cannot acquire the funds necessary to pay their interest bills.

This leads to a second certainty. At some point in the future the United States is going to have to shift from being a large net importer to being a large net exporter, and Japan is going to shift from being a large net exporter to being a large net importer. There is no uncertainty about the current patterns of trade. They are going to change.

While we know that the current patterns of borrowing and trading cannot forever continue, the timing of the shift is impossible to predict. How much will foreigners lend or Americans borrow before the lending and borrowing stops? No one knows, because the world is on brand new financial ice. The world's richest country has never been the world's biggest borrower. How much can it borrow before the lending stops? No one knows, or can know ahead of time. The lending may even have stopped in the time between the writing of this essay and the publication of this book.

If the United States can borrow as much as Mexico relative to its GNP, it can borrow about $650 billion and the problems will not occur until 1989. If it can borrow as much as Chile borrowed—130% of its GNP—the United States can borrow about $6,000 billion and the problems won't emerge until well into the twenty-first century. If it does so, however, like Chile at that time it will forever owe the rest of the world about 10% of its annual GNP in interest payments.

But maybe America can borrow even more than Chile. The United States borrows in dollars, and since it has the ability to print dollars, there is no default risk when lending to the United States. The only risk is the risk that one will be paid back in a currency that is worth much less than what one originally lent.

On the other hand, the American dollar is the de facto world reserve currency. This means that there are millions of investors holding hundreds of billions of dollars who are only in dollars for the sake of safety. They might bail out tomorrow morning. Those seeking safety do not normally lend to the world's most indebted borrower.

Anyone who tells you that they know how long the lending can last is telling you something that he or she simply cannot know. Current trading patterns are going to change, but no one knows when.

Economists make a distinction between what they call a hard and a soft landing. In the hard landing the United States quickly corrects its trade deficit and in the soft landing it slowly closes its trade deficits. A soft landing is better, with less short-run economic pain from readjustments, but it makes the long-run pain and readjustments much bigger and more painful.

Consider the economic arithmetic of a soft landing. Suppose that the

United States were to correct its balance of payments at the rate of $20 billion per year, a rate that would require the rest of the world to find alternative employment for 500,000 workers per year. In addition, assume that the interest rate on foreign borrowing averages 6% per year. Under these assumptions the United States does not balance its current account until the year 1999. By that time it will have accumulated an international debt of $1,400 billion and will owe annual interest payments of $90 billion.

This means that the United States, to balance its trade, must shift from a trade deficit of $170 billion per year to a trade surplus of $90 billion per year, and that instead of moving four million jobs back to the United States, six million jobs will have to be moved back. In that case, instead of declining by 4%, the American standard of living will decline by 6%.

Slow changes are better in terms of less immediate job loss in the rest of the world, but a price is paid in terms of a larger ultimate job loss.

Imaginary options

When faced with a difficult problem, it is simply human nature to look for a painless escape route. In this case the painless escape is the idea, often propagated inside and outside of the United States, that the country can simply abandon manufacturing and export enough services to balance its international accounts. If true, others would not lose their American markets and the United States would not have to suffer a sharp reduction in the value of the dollar to restore international competitiveness in manufacturing. Unfortunately, a brief look at the numbers will convince anyone that such an escape path does not exist.

If one subtracts earnings on direct foreign investment (counted as a service export, but more than balanced by the interest outflow on bonds that shows up in the capital rather than current account) and exports of military hardware (for some unknown accounting reason counted as service exports), the United States was in 1985 left with $55 billion in service exports. This compares with $460 billion in imports. There is no conceivable way that service exports can be expanded to pay for the volume of manufactured products that the United States now imports. A country the size of Switzerland might survive as a service exporter, but not one the size of the United States with its 245 million people.

More important, in the same year, 1985, the United States imported $58 billion worth of services. As in our manufacturing accounts, we had a deficit in our service accounts. If one looks at the components of the service accounts this is not surprising. The tourists' trade deficit is $12 billion: Americans like to take foreign vacations more than foreigners like to take American vacations. Or, take insurance. The United States owed $3 billion more in insurance fees than it earned from selling insurance to the rest of the world. In fact, the only part of the service account with a large surplus was the sales of technology (an $8 billion surplus). This, however, is the product of a past American lead in technology that is rapidly disappearing. There is every reason to believe that in the future Americans will export less and import more technology than they have done in the past. Earnings from licensing technology are apt to grow smaller with time. American service exports are not large enough, or competitive enough with the rest of the world, to carry the burden they would have to carry if the United States were to depend upon them to pay for its imports. It has no choice but to sell more manufactured exports.

This conclusion becomes inescapable if we look at agricultural exports. In 1979–80 the United States had an almost $30 billion trade surplus in agricultural commodities. In 1986 it is likely to have had a trade deficit in agriculture, and little of this shift in agriculture can be traced to the value of the dollar. The real causes are to be found in the green revolution (China, India, and Pakistan now all feed themselves) and the Common Market agricultural policies. In the 1970s the Common Market imported seventeen million metric tons of grain; in 1985 it exported three million metric tons. For the foreseeable future there is no agricultural trade surplus for the United States, and as a result manufactured exports must replace those lost agricultural markets.

The conclusion is inescapable. America's trade imbalances can only be rectified with manufactured products.

Undesirable options

Technically, it is certainly feasible to keep foreign products out of the American market and prevent the United States from slipping further into debt by protecting ourselves with tariffs and similar measures. While such protection of internal markets violates the spirit of international treaties such as the General Agreement on Tariffs and Trade (GATT), it is clearly possible, as many other countries have shown, to achieve the desired result without violating the letter of the law implicit in GATT treaties.

Foreign retaliation is offered as a reason for avoiding protectionism, but foreign retaliation, other than symbolic actions, is an empty threat in a world where the United States is running a $170 billion trade deficit. With American imports far exceeding American exports, the rest of the world has more to lose from the closing of American markets than the United States has to lose from the closing of foreign markets. No one declares a trade war when they are bound to lose it.

Protectionism is sometimes opposed on the ground that domestic industries relax and become inefficient once the threat of foreign competition is removed. While it is certainly possible to find examples of this phenomenon (the American steel industry is an example of an industry that has become relatively less efficient behind the walls of protection), it is also possible to find counterexamples. The farmers of the Common Market have dramatically raised their productivity while living behind the protection of the Common Market's agricultural policies. Protection does not lead to inefficiency if the protected industry is subject to internal competition. Inefficiency occurs when the protected industry has no domestic competition.

The real arguments against wholesale protection as an answer to the American trade and debt problems are political and military in nature. Wholesale protectionism is essentially a declaration of economic war, and one cannot declare an economic war on one's military allies and still expect to have military allies. Put bluntly, protection is inconsistent with America's status as a superpower running a worldwide military alliance.

Of course, technically it is also possible, again, for the United States simply to inflate its way out of its debt problems. American borrowing differs from the borrowing of all other countries in that America borrows in its own currency (dollars) while all other countries borrow in foreign currencies, usually dollars. Since the American government prints dollars, it is possible for the United States to print enough dollars to pay off its foreign debts.

Such a strategy is essentially one of inducing a sharp burst of inflation to make the value of foreign-held American bonds worthless. One of the consequences of this strategy, however, is that it also makes the value of American-held financial assets worthless. There is no way to reduce the value of foreign-held financial assets without at the same time reducing the value of American-held financial assets.

In the aftermath of such a strategy, real interest rates would also be apt to be very high. Foreigners would not want to lend, domestic demands would have to be cut back to levels consistent with domestic saving, and investment would sag.

Unlikely options

If one looks at real options for avoiding the black hole ahead of us, monetary and fiscal coordination among Europe, Japan, and the United States would seem to provide one possibility. What is economically needed, however, seems to be politically impossible.

The United States rightly tells West Germany and Japan that if they would vigorously stimulate their economies with monetary and fiscal policies they would provide a market for American exports that would allow the United States to balance its accounts without having to cut its imports (their exports). But Germany and Japan say no. Yet if one cannot stimulate when one has negative inflation, high unemployment, slow growth, and a large trade surplus, when can one?

At the same time, foreign growth cannot solve the American trade deficit problem. The amount that the rest of the world would have to grow economically to absorb $170 billion in extra American exports is

simply too large to be realistic. This is especially true since the rest of
the world's marginal propensity to buy American goods when foreign
incomes rise is just one-third that of America's marginal propensity to
buy foreign goods when American incomes rise.

Simultaneously, West Germany and Japan rightly tell the American
government to balance its budget. If it did, the United States would
need to borrow less of their money and lower interest rates could lead
to more domestic investment in Germany, Japan, and the United States.
But the United States says no. It refuses to raise the taxes that it would
have to raise if it were to balance its budget and reduce its absorption of
foreign funds and resources. While the advice is correct, balancing the
American federal budget by itself would not correct the trade deficit
problem. Those deficits are now built into the industrial structure of
both the United States and the rest of the world.

Both sides are right. Both actions are needed. Both actions would
help even if they would not solve the problems by themselves. The
problems flowing from the American trade deficit could more easily
be avoided if each would do what the other recommends. But neither
side is willing to bend, because their governments are elected not on
the strength of what they do for the world economy in the long run,
but for what they do in the short run to benefit their own national
economies.

Options to prolong

Curiously, most of the lending to the United States has taken the form
of investments in short-term financial assets such as Treasury bills or
commercial paper. Such investments do not yield the highest possible
returns; they are normally bought for reasons of safety and liquidity.
If bought in small amounts they have both characteristics, but if they
are purchased in the hundreds of billions, neither of these advantages
really exists. One simply cannot get out without severely reducing the
value of what one is trying to sell. If he gets paid back in dollars that
are worth much less than those he lent, the investor does not really
have either safety or liquidity in any meaningful sense.

In all probability, this pattern of short-term financial investments
emerged because such investments are the easiest to make if one unex-
pectedly has hundreds of billions of dollars to invest. Real investments in
corporations, plant and equipment, or real estate take much more local
knowledge and much more time to make. Given the passage of time,
one would expect to see a shift in the pattern of foreign investment
to either corporate equities or direct investments in real estate or plant
and equipment, since investments would simultaneously earn higher
rates of return and be a hedge against any future inflation caused by
further declines in the value of the dollar.

Such foreign investments would lead essentially to a situation in which Americans would be gradually selling America to foreign capitalists to get the extra resources necessary to raise their consumption levels above their production levels. American capitalists would sell out to, and be replaced by, foreign capitalists. New investments would be financed by and belong to foreign capitalists. A flow of interest abroad would be replaced by a flow of earnings and dividends abroad.

While a flow of dividends abroad reduces the American standard of living just as much as does a flow of interest payments, there are several advantages from an American perspective. To the extent that the foreign investments take the form of new investments rather than buying existing assets, they are essentially self-liquidating. The dividends owed would be financed by the new goods and services produced by the new plant and equipment made possible by the foreign investments.

Initially such investments would likely be made in the areas where foreign production was being displaced by the low value of the dollar and in which foreigners want to maintain their market positions. Japanese cars made in America would replace Japanese cars made in Japan. Such investments would also serve to increase internal price competition in the United States and limit future inflations. To the extent that foreigners have production technologies not existing in the United States, such technologies would also be brought to the United States and improve America's technical knowledge.

Eventually, if the dollar falls far enough, such investments might also be made in export industries. Foreign firms would make the United States an offshore production base just as American firms in the 1980s made foreign countries into offshore production bases to service the American market. Foreign managers essentially improve American knowledge of foreign markets.

There is a price to be paid, however. Top headquarters managerial jobs, research and development jobs, and design jobs tend to be disproportionally held in the home country of the controlling firms. Those Americans who might wish to hold such jobs would find themselves competing for a smaller supply of the very best high-paying jobs if American firms lose out to foreign firms as American producers.

When American capitalists sell existing assets to foreigners, the future price that must be paid is much larger. Essentially the country is transferring future income flows from the United States to the rest of the world in exchange for a higher immediate standard of living. In the future, Americans will have fewer claims on the goods and services produced in America, and foreigners will have larger claims on the goods and services produced in America.

To convert loans into equity is to extend the period of time when one's consumption can exceed one's production, but at the price of magnifying the eventual decline that must occur in a country's average standard of living.

The option of last resort

If all other options remain unemployed, the entire burden of adjustment will fall on exchange rates.

Abroad, a further sharp shift in exchange rates will be deflationary. The dollar will simply fall far enough to make foreign products unacceptably expensive on American markets. In Europe, Canada, and Japan this means the loss of millions of jobs. While old-fashioned Keynesian monetary and fiscal stimulus could be used to expand domestic demands to replace American demands, the new demand would come in very different industries from the present export industries. As a result, these countries would face a major change in their industrial structures and, during the transition from export industries to domestic industries, unemployment would be apt to occur.

Unemployment would also be apt to be higher than necessary given the reluctance of both Japan and West Germany to employ Keynesian antirecessionary policies vigorously. In the past both countries have been slow to employ expansionary policies when faced with recessions or deflationary circumstances. West Germany has been taking no action to reduce its currently very high unemployment rates, and Japan has done little to offset the slowdown in export growth springing from the rise in the value of the yen.

In the third world, a falling dollar would make it easier to pay dollar denominated loans, but much of this effect would be offset by the higher interest rates that would have to be paid on these loans as foreign lending to the United States diminished. The third world would also find it harder to offset the jobs they lose to a falling dollar, since structural shifts from one industry to another get progressively harder the poorer a country.

Inside the United States the effects of a falling dollar would be twofold. Some inflation would occur as the price of imports rises in parallel with rising foreign currency values. The magnitude of the resulting inflation depends on the amount the dollar must fall to balance exports and imports. If the dollar falls 30% and 12% of the GNP is imported, then 3.6 percentage points ($.30 \times .12$) of inflation would directly flow from imports. If rising prices for imports lead domestic producers of competing products to raise their prices, then this direct inflation must be combined with an indirect inflationary effect. Historically the indirect inflationary effects of external inflationary shocks have usually been bigger than the direct inflationary effects. The total inflationary effect of the OPEC oil price hikes, for example, were several times those that would have been predicted given the direct calculations.

Little inflation has thus far been produced by the falling dollar for two reasons. Falling oil and raw material prices have offset most of the effects of a falling dollar, and thus far, foreign producers have not raised their prices as much as one would have expected given the rising value of their currencies. Instead they have absorbed the impact of the falling dollar in lower profit margins on American sales. But neither of these factors can indefinitely offset the inflationary effects of a falling dollar. Eventually oil and raw material prices will quit falling, and eventually there are no profit margins left to be absorbed. Some inflationary pressure must occur as the dollar falls.

Since the current imbalance in the American balance of payments is outside the range of historical experience, no one knows or can easily estimate how much the dollar would have to fall to rebalance America's international accounts. As the following calculations indicate, however, the number is apt to be very large, indeed, large enough to scare everyone.

Consider the value of the yen to the dollar. In 1979–80 both Japan and the United States had balanced current accounts. Remembering that currency values affect trade with about a one-year lag, the currency values of 1978–79 produced the trade balances of 1979–80. In 1978–79 the yen stood at 210 to the dollar. Since that time, however, there has been 40% more inflation in the United States than in Japan and 15% less growth in manufacturing productivity. This means that the dollar would have to fall 55% from its 210 yen level to restore the relative production costs of 1979–80. This means a value of about 100 yen to the dollar.

Without the agricultural trade surpluses that existed in 1979–80, however, the United States also needs to export $30 billion more manufactured products today than it needed to export then. This will require a dollar low enough to generate the manufactured exports needed to replace the earlier agricultural exports and means an equilibrium value for the dollar of something less than 100 yen to the dollar.

In 1979–80 the United States also had a $15 billion trade surplus with Latin America. Since then Latin America has gone broke, and to repay its American bankers must for the foreseeable future have a $15 billion trade surplus with the United States. Here again the dollar must fall enough for the United States to sell an extra $30 billion in manufactured goods outside of Latin America to replace the exports that used to be sent there.

A lower price for oil helps both the Japanese and the American balance of payments, since they are both net importers, but it helps Japan much more than it helps the United States, for the United States still produces more than 60% of its own oil. The net result is a yen that has to rise further vis-à-vis the dollar to bring the Japanese accounts back into balance than it would have to rise if the Japanese were still buying expensive oil.

The shift in debtor-creditor relationships amplifies the same trends. In 1979–80 the United States was the world's largest net creditor and could pay for 14% of its imports with the earnings from its foreign investment. But today it is the world's largest net debtor and has to have a trade surplus to earn the interest that it owes its foreign lenders. Whatever the size of interest payments eventually owed, the dollar will have to fall far enough to generate the necessary surplus.

Econometric evidence also indicates that the United States' propensity to buy foreign imports as its income rises is three times that of foreign propensities to buy imports from the United States as foreign incomes rise. This means that unless the rest of the world grows three times as fast as the United States, the dollar needs to fall every year to balance these different income elasticities of demand. Here again the econometrics would point in the direction of a large decline in the value of the dollar. This has been confirmed by the very slow responsiveness of American exports and imports to the fall in the value of the dollar that has occurred since the spring of 1985.

A future expansion of manufacturing

As imports fall and exports rise, American manufacturing will expand, since neither agriculture nor services can do what must be done, but that observation does not lead to the conclusion that all of American manufacturing will recover. While manufacturing is often thought of as a high-wage industry, on average it is only slightly above average. In 1985 a manufacturing wage of $9.53 per hour compared with a wage of $8.57 per hour for all of private industry.

The United States wants not just a general recovery in manufacturing but a recovery in the high value-added, high-wage, part of manufacturing. But foreigners have an equal desire to keep exactly the same industries. As manufacturing inevitably moves from Europe and Japan to the United States, they will want to see the high-wage industries stay and the low-wage industries go.

What actually happens depends upon what Americans do. High-wage industries are usually capital-intensive industries employing highly skilled workers using the latest technologies. If capital is cheaper in the United States than it is in the rest of the world, if Americans are more skilled than workers in the rest of the world, and if new products and production processes are first developed in America, then high-wage, high value-added, industries will lead the expansion of American manufacturing. If none of these three factors is present, then low-wage, low value-added, industries will lead the recovery.

If we examine the first of these three factors, there is cause for concern. Given low American savings rates, the United States stands at a handicap when it comes to the cost of capital. Capital is more expensive here than it is in Europe and Japan. Capital costs suggest that capital-intensive production processes will tend to remain abroad.

The other two factors are more mixed. The United States has a larger college-educated pool of workers, but it also has a very different mix of such workers. It educates many fewer engineers, a slightly larger number of scientists, and many more people in the liberal arts and professions such as accounting. Among noncollege graduates, the American product is clearly inferior when it comes either to general academic achievements or to more specialized job skills.

When it comes to research and development (R&D) the United States is still by far the world's leader in developing new products, but has fallen behind when it comes to developing new processes for producing either old or new products. Total spending on civilian R&D is also now below that of West Germany, France, and Japan as a fraction of the GNP. The United States spends slightly less than 2% of its GNP on civilian R&D, while its competitors spend slightly more than 2% of their GNPs on the same activities.

Since high-wage manufacturing tends to be based on engineering expertise, America's relative lack of engineering manpower would seem to point to problems in expanding high-tech industries. This problem is compounded by the absorption of such people in the American defense effort. Neither West Germany nor Japan, America's two principal competitors, employs many of their engineers on such activities.

As a result, if the United States does nothing it is not likely that the recovery in American manufacturing will occur in the highest wage or value-added sectors of manufacturing. To the extent that these have gone abroad, they are likely to stay abroad, and they may continue to expand abroad even in the face of a falling dollar.

To hold the American position in high-wage industries will take more than a falling dollar. It will take a rate of growth of productivity in manufacturing equal to that of the rest in the world. When the United States was recovering from the 1981–82 recession in 1983 and 1984, U.S. manufacturing productivity briefly accelerated to world-class levels, but since that time it has once again been running at a rate roughly two-thirds that of Germany and half that of Japan.

To bring the American productivity growth rate up to that of the rest of the world will require higher savings and less consumption, so that we can invest more in plant and equipment. It will also require a better secondary-education system matched with some system of skill-training for the non-college-bound, and a different mix of college graduates with a higher proportion of engineers. R&D spending will have to come up to international standards as well.

Implications

Actions have inevitable consequences. Once in place, a large trade deficit or surplus and the resulting international indebtedness affect the future patterns of world trade. Every industrial country in the world is going to experience the pull created in the world economy by those surpluses or deficits. While the effects cannot be avoided, it is possible to minimize the adverse consequences. This will, however, require co-ordinated actions on a scale unprecedented in economic history.

The United States will have to agree to raise taxes to eliminate its budget deficit, while Europe and Japan will have to agree to take over America's role as the world economic locomotive. The United States will have to improve its competitiveness while the rest of the world copes with higher currency values and the need to shift structurally from export to domestic industries.

If positive actions are not taken to raise America's productivity growth and to increase its competitiveness, protectionism will come to look increasingly attractive. In the long run protectionism can only decelerate the rate of growth of productivity (who will improve their performance when they have guaranteed local markets?), but in the short run a policy that seems to protect one's job even if it means lower future productivity growth can look very seductive.

More likely than any of these developments will be others. Wishful thinking about services and agriculture will be combined with measured doses of protection and inflation. Requests will be made ineffectually for coordinated economic policies, but the United States will not balance its budget any more than Japan or West Germany will speed up their growth. Foreign investors will be met with xenophobia, and the fall of the dollar will lead to competitive depreciations. The United States will talk about accelerating its productivity growth and competitiveness, but it will do little of what needs to be done.

The world economy is fast entering an economic black hole. The structure and patterns of trading relations are about to undergo a sharp change. Getting out is becoming harder. And as with real black holes, no one knows exactly what goes on once we are too far into the black hole to leave it.

A surge in inequality

Much like the Hubbard Glacier in Alaska, the distribution of income and wealth in America were quiescent in the 1950s, 1960s, and most of the 1970s, with strong growth in average incomes but only small changes in relative measures of dispersion. The expansion of Social Security benefits dramatically lowered poverty among the elderly from more than twice the national average in 1967 (29.5% versus 14.2%) to less than the national average in 1985 (12.6% versus 14%), so that the national incidence of poverty fell slightly faster than one would have predicted given the general growth in real incomes, but otherwise the shares of total income going to different proportions of the population changed very little. Starting in the late 1970s, however, the distribution of income and wealth started to change very rapidly given its enormous mass. Like the Hubbard Glacier, the distribution of income and wealth is now in the midst of a surge—a surge toward inequality.

According to the United States Census Bureau, in 1985 the share of total income going to the top 20% of all families (43.5%) reached the highest level ever recorded (the data first began to be collected in 1947). In earlier periods the income share of this group had moved very narrowly between 40.5 and 41.5% of total income. Conversely, the income share of the bottom 60% of the population (32.4%) was at its lowest level in recorded history, down from slightly less than 36% of total income in the late 1960s.

If one looks at Federal Reserve Board data on the income distribution (data that include returns to wealth such as capital gains and retained earnings not counted in Census Bureau definitions of income), the movement toward inequality is even more pronounced. Between 1969 and 1982 the top 10% of the population raised their income share from 29 to 33% of the total, those between the 60th and 90th percentiles held even at 39% of total income, and the bottom 60% of the population saw their share of total income fall from 32 to 28%.

Federal Reserve Board distributions of wealth show that wealth is much more unequally distributed than income. The top 2% of the population have 14% of total income, but they have 28% of total net worth. Similarly, the 33% income share of the top 10% almost doubles to a 57% share of total net worth. In contrast, the bottom 50% of the population have 4.5% of total net worth. About half of America's top wealth holders got there through inherited wealth and half through self-generated wealth. In the top wealth group 98% are Caucasian.

The major forces producing rising inequality in the distribution of earnings are two in number—intense international competitive pressures coupled with high unemployment and a rising proportion of female workers.

International competitiveness

America's huge balance of trade deficit is merely the most visible symbol of a much more competitive international economy. Since manufacturing is relatively highly paid and tends to have a more equal distribution of earnings than other sectors such as services, noncompetitiveness in manufacturing directly leads to greater inequality in the distribution of earnings.

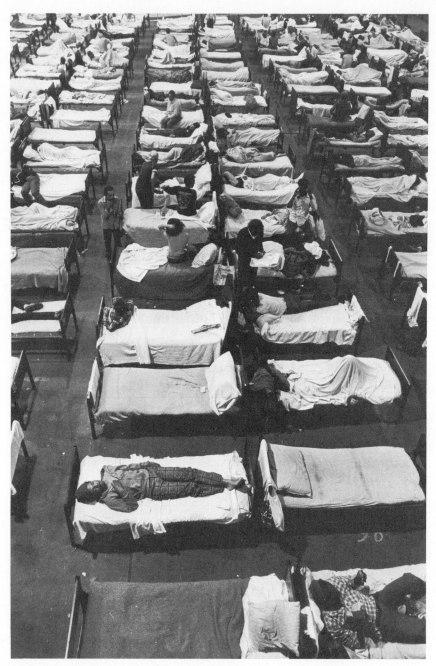

A shelter for homeless men in the Bronx, New York. *"Like the Hubbard Glacier, the distribution of income and wealth is now in the midst of a surge—a surge toward inequality."*

Using input-output techniques, it is possible to isolate the earnings distributions of America's exporting or import-competing industries and to compare their earnings distributions with those for the entire economy. When this is done, both exporting industries and the import-competing industries pay higher wages than does the economy as a whole. In 1983 the median exporting wage was $18,637 and the median import-competing wage was $19,583, while the entire economy generated a median wage of only $16,168.

In addition to paying higher wages, both export industries and import-competing industries also generated a more equal distribution of earnings. In 1983, 41% of the entire work force worked at jobs that paid less than $12,500 per year, but only 31% of those in exporting industries and 30% of those in import-competing industries earned less than this amount. While 56% of the total work force earned from $12,500 to $50,000 per year, 66% of those in exporting industries and 67% of those in import-competing industries earned this amount. But at the very top of the income distribution the percentages were essentially equal—2.6% of export work force, 2.7% of the import-competing work force, and 2.7% of the entire work force were paid more than $50,000 per year.

As a result, when exports fall and imports rise to produce a trade deficit, the distribution of earnings moves toward inequality. Jobs are lost in both export industries and import-competing industries and are replaced by jobs with lower, more unequal, earnings in the rest of the economy. This factor is the principal reason for the observed decline in male earnings. The industries that have been hit hardest by international competition—autos, steel, machine tools—are precisely those industries that have provided large numbers of upper middle-income male jobs. For women a service job does not mean a lower wage, but for men it does.

If one looks at earnings by industry or occupation, foreign competitive pressures have not so much shifted the relative earnings of different occupations or industries as they have increased the variance in earnings within each occupation or industry and forced workers down the earnings ladder. Some of this effect might have been offset if unemployment had been low and the nontraded sectors of the economy had been forced to raise productivity and wages to attract good workers, but high unemployment meant a plentiful labor supply where wages could if anything be lowered and dispersed more widely in the nontraded sector as well.

Female workers

Another part of the surge in inequality can be traced to women—or, more accurately, to society's economic treatment of women. Since women are paid much less than men and are much more likely to be part-time workers than men, a rising proportion of female workers automatically leads to a more unequal distribution of earnings. The average female worker makes just 52% of what the average male worker makes, and the average full-time year-round female worker makes just 65% of what the average full-time year-round male worker makes.

This combination of low wages and an increasing proportion of female-headed households (up from 28 to 31% of total households between 1979 and 1985 alone) has led to a low-income population that is increasingly dependent upon female earnings—the feminization of poverty. Women and children account for 77% of those in poverty, and half of the poverty population lives in female-headed families with no husband present. The average female worker earns just barely enough to get a family of four above the poverty line. To earn less than the average is to be in poverty. To do more than just escape from poverty requires a female job that is substantially above average.

The work behavior of women, however, is not just affecting the lower end of the income distribution. Women are increasingly influencing what a family must do if it wishes to have a middle-class standard of living. In 1984 there were eighty-seven million households in America. Of these, fifty million were traditional intact husband-wife families. Of the forty million intact husband-wife households with earnings (the rest were mostly retired), twenty-eight million reported earnings by both husband and wife. These families had a median income of $31,000— $22,000 earned by the husband and $9,000 earned by the wife.

Among working men, only 22% will earn $31,000 or more on their own and among working women only 3% will earn $31,000 or more on their own. As a result, few families are going to be able to afford that $31,000 middle-class life-style without both husband and wife in the labor force: in 1984 the average household income for those not in husband-wife families was only $12,000.

While the dominant family pattern is today a year-round full-time male worker and a part-year or part-time female worker, this pattern is rapidly shifting toward a life-style in which both husband and wife are year-round full-time workers. In 1984, eleven million families had two full-timers and these families had a median income of $39,000— $24,000 earned by the husband and $15,000 earned by the wife. As more and more families have two year-round full-time workers, those households without two full-time workers are going to fall farther and farther behind economically.

Rising female participation rates are also one of the factors leading the incomes of the highest earning families to grow much faster than the incomes of the average American family. If high-income males marry high-income females and low-income males marry low-income females, the net result is wider income gaps.

"Rising female participation rates are also one of the factors leading the incomes of the highest earning families to grow much faster than the incomes of the average American family."

While actual economic mating is not strictly selective, it is clearly highly selective. If one looks at the husband-wife group in which both are year-round full-time workers, a husband earning $6,000 to $7,000 per year (a minimum-wage male) is most likely to be married to a female earning $6,000 to $7,000 per year (a minimum-wage female). The middle-income male earning $20,000 to $25,000 per year is most likely to be married to a woman making $10,000 to $15,000 per year. She makes less than he does, but in comparison with other female earnings she is equally a median earner. This middle-income male's probability of being married to a woman earning more than $25,000 is, for example, just 9%. In contrast, the male earning more than $75,000 per year (the highest published male earnings category) is most likely to be married to a woman making over $25,000 per year (the highest published female earnings category)—45% are. Among such men, almost no working wives earn less than $10,000 per year.

So what? Who cares?

The distributions of income and wealth are surging toward inequality like the Hubbard Glacier, but also, like real surge glaciers, even a rapidly moving glacier moves only slowly. Economies can easily adjust to a shift in the distribution of purchasing power. They simply produce more low-income products, more high-income products, and fewer middle-income products. The discount (K-Mart) and upscale (Bloomingdale's) department stores thrive, while those in the middle (Gimbel's) go out of business. But who cares?

The 1960s public efforts to alter the distribution of income grew out of the political unrest of the civil rights movement. Black and Hispanic households still have incomes far below those of whites (only 59 and 70% that of whites, respectively), but the majority no longer seems to care and the minorities, if not happy, do not seem to be aggressively complaining.

The Japanese distribution of income is about half as unequal as that of the United States. Prior to taxes and transfers, West Germany has 28% of its population and the United States 27% of its population with less than half of the median income. After taxes and transfers, West Germany is left with only 6% of its population still with less than half of the median income while the United States is left with 17%. But so what? To say that Japanese and West Germans have or want less inequality is not to say that Americans want less inequality.

At the beginning of the Reagan administration, David Stockman announced that the distribution of income was not an appropriate subject for public remediation. That administration was overwhelmingly reelected and is still popular in the public opinion polls. Such polls also find most of the public generally satisfied with their economic circumstances.

Maybe no one cares. If so, Americans are now different from what they were in the past. The past one hundred years of American economic history is a history of government deliberately adopting policies to prevent the growing inequalities that all too often seemed to be arising. In the last half of the nineteenth century the Interstate Commerce Commission and the antitrust laws were designed to stop a growing concentration of wealth and to prevent that wealth from being used exploitatively; the railroads were not to be allowed to rip off the farmers, and the oil trust was not to be allowed to rip off the urban consumer. Mass compulsory public education was invented and designed to create an egalitarian distribution of human capital and more marketable skills so as to prevent large inequalities in earnings.

In the twentieth century, inheritance taxes and progressive income taxes were adopted to lessen inequalities. The rising inequalities of the Great Depression brought Social Security, unemployment insurance, and eventually medical insurance for the elderly and the poor to prevent people from falling out of the middle class when confronted with the harsh (old age, unemployment, illness) facts of life. Historically, government has played a major role in preventing surges in inequality. Economic surges toward inequality have always provoked political countersurges toward equality.

Whether the observed increases in inequality we are talking about here can be described as modest depends upon one's perspective (the bottom 20% of all families have seen their income share decline 18% since 1969), but regardless of whether they are labeled modest or large, they have not ended; the current surge is still under way, and no one can predict when it will stop.

Once the income distribution problem has become so acute as to create social or political unrest, it will be very difficult to solve. Politically it is a lot easier to prevent an increase in the income share of a dominant group than it is to adopt policies to take income away from that same dominant group. In economic health care, as in medical health care, prevention is always better than remediation—but, it must be admitted, just as seldom done.

Either prevention or remediation will require a return to the structural policies of the nineteenth century rather than the tax and transfer policies of the twentieth century. Whatever one thinks about the role of taxes and transfers in limiting inequality, they are clearly not the appropriate means for counteracting the current surge in inequality.

The heart of the solution will have to be found in a higher rate of growth of productivity and enhanced international competitiveness. Here the problem is not simply one of lowering the value of the dollar to regain a balance between exports and imports, although a lower valued dollar will have to be part of the cure until productivity growth can be enhanced. The American goal should not be to lower our standard of living but to raise our productivity, so that we can compete on world markets while paying wages and receiving profits second to none.

Working women are a fact of life. America has to find a way to make them a part of the solution rather than a part of the problem. If the United States wishes to avoid increasing inequality and the feminization of the lower reaches of the income distribution, it is going to have to do something to raise the earning capacities of women.

Families headed by females raise major sociological, religious, and ethical issues, but they also create an economic problem. They are never likely to provide an economic standard of living close to that enjoyed by intact two-earner families. This problem can be lessened, however, by adopting efficient social policies for insisting that fathers pay for their children even if they do not live with them.

To sum up: the United States is now in the midst of a surge in economic inequality. If history is any guide, this will sooner or later be met with a political countersurge to contain it. The nature of that countersurge remains buried, however, in the political ice.

The productivity problem

Productivity—output per hour of work—is the best general measure of a country's ability to generate a high and rising standard of living for each of its citizens. No country's citizens can for long enjoy a higher standard of living than they themselves produce, for no one can divide nonexistent output. To consume more, Americans have to produce more. Productivity measures America's ability to produce more of the goods and services, including leisure, that each of us wants.

Productivity is also a measure of the country's ability to compete as a high-wage country on world markets. To fall behind on productivity is to fall behind on introducing the new products and the new production technologies that give American products an edge on world markets. If American productivity is not equal to that of the best, the United States can compete only on the basis of wages that are lower than those of the world's productivity leaders. While it is certainly possible to compete on world markets based on low relative wage rates (most of the world does), I know of no American who wants to do so. Americans want to compete from a position of equality or superiority, not from one of inferiority.

Since World War II, productivity growth in the private economy has fallen from 3.3% (1947–65) to 2.4% (1965–72), to 1.5% (1972–78), and to 0.8% (1978–85). In 1983 and 1984 a cyclical upturn in productivity paralleled the upturn in output, but that upturn in no way reflected a change in fundamental trends. Productivity always rises rapidly at the beginning of a recovery as the costs of overhead workers in sales, finance, and administration are spread across more units of output. The 1983 and 1984 productivity gains were in fact much weaker than what would have been expected from historical experience, and in 1985 productivity grew at only 0.5% in the nonfarm business sector of the economy. America's poor productivity performance has lasted through four cyclical recoveries and is persisting through a fifth. Low productivity growth is not a problem on the way to being cured.

There are encouraging signs that American industry is now worried about its productivity performance and starting to take remedial measures, but as yet there is no statistical evidence that the problem is lessening, much less being whipped.

American productivity is best analyzed on a three-layer grid. The first grid consists of an industry-by-industry examination of productivity growth. The aim is to find those particular industry-specific problems that have led to lower productivity growth. While statistically all of the national decline can be traced to particular industries, to say that productivity has fallen in a particular industry is not to say that the cause is to be found in that industry. If the real cause of a poor productivity performance was too little capital or an unskilled, poorly motivated work force, these factors would show up as lower productivity in some industry, but the real problems would lie elsewhere. The job of the productivity analyst is to separate real industry-specific problems from those that only look as if they are industry-specific problems.

The second grid consists of the capital and labor inputs into the economy. What part of the decline in productivity can be attributed to reductions in either the quantity or quality of capital and labor going into the economy? Since higher real (inflation-corrected) earnings can only be generated by higher productivity, slowdowns in productivity growth must show up as slowdowns in income growth for some factor of production. As a result, such slowdowns in income growth can be used to attribute productivity declines to capital and labor. If real hourly earnings or returns to capital are down or growing more slowly, the earnings of these factors are down because they have become less efficient. (Technically, the economist is assuming that each factor of production is paid its marginal product and that less labor efficiency does not show up as less income for capital, or vice versa.)

As is the case with an industry-by-industry analysis, all of the slowdown in productivity growth can be attributed to deteriorations in either capital or labor, since declining productivity must be matched by declining incomes for some factor of production. As before, however, attribution is not necessarily causation. If the real productivity problem was an industry-specific problem, such as having to drill deeper (use more resources) to find fewer barrels of oil, then this industry-specific problem would show up as lower average earnings for capital and labor in the oil-drilling industry. To diagnose the problem as a capital-labor problem would be to misdiagnose it. Real capital-labor problems must be separated from phony ones.

The third grid is composed of adverse external shocks such as sudden large jumps in energy prices, the imposition of new environmental or safety rules, or droughts that lower farm output per unit of input. Some adverse shocks such as environmental regulations are controllable; others, such as droughts, are not. At this point, however, the goal is simply to determine what part of the observed decline is caused by factors external to the economy itself.

The productivity analyst must move across this three-layered grid searching for the ultimate causal factors. As is always true in economics, judgment is required before we can assign causation to different statistical results. Numbers are often true but misleading, or meaningless.

Specific industry problems

Statistically, the national decline in productivity can be disaggregated into slower productivity growth rates within individual industries and into shifts in output from high productivity industries to low productivity industries. If productivity growth rates are examined within industry, there is unrelieved gloom. No industry in the period from 1978 to 1985 had a higher rate of productivity growth than it did from 1948 to 1965, and while there were *no* industries with falling productivity in the first period, there were five such in the latter one. Each year these industries were slightly less efficient.

When industries are examined there seem to be five specific problems:

(1) The shift out of agriculture. From 1948 to 1965 the movement out of agriculture was strongly enhancing of national productivity growth. Although agriculture has had an above-average rate of growth of productivity since World War II, it had, and still has, a level of productivity well below that of other industries. In 1948 agriculture's productivity was just 40% of the national average. As a result, every worker released from agriculture and employed by other industries represented, on average, a 60 percentage point jump in productivity.

From 1948 to 1965, 9.1 billion man-hours of work (or 8% of the total number of hours worked in the entire private economy) left agriculture to enter industrial employment. By the early 1970s, however, this process was nearing an end, and after 1978 the number of people leaving agriculture was small relative to the entire work force.

As agriculture declined from 17 to 3% of all hours worked, national productivity growth was being enhanced. A very low productivity industry was shrinking, and its workers were taking jobs with much higher productivity. But this source of national productivity growth had to end—no industry can forever shrink. This shrinkage of agricultural employment explains about 12% of the observed drop in the national productivity growth.

Agricultural machinery, such as these potato-gathering machines, has drastically reduced man-hours needed in the industry. *"From 1948 to 1965 the [worker] movement out of agriculture was strongly enhancing of national productivity growth. . . . But this source of national productivity growth had to end—no industry can forever shrink."*

Identifying a cause does not, however, automatically lead to a solution. The United States cannot go back to the era when workers were leaving agriculture in massive numbers and contributing to national productivity growth. Agriculture no longer employs a large fraction of the labor force. America is faced with a new stage in its development. To get the old rate of productivity growth, new sources of productivity growth will have to be found.

(2) A mystery in construction. Where construction's productivity was once well above the national average, it is now 39% below the national average and 25% below its own 1968 peak. Construction productivity has been falling for most of the past fifteen years.

Because the construction industry builds the plants and installs the equipment used by other industries, a fall in construction productivity is much more important than its own size (6% of total hours of work) would indicate. If a country's construction industry becomes inefficient, the costs of installing plant and equipment rise for other industries; less plant and equipment can be purchased per dollar spent. These other industries consequently buy less plant and equipment and, having invested less, suffer from slower rates of productivity growth. With inferior construction productivity, U.S. Steel and Nippon Steel, for example, could buy identical steel mills and U.S. Steel would still not be able to compete, since it would cost U.S. Steel more to set up the mill in the United States than it would cost Nippon Steel to set up the same mill in Japan. As a consequence, construction productivity has major ripple effects on the rest of the economy.

If construction productivity had continued to grow at its 1948–65 pace instead of falling, 13% of the decline in national productivity would have disappeared. The decline in construction productivity is a major mystery, however. No one knows what caused it; no one knows how to reverse it. Various explanations for the decline in construction productivity have been advanced, but none of them is entirely convincing. Inefficient union work rules are one possibility, but this suggestion has to confront the fact that unionized construction is rapidly becoming a smaller and smaller fraction of total construction. If union work rules were the problem, one would expect to see productivity grow as unions become less important in the construction business. In fact, the decline in unionization and the decline in productivity have gone hand in hand.

To generate falling productivity from restrictive work rules it is also necessary to argue, not just that inefficient work rules exist, but that these inefficient work rules have been growing at a very rapid rate. Although such restrictive union practices certainly exist, there simply is not any evidence that they have been growing.

Some have suggested the problem is caused by statistical weaknesses in the way in which construction productivity is measured. Productivity is simply inflation-adjusted real output divided by hours of work. This means that to measure productivity, current dollar expenditures on construction must be deflated by some price index to yield real output. Since construction does not produce a homogeneous output, however, inflation is difficult to measure. If construction inflation was being systematically overestimated, then construction output would be simultaneously systematically underestimated, and construction productivity estimates would be too low.

There is some evidence to support such a conclusion. From 1954 to 1977 construction output was officially estimated to have risen 58%, but the use of construction materials (tons of steel, concrete, etc.) rose 133%. Few believe that 1977 buildings took more than twice as many materials as 1954 buildings. On the other hand, the government price index is basically an index constructed from data taken from some major private builders and buyers of construction. If government construction inflation estimates are wrong, the analyst must believe that major builders, such as the Turner Construction Company, and major users of construction, such as the American Telephone and Telegraph Company and the Bureau of Public Roads, do not know their own construction costs. Few observers want to make such an assertion.

Alternatively, construction productivity may have got bogged down in shifts from simple to complex outputs. Where the construction industry used to build simple interstate highways across the wide open spaces of Kansas, it is now building urban interstates, such as the proposed West Side Highway in New York City, where millions of wires and pipes have to be moved before construction can even begin. Where the construction industry used to build coal-fired or oil-fired electrical generating stations, it is now building complex bogged-down nuclear generating plants. Since construction output in the case of electrical generating plants output is measured in terms of kilowatts of installed capacity, long-drawn-out fights over safety show up as fewer plants completed and less output per hour of work in the construction industry.

Or, the decline may be a straightforward case where workers have got lazy and are simply doing less work per hour than their fathers before them. Within the construction industry most observers think that the decline is real but perhaps exaggerated in the government numbers.

Construction productivity is a major part of America's productivity problem, but no one knows what really caused the decline or what can be done about it.

(3) A geological blow in mining. The reasons for the decline in mining productivity are as clear as those in construction are mysterious. In 1983 mining productivity was 37% below where it was in 1972, but there was a simple explanation. Approximately 80% of the answer was found in oil and gas, the major mineral "mined" in the United States. The American oil industry is progressing up a rapidly rising cost curve because of geological depletion. There is a lot of oil yet to be found, but it is much more expensive to find it. Since output is measured not in feet drilled but in oil lifted out of the ground, productivity falls when production declines in old wells and when new wells yield less oil per foot drilled. Because of geological depletion, it takes many more hours of work to produce a barrel of oil. In addition, any expansion of drilling, such as that which occurred after the first and second OPEC oil shocks, adds hours of work to the mining industry well before it adds more output—oil or gas lifted. In 1983, with a cutback in marginal drilling activities, mining productivity rose 15.2%. This did not completely offset the 22% decline that had occurred from 1977 to 1982, but it went a long way.

The remaining 20% of the decline in mining productivity is to be found in the other minerals mined in the United States. Here environmental protection and occupational safety (third-grid effects) probably played a role; there is little evidence of rapid geological depletion of ore bodies. If open-pit mines have to be filled and the land restored to its natural contours, more hours of work are required to mine a ton of coal. If better ventilation and more tunnel supports are required to protect underground miners, more hours of work are necessary to mine a ton of copper.

To the extent that the productivity problem is caused by fewer ac-

An oil exploration and production rig in Texas. *"The American oil industry is progressing up a rapidly rising cost curve because of geological depletion."*

cidents or a cleaner environment, the measured productivity problem is less of a problem than it seems. In the past fifteen years, deaths in underground mining have been reduced from three to two per million hours of work. The air is better to breathe and there is less environmental damage than there used to be in mining areas. Neither of these is counted in conventional measures of mining output, yet they contribute to the well-being of American citizens. If the benefits of such factors had been included in mining productivity, it would not have declined as much as it did. Such outputs are not counted, since no one knows how to weigh the value of a life saved versus a ton of copper produced. Those interested in environmentalism and mining safety may be faulted for not finding the most efficient ways to get the desired results, but the heart of the productivity problem in mining is not to be found in environmentalism or safety. The measured effects are small, and even those small effects are to some extent a statistical artifact of defects in the way in which mining output is calculated.

If mining productivity had continued to grow at its 1948–65 rate of 4.3% per year, 6% of the national productivity decline would have disappeared. Most of this 6%, however, is an uncontrollable geological blow from Mother Nature: fewer pools of cheap oil yet to be found in the United States.

(4) The demand for electricity. Part of the national productivity decline flows from gas, water, and electrical utilities, where productivity growth

has fallen from $+6.3\%$ per year to -0.9% per year. If productivity had continued to grow at its old rate of 6.3% per year, 13% of the national productivity decline would have disappeared. While the causes of the decline in utility productivity are crystal clear, clarity does not automatically lead to an equally clear solution, unfortunately.

Utilities employ most of their workers installing and maintaining the distributing systems that deliver electricity, gas, or water to their customers. Relatively few workers are actually employed producing electricity, gas, or water. When the demand for utility output rises rapidly, productivity rises rapidly. Output is up, but more workers do not have to be employed, since the extra output can be sold through the existing distribution system. Conversely, when demand falls, productivity falls. Less output is being produced, but almost the same work force is necessary to maintain the distribution system. As a result, utility productivity is a direct function of the rate of growth of output. If output grows rapidly, as it did from 1948 to 1965, productivity grows rapidly. If output grows slowly, as it did from 1972 to 1977, productivity grows slowly. If output falls, as it did from 1977 to 1979, productivity falls.

The decline in utility productivity is in a class with oil depletion or agriculture when it comes to public remedies. There are none. If energy prices rise rapidly, energy consumption will fall and productivity must fall with it. Since energy prices seem to have peaked and are now falling, one would expect that utility productivity would rebound and continue to grow at the 3.6% rate of 1983 in the next few years. Barring another OPEC oil shock, the worst is behind us on the utility front.

Together, mining and utilities represent the direct "energy" blow (a third-grid effect) to productivity. The decline in oil-mining productivity is one of the reasons that energy prices are up, and higher energy prices lead to lower utility productivity. When these direct effects are added to the indirect effects (industry has to devote a larger part of its investment funds to saving energy rather than raising labor's productivity), the energy shocks probably explain about 20% of the national productivity decline. This 20%, however, is not an additional 20%. It is simply a different way of viewing the decline in mining and utility productivity.

(5) *Expanding services.* Services are the mirror image of agriculture. Agriculture was a rapidly declining low-productivity industry; services are a rapidly growing low-productivity industry. While agriculture's decline enhanced productivity growth, the expansion of services dampens it.

Services have been braking national productivity growth since World War II, but the brakes have been gradually tightening as service productivity falls farther and farther behind that of the rest of the economy. Back in 1948, when service productivity was 96% of the national average, moving a worker into services only lowered national productivity 4 percentage points. By 1983 service productivity had fallen to 61%

of the national average, and every worker who moved into services represented a 39-percentage-point decline in productivity.

Services have been growing very rapidly and since 1978 have been absorbing about two-thirds of all of the hours of work added to the private economy. Of these billion hours of new work, 36% went into health care, heavily into nursing homes, and 36% went into business and legal services (accountants, lawyers, consultants, etc.).

Health care in many ways is like safety and environmentalism. Nursing homes account for a major share of the growth of the health-care industry; yet bathing, feeding, and caring for grandmother is intrinsically a labor-intensive, low-productivity industry. If each of us took care of grandmother at home, as the Japanese do, grandmother would not show up as part of the productivity problem. Taking care of grandmother in a nursing home, however, has some advantages in terms of the well-being of the children who do not have to tie themselves to the care of an elderly sick person. Their well-being is not counted in conventional measures of health-care output.

The same problem exists in the rest of the health-care industry. Infant mortality has been cut in half over the last two decades, and life expectancy at age sixty-five rose three years in the decade of the 1970s—this as compared with a rise of only half a year every ten years in the decades of the 1950s and 1960s.

Lower infant mortality rates and longer life expectancy are worth having. As productivity is measured, however, hours of work devoted to this end will show up as declining productivity. More hours are worked without producing more output, since health-care output is measured in terms of treatments given rather than less illness or longer life expectancy. Even in cases where treatments fail, people feel better knowing that an effort is being made to save their lives. Such feelings may be assigned no value in productivity statistics, but they have value nevertheless.

At the same time, a country can be spending too much on health care and have a health-care industry which is a real as well as a statistical drag on national productivity growth. To determine this, however, it is necessary to examine the health-care sector and not just productivity statistics.

When it comes to the growing army of American business and legal consultants, there simultaneously is and is not a measurement problem. Since consultants give advice, it is difficult to measure their output directly. But if the quality of their advice is being underestimated in measures of service productivity, the unmeasured benefits will show up in higher productivity in the industries taking their good advice. The benefits cannot disappear. With an across-the-board slower rate of growth of industrial productivity, however, there is no evidence that consultants are having large positive effects which are incorrectly being attributed to industries other than their own. Legal and business services are being accorded a very slow rate of growth of productivity in the statistics, and they deserve it.

Legal services, for example, are mostly a zero-sum game. Suppose you fall down on my unshoveled sidewalk and sue me. If you win, you get to take some of my old output (income) away from me, but the process does not generate any new output that can increase the total income flowing to the two of us. Since the legal process consumes hours, the economy's hours of work are up without any equivalent increase in its output, and productivity is consequently down.

If service industries had not grown relative to the rest of the economy, 12% of the observed decline in national productivity would have disappeared. Alternatively, if service employment had grown, but service productivity had held pace with that of the rest of the economy (stayed at 96% of the national average), 9% of the observed decline in productivity would have disappeared.

Services illustrate the complexities of the productivity problem. Bathing and feeding old people may be intrinsically a low-productivity occupation, but every American wants to be bathed and fed when old. Lawyers may be a drag on productivity, but Americans are using them in prodigious numbers. Productivity statistics do not care whether you or some thief has your new stereo, but you care, and you hire an "unproductive" security guard. In 1985, 615,000 private security guards (up more than 40% in the previous eight years) were on private American payrolls. That is a lot of workers who in a more honest society could be productively employed making new goods and services rather than "unproductively" employed guarding old ones.

When the industry-specific first-grid effects from agriculture, mining, construction, utilities, and services are added together, they provide an explanation for slightly more than half the total slowdown in productivity growth. Where cures are possible they need to be applied, but to a great extent the United States needs new offsetting sources of productivity growth that up to now have not yet been found. Much of the decline that has been identified is irreversible and none is easily reversed.

The American problem is not so much correcting old bad habits as developing new good habits. Old veins of productivity ore have become depleted; new veins will have to be discovered if the country is to achieve the productivity performance it needs to match the international competition.

The capital-labor ratio

Inadequate investment in plant and equipment is a second-grid effect. Although Americans certainly invest too little, the problem is not quite as simple as it seems. Consider the following puzzle: In the years from

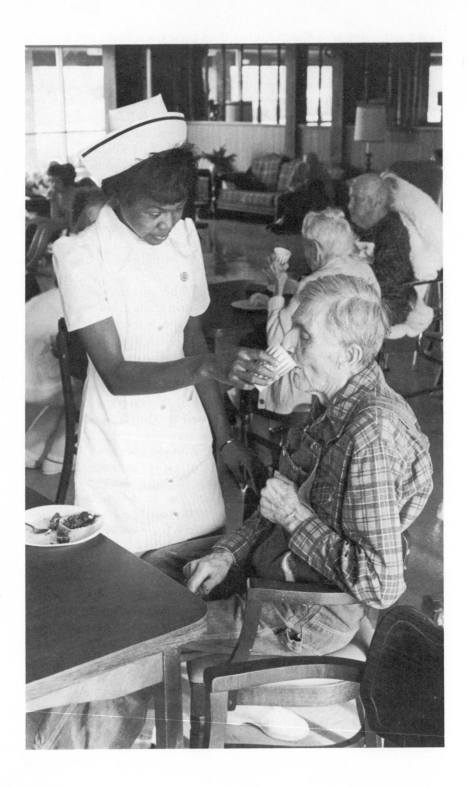

Work in service industries such as nursing home care (left), and private security (above) have accounted for two-thirds of all new work hours since 1978. *"While agriculture's decline enhanced productivity growth, the expansion of services dampens it."*

1948 to 1965, when productivity was growing at 3.3% per year, Americans invested 9.5% of the GNP in plant and equipment. In the years from 1978 to 1985, when productivity was growing at 0.8% per year, Americans invested 11.6% of the GNP. Investment went up 21% while productivity growth fell 76%. Why?

The answer is to be found in the baby boom. The average American works with $58,000 worth of plant and equipment. To reach average productivity levels, new workers must be equipped with $58,000 worth of plant and equipment. Implicitly the parents of the baby-boom generation were promising not just to bathe, feed, and educate their babies but to save $58,000 to equip each of their babies to enter the labor force twenty years later as the average American worker. For every wife who entered the labor force the family was implicitly promising to save another $58,000.

These implicit promises were not kept. Investment was up, but the labor force was growing much faster (up from 0.4% per year in the mid-1950s to 3% per year in the late 1970s). What was once a rising capital-labor ratio had become a falling capital-labor ratio—not because Americans were investing less, but because the labor force was growing much faster. With a falling capital-labor ratio, stagnant productivity should come as no surprise.

The amount of equipment per worker—the capital-labor ratio—is one of the key ingredients in any model of productivity growth. New equipment allows labor to produce more output per hour of work, but it is also a carrier of new technologies. To put new, more productive technologies to work, new equipment has to be built to embody the new technologies. New knowledge without new equipment is often useless. One cannot work with robots unless one has robots in the first place.

The observed slowdown in the growth of plant and equipment per worker explains about 22% of the national productivity decline.

The adverse effects of the baby boom were compounded by two energy shocks and by environmentalism. To the extent that investments are made to control pollution or cut energy usage, there are fewer funds left to raise labor productivity. There are no hard official estimates of how much of our plant and equipment has gone into energy-saving investments since 1972, although it must be substantial, but about 5% of American plant and equipment investment has gone into pollution and safety controls. If this investment is subtracted from the totals, the slowdown in the growth of plant and equipment per worker can explain something like 25% of the total slowdown—perhaps a little more if one remembers the role of capital as a carrier of new technologies.

The slowdown in the growth of America's capital-labor ratio, however, was not due to stupidity or irrationality. It was a perfectly rational market response to the economic facts of life. Firms invest to raise the capital-labor ratio when it is profitable to do so. Technical change brings about such investments, but they are also brought about by changes in the relative price of capital and labor. When the cost of capital falls relative to the cost of labor, firms find it cheaper to raise production by investing in capital than by hiring more workers. With fewer workers and more capital, output per hour of work rises. Conversely, when capital becomes more expensive relative to labor, firms find it cheaper to raise production by hiring more workers and the capital-labor ratio falls. With less capital and more workers, output per hour of work falls.

In the aftermath of a baby boom, simple supply and demand predict that as the supply of labor rises, wage rates fall. With wages down, capital becomes relatively more expensive. Firms shift technologies, replacing expensive machines with cheap workers. Labor productivity falls. From the point of supply and demand, the economy has been behaving precisely as it is supposed to behave. Economic signals have been calling for a reduction in the capital-labor ratio. Whereas the cost of labor (wages plus fringe benefits) was rising 1% per year relative to the cost of capital (a cost which includes the initial purchase price, the energy cost of operating the plant and equipment, and the interest cost of financing it) from 1948 to 1965, the relative price of labor was falling. Where American workers were once becoming expensive relative to machines, they are now becoming cheap relative to machines.

Given such a sharp shift in the movement of the relative prices of capital and labor, it is not surprising that there was a decline in the capital-labor ratio. Business firms were doing exactly what economic incentives were calling for. One can imagine other offsetting factors (a sharp increase in the savings rate) which if they had occurred would have offset the impacts of population growth, but these potentially offsetting factors did not occur.

In some ways the United States is over the hump with respect to the baby-boom generation. Most of them are now at work, and the growth of the labor force will slow appreciably in the late 1980s and 1990s as the baby-dearth generations following the baby-boom generation enter the labor force. Female labor force participation rates are also rising to levels where the growth in female participation must slow down. Both energy prices and interest costs also seem to be mitigating. As a result, some of the decline caused by a slower rate of growth of the capital-labor ratio should disappear without remedial action.

Looking forward, the United States should enjoy a productivity rebound into the 1 to 1.5% range without doing anything to achieve it. Such a rate, however, while better than what has been occurring, is not adequate. It does not come close to closing the productivity growth gap between America and its international competitors.

Even if the United States were living in a world by itself, 1 to 1.5% productivity growth rates would be inadequate if the country were to successfully absorb the baby-boom generation. Slow productivity growth is apt to produce unacceptable social and political results. With slow productivity growth, standards of living rise much more slowly than they have in the past. While Americans could get used to this new reality, the process of lowering expectations is not apt to be smooth. This is especially true for the baby-boom generation, which will end up with lifetime standards of living lower than those of both their parents and their children. (When older Americans bemoan the fact that their children will not be able to afford the house that they live in, this is precisely the problem to which they are implicitly referring.) A democracy only uneasily lives with what will see itself as a "deprived" generation.

Wanting a different result is a rational social desire, but not one which can be implemented by simply liberating free enterprise. The market is giving America the market solution, but it is a solution that Americans do not want to live with and do not have to live with if they are willing to organize themselves socially to change the parameters within which the market works. If Americans, for example, were to save much more, then capital's relative price would fall and labor would once again find itself working with a rapidly rising capital-labor ratio. Such changes do not happen automatically. Institutions and incentives have to be socially restructured to bring about the desired market result. One cannot fight the market, but one can channel it.

White-collar productivity

If the industry-specific problems and the capital-labor problems are added together, one has an explanation for about 75% of the observed decline in productivity growth. The remaining part of the problem is to be found in what might be called management inefficiency, but perhaps more accurately is seen as a basic failing of human nature. Human beings will almost always attempt to use new technologies in old-fashioned ways, and when they do so the beneficial productivity effects of those new technologies are often lost.

As mentioned, business productivity grew 0.8% per year between 1978 and 1985. Over that same period of time, the number of blue-collar workers on American payrolls declined by 1.9 million or 6%, while the real business GNP was rising by 16%. If one produces 16% more with 6% less, one has had a 22% gain in productivity, or an annual growth rate of 2.9%. When it comes to blue-collar productivity, the United States had a world-class rate of growth.

However, American firms were simultaneously adding ten million white-collar workers to their payrolls. This represented a 21% increase. If one needs 21% more employees to produce a 16% gain in output, one has had a 5% fall in productivity. Since in 1985 there were currently fifty-eight million white-collar workers and only thirty million blue-collar workers on American payrolls, the decline in white-collar productivity wiped out much of the gain in blue-collar productivity.

Viewed from this perspective, what the United States has is not a general productivity problem but an office productivity problem. The American factory works; the American office does not. Why? A good question, but one that is outside of traditional microeconomic analysis, where managers are assumed to be as efficient as it is possible to be.

Productivity comparisons with the rest of the world simultaneously reveal a white-collar productivity problem and some systematic failure of American managers to manage the office successfully. Studies of the relative cost of producing the Escort automobile in different countries show that 40% of the Japanese cost advantage is due to lower white-collar overheads in Japan than in the United States. When Japanese managers take over existing American enterprises they often dramatically reduce the number of white-collar workers. Too often they are reported to be getting higher productivity out of American workers than American managers. Something systematic must be wrong with American management.

Such comparisons have led to a lot of recent talk about reducing white-collar overheads in American industry but no action. In 1985 real output rose 2.1%. Yet the number of executives and managers on American payrolls rose by 5.6% and the number of what the Department of Labor now calls "administrative support staff" rose by 3.5%.

Why should the administrative support staff of American industry have to rise almost twice as fast as output, and why should the number of executives have to rise almost three times as fast? Why is there a recognition of the problem but no action?

This situation is even more puzzling if one remembers that the United States is supposed to be in the midst of an office automation revolution, and that investments in office automation have accounted for a large fraction of total business investment in recent years. New technology, new hardware, new software, and new skills are all going into the American office, but negative productivity is coming out. Why?

If one asks seriously why office productivity is falling while investments in office productivity are rising, one has to confront a set of factors that are left out of conventional economic analysis. Among them are power (American bosses exist to boss), style (a good boss should know everything and in principle have the knowledge to make all decisions), institutions (most middle-level managers get paid based on the number of people who report to them), peer pressure (it is harder to fire those who directly work with you than those at a distance), and beliefs (if the system is based solely upon individual effort, there is no need for group motivation, voluntary cooperation, or teamwork). None of these appears in what economists call "the theory of the firm." They simply are not important when it comes to efficiency.

Take the proposition that the best boss is the boss that has the most knowledge and can intelligently make the most decisions per day. In the late 1960s and early 1970s the business press (*Fortune, Forbes, Business Week*) set up bosses such as Harold Geneen of ITT as role models. According to them he was the "world's greatest business manager." His was a "managerial system of tight control" with "elements of a spy system." He "worked extraordinarily long hours and absorbed thousands of details about ITT's businesses." "Tales of Geneen's incredible stamina at these marathon affairs and of his brutality to any manager who dared to dissemble before him are retold today like epic poems." "Everything the company does is totally number-oriented." "His unique form of management allows him fingertip control over his vast empire." One could not decide if he was an ogre in a business suit, the greatest corporate manager of his time, an unimaginative numbers grubber, or a great leader of men.

Geneen and managers like him supposedly knew more about middle-level management jobs than the middle-level managers themselves knew, and they were famous for making thousands of rapid decisions. He was the prototypical boss who bossed. He was the macho manager whom lesser managers should attempt to emulate. Just as children copy the basketball styles and techniques of professional heroes, so do young business managers copy the styles and techniques of their ideal prototypes.

Such beliefs about the ideal boss may have long existed, but most managers could not have implemented them without the technological office revolution that is now under way. Previously firms had to decentralize and bosses had to defer decisions to those on the scene since there was no feasible way for them to know what they had to know to make good decisions. With the onset of a new information technology and the office revolution, bosses could implement that desired style. A lot more information could be gotten much more rapidly. Bosses could do a lot more bossing.

To do so, however, one had to build up enormous information bureaucracies. Information could be gotten, but only at the cost of adding a lot of white-collar workers; and, if there was an improvement in the quality of decision making from all of the information that could now be moved up the corporate hierarchy, the positive effects on output were smaller than the huge number of extra information workers that had to be added to the system. Information was moved faster from place to place, but productivity fell.

The problem is seen graphically in accounting. As mentioned, output rose 16% from 1978 to 1985, but the number of accountants on American payrolls rose 30%, from 1 million to 1.3 million. Computers made accounting more efficient, but that efficiency was not used to reduce the employment of accountants but to increase the frequency and types of accounting. Accounts that had formerly been evaluated every three months were ordered up every day. Whole systems of new accounts (management information systems, cost accounting, inventory control, financial accounting, etc.) that were previously impossible to calculate were invented and implemented. Yet there was no evidence that all of these new accounts with their increased frequency improved decision making enough to justify their cost. In fact, as the data at the beginning of this paragraph indicate, there was clear evidence to the contrary. Power and style, however, called for ordering up all of those accounts, and it was done.

The economy is rife with such examples. Banking enjoyed not just a computer revolution in accounting but a robot revolution (ATMs) in dealing with its customers, yet its employment went up faster than its real output, and productivity fell.

The institutional reasons for such an outcome are not hard to find. The ideal is perfect knowledge. No rational man is deliberately ignorant. To improve performance one must improve knowledge. To the local boss information seems to be a free good. Bosses order it from subordinates and the cost of acquiring it appears on the budgets of the subordinates. Subordinates in turn neither can refuse to provide it nor are they in a position to know whether it is worth the costs of acquisition. Costs are irrelevant and not even calculated since one must do what the boss orders. Both boss and subordinate are in a way imprisoned in standard operating procedures. What comes about is an institutional set of blinders and a double standard of management—there is a vice-president for factory productivity but none for office productivity.

Beliefs about how one *should* operate are important, since they condition what we do. Consider the conventional medical rule for stopping treatment—one may "do no harm." Employing every available procedure up to the point where it actively starts to harm the patient does not cost very much as long as there is not very much technology that can be employed in most illnesses. If technology develops and presents us with a lot of very expensive technologies with very marginal payoffs, however, the same stopping rule can become a very expensive stopping rule that society cannot afford to implement.

So it is with "know everything." As long as the technology did not exist to implement that stopping rule, it was not very harmful, but when a technology came along that in principle made it possible to know everything, that stopping rule became very expensive and led to the need for a very large number of white-collar workers to keep that information system working.

While those with efficient stopping rules will eventually drive those with inefficient stopping rules out of business, the efficient firms need not be American firms, and driving the inefficient out of business may take a long time. Despite international competitive pressures from foreign firms with lower white-collar overheads, American firms, as we have seen, are still adding white-collar overheads much faster than they are adding output. Beliefs about the "right" style change very slowly.

Factors of power emerge, since to do away with those white-collar workers is to delegate one's decision-making powers to others on the spot who have the information necessary to act without the benefit of an information system. To do so is to become a boss who does less bossing, but this is contrary to one's conception of one's own role. No one becomes a boss in order to do less bossing.

Participatory management may be an efficient method to cut the white-collar labor force and raise productivity, but it requires a reduction in the boss's power. Among the conventional words of wisdom it violates are that:

"The participative process doesn't always fit easily with traditional management methods and measurements."

"Fearing a loss of power, many middle managers torpedoed early participative programs."

"The higher up the corporate ladder, the tougher seems the shift to the participative mode."

"Information is power, and access to it remains a clear badge of rank to managers."*

---

*Bill Saporito, "The Revolt Against 'Working Smarter'," *Fortune*, 21 July 1986, 59–60.

Japanese managers have moved decentralization and participatory management into the mainstream of efficiency enhancement precisely because they had other badges of rank and systems of power. Their status did not flow from knowing the numbers better than their subordinates.

Consider shop-floor inventory control as it is done at the end of the shift on the Toyota assembly lines. Letting the assembly-line workers do inventory control may increase the variety in the tasks performed by blue-collar assembly-line workers, and may as a result increase their motivation to do a good job, but the major efficiency gains are not to be found in motivation among these blue-collar workers; they occur in the fact that their activity permits the complete elimination of a staff of white-collar inventory-control workers and the information system that is necessary to support their activities.

Efforts to allow shop-floor employees to purchase equipment directly rather than using purchasing agents has a similar payoff. Motivation may increase when workers want to prove that their purchasing decisions were good purchasing decisions, but the real efficiency gains are to be found in reducing the industrial engineers and their supporting staffs who used to be responsible for such purchasing decisions.

Traditionally, American plants have had "locked" numerically controlled machine tools, while the Europeans and Japanese have "unlocked" numerically controlled machine tools. The difference between locked and unlocked numerically controlled machine tools is whether blue-collar workers are allowed to change the programming (unlocked), or whether only a group of white-collar programmers is allowed to alter the programming. In the latter case, the machines are locked to prevent blue-collar workers from altering the system.

Efficiency would seem to be all on the side of the unlocked machines. A large staff of white-collar programmers does not have to be maintained, an information system does not have to be developed so that blue-collar operators can tell white-collar programmers that something has gone wrong, and downtime is reduced since the program corrections can be instantly made without waiting for the white-collar programmers to show up. But American firms have mostly opted for locked machines.

The issue seems to be one of power and control. With a locked machine management has more control and can set the pace of work. Locked numerically controlled machine tools were in fact sold as devices for capturing the initiative on the pace of work from assembly-line workers and increasing management control. In the words of *Iron Age,* a respected trade journal, "Workers and their unions have too much say in manufacturers' destiny, many metalworking executives feel that large, sophisticated Flexible Manufacturing Systems can help wrest some of that control away from labor and put it back in the hands of management where it belongs." If control is the issue, locked machines may dominate unlocked machines, but if enhanced productivity is the issue, it is clear that unlocked machines dominate locked ones.

In addition to the loss of power and control with shop-floor inventory control, shop-floor purchasing, and unlocked machine tools in the American system, managers face a direct reduction in their own salaries if they become efficient and reduce white-collar overheads. What manager is going to make such a shift in functions when he and his peers get paid according to the number of workers that report to them? To take actions to make the firm more efficient is to reduce one's own salary. It is also going to reduce one's own promotion opportunities, since a reduction in white-collar employees will reduce the number of bosses necessary to manage the system. When faced with a current and future reduction in their prospects, few are going to support enthusiastically any such shift in the standard operating procedures of American industry.

Or, consider word processors and the failure of office automation to yield the predicted gains in productivity. Not even in the companies that make office computers can anyone show hard data that such machinery pays off with higher productivity. The source of the failure is to be found in the interaction of a number of institutional realities.

As with shop-floor inventory control or shop-floor purchasing, management salaries are reduced when white-collar employees are eliminated. Even more important, to use office automation efficiently requires major changes in office sociology. The efficient way to use word processors is to eliminate secretaries or clerks and have managers type their own memos and call up their own files, but a personal secretary is an office badge of prestige and power. No one wants to give up that badge.

To shift to the new technology also requires managers without good keyboard skills to go through a transition period in which they look clumsy and get work done more slowly on the machines than when it was being done for them by others. Few bosses can maintain their prestige, power, and self-respect while publicly looking clumsy in front of their subordinates. They will order the assembly-line people to shift from human to robot welding, but they will not order themselves to shift from human to computer typing and filing. Those who might consider it face peer pressure not to fire those who are physically near them. If those like you can be fired, you can be fired. No one likes to be reminded of that fact of life; hence, American industry is much more ruthless when it comes to eliminating blue-collar workers than it is with white-collar workers.

Almost every American firm has a vice-president for factory productivity; almost no American firm has a vice-president for office productivity. In the 1981–82 recession 90% of the firms who laid off blue-collar workers laid off not a single white-collar worker.

In the American system, to fire managers below oneself is to open up the possibility of being fired by managers higher than oneself. A good illustration of the problem is to be found in the American armed forces. There are as many generals and admirals today with two million troops in uniform as there were in World War II with twelve million troops in uniform. Why? The answer is simple. What general or admiral wants to reduce the opportunities to become a general or admiral? If the existing generals were to reduce the number of middle-level officers, there would automatically have to be a cutback in the number of generals, for you could not have a system with more generals than colonels.

In Europe and Japan, where management salaries are more seniority dependent (not so dependent upon "merit" or the number of people reporting to one) and layoffs very rare, reducing white-collar overheads is not seen as such a personal threat to management as it is in the United States. Paradoxically, the real threat of firing managers ends up by producing a system with more managers than one in which there is little real danger of a manager being fired because improvements in efficiency have been achieved.

In experiment after experiment with participatory management, the problems have not been found among workers or in inefficient production but among middle-level managers who feel threatened. They *feel* threatened and block experiments with new, more efficient forms of production because they *are* threatened. The personal dangers in the American system are not imaginary but real. Personal rationality intervenes to prevent system rationality and system efficiency from being achieved.

Productivity gains are dependent upon the development as well as the use of new technologies. The pattern of research and development in American firms differs from that in Japan and Europe by having more process R&D and less new product R&D. Both ultimately end up producing higher productivity, but at every moment new process R&D has a bigger effect on productivity than new product R&D, since any economy is heavily weighted toward old rather than new products. Ultimately, new products become important, but new products are much easier to copy from the competition than new processes. One can buy a new product, tear it apart, and learn how it is made—a process called reverse engineering. One cannot reverse engineer a competitor's new process, however, since it is not possible to buy a copy of the new process to see how it works.

This structural difference is not caused, however, by American stupidity. It is endemic to the structure of organization. New processes require that you change old established ways of production. This requires managers who can manage people and persuade them to efficiently shift to new processes. If people were interchangeable parts, the view inherent in much of American management and American economics would be correct and such shifts would present no special problems, but people are not interchangeable. Sociologically, it is far easier to set up a new plant for a new product than it is to change production processes in old plants. In a system in which people are paid for the skills they use at work and are fired when improvements in efficiency make them superfluous, new process technologies are threatening to the incomes and employment of both workers and managers in those facilities. Unenthusiastic support (foot-dragging) on everyone's part can quickly turn a profitable new process technology into an unprofitable one.

Compared with the inherent human difficulties of managing new processes, mergers look like the easy route to economic success for both the firm and the managers. The firm expands in old markets without having to adopt new technologies, and the managers whose salaries are keyed to sales get big bonuses when sales rise as a result of a merger. But, for the economy as a whole, mergers do not lead to more productivity, while new process technologies do.

Here again, what is rational at the individual level is not rational at the social level. In an economy based on the principle that the engine of economic change is the individual operating alone, however, no one has the responsibility to insure that individual activity does in fact lead to improvements in system efficiency.

Standard operating procedures have a strong hold on the human mind. A Wang executive recently told me about an incident in which they investigated why a Wang Taiwanese facility had much lower production costs than the same American facility, even after correction for wage differences. They found that the differences were to be found in a lot of small standard operating procedures like the provision of telephones for every white-collar worker. Most white-collar workers make very few business phone calls each day and could easily use a central phone bank. American blue-collar workers are not provided with private phones. No one phone is terribly expensive, but when you add up the costs for thousands of white-collar workers, it becomes important. Phones are also part of the information system. Without them, one is not really hooked in. They are a symbol of white-collar power and importance, and taking them away from workers would be a traumatic affair. Replicate such procedures a few times, and we are talking about a significant savings in inputs, but the savings are not made because to do so would require a confrontation with those standard operating procedures and our view of ourselves.

In the end, the economic model that you believe to be true makes a difference. If you think of the recommendations for replacing today's wage system with a bonus system like that of the Japanese, replacing profit maximization with value-added maximization, or eliminating the fast track for young managers, you will not get far with a believer in microeconomics, who will tell you that none of those changes could possibly enhance productivity growth. That conclusion is not something he has to investigate empirically; it is something he knows.

People are paid in accordance with their marginal productivity. How one writes the check—hourly, monthly, or partly in the form of a bonus keyed to some measure of performance—is irrelevant. Human workers only look at the bottom line, the total sum they are being paid, and are not going to be affected by the institutional means whereby that sum is delivered to them.

A firm organized as a profit maximizer who hires and fires workers to maximize those profits has to be more efficient than a firm organized as a valued-added maximizing partnership in which the partners are not fired when sales decline. Efficiency depends upon the quality and quantity of inputs, not upon the institutional forms of organization. When redundant labor is fired rather than retained, the system has to be more efficient, since workers are more rapidly moved into the open labor market where supply and demand can allocate them to new activities.

From the microeconomic perspective a firm that quickly promotes what seem to be promising managers onto the fast track (the American pattern) should do better than one that keeps managers working as a cohort with roughly the same pay and a rotation of jobs and does not start the fast track until managers are in their forties (the Japanese pattern), since it learns earlier to take advantage of differences in talent.

But, from the perspective of real human behavior, motivation, voluntary cooperation, and teamwork make a difference, and the willingness to provide those key factors may well depend upon how people are rewarded. *Homo economicus* is not worried about unemployment and will not resist technical change to avoid it (he realizes that other jobs are easily available in the open market), but actual human beings may fear unemployment and resist technical change that threatens to throw them into unemployment. Having a colleague on the management fast track may well lower the work effort of those not on the fast track in the world of *homo sapiens,* though nothing of the kind occurs in the microeconomic world. Why should people work hard if it is already obvious that they have no chance to make it? Teamwork requires efforts to promote team harmony.

What one believes makes a difference. Human beings can have blinders that imprison them in low-productivity modes of behavior and analysis.

Across the board the message is the same. To cure its productivity problems the United States is going to have to change its standard operating procedures. Americans will have to save more; offices will have to be run differently. Americans often forget, when they sing hymns of praise to the ideal of competition, that competition forces change. To do it the American way may be to do it a losing way; to win may mean having to change standard American operating procedures.

The bottom line

Looking at the American economy in the mid-1980s, there are some simple observations worth remembering. The United States is now at a time in which much of the rest of the industrial world has caught up economically and is threatening to pass. To run with the economic pack in the years ahead will require internal structural changes to accelerate American productivity growth. If those changes are not made, the result is apt to be greater income disparities within the United States and a fall in the American standard of living relative to the most advanced developed countries. Rearranging the financial chairs on the deck of an industrial *Titanic* does little good. The only solution is to change one's standard operating procedure until one finds something that works.

What are the prospects? The truthful answer is that a prediction is both irrelevant and apt to be wrong. The prospects depend upon what we Americans are willing to do, and that depends upon what we want to do and how we react to our problems.

We the People: The Rulers and the Ruled

George Anastaplo

George Anastaplo has long been a student of our legal system. His career began in 1950 when, after graduating at the top of his law school class at the University of Chicago, he was denied admission to the Illinois Bar because of his opinions about the fundamental right of revolution. These opinions had led to questions being put to him about political affiliations, which questions he on principle refused to answer. Ever since an adverse ruling on his case (over strong dissent) by the U.S. Supreme Court in 1961, appeals for his admission to the bar have been made from time to time by prominent lawyers. Mr. Anastaplo himself prefers to let the matter stand, so that, as he says, "observers, including professors as well as students of law, may be obliged to . . . reflect upon their profession and the rule of law."

Mr. Anastaplo is professor of law at Loyola University of Chicago and lecturer in the liberal arts at the University of Chicago. Among his books are *The Constitutionalist: Notes on the First Amendment* (1971); *Human Being and Citizen: Essays on Virtue, Freedom and the Common Good* (1975); and *The Artist as Thinker: From Shakespeare to Joyce* (1983). He is also the author of a book-length series of lectures entitled *The United States Constitution of 1787*, printed in the Fall 1986 issue of the *Loyola University Law Journal* (Chicago, Ill.) and approved for publication by the Johns Hopkins University Press. His essay on the *Gilgamesh* epic appeared in last year's *The Great Ideas Today*.

Col. Mason. . . . Having for his primary object, for the pole-star of his political conduct, the preservation of the rights of the people, he held it as an essential point, as the very palladium of Civil liberty, that the great officers of State, and particularly the Executive should at fixed periods return to that mass from which they were at first taken, in order that they may feel & respect those rights & interests, which are again to be personally valuable to them. He concluded with moving that the constitution of the Executive as reported by the Committee of the whole be re-instated, viz. "that the Executive be appointed for seven years, & be ineligible a 2d time."

.   .   .

Dr. Franklin. It seems to have been imagined by some that the returning to the mass of the people was degrading the magistrate. This he thought was contrary to republican principles. In free Governments the rulers are the servants, and the people their superiors & sovereigns. For the former therefore to return among the latter was not to *degrade* but to *promote* them. And it would be imposing an unreasonable burden on them, to keep them always in a State of servitude, and not allow them to become again one of the Masters.

.   .   .

Mr. G. Morris. . . . In answer to Col. Mason's position that a periodical return of the great officers of the State into the mass of the people, was the palladium of Civil liberty he would observe that on the same principle the Judiciary ought to be periodically degraded; certain it was that the Legislature ought on every principle, yet no one had proposed, or conceived that the members of it should not be re-eligible. In answer to Dr. Franklin, that a return into the mass of the people would be a promotion, instead of a degradation, he had no doubt that our Executive like most others would have too much patriotism to shrink from the burden of his office, and too much modesty not to be willing to decline the promotion.

—In the Federal Convention, July 26, 1787

Prologue

The "People of the United States" are said, in the opening words of the Preamble, to announce themselves as the ultimate authority for the United States Constitution of 1787 which they purport to "ordain and establish."[1] It is also indicated in the Constitution that from these people are to come the officers of government who will provide these people with the governance required for their proper happiness.

The Americans of 1787 sensed in what capacities they were truly rulers and in what capacities they were to be ruled. Particularly instructive is the confident manner in which they set about the business both of ruling and of being ruled, recognizing what they were entitled to and what was expected of them. They knew as well how to make useful distinctions between themselves and other peoples of the world, both friendly and hostile.

Human beings are referred to in a variety of ways in the Constitution. They are thought of as capable of the most exalted conduct, even as precautions are taken against the devious promptings of mere self-interest. Human beings appear in a half-dozen secular capacities—as makers of constitutions (or full citizens), as electorates, as public servants, as beneficiaries of government, as resident aliens, as foreigners, and as enemies (both at home and abroad). A review on this occasion of the various, somewhat overlapping, ways in which human beings are regarded in the Constitution of 1787 permits us to talk about the entire Constitution in an instructive manner. An informed citizen's general familiarity with that Constitution is presupposed in this discussion, which relies considerably upon the very words of the Constitution.[2]

I. Human beings as makers of constitutions

The people as ultimate rulers assert themselves in the Preamble, thereby implementing the innate power proclaimed by them a decade before in the Declaration of Independence. They speak for themselves in the Preamble, but their concerns are not limited to the present generation. By looking out as they do for their "Posterity" they acknowledge vital connections across generations. Their concern for a "more perfect Union" reflects an awareness that the people have spoken and acted previously, and that they are returning in the Constitution to the objectives and efforts to which they have already formally devoted themselves on more than one earlier occasion.

To speak of "more perfect" is to acknowledge standards upon which the people depend for their integrity and to which they are naturally inclined. Such standards are reflected in the invocations in the Preamble of the great objects of the Constitution. All of these objects, when properly balanced and firmly secured, are in the service of the people's enduring happiness.

The people make their will known, for purposes of ratifying "this Constitution for the United States of America," through the mode of

Scene at the signing of the Constitution of the United States. *"The Americans of 1787 sensed in what capacities they were truly rulers and in what capacities they were to be ruled."*

Raising the Liberty Pole, 1776. *"The people as ultimate rulers assert themselves in the Preamble, thereby implementing the innate power proclaimed by them a decade before in the Declaration of Independence."*

ratification prescribed in Article VII of the Constitution. The mode prescribed was ratification by conventions which were to be chosen by, or on behalf of, the people in the various states. Among the things assented to by the people in ratifying this Constitution is the understanding implicit in the Constitution both of who the people are and of what they may do. Thus, "We the People" must be distinguished both from the delegates to the federal convention who wrote the Constitution and from the states (or state legislatures) which selected those public servants for the convention.

The people, as ultimate rulers, reserve the power to amend the Constitution pursuant to the disciplined modes provided for that purpose in Article V of the Constitution. They resemble in this capacity the people who originally framed the Constitution.

II. Human beings as electorates

It is only in a few places that provision is made in the Constitution for participation by the people, or rather by parts of the people, in the routine operations of the government.

Members of the House of Representatives are to be chosen "by the People of the several States, and the Electors in each State shall have the Qualifications requisite for Electors of the most numerous Branch of the State Legislature." (Article I, section 2). It is thereby recognized in passing that "the People of the several States" contribute to the selection of the legislatures of their respective states, which means that they play an indirect part as well in the choice by state legislatures of the "two Senators from each State." (I, 3.)

Nowhere else in the working of the Constitution do the people, or some of them, act with the immediacy that they do in their choice every two years of the House of Representatives. The choice of a President, on the other hand, proceeds by a much more complicated mode in which the part played by the people is dependent in its form and extent upon decisions by state legislatures (albeit the very legislatures that the people choose or help choose): "Each State shall appoint, in such Manner as the Legislature thereof may direct, a Number of Electors, equal to the whole Number of Senators and Representatives to which the State may be entitled in the Congress." (II, 1.)

How the people are distributed in the country is taken account of by the Constitution: "Representatives and direct Taxes shall be apportioned among the several States . . . according to their respective Numbers, which shall be determined by adding to the whole Number of free Persons, including those bound to Service for a Term of Years, and excluding Indians not taxed, three fifths of all other Persons." (I,

2.) This allocation of seats, we have seen, affects how many presidential electors each state is entitled to.

It should be evident upon reflection that the people—with their direct control of the House of Representatives, with their direct control of at least one house of each state legislature, and with their indirect control thereby of the selections of Senators and of the President—are ultimately in control of the operations of the general government.

The people as electorates indicate what they prefer by discussing men and measures not only in the course of election campaigns but all the time. The freedom of speech of this people was taken for granted well before the Constitution was prepared. It may be seen both in the calls for revolution prior to Independence and in demands for amendments after ratification of the Constitution. It may be seen as well in the command, "Each House [of Congress] shall keep a Journal of its Proceedings, and from time to time publish the same, excepting such Parts as may in their Judgment require Secrecy." (I, 5.) A reflection of this essential free-speech prerogative of the people may be seen in the guarantee provided for members of Congress that "for any Speech or Debate in either House, they shall not be questioned in any other Place." (I, 6.)[3]

III. Human beings as public servants

The people, as makers of constitutions, are particularly concerned to indicate how the men will be chosen who will exercise from time to time the powers entrusted to the general government.

It is from the people at large that these officers of government are likely to be taken. The Constitution provides both for the selection of specified primary officers (in the legislative, executive, and judicial branches of government) and for the authority in turn of those primary officers to create and to fill inferior offices.

The primary legislative officers are found in "a Congress of the United States, which shall consist of a Senate and House of Representatives." (I, 1.) We have seen how representatives are allocated among the states and how members of the House of Representatives are chosen. Qualifications are set for membership in that house with a view to a member's experience, national loyalty, and familiarity with his constituency: "No person shall be a Representative who shall not have attained to the Age of twenty five Years, and been seven Years a Citizen of the United States, and who shall not, when elected, be an Inhabitant of that State in which he shall be chosen." (I, 2.) The House of Representatives in turn "shall chuse their Speaker and other Officers." (I, 2.)

The other house of Congress, the Senate, "shall be composed of two Senators from each State, chosen by the Legislature thereof, for six Years." (I, 3.) "No Person shall be a Senator who shall not have attained to the Age of thirty Years, and been nine Years a Citizen of the United States, and who shall not, when elected, be an Inhabitant of that State for which he shall be chosen." (I, 3.) Although "the Vice President of the United States shall be President of the Senate," the Senate "shall chuse their other Officers, and also a President pro tempore." (I, 3.)

It is the Congress that is empowered "to constitute Tribunals inferior to the supreme Court," "to raise and support Armies," "to provide and maintain a Navy," and "to provide for organizing, arming, and disciplining, the Militia, and for governing such Part of them as may be employed in the Service of the United States." (I, 8.)

In various ways, the Congress is critical in determining who is chosen President, what he may do as President, and even whether he may remain as President. The mode of selection of the President and Vice President is provided for in detail in the Constitution, with Congress exercising the ultimate supervisory power here (II, 1). Qualifications are set for the President as for members of Congress: "No Person except a natural born Citizen, or a Citizen of the United States, at the time of the Adoption of [the] Constitution, shall be eligible to the Office of President; neither shall any Person be eligible to that Office who shall not have attained to the Age of thirty five Years, and been fourteen Years a Resident within the United States." (II, 1.)[4]

The President in turn "shall nominate, and by and with the Advice and Consent of the Senate, shall appoint Ambassadors, other public Ministers and Consuls, Judges of the supreme Court, and all other Officers of the United States, whose Appointments are not [in the Constitution] otherwise provided for, and which shall be established by Law." (I, 2.) Generally, though, "Congress may by Law vest the Appointment of such inferior Officers, as they think proper, in the President alone, in the Courts of Law, or in the Heads of Departments." (I, 2.) In addition, it is the President who "shall Commission all the Officers of the United States." (I, 3.)

A reminder of ultimate legislative supremacy among the three branches of the general government may be seen in the provision, "The President, Vice President and all civil Officers of the United States, shall be removed from Office on Impeachment for, and Conviction of, Treason, Bribery, or other high Crimes and Misdemeanors." (II, 4.) Furthermore, "the Congress may by Law provide for the Case of Removal, Death, Resignation, or Inability, both of the President and Vice President, declaring what Officer shall then act as President, and such Officer shall act accordingly, until the Disability be removed, or a President shall be elected." (II, 1.)

Legislative supremacy may be seen as well in the powers of Congress to shape the courts of the United States and to provide for their jurisdiction. The Supreme Court is established by the Constitution itself, but its size and most of its activities very much depend upon Congress. In addition, there will be "such inferior Courts as the Congress may from time to time ordain and establish." (III, 1.) These, then, are both the primary and the inferior officers of government provided for by the Constitution.

State governments are taken for granted, with state legislatures comparable to Congress (I, 2; I, 3), with an "Executive Authority" and a judicial power in each state (I, 2; I, 3; VI), with indirect indications (usually by restraints placed upon them) of what states may do besides contribute to national elections (I, 10; II, 1; IV, 4), and with the legislatures recognized as superior to the executives in their respective states (I, 3; IV, 4).

The supervisory power of the general government with respect to state governments is repeatedly indicated. Thus, "The United States shall guarantee to every State in this Union a Republican Form of Government." (IV, 4.) Thus, also, "The Senators and Representatives [in the Congress], and the Members of the several State Legislatures, and all executive and judicial Officers, both of the United States and of the several States, shall be bound by Oath or Affirmation, to support [the] Constitution." (VI.) We can see here the extent to which the governments of the United States and of the states are assumed to be compatible.

The officers of the general government and of the state governments are the generally recognized "rulers" in this country, but they in turn are ruled both by the Constitution established by the people and by the electorates' participation, which is assumed to be constant, in the political life of the country.

IV. Human beings as beneficiaries of government

It is the people (including their posterity) who are ruled, and for whose benefit primarily this Constitution is established and government is carried on. They are to enjoy "a more perfect Union," "Justice," "domestic Tranquility," "the common defence," "the general Welfare," and "the Blessings of Liberty." It is evident throughout the Constitution that the economic interests, temptations, and limitations of this English-speaking people are vital, as are their concerns about both personal and political safety.[5]

It is this people who are counted with a view to determining the allocation of members in the House of Representatives (I, 2), and on whose behalf various powers given to Congress should be exercised (e.g., I, 8). It is from this people that armies, a navy, and the militia are likely to be drawn, and among whom (or at least, for whose sake) "Authors and Inventors" should be encouraged (I, 8).

On the other hand, it is also among the people that there are most likely to be found offenders who should be subject to "Indictment, Trial, Judgment and Punishment, according to Law" (I, 3), including counterfeiters (I, 8), bribers and traitors (II, 4), and other felons (IV, 2). Such people fall lower than they should. Others reach higher than they should—and so it must be provided that neither the United States nor the states can grant any of the people a "Title of Nobility." (I, 9; I, 10.)

Aside from the grand objects set forth in the Preamble, little is said in the Constitution, either about precisely what benefits will accrue to the people from the Constitution, or about what limitations (in the way, for example, of criminal legislation or sumptuary legislation) will be placed upon them. These are left substantially to determinations by officers of government, national and state, established or recognized by the Constitution. It is taken for granted that these officers, aware of the direct and indirect control exercised over them, will take into account the interests and wishes of the people from whom they have come, and to whom they can be returned at any time.

We have been considering for the most part those "free Persons" within the United States who are eligible to serve as electors (I, 2). But there are other human beings within the country, besides the temporary representatives of foreign powers, who are referred to as well, including "those bound to Service for a Term of Years," "Indians [who are] taxed," and of course slaves (I, 2). All human beings permanently settled in the country (except "Indians not taxed") are included among "the People" for some purposes. They can be counted in determining representation; they too can benefit from the peace and prosperity to which they contribute.

Varying circumstances are expected to determine what measures should be resorted to by government to serve the interests, or the apparent interests, of the people. Considerable flexibility is left by the Constitution both for the people to shape their governments and to choose the officers thereof, and for the officers of government to serve the people they rule and are ruled by.

V. Human beings as resident aliens

The power given to Congress "to establish an uniform Rule of Naturalization" reminds us of the massive immigration upon which the United States has depended for more than two centuries (I, 8). Most immigrants were expected to qualify for citizenship in due time; their children, if born here, would be citizens from birth.

But it evidently was a different matter, as we have seen, for "the Indian tribes." (I, 8.) The ambiguity of the status of the Indians may be seen in the fact that some of them are regularly taxed (I, 2). A decade before, some of them could be condemned in the Declaration of Independence as "merciless Indian Savages, whose known Rule of Warfare, is an undistinguished Destruction of all Ages, Sexes and Conditions."

Also ambiguous is the status of the slaves who are alluded to in various guarded ways: as "other Persons" who would be counted as three-fifths for representation purposes (I, 2); as "such Persons as any of the States now existing shall think proper to admit" (permitting for twenty years a continuation of the international slave trade) (I, 9); and as persons "held to Service or Labour in one State, under the Laws thereof, escaping into another" (recognizing the right of owners to reclaim fugitive slaves) (IV, 2).[6]

That some immigrants, Indians, and slaves could be distinguished in these ways points up the status of fully "free Persons" that human beings aspire to acquire—the status of citizens who rule and are ruled in turn.[7]

VI. Human beings as foreigners

All this is not to deny that there may be "free Persons" elsewhere. Certainly, there are in the world "foreign Nations" (I, 8), "King[s], Prince[s], foreign State[s]" (I, 9), and "foreign Power[s]" (I, 10). Treaties may be made by the United States with such sovereigns (but not by the states, without the consent of Congress) (I, 10; III, 2; VI); "Ambassadors and other public Ministers" may be sent to them and received from them (II, 2; II, 3).

Commerce "with foreign Nations" and "with the Indian Tribes" may be regulated by Congress, as may the value in this country "of foreign Coin." (I, 8.) Relations between countries are governed by "the Law of Nations." (I, 8.) Of special concern seem to be "Cases of admiralty and maritime Jurisdiction" (III, 2), as well as the claims made in the courts of this country by "foreign States, Citizens or Subjects." (III, 2.)

Despite the determination to treat foreigners in this country fairly, to maintain proper diplomatic and commercial relations with other countries, and to defend the United States, the Constitution is not much concerned with what goes on in other parts of the world. Yet the American experiment has had, and was expected to have, a profound effect elsewhere as a numerous, growing, and ever more prosperous people developed themselves, thereby displaying to the world the possibilities of genuine self-government.[8]

Among the lessons taught by the American regime was that citizens of a free country need not identify themselves as "Subjects." That

"Indian Council," by Seth Eastman. *"The ambiguity of the status of the Indians may be seen in the fact that some of them are regularly taxed."*

designation was left, for the most part, for human beings elsewhere (III, 2). The American regime, "conceived in Liberty, and dedicated to the proposition that all men are created equal," offered a light to the world by means of which all might be enlightened and lifted up.

VII. Human beings as enemies (both at home and abroad)

The darker side of human relations was recognized, however, by the provisions in the Constitution for self-defense and war. Hostile human beings, both at home and abroad, are anticipated.

The provisions for armies, a navy, and militia, and for the President as Commander in Chief thereof, anticipate threats from the armed forces of other countries (I, 8; II, 2). Congress is given power "to declare War, grant Letters of Marque and Reprisal, and make Rules concerning Captures on Land and Water." (I, 8.) "Cases of Rebellion or Invasion" are anticipated (I, 9), so much so that the general restrictions upon the power of the states to engage in war are suspended when any state is "actually invaded, or in such imminent Danger as will not admit of delay." (I, 10.)

Related to the defense powers is the power in Congress "to define and punish Piracies and Felonies committed on the high Seas, and Offences against the Law of Nations." (I, 8.) These shade over into offenses against the criminal and other laws of the United States, including "Treason, Bribery, or other high Crimes and Misdemeanors" (II, 4), and culminating in "Insurrections," "Rebellion," or "domestic Violence." (I, 8; I, 9; IV, 4.) Even so, care is taken to define the most political of crimes: "Treason against the United States, shall consist only in levying War against them, or in adhering to their Enemies, giving them Aid and Comfort." (III, 3.) There is a recognition as well of charges of "Treason, Felony, or other Crime," pursuant to state laws, which the United States should respect (IV, 2).

The most challenging danger that the United States faced, however, was neither from enemies abroad nor from ambitious or corrupt men at home. Rather, danger threatened to come because of the slaves among them, those useful if not even friendly enemies from whom "domestic Violence" and "Insurrections" could be anticipated. The principles of the American regime tacitly called into question the slavery to which people of African descent were systematically subjected. It was sensed, therefore, that it was only natural that those human beings should rebel someday. It was no wonder, then, that their uprisings should be dreaded.

That is, sensitive citizens who tolerated slavery, and thus enjoyed the benefits of it, could not without reason attribute to the slaves among them the same kind of constant desires and explosive desperation they themselves would have had in like circumstances. This contributed to the eventual recognition that the nation could not endure half-slave and half-free—or, for that matter, as all-slave—without sacrificing its vital principles as well as its peace of mind.[9]

Epilogue

The existence of substantial slavery among them reminded the framers of the Constitution, if reminder they needed, of the lower aspects of human beings. They could see in the slaves themselves a multitude of markedly degraded human beings, and they could see in the exploitation of slaves the extent to which political principles and the sense of humanity can be sacrificed when either fear or greed dominates the ordering of a community.

The Constitution is liberally provided with sensible precautions taken against the conniving of which human beings are capable: the Chief Justice, not the Vice President who ordinarily presides over the Senate, conducts the trial of the President in an impeachment proceeding (I, 3); "No Senator or Representative shall, during the Time for which he was elected, be appointed to any civil Office under the Authority of the United States, which shall have been created, or the Emoluments whereof shall have been encreased during such time; and no Person holding any Office under the United States, shall be a Member of either House during his Continuance in Office" (I, 6); the President is limited to ten days during which he may veto bills passed by Congress (I, 7); such bills cannot be labeled an "Order, Resolution, or Vote" in order to circumvent Presidential review thereof (I, 7); "no Bill of Attainder or ex post facto Law shall be passed" (I, 9; 1, 10); "no Title of Nobility shall be granted" (I, 9; I, 10); the net produce of all duties and imposts levied by states purportedly to finance their inspection of imports or exports "shall be for the Use of the Treasury of the United States" (I, 10); "no Senator or Representative, or Person holding an Office of Trust or Profit under the United States, shall be appointed [a presidential] Elector" (II, 1); each presidential elector, in casting his two votes for President and Vice President, shall vote for one man who "shall not be an Inhabitant of the same State with [himself]" (II, 1); "the President of the Senate shall, in the Presence of the Senate and House of Representatives, open all the Certificates [of the votes from the states for President and Vice President], and the Votes shall then be counted" (II, 1); the day for presidential electors to give their votes "shall be the same throughout the United States" (II, 1); the President's compensation "shall neither be encreased nor diminished during the Period for which [he is] elected" (II, 1); all civil officers may be impeached and convicted for "Treason, Bribery, or other high Crimes and Misdemeanors" (II, 4); judges are to be shielded from

Emancipation Day, Richmond, Virginia, around 1890. *"Even the 1787 compromises with the slavery interests proceeded on the assumption that freedom was likely to fare better within an enhanced Union than it would with a dismantled Union."*

political or other improper influence by lifetime appointments as well as by an assurance of their compensation (III, 1); the jurisdictional prerogatives of the courts of the United States protect those who might be vulnerable in an out-of-state tribunal (III, 2); "The Citizens of each State shall be entitled to all Privileges and Immunities of Citizens in the several States" (IV, 2);[10] and "no new State shall be formed or erected within the Jurisdiction of any other State, nor any State be formed by the Junction of two or more States, or Parts of States, without the Consent of the Legislatures of the States concerned as well as of the Congress." (IV, 3.)

It is partly because the Constitution takes these (and other) precautions that we can be encouraged by its high-mindedness. That high-mindedness is reflected in the appeal to the finest human sentiments in the solemn oaths or affirmations required of the President (II, 1) and of all civil officers of the United States and of the states (I, 3; VI). It is reflected as well in the objects looked to in the Preamble and in the insistence upon various rights which protect liberty or respect equality (such as the assurance of the Writ of Habeas Corpus and of trial by jury) (I, 9; III, 2).[11] Even the 1787 compromises with the slavery interests proceeded on the assumption that freedom was likely to fare better within an enhanced Union than it would with a dismantled Union.

In sum, arrangements are made so that reason may rule.[12] A kind of faith is also looked to. Not only does constitutional government depend upon keeping the faith (as may be seen in the recourse to oaths), but even the proclamation of "We the People" is itself a matter of faith, a kind of revelation at work. The recognized prophets of this revelation are the thirty-nine men who signed the Constitution on September 17, 1787: they can be said to have been inspired to speak for the people.

The people of the United States naturally retain, as do human beings everywhere, the right, duty, and power to judge the Constitution itself and how it is being used: "whenever any Form of Government becomes destructive of [the proper ends of government], it is the Right of the People to alter or to abolish it, and to institute new Government, laying its foundation on such principles and organizing its powers in such form, as to them shall seem most likely to effect their Safety and Happiness." These words from the Declaration of Independence remind us that this people existed, or were believed to have existed and to have had rights, well before the Constitution of 1787 was drawn up in their name. Such words testify as well to a salutary public faith in the understanding that this people not only retain the right and power to control and reform any government they happen to establish but that they endure independent of the governments which they create from time to time as required by the occasion.[13]

[1]All of the quotations in the text are from the United States Constitution of 1787, except for the quotations from the Gettysburg Address at the end of Section VI and from the Declaration of Independence toward the end of Section V and at the end of the Epilogue. The citations in the text are to the Constitution (by Article and section). There is no indication, in my quotations from the Constitution, of omissions either at the beginning or at the end of the matter quoted; the original spelling, capitalization, and punctuation are retained. The discussion of constitutional arrangements in the text of this article does *not* take account of amendments since 1787.

See, for a systematic discussion of the original Constitution, George Anastaplo, "The United States Constitution of 1787: A Commentary," 18 *Loyola University of Chicago Law Journal* 15 (1986). That discussion seems to be the first book-length section-by-section commentary upon the Constitution of 1787 proceeding primarily from the original text itself. It is scheduled to be published in book form by the Johns Hopkins University Press in 1988. (There is appended to that commentary, which is cited hereafter in this article as *Commentary,* a selected bibliography of various of my publications on the Constitution.)

It should be emphasized at the outset of this article that the Constitution grants no power to the people: if the Constitution were to do so it would imply that the Constitution is superior to the people. Rather, the people indicate in and through the Constitution how they want various powers of government exercised and by whom. Among the powers authorized by the people are the powers of amendment to be exercised by Congress and the State legislatures pursuant to the modes set forth in Article V.

See, on the principles of the Constitution, Anastaplo, "Political Philosophy of the Constitution," in *Encyclopedia of the American Constitution* (1986).

[2]Gouverneur Morris observed in the federal convention, July 20, 1787, "The people are the King." The British king is, in contemplation of law, immortal. See William Blackstone, *Commentaries on the Laws of England,* I, 456–458 (1765). See, on the people, Anastaplo, *Commentary,* note 16. The "people" should be distinguished from the "masses." The masses are more likely to be thought of as susceptible only to being moved by forces (especially economic forces?); the people are more likely to be thought of as open to reasoned argument.

Not all of the terms I use in this article to categorize the capacities of human beings are eighteenth-century terms. The reader interested in further pursuing eighteenth-century usage with respect to "the people" in a constitutional context should find helpful the collection of references in this note to "people" in the federal convention at Philadelphia in 1787. This collection, which is extensive (but far from complete), is arranged by delegates. The spelling of names in the eighteenth century could be rather flexible. (The considerable work here of Peggy Andrews, a Loyola University of Chicago law student, is very much appreciated.)

Page references are to the Ohio University Press edition (1966) of James Madison's *Notes of Debates in the Federal Convention of 1787.* The numbers within parentheses indicate the number of references on a page when there are more than one.

Gunning Bedford (Delaware): 229, 230 (3).

Pierce Butler (South Carolina): 41, 73, 92, 240, 286, 366, 402, 519.

Daniel Carroll (Maryland): 642 (2).

William Richardson Davie (North Carolina): 226 (3).

Jonathan Dayton (New Jersey): 228.

John Dickinson (Delaware): 77, 82 (2), 84, 369 (4), 447 (2).

Oliver Ellsworth (Connecticut): 154 (2), 169, 189 (2), 345, 350, 351 (3), 378, 401 (2), 430, 483.

Benjamin Franklin (Pennsylvania): 53 (2), 62 (2), 65, 197, 251 (2), 371 (2), 404 (3), 420 (2), 426 (2), 653 (2), 654 (2).

Elbridge Gerry (Massachusetts): 39, 41 (4), 51 (2), 70 (2), 73, 74 (2), 84 (4), 86 (3), 89, 93, 106 (2), 107, 113, 197 (2), 250, 263, 327 (2), 328, 338 (2), 338, 345, 349 (3), 368, 377, 445, 452 (2), 453 (3), 482, 516, 529, 580, 603.

Nathaniel Gorham (Massachusetts): 212, 275 (2), 349, 376, 406, 432, 630, 636.

Alexander Hamilton (New York): 130 (2), 131 (3), 136 (4), 137 (2), 138 (3), 166, 170 (2), 172, 173, 215, 609 (3).

Daniel Jenifer (Maryland): 106, 179.

William Samuel Johnson (Connecticut): 211 (2), 278.

Rufus King (Massachusetts): 70, 71, 228, 261, 326 (3), 352 (2), 409, 410, 481, 598, 636.

John Langdon (New Hampshire): 377, 514 (2).

John Lansing (New York): 122, 155 (2), 156.

James Madison (Virginia): 40 (2), 41, 45, 56, 70, 75, 80, 83 (2), 86 (3), 111 (2), 113, 140 (4), 141, 143, 165 (6), 169, 193 (4), 194 (3), 213 (2), 214, 239 (4), 240, 259, 263 (2), 272, 273 (2), 293, 294 (4), 295, 301, 302, 309, 327 (3), 344 (3), 352 (2), 353 (2), 363 (2), 365 (4), 375, 403 (2), 419, 423, 424, 427, 438 (3), 440, 444, 525, 562, 563, 564, 595, 629.

Luther Martin (Maryland): 159 (5), 202, 203, 556 (2), 564 (3), 566.

George Mason (Virginia): 39 (2), 64 (4), 65 (2), 75 (4), 157 (3), 158 (5), 167 (2), 250 (2), 264, 266, 273, 274 (2), 308 (3), 348 (3), 370 (2), 371, 401, 416, 434, 443 (2), 444, 472 (2), 549, 552, 565, 630, 649, 651 (2).

John Francis Mercer (Maryland): 405 (4), 406, 451 (6), 470.

Gouverneur Morris (Pennsylvania): 235 (4), 240, 251, 255 (2), 256, 265, 271, 272, 278, 306 (2), 307 (2), 308 (3), 313, 322, 323 (4), 324 (5), 325 (2), 335, 339, 340, 351 (3), 367, 372 (2), 401, 402, 403, 407, 411, 453 (2), 468, 489, 491, 526, 545, 566.

William Paterson (New Jersey): 95 (3), 96 (4), 122, 123, 124 (2), 259 (3).

William Pierce (Georgia): 78.

Charles Pinckney (South Carolina): 73 (2), 181 (3), 182 (2), 183 (6), 184 (3), 185 (5), 186 (3), 187 (3), 307, 344, 450, 454, 566.

Charles Cotesworth Pinckney (South Carolina): 78 (3), 166 (2), 168.

Edmund Randolph (Virginia): 30, 33 (2), 46, 58, 93, 115, 128, 129, 155, 168, 171, 236, 264, 268, 326 (2), 349, 436, 448, 515, 642, 656, 657.

George Read (Delaware): 78, 195, 407, 485.

John Rutledge (South Carolina): 67, 167 (4), 405, 426, 448, 507.

Roger Sherman (Connecticut): 39 (2), 60 (2), 74 (2), 75, 86, 114, 160 (4), 161 (2), 170, 253 (2), 270, 306, 516, 628, 630.

George Washington (Virginia): 655.

Hugh Williamson (North Carolina): 190, 309 (2), 368, 422, 549, 582, 585 (2), 602.

James Wilson (Pennsylvania): 40 (3), 42, 48 (2), 49 (2), 50, 51, 56, 59, 60, 63, 74 (3), 82 (2), 83 (2), 85 (3), 97 (3), 124 (2), 125 (4), 126 (2), 162, 164 (3), 167 (2), 169 (2), 188, 189 (4), 252, 275, 287 (2), 296, 307 (5), 326, 336, 415, 454 (2), 455 (2), 464, 565, 578, 588.

[3]See, on freedom of speech and the Constitution, Anastaplo, *The Constitutionalist: Notes on the First Amendment* (Dallas: Southern Methodist University Press, 1971); Anastaplo, *Human Being and Citizen: Essays on Virtue, Freedom and the Common Good* (Chicago/Athens, Ohio: Swallow Press/Ohio University Press, 1975). See also Anastaplo, *Commentary,* note 21; "Censorship," in the *Encyclopædia Britannica,* 15th ed. (beginning with the 1985 printing); "Freedom of Speech and the Silence of the Law," 64 *Texas Law Review* 443 (1985); "William H. Rehnquist and the First Amendment," *Intercollegiate Review,* Spring 1987, p. 31; "What Is Still Wrong With George Anastaplo? A Sequel to 366 U.S. 82 (1961)," 35 *DePaul Law Review* 551 (1986).

[4]For the federal convention to be able to speak in 1787 of someone having been "fourteen Years a Resident within the United States" means that "the United States" must have been considered to have existed prior to 1776. Consider, also, the implications of this provision in Article VI of the Constitution, "All Debts contracted and Engagements entered into, before the Adoption of this Constitution, shall be as valid against the United States under this Constitution, as under the Confederation." See Anastaplo, *Commentary,* Lecture No. 15. See also note 10 below.

[5]Important for the shaping of the English-speaking peoples was the British constitutional system, the common law, and of course the thought of Shakespeare. See Anastaplo, *The Artist as Thinker: From Shakespeare to Joyce* (Athens, Ohio: Swallow Press/Ohio University Press, 1983), chap. 1; Anastaplo, *Commentary,* Lectures 1, 7, 10, and 11. See also note 10 below.

It is evident in the Constitution of 1787 that the people are very much concerned with how their money is taken from them by government and how it is spent (with the primary powers here intended to be vested in the House of Representatives). A corruption of this concern may take the form of turning citizens into mere consumers. See, on the proper shaping and guidance of the citizen body, note 13 below.

When one learns what has been done and said over millennia in ordering the lives of other great peoples, one may better see and hence more deeply appreciate what was said and done in this country between 1776 and 1789. I have been preparing in recent years introductions to ancient non-Western texts for the annual volumes of *The Great Ideas Today*. These introductions are to the *Analects* of Confucius (1984), to the *Bhagavad Gītā* (1985), to the *Gilgamesh* (1986), and to the *Koran* (forthcoming).

[6]See, on slavery and the Constitution, Anastaplo, *Commentary*, note 9. See also note 9 below.

[7]See, on the relation of liberty to equality in the American regime, Laurence Berns, "Aristotle and the Moderns on Freedom and Equality," in K. L. Deutsch and W. Soffer, eds., *The Crisis of Liberal Democracy: A Straussian Perspective* (Albany: State University of New York Press, 1987), pp. 156–59. See also Anastaplo, "Seven Questions for Professor Jaffa," 10 *University of Puget Sound Law Review* 507 (1987); *Commentary*, notes 14 and 15.

The dedication of the American people to equality is reflected in the equal status to be accorded to new states in the Union (IV, 3) as well as in the insistence upon preserving the equality of suffrage of all states in the Senate (Art. V). If great and quite evident disparities between states cannot affect their equality in certain respects, then why should disparities between human beings do so?

Classes of Senators are recognized (according to the years in which terms end), but no classes of people. Nor does wealth create any privileges or lack of wealth any disabilities. Nor was the Nineteenth Amendment needed to permit states (or, for that matter, the United States) to provide for woman suffrage.

[8]See, on the Universal Declaration of Human Rights, Anastaplo, "How to Read the Constitution of the United States," 17 *Loyola University of Chicago Law Journal* 1 at 55 (1983). This bears on the question of whether a people can properly be regarded as a natural unit. Consider, for example, the implications of the term "Naturalization" (as in Art. I, sec. 8 of the Constitution). Consider, also, Plato, *Republic* 414–415; *GBWW*, Vol. 7, p. 340. See, as well, note 10 below.

[9]See Anastaplo, "American Constitutionalism and the Virtue of Prudence: Philadelphia, Paris, Washington, Gettysburg" in L. P. de Alvarez, ed., *Abraham Lincoln, The Gettysburg Address and American Constitutionalism* (Irving, Tex.: University of Dallas Press, 1976), p. 77; "Abraham Lincoln's Emancipation Proclamation," in R. K. L. Collins, ed., *Constitutional Government in America* (Durham, N.C.: Carolina Academic Press, 1980), p. 421; "Slavery and the Constitution," 1986–1987 *Pepperdine Law Review* (forthcoming). See also note 6 above.

[10]We can be reminded, by the reference to "Privileges and Immunities," of constitutional understandings prior to the Constitution. See notes 4 and 5 above. See also the Ninth Amendment to the Constitution. Thus, the common law is very much taken for granted throughout the Constitution of 1787, that body of law in which both civil and criminal juries are critical. See note 11 below.

Among the principal benefits which government is to provide a people, it was believed by many, was the assurance of various personal rights and liberties. But however much the Bill of Rights (ratified in 1791) reinforces this belief, does not the Preamble remind us of the common good?

[11]The people's effective control over their government is enhanced by their participation in jury trials. See note 10 above. See also Anastaplo, *The Constitutionalist*, pp. 217–19.

[12]See Scott Buchanan, "The Constitution Revisited," *GIT* 1975, pp. 432, 460. See also the opening page of *The Federalist Papers*.

[13]Do the people truly govern only when they know what they are doing, and hence only when they are deliberately doing the right thing? We must be careful, that is, lest we make too much of the *will* of the people and not enough of a legitimacy grounded in sound moral and political judgment. See, on the merits of the "coordinated electorates" provided for by the Constitution, Anastaplo, *Commentary*, Lecture 16, Section VII. See, on a proposal for the abolition of television as a contribution to the restoration of the people to sound political health, Anastaplo, "Self-Government and the Mass Media: A Practical Man's Guide," in H. M. Clor, ed., *The Mass Media and Modern Democracy* (Chicago: Rand McNally, 1974), p. 161.

The need of the people for proper guidance, and their ultimate respect for such guidance, may be seen in the epitaph provided for the tombstone of a Charleston, South

Carolina, lawyer, James Louis Petigru, a Unionist who opposed Secession and a Constitutionalist who opposed Nullification:

JAMES LOUIS PETIGRU

Born at
Abbeville May 10th 1789
Died at Charleston March 9th 1863

JURIST.   ORATOR.   STATESMAN.   PATRIOT.

Future times will hardly know how great a life
This simple stone commemorates—
The tradition of his Eloquence, his
Wisdom and his Wit may fade:
But he lived for ends more durable than fame,
His Eloquence was the protection of the poor and wronged;
His Learning illuminated the principles of Law—
In the admiration of his Peers,
In the respect of his People,
In the affection of his Family,
His was the highest place;
The just meed
Of his kindness and forbearance
His dignity and simplicity
Unawed by Opinion,
Unseduced by Flattery,
Undismayed by Disaster,
He confronted life with antique Courage
And Death with Christian Hope.

In the great Civil War
He withstood his People for his Country
But his People did homage to the Man
Who held his conscience higher than their praise
And his Country
Heaped her honors on the grave of the Patriot,
To whom living,
His own righteous self-respect sufficed
Alike for Motive and Reward.

"Nothing is here for tears, nothing to wail,
Or knock the breast; no weakness, no contempt,
Dispraise or blame; nothing but well and fair
And what may quiet us in a life so noble."

James Petigru Carson, ed., *Life, Letters, and Speeches of James Louis Petigru* (Washington: W. H. Lowdermilk, 1920), p. 487. See also *ibid.*, pp. v–x (an appreciation by Gaillard Hunt).

PART TWO

Reconsiderations of Great Books and Ideas

Toward a Reading of *Capital*

Thomas K. Simpson

Thomas K. Simpson has broad concerns extending through the sciences
as well as the humanities. He has for many years been a senior tutor at St.
John's College, where he has had major responsibility for the development
of the laboratory program in physics as well as an opportunity to pursue
serious interests in both politics and philosophy. These interests have
led as well to his being made a consultant to the Museum of History and
Technology at the Smithsonian Institution, where he researched items in the
collection and wrote a guidebook to the exhibits in the Division of Electricity;
to service at the Franklin Institute, where he helped to evaluate the role of
a technological museum in contemporary society; and also, while on leave
from teaching, to an extended interval as consultant and witness in a major
consumer-action lawsuit.

Mr. Simpson studied engineering at Virginia Polytechnic Institute in
1944–45 and took his B.A. from St. John's in 1950, with military service
in between at the Applied Physics Laboratory in Silver Springs, Maryland.
Subsequently he earned an M.A. (1955) from Wesleyan University and a
Ph.D. in the history of science and technology from Johns Hopkins, where
his dissertation was a literary-critical study of James Clerk Maxwell's *Treatise
on Electricity and Magnetism*. A more recent essay by him on the *Treatise*
appeared in last year's *The Great Ideas Today*.

Marx's *Capital* is not a book "about economics," any more than Plato's *Republic* is a book about politics. Plato uses the *polis* as a metaphor through which to investigate the human psyche and its practices, and Marx examines the structure of capitalism in the same spirit to ask us the most fundamental questions about ourselves and our world. In this commercial age, the economic metaphor is the more telling, but the question in a broad sense remains the same: who are we, and what is our practical relation to the human good? The *Republic* is strangely displaced when it is read as a text on "political science," and can really be approached in its integrity only when it is read as a letter from Socrates to us. In the same way, I want to suggest, *Capital* cannot be left to the economists; it may indeed interest them least of all, for they have other ways of answering the kind of question which specifically concerns them. But taken as a letter from Marx to us, and read as a challenge to our sense of values and the daily operations of our society, *Capital* remains a telling and disturbing work.

For Marx, "capital" is an enveloping system: no less than Plato, he is asking fundamental questions about our cities, our sciences, and our practice of the human virtues. If he is right, we are upside-down people, imagining ourselves in one world but living in another. In the belief that he sees something about us that we don't, I propose to consider what he has to say, and to this end I will ask the reader to embark with me on a brief dialectical tour of the three principal volumes of Marx's *Capital*.

Let us from the outset agree to dissociate Marx for present purposes from the Soviet Union and any other societies that have adopted his name and claimed his heritage. We need not here judge the question, which social projects have misused his name and which have read him well. At best, these are questions we could take up only after we had ourselves taken on the discipline of studying his work earnestly and as openly as possible. *Capital* is, I believe, a great book, enormously complex, and strangely subtle in ways the world has not often taken time to consider.

There is a special urgency in such an undertaking today, for *Capital* has ranked high for a century now on the world's best-seller list; it hardly needs to be argued that we must do everything in our power to maintain a substantive dialogue with the reading public of the world. Even if we ourselves saw no promise in Marx's text, or any relevance to our own lot, the fact that others throughout the world do find it so compelling would suggest that Marx is still speaking to the world's concerns; this fact alone would demand that we come to comprehend *Capital,* and read it, if we can, at least as well as others do.

Once we have agreed to address Marx and his book in their own terms, we are ready for a proposition which I would like to assert now, at the outset of our investigation. Marx, I believe, is *on our side.* By "our side," I presume to mean the side of democracy, and of respect for the worth and dignity of every individual person. The reader may judge Marx differently, but the difference is likely to be a conclusion that, in the end, Marx has not too little confidence in human capabilities but too much—that he would grant us too much freedom, too much responsibility, that he credits too highly our powers of using our human skills to plan together rationally for the achievement of our common human goals—in short, that Marx is too democratic. In any case, I suggest that Marx is challenging us in *Capital* to go further—much further—along the way of democracy, down our own road, than we have gone ourselves.

Marx respects the central documents of the American tradition; these he sees as claiming and formally granting the equal rights of every individual. All that Marx believes and proposes he bases on the conviction that these rights have been won and must be defended and preserved. But as *formal* rights, they only launch the project of human freedom. The formal freedoms won by the American Revolution have yet to be implemented in a society that makes the corresponding real freedom a fact in the life of every member. A candid view of contemporary America can only remind us how far we have to go to achieve such a reality—and we are, too slowly, learning that we cannot in the modern world think of such matters in terms of one nation alone.

Marx may have more faith in us than we have in ourselves. He believes that it lies within the powers of modern industrial society—even *his* "modern" society of a hundred years ago—to make these freedoms *real.* As we shall see, this for him takes the form, not primarily of a redistribution of the world's present wealth, but of a transformation of society itself into a more rational human community, and the reorganization of the productive powers of modern technology so as to make real individual freedom and opportunity practicable. These are bold proposals, but as ideas they are rather simple, and they might be taken as nothing more, or less, than proposals for the implementation of the objectives of our own democracy—were it not that the image normally associated with Marx is totalitarian, so that the reader cannot believe they are what Marx really means. I propose that we listen to Marx himself, and see what he has to say.[1]

I think it is especially interesting that he writes, not as a Utopian or an idealist, but, he claims, as a scientist—a *dialectical* scientist. With this claim, he is challenging our concept of science itself; in effect, he finds that criticism of our ordering of political and economic society entails criticism of our practice of what we call "science" as well. A society and its sciences are, it seems, images of one another. We shall have to see, as we go along, how this might be understood. But for Marx it does seem to mean at least that he for his part understands *Capital* to be a work of science, and not just political rhetoric or speculation. We may thus have to reconsider our own concept of knowing, and of ourselves as knowers.

Marx may be right or he may be wrong (and we, in our lifetimes, may never know which). But his propositions stand in either case as fair challenges to our understanding. I hope that this present essay will help to open again the reading of *Capital*, which in our time of reaction is so difficult to undertake with that readiness to listen and, perhaps, to learn, that every great author must presuppose in order to be heard at all.

Formal and dialectical theory: the plan of this study

Marx is indeed confronted with a difficult concatenation of tasks. Both he, as author, and we, his readers, are totally embedded in an intricately woven historical era, the age of capitalism. True, he has arrived at it a little earlier than we, and assuredly there have been major shifts and changes from his time to ours, but essentially we share with him what Hegel would call the "spirit" of a common experience. The institutions we know, the language we speak, the social relations we have grown up to accept and work with as the terms and conditions of our lives, belong to the system of thought and practice which is capitalism: private property and its law, the modern city, the modern state, buying and selling, investment, profit and interest, and that kind of working-for-pay which we take for granted and call "having a job," "earning a living," or "pursuing a career." They are the *materials* of our lives (and it is just by virtue of his attention to the importance of the detail of these environing conditions of our lives that Marx is—appropriately—called a "materialist"). Yet though they are the material of our lives, we know, when we pause to reflect upon it, that they are products of history— they once *were not*—and they are, in principle, transitory. Capitalism is a brilliant and seemingly ever-more-total world; but it is a world that is a product of time and is thus in transience.

Thus, from a point *within* capitalism Marx proposes to develop a theory of capitalism. Already this is strange ground, for one expects to meet theories of objects that are permanent and about which we can be "objective"—and that are, as such, appropriate concerns of strict science. Marx will construct, instead, a formal theory of a transient object, and one with which we are totally and subjectively involved. Worse, though, the theory will be critical: that is, it will present its object, not only as transient, but as perverse—as inherently contradictory, and as an alienation of our humanity. And finally, if Marx is right, this science of a transient and perverse subject matter must be constructed from within that domain itself, using the language of an alienated dictionary and the experience and thought-structures of alienated minds, both his and ours. I think we can rightly characterize this as a dialectical enterprise, in the sense that it is fundamentally critical: it questions the very ground it stands on. It probes its own terms and our cherished concepts, and it reaches for higher ground, looking to the long scope of history, and speaking already in a language that must borrow problematically from what it conceives to be the human future.

I think we can conceive the work of *Capital*, then, in two distinct aspects. The first is that of the formal theory of capitalism, a science of this transient object, which will undertake to depict the operation of capitalism as a system, accurately and objectively, much as Newton depicted the motions of the heavens. For Marx, this will be, in effect, the science of a passing object, the truth of an error. It will view capitalism objectively, taking it provisionally in the way in which it presents itself in our time.

The second aspect is the critical theory, which undertakes to expose what Marx sees as the error of capitalism and locates it in a larger horizon of the past from which it came and, above all, in its potential historic destiny. Here the terms that are accepted by capitalism are criticized and their larger meanings revealed; the illusions generated by capitalism are identified and traced to their sources, and above all, perhaps, the workings of inner contradictions explored, by which capitalism is seen to be generating, within itself, its own antithesis. This we may call the dialectical theory of capitalism.

I suggest we can think of these two works of *Capital* as nested, one within the other—the *formal* theory, as a limited enterprise, contained within the encompassing *dialectical* theory. We might speak of the formal theory as "framed" within the dialectical. I do not mean to say that Marx addresses the two theories sequentially or in separation; elements of both are interwoven throughout the book. But they are in principle distinct, and we will do well here to take them up, as nearly as possible, one at a time. I propose, then, that we first address the formal theory and then consider the larger dialectical complication. Perhaps it is just as well that in practice things cannot be quite so neat, but we may take this plan as our guiding thread.

The cell form of capitalism: the commodity[2]

Indeed, at the very outset we meet a difficulty. Before the formal theory can unfold, we must establish a starting point, and this is not so easy. "Every beginning," Marx says, "is difficult." [GBWW, Vol. 50, p. 6b.] Marx must find the right point for the initiation of his own theory of capitalism for he cannot assume that everyone will start at the same place. His beginning point, he decides, must lie in the concept of the commodity and the commodity proves to be a paradoxical and elusive entity. To locate it, and thus to found the formal science, is already a dialectical task: that is, Marx must focus on a common concept, accepted within capitalism as altogether obvious, and examine it afresh with dialectical rigor. Only then will he be able to proceed securely with the formal science which builds on it. This dialectical examination he speaks of as an analytic procedure, likening it to microscopy. As the microscope reveals the cell as the common unit of living things, unseen by the unaided eye, so Marx's analysis identifies the commodity as the universal principle of the system of capitalism [GBWW, Vol. 50, p. 6b–c].

What happens to an object, Marx asks, when it becomes a "commodity"? Like a Socratic question about virtue, justice, or love, this one begins innocently enough but expands in significance as we pursue it. The beginning is with the distinction, already familiar in other authors before Marx, between "use-value" and "exchange value." The objects we employ in our lives have value for us because they serve our purposes: many are simply "useful" in that they meet necessity, providing food, shelter, or clothing; others we prize for their beauty and delight. All, as serving our human ends, have "use-value." The term is hardly adequate. Its referent is all the world of *quality*—of appetite, color, warmth, friendship, intelligence. Whatever we value and strive for belongs to this realm. It is important to reflect upon it here, for we are about to leave it behind.

Within our capitalist era, virtually every object we lay eyes upon has its price: most of the things we see about us have been objects of exchange and could, on some secondhand market, fetch a price again. Some have their price tags still on them: books tend these days to have selling prices printed on their dust jackets. Even a human life, it might seem, has its price: the courts are daily concerned to evaluate disabilities and deaths in terms of dollars and cents.

Things that are on the one hand needed, prized, or loved by human beings, but are at the same time made, bought, sold, and evaluated in money terms as objects of exchange, are commodities. In their qualitative role, serving human ends, they have use-value; yet as traded, bought, sold, and exchanged, they are reduced to equivalent *quantities*, and have exchange value. How does the world of quality thus turn into a world of quantity—and what does it mean for us, that it should do so?

Marx finds ingenious ways to examine this question in Chapter 1 of *Capital;* he weighs and scrutinizes what he calls the "forms" of the commodity and commodity exchange, dwelling first on one aspect, then another, and in the process the reader learns not only much about the commodity, but about Marx as well, and the meaning for him of "analysis." We meet a powerful, relentlessly critical mind, "analytic" not in the modern, algebraic sense but in some reconstitution of the Aristotelian patience with the particular. Out of it comes a steadily growing sense of the pervasiveness and significance of the "commodity" as founding idea of capitalist society: the transformation of quality into quantity, of all things into numbers which rate them in exchange.

I want to suggest that this first chapter of *Capital* sounds the note of Marx's whole work, and that his style seems to me to have something of the ancient about it, rejecting contemporary analysis and our modern, easy use of symbols, and insisting instead on finding the *content* of terms and transactions. He will take, for example, an ironic instance of an exchange—linen for Bibles—and work it out, back and forth, in arithmetic concreteness [*GBWW*, Vol. 50, p. 47d]. Modern readers may find themselves longing for an algebraic equation, or a graph or two, to summarize in a schema the relations which these details are tracing, but I think hardly in the thousands of pages of *Capital* does Marx ever really gratify that wish. He is on a different track, humanly and intellectually. And I think we can see a clue to this almost stylistic issue in the concept of the commodity, for what Marx is discovering in this "Commodities" chapter is the universal substitution of market magnitude for the distinctive qualities of those things in our lives which meet human needs, or answer human desires. In his own style, Marx will not follow that lead.

That substitution of quantity for quality, the manipulable symbol for a lost content, is exactly the questionable algebraic magic of the "Cartesian Revolution." That brilliant but disturbing exchange which is accomplished in the drama of the *Discourse on Method,* Marx in effect refuses to accept at face value. There, Descartes once and for all, on our behalf, doubts away the old world of quality, color, sound, and the human good and returns from the depth of his isolation with a new world of mathematical magnitude and formulable relation [*GBWW*, Vol. 31, pp. 44c–54b]. That is strikingly close to the universal transformation of use-value into exchange value of which Marx speaks, and Marx insists on reminding us of what we have lost. In his own manner and thought he is taking his stand outside that transformation; he will not reason as a Cartesian but stands resolutely and comfortably with the ancients in this, and perhaps with those of a future which will have passed through and beyond the Cartesian blackout.[3]

The commodity is not, of course, in itself a creation of modern capitalism. Marx catches Aristotle in reflection on this same mystery of the transformation of quality into quantity, in the markets of Athens. By what common measure, Aristotle asks in the *Nichomachean Ethics* [*GBWW*, Vol. 9, p. 381c], can five beds be equated to one house? Substantively, they are utterly unlike, yet they exchange in a specific numerical relation. Marx reports that Aristotle finds no adequate answer, and Marx in turn finds Aristotle's bewilderment appropriate and significant: the full, illogical logic of the commodity is the work of history, and in Athens there was at root, he says, no rational answer to Aristotle's conundrum.[4]

Only with capitalism has the commodity fought through to a completely coherent system of reckoning. We shall see in a moment Marx's solution to Aristotle's riddle, the foundation that Marx finds in capitalism for the ratios of universal exchange. But what is most striking in this passage is the evident satisfaction with which Marx accepts Aristotle as a colleague in the contemplation of the question: for both, the commodity is a dialectical problem, not an acceptable fact.

To help us in recognizing the profundity of the world change which the unbounded logic of the commodity has brought with it, Marx turns his inquiring irony to the contemplation of a chair. Its analysis, he says, "brings out that it is a very strange thing, abounding in metaphysical subtleties and theological niceties":

> So far as it is a value in use, there is nothing mysterious about it,
> whether we consider it from the point of view that by its properties
> it is capable of satisfying human wants, or from the point that those
> properties are the product of human labour.   [*GBWW*, Vol. 50, p. 31a.]

It begins as a thing of wood, "an ordinary sensuous thing." Yet:

> . . . so soon as it steps forth as a commodity, it is changed into something
> transcendent. It not only stands with its feet on the ground, but, in
> relation to all other commodities, it stands on its head, and evolves
> out of its wooden brain grotesque ideas, far more wonderful than
> "table-turning" ever was.   [Ibid.]

Where does this mysterious "value," which the chair possesses as a commodity, come from? It is nowhere visible to the eye, nor is it an object of touch; it is hardly related to use-value, since the items in the world that are most vital to us—the air we breathe, for example—often bear no exchange value at all. Marx's comic, Till Eulenspiegel chair figures the world turned upside down: it is a comic image of a tragic transformation, in which each object in our world converts itself from quality to quantity, from human service to the overriding demands of a universal, measuring market. If the wealth of our society indeed has taken the form of "an immense collection of commodities," then wealth has, per se, become stark *amount*, bearing, Marx says, "not an atom of use-value." We are at the threshold of a system of alienation of use-value and the human, the insight that for Marx is the key to understanding the entire world of capital.

Labor value[5]

We see that if Marx is to set forth a consistent theory of capitalism, he must first resolve Aristotle's conundrum and specify that common measure that will bring all things, as commodities, into quantitative relation.

Although I see no evidence whatever that Marx himself had this analogy in view, I would like to suggest another measuring task at the foundation of a formal science, which I think bears a striking and instructive likeness to the problem Marx faces at this point. I suggest that Marx is very much in the position at which Newton stood at the threshold of the *Principia*. Like Newton, Marx must choose a measuring unit that is well founded, and that will make a world intelligible. For Newton, this was the world of the planetary motions. For Marx, it is the world of capital.

At the outset of the *Principia*, Newton defines the quantity which he calls "mass"; this is a bold move, and one on which the integrity of his science entirely depends [*GBWW*, Vol. 34, p. 5a]. Correspondingly, Marx defines the unit of exchange value. There was nothing obvious about Newton's choice: indeed, "mass" is a concept remote from the familiar measuring processes in mechanics. We do not compare bodies by determining their masses; we put them on balances and determine their relative weights. Masses obey laws—Newton's "Laws of Motion" at the outset of the *Principia*—that are counterintuitive and that were, until recently, virtually unobserved in practice; according to Newton's first law, a body once set in motion will move with that same speed in a right line forever, whereas we all know that a terrestrial body will in fact shortly come to a stop [*GBWW*, Vol. 34, p. 14a].

Marx's definition of exchange value is almost equally difficult to grasp, and modern economists disdain it as unnecessary and contrived. I propose, however, that like Newton's "mass," Marx's definition of value is the cornerstone of a strict and powerful theory. The reason economists today do not appreciate this is, very possibly, that they have a different idea in mind of what a theory should be, and they do not demand an economics, as Marx did, that has the kind of rigor and coherence that distinguishes the *Principia*'s account of the heavens.

Marx asserts that the exchange value of a commodity is determined by the amount of human labor it contains. In saying this, he is repeating an opinion that was widely shared by such predecessors as Adam Smith and Benjamin Franklin. The difference is only that Marx carries the principle through with a precision and consistency that no one else had attempted. Marx states:

> That which determines the magnitude of the value of any article is the amount of labour socially necessary . . . for its production.

Further:

> Commodities, therefore, in which equal quantities of labour are embodied, or which can be produced in the same time, have the same value. The value of one commodity is to the value of any other, as the labour time necessary for the production of the one is to that necessary for the production of the other.

Finally as exchange values:

> . . . all commodities are only definite masses of *congealed labour time.*
> [*GBWW*, Vol. 50, p. 15b–c; italics added.]

Clarification of this concept to the point of scientific strictness presents a series of problems, which Marx carefully and systematically resolves. The first challenge is to clarify the notion of "socially necessary labour time." As Marx points out, if we simply define value as "labour time," it would follow that the product of a lazy or unskilled workman would be worth more than the same object produced by one who was energetic or skilled. It is for this reason that the unit of measure of labor time must represent a social average:

> The labour time socially necessary is that required to produce an article under the normal conditions of production, and with the average degree of skill and intensity prevalent at the time.   [*GBWW*, Vol. 50, p. 15b.]

Indeed, not only must the labor unit represent the social average for any given industry, with socially average skills and the level of development of machinery that customarily determines the productivity of labor in that branch of production; we must now speak of a unit of labor that is common among the whole variety of industries whose products enter into exchange in the total market system of an economic society. As a commodity, the object of labor becomes a certain quantity of exchange value, and as such, it has "abstracted," Marx says, "from the material constituents and forms which make it a use-value." It is:

> . . . no longer a table, a house, yarn, or any other useful thing. Its existence as a material thing is put out of sight. Neither can it any longer be regarded as the product of the labour of the joiner, the mason, the spinner, or of any other definite kind of productive labour. . . . There is nothing left but what is common to them all; all are reduced to one and the same sort of labour, human labour in the abstract.
> [*GBWW*, Vol. 50, p. 14b–c.]

The commodities all tell us, Marx says (and we may imagine ourselves gazing in bewilderment down the endless corridors of the supermarket or the discount store as we read these words) "that human labour power has been expended in their production, that human labour is embodied in them. When looked at as *crystals of this social substance,* common to them all, they are—values." [Ibid.; italics added.]

Newton, as we have seen, similarly founded his system on an act of radical and total abstraction—abstraction from every quality of physical substance but that invisible one, *mass:* not mass of copper, or of air, or of flesh, but of undifferentiated matter, a property exactly as unimaginable as Marx's "social substance." In either case, only such an act of penetrating abstraction would reach through to a unit sufficiently universal to weave together a single, coherent, and inclusive world.

I mentioned in passing that modern economists generally disdain this "labor theory of value" as unnecessary to their science, and I suggested that this is because they have a different idea of "science" itself. Let me suggest further what that alternative view of science might be, for I think that in this way we may locate more accurately what Marx is attempting, as well as the quite different, though perhaps equally legitimate, alternative aims of contemporary economics.

Two paradigms of science stand prominently before us in our Western tradition: that of Newton, to which I have been likening Marx's formal theory, and another, very different, that is represented first and perhaps best of all by Ptolemy in his *Almagest.*[6] The history of astronomy follows the trail of their divergent conceptions and purposes. Ptolemy's aim is, he says, to "save the appearances." He develops impressive, far-reaching mathematical methods (first cousin to Fourier analysis, one of the principal tools of modern mathematical physics) to achieve this purpose, but through it all, he regards the planets for his mathematical purposes merely as points of light; projected onto the celestial sphere, they are nowhere, and if they are made of anything, it does not concern his science of astronomy to consider that. His purpose is strictly and exactly limited: to find the mathematics of the observed motions of the heavenly bodies as geometric figures. Where and what they are, and why, concerns physics or theology, and these are neither of them the science of the *Almagest.*

It is such a paradigm that I believe the modern economist, like the modern quantum physicist, in effect looks to. To find a predictive mathematics that worked would be all that the contemporary scientist in either area would demand. Not so with Newton, or with Marx: each identifies his science with a right and penetrating determination of the substance he has taken as his object. Ptolemy, and our contemporary economist and quantum theorist, are quite reasonably content to *save* their appearances: Marx and Newton are determined to *penetrate* the appearances and save the underlying substance. Marx, I want to claim, is a "classicist," not only in his unwavering attachment to Aristotle and the tragedians, but in his perhaps intuitive attachment to the goals of what we now call "classical physics." Marx, like Newton, is most concerned with the right understanding of the substance on which the science is founded. It is in this sense that he said, "every beginning is difficult."

It is often remarked that *Capital* advances through descending levels of abstraction, and Marx himself makes clear that the beginning has been accomplished through an act of extreme abstraction from experience. Certainly the concept of "undifferentiated homogeneous labour time" is utterly remote from any particular, concrete labor process, just as a chair regarded as a "commodity" is utterly abstracted from anything one might sit on. In this sense, *Capital* begins at a pinnacle of abstraction, and the course of development of the work will be through a series of descents to successively lower levels until finally we find ourselves back, at the close of the formal theory, on the plane of the phenomena themselves—the daily phenomena, that is, of capitalism: actual market prices, profits, interest rates, and rents.

We must be on our guard, however, for there is another sense in which in Marx's case the concepts of "abstraction" and "descent" are complicated and even, perhaps, reversed. Marx is, after all, in his own view building a science of an alienated, illusory realm: he is setting out, as we said, to tell the truth about an error. The error begins with the commodity, in which use-value, about which we care, is supplanted by exchange value, which impersonally governs the motions of capitalism in its stead. Marx's formal science is the theory of exchange value, the false facade of use-value. Only with the dialectical theory, which I have envisioned as containing and "framing" this formal theory, will truth come into focus in its own right. The world whose theory we are now building, the world of commodities, even when these take forms of the most vivid phenomena in "concrete" detail—that world of market prices and the daily Dow Jones quote—this is itself an abstract world.

What is ultimately in fact substantive is the other face of the commodity, which capital in all its transactions leaves behind: use-value, human interest and purpose, and the concerns of the original "economics." Thus the further we go in constructing the edifice of capital, which is of course Marx's purpose in the contained, formal theory, the more complete is our severance from all relation to the genuinely human world, the only world that is ultimately "concrete." In this sense, by building a world of abstraction, we will only be sealing and confirming more completely our alienation from the concrete. We will "descend," then, to the detailed phenomena of an alienating, illusory, and abstract world, though nonetheless the very one in which we live, and with which we are most familiar. When we return to it under Marx's guidance, we will find that it looks very different; Marx will bring us back in a dialectically controlled reentry—with changed minds, if his enterprise has succeeded.

We must agree with Marx that our starting point, "socially necessary homogeneous labour time," is highly abstract, and difficult or impossible to visualize. How, then, can this elusive notion serve as a firm foundation for an applicable theory? If we cannot even visualize it, how can we expect to use it as our platinum-iridium measuring rod for the determination of exchange value? Efforts to characterize it more fully hardly make things any easier to grasp. Marx suggests, for example, as he often will do as the work progresses, that we think in terms of society as a whole. Will this help? He invites us to consider "the total labour power of society" as "one homogeneous mass of human labour power, composed though it be of innumerable individual units." Pursuing this suggestion, he asserts:

> Each of these units is the same as any other, so far as it has the character
> of the average labour power of society. . . .   [*GBWW*, Vol. 50, p. 15b.]

This may give some hint of a way to consider the question, but it surely does not resolve it. Do we have, then, a firm foundation for a science, or do we not?

Fortunately for Marx's science, the theory in no way depends on our ability to produce an exemplar—or a mental image—of this socially average labor power. The exact and scrupulous determination of the labor value of commodities is a practical measuring process which is in fact going on in the markets of capitalism at all times. Marx has precisely characterized a process, a relentless equipoise of product against product, by which the universally interconnected markets of capitalism are always appraising precisely the quantity we are interested in. As bargains are struck in the myriad daily purchases and sales of the commodity markets, what are in effect *measurements* are made which are more exacting, perhaps, than those of a bureau of standards. Overpriced products are discounted and must come down in their prices; those that are underpriced are quickly bought up, and their places are filled by others that are more realistically evaluated. The free market is the laboratory of capitalism. Marx has not dreamed up the definition of value: he has simply penetrated the secret of a historical fact. The weighing, evaluating, and appraising of commodities in terms of that single homogeneous unit is the underlying *fact* of the universal system of markets in capitalism; it is what is going on around us, every day. All products are in fact being brought into ratios with one another by the market process. Such a thoroughgoing technology of universal exchange did not exist in Athens, and Aristotle was rightly baffled by the problem of relating five beds to a house. History has solved Aristotle's problem, and Marx has simply interpreted that solution.

Capital and wage labor[7]

Marx is taking us on a revelatory tour of the world in which we live, whose name is "capitalism"—the reign of capital. What, then, is "capital"? Conventional wisdom answers in terms of things: a stock of goods, an investment in factories, processes, and tools—the means of production. Marx turns our attention instead to the form of organization of our society, the social relations under which we live. These are, of course, characterized by the institution of private property— more specifically, private property in the means of production. Yet this does not quite suffice to define our own era: means of production were owned before capitalism came to birth. Nor is it sufficient to speak of a class division, for there were classes of the rich and the poor, the few and the many, in ancient Greece. Only the combination of these two criteria catches the essence of our historical situation: exclusion of the worker from ownership of the tools with which he works, so that private property in the means of production is concentrated in one class, while the other, that of the workers, is obliged to come to these owners as wage labor in order to work at all. It is really, then, the *concentration* of ownership of the means of production—made possible by the universality of that supremely accumulable commodity, money, with its surrogate, credit—that gives rise to the specific social relations constituting our economic world.

It is often suggested that Marx writes of another era, that his analysis may have been appropriate in England of the nineteenth century, but that we have passed beyond the social conditions he describes. I think this perception, on the part of those who are indeed quite understandably struck by the conditions of long hours, undernourishment, and child labor which Marx describes, misses the central point of his definition of "capital." We are today a class society, and we live under the relations of capital as he describes them insofar as there are among us those who must seek employment by others in order to carry out our own productive work. This is true whether that employer is a person or an institution, and whatever form the "work" may take—wage labor or salaried employment, production or service. For "labor," at least to a first approximation, we may read "employment"; and "class" is still the central fact of capitalism in the sense that most of us must seek employment from others, in order to work and live. This concentration of ownership of the means of production has of course become much more extreme in our time, the age of vast corporations and multinationals, than it was when Marx wrote. And while we may be a mobile society, with opportunity for all, as our mythology reiterates, the fact of concentration of ownership remains impressive.[8]

When we enter into an employment contract, we transfer to another a certain right—the right to command a specified amount of our labor time, and to own the product of our work. This has nothing to do with the modality of the work—whether the agreement is friendly or not, whether we expect to enjoy the tasks we are given, whether in fact it may seem to us the very "opportunity," as we say, for which we have been waiting. It is a legal contract (written or not), the very foundation of our social order: our work, and our work product, by right belong to another. This means, as Marx points out, then, that our labor power has become a commodity, entering a market as other commodities do (the "job market," we do not hesitate to call it), which appraises the items offered for sale and strikes bargains with at least as much rigor and strategic care as in the traffic in hogs, or wheat futures.

The fundamental insight here is that all markets are inherently coupled in a single system, since money can flow freely from one to another. If on a given day we are a better bargain than hogs are, money will be siphoned out of hogs and put into us. Capitalism entails the universalization of the commodity-relation and, by virtue of the private ownership of the means of production, comes to include, among the other commodities, man himself.

The universal role of money, which has made unbounded accumulation possible and thus opened the way to capitalism, has likewise restructured the practice of commodity exchange in a fundamental way. Marx facilitates our thinking in these matters by means of a striking formula, which he has devised to represent in one linear chain of symbols the flow of an economic process. Commodity exchange is represented in this way:

$$C—M—C'.$$

A commodity, C, is brought to market and exchanged for money, M, while that money in turn is exchanged for a second commodity, C', for which the original commodity owner has greater need. Here, a human need has been satisfied. [*GBWW*, Vol. 50, p. 48a.]

It would represent a total change in social relationships if we were to write the same formula from a different point of view, starting now with money rather than with a commodity:

$$M—C—M'.$$

Let us call the one who enters the market carrying with him, not a product, but simply money, a "capitalist." Unlike the shoemaker, who comes to market to sell a commodity of which he has an excess in order to buy something for which he has a need, the capitalist comes to market with money. He buys in order to sell: that is, both the beginning and the end of his cycle will be money itself—initially M, and finally M'. There is, of course, something absurd on the face of this transaction—if goods trade at their values, as Marx has presupposed earlier, the beginning and end of the process consist of the same thing, and nothing at all has been achieved. Marx puts this puzzle in stark terms. The capitalist, he says:

> . . . must be so lucky as to find, within the sphere of circulation, in the market, a commodity whose use-value possesses the peculiar property of being a source of value, whose actual consumption, therefore, is itself an embodiment of labour, and, consequently, a creation of value.
>
> [GBWW, Vol. 50, p. 79c.]

Only in that case can M' be greater than M, and the capitalist's activity make sense. The quotation above concludes:

> The possessor of money does find on the market such a special commodity in capacity for labour, or labour power. [Ibid.]

To explain this claim, Marx makes a fundamental distinction, the roots of which I think must be found in his frequent mentor, Aristotle. The commodity in question is "labour power," not "labour." He buys the *potential* for labor; Aristotle's term would be *dynamis*, "potential-ity." The use-value of this potential is labor-in-act, *actual* labor: this corresponds to Aristotle's term, *energeia*, "activity." The difference, Marx says, speaking with a voice that sounds very much like Aristotle's *Physics* at this point, corresponds to the difference between the *faculty* of digestion and the *act* of digestion.[9] Now, the economic significance of this distinction in the grammar of economics is immense: for if the commodity is labor power, it will be priced like any other commodity at the cost of its production. The value it produces, on the other hand—its use-value as labor-in-act—will be all the value it can yield in the course of a working day. Between the cost of production of labor power and the value that labor power can produce when put to work lies the difference between M and M' in the formula for capital-ism—and hence, the fundamental principle of profit and "return on investment." Labor produces more value than it costs and, under the social relations we are describing, that added value belongs not to the laborer but to the owner of the means of production, the employer of the laborer.

Marx gives to this expansion of value the name "surplus value," and we may rewrite the formula for capitalism to give this explicit recognition:

$$M—C—C'—M'.$$

Here C includes the labor power, which is the magic commodity the capitalist purchases, while C' represents the greater value of the product which that labor produces in act—the difference $(C'—C)$, or equally $(M'—M)$, is the "surplus value" created in the process. This formula may be taken as the law of motion of capitalism, since the prospect of this expansion becomes the driving force of all investment. It is a law that seems to me strikingly analogous in principle to Newton's Second Law of Motion of the heavens:

$$M—C—C'—M' \qquad \text{(Marx)}$$
$$F = ma \qquad \text{(Newton)}.$$

Each is universal in its own domain. Newton's law sees a physical force giving rise to an increment of velocity in a given time; that of Marx speaks of a motivational force giving rise to an increment of money in a cycle of production. There is no acceleration in the heavens without what Newton calls a "motive" force; there is similarly no investment under capitalism without the prospect of gain, of which the employment of living labor is ultimately the only source. We are on the track of a dynamics of economic motion very much in the Newtonian, classical sense.

In the commodity-market equation $C—M—C'$, one quality was exchanged for another; the market process had a natural purpose and a limit with the completion of the transaction, in which something unneeded had been exchanged for something that was wanted. It made human sense. In $M—C—C'—M'$, which can be contracted from the point of view of the investor to $M—M'$, the alpha and omega are mere quantities. Money, which entered in the era of commodity exchange as a medium of exchange, has now become the goal. Quantity, rather than quality, rules the process. One quantity—however—as such, is like every other quantity: the process that once had a natural end and made sense is now inherently infinite, endless. Marx observes, of M and M':

> . . . both have the same mission to approach, by quantitative increase, as near as possible to absolute wealth. . . . The circulation of capital has therefore no limits.   [*GBWW*, Vol. 50, pp. 71d–72a.]

It is interesting that Marx here once again permits himself a long reference to Aristotle, in which he reviews the latter's thinking about this question of the conversion of quality to quantity in economics. Aristotle sees a degradation of "economics," from that art which aims at the provision of human goods (the Greek word, *oikonomike*, refers to the art of household management), to a mere art of moneymaking, which he names "chrematistic," after the Greek word *chremata*, "money":

> . . . in the case of Chrematistic, circulation is the source of riches. And it appears to revolve about money, for money is the beginning and end of this kind of exchange. Therefore also riches, such as Chrematistic strives for, are unlimited. Just as every art that is not a means to an end, but an end in itself, has no limit to its aims, . . . while those arts that pursue means to an end are not boundless, since the goal itself imposes a limit upon them, so with Chrematistic, there are no bounds to its aims, these

aims being absolute wealth. . . . By confounding these two forms, . . .
some people have been led to look upon the preservation and increase of
money *ad infinitum* as the end and aim of Œconomic.

[*GBWW,* Vol. 50, p. 72b; cf. Aristotle, *Politics, GBWW,* Vol. 9,
pp. 450d–51b.]

Marx has his reasons for wanting us to see our own image in this ancient
anticipatory portrait, as if Aristotle had sensed the oncoming dangers
of a possible society become frenetic with the search for unlimited,
and hence meaningless, chrematistic wealth, rather than the intelligent
search for the human good.

We have stepped, with Marx, a little distance outside the development
of his formal theory in order to gain perspective on its implications for
human life. If capitalism is indeed a set of social relations in which we
are ourselves immersed, we are likely to need all the help we can get
in comprehending our own situation. To this end, Marx relates a short,
ironic narrative.

A free bargain has been struck, he says, like any other bargain in
the marketplace, between a worker and his prospective employer. The
worker at this point is "free" in two senses, which Marx distinguishes:
he is "free" to strike whatever bargain he chooses, but he is also "free"
of a crucial possession—he is "free" of any ownership of the means
by which he might work. Within the terms of this double-edged "freedom," he strikes a fair bargain: he will be paid what it costs to feed,
clothe, house, and otherwise provide for himself and his family; this is
the cost of reproduction of his labor power. In return, his newfound
employer will own his labor power. On the conclusion of this transaction, we leave the free marketplace:

Accompanied by Mr. Moneybags and by the possessor of labour power,
we therefore take leave for a time of this noisy sphere where everything
takes place on the surface and in view of all men, and follow them both
into the hidden abode of production, on whose threshold there stares us
in the face: "No admittance except on business." Here we shall . . . at
last force the secret of profit making.

This sphere that we are deserting, within whose boundaries the sale
and purchase of labour power goes on, is in fact a very Eden of the
innate rights of man. There alone rule freedom, equality, property
and Bentham. . . .

On leaving this sphere of simple circulation or of exchange of
commodities, which furnishes the "Free-trader *Vulgaris*" with his view
and ideas, . . . we think we can perceive a change in the physiognomy
of our *dramatis personæ*. He, who before was the money owner, now
strides in front as capitalist; the possessor of labour power follows as
his labourer. The one with an air of importance, smirking, intent on
business; the other, timid and holding back, like one who is bringing his
own hide to market and has nothing to expect but—a hiding.

[*GBWW,* Vol. 50, pp. 83d–84c.]

Overdrawn, perhaps, angry and caustic as this little caricature may be, it forcefully epitomizes the class relation that emerges from the economic analysis: on the face of it, a fair bargain in the free market so much celebrated in the mythology of capitalism, but beyond the marketplace, the fact that possession of the means of production is divided in such a way that the labor power of the one must inevitably become the possession of the other, and hence, no actual symmetry in the "free" bargaining process.

This is not only a question of "impoverishment" or of a bargain which is unfair in the system's own terms: it is rather a problem of the status of human work. The worker whose product is another's is inherently alienated from his own product; and if he is alienated from that product, which by social and legal right inherently belongs, as a consequence of the bargain, to another, then he is *a fortiori* alienated from the work itself. This is the alienation of human activity.[10]

We, as members of corporate society, schooled from our earliest years in its ethic, take this altogether for granted—we expect to be free *outside* the workplace and have no concern for freedom of our work itself providing it is pleasant, "rewarding" (as we say), and leaves us at large during normal spare time and vacations. We have perhaps no conception of "free" work in Marx's sense. We do not perceive the class structure that causes us to make the unequal wage bargain, and we are rather affronted than otherwise to have it pointed out to us. We feel we are paid fairly, perhaps generously, for our working hours; Marx is simply showing, formally and carefully, a sense in which we are not. We are paid for the hour equivalent of the car, the home, the food, the clothing, the amusements. That is a certain fraction, calculable though not normally accounted for in our society, of the working time we spend on the job: a fraction which Marx calls the "rate of surplus value."

There are many ways to think of this rate of surplus value, and many ways in which it can be adjusted overtly or covertly in the struggle—implicit or explicit, but under capitalism inherently never-ending—over the wage contract. Marx examines these transformations with great care; here it is sufficient to point out that the rate he has in mind can be thought of as a division of the working day: so many hours for the reproduction of the labor power, so many hours of surplus value to the employer. But it is equally true that every minute of working time is divided in that same proportion.

In studying capital, it is essentially, according to Marx, a structure of social relations that we have to examine. Marx has to keep reminding himself as well as the reader, one feels, that it is not persons (despite his occasional caricatures) but types, in the sense of objective social processes, that we are exposing: they take individual form, certainly, in many ways, but the real object of analysis is a social structure of which the capitalist is, Marx says, simply a "representative."

At this point, I want to make a suggestion whose roots I think are hinted in Marx's text: the "capitalist" Marx is describing is often not a person at all. Marx sees very far into the future of the careening system he is describing, but we have come a hundred years further down that road, and the logic has carried itself to a phase he foresaw but could not himself fully contemplate. Today we can see that the "capitalist" Marx describes has become above all the corporation, that artificial person given legal license during the nineteenth century to enjoy immortal life, and to aggregate resources and move with a will vastly beyond that of the boldest member of any aristocracy of personal wealth.[11]

The *human* capitalist Marx describes is torn: he enjoys pleasures, with the result that use-value vies with exchange value, consumption vies with accumulation. As capitalist, he accumulates with a rigor inherited from Calvin, but he is only human and, like Faust, Marx says, he finds that "two souls . . . dwell within his breast"—a certain "fellow-feeling for . . . Adam" corrupts the logic of accumulation with which he is entrusted [*GBWW*, Vol. 50, p. 293c].

It is not so with the *corporation,* which as an impersonal being is able to carry through the logic Marx describes to a pure result: this death-less, artificial entity—this Leviathan, which in Hobbes's time appeared to be the State—makes, *can* make, no compromise with the logic of accumulation. It is, then, with the corporation that most of us enter into our contract of employment.[12]

Marx is quite blunt about what this means, which is that those of us who accept employment have sold ourselves. We are no doubt very happy to have done so, since the alternative, *un*-employment, is fraught with suffering and despair. We freely make our minds and our skills into commodities. We despise ownership of another person, which we rule out as "slavery," but without complaint we sell our working lives by segments to others we call "employers." In this sense we make ourselves slaves for the best part of our lives, the working core.

Here the wages or the salary, the nature and conditions of the work, are not the central point; it is rather the *status* of our human activity—as our own, or the property of another—of which Marx speaks primarily. If we are going to be slaves, it is nice, surely, to be well-cared-for house slaves with interesting tasks and many hours off around the fringes; but slavery is slavery. The central question is of the structure of the working relation, which under capitalism is, in principle, ownership of one's labor power by another and hence alienation of one's human activity. Better pay and all the amenities of attractive conditions of work become, Marx says, "golden chains" that bind us all the more firmly in servitude. It will not fit into our vocabulary to envision that "work" might, in a different system, become a domain of freedom.[13]

To return to the development of Marx's formal theory, we now have seen that the way from M to M' is through the employment agreement and the consequent claim on surplus value. It is now necessary to look more closely at that process. We have written:

$$M—C—C'—M',$$

where C initially denotes that magic commodity, labor power, which the capitalist purchases in order to generate surplus value. More generally, however, C must denote all the elements he must purchase in order to initiate a new cycle of production. Labor power must in any case always be among them, but the capitalist must also acquire the means of production to put that labor to work. In fact, by definition, the "capitalist" alone, through past accumulation, possesses money sufficient to purchase the means of production that will serve to put labor to work. So C really has two very different components—labor power itself, and the means of production.

Each of these categories of the capitalist's investment consists of commodities whose value is measured by the labor that has gone into their production, that is, labor power, whose value is the cost of its reproduction, and raw materials, factory buildings, and machinery, which are the products of earlier cycles of production. But these two categories function very differently, from the capitalist's point of view. The first is an investment in *living* labor, which will create new, expanded value; the other is a purchase of *congealed* labor, which can do no more than pass its own value on, proportionately, into the new product. These Marx calls, respectively, *variable* and *constant* capital. The latter he calls "constant" in the sense that, being already complete, it does not, like "variable" capital, grow. Constant capital then consists of "dead" labor which the entrepreneur brings to living labor in order to make new production possible:

> Capital is dead labour that, vampire-like, only lives by sucking living
> labour, and lives the more, the more labour it sucks.
>
> [*GBWW*, Vol. 50, p. 112c.]

One need not, perhaps, phrase it quite so vividly, but the principle is striking. We might say that M drives forward to M' as rapidly and efficiently as possible; it achieves this goal, which for capital can be its only goal, in setting current labor to work on the means of production, which are in turn the products of past labor. The means of production, apart from living labor, can produce no value.

What then does capitalism "produce"? In the defining formula, $M—M'$, we have seen that the product in the ordinary sense cancels out. By means of products, capital in the strict sense produces new accumulation: that is, the system reproduces itself, or, as we should say, the product of capitalism is the system itself, reproduced on an ever-increasing scale. Capitalism thus tends to expand into any sphere that had previously escaped its grasp, such as the family farm or the individually owned store or business, and it inherently seeks to press its way into any new areas of the world which afford an "opportunity" for investment. Whether it is a question of a retail chain or the third world, capital's concern can only be that passage from M to M'. The personal capitalist may have compromised with human concerns, but the ultimate capitalist, the corporation, bearing legal responsibility to its own stockholders, must ultimately justify every significant act in terms of prudent regard to return on initial investment. $M—M'$ is a principle built into today's corporate law, as every alert director keeps constantly in mind, or overlooks at his peril.

Circulation and the market[14]

The story of capitalism has to be told on two levels. The first is that of the individual entrepreneur, his production process, and his contract with labor; the second is that of society as a whole, the social relations and processes that arise from myriad individual transactions, and the final economic balance. On the individual level we meet the battle of competition and the sometimes fierce, always-thrusting individual drive that is the genius of capitalism and the motive force from which all other motions follow. Yet the perspective at this level is limited; it gives rise, in ways Marx describes, to the system of illusion under which "profit" seems merely an obvious return on "capital." From the individual standpoint, capital cannot be seen as the result of an intense and very recent social development. The laws of motion, by which those who think of themselves as agents are in fact caught up in cycles of greater social motions that govern them like forces of nature itself, remain invisible.

Marx has begun at this level, examining individual transactions and the individual production process, and there he has found, he is confident, the secret of capitalism in the expansive principle of surplus value. Gradually, however, he moves toward ever-larger views of the marketplace and the interaction of capitals in the overall circulation cycle, which will become the explicit subject matter of Volume 2. In this transition, he looks insistently for the relation between the individual drive and the social outcome, between the domain of the separate and the domain of the social, between the region of detail and vagary and the larger region of regularity and social perspective.

Each capitalist produces with the goal of sale in a specific market. There, his product enters into an exchange process in which, as we have seen, a continuous scrutiny is occurring, with the market appraising, perhaps on a daily or hourly basis, the socially necessary labor time incorporated in each item. From that arises, as a social judgment, a market price.[15] Since this price is a social average, if the individual capitalist can find any way at all to produce the same product more cheaply in his own particular factory—that is, if he can reduce the labor time incorporated in each item below the social average—he will be able to realize a higher-than-average rate of surplus value. He will thus gain a significant *differential* advantage over the market. Typically, he may do this by introducing some new machine, or by refinement of production that increases the productivity of his labor. Hence arises the compelling drive to analyze and improve the production process, or to expedite distribution and marketing in any way possible so as to reduce turnover time. This is the relentless force that was already dramatically transforming the factory and the means of transportation and communication in Marx's time—and is, perhaps even more dramatically, still doing so today. Marx stands in genuine awe of the social gains this energy has made possible.

Not only does competition drive each capitalist to achieve whatever differential advantage he can contrive, but it insures as well that every other capitalist will follow suit as rapidly as possible. Each new invention, each advance in the production or circulation process, must spread like a wave through the industry in a common effort to share in this new gain—and of course, as this occurs, the ever-watchful market will be reckoning the new socially-average labor time incorporated in the product at its new reduced level. A new market price will result, all differential advantage will be lost, but in the end the product will be cheaper and society will have registered a gain. Immediately, however, each capitalist will return to analyzing his process for opportunities to gain a new differential advantage and restart the cycle.

From this social perspective, one of Marx's principal (and most contested) insights now takes shape: the net effect of such cycles of improvement in the productivity of labor is to drive living labor out of the production process wherever possible, and to replace it with congealed labor in the form of machines and other forms of constant capital. From his individual standpoint, the capitalist cannot see that living labor is in fact the only source of surplus value. Thus, while each capitalist makes important transient gains during the interval in which his differential advantage lasts, the net effect for all is a lowering of the only real source of gain, which is living labor. In the limiting dream of total automation, there would be no source of surplus value, the social structure would cease to reproduce itself, and the system of capitalism would dissolve. This vision demands more careful formulation and criticism, of course, but it may serve for the moment as an example of a certain process. Not only an overall social result, but a long-term, historic law might arise from the unseeing, immediate individual interactions of marketplace competition.

As a city looks different from the air, the detail of daily life receding and relationships emerging which could never be apparent from the ground, so Marx's synoptic view of the production and circulation processes as a single social whole gives us access to new concepts and conclusions. Only from this higher ground can we see the market itself as simply an incident in the production and reproduction of social relations, indeed of society itself, which in this cycling of its greater year is taking new forms, shaping within itself new powers, contradicting its past, and giving birth, perhaps, to some very different future. The individual point of view sees the entrepreneur, as owner of resources, encountering the worker, who having no such resources is necessarily seeking a job. In that view, their relationship is taken as given: it appears in this sense as merely "accidental."

From the social perspective, by contrast, we can see that the case is very different. The same relationship appears as an outcome of previous cycles of accumulation, as itself a product of the system. It is not even necessary to go back to a distant past, to trace the history of the great capitalist fortunes, or to envision some original act of labor or of initiative in a "state of nature," as the origin of the fact of property.[16] Rather, in the social perspective, we can see the birth of the property relation reenacted before our eyes. Whatever an original fortune may have been, that first increment is soon a merely evanescent quantity with respect to the regeneration of surplus value and its accumulation which is occurring on a continuous basis. As new accumulation eclipses the old, what we see is the effect of the mere claim one segment of society has on the labor of another, by virtue of the institution of property in the means of production. We witness a perpetual separation of the social product into two portions, one going to the reproduction of the labor force, and the other to those who hold social claim to ownership of the means of production. "Capital" thus lies before us, not as a collection of *things,* or even as a static social relation, but as an ongoing *motion,* which is continuously reproducing the social relationships of a hierarchical society.

That sense of ongoing motion is perhaps nowhere more vivid in *Capital* than in the monumental Chapter 15 of Volume 1, on "Machinery and Modern Industry" [*GBWW,* Vol. 50, pp. 180ff.]. A reader who undertook no more than this chapter might get some sense of the magnificent shaping energies of capitalism, and the ambiguity of their outcome: new, unheard-of productive forces emerging on an almost daily basis, while at the same time what seems on its face a degradation of the role of man the worker, who was so recently still a craftsman and owner of his own tools, and to that extent, at least, still autonomous in the production process, comes about.

Marx describes in this chapter a vast concentration of resources, inexorable refinement of the labor process, and the substitution, at every turn, of machinery as surrogate for the human hand and human skill. Scale is decisive: large capital drives out small, centralization replaces scattered enterprises, transportation is revolutionized. Credit systems transform the market process into instant, ideal transactions that pare turnover time to the minimum—and make possible a concentration of investment in "cyclopean" machines which man can do no more than tend. Marx traces with fascination the development of machines that make machines, since even the human machine-maker appears as an annoying bottleneck in the burgeoning development of the industrial age.

All this can be said in a spirit of wonder and praise, since for Marx it is a vision of the almost unbelievable powers of man when those powers are organized on a social scale. Everyone wonders, of course, at the machines, and the rationalization of the production process; but from Marx's perspective such a rationalization holds meaning which others seldom articulate. On the individual scale we saw competition, the restless forces of private gain. On the social scale we see, by contrast, coming out of this, aggregations of capital, and *de facto* social organization and cooperation, however unwitting and unintended, on an unprecedented scale: the power of social labor. It is science and technology, of course, that in one sense make all of this possible. But science and technology are inherently social functions themselves, in which each investigator in due course shares in the gains of all, and can only work through access to the unfolding social product.

The interweaving of products and processes, circulating on a new, world scale, represents the construction of a totally new form of society. Competition and the accidents of the marketplace retreat in importance before the fact of unprecedented social organization and *de facto* rational cooperation. Capitalism reveals itself as giving birth in very fact to its opposite: competition is continuously generating unrecognized cooperation. Yet this new society-in-process, while it remains in the bonds of a hierarchical social order, is seen by Marx as fraught with deep contradiction: machines that save labor only cause us to work longer and under greater stress; machines that are works of great intelligence drain work itself of any intelligent involvement. Later, we will consider the implications of this double oracle: prospect, and denial.

Marx dismisses the usual analyses of the economic process given in terms of "supply and demand." This is not, of course, because of any lack of appreciation of the importance of the free market as the foundation of the system of capitalism: in all his analyses, Marx presupposes the free market. It is the free market, indeed, that continuously determines the values that underlie exchange. This is as true, we shall see, of the markets in capital itself, in money, and in land, as it is of those in labor power and the products of labor. But "market economics," though it has its use in relation to the immediate phenomena of the marketplace, does not yield that vision of the overall movements, laws, and problems which makes of economics the science Marx is seeking. Only the larger view, from which the transient phenomena of the market cancel out, can do that. It is the larger laws, not the passing turns of the market, which are Marx's concern in *Capital.*

Similarly, in place of the bourgeois term, "demand," Marx speaks of "social need." He defines this as the effective purchasing power of society as a whole—total effective demand—as backed up with the money necessary to effect a purchase. This is a somewhat different concept from the "demand" often thought of in connection with market economics, whose point of view is first of all that of the individual market transaction. Individual workers may need or "demand" all sorts of things, certainly far more than society is prepared to offer; but even when these desires are supported by occasional access to cash, and hence become "effective demands" on an individual basis, they must remain irrelevant to the overall economic accounting, except as vagaries which over time are canceled out. Social need is a class concept, and on balance only such a class approach to the market has significance for the formal science.

The social product is allocated to the working class, who are the bulk of the consumers, on the basis of the rate of surplus value; the drive to increase profit insures that this rate will be kept as high as conditions permit, and essentially a stable quantity. Therefore the flow of value into the category of purchases by workers, the reproduction of variable capital, is quite strictly determined. It consists of the basket of provisions required to reproduce the worker and his family under the conditions, including accepted standards of social expectation, in any given social era. *This* is "social need," and we can see why it is the operative concept in any really synoptic view. Its detail, in terms of brands, styles, fads, and the like, is indeed a matter for market determination and a question of prime concern to producers, investors, and advertisers—the immediate participants in the competition for sales. Over longer periods, because of the overall cheapening of products with improved methods of production, its content tends to improve. But its total amount in any given era is limited by the requirements of capital to command surplus value, and its basic composition (housing, clothing, nutrition, transportation, education, amusements, etc.), since it must meet fundamental human needs, can vary in any one period within only rather narrow limits.

Profit on capital[17]

We now move into Volume 3 of *Capital,* and at the same time we descend to a dramatically lower level of abstraction. We move, that is, closer to the detail of the world of capitalism, a world that, as Marx argues in this third volume, systematically hides its own essence in illusion and mystification. We began in Volume 1 by identifying the abstract elements of capitalism, in the commodity, in labor value, and in the secret of surplus value. As we move away from these, we will be reconstructing the phenomena of the daily life of capitalism, tracing always as we go their relation to that veiled essence that alone can render the phenomena intelligible.

It is ironic that *Capital* as generally known—as reprinted, for example, in the *Great Books of the Western World*—consists only of the first volume of the three Marx wrote. The result is that most readers are left at that initial level of abstraction, which cannot speak the full truth of the world in the world's own terms: it tells of the secret and essence of capitalism, but it has not yet taken on the crucial burden of working back to the ordinary events and familiar discourse of our economic lives. That is the special task of Volume 3. The importance of this is not only to make the connection in such a way that the theory of Volume 1 can actually be interpreted and applied, but also to illuminate the origin and nature of illusion itself. Marx traces here the systematic generation of false consciousness and the process that has since come to be called "reification," by which entities take shape in consciousness which have no objective counterparts in reality.[18] This must be a dark study, not only because it descends ever more deeply into shadows of distortion, but because a certain note of despair inevitably intrudes as it becomes apparent how total and almost indefeasible such systematic social illusion may be.

The first step in this descent is the transformation of the *rate of surplus value* into the *rate of profit.* This distinction arises because capital committed to an enterprise and tied up in it, as machinery, raw materials, or buildings, demands recognition. Capital, as such, contributes nothing new to the value of a product. But tied up as constant capital, it is prevented from utilization in other forms, in which it might be directly employing living labor and hence reaping surplus value. As capital, it is "owned," and no "owner" will forgo the opportunity to receive surplus value unless he receives adequate compensation. In fact, since his capital is crucially needed—for a certain minimum of constant capital is always required to put living labor to work—it might seem that he could demand whatever price he chose; but in fact, there is a limit.

Since the only source of any new value is the surplus value created in the labor process itself, the owner of constant capital can demand for it no more than a share of that new increment of wealth. The measure of this "share" is in turn determined by exchanges in a new kind of market that arises, *a market in capital itself.* In it, capital flows to investments that offer greatest return, with the result that overall, and to the extent that this market is universal and fully effective, all capital, constant or variable, tends to receive the same rate of return. "Profit" becomes the ratio of surplus value to the *total capital* invested in an enterprise. This will be less than the rate of surplus value, in which the numerator was the same, but the denominator was variable capital alone. The rate of profit will thus be lower than the rate of surplus value, as total capital is greater than variable capital, which directly employs labor.

We can see that the market in capital, which itself represents a major historical development in the unfolding logic of capitalism, must greatly alter the distribution of returns to investors from the production process. In the case of an industry that utilizes relatively small amounts of constant capital, the rate of profit would approach that of surplus value itself, its upper bound. On the other hand, a process that requires large amounts of constant capital will generate relatively little surplus value in relation to the capital invested—it will have a low rate of profit. However, through the operation of the capital market, neither investor will actually see the rate of profit his own enterprise would have generated if it operated alone. All industries are closely coupled through the capital market, and capital will thus flow out of the more profitable enterprise and into the less, until finally under the pressures of the competition of capitals, money invested in each becomes equally rewarded. As it thus comes to share in the average rate of profit, it continuously transfers surplus value from the intrinsically higher profit enterprise into the lower.

The effect of the capital market is thus to socialize the exploitation of labor: transfers of value occur constantly, through that market, from high-return to low-return industries, until all share in a common profit rate. This social process is not seen as such by the participants, but from the perspective of Marx's theory, we can now see how it would follow that in this way each capitalist would indeed become, as Marx puts it, "a shareholder in the whole social enterprise"—all are participants in a general "freemasonry of capital."[19] Since the operation of surplus value is, from the outset, unseen by the capitalist, he is even less aware of its transfer, and he does not perceive the immense and crucial social process in which he is taking part. To him, it seems that each capital investment itself generates its own expansion of value. What is in fact a social result, through which the highly technical operation of the market in capital has become generalized and effective on a world scale, occurs altogether "behind his back."

Since, with other things equal, capital tied up in an enterprise is rewarded in proportion as the turnover time of the process can be shortened (thereby absorbing more living labor in any given period of time), the production process is constantly being driven at the highest possible velocity. This calls for shortening of the circulation time whenever possible, the invention of methods of credit which circumvent delays in marketing, and pressures on commercial capital involved in commodity exchange. Communications, illustrated in the nineteenth century by such advances as the introduction, first, of packet ships, and later, of the telegraph and the ocean cables, are driven by the competition of the capital market: the effort to gain differential advantage through earlier access to market information, or to realize a higher-than-average rate of profit through an edge in turnover time. It is only the average rate of profit in an industry as a whole, over time, that the capital market establishes. Hence despite the "freemasonry of capital" that is thus ultimately assured for the industry as a whole, the individual entrepreneur still feels the same pressure as ever to gain any temporary advantage he can contrive.

The illusion that capital—which in fact simply *demands,* by virtue of its status as private property, to be rewarded—*creates* the value which flows to it, yields corresponding distortions throughout capitalist thought and accounting. Bookkeeping, whose art is the new rhetoric of capitalism and hence of our era, is conformed to profit, not to the underlying surplus value. Everywhere that capital, in whatever form, enters the production process, capitalist bookkeeping imputes to it the general rate of return on which it insists. The accountant makes this entry with no sense of duplicity or distortion, but rather in due recognition of what he has learned to call the "cost of capital." In his view, the "cost of capital" is no different from the "cost of labor" or the "cost of fuel": each he sees as a component of the "production price" of the product. Ultimately, this becomes incorporated in the price of the commodity, and the consumer pays for it accordingly, again with no more qualms than were felt by the accountant.

We see now that the actual commodity markets of capitalism are not, as we had assumed in Volume 1, assessing the *value* of the products in which they trade, but rather a *cost* based on a proportionate imputation of value to all elements of capital that have been involved in their production. Cost in this sense displaces value in all capitalist markets, and in economic theory as well. Price tends not toward true labor value, but toward a construct of capitalist bookkeeping that has the effect of transferring value in streams from high-profit to low-profit enterprises. We see now that the entire market operation, and with it, all thinking about the economic process, is systematically mystified in such a way that value and the source of value become invisible, just as the flows of value and the socialization of that flow remain unobserved.

Does this mean that, in practice, Marx's analysis, however true it might be at some level of abstract principle, has no real applicability? The question would seem to call for a thoughtful pause. We can see one thing, however: no matter what the participants themselves may think, if Marx was right in the fundamental analysis of Volume 1, then the law of value still governs the overall exchange. There is no source of profit other than surplus value, and the analysis of Volume 1 remains decisive: total profit in the entire market, having no other source, must finally equal total surplus value. Hence, other things equal, it is as true as before that the rate of surplus value is the underlying index that governs the return on all capital; it is only the purchase and exploitation of labor power that originally generates the returns in which, by whatever route, all ultimately share. And if that is true, then it is at least as important as before to recognize the fact, and to be able to penetrate the mists of illusion, to see through to the engine at the heart of the machine. One prime mover turns all the wheels, however they may imagine that they turn themselves. All that was said at the higher level of abstraction in Volume 1 remains true now, but its elements operate in Volume 3 increasingly behind the scenes, and the burden of tracing their operations through the hieroglyphs of economic practice becomes the more onerous.

What becomes apparent is the emergence of a systematic illusion, and we see at the same time how even that illusion itself is a necessary product of the very system that it serves to veil. We are speaking, not of a merely technical error, but of a coherent myth, a fundamental inversion of perception of what is going on in the universe of our experience. Capitalism constitutes an ever-ramifying *social* fabric, while at the same time it presents itself as individualistic and planless, indeed the very product of unfettered human nature.

Interest on money[20]

We now turn to the consideration of *interest,* and with it, take one more step downward from the clarities of the original abstract heights into the confusions of the realm most familiar to us, the daily phenomena of capitalism, with all its vicissitudes. We all know, as if it were one of the facts of nature, that money "draws" interest, and we view with concern anyone who keeps money in his possession for any length of time, without putting it "to work." With interest, Marx says, capital takes its ultimate fetish-form, in which it appears as if money itself were capable of generating value.

Interest is, of course, a pivotal phenomenon of capitalism, the out-come of its relentless effort to achieve the power to aggregate resources, through channels of credit, on short notice and into ever-larger con-centrations. Yet, by contrast with the rate of profit, the rate of interest obeys no inner law. Interest and profit must both, indeed, be carved from the same source in surplus value; a division must in some way take place between them. But for the determination of this point of division, there is here no rational principle. Competition, tradition, and the mood of the marketplace shift interest rates in a never-ending contest between lenders and entrepreneurs.

The illusion that arises with this division of function between profit and interest runs very deep. It seems as if the allocation of surplus value were measuring something fundamental in the economic process, as though two different *sources* of value were being tapped, and rewarded on some proportionate principle. "Interest" appears as a return on ownership per se, as though money tied up inherently generated a return. With this development of the capitalist market, it seems as if the original dream had been realized: money in itself seems to bear fruit, "as a pear tree bears pears." It is as if interest "grew" from money. Marx calls attention to the Greek word for "interest," *tokos*, which first means simply, "offspring."[21] It seems that the underlying formula of capitalism, $M—M'$, has now been realized without the annoying intervention of any production process whatever—that is, without the distraction of having to produce and distribute any product, in accord with the original more cumbersome, expanded formula,

$$M—C—P—C'—M'.$$

In turn, with interest now conceived as return to ownership per se, the function of the remaining profit of enterprise becomes seen as the return to a distinct function, as "wages of superintendence"—this despite the fact, which Marx and Adam Smith alike point out, that these functions of management are regularly in fact delegated to supervisory personnel, who as such have no share in ownership. Marx goes on to point out that the success of cooperative factories demonstrates that the capitalist's supposed role in actual production can be eliminated without its absence being especially noticed.[22]

Capitalist bookkeeping, which as we have already seen gives canonical form to a developing structure of illusion, now makes distinct entries: *interest* on borrowed funds, and *profit* on invested capital. The former appears as the "cost of money," and may be duly registered as a separate item even if the capitalist has advanced the funds himself, and no money has been borrowed. Confirmed in this perception by a coherent system of bookkeeping with its own terms and strict rules, the capitalist can hardly be held responsible for his error in imagining that money in itself contributes value to his product. Money is rewarded with interest in recognition of this magic efficacy to contribute new value by virtue of the mere passage of time—"asleep or awake, at home or abroad."[23] Preserving its myths, this world of illusion is intent on what becomes in effect a deliberate effort at self-deception: reproduction of its own ignorance of the realities on which it in fact rests.

Rent[24]

We now meet a yet further exaction from the production process, in the form of rent. Rent, Marx says, arises because "a monopoly to a piece of the earth enables the landowner to exact a tribute" in exchange for permission to use the land for the production of crops. There is a difference, however, between the "tribute" demanded by the landowner and the tolls taken by the capitalist and the banker. Although a demand is made for a return that does not arise from any actual contribution to the value of the product, at least in these two cases there is some basis in actual value: capital and money both represent value, definite amounts of crystallized labor time. When the landowner demands a payment for the use of unimproved land, however, his claim is not based on any actual value whatever: since it is not a product of labor, land *per se* has no value. Interest and profit represent returns on actual values; rent on unimproved land is a return on no value at all.

Any "value" that is set on unimproved land is, then, a purely irrational expression. Increasingly, as we move with Marx from the original surplus value through capital and interest to rent, we see social relationships of ownership distorting and veiling the actual underlying economic process, twisting the economy through the rhetoric of book-keeping into false measures of cost and price founded on arbitrary demands, detached farther and farther from the only source of value itself, human labor.

Marx is looking in particular at the English landowning class as he writes about rent (specifically, "ground rent"), but he points out as well that the same account could be given in other areas of an economy, such as mining. Because he founds his analysis systematically on first principles, it is not bound to the institutions of his own time; "rents" on unimproved properties in various forms are to be found through-out our contemporary society, and everywhere they occur, they are subject to Marx's finding of irrationality. Landed property, Marx says, "presupposes that certain persons enjoy the monopoly of disposing of particular portions of the globe as exclusive spheres of their private wills."[25] Agricultural land is certainly a prime instance of this, but any "portion of the globe" that has a use-value and can be "chained down" is a candidate for a rent—namely, a demand for payment for its use.

If we ask how large this rent might be, we see right away that we are confronted with an extreme case of the situation we met before. Once again, the only source of surplus value is the labor process; again, the question is that of division and distribution of the surplus value achieved there. The capital market decided the allocation to capital in the form of a rate of profit; the demand for interest yielded a fundamentally arbitrary division between the banker and the capitalist. In each case, however, the return took form of a *rate* calculable in relation to an actual value as denominator—the labor time that is crystallized in the capital or the loaned funds.

In the case of rent, there is no such denominator. Rent, as a return on what has in principle no value, is not a rate but a social exaction, worked out as an implicit or explicit confrontation between landlord and capitalist.[26] Once again, bookkeeping plays its responsive role: where before it imputed a rate of return to all money as such, it now—where there is no value on which to base a rate—reasons in reverse and *imputes* a value. In effect, it simply conjures up the missing denominator. A value is computed for the land, which is thus "capitalized" to justify the rent as if the latter were a rate. This, according to Marx, is the origin of the supposed "value" of land—it is simply a rent capitalized according to an assumed rate of return. Because social relations have exacted a rent, a value is attributed to the property. The house of mirrors is now very nearly complete.

Once the fiction has been established that land has a "value" and a "price," then by a kind of second imputation, or inversion of the inversion, bookkeeping will regard the use of this now valued land as a "cost" and will impute "rent" to it as a return on its facade of value. This becomes a new component in all pricing and in turn skews all market judgments to include a component toll to landownership. Marx acknowledges that it is extremely difficult to keep one's bearings in this labyrinth of fictions, all of which are so worked into our common experience that they feel to us like the most evident of truths.

With the theory of rent, Marx has essentially completed the inquiry that began with the identification of that abstract cell form, the commodity. We have before us now a new panorama of the phenomena of capitalism, not as mere empirical patterns or observed "laws," but as evidences of deeper social processes. What looks on the surface like fragmented thrusts of individual competitors on the track of separate advantage, reveals itself as governed by deep underlying social relationships, and we now see vividly before us social processes and cooperation just the opposite of the atomic market processes in terms of which capitalism pleases to think of itself.[27] A new society has been forged and is being advanced and perfected on a daily basis. It is a society with immense social and technological powers to achieve the human good, were the old mythology to be shed, and its real possibilities recognized—understood and mastered to serve rather than to threaten and possibly overwhelm us.

What has been revealed most clearly and consistently, if Marx's analysis is correct, is that, despite every illusion to the contrary, all rewards in our system are generated out of one underlying process of exploitation. The term "exploitation" refers simply to the basic principle for Marx, that labor is never paid at the value it produces, while the difference, that surplus value, is systematically transferred to reproduce a hierarchical society. It is a system that runs, not to achieve the human good, but to reproduce an arbitrary structure of inequality. The formal analysis has shown us that, if its terms are correct, we live in a perverse social order which, despite its persuasive rhetoric to the contrary, and despite all its promise and all our efforts, runs inherently to produce and to reproduce a twisted world.

Marx has traced to their origins the illusions that he believes altogether prevent us from seeing this truth about ourselves. Is he correct in this belief? It is not a small question, nor one confined to economic or political issues. If he is right, we are wrong about the very nature of freedom itself, and of our humanity. We think we are free, he says, but we are not; we think we understand ourselves and what we call our "human nature," but if Marx is right, we are still only on the way to the comprehension of what it would mean to be fully human. We have not yet formed a rational and cooperative society, whose members know, in practice, effective freedom and actual equality of opportunity. Yet if Marx's analysis is at all valid, we might be much closer to this than we permit ourselves to recognize.

Transition to a dialectical theory: the "Trinity Formula"

Having traveled such a long road in the development of his theory of capitalism, Marx now offers us, as a kind of antidote to all the deceptive mirrors we have looked into, a magic mirror of his own in which the whole work, with all its contradictions, can be reviewed with a new sense of perspective. I have attempted to distinguish throughout my own account of Marx between the "formal" and the "dialectical" theories, the former being, in principle—though not in any literal or sequential way—"framed" within the latter. It has often been difficult to preserve that distinction, since however they differ in principle and in their roles, the two run together throughout the work, the critical as a kind of subtext, we might say, to the formal. I think Marx wants to help us now in the transition from one mode to the other: from the "formal" to the "dialectical" reading of the work—and thus, in reflection, to put the formal theory in its dialectical frame. He does this in a remarkable chapter, in a sense the high point of Volume 3 or even of *Capital* itself, which he entitles, "The Trinity Formula."[28] Here, near the end of the work, we are invited to reconsider the entire account with new insight.

The reference of the chapter's title is to the Christian trinity, which Marx likens now to the three great elements of the conventional theory of capitalism, the theory that corresponds to capitalism's perception of itself—what Marx regularly calls, the "bourgeois theory." He recalls these elements in the pattern:

CAPITAL/INTEREST

LAND/RENT   LABOR/WAGES

where in each case an imputed "source" is paired with the mode of return that is assigned to it according to the distributive justice of this mythical order: thus, land "earns" rent, capital "earns" profit which generates interest, and labor "earns" wages. Marx says these elements are like the persons of the Holy Trinity: Father, Son, and Holy Ghost. Why does he say this? We know that he regards this bourgeois "trinity"—just as he regards the Holy Trinity—as a form of mystification. But why has he chosen this particular mode of parody? To arrive at an answer, we might remind ourselves that in earlier days, before *Capital,* when Marx was writing on these same subjects, he made clear that he saw the Christian mystery not simply as error. It is, he wrote, like capitalism itself, a mode of alienation—the Christian vision was not simply wrong, but an alienated perception of an important truth.[29] Christianity was seen then by Marx as an inverted perception of the vision of a longed-for human future—the Kingdom of Heaven as an alienated vision, projected into realms of eternity, of the liberated human community toward which mankind is striving in actual history. Behind the Holy Trinity, Marx claimed, lies a secret, and that secret is *man.* Where the religious consciousness has projected God, there lies in reality, hidden, a dawning recognition of the possibilities latent within the human community. The power of that veiled truth, refracted in one way and another, has been a primary moving force of Western history since the time of Christ.

In the same way, the capitalists' trinity, in Marx's view, contains a secret: behind the separate categories it asserts lies the one source of value from which they all flow—living human labor. This is so because, if Marx is right, "interest" and "rent" are, for all their separate pretensions, no more than shares in surplus value, which is what labor alone creates. This labor in turn Marx sees as having its ultimate fruition in human community—that which we are working for, he suggests, even if we don't realize it. Hence the analogy to the Holy Trinity is perhaps "not altogether fool," but a strong hint that behind the error lies an essential perception about ourselves and our society.

Of course the allusion to the Christian trinity in this connection is ironic, and boldly so. But irony is a mode that is inherent, and reveals itself in one way or another, in all dialectic. The path of dialectic lies through confrontation with contradiction. Marx collects the contradictions incorporated in the economic trinity, which we have seen along the way as the formal theory traced out the development of the three elements. There is in truth no relation between capital and interest, or between land and rent; and land itself has no value. How can such ratios be taken? Not by way of economic principles, which do not serve, but rather by way of social relations. The crucial error, underlying the apparent economic irrationality, is the social institution of private ownership of the means of production. In the formula, "LAND/RENT," for example, the noun "land," which seems to represent a fixed and definite *thing,* is in fact a surrogate for a historical social relation, landed property, property in "a portion of the globe." Similarly, "capital," which sounds like a *thing,* in turn represents a historical social relation which establishes certain persons as "owning" the means of production.

This substitution of a thing-word for what is in fact not a thing is the *reification* we spoke of earlier, and we might say now that the bourgeois trinity "reifies" land, labor, and capital, as necessary economic realities, where in fact by each of these ought to be meant a certain historical social relation—"ownership" in the case of land and capital; "nonownership" in the case of labor. The reified social relation, once recognized for what it is, links all the persons back to one center: living labor—not alienated "labor," the economic category to which "wages" are ascribed in the belief that it is thereby fully paid—but actual labor, which is never fully paid. This is the single source of all the categories.

We now see the relevance of the Holy Trinity. For the secret of that is the incorporation of the three "Persons" in one mystic unity. Correspondingly, behind the illusory distinction of the elements of the economic trinity there is an unseen principle of unity: the weave of economic society itself, which Marx sees as the social character of our labor. The weave of the markets in capital, money, labor, land, and all commodities, and the fine-tuning of densely intertwined production processes in every category have yielded, as we have seen, immense advancement in these forces of social labor, in the cooperative processes of science and technology, communication and transportation, and techniques of social planning and organization on unprecedented scales. The nature of labor has been entirely transformed to match this *de facto* socialization of the production process; out of it are coming, Marx sees, the makings of a new community of mankind.

On these terms Marx has shown that his vision of the future is to an important degree already with us, and yet wrapped in a cloak of invisibility, in the misconceptions and alienation of the present. Marx is not given to laying out blueprints of the future. Readers often feel disappointment in this; they want to know his prescription for human society. He does not indulge in such speculation, not out of avoidance of a task that would be a heavy one to undertake, but on principle. If history advances dialectically, the future does not come to us in blueprint form. We make our ways into it, reading the signs and shaping our advances as we go.

The future appears to us in the very pages of *Capital,* as we come to understand the unfreedom and illusion under which we now live and begin to read the signs of a possible human future—already so nearly in our hands, and yet so far from our grasp. Under the spell of the "Trinity Formula," Marx permits himself some reflections on the future toward which it points:

> Freedom, in this sphere [of human needs], can consist only in this, that
> socialized man, the associated producers, govern the human interchange
> with nature in a rational way, bringing it under their collective control
> instead of being dominated by it as a blind power; accomplishing it
> with the least expenditure of energy and in conditions most worthy and
> appropriate for their human nature.[30]

This is not an idle wish, Marx would have us believe, but a reading
of the evidence. Even in the bondage of the present "domination," if
we read through the opaque symbols of our current order, Marx has
shown us how many signs there are that we are already well on the way
to being, in fact, members of a cooperative and rational society, with
rapidly accumulating experience in "governing the human interchange
with nature in a rational way." Reality, Marx has endeavored to show
us, is working in the direction of freedom; it is myth and illusion, and
an anachronistic social order, that bar the way.

It would be the work of another essay to read *Capital* a second time,
systematically, as a work of dialectical science, and to examine and
develop the concepts which that phrase holds within it. It has been necessary here to walk once through the formal structure, noticing often
enough as we went along the contradictions and illusions that suggest
the further, dialectical reading. Here, in concluding the present study,
we can only look briefly at this question, to consider what it would
mean to speak of *Capital* as a "dialectical science," and to sketch what
a dialectical reading might entail.

Three stages in the dialectic of the dialectic[31]

We have spoken earlier of two models of "science"—that which aims
to save the appearances, and was exemplified by Ptolemy, and another,
exemplified by Newton and the *Principia,* which seemed the model that
Marx follows in *Capital* in its aspect as formal science. Now, however, I
am proposing a third, for I believe that the dialectical reading of *Capital* is not less "scientific" than the formal one, but rather that it very
much enlarges the sense and scope of "science." We would be right, I
believe, in speaking of *Capital* in its larger aspect as a work of dialectical
science. Though this thought cannot be adequately developed here, I
would like to suggest what it might mean. To do so, however, we must
take a moment to reflect on the notion of "dialectic" itself. For though
I have often referred to the concept in the course of this study, and
made certain claims about it in passing, I have not explained what I
understand it to mean.

Dialectic has had its own history in our Western experience; we
might speak of its own "dialectical" development—or of "the dialectic

of the dialectic." It will suffice for the moment if we take just three great benchmarks of dialectic as exemplars of this unfolding of the concept: the Platonic dialogues, of course; the Hegelian dialectic; and the dialectic of *Capital.*

Socrates remains the model of all dialectical teaching, we might agree—but how do we understand this? Perhaps, simply, that he teaches by means of *real questions.* Life stands or falls by the answer to a Socratic question, and the answer is always entirely up to us. It is the conviction underlying all dialectic, in any of its forms, that such fundamental questions of value, right, and human purpose—questions that have no "objective" answers, but that touch on matters closest to our lives—are not idle, but that in one way or another, we do have access to crucial means of moving toward their resolution.

On the other hand, the term "dialectic" suggests also a certain structure of inquiry, and we need to consider the relation between such a real question on the one hand, and the pattern of dialectic on the other: not only the vividness of the human questions that they ask, but a certain common form links Plato, Hegel, and Marx. As we say this, however, it is very important to avoid possible misunderstanding: though the thread that links these three stages of the dialectic is very real, and fundamental in particular to our understanding of Marx, to point to this common principle is not at all to assert that dialectic is not very much transformed in its passage from one stage to the next.

The dialogue *Meno* serves well as a paradigm of the dialectical motion in its Socratic mode, and I would invite the reader to take that volume from the shelf of the *Great Books* and reflect with me on it in relation to the very brief remarks which follow [*GBWW,* Vol. 7, pp. 174ff.]. In broad terms, we can see that it begins, as it should, with a question. It is not easy to say just what that opening question *is,* for as Meno asks it, it contains a nested set of complications that may well be endless. "Do you," he asks Socrates, "have it in you to say to me whether virtue can be taught, or if it is not teachable, whether it comes by practice; or if it neither comes by practice nor can be learned, whether it comes to men by nature or in some other way?"[32] I think it is characteristic of dialectic that the question itself is already questionable: we have questions in echelons, questions about the question. Is this a question about Socrates (as it seems grammatically to be), and his power, or is it about virtue, or about teaching . . . or about Meno himself? All these elements are so problematically interrelated that we sense that they must be, finally, just one question: who teaches, who learns, what is taught, what teaching is, and where the answers come from—a single package of perplexities.

Marx, similarly, asks us, as participants in the woven world of capitalism, to wonder with him who we are, what virtues we practice, and what source of light there might be for us from somewhere beyond this system within which we are enclosed, by which we might judge ourselves and it. Finding the real question about capitalism has been our first problem in approaching this attempt at a rereading: it is not, I have claimed from the outset, a book "about economics." But it is not so clear, on the other hand, where the boundaries of Marx's real subject matter do lie—his questions penetrate, as those of Socrates do.

To focus, then, for a moment on the *Meno* as paradigm of the dialectical form: the opening question is developed in a variety of artful ways that steadily reduce this brash young general, initially confident enough in the world's ways, to a state of what may be serious wonder and concern. He meets unexpected difficulty in defining virtue ("excellence"), though he had evidently never before doubted that he was himself a living model of it. His failure leads him to a certain, perhaps petulant, despair, and it is significant that here the dialogue comes to a dead stop—at its effective center—with an outcry from Meno that seems in its own terms unanswerable [*GBWW,* Vol. 7, p. 179]. Dialectic is impossible, he asserts, because we either (1) know the thing we are looking for already, in which case it is idle to be searching, or (2) we do not know what we are looking for, in which case it is even more idle to be searching, since we wouldn't know it if we found it. This is, presumably, a standard sophistic argument against learning and truth, but it defines a real problem, and here it may be that Meno is genuinely struck by it. Meno blames this *impasse* on Socrates, who he says is like the electric torpedo fish, which shocks anyone who comes upon it into numbness. This point of death of the argument—which appears, I am tempted to say, at the virtual center of all dialectic—is often referred to in Greek as the *aporia*—the sticking point, the point of no passage, the point of no return for the argument.

We cannot here trace that way by which Socrates at once opens a path for Meno—and, we must add, for us. It is by means of "recollection," Socrates half-mythically explains, that we are able to assert truths with conviction, as if we once knew them and were recovering them through a mist of forgetfulness. The *aporia* of the dialectic will always lead us into the darkest obscurity; but if all goes well, we will emerge empowered with knowledge we had not known we possessed. To be schematic about this, and as an aid in tracing something of this same pattern in Hegel and Marx, we may say that there are three parts to every dialectical motion.

   I. The opening question, a real question, which takes form through an intense searching in the mode of questions and answers, not yet fully articulate;

  II. The clarifying argument to the point of contradiction and despair; the question becomes articulate but, at the same time, leads to *aporia;*

III. The passage beyond the *aporia,* through yet more serious questioning, which yields whatever knowledge is humanly possible; not,
however, in the mode of syllogistic consequence, but drawing on
some larger source of human intuition, in the form of image,
myth and mystery.

If we were in this reminded of other tragic trilogies, such as the *Oresteia*
of Aeschylus and the Oedipus cycle of Sophocles, we would surely be
on the right track.[33]

Now, Hegel. The pattern of dialectic is in many ways the same, but
there is surely a fundamental difference as well, for we are in a different world: the Judeo-Christian world, the world of the omnipotent,
omniscient Creator God, God of love and sacrifice—the world infused
with the Holy Spirit. It would be hard to think of any aspect of life
that was not touched by this world change. The Hegelian dialectic thus
takes as paradigm not only Plato but the Christ story: Advent, Passion,
Resurrection. The dark moment of the *aporia* becomes the suffering on
the cross. Dialectic is the journey, not simply of the learning mind, but
of the subjective Self as Spirit, creatively acting to shape its own image,
and passing ultimately to freedom—not in objective knowledge—but
in self-consciousness. The argument unfolds, not in an afternoon, but
through the ages of history. The course of history now *is* the course
of the argument.

Hegel puts this in a pattern temptingly like the schema we outlined
earlier, but deeply altered as well:
 I. The Spirit *an-sich* (in itself, immanent), thrusting forward in dialectical search for its own identity;
 II. The Spirit *für-sich* ("for" itself), objectively determinate in the
world, and suffering all the consequences of the estrangement
from itself;
 III. The Spirit *an-und-für-sich;* the mystery of the Resurrection, which
restores the Spirit to itself without denial of its objectification.

The third stage is expressed in a German word of double meaning,
Aufhebung, at once both "cancellation" and "uplifting." "Transcen-
dence" is a word that is often invoked by translators to suggest something of the magic of this third phase.

It would be worth the reader's turning to a paragraph in the *Philosophy of History* in which Hegel images this life of the Spirit in terms of
the passage of the sun in the course of one great day of the history of
the Spirit in the Western world [*GBWW*, Vol. 46, p. 203a]. The first
phase (or "moment," in Hegel's terminology) is that of the dawn, but
no ordinary dawn: to suggest the sense of that immanence (the Spirit
an-sich), Hegel visualizes the experience of a blind man who has for the
first time been granted sight (I). He is engulfed in the light of the rising

sun: no objects are yet differentiated; it is a single, whole experience. By midday (II), however, objects are differentiated, the magic is dispelled, and all is explicit and objective; the Spirit is alienated, distanced from itself, *für-sich*. In the life of mind, this is the phase of objective, syllogistic reasoning, which Hegel interestingly likens to attaching labels to a skeleton. Yet by evening (III), Hegel says, man "has erected a building constructed from his own inner sun" [ibid.], a vision of his own Spirit, and in this late light, Spirit knows itself in the illumination of its own, greater sun. This is *self-consciousness,* and that, for Hegel, is freedom, the culmination of the dialectic.

The dialogue which, for Plato, has been in a sense timeless, essentially the same in every repetition, has now entered time and become History itself, one epoch perishing, to be transcended by another in the advance of an argument that has become our collective inquiry—the learning process of Western man. If there is indeed real *progress* in the evolution of mankind and the development of our human culture, must it not be the case that Hegel is right, in some fundamental way?

Finally, Marx—and the bearing of this long tale on the dialectical reading of *Capital.* It seems to me that without having reached some understanding together of this dialectical tradition, we could not recognize the nature and magnitude of the task Marx may be setting for us, his readers. Commentators often speak of Marx as having rejected Hegel's thought, while using his "method." It is true that Marx does explicitly reject Hegel's philosophy in certain important ways, while incorporating the form of the dialectic. But dialectic is never simply a "method." Such a tortured procedure, through the negation which marks the second phase, makes sense only if the human situation is itself perceived as dialectical, only if the human circumstance demands and justifies such a process—as to which all three of our "dialectical" authors must be in some deep agreement. What is it about our world that leads Marx to conceive it—as did Plato and Hegel before him— as a dialectical problem, and in what way, in *Capital,* do we meet the threefold structure of the dialectical investigation?

Marx has found that capitalism is a social structure in motion, in history, generating and regenerating its own progression, and changing as it goes. We, his readers and fellow human beings, are, like Marx himself, immersed in that world and in the stream of that unfolding history. Its terms and symbols are ours. Yet at the same time, it is eminently questionable: *what is it,* and hence also, *who are we,* as participants—our selves and our lives embedded in it? This last is certainly not an idle question, certainly not an "objective" one, but a truly Socratic question; it is our subjective selves that Marx places in doubt. The dialectical question is always one of life and death. *Capital* is such a dialogue, with the opening question addressed to us.[34]

Perhaps Aristotle has asked the opening question in its root form:

what is the relation between *economics* and *chrematistic?*—that is, in terms of our own time, what is the relation between human ends (use-values) and the system of capitalism (the universe of exchange values)? From the immediacy of the concrete economic life that is so familiar to us that we cannot criticize or even really see it—phase I of Hegel's schema—*Capital* has proceeded to separate and trace the abstract forms that are in fact at work. Marx's formal theory serves to reveal the systematic network of abstractions that constitutes the system of capitalism; we recognize the objective abstractions of Hegel's phase II in the reified entities of the bourgeois trinity. As we penetrated deeper and deeper into this labyrinth, two things were happening: exchange value as an abstraction from all judgment of human value became total, and at the same time a system of illusion was shaping itself in such a way that all traces of the derivation of the system from its human base were swallowed up. That is, for Marx, the depth of the labyrinth—we have ceased at this point even to ask the question of human goals, have ceased even to recognize how far we have strayed from them. That is where he finds us today, and in the three volumes of *Capital* he has taken the full measure of our darkness: the depth of the *aporia.* Our systems and our machines, including those of war, dictate to us: we can no longer bend them to our human purposes. It is at this point that Marx utters the sober words: "It might seem that we must abandon all hope. . . ."[35] What light is there which will illuminate our present darkness?

If Socrates invokes the Forms, and Hegel invokes the Spirit, what power can Marx turn to that will bear the dialectical burden of a resurrection of the human, in some new form, in the midst of a world in which quantity has seemingly so totally devoured quality? I think in fact we have seen the answer unfolding as the account of capitalism progressed. In the *Meno,* we sensed the operation of the mystery of "Recollection"—that is, the mystic advent of knowledge from a source that was in no way evident—as the dialogue unfolded. So in *Capital,* as the picture of the system of capital was drawn more and more completely, Marx has been continually indicating that something else is happening, not evident on the surface of the system itself. This is, as he has traced in concrete and material terms, the increasing socialization of the processes, the socialization of labor, the structures of credit and the markets, all the devices of science and engineering, of communication and distribution. It all derives, to appearances, as a weaving of mere impulses toward private gain. But despite such apparent competition and separation, we are as human beings in fact learning, albeit in some sense despite ourselves, ever more ways to function cooperatively and socially.

Like any answer to a genuine dialectical question, this new society of rational and cooperative effort is too urgent for us to perceive neutrally, as mere *observers;* rather, it appears as an answer to alienation, which has become an anguish for us in our time. A dialectical question takes the shape of a crisis which we suffer (I); to ask the question is to cry out for release from a bondage.[36] What Marx is trying to show us, as the dialectical subtext to our culture of competition, automation, and strife, is a possible answer to the longing of the denial that is our modern world. Out of the depth of the negation (II) arises a new prospect (III): not simply as a denial of the alienation, a negation of the negation, but as a positive affirmation of an access to a human community that had never existed before. I have suggested that the question which we launch returns to us: we are set to wonder about our own identity. Could we be members of such a human community? I think that *Capital* is leading us in the direction of what might be a surprising answer: we are rational and social human beings in ways we had perhaps thought impossible.

This same pattern can be seen, arguably, in terms of a long motion of human history, one that I think is the underlying clue to the meaning of *Capital* for Marx. In Athens (I), the *polis* was a sketch of a human community: not yet recognizing human rights, human equality, the full worth of the individual human being. It was still a slave society—yet, nonetheless, a society that saw itself in human terms, shaped to human purpose and the human good. Quantity was still instrumental to quality.

We have now in capitalism the full development of the opposite (II): the farthest extreme of departure from the human and the qualitative, and from the sense of human community—the *aporia* of our Western history. Yet even here something is brewing which is new on the face of the earth, a new sense of our common humanity, and of a new human society which would give reality to it.

This would be the *Aufhebung* (III): the cancellation of the present alienation, and the affirmation of something that we cannot yet know in detail or clarity but can begin to perceive: a rational human society which Marx calls, tentatively, not "political," but an "association." In it would be realized the value and separate identity of each individual, whose formal recognition has been the triumph of our own political heritage. But this equality and these freedoms would be brought into actuality by recovering the sense of community that was the legacy of Athens, and which we have so nearly lost.

Marx sees, then, first, the affirmation of the human community in the *polis,* where individual rights and the equality of all human beings were not yet known; second, the recognition of these rights and the formal commitment to human freedom in our own society, where on the other hand we have gained rights only by denying the human community— we have gained formal freedom only by separating ourselves from one another and substituting quantitative processes for a common rational judgment of our human purpose. The third phase of our Western history is already with us, but we have not seen it: the incorporation of the community of the *polis* with the technology of the modern world, in the realization of that individual freedom in which we so strongly believe, but which our present society still contradicts at every turn. True substantive individual freedom is now a realistic possibility. This, I think, is the constant suggestion of the pages of *Capital.*

Dialectical science

Is Marx, we must ask, writing *science,* or is he painting yet one more dream-picture of a future for mankind? The question would hardly come up, if it were not for Marx's surprising claim that this is indeed a work of science, and by no means mere speculation or political persuasion.[37] Evidently, Marx is challenging our idea of "science" in a way that requires us to go back to its foundations if we are to follow his thinking. Such an investigation, of the possibility of a *dialectical* paradigm of science itself, would be altogether beyond the compass of our present study. Yet if Marx is claiming that *Capital* in its dialectical aspect is at the same time to be understood seriously as a work of *science,* then we can hardly omit consideration of this claim altogether from our own "reading" of the book.

I think it will be possible here to take just the briefest measure of what Marx's claim concerning the scientific character of the dialectic— or the dialectical character of the sciences—might entail. It may be that if there is indeed a formal, Newtonian theory of capitalism housed in *Capital* within a dialectical framework, as we have discussed, the scientific character of the work belongs more to the dialectical frame than to that objective, formal theory. Can a work be at the same time "dialectical" and "scientific"?

There is an image of "good" science, shared by both our Ptolemaic and our Newtonian models, for which the criteria run something like this: the theory is based on explicit assumptions expressed in univocal language; the reasoning from first principles is sound; the conclusions reached are capable of being tested in the observatory or the laboratory and are thus confirmed or disconfirmed by observation or experiment. Nature renders a dispassionate judgment; and a theory of this kind can be regarded as objectively true just insofar as experiments have been devised and carried out to put it to empirical test.

I am oversimplifying, of course, but in broad terms this is the paradigm that accounts, we tend to feel, for the brilliant success of the sciences in the past three centuries. As theories fall and are replaced, with what seems increasing rapidity, we become more sophisticated in our recognition of the fallibility of any one theory, and yet the paradigm of "science" itself remains firm among us: in fact, the more fallible the individual theory, the more crucial the adherence to strict method in the overall community of the sciences might well seem.

What *was* that idea, which was born into the world in the course of those events that we call the "Scientific Revolution"? The crux, I think, is the concept of "objectivity," which has already appeared so often in this study. It is a notion which seems so persuasive to us that we embrace it in all aspects of our society, whether in our journalism or our personal lives, with nearly the same conviction with which we insist on it in our laboratories.

Let me for a moment, for the sake of reflection, paint the alternative picture. Perhaps the world does not really come apart, as the criterion of "objectivity" presupposes, into two distinct parts—the realm of the observed and the realm of the observer. Perhaps the "subjective" and the "objective" are inherently and inseparably joined in a single fabric, and perhaps this fabric is itself the work of time, the weave of history. When we enter the laboratory and arrange an experiment, perhaps we are fashioning images of ourselves and our historically conditioned expectations—in the forms of the apparatus, shaped by the machines of our time from the materials we have wrought from the earth and cooked up in our processes of production; in the devices of measurement, fitted to notions of time and distance and all the entities of our current speculations—indeed, to our paradigmatic vision of the nature of "theory," or of "knowledge" itself. Marx says, "We hear with a human ear, and see with a human eye."[38]

Our very senses and the entities they perceive are themselves products of human history. They pick out, form up, and thus "detect" what we have learned to sort, attend to, and speak of. These comments are obvious enough, perhaps banal, but their consequences for the idea of "science" may be profound if we take them altogether seriously, as it appears that Marx does. What we "measure," "observe," "record," and "prove" or "disprove" in the laboratory belongs inextricably to that same web of human history in which we ourselves are involved—when we seek the object, we, to a large extent, find the subject. When we turn to Nature for final judgment, we meet, often enough—ourselves. "Man makes Nature," Marx says, meaning, I think, that everywhere we turn, we meet ourselves in domains of our own shaping and making.[39]

Of course, there is a vast component of the "objective" in the work of the laboratory; such "objectivity," we tend to say, "built the atomic bomb." Yet we must check ourselves; we know better. "Objectivity" alone did not build the bomb, nor the deadly train of terrors which continue to follow in the path it opened. What we call "objectivity" melds with the social and the human in ways we have not very well learned to disentangle. The bomb was the combined product of inextricably interrelated "objective" and "subjective" factors. What we think of as "objective" science is, perhaps, *inherently* "framed" within a context of larger social institutions and the movements of human history, much as I have claimed the formal theory of *Capital* is "framed" within a dialectical critique.

It is not hard to see that our image of "objective" science is very closely wedded to the idea of capitalism: scientific truth, we learn to believe, is quantitative, and objective realism is identified with power; the structure of truth, we believe, is hierarchical. Any other forms of truth—that is, most of the truths which really matter to us, humanly speaking—tend to be misprized among us as matters of "opinion," or (worse) as "value judgments."

Our very idea of "objective" science is a product of the dialectic of history, of course: it has emerged from a certain human experience, a certain human preoccupation, and it will pass, as experiences broaden and we gain fuller recognition of what a "human" preoccupation might really be. Dialectical science, which looks at the rise and transformations of "objective" science, takes a much larger field of view. It sees all that "objective" science sees, but it sees as well the extent to which so-called objective science is the dialectical work of time: how its preoccupations, its univocal terms, its underlying ideas flow, shift, and are transformed; how science takes the image of the social processes of an age: how it serves them, is rewarded by them, and is in time transcended. Because "objective" science does *not* see all this; because it takes its terms as "univocal," because it thinks its intentions are indifferent to the biases of institutions and purposes, which in fact fund and house and nourish it, because it does not see the colorations of the minds and passions which give it being, it is not "objective" at all, but in its presumed objectivity, to that extent, merely naïve.

The picture cannot see the frame. Only the whole view would take the measure of truth. Marx strives in *Capital* for this wholeness of view: that is, for the more complete science. And we might reflect that if, with respect to the political and the social, he is showing us the way to a recovery of a transformed ancient *polis* in the modern world, so with respect to the concept of science, he is showing us the way to a recovery of the principle of *dialectic* in relation to our modern truths. It must be important to observe that the two—the social and the scientific—are strictly parallel enterprises. If Marx is right, our limited idea of "science" and our limited idea of "society" mirror each other, in their pallor.

The customary term "dialectical materialism" seems to serve well to express the union in *Capital* of the ancient dialectical and the modern scientific traditions. It is a work of science, but it is not, on the other hand, an "objective" work. If it were objective, if it were merely examining the *fact* of capitalism "scientifically," in the manner of the formal, Newtonian theory . . . it would *not* be scientific. It is in fact a human work in which alienation appears as an affront, outrage surges in its prose, and the prospect of something coming to birth appears with the urgency of prophecy. What do we want to "know," and what does "learning" feel like? Dialectical materialism recognizes that our concern is with the forging, in history, of our own humanity: we have not yet learned what it is to be human, and that must be the governing question for our science. It is not as though we had the option of setting it aside—bracket it, for separate consideration. Without our recognizing it, this one question of ourselves infuses and informs all our sciences.

The question of our identity is urgent upon us. Though we no longer eat each other, we currently tear ourselves limb from limb—men, women, and children—with daily and procedural indifference, by means of our "objective" sciences, and in the name of "freedom," a word whose meaning we evidently do not yet quite understand. It is in the process of working our way out of this dark complex of circumstances that we must come to find ourselves: the "knowing" is not simply a "theoretical" matter, but rather a question of shaping our practices—above all, surely, our practice of the sciences—little by little confirming our horror at our mistakes, little by little finding ways to do better. Learning in this unfolding, dialectical practice is what Marx in some places calls *praxis:* not simply theory or simply practice, not simply "objective" nor simply "subjective," but a process of bringing our humanity into being in and through conscious practice.[40]

The emphasis in dialectical "materialism" is on the principle that we can come to grips with this only in the detail: the detail of the conditions under which our world lives—the society, the language, the physical equipment, the myths, the arts, the health or disease, nourishment or starvation, peace or war, wealth or poverty, which are the "material" of our actual lives. "Learning" is not a question of general ideas, simply, but of the detail and suffering of human *praxis,* in, through, and beyond the concepts, the theories, the equations, and the terrible misunderstandings and consequences in which our "sciences" are entwined.

Conclusion

I suggested at the outset that *Capital* was not a work on economics but was really directed at other and larger questions. I think we have seen that Marx has really laid his question at our own doorstep and challenges our concept of ourselves. Are we the separate, competitive beings envisioned by Hobbes and Locke, and presupposed by Adam Smith, or are we in some fundamental way members of a larger society? Aristotle thought we were political "by nature"; our current view is that the polity is a work of our own making, and that it serves to bring together persons who are initially and primarily alone. Aristotle thought that outside of society we were either beasts or gods; our mythology has it that we were free in our separation, and that we form and join societies in order to preserve that original freedom. I do not think we have really resolved this question. There is, I think, a deeply felt conviction that something is missing in our modern societies, and it may be . . . the sense of society itself. It would not be a particularly original observation to remark that we moderns feel lost and insecure; we feel a need to "belong" but are not sure what we are prepared to belong to. We try to fill this gap in religious communities and in networks and organizations of all kinds. They express something we are aware we are seeking, but they are all filling in, in their various ways, for a missing center.

Marx, I think, is suggesting that we have misplaced our conception of freedom. We do not become free, he is saying, in isolation: rather, we can only be free in common. All our recent intuitions warn us against this approach: we have seen too vividly the consequences of totalitarian social impositions of "freedoms" that convert to nightmares. But *Capital* is not advocating totalitarian solutions; Marx's vision—right or wrong, possible or impossible—is of a creative individual freedom in practice, achieved within and through membership in a conscious and rational society.

Marx is, perhaps, too much of a democrat. He tries hard and in detail, even from his vantage point of a hundred years ago, to show us that we are already doing many of these things: we do have these capabilities, we really do think together and plan, we can formulate a common end, can amass great social powers and inventiveness, determination, and skill to accomplish social goals, and can in the process achieve new levels of individual freedom in practice. Perhaps in all this he remains unpersuasive; the cautious reaction is to point out that something called "human nature" will not admit cooperation or common reasoning to be a human good. We will, caution pronounces, pursue private ends, tear and maul one another, or lose all interest if we can see no separate gain. Perhaps in this we do injustice to ourselves.

One word has been strikingly absent from this discussion—the word *revolution*. It is not a word which comes up much in the text of *Capital*. Surely *Capital* is a revolutionary text, as all dialectic is; and it is clear, too, that *Capital* is revolutionary in a way that Plato's *Dialogues* are not (though it is a curious thought, and a testament to our English freedoms, that Socrates was executed as a threat to the polity, while Marx died a natural death as a father and a husband). The difference, I think, is that while Socrates mortally affronts Athens with his insistence that it has its values upside down, he sees this as a tragic circle out of which, in the long run, no society can hope to escape, and his arguments therefore do not suggest revolutionary change. *Capital* on the other hand is implicitly revolutionary, because Marx says we are stronger and better than we know, and we have it in us to constitute a society that affirms our humanity in ways we have not yet realized. In this sense,

Socrates belongs to the tragic tradition, and Marx to the prophetic.

Throughout the world, for a century now, people have been reading *Capital* as a message of hope. The spectrum of interpretations has ranged from the most esoteric formulations of "the dialectic" to discussions of revolutionary block committees dedicated to life-and-death struggle against the oppressions of the modern world. I am suggesting that we cannot afford to remain illiterate in relation to this world discourse. I urge readers of the *Great Books of the Western World* to take down Volume 50 from its very likely neglected place on the shelf and see what they can make of this remarkable package of propositions about ourselves.

---

[1] In *Capital,* Marx envisions "a higher form of society, a society in which the full and free development of every individual forms the ruling principle." [*GBWW,* Vol. 50, p. 292d.]

[2] Marx discusses the "commodity" in Part One of Volume 1 of *Capital* [*GBWW,* Vol. 50, pp. 13a–37c]. In general, the discussion in this essay will follow the order of the argument in *Capital* itself, and I will try to let the reader know, in footnotes to the headings of this study, where we are in Marx's text. In this way, the interested reader might wish to use this study as a partial guide to reading selected sections of *Capital. Capital* is usually thought of as consisting of three volumes, of which only the best-known, the first, is reprinted in *Great Books of the Western World,* in the translation of Samuel Moore and Edward Aveling. Only this first volume was seen through publication by Marx himself; Volumes 2 and 3 were edited and published by Friedrich Engels. Since the present "reading" will include all three volumes, reference will be made to the last two volumes in another edition, translated by David Fernbach, with valuable introductions by Ernest Mandel (New York: Vintage Books, 1978, 1981). There is a "Volume 4" of *Capital* (in three volumes!), edited by Karl Kautsky under the title *Theories of Surplus Value* (Moscow: 1963–71); it is of special interest to readers of the *Great Books,* since it includes the critique which results from Marx's intensive reading of Adam Smith.

[3] It may be helpful to point out, at the outset, that Marx was in certain ways in fact a "classicist." His doctoral dissertation was on Democritus: my own sense of this is that he was especially interested in the concept of free will or spontaneity, represented in Democritus's theory by the "swerve" of the atoms. (Lucretius includes this in *De rerum natura* [*GBWW,* Vol. 12, p. 17d].) Marx knew Greek well, and his biographers report that he read Aeschylus regularly, throughout his life. ("According to Lafargue Marx read Aeschylus in the original Greek text at least once a year." (Franz Mehring, *Karl Marx* [Ann Arbor: 1962], p. 503); Marx listed Aeschylus as one of his three "favorite poets"— the others, Goethe and Shakespeare.)

[4] [*GBWW,* Vol. 50, pp. 59–60.] Aristotle says, in the *Nichomachean Ethics,* "Now in truth it is impossible that things differing so much should become commensurate. . . ."

[*GBWW*, Vol. 9, p. 381c.] Aristotle sees need ("demand") bridging the gap in practice, but what interests Marx is that Aristotle recognizes the lack of a common measure *in principle*. What was lacking, Marx says, was the concept of *human* equality, as the needed common unit of measure.

⁵The fundamental principles of Marx's labor theory of value are set out in the opening chapter of Part One, on commodities, to which we have already referred in general [*GBWW*, Vol. 50, pp. 13a–37c]. The labor theory of value is discussed, with reference to John Locke and Adam Smith, in the *Syntopicon* article on LABOR, to which the reader may wish to refer [*GBWW*, Vol. 2, pp. 926b–27b, 936b–c]. Marx certainly read with great interest such passages in Smith as this: "Labour, therefore, it appears evidently, is the only universal as well as the only accurate measure of value. . . ." [*GBWW*, Vol. 39, p. 16a.]

⁶Ptolemy confronts a crisis when he finds that two different hypotheses will account for the same phenomena, namely, the epicycle and the eccentric. His comment is, ". . . all the appearances can be cared for interchangeably according to either hypothesis." That being the case, he concludes it is reasonable to opt for the simpler one [*GBWW*, Vol. 16. pp. 89b–93a]. On the idea of SCIENCE, *see* the *Syntopicon* [*GBWW*, Vol. 3, pp. 682a–705b]. This article points out that Marx in effect takes England as his laboratory [ibid., p. 686b–c].

⁷*GBWW*, Vol. 50, pp. 69a–151c.

⁸Many studies, dating from those of the Temporary National Economic Committee in the 1930s, have shown this; recent studies seem only to confirm the old findings. One analysis, for example, found that in the realm of personal ownership of corporate stock—close to our present concern—83 percent was in the hands of the top 5 percent of the population (cited in Richard Parker, *The Myth of the Middle Class* [New York: Liveright, 1972], p. 212). The subject, admittedly, is one which invites bottomless discussion on the part of professional economists and sociologists, but data of this kind abound, which strongly indicate the unequal division of wealth, power, and opportunity in our society.

⁹I am thinking in a general way of the fundamental account of motion in Aristotle's *Physics*, Book III. Marx's understanding of our freedom as being experienced in *activity* ("self-activity" is a term he uses often) is suggestive of Aristotle's emphasis on *act (energeia)*. [*GBWW*, Vol. 8, pp. 278ff.]

¹⁰The term "alienation" (or "estrangement," German *Entfremdung*) is very important in the early writings of Marx, in such essays as that on "Alienated Labor." It is a classic question among scholars whether Marx had fundamentally changed his mind by the time he wrote *Capital*. I think that, while he may have avoided the term to adjust his vocabulary to new tasks and a new readership, the concept remains fundamental to a reading of *Capital*, and there is no abandonment of the earlier position in the later work. Rather, it is applied in new ways to a specific task in hand.

¹¹It is hard to appreciate adequately the significance of the legal processes that brought the corporation into our midst, as a dubious quasi-citizen of the polity. It was the "Dartmouth College Case" (1819) in which the Supreme Court took a decisive move in this direction; Chief Justice John Marshall wrote these awesome words: "A corporation is an artificial being, invisible, intangible, and existing only in contemplation of law. Being the mere creation of law, it possesses only those properties which the charter of its creation confers upon it. . . . Among the most important are immortality, and, if the expression be allowed, individuality. . . ." (Selected and edited by the staff, Social Sciences 1, the College of the University of Chicago, *The People Shall Judge* [Chicago: University of Chicago Press, 1949], Vol. 1, p. 460.)

¹²It is worth turning to Hobbes's account of Leviathan, which one can't help but feel Marshall must have been reading: "This is the generation of that great LEVIATHAN, or rather, to speak more reverently, of that mortal god . . . *one person, of whose acts a great multitude, by mutual covenants . . . have made themselves every one the author. . . .*" [*GBWW*, Vol. 23, p. 100d.] Hobbes of course is characterizing the *state* as he understands it, but the concept has now far outrun his intentions. Marx, already in his time, is deeply impressed by the corporation (the "joint-stock company"), which he sees as a necessary stage in the transition to ownership by the producers themselves, i.e., as directly social property. He speaks of it as "an abolition of capitalist private industry on the basis of the capitalist system itself." (*Capital*, Vol. 3, p. 570.) A similar perception of the corporation as the socialization of the institution of private property was expressed by Adolf Berle in Berle

and Means, *The Modern Corporation and Private Property* (New York: Macmillan, 1982).

[13]Throughout the essay on "Alienated Labor" runs the principle that our work ought to be free, and that our free activity is our real work, ". . . for what is life but activity?" Our "free, conscious activity" is our end in life, which is denied under alienation. The term "spontaneity" is often used by Marx in the earlier writings to characterize the radical freedom he is talking about: our activity in our work *ought* to be our "own spontaneous activity." Marx is, again, very close in spirit to Aristotle in seeing *free* work as an end in itself (as in *activity, "energeia"* in Aristotle), whereas alienated work is a mere means, and external. Admittedly, with the introduction of the *free will,* the concept of "freedom" may have undergone a sea change between Aristotle's time and ours.

[14]In general, the question of circulation is the topic of Volume 2, where Marx draws upon the work of François Quesnay, who developed "tables economiques." Marx's tables balance the overall exchange between sectors of the economy and thus become most interesting models for the kind of planning of an economy which he visualizes for the rational society of the future. (*Capital,* Vol. 2, pp. 468–97, on "simple reproduction"; and ibid., pp. 565–99, on "reproduction on an expanded scale.")

[15]As we shall see, the outcome of this market evaluation is not that the sale price is literally equal to the "value"; things prove much more complicated than this, but as a component of the sale price, the judgment of *value* by the market is nonetheless presupposed [p. 102].

[16]Locke envisions, in a kind of myth of the state of nature, the origin of the right of private property in an act of individual labor [*GBWW,* Vol. 35, pp. 30b–36a]. Rousseau similarly refers the question to an imagined original state but sees this primal claim to a right of private property as an outrage against mankind [*GBWW,* Vol. 38, p. 348b]. These views are part of the discussion of WEALTH in the *Syntopicon* [*GBWW,* Vol. 3, pp. 1038a–49c].

[17]*Capital,* Vol. 3, pp. 117–99, 241–306.

[18]The term "reification" is developed by György Lukács, one of the most interesting interpreters of *Capital,* in his *History and Class Consciousness* (Cambridge, Mass.: MIT Press, 1971). *See,* for example, the essay "Reification and Class Consciousness, I: The Phenomenon of Reification," pp. 83–110. Marx uses the term "fetishism" to characterize this conversion of a relationship into a thing; this is already apparent in the discussion of the commodity, but Marx reflects on the process in the third volume (*Capital,* Vol. 3, p. 516).

[19]*Capital,* Vol. 3, p. 312.

[20]*Capital,* Vol. 3, pp. 459–573.

[21]*Capital,* Vol. 3, p. 517.

[22]*Capital,* Vol. 3, p. 511.

[23]*Capital,* Vol. 3, p. 517.

[24]*Capital,* Vol. 3, pp. 751–87; 882–916. Note that these readings do not address the question of "differential rent," which in the overall theory becomes very important as a development of the "marginal" principle, but which it has not been possible to include in the present essay.

[25]*Capital,* Vol. 3, p. 772.

[26]*Capital,* Vol. 3, pp. 772–78.

[27]The seed of this perception, that a larger, systematic social result arises from the operation of many individual actions, each of which considers only a separate advantage, can be found (like so many of Marx's ideas) in Adam Smith, who says of the individual entrepreneur, ". . . he intends only his own gain, and he is in this, as in many other cases, led by an invisible hand to promote an end which was no part of his intention. . . ." [*GBWW,* Vol. 39, p. 194b.] But where Smith sees in this a *limitation* of our human abilities—we will make things very much worse if we try to plan for a social goal—Marx understands this as a dialectical *prospect:* we have powers we have not recognized or utilized. Marx speaks of Adam Smith's "invisible hand" in these terms: ". . . trade . . . rules the whole world through the relation of supply and demand—a relation which . . . hovers over the earth like the fate of the ancients, and with invisible hand allots fortune and misfortune to men . . . ." (*German Ideology* [New York: International Publishers, 1970], pp. 54–55).

[28]*Capital,* Vol. 3, pp. 953–70.

[29]Marx discusses his understanding of the role of religion in early essays, for example,

"On the Jewish Question" (*Karl Marx: Early Writings,* ed. T. B. Bottomore [New York: McGraw-Hill, 1964], pp. 3–40). Marx's famous characterization of religion as "the opiate of the people" does not mean that it is stupefying, but that it projects a vision of the human community in alienated—remote—form. Marx speaks in the same terms in *Capital:* "The religious world is but the reflex of the real world." [*GBWW*, Vol. 50, p. 35b.]

[30]*Capital,* Vol. 3, p. 959.

[31]In connection with this account of dialectic, the reader might like to compare the discussion in the article DIALECTIC in the *Syntopicon* [*GBWW*, Vol. 2, pp. 345ff.], where somewhat different "benchmarks" are employed.

[32][*GBWW*, Vol. 7, p. 174a.] I have taken the liberty of supplying my own translation, to catch what I think is the literal, or sub-literal, intention of the Greek.

[33]We may be reminded as well of the dark moment in the *Phaedo,* the dialogue in which we witness the last hours, and the death, of Socrates. At a certain point, the argument, and with it, possibly, all the powers of dialectic to lead us to the truth, seem to have failed. A silence falls over the group at this apparent death of the argument, prefiguring Socrates' own death [*GBWW*, Vol. 7, pp. 236a–37d]. In the mythology of the dialogue, this dark moment is the depth of the labyrinth of Crete. The rescuing dialectic of the third phase becomes the thread of Ariadne, by which Theseus is led back to the light.

[34]The opening question of the dialogue *Gorgias* is perhaps really the essential opening question of all dialectic. Socrates suggests that they ask of Gorgias, an eminently successful and celebrated orator, "Who he is?" (*hostis estin*) [*GBWW*, Vol. 7, p. 252a]. This becomes the occasion of a tragic fall, in which he is revealed—to himself as well as the assembled company—as having led an unjust life.

[35]*Capital,* Vol. 3, p. 252.

[36]It seems likely that the threefold pattern of dialectic is indeed reflected (or founded) in the traditional structure of the Greek tragedies in the form of trilogy. Thus Aeschylus's trilogy, the *Oresteia,* opens with what might seem the universal outcry of suffering mankind: "I pray the gods for release from these labors . . ." [cf. *GBWW*, Vol. 5, p. 52a]. Only after the depths have been sounded of the tragic events of the first and second plays does the "release" in fact come, in the form of the transformation of the Furies into benign spirits, and the foundation of the Athenian polity in a system of justice. These identities are suggested in the closing scene of the *Symposium* [*GBWW*, Vol. 7, p. 173a–c].

[37]The claim is made, for example, at the outset, in the Preface to the First German Edition: ". . . it is the ultimate aim of this work to lay bare the economic law of motion of modern society. . . . My standpoint, from which the evolution of the economic formation of society is viewed as a process of natural history. . ." [*GBWW*, Vol. 50, p. 7b–c.]

[38]"The eye has become a *human* eye when its *object* has become a *human,* social object, created by man and destined for him. The senses have, therefore, become directly theoreticians in practice. . . . It is evident that the human eye appreciates things in a different way from the crude, non-human eye, the human *ear* differently from the crude ear." ("Private Property and Communism," in Bottomore, ed., *Karl Marx: Early Writings,* p. 160.)

[39]Marx says of the naïve materialist: "He does not see how the sensuous world around him is, not a thing given direct from all eternity, remaining ever the same, but the product of industry and of the state of society; and, indeed, in the sense that it is an historical product, the result of the activity of a whole succession of generations, each standing on the shoulders of the preceding one. . . . Each of the objects of the simplest 'sensuous certainty' are only given him through social development, industry and commercial intercourse." "Feuerbach . . . mentions secrets which are disclosed only to the eye of the physicist and chemist; but where would natural science be without industry and commerce? Even this 'pure' natural science is provided with an aim, as with its material, only through trade and industry, through the sensuous activity of men." (*German Ideology,* pp. 62–63.)

[40]Marx sets forth the notion of *praxis* in the *Theses on Feuerbach.* For example, from the Second Thesis: "The question whether objective truth can be attributed to human thinking is not a question of theory but is a *practical question.* Man must prove the truth, i.e. the reality and power, the this-sidedness of his thinking in *praxis.* . . ." (*German Ideology,* p. 121.)

On Reading the *Summa:* An Introduction to Saint Thomas Aquinas

Otto Bird

Born and raised in Ann Arbor, Michigan, Otto Bird attended the university there, graduating in 1935 with honors in English. He added a master's degree in comparative literature the following year. He took his doctorate in philosophy and literature at the University of Toronto in 1939.

From 1947 to 1950 he served as associate editor of the *Syntopicon* for *Great Books of the Western World,* working with Mortimer Adler. In the latter year he joined the faculty at the University of Notre Dame, where he was founder and director of the general program of liberal studies until 1963. He was executive editor of *The Great Ideas Today* from 1964 to 1970, when he was appointed university professor of arts and letters at Notre Dame, from which he retired in 1977. In 1986 he was distinguished visiting professor of the humanities at the University of Dallas.

He has written four books, *The Canzoné d'Amore of Guido Cavalcanti with the Commentary of Dino del Garbo* (1942), *Syllogistic Logic and Its Extensions* (1964), *The Idea of Justice* (1967), and *Cultures in Conflict* (1976), besides articles on the history and theory of the liberal arts. In addition, he was a major contributor to the *Propædia,* or Outline of Knowledge, of the current (fifteenth) edition of the *Encyclopædia Britannica.*

Mr. Bird now spends much of the year in Shoals, Indiana, where he has built a house and grows grapes for making wine. He continues to be active in editorial projects of Encyclopædia Britannica, Inc., and remains consulting editor of *The Great Ideas Today.* He has contributed to many of our volumes. His essay on Euclid appeared last year.

Someone opening and paging through the *Summa Theologica* for the first time is almost certain to be puzzled, if not disconcerted and even repelled. Page after page contains the same unvarying subdivisions, sections entitled "Articles," each of which begins with an interrogative sentence, asking whether such and such is so. The one-volume Latin edition contains 2,777 pages plus an additional 69 pages of indices, listing all 3,112 of these Articles. Reading the text, we find that the same procedure is followed in every one of these Articles, unvarying, stereotyped, monotonous. The language too is plain, unadorned, impersonal—almost entirely lacking any appeal to the imagination. If the reader comes to the text expecting to find high thoughts expressed in high and moving language, he is bound to be disappointed. We may well ask why anyone would ever want to adopt such a style and method of writing.

To this, the first and simplest answer is that Thomas was following and improving upon the methods used in the schools in which he spent his entire life. At the age of five he was placed in the monastic school of the Benedictines at Monte Cassino, and during the rest of his life he studied and taught at various universities and houses of study in Naples, Paris, Cologne, and the cities in Italy where the papal court was located. About the only time he was not in the schoolroom was when he was in church or walking from one school to another; the trip from Naples to Paris, for example, took two months, and he seems to have made it at least four times. Furthermore, practically all of his many writings not only grew out of the practice of the schools but were also addressed to their members, which is to say that they were intended for a specialized and highly trained audience. In this respect his work differs greatly from that of Saint Augustine, for example, who, when he was not addressing his own parishioners and through them all Christians, was writing for a generally cultivated audience.

Thomas refers to the methods used in the theological schools of his day in declaring that he intended to improve upon them. In the general prologue to the *Summa* he notes that beginners in theology have been hampered in their study by two of the methods then in use. One is that of expounding and explaining a text (*librorum expositio*), in which one has to follow the plan of the book being read. The other is that of disputing and discussing questions raised during the reading of the text (*occasio disputandi*). Both methods, he claims, weary and confuse the student in that they fail to follow the order and organization proper to the subject matter and discipline of theology (*ordo disciplinae*).

The "beginners" (*incipientes*) he is talking about here and addressing were students who had graduated from the faculty of arts in the university and entered the faculty of theology. In other words, in our terms, they were graduate students, and those at the University of Paris in the thirteenth century had already studied much logic and a lot of Aristotle. By the time that Thomas became such a beginner in 1252 the course in theology had become established and fixed in a form that was to remain the same down to the Renaissance and the Council of Trent. It consisted of a four-year course of studies in which during the first two the beginner was a "Biblical Bachelor" (*Baccalaureus Biblicus*) engaged in a cursory reading of the entire Bible, both Old and New Testaments. During the final two years he was a "Sententiary Bachelor" (*Baccalaureus Sententiarius*), because he was engaged in teaching the *Four Books of Sentences* compiled by Peter Lombard in Paris in about 1150. The teaching of this text was not restricted, as it was on the Bible, to exposition and commentary (*lectio, expositio*) but could wander away from it to investigate and discuss questions suggested by the reading of the text, the *disputatio*. Once the four-year program was satisfactorily completed, the bachelor was declared a *Magister in Sacra Pagina* and licensed to teach in any faculty of theology.

Thomas spent his four years as a bachelor in theology at the University of Paris, and we still possess the *Commentary on the Sentences* that he then wrote. This work can throw considerable light upon the great *Summa* that he began in 1267 and was still writing when he died in 1274. That is so not only because of the influence it exercised with regard to both matter and method but also because the completion of the *Summa* that is now contained in the *Supplement to the Third Part* consists of materials excerpted and rearranged from the *Commentary on the Sentences*. Comparing the *Supplement* with the *Commentary*, we can see how the former was put together by conforming to the method adopted for the *Summa*, and how it makes an improvement in clarity. For that purpose we will look at the initial questions dealing with the resurrection, beginning with Question 75 of the *Supplement* (*GBWW*, Vol. 20, p. 935a).

The corresponding place in the *Sentences* occurs in the fourth book. There, in accordance with the plan of the book, the relevant scriptural passages on the resurrection are cited first, after which selected passages on the subject are quoted from the fathers of the church. These judgments constitute the "sentences" from which the work derives its name.

Those of Saint Augustine are much the most frequent, some ten times as many as those from any other authority, according to one count.

Thomas's *Commentary,* like those of other commentators, is much more complex. The Lombard text is divided up into sections called *Distinctiones,* which in turn are divided into *Quaestiones.* Each of these consists of *Articuli,* which in turn are subdivided into *Quaestiunculae,* which form the smallest part. Thus, in his *Commentary* on the 43rd Distinction of Book IV, after quoting the text from the *Sentences* on the resurrection and noting how it can be divided, Thomas has one Question with five Articles, each of which contains three or four *Quaestiunculae.* These consist of arguments, usually from some church fathers, often disagreeing with one another. After all of these have been stated, Thomas then gives his own solution or decision about each of them. Thus he proceeds from one Article to another. Merely from this description of it one can see why the *Summa*'s prologue complains of "the multiplication of . . . questions, articles, and arguments."

After the death of Thomas, his first editor could bring about a considerable simplification merely by excerpting and rearranging Thomas's words in his commentary according to the plan he had established in the *Summa.* Thus the 5 Articles under Question I of Distinction 43 are made into 5 Questions of the *Supplement* (QQ. 75–78 and 87), and the *Quaestiunculae* become their respective Articles. The work was obviously much of a "scissors-and-paste" job, the signs of the original being indicated by frequent references to words of the Master, i.e., Peter Lombard, or merely to "the text" (PART III SUPPL., Q 76, A 2, ANS; *GBWW,* Vol. 20, p. 941c).* It should also be remembered that they are words taken from his earliest work and, consequently, do not reflect his mature thought such as we have it in the rest of the *Summa.*

The method and plan of teaching the *Sentences* is obviously complex and cumbersome. Why then was it adopted and continued in use for more than three centuries as the basic way of teaching theology? (One effect of this use was that Thomas himself until the mid-sixteenth century was known more for his comment on Peter Lombard than for his revolutionary *Summa.*) Here again, the simplest answer is to be found in the practice of the schools and the preferred mode of the disputation. The books we have of that practice are but written records of what, as actually carried on, was an oral and not a written tradition. To understand and come to appreciate the intent of these books, including the *Summa* itself, it helps greatly to know the what and the how of their disputations.

---

*Such is the style of citation adopted for the *Summa* in the *Syntopicon.* But henceforth for the sake of brevity I will omit the Q and the A, as well as any except a numerical reference to the Part of the *Summa.*

The disputation

There are extant many records of disputations held in the medieval universities, including those that Thomas himself held. From these as well as from the laws and rules by which the universities were governed, especially those of the University of Paris, much can be learned about the actual conduct of these disputations. From such sources we can gain some insight into the actual life that lies behind the conception and writing of the *Summa*.

The disputation constituted the most solemn public academic exercise held in the university. On the day one was to be held, all other activity in the university was canceled so that all might be free to attend. There were two kinds of disputations, the ordinary and the extraordinary. The latter were called *Quodlibetales,* in that they were held only at special times on which occasions a master would announce his intention to entertain any question (i.e., theological) that anyone wanted to offer and engage in argument about it. The ordinary one that was a regular part of the academic program was the Disputed Question (*Quaestio Disputata*). In this case a master would announce in advance a subject, i.e., the *quaestio,* which he proposed to discuss and, along with it, the points of inquiry under which he would consider it.

The dispute lasted for two days. The first day provided the public occasion that was open to the entire university, indeed to the public at large, and could last from six to eight hours. At this time the master presided only, and his students, one or more of them, were responsible for presenting the arguments and meeting any questions or opposed arguments; the master would intervene only if the discussion got off the track, as it were, or if he wanted to come to the aid of his student. Reporters took down in writing the arguments advanced and then, apparently on separate sheets, the answers given to them.

The second day of the dispute was private, inasmuch as the master met only with his own students, went over the arguments of the previous day, developed his own position on the question, and offered answers to the arguments contrary to his own position. This session in turn became public since the master was required to turn over to the university authorities within ten days his written version of the two-day disputation. It is such reports as these that exist today as *Quaestiones Disputatae* or *Quodlibetales,* as the case may be.

These reports, even though they have been revised and edited by the master, take us as close as we are likely to get to the actuality of a medieval disputation. We have many of Thomas's own, since he was willing and able to engage in both kinds of disputation. The *Quodlibetales* were especially demanding, and some masters never offered to hold one. Thomas seems to have disputed once or twice a month while at Paris.

He held ten disputations, for example, on the power of God, and the text of the report still reveals something of how it was conducted. In the Article of one Question (Q. 4, A. 2) we find thirty-four arguments presented on one side of the question and ten on the opposite side; often two opposing arguments appear side by side without being separated into distinct groups. This indicates that the respondent frequently gave his answering argument as soon as an opposing argument was advanced, as is shown by the text noting that "the answerer said" (*sed dicit respondens*), which is then followed by a counterargument. With so many arguments being advanced both *pro* and *con,* it is not surprising that a dispute could last for an entire day and require a second day for the master to state his own position.

It bears noting that the two days of the disputation served quite different functions. The first day was given over to a wide-open discussion of the matter proposed, primarily by the students, although it was not limited to them. The master was charged not only with training future teachers but also with advancing the cause of his theological discipline. He was engaged in research as well as teaching. Hence his work on the second day was known as the "determination" (*determinatio*), in which he declared to the best of his ability what he took to be the truth of the matter under discussion.

Quaestio and Articulus

If now, with that practice in mind, we look at the form of the written work with which Thomas hoped to improve the teaching of theology, we can see why the *Summa* has the form that it has. It is an abbreviated version of the disputation. The stereotyped phrases can even be viewed as stage directions telling one how to undertake such an inquiry by way of disputation.

The structure of the Article reveals its origin. However, it should be noted at once that although the Article may be the elementary unit, it is not the basic one. That position is filled by the *quaestio;* for as in the disputation, it is the *quaestio* that identifies the immediate subject of inquiry. Indeed "inquiry" would be a more accurate translation than "question" as marking its root in *quaerere,* meaning to search or inquire. Further, the *quaestio* is not even phrased as an interrogative. Thus the very first Question introducing the *Summa* as a whole reads: *De sacra doctrina qualis sit, et ad quae se extendat,* or literally, "Concerning sacred doctrine, what kind it is, and to what it extends." The ten Articles which it contains are all addressed to that subject. (That Articles are parts belonging to the Question as a whole is clear from the discussion of the meaning of *articulus* in II-II,6, Ans.; *GBWW,* Vol. 20, p. 384d.)

In structure, the Article is shown to consist of four distinct parts:

1. It begins by posing a question, a sentence in interrogative form that presents an alternative by starting with the particle "whether" (*utrum*).

2. Arguments are then presented for each side of the alternative: several arguments for the side opposed to that which Thomas himself will maintain, and for that reason often called "objections"; but usually only one argument for the other side of the issue, being introduced by the words, "On the contrary" (*sed contra*).

3. Thomas's own solution to the problem that has been proposed is then stated. This part begins with the words *respondeo dicendum quod,* which are usually translated by "I answer that." As will be seen, however, there is reason for keeping the whole expression as "I answer that it must be said that." This part is called the body of the Article.

4. Notice is then taken of the preliminary series of arguments by meeting them as objections. Usually these answers apply only to the first series, since the argument cited in the "on the contrary" almost always coincides with the position taken in the body of the Article. However, there are instances in which answer is also given to the contrary argument; in the first part I have counted some sixteen such instances.

Setting out its parts in this way at once reveals that the Article in form is intended to resemble the oral disputation. The initial question raises a problem that is discussible, in that arguments can be advanced both *pro* and *con.* The presentation of such opposing arguments corresponds to the first day of the disputation, although in a much shortened form. The body of the Article and the replies to the objections correspond to the work of the second day on which the master gave his determination of the issue.

So much, however, provides only the historical background behind the literary form. It does not say why it was prized by its users or what justification there is for it as an intellectual instrument. The scholastic thinkers like their master, Aristotle, were explicit about the methods they used, as Thomas was himself, and they have much to say about both points that can help us to understand their writings.

The dialectical question

The first thing about an Article, as already noted, is that it begins with a question, and that question is so framed as to admit of an alternative, either *pro* or *con.* This is accomplished by introducing the question with the particle "whether." Such is the claim made by Aristotle (for the Greek *poteron*) and that Thomas makes for the Latin *utrum* in his comment upon the Aristotelian passage (*Metaphysics* X,5,1055^{b}32–1056^{a}3; *GBWW,* Vol. 8, p. 583a). Thomas writes:

We always use the word in connection with opposites. Thus we question whether something is white or black, which are opposites of contrariety, or whether it is white or not white, which are opposites of contradiction. But we do not ask whether a thing is man or white except on the supposition that it cannot be both man and white. Then we would question whether a thing is white or man as we would whether it was Socrates or Cleon coming down the street, supposing that both could not come at once. But this mode of questioning about things that are not opposites has no necessity of any kind, but is only according to supposition. Therefore, we use the word "whether" only about things that are opposite from necessity, and about other things only according to supposition, because it is only opposites by nature that cannot exist simultaneously.

The particle "whether" indicates what kind of question is being asked, namely the kind that Aristotle calls a "dialectical question." Such a question, he writes in *On Interpretation* (11,20ᵇ23–30; *GBWW*, Vol. 8, p. 31d), is one that leaves one free to take either side of a contradiction. Thus, to ask what a thing is, such as man, is not a dialectical question, since it admits of only one possible answer, granting that a nature is one and not many. But once a definition is given, it becomes possible to put a question about the nature into a dialectical form. We need only ask, "Whether such is the definition of man." Thomas asks many such questions about definitions in the course of the *Summa*, usually by asking whether the definition offered is fitting or proper (*conveniens*).

Questioning the kind of question we have to deal with is more important than it may appear. For in effect it involves determining what is discussible and thus concerns the matter of what is asked and not merely the form of the asking. Some questions are such as not to present a matter that is discussible, as Aristotle points out in distinguishing questions that are not dialectical (in *Topics* I,11,105ᵃ1–9; *GBWW*, Vol. 8, p. 148c). Questions where there is nothing to be gained from discussion are: (1) Those regarding moral duty, where it is punishment, not argument, that is required, as in "Whether one ought to honor the gods and love one's parents." (2) Those regarding matters of fact, where it is perception, not reason, that is needed, such as, "Whether snow is white." (3) Questions that are either too close or too far removed from rational proof, as being either too obvious or too difficult.

Thomas is not as stringent as Aristotle with regard to the discussible. In his discussion of piety, for example, he is perfectly willing to discuss what is owed to parents (II-II,101,1).*

---

*No page reference to *GBWW* is given here since the text occurs in a part of the *Summa* that has been omitted. *GBWW* omits II-II,47–178, containing 588 Articles, covering the discussion of prudence, justice, fortitude, temperance, and special states of life arising from special graces, such as prophecy, tongues, miracles, III,27–59 (174 AA.) on the life of Christ, and III,66–90 (186 AA.) + Supp. 1–68 (289 AA.) on each of the seven sacraments.

Granting that not all questions are discussible, one might still ask whether there is any value to be got from discussing those that are discussible. Does discussion have a solid intellectual value in the search for truth apart from its psychological, pedagogical, or social utility? With this we come to consideration of the place and function of the opposing arguments in the Article.

The disputative part

Just as the phrasing of the question that introduces an Article always has the same form, so too does the presentation of the arguments *pro* and *con*. It begins with the words *sic proceditur*, which are usually translated by "we proceed thus." However, a detailed analysis of the vocabulary of argument in Thomas's day has shown that this translation is not as accurate as it might be. For by his time the verb *procedere* had acquired a technical usage in argument equivalent to "infer" or "conclude" and, in a slightly more extended sense, to "reason, argue, or dispute." The form in which the arguments are introduced is thus equivalent to *sic disputatur* and is, accordingly, better translated as "thus it is argued or disputed."

The first series of arguments clearly stakes out a position on one side of the issue, usually that opposed to the one Thomas will take: "Whether God exists? . . . It seems that God does not exist," and arguments are presented to that effect, one from the existence of evil, and another from parsimony in that God is not needed to explain anything (I,2,3, Obj. 1-2; *GBWW*, Vol. 19, p. 12c-d). Thus, these count as objections. Then the position on the other side of the issue is stated: the argument "on the contrary," meaning the opposite side of the issue, and not except indirectly contrary to the arguments just stated; the arguments directly opposed to these are not given until Thomas has stated his own argument in the body of the Article.

Usually only one argument appears in the "on the contrary" position, most often in the form of a quotation from some authority. But, as already noted, in an actual disputation, many arguments were presented on this side as well as on the other. Presumably, the reduction in the number of these arguments is for the sake of simplification. Why this argument is usually a citation from some authority is better postponed until we consider the function of authority.

But what is the point, the value, of beginning an investigation by raising a question and then considering arguments on both sides of it? Here again Aristotle's discussion of method and Thomas's comment on it are illuminating. The passage occurs near the beginning of the third book of the *Metaphysics* (995^a4-^b4; *GBWW*, Vol. 8, p. 513b-d) on which Thomas comments as follows:

Those who want to investigate the truth should at the start question well (*bene dubitare*), i.e. to reach well into what is questionable. The reason for this is that investigation of the truth afterwards is nothing else than the solution of the things that were questionable before. But it is obvious that in the untying of bodily bonds one who is ignorant of the knot cannot untie it. But a question (*dubitatio*) about a thing is related to the mind just as a knot is to the body and has the same effect. For one who is in a state of questioning about a thing is like one who has his mind bound and cannot proceed along the way of speculation. Therefore, just as one who unties a bodily knot must first inspect the knot and the way it is tied, so he who would solve a problem must first look into (*speculetur*) all the difficulties and their causes. . . . Secondly, those who would inquire into the truth without first considering the question are like those who do not know where they are going. And as the termination of the journey is that which is aimed at by the traveller, so the solution of the question (*exclusio dubitationem*) is the end aimed at by the one inquiring into the truth. It is obvious that one who does not know where he is going cannot get there except by chance. Therefore, neither can one inquire directly into the truth unless he first sees the question. . . . Thirdly, from the fact that one does not know where he is going it follows that when he arrives at the place aimed at he still will not know whether to remain there or go further; so also one who does not first know the question, the solution of which is the end of the inquiry, will not know when he has found the truth sought for, since he does not know the end of the inquiry which is manifest to one who has first known the question. . . . The fourth reason [for questioning well] is taken from the side of the hearer, for a hearer must judge of things heard. But in matters of judgment (*in judiciis*) no one can judge unless he hears the arguments of both parties. The same holds for one who would learn philosophy, and he will do better in judging if he hear all the arguments as though they were adversaries in a dispute (*quasi adversariorum dubitantium*).

After thus explaining the text of Aristotle, Thomas notes that the account fits the method of Aristotle in "almost all his books," and he calls it that of "dialectical disputation." Aristotle expressly praises dialectic for enabling one to see both sides of a problem through raising questions, thus making it easier to see where truth or falsity lies (*Topics* I,2,101ᵃ34–ᵇ4; *GBWW,* Vol. 8, p. 144a).

The first part of the Article, from the statement of the question through the presentation of the two series of arguments, is manifestly an example of the same method. It is a stylized, shorthand version of it, but every argument just adduced from the text of Aristotle will apply. The question and opposing arguments pose a problem and present a difficulty for the mind. The opposing arguments bind the reader's mind, tying him in a knot of contradiction, and if he is to get free, he has to become a judge. A judgment is called for and an inquiry must be made so as to reach a verdict that will settle the case.

The sources of these preliminary arguments, which in many cases have been identified, show that Thomas in the *Summa* was engaged in an ongoing discussion with his contemporaries; for it is seldom that the objections have been invented by Thomas himself. Yet for him, as for his reader now, the function of the opposing arguments is to open up a problem for discussion. This is especially true when all of the Articles of a single Question are taken together. For they then indicate how the main problem posed in the *quaestio* can be broken down into subsidiary points for investigation. So the Question concerning God's existence is not just whether He exists, but whether His existence calls for any proof at all (I,2,1), and if it does, whether proof can be arrived at (I,2,2), and if so, how (I,2,3).

The determination

With the words *respondeo dicendum quod* we come to the answer that the master in theology proposes to give to the question. Here again the beginning words are always in a standard form. It is customary to translate the Latin words by "I answer that," which implies that one of the words is redundant. Yet each of the words performs a different function. The *respondeo* refers back to the initial question and indicates that we will have an answer to it. The *dicendum* refers to the licensed master as the one alone qualified to determine "what must be said" on a theological matter. We are faced with a case on which judgment must be rendered between two opposing sides. Hence the need for a competent judge who possesses the authority and jurisdiction to render a judgment on the matter.

The answer is set off from the previous arguments, not only in being much longer, but also in being intended to settle the question. But in addition to the weight of his authority, the settling depends on the reasons that the judge provides and their ability to end the indeterminacy of mind in which the opposing arguments have left it. As Thomas notes about the function of a judgment, it must satisfy a desire as well as provide a conclusion for the reason (I,83,3, Reply Obj. 2; *GBWW*, Vol. 19, p. 439b–c). The final seal on the determination is provided by the ability of the answer to meet objections to it, showing where and how they are right as well as wrong.

Subjects and principles

In the first Question of the *Summa,* Thomas sets forth his conception of what theology ought to be. That he was conscious of his innovation is indicated by his criticism of the way in which Christian theology had been organized previously. In discussing the subject of theological science (I,1,7; *GBWW,* Vol. 19, p. 7a–c), he refers to three forms of organization: that of Lombard's *Sentences,* based on the Augustinian distinction between things and signs (*On Christian Doctrine* I,2,2; *GBWW,* Vol. 18, p. 624d); that of Hugh of Saint Victor in the twelfth century, based on the work of salvation or reparation; and that of several early thirteenth-century theologians who had organized theology about "the whole Christ," that is, about Christ as head and the faithful as members that compose the mystical body that is the church.

Thomas criticizes all three methods for "looking to what is treated of in this science" instead of "to the aspect (*ratio*) under which it is treated." He illustrates the distinction by comparing theologizing to seeing. Just as we see both man and a stone as colored objects, inasmuch as what is colored is the proper object of sight, so theology considers its objects "under the aspect of God (*sub ratione Dei*), either because they are God Himself, or because they are ordered to God as their beginning and end." All the matters covered in the theologies just referred to will be taken up, but they will be organized about God as their proper subject. Hence, it is fitting that this science should be called "theology," that is, "discourse about God (*sermo de Deo*)."

To some of his contemporaries Thomas's claim that theology could be a science was as monstrous as it is to many today. Science rests on what is seen to be evident to sense and reason. But faith in the words of Saint Paul, which Thomas accepts, is defined as "the substance of things to be hoped for, the evidence of things that appear not" (Heb. 11:1). Seeing is not believing in this case, and Thomas asserts unequivocally that "it is impossible that one and the same thing should be believed and seen by the same person. . . . Consequently faith and science are not about the same things" (II-II,1,5, Ans.; *GBWW,* Vol. 20, p. 383d). Yet Thomas also declares just as unequivocally that theology is a science which yet has as its first principles on which it is based the articles of faith (I,1,7, Ans.; *GBWW,* Vol. 19, p. 7b). By articles of faith he understands the "primary matters of faith" (*prima credibilia*), which are set forth in the creeds of the Catholic Church, such as belief in the existence of God, His providential concern for mankind, and the divinity and humanity of Jesus Christ (II-II,1,7, Ans.; *GBWW,* Vol. 20, p. 386a–b).

Thomas thus seems to be both affirming and denying that theology is both a faith and a science. How can he do so without contradicting himself? The answer he provides depends upon his conception of the nature of science and of the relation that sciences can have to one another. The conception of science to which he appeals is one that is still held, although it also existed in antiquity—that, namely, of an axiomatic system. The characteristic feature from which it derives its name is its structure: certain propositions are taken as axioms, which function as first principles in the sense that from them, with the help of certain definitions and the application of logical rules, propositions can be derived that constitute the theorems or laws of the science.

The nature of the axioms and the way they are obtained serve to distinguish different kinds of science. Some, as is noted (I,1,2, Ans.; *GBWW,* Vol. 19, p. 4b), such as arithmetic and geometry, proceed from principles known by the natural light of the intellect, whereas others take as axioms propositions that have been established by other sciences. Examples of the latter are optical perspective, which takes as axioms theorems proved by geometry, and music, or harmonics, which proceeds from principles established by arithmetic. Thus no science proves its own axioms; it either sees that they are so or else takes them on the authority of a higher science. Theology is a science of the latter kind, for "just as music believes (*credit*) the principles given to it by arithmetic, so sacred doctrine believes the principles revealed to it by God." In both cases there is an act of belief or trust, although in the one it is belief in something proven by another science and in the other a belief that God has revealed Himself to man.

The revelation of God, however, is contained in Sacred Scripture. It would seem then that the Bible would have to supply the principles as well as the matter of Thomas's theology. Yet one need read but a few pages in the *Summa* to find much that cannot be found anywhere in the Bible; indeed, in many places there are more references to Aristotle than to any of the sacred writers. How then can Thomas maintain that his doctrine is based on revelation? He does so by making a distinction, which occurs in one brief sentence, and since the sentence is often not well translated, it merits careful consideration. It occurs in answer to the question of whether sacred doctrine is one science (I,1,3, Ans.; cf. *GBWW,* Vol. 19, p. 4d):

> Because Sacred Scripture considers things according as they have been divinely revealed (*revelata*), everything whatsoever that is divinely revealable (*revelabilia*) shares in the one formal aspect of this science. And therefore is comprehended under sacred doctrine as under one science.

The controlling distinction is clearly that between what has been revealed and what is revealable or could be revealed. The latter at once opens the way to a much wider field of rational speculation than if it were confined entirely to the revelation given in the Bible. In fact, it opens the way to any truth, however obtained, that bears upon God Himself, or as the beginning and end of creatures.

How much that category takes in is indicated by the ten Articles of the first Question devoted to the nature of sacred doctrine. They include the philosophical sciences that deal with God, man, and the nature of reality; with human acts; with any knowledge bearing on such matters as it compares with the truths of revelation; of argument according to the rules of logic; of the proper use of metaphor; and of literary criticism as applied to the interpretation of Scripture.

As Thomas works it out, theology has a fourfold task: to seek to understand and protect the mysteries revealed that are beyond the reach of human reason; to prove by reason whatever is rationally demonstrable within the revealable; to draw out the implications within the revealed; and to organize all into a clearly articulated rational structure. This last task requires much more than the deduction of implicit and previously unstated conclusions. The *Summa* is a vast rational structure, but strictly formal deduction is but a small part of it. It employs many other forms of reasoning, informal as well as formal, reductive as well as deductive. Although its ideal may be the scientific model of a deductive axiomatic system, much of its reasoning is reductive and hypothetical rather than deductive. Thomas notes this fact when he compares the theory of the Trinity with the Ptolemaic theory of the motion of the heavens. In both, the logic employed is not that of "furnishing a sufficient proof of a principle, but as confirming an already established principle, by showing the congruity of its results, as in astrology [i.e., astronomy] the theory of eccentrics and epicycles is considered as established because thereby the sensible appearances of the heavenly movements can be explained; not, however, as if this reason were sufficient, since some other theory might explain them." It is in this way that "reasons avail to prove the Trinity; because, that is, when assumed to be true, such reasons confirm it" (I,32,1, Rep. 2; *GBWW*, Vol. 19, p. 177c).

It is as science, and especially in its argumentative mode, that Thomas's theology departs most widely from a scriptural theology. For a theology of the latter kind, especially as exhibited in its source in the Bible, is primarily narrative in proceeding by story and history. In dealing thus with individuals and particular events, this fact is cited as an objection against the possibility of theology being a science. Thus in the Gospels, when Jesus is asked who is one's neighbor, he responds by telling the story of the good Samaritan (Luke 10:30–37). For Thomas such stories can at most only provide illustrations of some argument by way of example (I,1,2, Rep. 2; *GBWW*, Vol. 19, p. 4c). Hence when he discusses love of neighbor, he raises a series of questions regarding proximity and whether one should be loved more than another because of consanguinity, moral character, generosity, indigence, etc. (II-II,26,1–13; *GBWW*, Vol. 20, pp. 510b–20d).

Sacred Scripture and authority

Yet the *Summa* remains a profoundly scriptural work. One must remember that the beginners in theology for whom it was written had already completed two years of graduate study of the Bible. Then, as we have just seen, its first principles are the articles of faith, and these have their source in Sacred Scripture. In fact, Thomas takes it as a rule that nothing is to be said about God "which is not found in Holy Scripture either explicitly or implicitly (*per verba vel per sensum*)" (I,36,2, Rep. 1; *GBWW*, Vol. 19, p. 193c). Also, the *Summa* itself contains what amounts to extensive commentary on certain parts of the Bible, especially:

On the Work of the Six Days in Genesis
    (I,67–74 in 21 Articles)

On the Old Law
    (I-II,98–105 in 46 Articles)

On the Life of Christ
    (III,27–59 in 174 Articles)

Sacred Scripture may provide the rule and norm of theology, but Thomas claims it is necessary to go beyond the express words: "If we could speak of God only in the very terms themselves (*secundum vocem*) of Scripture, it would follow that no one could speak about God in any but the original language of the Old or New Testament." Furthermore, the need to preserve the truth of revelation has "made it necessary to find new words to express the ancient faith about God" by disputing heretical interpretations of it (I,29,3, Rep. 1; *GBWW*, Vol. 19, p. 165a).

Another reason is the fact that more has been claimed to be the revelation of God than in fact has been revealed. To identify the true and genuine and distinguish it from the false and fraudulent, it is necessary to identify the canonical books, and that task demands more than the Bible itself can provide—a task accomplished within the tradition of the church by its early fathers. For this reason, their teaching ranks in authority almost equal to that of the sacred page itself. It also explains in part why the words of an "authority" appear so frequently in the *Summa*.

Auctoritas in scholastic teaching has a wider and even more primary meaning than the power of jurisdiction that can "authorize" something, although it carries that meaning too. It means a source, an original fountain of knowledge and teaching. Thus in theology Sacred Scripture is the primary authority. But the writings of the early fathers of the church also provide proper and internal authority, although not final, and their writings were read with reverent care. Thus Thomas writes of the Greek father Gregory Nazianzen that his "authority in Christian doctrine is of such weight that no one has ever raised objection to his teaching, as is also the case with the doctrine of Athanasius" (I,61,3, Ans.; *GBWW*, Vol. 19, p. 316c). The words of a master in theology, however, have no such weight. For although only a master had the right to determine a disputation, he did not count as an authority (II-II,5,1, Rep. 1).* This was true even of Peter Lombard, who was known as The Master.

Yet the texts set by the university for the teaching of a subject were considered to enjoy some degree of authority and were cited accordingly. This was true especially of Aristotle, known as The Philosopher, as is evident from the many references to his works in the *Summa*.

The place and importance given to authority in the *Summa* depend on the unique function that it has in revealed theology. In general the argument from authority is "the weakest form of proof," but it is "most proper to this doctrine, since its principles are obtained by revelation, and thus we must believe the authority of those to whom the revelation has been made. . . . For although the argument from authority based on human reason is the weakest, yet the argument from authority based on divine revelation is the strongest." For sacred doctrine, appeal to the authority of the canonical books of Scripture provides a "necessary argument," whereas citing the authority of any other learned men in theology or any other science can never provide anything more than "extrinsic and probable arguments" (I,1,8, Rep. 2; *GBWW*, Vol. 19, p. 8b–c). And in the matter of philosophy, Thomas declares in his comment on Aristotle's *On the Heavens* (I,22) that the purpose of the study is not to find out what men have thought but rather to discover the truth about things, so that in citing words of Aristotle he cites them because he believes them to be true and not because they are Aristotle's.

Ordo disciplinae

So far we have yet to see how Thomas plans to reorganize the discourse about God so as to meet the demands of knowledge and teachability. As we have seen, he finds that previous theologies have not done as well as they might have, especially in that they have failed to see how theology as a science demands that it should be ordered. Hence he devotes considerable care to make explicit how he will divide up his vast subject so as to make perspicuous his plan of organization. He does so by means of the prologues that he affixes to each Question. Every one of the 611 has such a prologue, although in most cases it does no more than give the heads or Articles under which he proposes to investigate the problem. However, a few of them are of major importance for indi-

---

*The text in *GBWW*, Vol. 20, p. 411a, omits the negative and should read: ". . . the words of Hugh of S. Victor are those of a master, and have NOT the force of an authority. . . ."

cating the crucial divisions of the whole work and thus for manifesting the *ordo disciplinae* as he conceives it. These divisions are the following:

The whole into 3 parts, as outlined in I,2, the prologue

Part I into 3 parts, as outlined in I,2, the prologue

Part II into 2 parts, as outlined in I-II,6, the prologue

Part I-II into 3 parts, as outlined in I-II,6, the prologue

Part II-II into 2 parts, as outlined in II-II, the prologue

Part III into 3 parts, as outlined in III, the prologue

The fact that the division of the work as a whole is not given until the second Question is itself significant. It indicates that the first Question serves as an introduction to the whole *Summa* and not just to its first part. As we have seen, it deals with the second-order consideration of the kind of knowledge theology is and the method to be followed in its pursuit. Theology itself does not get to work until the second Question, where in its prologue we learn how the entire field of theology can be surveyed and major areas marked out and related so as to determine the order in which they can be covered.

Accordingly, we read that the *Summa* will treat first "of God," second "of the rational creature's movement towards God," and third "of Christ, Who as man, is our way to God" (*GBWW,* Vol. 19, p. 10c). Each of these main parts (except for the third, which Thomas failed to complete) is ended by a special ritualistic acclaim "to Him, who is above all God for ever blessed. Amen" (I,119,2, Rep. 4; *GBWW,* Vol. 19, p. 608d; and II-II,189,3, Ans. 3; cf. *GBWW,* Vol. 20, p. 700d).

Part I contains 119 Questions, 584 Articles.

Part II, 303 Questions, 1,536 Articles.

Part III, 90 Questions, 549 Articles plus.

Part III, Supplement with 99 Questions, 443 Articles.

Although there are clearly three principal parts, there has been controversy over their relation to one another and the reason for it. Some have even thought it little short of scandalous for a Christian theology to postpone until the final part the consideration of Christ, who is the Savior and cause of divine grace in the world. In answer to this complaint, it has been claimed that, based on the principle that grace builds upon nature to complete and perfect it (I,1,8, Rep. 2; *GBWW,* Vol. 19, p. 8c), Thomas treats first of nature and then of grace, starting with the nature of God and of his creatures, angels and men, and of man's free actions, before taking up the consideration of grace as providing a transition to consideration of the theological virtues, and so on to the treatment of Christ as the giver of grace and of the sacraments as their channel. While this much is true, it cannot be said that nothing is said about grace until the questions dealing with it at the end of Part I-II. As we have just seen, the relation between grace and nature is referred to in the very first Question, and many such references will occur before the Questions directly concerned with its nature.

Another way of explaining the relation between the three parts is to base it on the distinction between nature and history. Thomas maintains that human nature is one and the same for all men throughout time; hence he can consider that nature before discussing the intervention of God in historical time by the advent of Christ. The trouble with this argument is that history as an entrance into time occurs much earlier than this in the *Summa*. It is there in the First Part in the account of the Creation, as well as in the Second Part in the discussion of the first sin, both of which Thomas takes to be historical events.

Another explanation sees in the relation of the Parts a reflection of the Neoplatonic notion that all things follow a process of *exitus-redditus,* an exit from and a return to the first principle of all, but such an explanation seems to over-Platonize the Aristotelian inclinations of Thomas.

Still another finds in the relation of the Parts a reflection of the threefold presence of God in the world as creative power bringing all things into existence, as grace offering to man the opportunity to freely choose the essential means to return to God, by accepting Christ as the way, the life, and the truth.

All of these explanations say something important about the *Summa*. But the most convincing account of the relation between the three Parts would seem to be this: that we start from a vision of God in Himself and of creation as it came forth from the creating God (Part I); that we proceed to the vision of God as a possibility open to His rational creatures through the free adherence of their will (Part II); that we conclude by accepting Jesus Christ as His son and the Church that He established as the means of attaining eternal life and union with God (Part III).

The "Treatises"

The largest division after that into the three Parts is the one made in many editions into "Treatises," as in the Treatise on God, on Man, on the Last End, on Law, on the Sacraments, etc. Such a division is not one that Thomas makes in the text of the *Summa*. In fact he seldom uses the term, *tractatus,* in discussing his analysis of the field of theology. I have not found that he ever uses it as his editors do. He does refer to the "treatise on Morals" (I,83,2, Rep. 3; *GBWW,* Vol. 19, p. 438d), but this refers to the whole second Part and not to any of the sections editors have labeled "Treatises." Translators also sometimes use the word where the Latin equivalent does not occur in the text. Thus a translation of the prologue to II-II begins by speaking of the "general treatise of virtues and vices," whereas the Latin has only "general consideration" (*communem considerationem*) (*GBWW*, Vol. 20, p. 379a). The words *tractatus resurrectionis* do occur, but they do so in the prologue to the Supplement to the Third Part (*GBWW*, Vol. 20, p. 885), which is the work of the first editor and not of Thomas.

This division into Treatises can be misleading on at least two counts. First, it tends to destroy the unity and integrity of the *Summa* as a single book by making it, as it were, into a collection of books. Second, it may lead the reader to suppose that a given Treatise contains all the *Summa* has to say, or whatever is most important, on its subject. But this is not the case. For example, what is called the "Treatise on the Angels" contains QQ. 50–64 of the First Part, and yet there is much of importance about the angels contained in QQ. 106–113 in the "Treatise on the Divine Government," dealing with such matters as the speech of angels, their hierarchies, their mission and action on men, etc.

The division into Treatises may be historical accident arising from the need that Thomas's confreres had for the use of his *Summa*. There is some reason for thinking that he may have undertaken that work at the request of his religious superior. The Dominican order had been licensed by the pope as confessors as well as preachers, and the early Dominicans relied heavily upon works dealing with sins. To overcome such one-sided emphasis, it is thought that Thomas may have been asked to place the consideration of sin within the overriding theological consideration of man and his relation to God. That may well have been the instigating reason for the writing of the *Summa,* but if so, it seems to have failed to achieve that immediate purpose, for the manuscript evidence reveals the existence of many more copies of Part II-II, which deals with individual sins, than of any other part.

The First Part

Much of interest can be learned about theology from the way that each of the three main Parts is divided, so it is worth considering in some detail the rest of the major prologues.

Immediately after the plan of the whole is set forth, we find that the First Part on God will also be divided into three according as it treats of:

The Divine Essence:	25 QQ. 149 AA.
The Distinction of Persons in God:	17 QQ. 74 AA.
The Procession of Creatures from God:	76 QQ. 350 AA.

In accordance with the principle that God is the subject of theology and its first principles His revelation, the plan of this part reflects its scriptural origin. Concerning the essence of God, the crucial text is that in which to Moses "it is said in the person of God: *I am Who am* (Exod. 3:14)" (I,2,3; *GBWW,* Vol. 19, p. 12d). For the Trinity of persons the New Testament provides the basic text, where "It is said (I John 5:7): *There are three who bear witness in heaven, the Father, the Word, and the Holy Ghost"* (I,36,1; *GBWW,* Vol. 19, p. 191b). Creation, according to Thomas, is the work of the "whole Godhead" *(totius divinitatis),* for in common with the church fathers he found references to the Trinity in such words of Genesis as "Let us make man in our image (Gen. 1:26). This complementarity between the Old and New Testaments is reflected elsewhere in the *Summa,* as in placing consideration of the Old Law before that of the New, and of God and all creation before that of Christ.

The conception of nature, as already mentioned, functions as a controlling principle in the plan of the work. One of the clearest examples appears in the way the subject of law is treated (I-II,90–108). It begins with three Questions in general on the essence or nature of law, its kinds, and its effects, before moving on to each of the particular kinds, starting with the eternal law as proper to theology, then the natural law, followed by human positive law, and concluding with divine positive law in the Old and New Testaments in some 11 Questions and 58 Articles. In short, the general procedure is to go not only from the general to the particular but also from nature to history, since history, like grace, presupposes nature.

A particularly interesting and significant application of this principle can be seen in the way that the work of material creation is analyzed. Based on the description given in Genesis, the analysis begins with a general Question on the work of corporeal creation (I,65), then one to consider the order in which distinct things were produced (I,66), before treating the work of each day in particular, concluding with final Questions on the work of the seventh day and what is common to all of them (I,73–74). The significant thing is, however, that when we come to the sixth day on which man was created, hardly any account is given of him. The scriptural account is abandoned, and we do not find a return to it until much later, in the treatment of the first man and woman and of Paradise in I,90–102, and still later of the first and original sin (I-II,81–83).

The first interruption occurs after I,74 and runs for 15 Questions and 89 Articles, dealing with the nature of man as a rational soul united with a body and having powers of intellect, sense, and appetite, capable of certain kinds of knowledge. Thus, before returning to the scriptural account of man in Paradise, Thomas considers what man is as a creature coming forth from the hand of God. So too, he does not take up the problem of the first sin until he has investigated the nature of human acts issuing from freedom of will and choice, which alone allow the possibility of sin, that is, after some 80 Questions and 434 Articles.

The plan and structure of the *Summa* manifest basic principles of Thomas's thought such as that man has a nature that is one and the same for all of mankind through all time, from that of the first man to the present; that it is possible by the use of our knowing powers to discover what God has made, what he meant it to be, and hence also to learn something about God; and, finally, that this knowledge so rationally achieved is not only not incompatible with but is even furthered by the revelation of God communicated through the Sacred Scriptures.

The nature that is the object of Thomas's investigations, however, is not limited to that of mankind. In the First Part alone there is extensive consideration of the nature of God as well as of those creatures that are purely intellectual and spiritual, the angels. Thomas came to be known in the schools as the Angelic Doctor, as though he approached as nearly as possible from the human side what it is like to be a pure intellect. Also, however, from the extent of his treatment of them it is clear that he delighted in speculating about what it would be like to be such a pure intellect: 24 Questions and 118 Articles in Part I.

The Second Part

We already know from the first general division that this part will treat of man's movement toward God. The prologue to it now further specifies that it will consider man as the image of God. It thus not only refers the whole discussion back to God, as is proper to theology, but it also investigates the very traits that man images in God the exemplar: "that is, man, according as he too is the principle of his actions, as having free choice and control (*potestatem*) of his actions" (I-II, Prol.; *GBWW*, Vol. 19, p. 609).

However, it is not until the sixth Question that the plan of the whole Second Part is given. Hence the first five Questions serve as an introduction to this whole Part. These five Questions, consisting of 40 Articles, concern the nature of happiness as the last end or goal of all men and maintain that it cannot be anything other than God Himself, since no created partial good can satisfy man's desire for happiness. The analysis is heavily dependent upon the ethics of Aristotle, as it will continue to be throughout the account of the moral life, but that ethics has been utterly transformed by being ordered to a radically new end, that of the infinite God.

The discussion of happiness is also set off from the rest of the Second Part in that it concerns an area of life in which man is not free, since man cannot *not* desire to be happy. All the remainder of the moral Part deals with man as a free agent and the acts by which he can obtain, or be prevented from obtaining, happiness. This consideration is divided into two main parts: "Because operations and acts are concerned with things singular, consequently all practical knowledge is incomplete unless it take account of things in detail (*in particulari*)" (I-II,6, Prol.; *GBWW*, Vol. 19, p. 644a). Thus the First of the Second Part deals with morals in general, while the Second deals with morals in particular. Of these two the Second is much the larger, consisting of 189 Questions and 917 Articles, compared with the First's 114 Questions in 579 Articles. Yet it is the First that is more complex in organization, as can be seen by looking at schematic outlines of the two.

Part I-II
    I. Of human acts
        1. Acts proper to man
           a. Voluntary free acts   I-II,6–17
           b. Goodness and badness of acts   I-II,18–21
        2. Acts common to man and animals: Passions
           a. In general   I-II,22–25
           b. In particular   I-II,26–48
             (love, hate, pleasure, sorrow, fear, anger)
    II. Intrinsic principles of human acts
        1. Habits in general   I-II,49–54
        2. The virtues   I-II,55–70
           (intellectual, moral, theological)
        3. Vice and sin   I-II,71–89
    III. Extrinsic principles of human acts
        1. Law   I-II,90–108
           (eternal, natural, human, Old, New)
        2. Grace   I-II,109–114

Part II-II
    I. Of the virtues
        1. Theological virtues   II-II,1–46
           (faith, hope, charity)
         2. Moral virtues   II-II,47–170
           (prudence, justice, fortitude, temperance)
    II. Of particular states of life
        1. Of special graces   II-II,171–178
           (prophecy, tongues, miracles)
         2. Of the active and contemplative life   II-II,179–182
         3. Of the states of life   II-II,183–189
           (religious life, episcopacy)

However, the plan for Part II-II does not appear so simple when one comes to see how it has been obtained, as is set forth in its prologue. The first simplification is clear enough: it is based on the distinction between the moral life that is common to all men and that of men occupying special position, such as a bishop or one who lives in a religious order. The second simplification consists in reducing the inquiry into the common moral life into consideration of just seven virtues: the theological virtues of faith, hope, and charity, and the moral virtues of prudence, justice, fortitude, and temperance. The reason behind this move is to avoid having "to say the same thing over and over again" as would be required if each virtue with the corresponding gift of the Holy Spirit, vice, and precept were to be treated separately. It is here that the complicating factor occurs. For Thomas proposes "in treating about each cardinal virtue . . . [to] treat also of all the virtues which, in any way whatever, belong to that virtue, as also of the opposite vices" (II-II, Prol.; *GBWW,* Vol. 20, p. 379).

How considerable a complication this decision entails can be seen merely from a list of the subjects that are added to the five principal Questions on charity (II-II,23–27): Of joy, peace, mercy, beneficence, almsdeeds, fraternal correction; hatred, acedia, envy; of sins contrary to peace, contention, schism, war, strife, sedition, scandal; of the precepts of charity; of the gift of wisdom and of folly opposed to wisdom, which amount in all to 19 Questions, 89 Articles.

The treatment of justice is by far the most complex and extensive: 66 Questions with 303 Articles (II-II,57–122). This is not surprising, since justice is considered to be preeminent (*praeeminet*) among moral virtues (II-II,58,12). It includes not only man's duties to other men but also his duties to God. Hence the virtue of religion belongs to it, along with associated virtues such as devotion, prayer, adoration, and sacrifice, as well as the contrary vices, amounting to 42 Questions. Justice thus includes, or is summed up, in the command of love of God and neighbor, while the final Question on justice is devoted to consideration of the Ten Commandments.

The Third Part

We already know from the previous announcement that this part is to be devoted to the consideration of Christ as man's way to God. Yet it must not be supposed that God's help to man is introduced only here in the final Part. At three significant points in the analysis of the moral life, Thomas notes both the need and the promise of that help. First, in treating of happiness as constituting the perfection of man, he devotes an entire Question to the problem of its attainment, in which he claims that man enjoys the help of God in achieving what he cannot achieve by his own efforts (I-II,5,1–8; *GBWW*, Vol. 19, pp. 636d–43d). Second, in discussing the consequences of good human acts, he declares that God recognizes them as meritorious and deserving of reward (I-II,21,4; *GBWW*, Vol. 19, pp. 719d–20c). Third, the final sections of Part I-II on the New Law and on grace, which are the work of Christ, claim that by cooperating with divine grace man may be assured of attaining his last end (I-II,114,1–10; *GBWW*, Vol. 20, pp. 370c–78c). However, the analysis of the moral life is mainly, if not exclusively, concerned with the nature of things, in fact or promise. It is only in this Third Part that we turn from nature to history and consider the life and work of Jesus Christ. Accordingly, as set forth in its prologue, this Part considers:

The Saviour Himself: III,1–59, 325 AA.

The sacraments by which salvation is attained: III,60–90 + Supp. 68, 513 AA.

The end of immortal life which is attained
    through Him by the resurrection: Supp. 69–99, 153 AA.

The treatment of Christ, as the prologue indicates, is divided into two sections. Of these, the first deals with the mystery of the Incarnation in the union of the human and divine nature in one person (III,1–26; *GBWW*, Vol. 20, pp. 701–846); the second has to do with the mystery of the life and acts of Christ, beginning with a consideration of the Blessed Virgin and ending with the resurrection of Christ, His ascension, and sitting at the right hand of the Father, endowed with the power of judgment (III,28–59). In his account Thomas follows the course of the life as it is told in the Gospels. But his emphasis is upon the perfection of human nature in Christ rather than upon his saving death, an emphasis that derives, perhaps, from the claim that God makes possible the attainment of man's perfection. An example of such an emphasis may be seen in the way the discussion of Christ's subjection to the Father and his prayer (III,20–21; *GBWW*, Vol. 20, pp. 821b–27c) draws upon and reflects the analysis of the virtues of devotion and prayer in the treatment of justice in the Second Part (II-II,82–83).

Discussion of the sacraments follows the plan adopted for the Second Part by beginning with a general consideration in Questions 60–65 (*GBWW*, Vol. 20, pp. 847–85) and then analyzing each of the seven sacraments in particular. Thomas had completed his examination of baptism, confirmation, the eucharist, and begun that of penance when death brought an end to his writing with III,90. His plan for the treatment of penance had been stated in III,84, prologue, and from this it was possible to continue with what he had written about it in his commentary on Peter Lombard. The same procedure was followed for the remaining sacraments of extreme unction, holy orders, and matrimony, as well as for the resurrection of the body and the attainment of eternal life. This work was done perhaps by one of the secretaries to whom Thomas dictated his work. The additions as published in the *Supplement to the Third Part* are considerable, amounting to 99 Questions out of the 611 of the *Summa* as a whole, and 452 Articles out of 3,112. And since these Articles were put together out of his earliest large work, they lack the presence of the mature thinker.

On coming to terms

Reading the *Summa* requires more than coming to understand and accept the stylized form of the disputative mode of writing, the detailed articulation of structure, and the constant citing of authorities. There is the still greater difficulty of getting a grasp on the terms that are used. The language is simple and the syntax clear, but the terminology is specialized and technical. It may have been the common language of the schools in which Thomas taught and of the "beginners" for whom he wrote: the result of a centuries-old tradition of speculation by both Latin and Greek theologians seeking understanding of their faith with the addition of an intensive and prolonged study of the works of Aristotle. Thomas uses that language as though it were his native tongue, but for the reader today it is one that has to be learned and acquired.

However, the difficulty can be exaggerated, for in many instances Thomas takes care to explain the meaning of terms that are strange to us. In discussing the Trinity, for example, he asks "whether *Person* is the same as *Hypostasis, Subsistence,* and *Essence*" and then analyzes the meaning of each and explains how they differ (I,29,2; *GBWW,* Vol. 19, pp. 163–64). A good example of the precision with which he works is evident, in another example, from the way he distinguishes between distinction, diversity, difference, disparity, separation, and division (I,31,2; *GBWW,* Vol. 19, pp. 172c–73c).

Often terms from the specialized Aristotelian vocabulary are used first without any explanation of their meaning, such as form, matter, substance, accident, act, potency, nature. But then on a later occasion a detailed explanation of them is provided. The reader, by continuing, will eventually meet that explanation. Failing that, recourse to an index of terms can be of great help, such as the *Syntopicon* or any Thomistic index. For the meaning of "nature," for example, the *Syntopicon* lists six references to the *Summa* where detailed accounts of that term are given (*GBWW,* Vol. 3, p. 235b). Then too, another source can be found in the lexicon of terms in Book Five of Aristotle's *Metaphysics* (*GBWW,* Vol. 8, pp. 534d–35c).

A difficulty of a different order arises if we attempt to read according to the principle that Thomas lays down, which is to look for the truth and not what a man thinks. The *Summa* contains a great deal of philosophical speculation, much also that is scientific in claiming to state how things are. Aristotle is quoted many times, but on the ground that what he says is true and not because he said it. Thomas uses his statements in thinking about his faith from the conviction that knowledge of any truth will further knowledge of God as the source of truth. But what if it does not, being in fact false? What should a reader do when he finds Thomas is mistaken about the truth of things?

Take his consideration of the work of creation as described in Genesis. Since the words of Scripture must be understood to be in accord with the way things are, to understand the creation of light we must understand the nature of light, and Thomas then proceeds to say that light is not a body and its motion is instantaneous (I,67,2; *GBWW*, Vol. 19, p. 350c–d). One might argue about whether or not it is a body or matter, for that depends on what matter is, which is as much a philosophical as a scientific question. But that light is not instantaneous but has a definite velocity is a scientific fact. Following Thomas's principle to look for the truth and not what men say, we should presumably lay aside his work at this point and inquire further into the nature of light: a task obviously not easily or readily undertaken if one is interested in reading the *Summa*.

Of course, many references to what is taken to be the fact of the matter are offered only by way of example and illustration to clarify a philosophical or theological notion, such as that fire rises because it seeks its natural place in the fiery heaven, or that all the heavens revolve about the earth as center. But, since they are offered only as illustrations, the reader need only take them on supposition; that is, if things were so, light would be thrown upon the point at issue.

A difficulty of still another kind occurs with regard to the faith that Thomas has and is seeking to illuminate. The knowledge that he is concerned with is said to be practical as well as speculative, concerned with doing as well as knowing, of what we should do to get to God (I,1,4; *GBWW*, Vol. 19, p. 5a–b). Yet it is based on the Catholic faith, and the action it aims at is action in accordance with that faith. What then is a reader to do who does not share the same faith with Thomas?

One possible answer is offered by the explanation that the *Summa* gives for the theory of the Trinity. It is compared, as already noted, to the Ptolemaic theory of the heavens. The theory does not prove that the heavens in fact so operate as it describes, but, granting its principles, it will "save the appearances" in the sense of showing how they might move, and, in doing that, it says many true things about the movements of the heavenly bodies, sufficient, for example, to predict where they will be in the future, when an eclipse will occur, etc. So in its explanations of the Catholic faith the *Summa* has many true things to say about God, the world, and man, even things that may influence a person in his beliefs and actions.

Yet Thomas also holds that theology is more speculative than practical, inasmuch as it is more concerned with divine things than with human actions, and the *Summa* is replete with rational speculation about all manner of things, including the importance and delight of speculation itself. A good example is the account that is given of the angels, which is all but pure speculation, the intellectual significance of which has been shown recently by Mortimer Adler in his book *The Angels and Us*.

Despite Thomas's disclaimer, there is also something to be said for reading an author to find out what he thought. In fact, Thomas manifested such an interest in one quite important instance. In his day there was a work attributed to Aristotle known as the *Liber de causis*, which enjoyed an authority equal to that of the genuine works. Thomas doubted the truth of that attribution, and in his commentary on it he showed that it could not be, for comparing passage after passage in it with the work of the late Neoplatonic philosopher, Proclus, he showed that the work came from this later thinker. Clearly, in this instance he was interested in the history of what men have thought, or in what is called the history of ideas. And, indeed, since we are influenced in our own thinking by what other men have thought, it is to our own benefit to seek to know better what others have thought.

On some matters, of course, historical truth is the only one that can be found; e.g., that the sun revolves about the earth was, at the time Thomas wrote, the best scientific theory available. Such a reading holds for matters of law as well as of science. Laws dealing with usury, marriage, and penance, for example, are no longer laws, and hence Thomas's exposition of them now has at most a historical interest in showing what those laws were and how they could be explained and justified.

The teaching instrument

The purpose of the *Summa* is to teach, as is stated in the general prologue. It is natural to ask, then, how well it is designed to serve as an instrument of teaching. Any teaching involves three elements: subject matter, teacher, and student; and the success of the teaching is measured by the success of the student in handling the subject matter. For this, competence in the teacher is required, not only in command and organization of the subject matter, but also in the ability to engage the student in the activity of learning.

That the *Summa* meets the first requirement is evident from the coverage of its subject matter and the perspicuity of its structure, although here, of course, most depends on the value of what it has to say. How well it meets the second requirement depends on how well its method succeeds in actively engaging the mind of its readers.

As Thomas discusses in his analysis of teaching (I,117,1; *GBWW,* Vol. 19, pp. 595d–97c), the teacher can never be the primary or principal cause of learning in the student. Learning is like healing in that it may be achieved in two different ways. At times the sick person manages to recover his health by himself through the natural healing processes of the body, whereas at other times he requires the aid of a doctor and the medical art. So too the ignorant person may succeed through his own efforts to acquire the knowledge that he previously lacked, whereas in other cases he may need the help of a teacher and the teaching art. In both instances, however, the primary agent is the patient or student, the doctor and teacher being at most secondary and cooperative agents. If the patient fails to respond to the doctor and his art, he will not recover his health; if the student does not become active in the learning process, he will not learn.

Thomas points out that there are two ways in which the teacher can aid the student: "First, by proposing to him certain helps or means of instruction (*instrumenta*) which his intellect can use for the acquisition of science. . . . Second, by strengthening the intellect of the learner. . . ." By these criteria, how well does the *Summa* fulfill the needs of a teaching instrument? How well adapted is it to engage the mind in the activity of learning? Given the kind of knowledge that it is concerned with—that is, a science considered as a movement from principle to conclusion, as finding an answer to a question that admits of opposed answers—how fit is it for generating such a discourse of reason?

Phrased in such terms, the question all but answers itself. The Article is an imitation of a disputation, and, as such, it seeks to engage the reader in the process of arguing. But for such a purpose the weakness of a written discourse is that one person, the writer, gets to do all the talking while the reader is left a passive listener. The Article by its form is designed so as to all but compel the reader to engage in discussion, if only to the extent of seeing that there are opposing positions with regard to the problem raised by the opening question. Ideally, then, to use it as an instrument for "strengthening the intellect," we should propose an answer after reading the opening question; then we should read and respond on our own to the opposing arguments that are stated, before proceeding to consider how the question is determined and resolved in the body of the Article and in the answers to the objections. In this way we could test whether the question has truly been resolved, so that the mind can rest in its judgment.

In its own way the Article may be viewed as a much shortened version of a Socratic dialogue, or better perhaps as the stage directions for conducting one. It is intended to have a maieutic function of bringing ideas to birth. But, going further, Thomas like his master Aristotle believes that it is possible to attain an assured truth. Reading the *Summa* then should be not only an exercise in thinking but thinking itself, and the Article in its way conforms to the description of thinking that Plato puts in the mouth of Socrates in the *Theaetetus* (189e–190a; *GBWW,* Vol. 7, p. 538a):

> Thinking appears to me to be just talking—asking questions of herself
> and answering them, affirming and denying. And when she [the soul]
> has arrived at a decision, either gradually or by a sudden impulse,
> and has at last agreed, and does not doubt, this is called her opinion.
> I say, then, that to form an opinion is to speak, and opinion is a word
> spoken,—I mean, to oneself and in silence.

Documentation

This essay is a revised and much expanded version of one published under the title, "How to Read an Article of the *Summa*," in *The New Scholasticism,* XXVII, 2 (April 1953), 129–59.

The Latin text has been cited according to the one-volume edition *Summa Theologiae,* Alba-Roma, Editiones Paulinae, 1962.

The translation cited is that of the Fathers of the English Dominican Province, revised by D. J. Sullivan, included in *GBWW,* Vols. 19–20.

The best historical introduction to the work of Saint Thomas remains that of M. D. Chenu, *Introduction a l'étude de Saint Thomas D'Aquin,* Paris, 1950, translated as *A Guide to the Study of Thomas Aquinas,* Chicago, 1964, but it needs correcting in places, especially with regard to the overall structure of the *Summa* by G. T. Lafont, *Structure et méthode dans la Somme Théologique de Saint Thomas d'Aquin,* Paris, 1961.

The latest English translation with accompanying Latin text and voluminous notes and commentaries is that by the English Dominicans under the general editorship of Thomas Gilby, *Summa Theologiae,* New York and London, 1967, in sixty volumes.

PART THREE

Special Features

The Invention of the Presidency

Marcus Cunliffe

Marcus Cunliffe, who was educated at Oriel College, Oxford, and at Yale (as a Commonwealth Fellow), is well known as a historian who has devoted a distinguished career chiefly to American studies, including American literature. He held posts at two English universities before he was appointed University Professor in 1980 at George Washington University, Washington, D.C., where he now teaches. At various times he has been visiting professor at Harvard, The City University of New York, and the University of California at Berkeley; he has also held fellowships at the Center for Advanced Study in Behavioral Sciences at Stanford (1957–58) and at the Woodrow Wilson International Center for Scholars in Washington (1977–78).

Professor Cunliffe maintains a vigorous lecture schedule, which has taken him to India, Nepal, Sri Lanka, Lebanon, Turkey, Tunisia, Cameroon, Tanzania, Kenya, Yugoslavia, Japan, and Finland, as well as to all the countries of Western Europe. He has also written many books and articles. Among the former are *The Literature of the United States* (1954; rev. ed. 1986), *George Washington: Man and Monument* (1958; rev. ed. 1982), and *American Presidents and the Presidency* (1969; rev. eds. 1972, 1976, 1987). His current interests and researches are in the subject of monarchy and republicanism in the American context, and in the conceptions of private property held by Americans over the course of their history.

Introduction

The bicentennial celebrations of the American Revolution, and of the subsequent era of constitution-making, tend not surprisingly to be cheerful and patriotic in tone. The colonists' freedom-loving and self-governing capacities are pointed out, along with both their practicality and their innovative boldness. We learn how the Americans, while fighting a long war against the military, naval, and commercial might of Great Britain, created a national league of republics, under the Articles of Confederation. We learn further that the Founding Fathers, concerned to strengthen the unity and executive energy of their first experiment, boldly replaced the Articles with the new Constitution of 1787. This Constitution, ratified by the states after some exhaustive debate, took effect in 1789, with George Washington as first President of the United States. America's is, we are often reminded, the oldest surviving written instrument of government in the modern world. True, it has been amended now and then, but not fundamentally changed, as if it had a kind of sanctity about it. Indeed, almost from the first, with the addition of the first ten Amendments, or Bill of Rights, ratified in 1791, even some of the document's previous critics joined in a chorus of praise that has been described as "Constitution-Worship."[1]

While not every incumbent has matched the inspiring example set by General Washington, the office of President has survived and apparently thrived along with the other elements sketched out in 1787 at the Philadelphia convention. From time to time, no doubt, there is talk of serious deterioration. In the early 1970s Arthur Schlesinger, Jr., and other pundits expressed alarm at the recent growth of an "imperial" or "runaway" presidency.[2] Jimmy Carter as presidential candidate owed some of his early success to public alarm over the alleged high-handedness of Lyndon Johnson's administration, and the underhandedness of Richard Nixon's. Within a few years, however, journalists and political scientists alike were calling for stronger, not milder, presidential leadership, as if the Johnson-Nixon era belonged to ancient history. For contemporary discussion of the Constitution in general, and of the presidency in particular, is present-minded rather than skeptical, and in emphasizing the Founders' sagacity, it pays relatively little attention to the actual circumstances of the Revolution and its aftermath.

This essay, focusing upon the "invention" and early evolution of the presidency, an office seemingly unknown in previous world experience, goes back to the eighteenth-century context. We shall consider the omnipresence of monarchy and the contrasting doubts as to the viability of republicanism. We shall note that there was in effect no executive branch under the Articles of Confederation. Not only was the creation of a federal executive, under Article II of the 1787 Constitution, a radical departure from the Articles; it was to some a horrifying reversion to the very forms of monarchy that the Declaration of Independence had cast out, as recently as 1776. During the 1790s, Thomas Jefferson and many of his Republican associates claimed that the rival, Federalist administrations of George Washington (1789–97) and John Adams (1797–1801) meant to restore a kind of elective monarchy, or "monocracy," not fundamentally different from that of England's Hanoverian King George III.

How and why *did* the United States repudiate the royal connection in 1776? Why the hiatus of 1776–87, during which there was no separate executive? Did the 1787 delegates, or some of them, consciously or unconsciously provide their country with a revised, nonhereditary version of the old British monarchy they had lately repudiated? Or, whether by intent or outcome, did the Founding Fathers make a clean break with the past? Inventions, as we know, commonly take a while to evolve from the very forms they supersede. Early automobiles were thus known as "horseless carriages," and their design (with its significantly named "coachwork") at least outwardly continued to resemble the horsedrawn vehicles they had rendered obsolete. In relation to monarchy, was the American presidency an analogous "horseless carriage"? As with early automobiles, is it more relevant to stress the resemblance to antecedent structures, or to the vital novelties they presage? Much, though not all, of this essay is concerned with that side of eighteenth-century American thinking which instinctively consulted the past for guidance as to the future.

1. The prevalence of monarchy

Throughout the known world of the 1760s and 1770s, hereditary monarchy was the almost universal type of government. This was the case whether the sovereign was dubbed emperor or king (or their female equivalents), tsar, prince, duke, sultan, shah, caliph, shogun, sheikh, rajah, or—among the North American Indians—sachem or sagamore.

Their subject peoples well knew that royal regimes might be less glorious in practice than in theory. Nevertheless, hereditary monarchy was seen as the indispensable norm. Long reigns were taken as guarantees of stability, and possibly of divine approval. Among such splendid reigns

"Declaration of Independence in Congress, at the Independence Hall, Philadelphia, July 4th, 1776," by John Trumbull. *"Not only was the creation of a federal executive, under Article II of the 1787 Constitution, a radical departure from the Articles; it was to some a horrifying reversion to the very forms of monarchy that the Declaration of Independence had cast out."*

were those of Frederick the Great, ruler of Brandenburg-Prussia from 1740 to 1786, Maria Theresa of Austria (1740–80), Catherine of Russia (1762–96), and the all but unending spans of Bourbon France (Louis XIV, 1643–1715; Louis XV, 1715–74). In Great Britain, George II occupied the throne from 1727 to 1760. His grandson, George III, who succeeded George II, was to reign officially for sixty years, although in the final decade 1810–20 formal duties were undertaken by the Prince Regent, the future George IV.

In the received wisdom of the eighteenth century, the road to success was the royal road. As pundits interpreted the historical record, this had almost invariably been so. The royal heroes of misty antiquity were thought to have descended from the gods. Elements of ancient magic clung to modern monarchs. They were for example credited with the power to achieve instantaneous cures for the "king's evil" (scrofula) through the lightest physical contact with the afflicted person. Belief in the efficacy of the royal touch lingered into the early eighteenth century; Queen Anne still now and then "touched" her subjects.[3]

Royalty was symbolized and venerated in recreation and mythology. Thus, the old game of chess presented a fixed monarchic order. Pawns were like humble foot soldiers, available for sacrifice. Mobile knights and foursquare castles served their crown, aided by the oblique excursions of the church's bishops and by the privileged activity of the queen. All owned an ultimate duty to protect the king, who could be threatened yet who remained inviolable.

Again, in a pack of playing cards, the most valuable—except for the mysterious ace—were generally the "court" cards: king, queen, jack or knave (i.e., prince). Children absorbed a sense of the rightness of royalty from nursery rhymes. "The king was in his parlor. . . ." When Humpty-Dumpty had his great fall, the recourse was to the greatest power in the land: "all the king's horses and all the king's men." In fairy-tales, the ultimate reward for eager, upwardly mobile young men is half the kingdom and marriage to the king's daughter; and beauteous if lowly maidens, as with Cinderella, find a Prince Charming.

In the Scriptures, too, the imagery was for the most part deeply regal. God and his son Jesus are each *Lord,* and often *King.* True, Jesus resists such tribute for himself, and the title *King of the Jews* is applied to him in bitter irony. True, too, occasional texts are cautionary (*Put not your trust in princes;* Ps. 146:3). But many another verse equates divinity with majesty and must have reinforced the inclination of Bible-readers to think in the same terms. In the medieval world contemplated in Dante's treatise *De monarchia* (ca. 1313), Rome was the headquarters of the Church Catholic; the Holy Roman Empire with its Emperor and princely Electors formed a secular counterpart. For Dante the perfect system would involve the joint sway of a universal Emperor and a universal Pope. God himself, it was reasoned, had established hereditary monarchy as the nearest earthly resemblance to the kingdom of heaven.

By the time of Queen Anne the old extreme claims of divine origin and divine right were no longer being advanced, in Anglo-America at any rate. They were hardly necessary, we may think, when sovereigns enjoyed so much other actual and metaphorical support. God is "our Father." Monarchs similarly were still spoken of as *Patres Patriae,* fathers of their people—a position of natural authority, understandable to everyone. Moreover, as children are nurtured by their parents so the father is head of the household, and offspring owe him respect. And so it was with kings.

Nevertheless, in the world of around 1760, monarchy did not seem antiquated. On the contrary, vigorous rulers (in Spain, France, Habsburg Austria, and Tsarist Russia) appeared to be centralizing and modernizing agents, struggling on behalf of their whole people to curb the excessive parochial privileges of aristocrats and churchmen. The enlightened Frenchman Voltaire was among those who upheld the so-called royal thesis or *thèse royale,* according to which only the monarch represented his people in all their classes or estates.

Some of these sovereigns, such as Frederick of Prussia, have been spoken of as "enlightened despots."[4] They were certainly capable of capricious and even brutal autocracy. Yet ancestral arrogances were on the wane, and for Voltaire, Montesquieu, and other European *philosophes,* as well as for a number of Anglo-American philosophers and jurists, the best existing, possibly the best conceivable, pattern of government had been hit upon, by a happy blend of wisdom and of trial and error, across the Channel in Great Britain.

Since there was no written English constitution other than the Parliamentary Act of 1689, "for declaring the rights and liberties of the subject and settling the succession of the crown," which was known as the Bill of Rights, explanation as to what the nature of that constitution was varied. The English Bill of Rights, coming after decades of civil strife, Cromwellian republicanism, Stuart restoration, and disputed succession, offered the throne to William and Mary on nothing more than the assumption that William, Prince of Orange, would realize he owed his elevation to Parliament, and that he would with his wife, Queen Mary, rule over a genuinely constitutional, or (in John Locke's word) "moderated" monarchy.[5]

This precarious-seeming settlement endured and even became hallowed, though it was challenged by rebellions at thirty-year intervals: that of the Duke of Monmouth (natural son of Charles II) in 1685, of the Jacobite or Stuart "Old Pretender" in 1715, of the "Young Pretender" Charles Edward Stuart in 1745–46, and eventually that of the American mainland colonies in 1775–76. Early in his reign, George III spoke of the British patchwork of precedents and restraints as "the most beautiful combination that ever was framed." This was the standard tribute, even down to the choice of epithets. Arguing against Lord North in the House of Commons in 1782, William Pitt was to acclaim his country's system as "the most beautiful fabric of government in the world," and he was echoed by his adversary: "the most beautiful fabric," said North, "that had ever existed perhaps from the beginning of time."[6]

Such panegyrics were to be reserved in later days for the 1787 American Constitution—a wonderful piece of creative thought, according to William Ewart Gladstone, the Victorian statesman. But in the mid-eighteenth century it was the "mixed" English constitution that drew the chorus of praise. Ancient writers—Aristotle, Cicero, Polybius—quite commonly asserted that there were three basic patterns of rule: rule by one (monarchy), by the few (aristocracy), and by the many (democracy). They recognized the potential defects of each model and tended to conclude that the very best form would somehow blend or

mix elements of each. The English secret was explained as a balance
in which each of the three fundamental parts—monarch (or executive),
aristocracy (or House of Lords), and "people" (House of Commons)—
restrained the others. "Herein," Sir William Blackstone, the celebrated
jurist, wrote, "consists the true excellence of the English government":

> In the legislature, the people are a check upon the nobility, and the
> nobility a check upon the people; by the mutual privilege of rejecting
> what the other has resolved: while the king is a check upon both. . . .
> And this very executive power is again checked and kept within due
> bounds by the two houses, through the privilege they have of inquiring
> into, impeaching and punishing the conduct (not indeed of the king,
> which would destroy his constitutional independence; but, which is more
> beneficial to the public) of his evil and pernicious counsellors.

The parts of government, Blackstone concluded, were "like three
distinct powers in mechanics," producing a wholly effective resultant
force:

> They jointly impel the machine of government in a direction different
> from what either, acting by itself, would have done; but at the same time
> in a direction partaking of each, and formed out of all; a direction which
> constitutes the true line of the liberty and happiness of the community.[7]

The actual constitution, it need hardly be said, seemed less idyllic
to those who worked the machine, and much less static than people
pretended. Nevertheless it was praised and wondered at far and wide,
not least in North America. And the colonists showed no uneasiness at
welcoming the kingly part of the mechanism. A treatise of 1717 by John
Wise, pastor of Ipswich, Massachusetts, avowed that of all the "Mixt
Governments" in the world, the best appeared to be "that which has
a Regular Monarchy (in distinction to what is called Dispotick) settled
upon a Noble Democracy as its Basis":

> It is said of the *British* Empire, That it is such a Monarchy . . . as by
> most Admirable Temperament affords very much to the Industry,
> Liberty, and Happiness of the Subject, and reserves enough for the
> Majesty and Prerogative of any King, who will own his People as
> Subjects, not as Slaves. It is a Kingdom, that of all the Kingdoms of the
> World, is most like to the Kingdom of Jesus Christ, whose Yoke is easie,
> and Burden light.[8]

The constitution of Great Britain was extolled by Americans in language practically identical to that of the mother country, and with the
same references to authors ancient and modern. "Limited" monarchy
was lauded: "under the mild . . . Administration of a *limited* Prince,
every Thing looks . . . smiling and serene." Sermons preached by

Independence blamed the King himself, not his ministers, for the tally of British injustices, but this turn against his person occurred only at the eleventh hour. By and large, until the 1770s, American radicals professed to regard the Crown as their ally rather than their enemy; they sharply distinguished, as Blackstone had done, between a sovereign incapable of wrong and "evil and pernicious counsellors" who could be put on trial by impeachment for their sins.

In short, according to one eminent historian, before 1776 "the Americans were not republicans in either a formal or an ideological sense," although "within a few months they were, and have remained so ever since."[15] Our next section examines this astonishing apparent last-minute change of heart and mind. It will, however, leave open the question of whether "monarchy" altogether disappeared here.

2. The repudiation of monarchy

In the nineteenth century, patriotic American historians like George Bancroft insisted that the Revolution, with its essentially republican dynamism, had been progressive and foreordained. Opting for independence, said Bancroft, "the people of the continent obeyed one general impulse, as the earth in spring listens to the command of nature and without the appearance of effort bursts into life."[16]

Modern scholarship, as practiced by Edmund S. Morgan, Bernard Bailyn, Gordon S. Wood, Jack P. Greene, and others, is more circumspect. Bancroft's successors recognize that there was less joyous unanimity than he supposed. Yet on the whole most of them would concur that the Revolution was bound to come, sooner or later, with or without a prolonged military contest, and bound to result in a settlers' republic. In reaching this position they have reexamined the emergence and meanings of the term "republican." It may be useful to distinguish two main usages.

The first and broader of these is roughly equivalent to "democracy." It relates to the contrast between British and American social styles of the era. We may speak of it as "implicit" or perhaps "informal" republicanism: a condition of life rather than a creed: "independence" as a characteristic attitude on the part of ordinary colonial Americans— or at any rate the white male property-owners among them. Implicit republicanism can be regarded as a demeanor rather than an ideology, a way of behaving not necessarily described as "republican" by those whose conduct would later merit the epithet.

The second aspect may be called "occluded republicanism." This refers to the realm of explicit ideas—to principled protest, profoundly rooted in the libertarian tradition of Anglo-America. It is explicitly republican in drawing upon a literature which values mixed or constitutional governments to the extent that they are based on the consent of the governed; which would limit the power of the powerful; and which borders upon a doctrine of popular sovereignty. It is, before 1776, "occluded" because in most Anglo-American "Commonwealth" writing, republicanism as such—the rejection of monarchy—was formally taboo. "Occluded" suggests something shut away from sight or use. Oxygen, for example, is an occluded element in air and in water. In water this occluded chemical component can be released or separated out by means of electrolysis—the passage of an electric current. But it is not self-evidently present, in fact seems in immediate commonsense observation to be self-evidently absent. Oxygen was indeed not discovered as an element until the late eighteenth century—in part, unwittingly and yet fittingly, through the experiments of Joseph Priestley, an English dissenting semi-republican who emigrated to the United States. Occluded republicanism, then, is republicanism that required a kind of electric shock to be disclosed.

Implicit republicanism, to deal with this form first, has been detected by some historians as far back as the first Puritan settlements of New England. Many years before the Revolutionary crisis, it was predicted, whether with alarm or dispassionately, that one day the colonies would seek the full independence implicit in their everyday circumstances. Nowhere did this seem more likely than in those Presbyterian or Congregational churches whose organization differed increasingly from that of the Church of England which the Crown was sworn to uphold. The American Samuel Johnson, a former Presbyterian who had gone over to the Anglicans, told the Bishop of London in 1725: "It has always been a fact, & is obvious in the nature of the thing, that anti-Episcopal are of course antimonarchical principles." According to the historian Carl Bridenbaugh, "religion provided the foundation for early American nationalism. . . . Republicanism in church quite as much as in state was the form of polity congenial to these people."[17] In political life, too, historians contend, perhaps Americans "long before 1776 concluded from the efficiency of colonial self-government that government without a king or nobles would do for them."[18]

So implicit republicanism could be identified before the 1760s, if the term is taken to embrace self-reliance; physical remoteness from England; awareness of the lessening advantages of the connection with England (especially after the collapse of the French empire in North America); and an indifference to some of the preoccupations of the mother country that could shift into impatient dislike.

No English monarch ever set foot in the American colonies, though some (Virginia, Carolina, Georgia) were named after monarchy. There were appreciable divisions of status and wealth in America, and these hardened during the eighteenth century. A colonial ruling class enjoyed esteem and authority. But they did not comprise an aristocracy in the

English mold. Their influence and family networks were mainly local, with little intermarriage between colony and colony. Primogeniture, or inheritance of the principal estate by the eldest son, was less observed than in England. The only men of title to be met with in America were British-born governors, or a rare figure such as Lord Fairfax, proprietor of the "Northern Neck" in Virginia.

Opportunities for ambitious Americans to rise in political, military, clerical, or legal circles of the British Empire were limited. An occasional American secured a governorship. Jonathan Belcher, under the patronage of Viscount Townshend, was appointed governor of Massachusetts and New Hampshire in 1730. But only one in five of all the royal governors in British America was American.[19] Governors had in any case almost no patronage to bestow on their own account, and those who did often seemed out of earshot. In Virginia the shrewd young George Washington met with scant success in his efforts to impress Governor Dinwiddie, or his neighbor Lord Fairfax, or the senior British army officers who would he hoped recommend him for a regular commission. There were judgeships; but in the 1760s and 1770s these, like the newly created tax offices, were denounced by other colonists as posts for lackeys and embezzlers. Nor were prospects bright in the Anglican church, even for men such as the Rev. Samuel Johnson: poor pay, modest prestige at best, no chance of high rank.

In some ways, Americans had more free scope—for instance, to speculate in land, to control colonial legislatures—than people of comparable wealth in Britain. They had less access to the top people of the Empire than their counterparts in, say, Scotland or Ireland. On the other hand, the aspiring American was less distracted than they by visions of patronage. In common with the Scot, the Anglo-Irishman, and the English dissenter, the American colonist can be viewed as a semi-outsider, a dweller on the imperial periphery. The difference was that while the desire to shine attracted some of these toward the center, the Anglo-American also felt the tug of a contrary, centrifugal impulse. So long as centripetal and centrifugal pulls were in equilibrium, the American saw no serious need to quarrel. He tended, we may say, to be of an "independent" disposition, like the independent or "country" persuasion in English domestic politics. In short, it is arguable that full American autonomy, growing out of informal, de facto or implicit republicanism, was only a matter of time; and that when the time came, the British apparatus of Crown, Parliament, and Church would strike America's elites as irrelevant, if not a positive hindrance, to their trading and governing independency.[20]

Recent scholarship likewise emphasizes the ideological basis of colonial resistance that we have called "occluded" republicanism. According to such an interpretation, Americans were particularly responsive to a mass of libertarian theory in the "Commonwealth" or "Real Whig" tradition, together with covenant theology and other religious formulations from the Puritan heritage. Educated Americans drew upon classical sources such as Cato and Cicero, and upon various European philosophers and jurists (Machiavelli, Grotius, Beccaria, Montesquieu, the historian Delolme, and so on), but above all from the works of English and Scottish libertarians of several persuasions.

What they had in common, and what appealed to American readers, was the stress on liberty. They tended to regard constitutional history as a long, vigilant struggle to recover lost freedoms or preserve them. British opposition writers of the eighteenth century harped upon the symptoms of national decay. At the center, in their view, was a possibly fatal corruption. A crucial danger was the tendency of rulers to create standing armies—permanent military forces set apart from the people. These critics did not call for any wholesale revision of the social and economic order. Nor did they envisage a "republic" after the abandonment of the 17th-century Commonwealth. Their reforms, though, rested upon "republican" principles of the kind explored by Machiavelli and the English political theorist James Harrington. A sound constitution, that is, required "virtue" in the body politic. Hence the enthusiasm for a widened franchise; a redistribution of constituencies so that the population would be equitably represented; annual elections, to replace the seven-year parliaments introduced by an act of 1716; and in general, as recommended in Harrington's *The Common-wealth of Oceana* (1656), a frequent "rotation" of men in and out of office.[21] It can be seen why, as is claimed, after the accession in 1760 of George III, the opposition in England and the conduct of the government supplied Americans with causes for disquiet. The policies of George III's ministers were easy to interpret as a calculated plan to rob the colonies of hard-won rights.

A debate stirred up by John Wilkes, William Pitt, James Burgh, Charles James Fox, Edmund Burke, the historian Catharine Macaulay, and other British figures of mid-century prompted Americans to join in questioning the very fabric of British constitutionalism. What *was* the Empire, whose nature had never been legally expounded? Whom did the constitution cover—Scots, Irish, nonconformists, Catholics, Jews . . . Americans? If Lords and Commons were distanced from the people by the hereditary principle and a haphazard, inadequate franchise, what of the monarchy? Historians can point to a good deal of latently republican Anglo-American comment. A common deduction to be drawn was that whatever the notional benefits of the British mixed monarchy, it was laudable mainly in comparison with the deplorable absolutism of other Old World monarchies; and that whatever the merits of particular kings and queens, England's royalty had not always deserved or received respect. At least three medieval kings had been murdered.

Concessions such as Magna Carta had been won in the teeth of royal objections. Could it be that English liberties had usually been achieved not because, but in spite, of royal wishes?

One of the most trenchant American critiques was a Boston sermon of 1750, preached by Jonathan Mayhew on the anniversary of the execution of Charles I. Mayhew was angered by the Anglican tendency to portray Charles as a royal martyr: Mayhew saw him as a tyrant who deserved to die. If a government were good, said Mayhew, its precise design was unimportant—"whether the legislative and executive power be lodged in . . . *one* person . . . ; whether in a *few* . . . ; whether in *many,* so as to constitute a *republic;* or whether in *three co-ordinate branches.* . . ." Mayhew's somewhat skeptical remarks on monarchy were criticized, especially by American Episcopalians. But he was also widely commended, and his tone was adopted by other commentators. In a pamphlet of 1764, the Boston lawyer James Otis, after paying the customary tribute to the "present happy and most righteous establishment," made plain that it was "built on the ruins" of Stuart misconduct. Dethroned, and exiled in France, James II "died in disgrace and poverty, a terrible example of God's vengeance on arbitrary princes!" The rightness of rebellion against James II, "tyrannic" and "weak," was also stressed in another American pamphlet, William Hicks's *The Nature and Extent of Parliamentary Power Considered* (1768).

The majesty of majesty was indirectly queried in other ways. The familiar contrast between Britain and other monarchies appeared at first sight to reinforce allegiance to the Hanoverians. If all went well, said Otis, the British monarchy "will remain in . . . full vigor at that blessed period, when *the proud arbitrary tyrants of the continent* shall either unite in the deliverance of the human race, or resign their crowns. . . ." Richard Bland, a Virginian, commented in his *Inquiry into the Rights of the British Colonists* (1766): "The Colonies are subordinate to the Authority of Parliament; subordinate . . . in Degree, but not absolutely so; For if by a Vote of the British Senate [Parliament] the Colonists were to be delivered up to the Rule of a French or Turkish Tyranny, they may refuse Obedience . . . , and may oppose the Execution of it by Force."[22]

But the sense of these seemingly complaisant contrasts could be turned round. They made it difficult to sustain the opinion that the institution of monarchy was inherently right. On the contrary: monarchy was inherently dangerous, and only to be venerated where its prerogative was safely contained. All rested on the supposed superiority of the mixed English constitution. Once this was denied, and George III's conduct became suspect, parallels rather than contrasts with "French or Turkish Tyranny" were indicated. Indeed, in a clash with Governor Bernard of Massachusetts over an alleged infringement of the powers of the legislature, Otis maintained that if such abuses were allowed, "it would be of little consequence to the people whether they were subject to George or Louis, the King of Great Britain or the French King."[23]

In the light of all this, it might appear mere common sense—to borrow the expressive title of Tom Paine's great tract of January 1776—that the Americans should have found so little difficulty in repudiating monarchy, and such satisfaction in identifying themselves with the noble old memories of republican virtue and independence. Jefferson's observation, in 1777, was that "Americans seem to have deposited the monarchical and taken up the republican government with as much ease as would have attended their throwing off an old and putting on a new suit of clothes." John Adams, writing in the excitement of the previous year, admitted the "Suddenness" of the change, but he also asserted that the "Alteration in the Prejudices, Passions, Sentiments, and Principles of these thirteen little States" had been so complete "as to make every one of them completely republican. . . . Idolatry to Monarchs, and servility to Aristocratical Pride, was never so totally eradicated, from so many Minds in so short a Time."[24]

We can see how, to recapitulate, Americans in their everyday circumstances may have developed an implicit republicanism that anticipated the actual, explicit declaration of republican independence of 1776. We can see too how the theory of republicanism, occluded in Anglo-American discourse, was nevertheless preserved as a body of lore with powerfully libertarian significance. One can understand how, in the mother country, habits of deference, the sway of the great landed families, royal and ministerial patronage, expanding commerce and empire, the shakiness of regimes elsewhere, restraints on freedom of utterance, conventionality, complacency—a whole congeries of reasons—may have inhibited any fundamental criticism of a social order capped and symbolized by the Crown.

In this regard, it becomes plausible to expect that criticism would be expressed, if at all, covertly and indirectly, by means of satire, scandal, and parable. So it was. Bible texts were useful for such purposes. The history of the Jews, as invoked by Mayhew and also by Tom Paine, could be interpreted as a cautionary tale. In the Old Testament, I Samuel recounts how the people of Israel asked the prophet Samuel to give them a king. He was displeased, and so was God, by the Israelites' craving for a secular leader. Samuel warned that a king (Saul in this instance) would "take your sons, and appoint them for himself. . . . And he will take your daughters. . . . And he will take your fields, and your vineyards, and your olive yards, . . . and give them to his servants. . . . And ye shall cry out in that day because of your king which ye shall have chosen you; and the Lord will not hear you. . . ." Paine, repeating the familiar story in "Common Sense," [GIT 1976, pp. 313–335] claimed that "these portions of scripture . . . admit of no equivocal

COMMON SENSE;

ADDRESSED TO THE

INHABITANTS

O F

AMERICA,

On the following interesting

SUBJECTS.

I. Of the Origin and Design of Government in general, with concise Remarks on the English Constitution.

II. Of Monarchy and Hereditary Succession.

III. Thoughts on the present State of American Affairs.

IV. Of the present Ability of America, with some miscellaneous Reflections.

Man knows no Master save creating HEAVEN,
Or those whom choice and common good ordain.

THOMSON.

PHILADELPHIA;

Printed, and Sold, by R. BELL, in Third-Street.

MDCCLXXVI.

Title page of the first edition of Tom Paine's *Common Sense.* "Thanks to Paine, 'the powers, and even the name of a king was rendered odious in the eyes of the numerous colonists who had read . . . the history of the Jews. . . .' "

construction. . . . the Almighty hath here entered his protest against monarchical government. . . ." David Ramsay's subsequent *History of the American Revolution* (1789) maintained that, thanks to Paine, "the powers, and even the name of a king was rendered odious in the eyes of the numerous colonists who had read . . . the history of the Jews. . . ." Paine's references to "the oppressions to which they were subjected in consequence of their lusting after kings to rule over them, afforded an excellent handle for prepossessing the colonists in favor of republican government. Hereditary succession was turned into ridicule."[25]

Occlusion? A tall story by Antiphanes, from North's *Plutarch,* is attractively apposite. "In a certain city," according to this ancient fabulist, "the cold was so intense that words were congealed as soon as they were spoken, but . . . after some time they thawed and became audible; so that the words spoken in winter were articulated next summer." The language of republicanism may likewise have thawed out, in America's heat, while remaining largely insulated across the Atlantic. None of Tom Paine's contentions, scriptural or otherwise, was novel. From about 1770, as Pauline Maier has shown, the colonists were increasingly ready to voice disapproval of monarchy in general, and George III in particular, along with their complaints of Parliamentary misrule. "A good King is a miracle," wrote an American in 1774—probably with ironical intent. On the eve of the Revolution, Calvinist rhetoric even came close to identifying King George as Antichrist.[26]

Historians, and Paine's contemporaries, nearly all agree that his special contribution was to demythologize or debunk the institution of monarchy, in the process of seeking to convince Americans that freedom and prosperity would go hand in hand, once they had severed the ties with Britain. Historically, for Paine in "Common Sense," kings are "ruffians" who have imposed themselves and their lineage upon the rest of mankind. Set apart from ordinary people, they know nothing of the real world, "and when they succeed to the government are frequently the most ignorant and unfit of any throughout the dominions." Hereditary succession could only be justified if it ensured "a race of good and wise men." Instead it produces fools and bullies. Sometimes the throne is occupied by children, sometimes by rulers who have become senile.

As for the British monarchy, from which Paine draws most of his examples, it is an absurdity. For him, a "strong" king is a despot and a constitutional king is superfluous. In England, "a king hath little more to do than make war and give away places. . . . A pretty business indeed for a man to be allowed eight hundred thousand a year for, and worshipped into the bargain!" A few pages later Paine shifts from poking fun at this useless ceremonial figure, so as to renew previous charges that "the corrupt influence of the crown" has "swallowed up the power, and eaten out the virtue of the House of Commons (the republican part of the constitution). . . . Why is the constitution sickly but because monarchy hath poisoned the republic. . . ?" George III is the "royal brute," "an inveterate enemy to liberty," a "sullen-tempered Pharaoh." If the colonies remain under his sway, George III "will suffer no law to be made here but such as suits *his* purpose." This is the language of deliberate insult, proud in its affront, pushing to the point of no return. It is the language of a kind of exorcism, of metaphorical regicide. It cries: THE KING IS DEAD: LONG LIVE THE REPUBLIC![27]

Much evidence, however, can be cited to bolster the claim that the American colonies were actually republican, or temperamentally disposed to be so, before the break signalized by Paine's pamphlet and the Declaration of Independence of the same year, 1776. The continued protestations of reverence for His Majesty can be understood as forms required by courtesy and legal custom. Petitioners to the king, anxious to secure a hearing, would for obvious reasons take care to abide by the rules. It would not follow that they were feeling obsequious awe, any more than one should take literally the announcement by a correspondent that he is "your obedient servant." In a 1768 letter from London, deploring recent riots there, Benjamin Franklin remarked with outward piety that "some Punishment seems preparing for a People who are ungratefully abusing the best Constitution and the best King any Nation was ever blessed with." But this praise is at once undercut. The English, Franklin adds, are "intent on nothing but Luxury, Licentiousness, Power, Places, Pensions and Plunder."[28]

The colonists, it can therefore be argued, lived under a monarchy because that was the norm but were not ardent monarchists. The repudiation of the king in 1775–76, blaming him for misgovernment instead of his ministers, can then be seen as the ultimate act of defiance mainly in a chronological sense. The crucial denial, we may think, concerned the authority of Parliament over the colonies. Once that denial had been militantly affirmed, and petitions to the Crown proved ineffective, the final rejection of monarchy was logically bound to follow.

Is the theory then wrong that while Americans have been republican ever since 1776, they were not republican before then? That depends on how one defines the essential but slippery concept of "republicanism," which has become so much a debating point in late twentieth-century American historiography. Our concern in this article is with the historical origins of the American presidency. The questions to which we shall recur are:

—what positive and negative features did the colonists associate with monarchy, and more especially that of Great Britain?

—why did they not institute their own royal line, when monarchy was so prevalent a feature of the era?

—positively or negatively, to what extent did Americans have monarchy in mind when establishing the office of President in the Constitution of 1788?

Colonists pull down a statue of George III. *"From about 1770 . . . the colonists were increasingly ready to voice disapproval of monarchy in general, and George III in particular, along with their complaints of Parliamentary misrule."*

Among present-day historians, Jack P. Greene makes a strong case for the view that many colonists were much less hostile or insouciant than Paine or such leaders of revolt as Samuel Adams and Thomas Jefferson. They were torn, he says, between proto-republican leanings and a deep Englishness. This Englishness meant several things, among them a belief that outright republicanism was liable to lead to anarchy and thence to despotism. They well recalled that in the English experiment with republicanism of the 1650s, Oliver Cromwell had begun to comport himself like an autocrat; his investiture as Lord Protector closely resembled a coronation, and when he died in 1658 his funeral effigy bore a royal crown. Perhaps then the Americans opted for a republic in 1776 mainly or in part because there was nothing else to do. Full independence necessitated the rejection of allegiance to George III. To have sought another sovereign would have been impossible (though the notion was toyed with subsequently). In breaking with Britain, the Americans were obliged to break with monarchy as such, and by their own logic were debarred from choosing a king, hereditary or elective, from among themselves—though for some this truth may have taken several years to sink in.

Old forms can have stubborn roots. If some of monarchy's roots were shallow in America, the institution was in certain other respects deeply important. Against its negative connotations must be set the Crown's symbolic appeal. It stood traditionally for legitimate authority, pledged faith, the lofty detachment pictured in Bolingbroke's vision of a "Patriot King"; it stood as well for the Protestant cause, imperial might, the achievements and character of Great Britain—all the handsome heritage embodied in the English word "majesty." Greene suggests that this symbolic fealty could not be cast off by Americans without "a major desacralization of the existing moral order which bound the colonies so tightly to Britain." Hence, obviously, the importance of Paine's almost blasphemous diatribe. Hence too, possibly—a point to be taken up again later—the intense dislike of Paine expressed subsequently by so many Americans.[29]

Clearly the bulk of colonists by about 1770 were more opposed than the English to social and religious hierarchy, and more insistent upon the principle of government by consent of the governed. However, few if any Anglo-Americans of the immediate period anticipated Paine in outright, confident advocacy of republicanism. Even "Common Sense" offers only "hints" and "straggling thoughts" on the organization of a continental republic. Paine's praise of republicanism is largely rhetorical and anecdotal. The lack of specific analysis is equally striking in Paine's "Crisis" papers of 1776–83. They contain further diatribes against kingship but merely incidental references to alternative systems. In the "Crisis" Paine speaks of the American "people" or "nation," not of the "republic."

In the 1770's, Paine was of course antipathetic to government *as such*. Government was the "lost badge of innocence," and its faults were aggravated in proportion to its remoteness, expensiveness, and intrusiveness. Paine's prejudices, if that is what they were, were widely shared in the early Revolutionary era. Understandably enough, they were reactions to the perceived faults of the "poisonous" elements in the British constitution, heightened by a considerable initial uncertainty among the Revolutionary leaders as to whether they represented one nation or a confederated plurality of "these United States."

The well-known consequence was the new nation's (or nations') first instrument of government, the Articles of Confederation, drawn up by the Continental Congress in 1776–77 but not ratified until 1781. Under the Articles, each state retained its "sovereignty, freedom, and independence, and every power, jurisdiction, and right, which is not by this Confederation expressly delegated to the United States in Congress assembled." There was no executive branch. A figure known as the President of Congress was merely the chairman of the "Committee of the States" appointed to manage affairs when Congress was in recess— "provided that no person be allowed to serve in the office of president more than one year in any term of three years." This was no doubt a good republican formulation, along the lines of Harrington's *Oceana*. By design, it could hardly have been further from the despotisms of France and Turkey (as perceived in Anglo-American libertarian discourse), or even from the mixed or moderated monarchy of the old mother country.[30]

3. The reform reformed

The Declaration of Independence of July 1776 renounced the British connection, and in so doing it denounced King George III. During the next few years the thirteen former mainland colonies strove to vindicate their decision; nineteen other British colonies, including Upper and Lower Canada, Bermuda, and Jamaica and other islands in the Caribbean, remained "loyal" to the Crown. The warring United States operated under the direction of the Continental Congress, and though the nation's first written constitution, the Articles of Confederation, was not ratified until 1781, the victory signaled by the Peace of Paris in 1783 appeared to show that the thirteen more or less sovereign states had all the government they needed.

In the war years there was considerable discussion of political and constitutional issues. Most of this went on in individual states, especially when they were formulating their own particular instruments of government. Moreover, although these constitution-making debates were often quite profound—for example, in Virginia, Pennsylvania,

Lord Protector Oliver Cromwell refuses the British crown in 1657. *"In the English experiment with republicanism . . ., Oliver Cromwell had begun to comport himself like an autocrat."*

and Massachusetts—the historical and theoretical allusions introduced by delegates and legislators were much influenced by fears and hopes based upon practical experience. Each state in some degree reproduced the structures of pre-Revolutionary days. In place of the former royal or proprietary governor came a new yet not greatly dissimilar breed of chief executives. In most states they were still known as "governors" ("presidents" in Pennsylvania, Delaware, and New Hampshire, and in the 1776, though not the 1778, constitution of South Carolina).

Some of these governors were conspicuous authority figures; a number of them also served in the Continental Congress. Within the period 1775–83, as Jackson Turner Main has shown, governors were far from negligible (with the exception of Georgia). True, the drafters of the state constitutions tended to stress the primacy of the legislature over the executive branch, largely because of a determination not to perpetuate quasi-monarchical hierarchies. In eight states the governor was selected by the legislature. In several, such as Pennsylvania and New York, he was boxed in by executive councils. Ten states limited his term of office to one year. Only two, New York and Delaware, stipulated a three-year term of office. Edmund Randolph, governor of Virginia in 1786–88, spoke of himself modestly as "a member of the executive." On the other hand, in the executive branches analyzed by

Main, governors tended to be reelected, averaging nearly four years in office. The formidable George Clinton, first elected governor of New York in 1777, held on to his post until 1795 and came back for several more years in 1800.[31]

At the state level, conceptions of executive authority and actual conditions are not always easy to interpret. What can be said is that, in rhetoric at any rate, Americans professed abhorrence of anything that smacked of kingly rule. The indictment of George III in 1776, embodied in the Declaration and in "Common Sense," was endlessly reiterated in American pamphlets, poems, and sermons. The Declaration called him a "prince, whose character is . . . marked by every act which may define a tyrant. . . ." In a publication of 1782, Benjamin Franklin proclaimed that "this King will . . . stand foremost in the list of diabolical, bloody, and execrable tyrants." A few years later, a poem by Philip Freneau paid tribute to Paine as the great exposer of monarchy:

> From Reason's source, a bold reform he brings,
> In raising up *mankind,* he pulls down *kings,*
> Who, source of discord, patrons of all wrong,
> On blood and murder have been fed too long. . . .

The United States was set on the right course:

> So shall our nation, form'd on Virtue's plan,
> Remain the guardian of the Rights of Man,
> A vast Republic, famed through every clime,
> Without a king, to see the end of time.

There was fierce criticism of any institution, above all a new one, that appeared to rest upon privileges of birth or wealth. One of the biggest uproars, during the 1780s, was occasioned by the establishment of the Society of the Cincinnati, of which George Washington was persuaded to become the first president. The Society incurred censure because its membership was confined to military *officers* (American or French) who had served in the War of Independence, and because their subsequent male heirs would inherit membership. Washington himself was surprised and dismayed by the chorus of disapproval—surprised in part, perhaps, because he himself was childless. He was quick to protest, no doubt sincerely, that "Monarchial ideas" were and should be foreign to Americans. He assured a correspondent in January 1784 that "it appears to be incompatible with the principles of our national constitution to admit the introduction of any kind of Nobility, Knighthood, or distinctions of a similar nature, amongst the Citizens of our republic."[32]

The "republican" element in American thought and behavior took the shape of avowed detestation of centralized government, kingship, the refinements and decadences attributed to courtiers and noblemen (the latter, said Paine, actually persons of "no-ability"), and of extreme forms of opulence or poverty. Such republicanism tended to embody an alarmed suspicion that the Revolution was not only incomplete but threatened by people who still hankered after the fleshpots of the old order. After all, the War of Independence had been fought in alliance with the Bourbon and Catholic King Louis XVI, the symbol of an appreciably more authoritarian and more alien regime than that of Protestant George III. At the time of the 1783 peace treaties, no American had yet worked out a convincing, systematic rationale for the new American polity (or polities). "Republicanism," despite its gallant old associations, was hard to envisage in the modern world. According to traditional testimony, republics were usually short-lived. They were proverbially ungrateful to their public servants and therefore chronically short of able, honest leaders. They could not function over a large extent of territory.

Such misgivings were painfully and confusingly augmented in the 1780s, when it seemed increasingly clear—even to men like Paine—that the national government established under the Articles of Confederation was inadequate, and that the Americans might have gone too far in their hostility to executive control. But what form of executive authority was desirable, or feasible? The defects of the Articles were acknowledged by almost every articulate person. The remedies were far harder to define or to agree upon. George Washington, living at Mount Vernon in retirement from his military command, exchanged letters throughout the Confederacy with other prominent and worried citizens. They discussed rumors that the confusion was leading their fellow countrymen backward. "I am told," Washington wrote in the summer of 1786, "that even respectable characters speak of a monarchial [*sic*] form of government without horror. . . . what a triumph for the advocates of despotism to find that we are incapable of governing ourselves, and that systems founded on the basis of equal liberty are merely ideal and fallacious."[33]

There is no need to recount the stages by which the disquiet of prominent Americans brought fifty-five of them to Philadelphia in 1787 (though only twenty-seven were present at the first meeting, on May 25), as delegates to a convention. The Continental Congress had agreed to sanction such a meeting, so as to amend as necessary the Articles of Confederation and thereby achieve a "more perfect Union." With some reluctance, George Washington attended as a Virginia delegate. The assembly, meeting in Independence Hall, unanimously voted that he should chair the proceedings. Among the rules they agreed upon was one of confidentiality. Their debates were to be carried on behind closed doors and not disclosed to outsiders. As everyone knows, the Philadelphia convention concluded (in mid-September, with one longish August adjournment) by scrapping the Articles and substituting an altogether new Constitution. The new instrument would require to be ratified by at least nine of the thirteen states—each of which began to make preparations for a ratifying convention.

What concerns us is the part of the prolonged Philadelphia deliberations that resulted in the creation, under Article II, of a separate executive branch to be headed by a President of very different complexion from the ad hoc, temporary "presidency" of the Articles of Confederation. It was, of course, only one among several weighty issues. Nor can we be sure exactly what was said, and with what nuances; we are obliged to rely on the notes kept by a handful of delegates—those of James Madison of Virginia being the fullest. There is, however, enough corroboration among these jottings, and from other papers and reminiscences, to reconstruct the *what* and *when* if not always the *why* and *wherefore*.[34]

The proceedings took on weight on May 29, 1787, in an opening speech from Edmund Randolph of Virginia. After outlining what he deemed the main weaknesses of the Articles of Confederation, Governor Randolph emphasized the need to build upon "the republican principle." He offered a series of proposals that were to be known as the Virginia Plan, entailing such wholesale alteration of the Articles that they were virtually annulled. As Madison jotted down the Randolph resolutions, there was to be a "National Legislature" of two houses, and a "National Executive" chosen by the Legislature. The Executive's term of office was left open, but not to be renewable. "Besides a general authority to execute the National laws," Madison noted, "it ought to enjoy the Executive rights vested in Congress by the Confederation." (At this stage the proposed new branch was an "it," not a "he.")

Randolph had left open the question of whether one man or a group were to be in charge. A few delegates—for instance, George Mason of Virginia, speaking on June 4—argued for a plural executive: Mason recommended a triumvirate or *troika* of three people. But quite early in the Convention, there seemed a firm majority in favor of a "Single Executive." At this stage the tentative decision was also for an "Executive Magistracy" elected by the national legislature for seven years, and thereafter ineligible—Randolph's formula. How this chief magistrate was to be elected remained, however, the most vexed issue of all the debates over the executive branch. What Madison called the "mode of appointment" was eventually, as everyone knows, resolved through the device of the Electoral College, with resort to Congress only in the case of a deadlock (as was to occur in 1800 and 1824). The details, he recalled, were not arranged until "the latter stage of the Session," and so "not exempt from a degree of the hurrying influence produced by fatigue and impatience."

Early and late in the Convention, various speakers confessed to serious doubts as to the wisdom of what was being attempted. Some, like Mason, were worried that, in the admitted need for a "strong

Edmund Randolph, governor of Virginia. *"He offered a series of proposals that were to be known as the Virginia Plan, entailing such wholesale alteration of the Articles that they were virtually annulled."*

Executive," the government might well "degenerate . . . into a monarchy." Others, such as John Dickinson of Delaware, appeared to be arguing that a "limited monarchy" on the British model was perhaps the best form of government. The misgivings voiced during and after the Philadelphia convention will be discussed in the next section. What should be stressed here is that, despite their inner anxieties, Mason, Dickinson, and their fellows all paid at least lip service to Randolph's emphasis on "republican principles." The American people, it was reiterated, would not stand for *un*-republican forms.[35]

Week by week, in the process of inventing what was essentially a new national government, the men in Independence Hall invented a new chief executive office. Those who, like William Paterson of New Jersey, represented the small states and supported the initial notion of a plural executive of restricted powers, lost out to such eloquent figures as Gouverneur Morris and James Wilson of Pennsylvania, Rufus King of Massachusetts, and Charles Pinckney and John Rutledge of South Carolina. Wilson and Rutledge were members of the important five-man Committee on Detail, charged with drafting the actual Constitution. It was they, for example, who probably decided to call the executive "President" instead of "Governor"—the latter title having been previously mentioned by Edmund Randolph and by New York's Alexander Hamilton. Another committee, on Style and Arrangement, was headed by Gouverneur Morris. Aided by Hamilton, Madison, and Rufus King, he was able to select what they deemed to be the wording best calculated to appeal to the Convention, and to the waiting public throughout the Union.

The document was finally ready on Sept. 17, 1787, when of the forty-two delegates still present, thirty-nine affixed their signatures.

Two key factors contributed to the evolution of the 1787 Constitution. The first was that most of the delegates had already, within quite recent memory, gained experience in the construction and operation of state constitutions. Consciously or unconsciously, this experience acted upon the debaters at Philadelphia. In Max Farrand's view, the New York state constitution of 1777 seemed particularly relevant in matters relating to the procedures for succession in the event of presidential death or removal, and in the enumeration of executive powers and duties, all of which appear to echo the New York gubernatorial provisions. The German scholar Willi Paul Adams concludes a careful study of the first state constitutions with this verdict:

> The office of the president was comparable to that of a governor. . . .
> The Presidential system did not develop in America because Americans wanted a substitute for the king. If that is what they had wanted, a more exact copy of the British system with a prime minister, a cabinet responsible to the legislature, and a head of state elected for life would have served them better. The presidential system at the federal level can be ascribed much more to the beliefs of the authors of the first state constitutions that free government, stability, and efficiency were most likely to be found with the combination of governor, assembly, and courts to which they were accustomed from colonial times, and to the fact that the architects of the Federal Constitution adhered to the outlines of the familiar building plan.[36]

A second crucial factor was the participation of George Washington. He was present *and* a presence. Together with the aged Benjamin Franklin, a delegate at the Convention, he enjoyed a unique standing in America. General Washington had served for eight and a half years as commander in chief of the Continental forces, declining to accept remuneration other than his expenses. As commanding general he had shed his initial Virginia localism and become a convinced nationalist. He had also revealed a scrupulous regard for the principle of civilian control of the military. After returning his commission to Congress at the end of 1783—an act of great symbolic appeal—Washington, like the semilegendary Roman part-time soldier Cincinnatus, had returned to his former occupation as an agriculturalist. At Philadelphia, although he made plain his support for a more energetic national government, voting now and then with the other Virginia delegates, he chaired the sessions with an austere authority that vastly impressed his companions. They trusted him. They took pride in the thought that America could produce a man of such caliber; his very existence seemed to vindicate the cause of republican independence. Everyone was aware that if the new Constitution were to be ratified by the states, Washington was both the inevitable and the ideal choice as the nation's first chief magistrate. Among the delegates, Pierce Butler of South Carolina afterward confessed that he did not think the powers vested in the presidency "would have been so great had not many of the members cast their eyes towards General Washington as President, and shaped their Ideas . . . by their opinions of his Virtue."[37]

In the outcome, Article II did entrust considerable authority, actual and potential, to the head of the proposed executive branch. This person, chosen by an Electoral College, was to be installed for a four-year term, and to be eligible for reelection. He could be removable, but only through the old English device of impeachment, involving a trial by the legislature. He could veto legislation, though a veto could be overridden by a two-thirds vote of Congress. He would have a main say in selecting the heads of executive departments, judges, diplomats, and other federal officers; would have similar though not absolute power in the conduct of foreign affairs; and was allowed additional prerogatives such as the right to "grant reprieves and pardons for offences against the United States, except in cases of impeachment."

Such was the document that emerged from Philadelphia in September 1787, to endure close scrutiny in state conventions and engender a considerable literature, pro and con, throughout the United States. The most famous of the post-Philadelphia arguments were developed in what is still accepted as the classic analysis of American constitutionalism, *The Federalist Papers,* or *Federalist* for short. It consists of eighty-five essays, which appeared in New York newspapers from the end of October 1787 to the end of May 1788, under the signature of "Publius." The first thirty-six pieces came out in book form, as volume 1 of the *Federalist,* in March 1788; the remainder appeared, as volume 2, on May 28. Alexander Hamilton was the architect of the plan. As things worked out, he and James Madison divided the labor between them. Their third associate, John Jay of New York, was able only to furnish five articles out of the total.[38]

In some degree *The Federalist Papers* could be described as propaganda, ammunition for supporters of the Constitution to be used against its many critics in the state of New York. A number of the essays were written to counter specific assertions by opponents. The "Anti-Federalist" complaints against Article II are examined in the next section. For us at this point, the *Federalist* may best be cited simply as the outstanding justification for establishing a single executive leader within

*"After returning
his commission to
Congress at the end
of 1783 [depicted
here in a painting by
John Trumbull]—an
act of great symbolic
appeal—Washington,
like the semilegendary
Roman part-time
soldier Cincinnatus,
had returned to his
former occupation as an
agriculturalist."*

an undeniably strengthened national government. The "Publius" authors had several tasks to perform. They strove, for instance, to show that the delegates had not exceeded their authority in scrapping rather than amending the Articles. In Number 9, Hamilton insisted that a confederated republic would avoid the fatal defects Montesquieu had ascribed to *small* republics. Madison followed up the point in Number 10, claiming that the reformed United States would be a republic rather than a democracy (the latter system, according to countless theorists, being unworkably close to chaos), or at least a *representative* democracy in which government would be delegated "to a small number of citizens elected by the rest." Madison also contended that representation was the feature that would enable the Union to function over a vast extent of territory as a confederated republic, deriving strength and not weakness from its sheer size.[39]

Among such brilliantly reasoned expositions, the essays (nos. 67–77) devoted to the executive branch, all written by Hamilton, are no less compelling. Number 67 ridicules the grumblers who pretend that the "intended President of the United States" is "not merely as the embryo, but as the full-grown progeny, of that detested parent," monarchy [*GBWW*, Vol. 43, p. 203b]:

> The authorities of a magistrate, in few instances greater, in some instances less, than those of a governor of New York, have been magnified into more than royal prerogatives. . . . He has been shown to us with the diadem sparkling on his brow and the imperial purple flowing in his train. He has been seated on a throne surrounded with minions and mistresses. . . . The image of Asiatic despotism and voluptuousness have scarcely been wanting to crown the exaggerated scene. We have been taught to tremble at the terrific visages of murdering janizaries, and to blush at the unveiled mysteries of a future seraglio. [*GBWW*, Vol. 43, p. 203b–c.]

In reality, Hamilton seeks to demonstrate, the office is properly "republican." The method of appointment, for example (no. 68), avoids all risk of those "most deadly adversaries of republican government" which he enumerates as "cabal, intrigue, and corruption." The electors are expressly separated from the national legislature in the first place, within their individual states:

> The process . . . affords a moral certainty that the office of President will never fall to the lot of any man who is not in an eminent degree endowed with the requisite qualifications. Talents for low intrigue and the little arts of popularity may . . . suffice to elevate a man . . . in a single State; but it will require other talents, and a different kind of merit, to establish him in the esteem and confidence of the whole Union. . . . [*GBWW*, Vol. 43, p. 206b–c.]

Next (no. 69), Hamilton turns to a detailed comparison of the proposed president and the British sovereign. The only common feature, according to Hamilton—"Publius"—is that both societies have a single executive. The "king of Great Britain" is, however, a "*hereditary* monarch, possessing the crown as a patrimony descendible to his heirs for ever." True, the President would be reeligible; but then, so is the governor of New York. The king is "inviolable": the President could be impeached and removed from office, and "would afterwards be liable to prosecution and punishment in the ordinary course of law." Laying out further contrasts, Hamilton sums up. The President, he says, would have a qualified legislative veto, the king an *absolute* negative:

> The one would have a right to command the military and naval forces of the nation; the other, in addition to this right, possesses that of *declaring* war, and of *raising* and *regulating* fleets and armies by his own authority. The one would have a concurrent power with a branch of the legislature [the Senate] in the formation of treaties; the other is the *sole possessor* of the power of making treaties. The one would have a like concurrent authority in appointing to offices; the other is the sole author of all appointments. . . . The one has no particle of spiritual jurisdiction; the other is the supreme head and governor of the national church [the Church of England]! . . .

Hamilton's final thrust:

> What answer shall we give to those who would persuade us that things so unlike resemble each other? The same that ought to be given to those who tell us that a government, the whole power of which would be in the hands of the elective and periodical servants of the people, is an aristocracy, a monarchy, and a despotism. [*GBWW*, Vol. 43, p. 210b–c.]

In Number 70 Hamilton seeks to refute the view that "a vigorous Executive is inconsistent with the genius of republican government." All sensible people, he maintains, will agree that such energy is necessary. The question then is how to combine "energy" with "safety in the republican sense." A single executive is essential for the "decision, activity, secrecy, and despatch" on which successful government depends. The other essential, "safety in the republican sense," rests upon "due dependence on the people" and on "due responsibility." These, Hamilton suggests, are actually impaired where there are several people occupied in making policy, and the zones of responsibility are blurred: "all multiplication of the Executive is rather dangerous than friendly to liberty." [*GBWW*, Vol. 43, pp. 210d–13d.]

Federalist Number 71 is concerned with the length of the presidential term. Hamilton argues that on the one hand, "a duration of four years will contribute to the firmness of the Executive in a sufficient degree," while on the other hand "it is not enough to justify any alarm for the

THE

FEDERALIST:

A COLLECTION

O F

E S S A Y S,

WRITTEN IN FAVOUR OF THE

NEW CONSTITUTION,

AS AGREED UPON BY THE FEDERAL CONVENTION,
SEPTEMBER 17, 1787.

IN TWO VOLUMES.

VOL. I.

NEW-YORK:

PRINTED AND SOLD BY J. AND A. M'LEAN,
No. 41, HANOVER-SQUARE,
M.DCC.LXXXVIII.

"The most famous of the post-Philadelphia arguments were developed in what is still accepted as the classic analysis of American constitutionalism, The Federalist Papers. . . . Alexander Hamilton [above, right] was the architect of the plan. As things worked out, he and James Madison [above, left] divided the labor between them."

public liberty." [*GBWW*, Vol. 43, p. 216a.] Next (no. 72) he passes to the reeligibility problem. On the face of it, he concedes, there is much to be said for "continuing the chief magistrate in office for a certain time, and then" (as Harrington's *Oceana* had advocated) "excluding him from it, either for a limited period or for ever after." But to shut out leaders so arbitrarily would be to disappoint the worthy and tempt people to "peculation" or even "usurpation." "Would it," he asks, "promote the peace of the community or the stability of the government to have half a dozen men who had had credit enough to be raised to the seat of the supreme magistracy, wandering among the people like discontented ghosts, and sighing for a place which they were destined never more to possess?" Why waste talent and experience? There is, "Publius" announces, "an excess of refinement in the idea of disabling the people to continue in office men who had entitled themselves . . . to approbation and confidence; the advantages of which are at best speculative and equivocal, and are over-balanced by disadvantages far more certain and decisive." [*GBWW*, Vol. 43, pp. 216d–18d.]

In Number 73, Hamilton displays his occasional tendency to weaken a case by producing too many arguments in favor of it—arguments apt to collide with one another. The main theme of Number 73 is the soundness of the provision for the "qualified negative" of the presidential veto. We are told that the President needs a veto to defend the executive branch, which might otherwise be stripped of his constitutional powers by successive legislative encroachments. It is also a protection against bad laws. Hamilton denies the assumption that the collective wisdom of many lawmakers is superior to that of a single person. Legislatures are subject to error and to the pressure of time. Does "the power of preventing bad laws" carry the unfortunate corollary power "of preventing good ones"? Possibly; but then, legislators pass too many laws, so the injury that might be done "by defeating a few good laws will be amply compensated by the advantage of preventing a number of bad ones." Besides, executives in soundly formed governments hesitate to challenge legislatures, especially when two houses (here the House of Representatives and the Senate) have maturely considered a measure. After all, says Hamilton (ignoring his contrary remarks about royal vetoes in no. 69), even the "powerful and . . . well fortified" British monarch has not dared a veto for "a very considerable period" (actually, not since the reign of Queen Anne, 1702–14). If such a personage is obliged to hold back, "how much greater caution may be reasonably expected in a President of the United States, clothed for the short period of four years with the executive authority of a government wholly and purely republican?" [*GBWW*, Vol. 43, pp. 219b–20c.]

Hamilton goes on to urge the desirability of a qualified veto, which can be rejected by a sufficient legislative majority. It is less peremptory and more persuasive than an absolute negative. Furthermore, the state of New York has allowed gubernatorial vetoes, requiring them to emanate from a council of the governor and senior judges. The Philadelphia delegates—rightly in Hamilton's view—in accepting the general principle of executive veto, preferred the precedent of Massachusetts in eliminating the judicial voice and leaving the decision solely to the governor.

The remaining four *Federalist Papers* devoted to the executive branch (nos. 74–77) are equally, though a trifle miscellaneously, ingenious in defending such prerogatives as the pardon power, or various joint activities such as treaty-making (no. 75) and appointments (nos. 76–77) in conjunction with the Senate. Here too, as before, Hamilton rather ambiguously cites British parliamentary circumstances, both as cautionary tales (corruption, etc.) and as good lessons to be followed (wise and libertarian legislators—see the final paragraph of no. 76). In his usual lucid fashion, he briefly recapitulates, at the end of Number 77, the contention that the executive department balances energy and "safety" in the most sagacious and comforting blend. "What more could be desired by an enlightened and reasonable people?" [*GBWW*, Vol. 43, p. 229c–d.]

4. Criticisms and misgivings

As Hamilton well knew, a good many Americans in 1787–88 did desire more, or perhaps less. He and Madison had performed brilliantly as spokesmen for the ratification of the Constitution. Hamilton in particular had sought to rebut objections expressed in tracts and newspapers, and in the speeches reported from the state conventions. Though Hamilton did not mention the work he had in mind, he did for instance refer (no. 68) to the writings of a relatively "plausible" opponent, since on one issue they seemed to agree with "Publius." [*GBWW*, Vol. 43, p. 205b.] (The work in question was *Letters from the Federal Farmer to the Republican,* whose anonymous author may have been Richard Henry Lee of Virginia.) It was embarrassing that some of the most vocal critics, such as Edmund Randolph and George Mason in Virginia, and Luther Martin in Maryland, had actually been delegates at Philadelphia. Among the ranks of the "Anti-Federalists"—the label gradually if confusingly attached to them—were eminent Americans like Governor Clinton of New York and Patrick Henry (whom Randolph succeeded in November 1786 as governor of Virginia).

"Publius," the result of a close collaboration between Hamilton and Madison, both then resident in New York City (Madison as member of the Continental Congress), was in the main unified and tightly constructed. There was no corresponding *Anti-Federalist Papers.* Though scholars have compiled anthologies of Anti-Federalist testimony, the results are in their nature somewhat scattered and diverse. There were people who disapproved of the entire proceedings. More commonly, dislike was expressed of certain features. Apart from protests at the high-handed discarding of the Articles, the commonest general criticism was that the Philadelphia Constitution embodied a "consolidated," national government, not sanctioned or desired by Americans. It subverted the principle of states rights and was in an ominous broad sense "monarchical." Within this broad complaint, attacks were directed against particular aspects of Article II of the new Constitution.[40]

Some of the most sweeping hostility was contained in a set of essays first printed in the *New-York Journal* under the pen name "Cato," and usually—though, it seems, wrongly—attributed to Governor Clinton. Hamilton clearly read and sought to refute them. "Cato" contended that any chief executive holding office for any "considerable duration" was dangerously prompted to oppress his fellow citizens and raise himself "to permanent grandeur on the ruins of his country." The proposed President seemed to fit these alarming criteria:

> His eminent magisterial situation will attach many adherents to him,
> and he will be surrounded with expectants and courtiers, his power of
> nomination and influence over all appointments, the strong posts in each
> state comprised within his superintendence, and garrisoned by troops
> under his direction, his control over the army, navy, militia, and navy,
> the unrestrained power of granting pardons for treason, which may be
> used to screen from punishment those whom he had secretly instigated
> to commit the crime, and thereby prevent a discovery of his own guilt,

his duration in office for four years: these, and various other principles evidently prove . . . that if the president is possessed of ambition, he has power and time sufficient to ruin his country.

"Philadelphiensis," writing in the Philadelphia *Independent Gazeteer,* was if anything even more hostile to the Constitution:

> Who can deny but the *president general* will be a *king* to all intents and purposes, and one of the most dangerous kind too; a king elected to command a standing army? . . . A quorum of 65 representatives, and of 26 senators [the number who would form the first new Congress], with a king at their head, are to possess powers, that extend to the *lives,* the *liberties,* and *property* of every citizen of America. This novel system . . . , were it possible to establish it, would be a compound of *monarchy* and *aristocracy,* the most accursed that ever the world witnessed.

William Grayson, in the Virginia ratifying convention, described the Constitution as "a republican government founded on the principles of monarchy." Patrick Henry, in the same convention, charged that the intended "great and mighty President" would be "supported in extravagant magnificence; so that the whole of our property may be taken by this American government, by laying what taxes they please, giving themselves what salaries they please, and suspending our laws at their pleasure." The Constitution, said Henry, had some "horribly frightful" features; "it squints toward monarchy; and does not this raise indignation in the breast of every true American?" Like "Cato," he feared that an ambitious and unscrupulous chief, backed by the army, would seek to "render himself absolute." In face of that dreadful prospect, "I would rather infinitely . . . have a king, lords, and commons, than a government so replete with such insupportable evils."

More mildly, the "Federal Farmer," not against a single executive as such, was perturbed by the proposal for reeligibility. He preferred a longer period, such as the seven years originally envisaged, rather than a repeatable four-year term:

> When a man shall get the chair, who may be re-elected, from time to time, for life, his greatest object will be to keep it; to gain friends and votes . . . ; to associate some favourite son with himself, to take the office after him: whenever he shall have any prospect of continuing the office in himself and family, he will spare no artifice, no address, and no exertions, to increase the power and importance of it; the servile supporters of his wishes will be placed in all offices, and tools constantly employed to aid his views and sound his praise.

This was likely to be the situation with "nine tenths of the presidents; we may have, for the first president, and, perhaps, one in a century or two afterwards (if the government should withstand the attacks of others) a great and good man, governed by superior motives; but these are not events to be calculated upon in the present state of human nature." Like Patrick Henry, the "Federal Farmer" professed to believe it "would be almost as well to create a limited monarchy at once, and give some family permanent power and interest in the community, . . . as to make a first magistrate eligible for life, and to create hopes and expectations in him and his family, of obtaining what they have not. In the latter case, we actually tempt them to disturb the state. . . ." Thomas Jefferson too, writing to Madison, avowed that while he by and large approved the new Constitution, he feared the President was apt to become a chief magistrate for life (and so, in implication, an elective monarch, as in Poland but with greater power).[41]

Every American schoolboy or schoolgirl is supposed to know the happy outcome. In the standard old textbook version, the new Constitution *was* ratified, initially by eleven of the thirteen states, and soon by all of them, after a good deal of American plain speaking. Fears that the proposed new government tilted toward monarchy and aristocracy were allayed by the understanding that a federal Bill of Rights would be introduced (the first ten Amendments to the Constitution, passed by Congress in September 1789 and ratified by the necessary three-fourths of the states by December 1791). George Washington, the unanimous choice of the brand-new Electoral College, duly took office in April 1789, and with becoming republican propriety retired at the end of his second term, timing his *Farewell Address* in September 1796 to coincide with the ninth anniversary of the Philadelphia signing.

Young Americans who do their homework are likewise deemed to know that political parties appeared more quickly than had been anticipated, or even wished for. What was more characteristically American, though, than that the politicians abided by the constitutional rules, ensuring a smooth presidential transition, to John Adams in the 1796 election and his opponent Thomas Jefferson in 1800? Or that the Twelfth Amendment (ratified 1804) should have briskly tackled the problem, raised by the 1800 election, of differentiating between the votes cast for the President and those for the Vice-President?

This story is not untrue; and its positive features will be discussed later. Yet it is not the whole truth. The 1790s was a decade in which ferocious controversy continued as to the republicanism or otherwise of the Washington and Adams administrations. In conceding that the Philadelphia delegates had "shaped their Ideas of the Powers to be given to a President" by their admiration for Washington, Pierce Butler admitted too that the presidential powers were "full great, and greater than I was disposed to make them." He added, disquietingly: "So that the Man, who by his Patriotism and Virtue, Contributed largely to the Emancipation of his Country, may be the Innocent means of its being, when he is lay'd low, oppress'd." Fifteen years later, in a U.S. Senate debate on the Twelfth Amendment, Butler asserted that, having been present at Philadelphia, "he could take it upon him to say what was the intention of the Constitution; the framers of that instrument were apprehensive of an elective Chief Magistrate; and their views were directed to prevent the putting up of any powerful man."[42]

Were Washington and his successor John Adams too "powerful" as presidents? Yes, according to some of their contemporaries. Or rather, John Adams was accused by Jefferson and others of a not-so-secret preference for monarchy; and Washington was thought by some to be allowing this dangerous tendency to gain a footing under the new Constitution. Debate on the issue began early in Washington's first administration, though Adams bore the brunt of criticism. Presiding over the Senate as Vice-President, he referred to Washington's inaugural address as the President's "most gracious speech"—language associated with British royalty. Adams also felt that the President should be given an honorific title, for formal purposes, such as "His Highness the President of the United States of America and Protector of the Rights of the Same." According to the journal kept by Senator William Maclay of Pennsylvania, several colleagues appeared to favor these suggestions—some wishing to allude to Washington as "His *Elective* Highness." Maclay and a number of Jeffersonian associates were outraged. "The abolishing of royalty, the extinguishment of patronage and dependencies attached to that form of government, were the exalted motives of many revolutionists. . . . Yet there were not wanting a party whose motives were different. They wished for the loaves and fishes of government, and cared for nothing else but a translation of the diadem and scepter from London to Boston, New York, or Philadelphia; or, in other words, the creation of a new monarchy in America, and to form niches for themselves in the temple of royalty." Such attitudes, in Maclay's view, were especially prevalent among the former army officers who had been active in establishing the Society of the Cincinnati.

The titles problem was quickly resolved along republican lines, and Adams made to seem foolishly fussy, if not worse. A couple of months later, Maclay's suspicions were again aroused when the Senate debated whether the President, empowered by the Constitution to appoint federal officers, also had the right to dismiss them. Maclay professed considerable uneasiness when the question was resolved in favor of the executive branch. On a number of other matters he recorded his conviction that in the Senate at any rate, "revolutionists" might be outnumbered by closet royalists. In December 1790, for instance, Maclay dressed in his best clothes to attend the presidential entertainment known as a levee. Conceding that it was in itself "innocent" enough, he grumbled that levees were monarchical rituals:

> This certainly escapes nobody. The royalists glory in it as a point gained. Republicans are borne down by fashion and a fear of being charged with

a want of respect to General Washington. If there is treason in the wish
I retract it, but would to God this same General Washington were in
heaven! We would not then have him brought forward as the constant
cover to every unconstitutional and irrepublican act.[43]

Maclay left the Senate in 1791, but fears of the kind he had expressed
by no means died away. Although he himself disliked public controversy, Secretary of State Thomas Jefferson became increasingly alarmed
by the centralizing pressures of Washington's Federalist administration.
So, in the House of Representatives, did James Madison. Identified as
"Republicans," they frequently and explicitly equated Federalism with
royalism. Although Jefferson paid sincere tribute to Adams's scholarship and essential integrity, he let drop in conversation and in private
correspondence (both of these apt to become public) his belief that
Adams had departed from the sturdy republicanism of the 1780s. For
Adams's own words, indeed, the Jeffersonian Republicans could turn to
his three-volume *Defence of the Constitutions of Government of the United
States of America* (1787), which appeared to extol hierarchical and mixed
polities such as that of the former mother country, and his *Discourses on
Davila* (1791), which likewise leaned toward Great Britain rather than
to the France that was embarked upon what was to prove a root-and-
branch Revolution.[44]

If John Adams struck the Republicans as a theoretical monarchist,
Alexander Hamilton, and others close to the Washington administration, looked to them like unscrupulous enemies of the infant republic.
In a long complaint to President Washington of May 23, 1792, Jefferson alleged that Treasury Secretary Hamilton's financial measures
were designed to produce a corruptly centralized system, aiming at "a
change, from the present republican form of government, to that of a
monarchy, of which the English constitution is to be the model." These
"Monarchical federalists" had dreamed of such a development at the
time of the Philadelphia convention; "to effect it then was impracticable, but they are still eager after their object."

Within a few years, Washington himself was under fire, directly in a
few instances, obliquely in several more. Thomas Paine had dedicated
the first part of *The Rights of Man* (1791) to the President, as "a small
treatise in defense of those principles of freedom which your exemplary
virtue hath so eminently contributed to establish." By 1796 Paine had
changed his mind about the exemplary virtues. In an "Open Letter"
Paine singled out the fundamental defects in the executive branch of
the new national government. "I have always," Paine claimed with less
than complete accuracy, "been opposed to . . . a single executive. Such
a man will always be the chief of a party. A plurality is far better; it
combines the mass of a nation better together. And besides this, it is
necessary to the manly mind of a republic that it loses the debasing

195

Secretary of State Thomas Jefferson (left) and Treasury Secretary Alexander Hamilton (center) confer with President Washington. *"Jefferson alleged that . . . Hamilton's financial measures were designed to produce a corruptly centralized system aiming at 'a change, from the present republican form of government, to that of a monarchy.'"*

idea of obeying an individual." Washington was the unworthy figure to whom Americans were now supposed to reverence:

> You commenced your Presidential career by encouraging and swallowing the grossest adulation, and you travelled America from one end to the other to put yourself in the way of receiving it. . . . As to what were your views, . . . they cannot be directly inferred from expressions of your own; but the partisans of your politics have divulged the secret.
>
> John Adams has said (and John it is known was always a speller after places and offices, and never thought his little services were highly enough paid—John has said, that as Mr. Washington had no child, the Presidency should be made hereditary in the family of Lund Washington [a distant cousin who ran the Mount Vernon estate during the President's absences]. John might then have counted upon some sinecure himself, and a provision for his descendants. He did not go so far as to say, also, that the Vice-Presidency should be hereditary in the family of John Adams. He prudently left that to stand on the ground that one good turn deserves another.

Washington's ability and honesty were impugned by other American pamphleteers. And in fact, when Paine attacked him, in July 1796, there was still a fairly widespread expectation that Washington might opt for a third presidential term, as some Federalist supporters were begging him to do. A sarcastic editor in Savannah, Georgia, composed a mock prayer: "Our President which art in office, illustrious be thy name; thy election come, our will be done, resign for none on earth, until thou art called to heaven. . . ." Vice-President Adams, indiscreetly describing himself as "heir apparent" in a letter to his wife, Abigail, was concerned for a while that his turn might never come.[45]

Much of the anger of Republicans in 1795–96 was directed against the Jay Treaty with Great Britain, which they felt sacrificed American interests (and friendship with the nation's ally, France) out of feeble, or possibly treacherous, "Anglomania." When John Adams did after all succeed Washington as President, in 1797, the opposition found further reasons to mistrust the Federalists. Jefferson had vastly offended Adams, as well as Washington, by sending a letter to the Italian liberal Philip Mazzei, of which some damaging lines got into print:

> In place of that noble love of liberty, & republican government which carried us triumphantly thro' the war, an Anglican monarchical, & aristocratical party has sprung up, whose avowed object is to draw over us the substance, as they have already done the forms, of the British government. The main body of our citizens . . . remain true to their republican principles. . . . Against us are the Executive, the Judiciary, two out of three branches of the legislature, all the officers of the government, all who want to be officers, all timid men who prefer the calm of despotism to the boisterous sea of liberty . . .

and various other cowardly or corrupt groups. Jefferson added words that were particularly insulting:

> It would give you a fever were I to name to you the apostates who have gone over to these heresies, men who were Samsons in the field and Solomons in the council, but who have had their heads shorn by the harlot England.

Such an allusion must surely refer to Washington himself, and to his closest associates. After these dire comments, Jefferson seemed almost to be groping for comfort when he assured Mazzei that nevertheless America would survive and thrive: "We have only to awake and snap the Lilliputian cords with which they have been entangling us during the first sleep which succeeded our labors."[46]

The passage of the Alien and Sedition Acts (1798) by John Adams's administration prompted his Vice-President, Thomas Jefferson, and also James Madison, who had left Congress the year before in protest against the Jay Treaty, to engineer two direct challenges to federal authority in the shape of the Virginia and Kentucky Resolutions. The Virginia protest, drafted by Madison, repeated the Republican claim that Federalist machinations were subverting the Constitution:

> The disproportionate increase of prerogative and patronage must evidently either enable the chief magistrate of the Union, by quiet means, to secure his reelection . . . and finally to regulate the succession as he might please; or, by giving so transcendent an importance to the office, would render the election to it so violent and corrupt, that the public voice itself might call for an hereditary in place of an elective succession. Whichever of these events might follow, the transformation of the republican system of the United States into a monarchy, anticipated . . . from a consolidation of the states into one sovereignty, would be equally accomplished. . . .

The only uncertainty remaining would be whether the result would be "a mixed or an absolute monarchy." Sure enough, Matthew Lyon, a Republican congressman from Vermont, was tried and found guilty under the Sedition Act. One charge was that in his newspaper, *The Scourge of Aristocracy,* he had brought the President and government of the United States into contempt by inveighing against the administration's "continual grasp for power, . . . unbounded thirst for ridiculous pomp, . . . and selfish avarice." Lyon received a stiff fine and a four-month jail sentence—later canceled when Jefferson became President in 1801.[47]

Jefferson and Madison remained convinced in old age that they had staved off an ominous anti-republican drive by their political opponents. Putting together the reminiscent notes known as the *Anas,* in 1818, Jefferson recounted his version of American history, from the Philadelphia convention on through the next quarter-century, as a struggle between republican patriots and "the advocates for monarchy." He claimed to have been appalled, on returning to the United States from France in March 1790, to assume office as Secretary of State, to find that the fashionable conversation in New York belittled the Revolution. "Politics were the chief topic, and a preference of kingly, over republican, government, was evidently the favorite sentiment." The arch-villain, in Jefferson's recollection, was Alexander Hamilton. At Philadelphia, Hamilton had argued for a half-royal, half-republican government, with the executive and upper house in power for life. Hamilton, Jefferson asserted, was "not only a monarchist, but for a monarchy bottomed on corruption." Adams, on the other hand, "originally a republican," had been unduly influenced by "the glare of royalty and nobility, during his mission to England." As for President Washington—in Jefferson's version—he was an upright man who had become subject to manipulation by Federalists after Jefferson resigned the secretaryship of state at the end of 1793:

> His memory was already sensibly impaired by age, the firm tone of mind for which he had been remarkable, was beginning to relax, its energy was abated; a listlessness of labor, a desire for tranquillity had crept on him, and a willingness to let others act and even think for him.

James Monroe, who followed Jefferson and Madison in the sequence of Virginia presidents, clung to a similar interpretation of the formative era. He remembered the 1790s as a period when the nation was threatened with an insidious, camouflaged yet nevertheless real slide toward monarchy, from which it had been saved by the vigilance of the Republicans. In about 1810 the poet Joel Barlow, an early convert to Jeffersonian principles, began at Jefferson's instigation an effort to counter John Marshall's Federalist *Life of George Washington.* Barlow's abortive project was to write a true history of the era, so as to reveal the average American Federalist as a "monarchist: a doubtful friend if not an enemy of republican principles, and of all representative government." Mercy Otis Warren of Massachusetts, in her three-volume *History of the Rise, Progress and Termination of the American Revolution* (1805), claimed that Federalist supporters of Washington, "after the poison of foreign influence had crept into their councils, . . . created a passion to assimilate the politics and the governments of the United States nearer to the model of European monarchies than the letter of the constitution, by any fair construction would admit."[48]

Worries about the nature of the presidency thus persisted among Jeffersonian Republicans even when their Federalist enemies ceased to occupy the White House—indeed, disintegrated as a force in national politics. These concerns continued, however, to be voiced by Americans of varied political and class orientation. Federalists counterattacked their opponents by maintaining that the supporters of Jefferson were atheists, Jacobin revolutionaries, demagogues scheming to corrupt a good-natured yet gullible electorate. In 1803 Uriah Tracy, Federalist Senator from Connecticut, warned that the "vastly extensive" powers entrusted to the executive were bound to excite "avarice and ambition" among aspiring politicians. A few years later, Tracy's Connecticut colleague Senator James Hillhouse argued that the 1787 Constitution had made a fundamental error in "setting the people to choose a King." Presidential electioneering would eventually "terminate in civil war and despotism."

Between 1809, when Jefferson left office, and 1829, when Andrew Jackson entered the White House, over a hundred proposed constitutional amendments—half the entire total—related to Article II. Some sought to limit the President to a single term, some to restrict office to two terms. Much dissatisfaction was expressed with the electoral college. One plan even suggested choosing chief executives by lot. Presidential patronage increasingly perturbed observers of the process. Thomas Hart Benton of Missouri warned in 1824:

> The time will come, when the American President, like the Roman
> Emperors, will select his successor, take him by the hand, exhibit him to
> the people, place him upon the heights and eminences in the Republic
> . . . , make him the channel of all favor, and draw the whole tribe of
> parasites and office hunters to the feet of the favorite.

Georgia's vehement spokesman Senator George McDuffie, convinced that Washington, D.C., was a seedbed of corruption, predicted in 1826 that within half a century, "the great aggregate of Executive patronage in this country will be . . . greater than it was in England in the days of Sir Robert Walpole."

President Andrew Jackson was portrayed by his critics as just such a monster—a would-be Napoleon with scant regard for constitutional niceties. Jackson, in the Whig version of events, was a bully, an ignoramus, and a liar. Pretending to believe in a limitation of federal and executive powers, he concentrated prerogative within the White House and his circle of "courtiers." Professing to believe in one-term presidencies, he got himself elected for a second term. Jackson then secured the succession for his tame nominee Martin Van Buren. Van Buren was not only Jackson's tool: he was, according to abusive Whig journalists in 1836, "a proud, rich nabob, who dashes through our streets . . . with all the pomp and parade of an heir apparent." One of Jackson's grounds for offense was his claim that he and he alone within the American system represented the entire nation; he alone, therefore, was entitled to divine America's wants and needs.[49]

In short, if we pay attention to negative testimony, whatever the general agreement that the Constitution was a stupendous achievement,

Andrew Jackson's first inauguration, on the steps of the Capitol, 1829. *"President Andrew Jackson was portrayed by his critics as . . . a would-be Napoleon with scant regard for constitutional niceties."*

much uneasiness remained throughout the formative decades as to the wisdom of the provisions under Article II.

5. Republican monarchy

Previous sections of this essay have suggested that:

for Anglo-American policymakers and political philosophers, on the eve of 1776, hereditary monarchy was by far the most successful system;

of the extant forms, the British "mixed" or "moderated" monarchy commended itself as superior to all others;

republicanism, while sometimes admired in the abstract, was generally regarded as too dependent on individual and communal virtue, and feasible only for limited periods within geographically compact communities;

American impatience with and mistrust of British suzerainty led to a repudiation of colonial status, a repudiation of remote and hierarchical government per se, and the creation of a decentralized group of American republics, described in a rather ad hoc way as the "United States" (a designation rather than a name);

dissatisfied with the resulting loose structure, the leaders who organized the Philadelphia convention in 1787 replaced the Articles of Confederation with a new, more centralized government that also made provision for a single executive, the President, with George Washington in mind as first incumbent;

this change was not made without considerable protest, often expressed as a fear that the United States was reverting to monarchy, in betrayal of the republican principles of the Revolution;

although the Constitution itself was quite swiftly accepted as a legitimately "republican" document, and indeed soon revered, the nature of the presidency remained a matter for controversy during the formative decades after the Constitution took effect in 1789; and in this controversy, the "monarchical" propensities of the executive branch continued to be emphasized.

How are we to reconcile these seemingly fluctuating and even contradictory viewpoints? The principal character in Saul Bellow's novel

The Dean's December (1982) remarks of another person: "He accused me of abyssifying and catastrophizing. We have a weakness for this." Were the Anti-Federalists, and subsequent critics of the presidency, indulging a national appetite for "abyssifying and catastrophizing"? There is a Chinese saying: "One dog barks at nothing; the other dogs bark at him." Are we to dismiss the misgivings outlined above as mere pessimistic melodrama? Or do they deserve to be taken seriously? Is there, perhaps, a deeper significance in the tendency of commentators on the presidency, right down to the present day, to fall back upon the accusatory metaphors of the Revolutionary era whenever some activity within the White House antagonizes them?

On the way toward some speculative conclusions, a number of relatively noncontroversial points are worth making with reference to the invention of the presidency and its early evolution.

One simple yet vital observation is that the achievement of American independence, and a stable form of government, was no light task. Apart from the difficulties of reaching agreement on a new, federal, republican apparatus, the external circumstances of the day—a war of independence followed not long after by the gigantic upheavals of the French Revolution and the worldwide conflicts of the Napoleonic empire—placed huge strains upon the young United States. Counterrevolutionary impulses inevitably affected the Americans' confidence in their own modestly republican experiments. The issue of neutrality in the struggles between Great Britain and France was bound to engage and embitter Federalists and Republicans at the time of the Jay Treaty.[50]

Again, the debaters of 1787 and afterward were not concerned solely, or sometimes even principally, with the presidency as such. They had many things on their minds. James Madison, in a long letter to George Washington (April 16, 1787), foreshadowing the themes he felt must be examined when the delegates came to Philadelphia, spoke of the need for a "due supremacy of the national authority" that would stop short of "a consolidation of the whole into one simple republic." But he confessed he had no firm ideas about the desirable shape of the decision-making mechanism:

A National Executive must also be provided. I have scarcely ventured as yet to form my own opinion either of the manner in which it ought to be constituted or of the authorities with which it ought to be cloathed.[51]

Even the sagacious Madison was feeling his way, on the very brink of the Philadelphia assembly. And when Madison and his contemporaries spoke of "monarchy," they might use the term in several different senses. Sometimes it was associated with, say, "aristocracy" or "monopoly"; sometimes it was a shorthand way of alluding to a branch of government, sometimes to the attributes of any sort of "consolidated," or centrally controlled, system.

It is hard to tell whether Thomas Jefferson, who detested European monarchy and frequently used the word as a near-synonym for Federalist "monocracy," actually believed that opponents of the Hamilton stamp wanted to restore kingship to America. To the extent that he was sincere, was his judgment warped by the crisis atmosphere of the 1790s? Both sides bandied epithets with a truculent relish that was not to disappear, even in calmer times, from the nation's political scene. In Joel Barlow's fragment of history we can see him struggling to be judicious, without conceding that the Jeffersonians were resorting to smear tactics:

> By monarchist . . . I do not necessarily mean royalist, or the adherent
> of a kingly government exclusively. *Monarchia* . . . signifies one integral
> dominion. In this country it would signify an amalgamation of the
> several states into one great state; which great state, administered by a
> single magistrate, whatever were his title, would be a monarchy, in the
> sense in which I use the word.

In 1810, mutual suspicions were no longer quite so ferocious. Barlow also announced that he was "far from ascribing any dishonest views to the monarchists of the United States. I consider them as sincere in acting from their opinions as I wish them to consider me in announcing my own. . . . They doubtless believe that a monarchy is the best form of government. I believe a federal and representative system the best, especially for this country."

That qualifying phrase perhaps relates to Barlow's own evolution. As late as 1787 he had dedicated his epic poem *The Vision of Columbus* to the French king Louis XVI, who had graciously responded by purchasing twenty-five copies of the work. The passionately republican phase of Barlow's life began a few years later, at a moment when his erstwhile literary acquaintances, the Connecticut Wits, were moving in the opposite ideological direction, *away from* confident radical republicanism. Barlow's remarks may embody, too, a Republican annoyance at the misleading appropriation of the appellation "Federalist" (i.e., decentralized) by the other side.[52] Certainly, despite his disclaimers, "monarchy" had become a pejorative term, as "republican" had by degrees become for Americans a term in affectionate rhetoric; and certainly Barlow and Jefferson both had a fine sense of word nuances.

There is then probably a tinge of artfulness in the choice of political language attributable to Federalists and Jeffersonians. Both could honestly affirm themselves patriotically "republican," and honestly, if exaggeratedly, fear the worst if the policies of their opponents should carry the day. George Washington's gentleman-demeanor, while it might irk a disgruntled figure such as Maclay, no doubt struck Washington himself not as "monarchical" in any meaningful respect, but simply as appropriately dignified. One of the conceptions known to and

President Washington leads the minuet. *"George Washington's gentleman-demeanor, while it might irk a disgruntled figure such as Maclay, no doubt struck Washington himself not as 'monarchical' in any meaningful respect, but simply as appropriately dignified."*

praised by most educated Americans was Viscount Bolingbroke's "Patriot King"—a leader of perfect integrity and aplomb. Jefferson, who was among the readers of Bolingbroke, deliberately sought a "republican" tack when he became President, by abandoning the formalities practiced by Washington and Adams. But his casualness brought condemnation; and despite growing social egalitarianism, James Monroe and other subsequent presidents restored a measure of formality to White House functions. John Adams, a somewhat prickly person, was no "monarchist" in a literal sense (as distinct from that explained by Barlow). On the other hand, he did grow more conservative with age, and with the times. He did cling with a stubborn, intellectual's vanity to his own skeptical views of human nature. And Adams did, correctly if rashly, insist that it was tenable to establish a typology according to which republicanism and limited monarchy were not necessarily incompatible. He agreed with Tom Paine on this, if not on much else: the better parts of the British government were inherently "republican." The British system was mixed. So was the American. *Ergo* (an *ergo* inimical to Adams's critics), there was no absolute difference between a constitutional monarch and a reeligible President.[53]

Some of what happened was fortuitous, though not unappreciated by contemporaries. The absence of surviving male heirs for Washington, Jefferson, and Madison reduced the likelihood that sons might in due course follow their fathers into the White House. We know that Washington for one was keenly conscious of this element. In a discarded draft of his first inaugural address, Washington explicitly cleared himself of dynastic ambition. The Divine Providence, he said (a little wistfully?)

> hath not seen fit that my blood should be transmitted or my name
> perpetuated by the endearing, though sometimes seducing, channel of
> immediate offspring. I have no child for whom I could wish to make a
> provision—no family to build in greatness upon my country's ruins.

A scurrilous Republican legend, circulated during the Adams *vs.* Jefferson presidential campaign of 1800, alleged that John Adams had once planned to marry one of his sons to a daughter of George III—several of whom were indeed available—and so start a new Anglo-American royal dynasty. According to the story, George Washington had got wind of the scheme and threatened to run Adams through with his sword if he persisted in the vile enterprise. And, after all, a son of John Adams, John Quincy Adams, *did* reach the presidency a quarter of a century later.

Reacting to public pressure, individual instinct, domestic circumstances, and the state of party politics, the early presidents tended to oscillate between the "dignified" and the "efficient" (a distinction between the parts of government that was to be drawn by the English analyst Walter Bagehot): this alternation is still sometimes discernible in the late twentieth-century presidency. One inherently republican precedent set by Washington was that of what Michael J. Heale calls the "Mute Tribune." In other words, the man must not seek the office: it must seek him, while he maintains an air of lofty disinterest. Such a demeanor accorded well, of course, with Washington's actual temperament. It was, though, made easier for him, if not for subsequent candidates, by the fact that there were no national parties when he first became President, and also that there were no rivals challenging him. He was indeed not a "candidate" and therefore did not have to pretend to be indifferent to political maneuvers. The disappearance of the national Federalist party, during the "Era of Good Feelings" of 1815–25, likewise helped to prolong the supposition that the chief executive was the supreme embodiment of civic virtue: that each President would handsomely reenact the selfless commitment of George Washington, before retiring once more to bucolic simplicity.[54]

The pattern of simplicity was enshrined too in folklore, as a set of anecdotes illustrating the modesty and accessibility of the nation's chief magistrates. An early instance is related by the English actor-manager John Bernard, who lived in the United States from 1797 to 1819 and claimed to have been introduced to Jefferson by President Washington. Jefferson, he says, told him of this incident, which occurred shortly after Jefferson came to the White House. While out riding, "in his usual plain attire," the President was accosted by a blunt Connecticut farmer, down South to visit a brother. The Yankee promptly announced that he had voted for Adams and mistrusted the tyrannical, extravagant Jefferson (having no idea of the other man's identity). After a while, they came in sight of the White House. The farmer was highly indignant:

> "There's a house as big as Noah's ark. At the smallest count, there's
> thirty rooms in it. What can any careful chap . . . want with more
> than *six*? I ha'nt got more than *four*. I say this Jefferson's wasting the
> people's money, and Congress is winking at it . . . ; and I ain't afraid
> to affirm that it's my guess the inside of that house shows just as much
> wastefulness as Jefferson a-horseback."

Thereupon, Jefferson, still incognito, offered to show the house to the stranger. But as he approached the entrance,

> some gentlemen, who were engaged to dine with him, stepped
> forward and exclaimed, "Good morning, president. . . ." At the word
> "president" the farmer . . . drew up so short he was near flying over
> his steed's ears. He turned and stared at Jefferson with a mixture of
> curiosity and alarm. . . . In another instant he had struck his spurs into

his horse and was flying away . . . , fully convinced he should in some way pay for his temerity. "Hallo, friend!" shouted Jefferson, "won't you go over the house?" "No, thank ye, president," was the reply; "I'll look in when I come back."[55]

Perhaps the story is not quite as "republican," or "democratic," as it purports to be; Jefferson, much more of a gentleman than his interlocutor, could almost be a monarch in disguise. Nevertheless, the anecdote was to become characteristic of descriptions of public receptions, importunate office seekers, and casual foreign tourists, all given easy access to what in Europe would have been a closely guarded palace. Some of the foreigners remarked on the lack of ceremony within the White House, or on how a particular President received them at his working desk, in business clothes, instead of from a throne.

A further fortuitous aspect of the early presidency is that peace returned to the world in 1815, with a spectacular final American triumph at the end of the "second war of independence," the War of 1812, with the victory of Andrew Jackson over a British veteran army in the Battle of New Orleans. Exultant and relieved Americans, whose previous exploits in the war had been less astounding, took the victory as additional proof of the superiority of their institutions to those of the repudiated former mother country. Jackson, the self-taught amateur warrior, had worsted a titled professional soldier, Sir Edward Pakenham, brother-in-law of the famous Duke of Wellington, who was shortly to defeat Napoleon Bonaparte at Waterloo. In patriotic logic, Jackson was thus world champion, and his Kentucky riflemen supremely invincible. Jackson's amazing success at New Orleans was to propel him into the White House.

In the years after 1815, however, America was free from foreign crises, and domestically master of her own destiny. Put more prosaically, presidents had not a great deal to do during the next few decades, unless they chose to exert themselves, as did James K. Polk in pushing his country toward war with Mexico in 1846–48. That latter year saw the publication of Frederick Grimke's reflective discussion, *The Nature and Tendency of Free Institutions,* including a chapter on monarchical government, which represented a survival of somewhat outmoded "superstition." Grimke was matter-of-factly cheerful in dealing with the American presidency. He applauded the wholesome tendency in the United States to "elevate men of moderate talents." Their very ordinariness was all to the good. "A president who possesses pre-eminent abilities has a sort of magical control over his party" (was Grimke harking back to President Jackson's hold over his Democratic followers?). But with the average incumbent, "instead of molding public opinion to his wishes, public opinion controls him and stops him in the commencement of his career."[56]

Jimmy Carter (top, with wife Rosalynn and daughter Amy) and Ronald Reagan (bottom, with wife Nancy) during their presidencies. *"The early presidents tended to oscillate between the 'dignified' and the 'efficient' . . . . : this alternation is still sometimes discernible in the late twentieth-century presidency."*

Again, "abyssifiers and catastrophists" had foretold the emergence of the projected federal capital as a den of iniquity. Perhaps they were not altogether wide of the mark, looking far into the future. But in the early decades of national government, Washington, D.C., was a pathetic sight. According to the Anti-Federalist vision of "Cato," the federal district would soon reveal the inherent monarchical vices—*"ambition with idleness—baseness with pride—the thirst of riches without labor— aversion to truth—flattery—treason—perfidy—violation of engagements— contempt of civil duties—hope from the magistrate's weakness; but above all, the perpetual ridicule of virtue."* In Jefferson's administration, however, as described by the Irish poet Thomas Moore, the "embryo capital" was a wilderness. A Philadelphia editor derisively observed: "The Federal city is in reality neither town nor village; it may be compared to a country seat where state sportsmen may run horses and fight cocks. . . . There sits the President . . . like a pelican in the wilderness, or a sparrow upon the housetop." Although Washington grew with the years, it grew slowly. Charles Dickens was not much impressed when he saw it in 1842, nor was Anthony Trollope on a visit twenty years later than that. But at least it was not the glittering lure envisaged by many a pessimist. Arguably, the sheer charmlessness of Washington, D.C., was fortunate for the country in the crucial formative era. Presidents and their aides joined with members of Congress in escaping the steamy summer of the capital, staying away as long as possible. While the town was, so to speak, in session, the inhabitants talked politics, which was better for America than talk of dynastic alliances and coups d'état.[57]

Such considerations, it will be seen, are matters of accident, or perhaps geography. They may have little or nothing to do with political theory, as indulged in by Jefferson, Adams, and Madison in their more philosophical moments. They are however an important part of the total picture, which we may now attempt to pull together in assessing the manifold hopes and fears, speculations and memories, that went into the invention of the American presidency.

Conclusions

Let us first recapitulate the elements of novelty and precedent-breaking that can be regarded as truly "inventive" in the creation of the presidency. There was surely a bold spirit of innovation—a *Novus Ordo Seclorum* or new order of the centuries—in the America of 1776, at least to judge by the declarations of the leaders in the move for independence. There was an emphatic repudiation of monarchy, British and otherwise. There was a repudiation too of the "modernizing" activities of Europe's "enlightened despots," who were centralizing autocrats. America under the Articles of Confederation was to be broadly democratic and decentralized. The American alternative to centralized monarchy, localized republicanism, was (as outlined by Madison in the *Federalist*) a bold reversal of received wisdom as to the nature of republics.

No less boldly, pragmatic Americans (it can be argued) replaced the Articles when they proved inadequate. In search of a "more perfect Union," they may be said to have reinvented the initial invention. Entirely fresh, within the 1787 Constitution, was Article II—so fresh, indeed, that even such bravely innovative democrats as Patrick Henry were resistant to further change. However, the test of experience soon reassured Patrick Henry and many initial doubters such as he. They could perceive that the nation's new chief magistracy was, when properly defined, a "republican" institution, designed to combine simplicity and integrity. Joel Barlow, referring to the reelection of George Washington in 1792, said:

> The people, being habituated to the election of all kinds of officers, the *magnitude* of the office makes no difficulty in the case. The president of the United States, who has more power while in office than some of the kings of Europe, is chosen with as little commotion as a churchwarden. There is a public service to be performed, and the people say who shall do it.

Barlow's countrymen could share his evident satisfaction in the performance of the first President, whether they called themselves Federalists or Anti-Federalists at this stage. The wealthy Massachusetts Federalist Theodore Sedgwick wrote of Washington, in a letter of July 1789: "he has a personal dignity I have not seen in any other man, while the unaffected simplicity of his manners makes one easy in his presence." Washington was well aware that "the first transactions of a nation, like those of an individual upon his first entrance into life, make the deepest impression, and . . . form the leading traits in its character."[58] By retiring after two terms, Washington set one vital precedent that was to be honored by every other President, willingly or not, except for Franklin D. Roosevelt in the special crisis-circumstances of 1940. In other ways, however, the office adapted itself as fresh conditions demanded change—notably, for instance, in response to the emergence of the political parties, whose existence Washington had been loath to acknowledge. To the extent that there were older models for the presidency to build upon, these again are asserted to have been *American* in provenance. The presidency, that is, has often been seen as deriving from the colonial and then state governorships, instead of from supposed British or European ancestry.

On the other side of the argument, there are some of the awkward considerations we have already touched upon, such as the intense and lingering suspicion that Article II did not so much reinvent a fittingly American form of government as negate the republican spirit of the

1770s and early 1780s. Even a staunch Federalist could confess uneasiness at tinges of monarchical behavior, along with Maclay. A devoted admirer of George Washington, Sedgwick nevertheless was disquieted by some aspects of the President's Birthday Ball staged in February 1791 in Philadelphia: "When the president entered . . . , the tune called his march struck up, and he was saluted with three Huzzas. A ceremony more proper in my opinion for savages than the first citizens of the first city in America." And still more of course did people of Sedgwick's stamp dislike what they regarded as the demagogic exploitation of the office by a Jefferson or a Jackson.

Vocabulary, to repeat, blurs our understanding of how Americans felt about the new chief magistracy. The White House became the presidential residence in 1800. In the next decade it was occasionally referred to, quite neutrally so far as one can tell, as the "President's Palace." Noah Webster, the lexicographer, in the 1828 enlarged version of his *Dictionary* (borrowing perhaps from Samuel Johnson's earlier compilation?) offers "monarch" as a synonym for "president." We cannot be altogether sure of the exact shades of meaning, or of the shifts in meaning, in such words. We know, for example, that the Massachusetts Federalist Fisher Ames became increasingly scornful of American political democracy. We know that he was pleased when Washington and Adams were reelected in 1792. It is hard, though, to tell just what sort of satisfaction he was voicing when he said of that result that the "old King and his second" were in again. Washington received all the electoral votes. If the United States did not have an "elective kingship," what did it have? Whatever the answer, Ames was plainly content in 1792. Twenty years on, when Madison was reelected in the presidential contest of 1812, a Federalist journal printed a verse that was quite plainly *dis*approving of the kingly comparison:

> The day is past—the election o'er
> And Madison is King once more![59]

Even if the Philadelphia delegates built Article II by analogy with their experience of state governorships, they had additional and different prerogatives in mind. There was general agreement that, in the conduct of foreign policy, the need for "energy," "secrecy," and "despatch" necessarily concentrated authority within the executive branch, though with consultative assistance from the Senate and financial sanction from Congress. In *Federalist* Number 64, John Jay, discussing relations with foreign powers, was at pains to suggest that the Senate would be very actively involved. Possibly he was seeking to allay criticism that the President would have too free a hand in this area. Whatever interpretation we put on such debates, it seems undeniable that, potentially at least, the new chief magistrate would in international affairs have responsibilities on another level from that of gubernatorial business.

Equally undeniable, if not always fully understood at the time, was an implied symbolic role to be filled by the President and no one else. At Philadelphia on July 19, 1787, Gouverneur Morris of Pennsylvania said:

> One great object of the Executive is to controul the Legislature. . . . It is necessary then that the Executive Magistrate should be the guardian of the people, even of the lower classes, agst. Legislative tyranny, against the Great & the wealthy who in the course of things will necessarily compose—the Legislative body. . . . The Executive ought therefore to be so constituted as to be the great protector of the Mass of the people.

Here is a bold avowal, and by a conservative, that the President speaks for everybody. That doctrine, still more boldly reaffirmed by President Andrew Jackson, has been described (and sometimes regretted) as opening the door to a "plebiscitarian" democracy in which the occupant of the White House acts as "republican monarch," in a manner comparable to France's Napoleon III or, in the twentieth century, Charles de Gaulle. It will not do to attribute the origins of such a potentially dictatorial creed to crypto-monarchical Federalists yearning to be back under the British flag. In 1794 the deeply Anti-Federalist John Taylor of Caroline urged upon President Washington that he rise above partisanship and embody the aspirations of the American people as a whole. Ironically, however, Taylor's model for such lofty representativeness was the "Patriot King" as sketched by the English Tory Lord Bolingbroke. Ironically too, according to Benjamin Harrison, a hundred years after John Adams's wrangle over presidential titles, ordinary citizens who wrote to the President still sometimes addressed him as plain "Mister," but also quite often as "His Excellency" and sometimes as "His Majesty."[60]

From this mass of somewhat contradictory evidence, it seems reasonable to conclude that the office itself perhaps originated under contradictory and not entirely straightforward circumstances. Few if any delegates at Philadelphia envisaged an actual return to monarchy, still less to British suzerainty. Hamilton and one or two others may secretly have wished for such a development, but they knew it was out of the question. What they intended to create by way of a single executive was not a slavish copy of the British mixed monarchy. They could not agree, or foretell, just what was being established. They wanted Americans to close their eyes and think of George Washington. In acts of salesmanship such as the *Federalist Papers,* they perhaps disguised from themselves and from their readers the extent of overlap between a constitutional monarchy and the "rising empire" of the United States. Necessarily, in rhetoric they exaggerated the differences. After 1776, "monarchy" became increasingly a term of opprobrium, to contrast with "republic" and then with "democracy."

Conceivably, though, somewhere within the semantic shifts there remained a half-buried respect for the old English constitution upon which so much praise had been lavished in the decades before 1776. Americans continued to play chess and cards, in which royalty ruled the roost, and to use words like "noble" and "majestic," whose connotations were nonrepublican. Tom Paine had helped to "kill the king" with his fierce debunking mockery of tradition and hierarchy. But perhaps the subsequent extraordinary revulsion from Paine in the United States—almost universal, except for Jefferson and a handful of others—has to be understood in part as a distaste for a person who, like, say, a hangman or a slave trader, has performed a task that his society finds deeply distasteful, and only valuable on rare occasions.

Perhaps too the presidency, in common with many another invention, was as much an evolution as a revolution. The "horseless carriage" designed under Article II at Philadelphia was bound to reflect some features of other executive structures with which the delegates were familiar. It could not but mirror certain aspects of the world of Westminster and St. James's Palace, although the Founding Fathers were inhibited from saying so.

But we should not yield to the temptation of believing that the Americans merely produced a modified, concealed imitation of the British executive. Horseless carriages have a different motive power from their venerable prototypes. Why then the continuing parallels, drawn again and again from the 1780s to the 1980s, between presidents and kings? In part, we may think, because the United States has achieved the power and wealth that its founding spokesmen associated with the corruptions of courts. And in part, perhaps, because all leaders are prone to error; because, in all societies that permit dissent, ordinary citizens are prone to vent their dissatisfaction; and because the language of political vexation, despite its rich textures, still draws upon basic images that go back to the Old Testament, Shakespeare, ancient Rome, and even further in the mists of time.

---

[1]Frank I. Schecter, "The Early History of the Tradition of the Constitution," *American Political Science Review* 9 (November 1915): 707–34.

[2]Arthur M. Schlesinger, Jr., *The Imperial Presidency* (Boston: Houghton Mifflin, 1973); George E. Reedy, *The Twilight of the Presidency* (New York: Mentor, 1971); James David Barber, "The Nixon Brush with Tyranny," *Political Science Quarterly* 92 (Winter 1977–78): 581–605.

[3]Marc Bloch, *Les rois thaumaturges* (1924; repr. Paris: Colin, 1961).

[4]Fritz Hartung, *Enlightened Despotism* (London: Historical Association, 1957)—a phenomenon he prefers to call "enlightened absolutism." Peter Gay, however, is critical of all such labels: *see* his *The Enlightenment: An Interpretation*, vol. 2, *The Science of Freedom* (London: Weidenfeld & Nicolson, 1970), 682–89.

[5]E. Neville Williams, ed., *The Eighteenth-Century Constitution, 1688–1815* (Cambridge: University Press, 1960), 10–17; Locke, *Second Treatise*, chap. 14, para. 159, in Peter Laslett, ed., *John Locke: Two Treatises of Government*, rev. ed. (New York: Mentor, 1965), 392. Laslett believes that Locke wrote this section as early as 1679. For a good brief analysis, *see* Richard Pares, *Limited Monarchy in Great Britain in the Eighteenth Century* (London: Historical Association, 1957).

[6]G. H. Guttridge, *English Whiggism and the American Revolution* (Berkeley and Los Angeles: Univ. of California Press, 1942, repr. 1963), 17; J. R. Pole, *Political Representation in England and the Origins of the American Republic* (New York: Macmillan Co., 1966), 435.

[7]Colonial familiarity with Blackstone is demonstrated in H. Trevor Colbourn, *The Lamp of Experience: Whig History and the Intellectual Origins of the American Revolution* (Chapel Hill: Univ. of North Carolina Press, 1965). Blackstone's *Commentaries on the Laws of England* were first published in London (4 vols., 1765–69), though delivered as lectures at Oxford in 1758. This quotation is from Williams, *Eighteenth-Century Constitution,* 74–75.

[8]John Wise, *A Vindication of the Government of New England Churches,* in Edmund S. Morgan, ed., *Puritan Political Ideas, 1588–1794* (Indianapolis: Bobbs-Merrill, 1965), 266–67.

[9]Clinton Rossiter, *Seedtime of the Republic: The Origin of the American Tradition of Political Liberty* (New York: Harcourt, Brace, 1953), 142–43. On Tennent and Davies *see* Winthrop D. Jordan, "Familial Politics: Thomas Paine and the Killing of the King, 1776," *Journal of American History* 60 (September 1973): 300–301; and Alan E. Heimert, *Religion and the American Mind, from the Great Awakening to the Revolution* (Cambridge, Mass.: Harvard University Press, 1966), 304.

[10]Otis quotation is from his *Rights of the British Colonies Asserted and Proved,* cited in Edwin G. Burrows and Michael Wallace, "The American Revolution: The Ideology and Psychology of National Liberation," *Perspectives in American History* 6 (1972): 191; Richard L. Bushman, *King and People in Provincial Massachusetts* (Chapel Hill: Univ. of North Carolina Press, 1985), 4–5, 248–52; Jack P. Greene on the "desacralization" necessary for Americans to reject their tie to the British monarchy, in "Paine, America, and the 'Modernization' of Political Consciousness," *Political Science Quarterly* 93 (Spring 1978): 80–83, as well as some of his other important essays.

[11]Max Beloff, *The Age of Absolutism, 1660–1815* (New York: Harper Torchbooks, 1962), 148–51. The complexities of the Polish scene are recounted in W. F. Reddaway et al., eds., *The Cambridge History of Poland, 1697–1935* (Cambridge: University Press, 1941). Vol. 1 of Edward Gibbon's *Decline and Fall of the Roman Empire,* published in the fateful year 1776, has a brisk defense (chap. 7) of "hereditary monarchy." [*GBWW,* Vol. 40, pp. 68b–79d.] Conceding that at first sight the notion seems absurd, he insists that "the acknowledged right extinguishes the hopes of faction, and the conscious security disarms the cruelty of the monarch. To the firm establishment of this idea, we owe the peaceful succession, and mild administration, of European monarchies. To the defect of it, we must attribute the frequent civil wars, through which an Asiatic despot is obliged to cut his way to the throne of his fathers." Imperial Rome in its decline was even worse: "The right to the throne, which none could claim from birth, every one assumed from merit."

[12]Willi Paul Adams, "Republicanism in Political Rhetoric before 1776," *Political Science Quarterly* 85 (September 1970): 417.

[13]A typical Shakespeare pronouncement is voiced by Portia in *The Merchant of Venice* (4.1), for whom the quality of mercy

> is above this sceptr'd sway;
> It is enthroned in the hearts of kings,
> It is an attribute to God himself;

The conception of a Patriot King, eloquently expressed by the Tory radical Viscount Bolingbroke, is nicely related to American colonial opinion, and American ambivalences as to monarchy, in William D. Liddle, "'A Patriot King, or None': Lord Bolingbroke and the American Renunciation of George III," *Journal of American History* 65 (March 1979): 951–70. Montesquieu is available in many editions [including *GBWW,* Vol. 38]; and *see* Paul M. Spurlin, *Montesquieu in America, 1760–1801* (Baton Rouge: Louisiana State University Press, 1940), and Thomas L. Pangle, *Montesquieu's Philosophy of Liberalism* (Chicago: University Press, 1973).

[14]On Burgh, *see* Adams, "Republicanism in Political Rhetoric," 403–4, and for a full discussion, Oscar and Mary Handlin, "James Burgh and American Revolutionary Theory," *Massachusetts Historical Society Proceedings* 73 (1961).

[15]Cecelia M. Kenyon, "Republicanism and Radicalism in the American Revolution: An Old Fashioned Interpretation," *William and Mary Quarterly,* 3rd ser., 19 (1962): 165.

[16]Quoted in Merrill Jensen, "Historians and the Nature of the American Revolution," in Ray A. Billington, ed., *The Reinterpretation of Early American History: Essays in Honor of John Edwin Pomfret* (New York: Norton, 1968), 115.

[17]Arthur L. Cross, *The American Episcopate and the American Colonies* (Harvard: 1902; repr. Hamden, Conn.: Archon Books, 1964), 106–8, 120; Carl Bridenbaugh, *Mitre and Sceptre: Transatlantic Faiths, Ideas, Personalities, and Politics, 1689–1775* (New York: Oxford University Press, 1962), 338.

[18]Willi Paul Adams, "Republicanism in Political Rhetoric," 421. Adams also cites J. R. Pole, *The Seventeenth Century: The Sources of Legislative Power* (Charlottesville: Univ. of Virginia Press, 1969), 69: "The American colonists developed the characteristics of what would later be known as a republican form of government many years before they were to claim to be republican in principle."

[19]Bernard Bailyn, *The Origins of American Politics* (New York: Knopf, 1970), 89.

[20]John G. Murrin, "The Great Inversion, or Court versus Country: A Comparison of the Revolution Settlements in England (1688–1721) and America (1776–1816)," in J. G. A. Pocock, ed., *Three British Revolutions: 1641, 1688, 1776* (Princeton: Princeton University Press, 1980). Core-periphery ideas were formulated by the sociologist Edward Shils, developed by Pocock, in "British History: A Plea for a New Subject," *Journal of Modern History* 47 (December 1975): 601–21, and have been applied by Bernard Bailyn, for example in his *The Peopling of North America: An Introduction* (New York: Knopf, 1986). The inference that American independence was, so to speak, in the nature of things, may fairly be drawn from the work of a wide variety of present-day historians of the American Revolution, no matter what their disagreements on specific factors. It is also an underlying theme in most interpretations of *pre*-Revolutionary America, e.g., Alan Rogers, *Empire and Liberty: American Resistance to British Authority, 1755–1763* (Berkeley and Los Angeles: Univ. of California Press, 1974).

[21]*See* Bernard Bailyn, *The Ideological Origins of the American Revolution* (Cambridge, Mass.: Belknap Press of Harvard University Press, 1967); Caroline Robbins, *The Eighteenth-Century Commonwealthman* (Harvard, 1959); Richard Buel, Jr., "Democracy and the American Revolution: A Frame of Reference," *William and Mary Quarterly,* 3rd ser., 21 (1964): 165–90; Heimert, *Religion and the American Mind;* Edmund S. Morgan, "The Puritan Ethic and the American Revolution," *William and Mary Quarterly* 24 (1967): 3–43; J. G. A. Pocock, *The Machiavellian Moment: Florentine Political Thought and the Atlantic Republican Tradition* (Princeton: Princeton University Press, 1975), 506ff.; Robert E. Shalhope, "Toward a Republican Synthesis: The Emergence of an Understanding of Republicanism in American Historiography," *William and Mary Quarterly,* 3rd ser., 29 (January 1972): 49–80; and some of the contributions to Jack P. Greene and J. R. Pole, eds., *Colonial British America: Essays in the New History of the Early Modern Era* (Baltimore: Johns Hopkins University Press, 1984), and in *American Quarterly* 37 (Fall 1985): special issue ed. by Joyce Appleby, "Republicanism in the History and Historiography of the United States."

[22]Mayhew's *Discourse concerning Unlimited Submission and Non-Resistance to the Higher Powers* is reprinted in Morgan, ed., *Puritan Political Ideas,* 304–30; and *see* Bridenbaugh, *Mitre and Sceptre,* 99–103. Otis's *The Rights of the British Colonists Asserted and Proved* (1764), and the pamphlets by Hicks and Bland, are in Merrill Jensen, ed., *Tracts of the American Revolution, 1763–1776* (Indianapolis: Bobbs-Merrill, 1967), 21, 37, 122, 182.

[23]Quoted in Richard Koebner, *Empire* (Cambridge: University Press, 1961), 133.

[24]Cited in Gordon S. Wood, *The Creation of the American Republic, 1776–1787* (Chapel Hill: Univ. of North Carolina Press, 1969), p. 92.

[25]Quotations from "Common Sense" in Philip S. Foner, ed., *The Life and Major Writings of Thomas Paine,* 2 vols. (Secaucus, N.J.: Citadel Press, 1974), vol. 1, 9–12. In the later *Age of Reason* (part 2, 1795; *see* Foner, vol. 1, 517ff.), Paine as a deist is much more skeptical of scriptural evidence: "It has often been said, that anything may be proved from the Bible. . . ." Ramsay's *History* is excerpted in Morton and Penn Borden, eds., *The American Tory* (Englewood Cliffs, N.J.: Prentice-Hall, 1972), 103–4.

[26]*See* Pauline Maier, *From Resistance to Revolution: Colonial Radicals and the Development of American Opposition to Britain, 1765–1776* (New York: Knopf, 1972), especially 198–227 and 255–70, and the same author's "Beginnings of American Republicanism, 1765–1776," in *The Development of a Revolutionary Mentality* (Washington: Library of Congress,

1972), from which these references are drawn. On Calvinist imagery *see* Heimert, *Religion and the American Mind,* 408–11, and the detailed discussion in Nathan O. Hatch, *The Sacred Cause of Liberty: Republican Thought and the Millennium in Revolutionary New England* (New Haven: Yale University Press, 1977), 21–22 and 51ff.

[27]There are many available texts of "Common Sense." The fullest current collection is the two-volume set edited by Philip S. Foner, vol. 2 of which contains some of the essays and verse Paine wrote in Philadelphia before "Common Sense." Harry Hayden Clark, ed., *Thomas Paine: Representative Selections* (New York: Hill & Wang, 1961) is a useful compilation. On the impact of "Common Sense" *see* Bailyn, *Ideological Origins of the American Revolution,* 258–91, and his essay in *Fundamental Testaments of the American Revolution* (Washington: Library of Congress, 1973); Jordan, "Familial Politics," 294–308; Greene, "Paine, America, and the 'Modernization' of Political Consciousness," 80–83; Eric Foner, "Tom Paine's Republic: Radical Ideology and Social Change," in Alfred F. Young, ed., *The American Revolution: Explorations in the History of American Radicalism* (DeKalb: Northern Illinois Univ. Press, 1976), esp. 198–201, and the chapter on "Common Sense" in Eric Foner's *Tom Paine and Revolutionary America* (New York: Oxford University Press, 1976).

[28]To John Ross of Philadelphia, May 14, 1768, in William B. Willcox, ed., *The Papers of Benjamin Franklin* (New Haven: Yale University Press, 1959–   ), vol. 15, 129.

[29]Jack P. Greene, in *The Development of a Revolutionary Mentality,* and his essay in Stephen G. Kurtz and James H. Hutson, eds., *Essays on the American Revolution* (Chapel Hill: Univ. of North Carolina Press, 1973); Roy Sherwood, *The Court of Oliver Cromwell* (London: Croom Helm, 1978).

[30]Text of Articles of Confederation in H. S. Commager, ed., *Documents of American History,* 4th ed. (New York: Appleton-Century-Crofts, 1948), 111–16; Merrill Jensen, "The Articles of Confederation," in *Fundamental Testaments of the American Revolution* (Washington: Library of Congress, 1973), 49–80.

[31]*See* Marcus Cunliffe, *American Presidents and the Presidency,* 2nd ed. (New York: McGraw-Hill, 1976), 21–22; Jackson Turner Main, *The Sovereign States, 1775–1783* (New York: New Viewpoints, 1973), 190–91.

[32]Franklin and Freneau references: *see* Marcus Cunliffe, "The Two Georges: The President and the King," *American Studies International* 24, no. 2 (October 1986): 53–54, 62. On the Cincinnati, James T. Flexner, *George Washington in the American Revolution, 1775–1783* (Boston: Little, Brown, 1968), 513–14, and Wood, *The Creation of the American Republic,* 399–400. Washington's letter, to Jean de Heintz, Jan. 21, 1784, is in the 39-vol. set *Writings of George Washington,* ed. John C. Fitzpatrick (Washington: Government Printing Office, 1931–44), vol. 27, 310.

[33]Washington to John Jay, Aug. 1, 1786, in Fitzpatrick, ed., *Writings,* vol. 28, 503.

[34]Material by Madison and other delegates is assembled in Max Farrand, ed., *The Records of the Federal Convention,* rev. ed., 4 vols. (New Haven: Yale University Press, 1937); and *see* Marcus Cunliffe, "Elections of 1789 and 1792," in Arthur M. Schlesinger, Jr., ed., *History of American Presidential Elections, 1789–1968,* 4 vols. (New York: Chelsea House, 1971), vol. 1, 3–12.

[35]Farrand, ed., *Records,* vol. 1, 18–114. Madison apologia (in letter to Jefferson) cited in Cunliffe, "Elections of 1789 and 1792," vol. 1, 3.

[36]Max Farrand, *The Framing of the Constitution of the United States* (New Haven: Yale University Press, 1913), 128–29; Willi Paul Adams, *The First American Constitutions: Republican Ideology and the Making of the State Constitutions in the Revolutionary Era* (Chapel Hill: Univ. of North Carolina Press, 1980), 290–91; Charles C. Thach, Jr., *The Creation of the Presidency: A Study in Constitutional History, 1775–1789* (1923; repr. Baltimore: Johns Hopkins University Press, 1969), 176.

[37]Butler comment, in letter to Weedon Butler, May 5, 1788, reproduced in Farrand, ed., *Records,* vol. 3, 302. Other contemporaries made the same point about trust in Washington. Several, including people suspicious of a strengthened national government, are cited in Jackson Turner Main, *The Antifederalists: Critics of the Constitution* (Chapel Hill: Univ. of North Carolina Press, 1961), 253–54. Thus, the Hartford *Conn. Courant* for Feb. 4, 1788, published a purported extract from a private letter: "Should the new Constitution be adopted, General Washington will unquestionably be the President, and Governor Hancock [of Massachusetts] Vice-President of the Union. With these great

men at the head of government, all Europe will again acknowledge the importance of America" (Main, 254n.).

[38]There are many editions of the meditations of "Publius." Among the best is the text painstakingly collated by Jacob E. Cooke, ed., *The Federalist* (Middletown, Conn.: Wesleyan University Press, 1961). It forms the basis, for instance, of the paperback *Federalist Papers,* edited by Garry Wills (New York: Bantam, 1982). Wills's commentary upon *The Federalist* is entitled *Explaining America* (New York: Doubleday, 1981). Other discussions include Douglass Adair, *Fame and the Founding Fathers* (New York: Norton, 1974); David F. Epstein, *The Political Theory of the Federalist* (Chicago: Univ. of Chicago Press, 1984); and Albert Furtwangler, *The Authority of Publius: A Reading of the Federalist Papers* (Ithaca, N.Y.: Cornell University Press, 1984).

[39]Madison's idea of a large republic was adapted, with important modifications, from the Scottish philosopher David Hume: *see* Adair and Epstein, cited in note 38, and also Gerald Stourzh, *Alexander Hamilton and the Idea of Republican Government* (Stanford, Calif.: Stanford University Press, 1970). That Madison had been mulling the notion in advance of the Philadelphia convention is clear from his April 1787 essay, "Vices of the Political System of the United States," reprinted in Marvin Meyers, ed., *The Mind of the Founder: Sources of the Political Thought of James Madison* (Indianapolis: Bobbs-Merrill, 1973), 93: "It may be inferred that the inconveniences of popular States, contrary to the prevailing Theory, are in proportion not to the extent, but to the narrowness of their limits."

[40]There is a recent scholarly edition of *Letters from the Federal Farmer to the Republican* by Walter H. Bennett (Montgomery: Univ. of Alabama Press, 1978). Cecelia M. Kenyon has put together an excellent collection, *The Antifederalists* (Indianapolis: Bobbs-Merrill, 1966), drawing upon such important older sources as Jonathan Elliot's *Debates in the Several State Conventions on the Adoption of the Federal Constitution,* 2nd ed., 5 vols. (Philadelphia: Lippincott, 1896). Some of the quotations that follow are taken from Kenyon.

[41]Kenyon, *Antifederalists,* 302–22; Morton Borden, ed., *The Antifederalist Papers* (East Lansing: Michigan State University Press, 1965), 197–99, 212–13; E. W. Spaulding, *His Excellency George Clinton* (New York: Macmillan Co., 1938), 175–83; and (on Clinton and the authorship of "Cato") Linda De Pauw, *The Eleventh Pillar: New York State and the Constitution* (Ithaca, N.Y.: Cornell University Press, 1966), 283–92. *See also* Herbert J. Storing, ed., *The Complete Anti-Federalist,* 7 vols. (Chicago: University of Chicago Press, 1981), a vast compendium, conveniently summarized in vol. 1, *What the Anti-Federalists Were For.* Jefferson's comments to Madison on the new Constitution are in a letter dated Dec. 20, 1787 (he had written in similar terms to John Adams, also from Paris, Nov. 13, 1787). These letters are handily available, in a scholarly text, in Merrill D. Peterson, ed., *Thomas Jefferson: Writings* (New York: Library of America, 1984), 912–18.

[42]Pierce Butler to Weedon Butler, May 5, 1788, in Farrand, ed., *Records,* vol. 3, 302; debate in U.S. Senate, Dec. 2, 1803, excerpted from *Annals of Congress,* in Farrand, vol. 3, 404.

[43]Edgar S. Maclay, ed., *The Journal of William Maclay, 1789–1791* (1890; repr., New York: Ungar, 1966), 10–29, 110–17, 351; James H. Hutson, "John Adams' Title Campaign," *New England Quarterly* 41 (March 1968).

[44]*See* Joyce Appleby, "The New Republican Synthesis and the Changing Political Ideas of John Adams," *American Quarterly* 25 (December 1973): 578–95.

[45]Jefferson letter in Peterson, ed., *Jefferson: Writings,* 985–90; Paine "Open Letter" in Clark, ed., *Thomas Paine: Representative Selections,* 387–408; other allusions from Stephen G. Kurtz, *The Presidency of John Adams* (Philadelphia: Univ. of Pennsylvania Press, 1957), 78–80, 86–87.

[46]Jefferson to Mazzei, Monticello, April 24, 1796, in Peterson, ed., *Jefferson: Writings,* 1035–37.

[47]*See* Meyers, ed., *The Mind of the Founder,* 297–313. Lyon reference in Nicholas N. Kittrie and Eldon D. Wedlock, Jr., eds., *The Tree of Liberty: A Documentary History of Rebellion and Political Crime in America* (Baltimore: Johns Hopkins University Press, 1986), 87–88.

[48]Jefferson, letter to Benjamin Rush, Jan. 16, 1811, and *Anas* in Peterson, ed., *Writings,* 665–66, 670–73, 1235–36. On Barlow, *see* Christine M. Lizanich, "'The March of this Government': Joel Barlow's Unwritten History of the United States," *William and Mary Quarterly,* 3rd ser., 33 (April 1976): 315–29. On Mercy Otis Warren, *see* William Raymond Smith, "Mercy Otis Warren's Radical View of the American Revolution," in Lawrence Leder, ed., *The Colonial Legacy,* vol. 2, *Some Eighteenth Century Commentators*

(New York: Harper and Row Torchbooks, 1971), 219–25; Lester H. Cohen, "Mercy Otis Warren: The Politics of Language and the Aesthetics of Self," *American Quarterly* 35 (Winter 1983): 480–98.

[49]Michael J. Heale, *The Presidential Quest: Candidates and Images in American Political Culture, 1787–1852* (London and New York: Longman, 1982), 15–16, 23–31, 196; and *see* Marcus Cunliffe, *The Presidency*, rev. ed. of *American Presidents and the Presidency*, 1968 (Boston: Houghton Mifflin, 1987), chap. 5 on "Suspicion of the Presidency."

[50]*See*, e.g., John R. Howe, Jr., "Republican Thought and the Political Violence of the 1790s," *American Quarterly* 19 (Summer 1967): 145–65; Lance Banning, "Republican Ideology and the Triumph of the Constitution, 1789 to 1793," *William and Mary Quarterly*, 3rd ser., 31 (April 1974): 167–88.

[51]Meyers, ed., *The Mind of the Founder*, 93–98.

[52]Lizanich, "'The March of this Government,'" 320–21; Marcus Cunliffe, "'They Will All Speak English': Some Cultural Consequences of Independence," in Ronald Hoffman and Peter J. Albert, eds., *Peace and the Peacemakers: The Treaty of 1783* (Charlottesville: Univ. of Virginia Press, 1986), 145–46.

[53]Richard Hofstadter, *The Idea of a Party System: The Rise of Legitimate Opposition in the United States, 1780–1840* (Berkeley and Los Angeles: Univ. of California Press, 1969), 84–86; Linda K. Kerber, *Federalists in Dissent: Imagery and Ideology in Jeffersonian America* (Ithaca, N.Y.: Cornell University Press, 1970; repr. 1980), esp. 193–201; Lance Banning, *The Jeffersonian Persuasion: Evolution of a Party Ideology* (Ithaca, N.Y.: Cornell University Press, 1978); Appleby, "New Republican Synthesis"; John R. Howe, Jr., *The Changing Political Thought of John Adams* (Princeton: Princeton University Press, 1966); on Bolingbroke, passim, Ralph Ketcham, *Presidents Above Party: The First American Presidency, 1789–1829* (Chapel Hill: Univ. of North Carolina Press, 1984); on George Washington and gentlemanliness, *see* Robert H. Wiebe, *The Opening of American Society: From the Adoption of the Constitution to the Eve of Disunion* (New York: Knopf, 1984), 40–47.

[54]Heale, *The Presidential Quest*, chap. 1; Cunliffe, "Elections of 1789 and 1792," in Schlesinger, ed., *History of American Presidential Elections*, vol. 1, 3–32. Addressing the impending presidential contest between Adams and Jefferson, a Pennsylvania Republican handbill of October 1796 claimed that *"Thomas Jefferson . . . first framed the sacred political sentence that all men are born equal. John Adams says . . . that some men should be born Kings, and some should be born Nobles. Which of these . . . will you have for your President? . . . Adams has Sons who might aim to succeed their father; Jefferson like Washington has no Son."* Cited in Noble E. Cunningham, Jr., *The Jeffersonian Republicans* (Chapel Hill: Univ. of North Carolina Press, 1957), 99.

[55]John Bernard, *Retrospections of America, 1797–1811* (New York: Harper & Brothers, 1887), 240–42.

[56]Frederick Grimke, *The Nature and Tendency of Free Institutions* (1848), John William Ward, ed. (Cambridge, Mass.: Belknap Press of Harvard University Press, 1968), 259–65, 570–71.

[57]"Cato" quoted in Kenyon, ed., *Antifederalists*, 304–5; Thomas Moore, *Complete Poetical Works* (New York: Crowell, 1895), 142–47; James Sterling Young, *The Washington Community, 1800–1828* (New York: Harcourt, Brace, 1966), 41.

[58]Joel Barlow, *Advice to the Privileged Orders in the Several States of Europe* (1792; repr., Ithaca, N.Y.: Cornell University Press, 1956), 16; Richard E. Welch, Jr., *Theodore Sedgwick, Federalist: A Political Portrait* (Middletown, Conn.: Wesleyan University Press, 1965), 58n.; Washington, letter to John Armstrong, April 25, 1788, in Fitzpatrick, ed., *Writings*, vol. 29, 464–65.

[59]Welch, *Sedgwick*, 103n.; W. Bernhard, *Fisher Ames* (Chapel Hill: Univ. of North Carolina Press, 1965), 209–10; and (on Madison) Denis T. Lynch, *An Epoch and a Man* (New York: Liveright, 1929), 114.

[60]Gouverneur Morris, as reported by Madison, in Farrand, ed., *Records*, vol. 2, 52; reference to Taylor of Caroline in Banning, *The Jeffersonian Persuasion*, 199–200; information on presidential correspondence in Benjamin Harrison, *The Constitution and Administration of the United States of America* (London: David Nutt, 1897), 165. For a general analysis of plebiscitarian tendencies, brought down to the present day, *see* Theodore J. Lowi, *The Personal President: Power Invested, Promise Unfulfilled* (Ithaca, N.Y.: Cornell University Press, 1985); and *see* Richard Rose and Dennis Kavanagh, "The Monarchy in Contemporary Political Culture," *Comparative Politics* (July 1976): 548–76.

READING LIST

(*Note:* this list is a selection of key articles and books. For additional and more detailed information, consult the footnotes. The list does however supplement the footnotes by adding a few titles of newly announced material, not available when the article was written.)

ADAMS, WILLI PAUL. "Republicanism in Political Rhetoric before 1776." *Political Science Quarterly* 85 (1970): 397–421.
———. *The First American Constitutions: Republican Ideology and the Making of the State Constitutions in the Revolutionary Era*. Chapel Hill: Univ. of North Carolina Press, 1980.
ARENDT, HANNAH. *On Revolution*. London: Faber and Faber, 1963.
BAILYN, BERNARD. *The Ideological Origins of the American Revolution*. Cambridge, Mass.: Belknap Press of Harvard University Press, 1967.
BANNER, JAMES M. *To the Hartford Convention: The Federalists and the Origins of Party Politics in Massachusetts, 1789–1815*. New York: Knopf, 1970.
BANNING, LANCE. "Republican Ideology and the Triumph of the Constitution, 1789 to 1793." *William and Mary Quarterly*, 3rd ser., 31 (April 1974): 167–88.
———. *The Jeffersonian Persuasion: Evolution of a Party Ideology*. Ithaca, N.Y.: Cornell University Press, 1978.
BERNSTEIN, RICHARD B., with RICE, KYM S. *Are We To Be a Nation? The Making of the Constitution*. Cambridge, Mass.: Harvard University Press, 1987.
CUNLIFFE, MARCUS. *The Presidency*. (1968) Rev. ed. Boston: Houghton Mifflin, 1987.
———. "The Two Georges: The President and the King." *American Studies International* 24, no. 2 (October 1986): 53–73.
The Development of a Revolutionary Mentality. Washington: Library of Congress Bicentennial Symposium, 1972.
DUNBAR, LOUISE. *A Study of "Monarchical" Tendencies in the United States from 1776 to 1801*. 1922. Reprint. New York and London: Johnson Reprint, 1970.
DUTCHER, GEORGE M. "The Rise of Republican Government in the United States." *Political Science Quarterly* 55 (1940): 199–216.
FARRAND, MAX, ed. *The Records of the Federal Convention*. 4 vols. New Haven: Yale University Press, 1911. Rev. ed. 1937. Reprint. in 3 vols., 1987, with new 4th supplementary vol., ed. James H. Hutson.
FLIEGELMAN, JAY. *Prodigals and Pilgrims: The American Revolution Against Patriarchal Authority, 1750–1800*. New York and Cambridge: Cambridge University Press, 1982.
FONER, ERIC. "Tom Paine's Republic: Radical Ideology and Social Change." In Alfred E. Young, ed., *The American Revolution: Explorations in the History of American Radicalism*, 188–232. DeKalb: Northern Illinois University Press, 1976.
———. *Tom Paine and Revolutionary America*. New York: Oxford University Press, 1976.
Fundamental Testaments of the American Revolution. Washington: Library of Congress Bicentennial Symposium, 1973.
HEALE, MICHAEL J. *The Presidential Quest: Candidates and Images in American Political Culture, 1787–1852*. London and New York: Longman, 1982.
HOWE, JOHN R., JR. "Republican Thought and the Political Violence of the 1790s." *American Quarterly* 19 (August 1967): 145–65.
———. *The Changing Political Thought of John Adams*. Princeton: Princeton University Press, 1966.
HUTSON, JAMES H. "John Adams' Title Campaign." *New England Quarterly* 41 (March 1968): 30–39.
JENSEN, MERRILL, ed. *Tracts of the American Revolution, 1763–1776*. Indianapolis: Bobbs-Merrill, 1967; includes Paine's *Common Sense*, and also the reply, *Plain Truth*, by James Chalmers.
JORDAN, WINTHROP D. "Familial Politics: Thomas Paine and the Killing of the King, 1776." *Journal of American History* 60 (September 1973): 294–308.
KENYON, CECELIA M., ed. *The Antifederalists*. Indianapolis: Bobbs-Merrill, 1966.
KERBER, LINDA K. *Federalists in Dissent: Imagery and Ideology in Jeffersonian America*. Ithaca, N.Y.: Cornell University Press, 1970. Reprint. 1980.

KETCHAM, RALPH. *Presidents Above Party: The First American Presidency, 1789–1829.* Chapel Hill: Univ. of North Carolina Press, 1984.

LIDDLE, WILLIAM D. "'A Patriot King, or None,': Lord Bolingbroke and the American Renunciation of George III." *Journal of American History* 65 (March 1979): 951–70.

MAIER, PAULINE. *From Resistance to Revolution: Colonial Radicals and the Development of American Opposition to Britain, 1765–1776.* New York: Knopf, 1972.

MALSBERGER, JOHN W. "The Political Thought of Fisher Ames." *Journal of the Early Republic* 2 (Spring 1982): 1–20.

MEYERS, MARVIN, ed. *The Mind of the Founder: Sources of the Political Thought of James Madison.* Indianapolis: Bobbs-Merrill, 1973.

POCOCK, J. G. A. *The Machiavellian Moment: Florentine Political Thought and the Atlantic Republican Tradition.* Princeton: Princeton University Press, 1975.

———, ed. *Three British Revolutions: 1641, 1688, 1766.* Princeton: Princeton University Press, 1980.

POLE, J. R. *Political Representation in England and the Origins of the American Republic.* New York: Macmillan Co., 1966.

———, ed. *The American Constitution: For and Against.* New York: Hill and Wang, 1987.

ROBINSON, DONALD L. *"To the Best of My Ability": The President and the Constitution.* New York: Norton, 1987.

ROSSITER, CLINTON. *Seedtime of the Republic: The Origin of the American Tradition of Political Liberty.* New York: Harcourt, Brace, 1953.

SHALHOPE, ROBERT E. "Toward a Republican Synthesis: The Emergence of an Understanding of Republicanism in American Historiography." *William and Mary Quarterly,* 3rd ser., 29 (January 1972): 49–80.

SMELSER, MARSHALL. "The Jacobin Phrenzy: The Menace of Monarchy, Plutocracy, and Anglophilia, 1789–1798." *Review of Politics* 21 (1959): 239–58.

SMYLIE, JAMES H. "The President as Republican Prophet and King: Clerical Reflections on the Death of Washington." *Journal of Church and State* 18 (1976): 233–52.

STORING, HERBERT J., ed. *The Complete Anti-Federalist.* 7 vols. Chicago: Univ. of Chicago Press, 1981. Vol. 1, *What the Anti-Federalists Were For,* summarizes the source material in the other volumes; vol. 7 is an index.

STOURZH, GERALD. *Alexander Hamilton and the Idea of Republican Government.* Stanford, Calif.: Stanford University Press, 1970.

THACH, CHARLES C., JR. *The Creation of the Presidency, 1775–1789: A Study in Constitutional History.* 1923. Reprint. Baltimore and London: Johns Hopkins University Press, 1969.

UPHAUS, JUNE E. "The Attitude of the Colonists toward the King and Royal Power during the Decade of Controversy." Master's thesis, Indiana University, 1960.

WHARTON, LESLIE. *Polity and the Public Good: Conflicting Theories of Republican Government in the New Nation.* Ann Arbor, Mich.: University Microfilms International, 1980.

WOOD, GORDON S. *The Creation of the American Republic, 1776–1787.* Chapel Hill: Univ. of North Carolina Press, 1969.

YAZAWA, MELVIN. *From Colonies to Commonwealth: Familial Ideology and the Beginnings of the American Republic.* Baltimore and London: Johns Hopkins University Press, 1985.

The Great Books of the East

Wm. Theodore de Bary

William Theodore de Bary is among the foremost authorities in the United States today on Eastern cultures, with extensive writings on Chinese thought, especially Neo-Confucianism. He has been associated throughout a distinguished career with Columbia University, New York City, where he was educated, and where at various times he has been Executive Vice President for Academic Affairs and Provost (1971–78), Chairman of the University Senate's Executive Committee (1969–71), Carpentier Professor of Oriental Studies (1966–78), Chairman of the Department of East Asian Languages and Cultures (1960–66), and Chairman of the University Committee on Oriental Studies (1953–61). Since 1979 he has been John Mitchell Mason Professor of the University. Among his books are *Neo-Confucian Orthodoxy and the Learning of Mind and Heart* (1981), *The Liberal Tradition in China* (1983), and the soon-to-be-published *East Asian Civilizations: A Dialogue in Five Stages.*

    Barbara Stoler Miller ("Kālidāsa's *Śakuntalā*"), who studied at Columbia and at the University of Pennsylvania, from which she received a doctorate in Oriental Studies, Indic Division, has taught for many years at Barnard College, where she is Professor of Oriental Studies, and where she has at various times (including the present) served as chairman of her department. She has done extensive research in India, notably on Sanskrit studies, and has translated and edited many works from that language, among them *Śakuntalā* in this year's *The Great Ideas Today.*

    Robert A. F. Thurman, who writes here on "*The Teaching of Vimalakīrti,*" is Professor of Religion at Amherst College. He is noted for his interest in Buddhism, having spent three years in Buddhist monasteries and having helped to found the American Institute for Buddhist Studies, of which he has been president since 1976. Educated at Harvard, where he took a degree in Sanskrit and Indian studies, he is the author of *Holy Teaching of Vimalakirti* (1977), among other books and numerous lengthy articles.

Irene Bloom ("A Note on the *Mencius*") has degrees from the Department of East Asian Languages and Cultures at Columbia and has held various teaching posts there and at Barnard College, where at present she is Adjunct Assistant Professor of Oriental Studies. Her field, too, is that of Chinese thought. Her most recent book, *Knowledge Painfully Acquired* (1986), is a study in 16th-century thought.

Burton Watson ("T'ang Poetry: A Return to Basics") has studied both at Columbia and at Kyoto University in Japan. He has taught Chinese and Japanese both in this country and in Japan, where he now lives and works as a translator. Among his books are *Early Chinese Literature, Chinese Lyricism,* and *From the Country of Eight Islands: An Anthology of Japanese Poetry* (with Hiroaki Sato).

C. T. Hsia ("*A Dream of Red Mansions*") took degrees in English literature from Yale before going on to become Professor of Chinese, first at the University of Pittsburgh and, since 1969, at Columbia, where he teaches in the Department of East Asian Languages and Cultures. He is the author of a history of modern Chinese fiction and also of *The Classic Chinese Novel: A Critical Introduction* (1980), besides numerous publications in Chinese.

Edward Seidensticker ("*The Tale of Genji*") is a specialist in Japanese literature, particularly the modern novel, who taught at Sophia University (Tokyo), at Stanford, at Michigan, and at Columbia before he retired in 1986 to live in Honolulu. He has translated many works, among them *The Tale of Genji* (1976), and has also written books of his own, including *Genji Days* (1977) and *This Country, Japan* (1979).

Donald Keene ("*Tsurezure-gusa*") is one of the world's leading authorities on Japanese language and literature, a field in which he has written widely. Most of his career has been spent at Columbia, where he is now Shincho Professor of Japanese Literature, and where the Donald Keene Center of Japanese Culture has been named in his honor. He also spends part of each year in Japan. Elected in 1986 to the American Academy and Institute of Arts and Letters, he is the author of several works about Japanese literature, both modern and of earlier times, and is the editor as well of two much-used anthologies of Japanese literature in English. He has also published numerous articles in the Japanese language.

In the interests of uniformity, the spellings of Eastern names and terms in the following essays have been made to agree with the usage of the *Encyclopædia Britannica,* which does not always correspond to present scholarly usage among the contributors.

The "Great Books" may not be one of the "Great Ideas" listed within the front cover of this volume, but the idea of books so challenging to the mind, so close to the human heart, and of such impressive depth or stature as to command the attention of generation after generation is certainly not confined to the Western world. Each of the major Asian civilizations has had its canonical texts and literary classics. Significant differences appear, however, in the way the classic canon is defined—by whom, for what audience, for what purposes, and in what form.

To Muḥammad, "the people of the book" was an important concept for locating the spiritual roots of Islām in an earlier prophetic tradition, and for affirming a common religious ground in the Bible among Jews, Christians, and Muslims.[1] Yet it is by no means clear that the books of the Old Testament, or such of the New as he in any way recognized, were thought to be essential reading for his own followers, let alone for the other "people of the book." The same could be said of other writings in the Western tradition. Anyone who today reads the great Muslim philosophers and theologians would know that they, no less than Saint Augustine and Saint Thomas, engaged in significant dialogue with the Greek philosophers and were long ago party to the "Great Conversation" that Mark Van Doren, Lyman Bryson, and Jacques Barzun used to talk about at Columbia and on CBS radio. While the contributions of Islāmic philosophers were rarely acknowledged in the discussions Bryson held on CBS's Sunday morning "Invitation to Learning," a recently published series on Western Spirituality recognizes that they do indeed belong in this company.[2] But it is doubtful that, in the Muslim world itself, the writings of Plato and Aristotle would have been thought essential reading for any but the scholarly few who studied al-Ghazālī, Avicenna, Averroës, or Ibn Khaldūn. As much could be said of other Eastern cultures. Hindus had their own sacred scriptures, some lines of which would be on the lips of pious Indians, but for the most part these texts were considered the sacred preserve of learned pundits, not to be read—much less discussed—by the faithful. Among the latter, oral texts had far more currency than written ones did. In China too there were the classics of the Confucian tradition, again the property principally of a learned elite, though Taoist works like the *Lao-tzu* and *Chuang-tzu* also figured in cultivated discourse among the literati and thus in a sense qualified as great books, even if not as canonical literature.

In Japan, eminent Buddhist monks like Saichō and Kūkai in the ninth century advanced the idea that, for those who would occupy positions of social as well as clerical importance, a proper training should include the reading of at least some Confucian classics, together with the major scriptures of Mahāyāna Buddhism. So assiduously cultivated in Heian Japan was this classical study that even court ladies like Murasaki Shikibu and Sei Shōnagon, great writers in the vernacular Japanese literature of the eleventh century, had themselves read the major Confucian classics, along with the monumental Chinese histories and leading T'ang poets, and would have disdained as uncouth and illiterate anyone who had not done the same. Important later writers in Japan, as diverse as the monk-essayist Kenkō in the fourteenth century, the teacher of military science Yamaga Sokō in the seventeenth century, and the great nativist scholar Motoori Norinaga in the eighteenth century, all had read the classic Confucian and Taoist texts as part of their mixed cultural inheritance, whether or not they identified themselves with either of the traditions from which these works derived. Thus the latter were read by non-Chinese too as great books commanding attention, even when not compelling assent.

In this respect the Japanese (along with the Koreans and Vietnamese, who shared the same Confucian, Taoist, and Buddhist literature) may have been more accustomed to multicultural learning than some other Asian peoples who rarely recognized as classics the major works of traditions other than their own. As a general rule, certainly, the traditions transmitting these texts were apt to be socially circumscribed and more or less culture-bound within the limits of a common "classical" literature. As religions, their appeal might be more universal, but in the transmission of texts they stood out as high classical traditions— "great traditions" for the few rather than little traditions shared in by the many. Their "great books" were most often scriptures preserved and read by particular religious communities or classics cherished by the bearers of high culture. The reason for this was in the main that most classics and scriptures were preserved in difficult classical or sacred languages. Thus even popular works in the vernacular tended in time to become inaccessible, because spoken tongues, more subject to change (i.e., less fixed and disciplined than classical languages), tend toward their own kind of obsolescence. The recognized "classics" of popular fiction, too, as well as philosophical and religious dialogues in the vernacular (such as Zen dialogues or Neo-Confucian "recorded conversations"), could be so studded with colloquialisms as to present difficulties for readers of a later age.

One can hardly exaggerate the persistence and pervasiveness of this problem in communication. Modern writers sometimes assume that the restricted readership of classical literature in Asian societies is mainly attributable to an exclusivity or possessiveness on the part of the custodians of the high tradition. Their monopoly of learning, it is supposed, gave them a vested interest in preserving sacred knowledge as something precious and recondite, out of the ordinary man's reach. The Confucian literati, one is told, both jealously guarded the purity and reveled in the complexity of a written language the masses were not supposed to touch. Buddhist monks of Heian Japan, historians often say or imply, deliberately mystified religious learning so as to insure their own dominance over credulous masses.

Such imputations are not without some basis, as in the case of those Confucian literati in fifteenth-century Korea who resisted the development and use of a new alphabet for their native language because it would compete for attention with Chinese language and literature—an argument not unmixed with the concern of some to maintain their own privileged position as dispensers of the Chinese classical tradition.

Yet there are contrary cases. The leading Japanese monk Kūkai, himself a spokesman for the so-called Esoteric School of Buddhism, advocated public schooling in the ninth century, and Chu Hsi, the great Neo-Confucian philosopher of the twelfth century, was a strong advocate of universal education through public schools. Chu devoted himself to editing and simplifying the classics with a view to making them more understandable for ordinary persons. Since other leading Neo-Confucians after Chu Hsi took up this cause in their writings, the limited success of their efforts must have been due to factors other than the lack of good intentions. Chief among these were, probably, the perception of peasants in a predominantly agrarian society that learning yielded few economic benefits unless one could convert it into official position or status, and the government's lack of interest in the matter beyond the needs of bureaucratic recruitment. In such circumstances, for those with little leisure to dispose of, the difficulties of mastering the great books in classical languages might not seem worth the costs.

In some ways Chu Hsi, as an educator trying to reach beyond his immediate scholarly audience, was the Mortimer Adler of his time, but he would probably have thought Adler's reading list of *Great Books* too ambitious. His goal was to reach the aspiring youth of every village and hamlet in China, for which he recommended a shorter list: a program based on the Confucian Four Books and his own compact anthology of Sung dynasty thought, the *Reflections on Things at Hand (Chin-ssu Lu)*. Chu's competition in those days, the Ch'an (Zen) masters, were offering enlightenment at no cost in terms of reading, and Zen painters even portrayed sages tearing up the scriptures. Too much book learning was already seen as injurious to the health, and Chu Hsi himself, as well as his Neo-Confucian predecessors, favored careful reading of a few books, as well as reflection over them and discussion with others, instead of a superficial acquaintance with many. Hence he was modest in his initial demands, trying to keep his reading program simple and within people's means and capabilities.

In his efforts along this line, Chu very early reached the Aspen phase of his great-books movement, when snippets and selections would often have to serve in place of whole books if the reading were to be done by other than scholars. Two of his Four Books, in fact, were selected short chapters from the classic *Record of Rituals:* "The Great Learning" and "The Doctrine of the Mean." These he further revised and edited in order to make them more coherent, systematic, and integral texts—shaping them according to what, in his mind, the classic form must have been.

Chu Hsi also had his rough equivalent of Aspen in sylvan retreats such as the historic White Deer Grotto near Mount Lu, at the deep bend in the Yangtze River, where he conducted colloquia on the Confucian classics for his students and other literati of the day. But so concerned was he with the larger educational needs of his society, and with developing a cradle-to-the-grave approach for the individual, that he even directed the compilation of a preparatory text called the *Elementary Learning (Hsiao hsüeh),* as a guide to the training of the young before they took up the Four Books and Five Classics.

For all of these efforts at providing a *Reader's Digest* of the Confucian classics, Chu never attempted to translate his scriptures into a Vulgate. Even the *Elementary Learning* was composed of so many excerpts in classical Chinese that it would serve better as a teacher's manual than as a primer. Followed or accompanied by the Four Books, and then by the Five Classics, it became part of the standard classical curriculum throughout East Asia and had a remarkable diffusion in premodern times, yet always within the severe limits which the classical Chinese language imposed on its adaptability to popular audiences and changing times. In China this system lasted down to 1905, when the pressure to adopt Western scientific learning brought the scrapping of Chu's humanistic core curriculum based on the Chinese classics.

Half a world away and by a curious historical coincidence, at about the same time that Chinese classical learning was being abandoned, American college education was being cut loose from its old moorings in classical studies. At what was sometimes called the new "Acropolis on the Hudson," which Columbia presidents Seth Low and Nicholas Murray Butler were erecting on Morningside Heights in the early decades of this century, the old language requirements in Greek and Latin, along with the reading of the classics in the original, were giving way to a new educational approach. John Erskine, following George Woodberry, championed the idea that all the benefits of a liberal education in the classics need not be lost, even if Greek and Latin were no longer obligatory, provided that undergraduates could read and discuss the classics in translation. This was the germ of Erskine's Honors course, first offered just after World War I, out of which grew the later Great Books movement.

Erskine's original idea, as he explained the Honors course, was nothing very grand:

> The ideas underlying the course were simple. It was thought that any fairly intelligent person could read with profit any book (except, of course, highly specialized science) which had once made its way to fame among general readers. Even without the introductory study which usually precedes our acquaintance with classics in these various fields, any reader, it was thought, can discover, and enjoy the substance which has made such books remembered. It was thought, also, that a weekly discussion of the reading, such an exchange of ideas as might occur in any group which had read an interesting book, would be more illuminating than a lecture. It was thought, also, that the result of such reading and discussion over a period of two years would be a rich mass of literary information, ideas and principles, even emotions.[3]

Erskine was well aware that such a procedure challenged prevalent scholarly conceptions concerning proper methods of serious study. In the same essay quoted above, written as a preface to a reading list for the Colloquium, he argued:

> Many scholars might object to certain implications in such a reading list as this. They might think that if we read, without assistance, Homer and the Greeks, Virgil and the other Romans, Dante and the other men of the Middle Ages, we shall probably get a false idea of each period, and we may even misunderstand the individual book. To a certain extent this is true. Undoubtedly we get a better historical approach to anything that is old if we have the time to study its environment and its associations. But in art it is not the history of a masterpiece which makes it famous so much as qualities of permanent interest. It is precisely those qualities which we recognize first when we take up an old book without prejudice, and read it as intelligently as we can, looking for what seems to concern our times. I personally would go rather far in protest against the exclusively historical approach to literature, or any other art. . . . As a matter of fact, the literature which grows up around a famous book is often composed less because the book needs the aid of interpretation than because it has inspired admiration, and man likes to express his affection. We all write essays about our favorite authors. It is well, however, if the world reads the favorite author, and mercifully forgets the baggage with which our approval has burdened his reputation.[4]

Erskine's claims bespoke his confidence in the intrinsic value of the works themselves and their ability to speak directly to the individual about human life in the broadest terms. An artist and musician himself, as well as a critic, he distinguished this kind of reading from anything that would serve as an introduction to "different fields of knowledge." "It is the critic," he said, "not the artist, who invents distinct fields of knowledge." To which he added that "in life, these fields all overlap. . . . Great books read simply and sensibly are an introduction to the whole of life; it is the completeness of their outlook which makes them great."[5]

In Erskine's day, and for some time thereafter, the term "great books" was not well established at Columbia, and the further idea of "A Hundred Great Books" must have been a later revelation from on high to those who created St. John's College. Erskine himself disavowed any claim to having defined, in his list, any fixed number of such classics. In the direct successor to the Honors course, known in the thirties as "The Colloquium on Important Books," the works read were referred to as classics, important books, or major works, but only occasionally as "great books." Even Mark Van Doren made sparing reference to the term in his *Liberal Education,* published in 1944, and not often enough for it to gain entry in the index to the book.

The terminological issue is not itself important, but a syllabus for the Colloquium prepared in 1934 by J. B. Brebner (representing a stellar staff that included Mortimer Adler, Jacques Barzun, Irwin Edman, Moses Hadas, Richard McKeon, Lionel Trilling, Rexford Guy Tugwell, Mark Van Doren, and Raymond Weaver, among other distinguished scholars and teachers) was entitled "Classics of the Western World." This parochialism had not gone unnoticed. More significant than the word "classics" is the fact that even prior to the establishment of the required Humanities A, its advocates and collaborators were conscious of the geographic limits of the Columbia program at that time. I can testify myself to the feeling among prominent leaders of the College faculty in the late thirties that something needed to be done about expanding the horizons of the general education program, including both the older Contemporary Civilization course and Humanities A, so as to bring Asia into the picture. Perhaps the most significant aspect of this progressive ferment was that it arose among scholars and teachers who had no professional interest in Orientalism.

Indeed, as matters stood at Columbia in those times, classical Orientalism was in serious decline, if not almost defunct. It had no articulate spokesmen among the College faculty, and since its fortunes had been closely tied to biblical studies, Semitic languages, and the old language requirements, it had few vested interests left to defend or assert once the new liberal education had taken over.

The advocates of the new Oriental Studies program were amateur types, liberal-minded gentlemen who took education, and not just their own scholarly research, seriously. Typical of them were Van Doren himself; his colleague Raymond Weaver, an authority on Herman Melville with a deep appreciation also of Japanese literature; Burdette Kinne, an instructor in French with a passion for everything Chinese; Harry J. Carman, a professor of American History and New York State dirt farmer who wanted to see Asian civilizations brought into the Contemporary Civilization program.

When the first Oriental Humanities course was set up in 1947, about as soon after World War II as one could have mounted such a venture, the lead was taken in this experimental course by such scholars as Moses Hadas, the Greek classicist; Herbert Deane, a political scientist specializing in Harold Laski and Saint Augustine; James Gutmann in German philosophy; and Charles Frankel, the philosopher of Western liberalism. Naturally enough, on putting together the reading list for their first "Oriental Colloquium" (as it was initially called) Deane and Hadas consulted specialists on the Columbia faculty more learned than themselves in the several traditions to be included within the scope of the course. From the start, however, the reading and discussion of the Oriental classics were to be guided by the principles of the earlier Honors course, as stated by Erskine above, and not by the kind of textual study which had long dominated the classical Orientalism of the nineteenth and early twentieth centuries.

The course's distinctive character arose in large measure from the fact that it was conceived as part of a liberal education (later to be called by some "general education") and was designed to supplement a core curriculum already set in place for the first two undergraduate years. In this program priority had already been given to the study of Western Civilization and the "classics of the Western World" (as the Erskine/Brebner syllabus put it). This entailed no disadvantage, since students came to the new course as a natural next stage in their general education—already familiar with the ground rules of the reading-discussion method and prepared to take an active part in a discourse well under way. It did mean, however, that the choice of Oriental classics would, in turn, be governed by the same high degree of selectivity as in the Western case and yet further still, by the need to exercise this selectivity in respect to several major Asian traditions at once—indeed all that might be included in the so-called non-Western world. In other words, it demanded a rare combination of both breadth and selectivity, much in contrast to the kind of specialized study traditional Orientalism had favored; it went beyond even what advocates of the Great Books—for all their high standards of selectivity—would have suspected was necessary.

Exercising this selectivity in the multicultural East was far more difficult than it had been within the bounds of the more unified Western tradition. There was an added complication in that, though the "East" had something like "great books," it had nothing that could be called the Great Books of the East. Such a conception would have been a

Western idea, both in seeing the East as one, and in imagining that there had been a common tradition shared by the peoples of this "East." Each of the major Asian traditions tended to see itself as the center of the civilized world and to look inward—spiritually and culturally— toward that center rather than outward on the world or on each other. The famous "Sacred Books of the East," as published at Oxford, was a Western invention. It sprang from the minds of nineteenth-century scholars in Europe as their intellectual horizons reached out with the West's expansion into Asia. "Asia" was itself a mere geographic designation representing no common culture or moral bond among the peoples of that continent until, in modern times, a new unity was found in their common reaction to that same expansionism.

There being no common tradition in Asia to define the Great Books of the East, a reading list had to be constructed synthetically out of largely separate and discrete traditions—a construction made all the more difficult and delicate, in the absence of any Eastern canon, by the risk that the very process of its devising might be contaminated by Western preconceptions. Instead therefore of searching for "Eastern" equivalents of Western classics, we were looking for what each of the several Asian traditions honored themselves as an essential part of their own heritage.

Seemingly the least problematical way of doing this was to identify the scriptures already well known within the distinct ethicoreligious traditions of Islām, Hinduism, Buddhism, Confucianism, Taoism, etc. Similarly one could find recognized classics of the literary and intellectual traditions, though these might or might not run parallel to the religious traditions. This method, proceeding inductively from the testimony of Asians themselves rather than deductively from some Western definition of a classic norm or form, has produced what might appear to be an odd assortment of genres. Great poetry exists in each of the major traditions, though it varies considerably in form. Epics can be found in Iran and India that bear comparison to the *Odyssey, Iliad,* and *Aeneid,* but there is nothing like them in China and Japan. The same is true in reverse of the haiku or Nō drama, classic forms in Japan but found nowhere else. Histories as monumental in their own way as those of Herodotus and Thucydides have been produced in the Islāmic world by Ibn Khaldūn and in China by Ssu-ma Ch'ien but by no one in traditional India or Japan.

Perhaps the greatest diversity, however, is exhibited among the religious scriptures, some of which can barely be regarded as "texts" in any ordinary sense of the term (for instance, although the *Platform Sūtra* of the Sixth Ch'an Patriarch is presented in one sense as authoritative scripture, in another sense it points to an abjuration of all scripture). For the purposes of our reading program, however, all this variety has had to be taken in and, more than that, welcomed, as a healthy challenge to Western conventions of discursive and literary form, if there were to be any real dialogue with the multiform East.

Other problems of selection arise from the choice of four major traditions to represent the "East." The four we have identified—the Islāmic world, India, China, and Japan—betray a lack of geographic and cultural congruence among themselves. The Islāmic world, which covers almost half of Asia and North Africa as well, includes Iran, with its own language, civilization, and indigenous religious traditions (Zoroastrianism and Manichaeism). Our "coverage" of India includes Buddhism as well as Brahmanism and Hinduism, and in China and Japan Buddhism as well as Confucianism and Taoism. Thus religion cuts across cultures, while it may also provide the underlying continuity in a given culture. For the most part, however, it is in literature that each tradition best reveals its distinguishing features and basic continuity. Hence each has had to be represented by enough classic examples to show both the unity and diversity of the traditions, and to demonstrate how the great religions have assumed a different coloration in each historical and cultural setting, while also revealing the distinctive aesthetic and intellectual qualities of the tradition.

If for instance the case for Islām and our understanding of the Qur'ān [Koran] depend heavily on how one views the distinctive claims made for that work as prophecy and for Muḥammad as the "seal of the prophets," the significance of those claims cannot be judged from a reading of the Qur'ān alone, without seeing how the matter is dealt with later by al-Ghazālī in relation to Greek philosophy and Ṣūfī mysticism, or by Ibn Khaldūn in relation to the patterns of human history. The contrasting claim of Hinduism, that it transcends any such particular revelation and can accommodate all other religions, may be difficult to evaluate except in some relation to Islām or to the Mahāyāna Buddhist philosophy that Śaṅkara is variously said to have refuted and assimilated into the Vedānta.

These religions or teachings, as represented by the texts we read, may not always have acknowledged each other openly, but if we know or even suspect that there was indeed an unspoken encounter among them, some reconnaissance of the alternative positions is requisite to an understanding of any one of them. By this I mean, to be more specific, that one cannot enter into any serious encounter with the early Buddhist *sūtra*s unless one has read the Upanishads, nor can one later come to grips with Śaṅkara if one knows nothing of the major Mahāyāna texts. Likewise, in China, while it is obviously unthinkable that one would take up such major Confucian thinkers as Mencius and Hsün-tzu without first having read the *Analects* of Confucius [*see GIT* 1984], it would be no less an error to do so without reference to Lao-tzu and Chuang-tzu.

In China, though the inception of the Confucian tradition is most directly accessible through the *Analects*, if one stopped there and went no further into any of the later Confucian thinkers, one would get only an archaic, fossilized view of Confucianism. Only by going on to the Neo-Confucians Chu Hsi and Wang Yang-ming can one begin to appreciate how the classic teachings underwent further development in response to the challenge of Buddhism and Taoism. In the West it would be like reading the Old Testament without the New, or the latter without Saint Augustine, Saint Thomas, or Dante. Yet it can equally well be argued that the encounter among the so-called Three Teachings in China is even more vividly brought to life in such great Chinese novels as the *Record of a Journey to the West* and the *Dream of the Red Chamber*. Thus reading classic fiction can give access to the dialogue in China on levels not reachable through the classical and neoclassical philosophers.

The same—and more—can be said for Japanese literature as a revelation of Buddhism's encounter with the native tradition. Often that tradition is identified with Shintō, but as there were no written texts or scriptures antedating the introduction of the Chinese script, the best one can do is look to the earliest literature in Japanese—such works as the *Man'yō-shū, The Tale of Genji,* and the *Pillow Book,* to name only a few of the finest examples—if one wishes to get, in the absence of open doctrinal debate, a more intimate glimpse of what is going on in the Japanese mind and heart behind the outward show of polite professions. This indeed is where the real struggle has taken place among the deep-seated aesthetic preferences and emotional inclinations of the Japanese as they strove to assimilate the more ascetic or moralistic doctrines imported from the continent. There too one may get a sense of the cultural situation into which Zen Buddhism was later introduced and judge from the outcome how much of contemporary Zen is actually Japanese or Chinese rather than Buddhist.

In sum, unless other guests are invited, there will be no party for us to join—no way to renew the conversation with any of the great works or thinkers of the past without having others present who had engaged in the original dialogue. How long the list of participants may become is always a matter for local discretion, but in no case can just one or two works generate a real conversation. In the silence of Zen there may be such a thing as one hand clapping, but in the discourse we are entering into there is no book that speaks just to itself.

In this way, working through the natural, original associations among the recognized classics of the Asian traditions, one arrives, by the inductive process I referred to above, at a provisional set of the Great Books of the East. Admittedly a modern creation, it is put together from materials quite authentic to one or another of the Asian traditions. The linkages so identified within and among these traditions, though often obscured or suppressed in the past by cultural isolationism and national or religious chauvinisms, are nonetheless real and meaningful. According to this understanding, "The East" is no mere fabrication, made to serve as a foil for the West. Rather it is an East that has emerged in its true reflected colors only since it came to be observed in a modern light.

Rabindranath Tagore, the charismatic cosmopolitan from Calcutta who thought of himself above all as a citizen of the world, was perhaps the first to appreciate this. In his new perception of the "East," brilliantly articulated in an essay on "The Eastern University" but only incompletely realized in his Viśva-Bhārati University at Śantiniketan, he saw the need for a multicultural curriculum in which the several Asian traditions would complement one another, highlighting each other's distinctive features in a way no solitary exposure could do.

Regrettably, the direction of modern education, whether in India or elsewhere in Asia, has taken a different turn, emphasizing technical learning and specialized training at the expense of any kind of humanistic education, Eastern or Western. In this situation, as in our own, the humanities are taught as discrete disciplines and each national tradition is a separate subject of specialization, a field in which to practice the new humanities technologies. The usual result of this process is that nothing can be seen whole, and every great work is subjected by analysis to unmitigated trivialization. In most Asian universities today it is only the student majoring, say, in Sanskrit, Chinese, or Japanese studies who learns anything of the classics of his own tradition, and even then it will most likely be to specialize in a single text.

Against this pessimistic estimate of the present situation, a more positive view may be offered that microscopic studies of this kind are the necessary building blocks for the construction tomorrow of a macroscopic, global edifice of human civilization. Why then at this late stage should one bother to establish an intermediate position, a regionalized view of the humanities, when nothing less than a total worldview is called for? Given the inherent tendency toward universalization of all scholarly disciplines, it would be perverse—and no doubt unavailing— to resist the incorporation within them of Asian materials. Recognizing too the impacted state of the college curriculum, and the difficulty of finding any time in it for Asia as such, one can hardly afford to pass up opportunities for the inclusion of Asia in world history or world literature courses which already provide a place for it in the core curriculum.

Even so, while accepting these as facts of academic life, I would still argue the need to make a place, at some point in the curriculum, for a course which includes the "Great Books of the East" or the "Oriental Humanities." My ground for so arguing is the very same need to face squarely the implications of the global view already projected. This to me requires, not necessarily that an equal priority be given to Asia and the West, but only that there should be some parity of treatment for them in the overall program. To understand why I make this distinction between priority and parity, however, it may be well to step back a bit and look at some basic premises.

Learning, as everyone is aware, works from the known to the unknown. Just so, some degree of self-understanding is prerequisite to an understanding of others, and by extension an understanding of one's own situation or one's own past may be accepted as a precondition for understanding another's. I have acknowledged this in reporting our experience with the Oriental Humanities, which shows how much deeper and more meaningful the new learning experience can be for those who have first come to an appreciation—or even just a keener awareness—of their own tradition. The same principle, I would readily concede, applies in reverse to the Asians' understanding of the West, which may be just as advantaged or handicapped, depending upon how well they have come to know their own culture. Those who have been deprived by an almost total uprooting from their own cultural traditions, as in China during the long blight of the Maoist era and especially during the Cultural Revolution, may be no less disadvantaged in understanding the West for all the hunger to learn from it which they now show. Not to come to terms with one's past, or in some degree to master one's own tradition, is to remain a hostage to it, even though unconsciously so, and thus not to become fully master of oneself. In such a condition, being unable to take responsibility for oneself and one's own past, one is in a poor position to become truly responsive to others'.

All this may verge on rhetorical overkill, but to me such considerations are bound to enter into what I have referred to above as "parity of treatment." If one can appreciate what it would mean for the *Great Books of the Western World* to be represented only by Plato's *Republic* or the Book of Job—a meaningless question for anyone who had not read considerably more of the *Great Books* than that—one can begin to appreciate why a reading of the *Analects* alone might not do sufficient justice to the Confucian tradition; why the *Dhammapada* by itself would be inadequate to represent Buddhism; and why one would face an impossible dilemma if one had to choose between the *Dream of the Red Chamber* and *The Tale of Genji*, *Śakuntalā* [*see* elsewhere in this volume] or the Nō drama, the *Rāmāyaṇa* or Tu Fu, as candidates for infiltration into a humanities sequence or world literature course otherwise based on the Western tradition. If the selectivity which is always a prime factor in the design of general education programs should be taken to rule out more than token representation for the East, and if to include the *Analects* (or as some generous souls even proposed twenty years ago, Mao Zedong) would mean dropping Thomas Aquinas, John Locke, or Immanuel Kant from the list, one must wonder whether the result would do justice to either East or West.

Even putting the question in this way, I do not rule out the possibility of accepting such unpalatable choices, if only to serve the educational purpose of getting an East-West dialogue started. It all depends on knowing where you want to go and how, by what stages and means, you hope to get there. For this it is important to recognize that the risks of distortion or misrepresentation are great. If one knows how painfully abbreviated is even the usual one- or two-year sequence in the Western humanities, or how deficient the student's familiarity often is with the great works of his own tradition, one will not rush to a solution which only compounds the difficulty.

Whatever is to be done, it seems to me, should be governed by two considerations. The first is that the reading and understanding of a text should work, as much as possible, from the inside out rather than from the outside in. Granted that we are indeed outsiders looking in, we must make the effort to put ourselves in the position or situation of the author and his audience. This means that no reading of an Eastern text should be undertaken which is so removed from its original context as to be discussable only in direct juxtaposition to something Western. Such a reading leads almost inevitably to one-sided comparisons and does not serve genuine dialogue. Party to this new dialogue must be enough of the original discourse (i.e., writings presenting alternative or contrasting views) so that the issues can be defined in their own terms and not simply in opposition to, or agreement with, the West. If a world literature course or humanities program can include enough works of the original tradition to meet this test, the risks run may be worth taking.

Since the inclusion of more than a few such works will put a strain on any reading program that is part of an already crowded core curriculum, a second set of considerations will likely come into play: how can a total learning process be conceived which makes the best use of scarce resources (deployment of instructional staff, provision of texts and teaching materials), and above all of the student's time, to provide a properly balanced and truly global program?

Most persons who face this question will be teachers and administrators in colleges and universities, but I do not mean to limit the discussion to academics. The need for global education is widely felt and cannot be met simply within the framework of the college curriculum. Granted that the undergraduate years are where the process should start, it is neither reasonable nor realistic to suppose that an adequate liberal or general education can be compressed simply within the typical four-year college program. I have long believed that there is a need for general education even in graduate schools, and for more reasons than just to provide remedial instruction in matters neglected by many colleges (including the Asian humanities, and much else that is antecedent to civilization). But this is not the place to argue the point, and whatever might be undertaken in graduate schools would still not do the whole job.

The Great Books program, however—or some version of it—does seem to me a possible vehicle for introducing the Asian humanities to the West, preferably a program starting in college, but in any case extending into adult or continuing education. To my knowledge, the Great Books program was the first to recognize that the gaining of a liberal education would need to be a lifelong learning process, and it was also the first to develop a practical format and procedure for its realization, including the three most essential components: appropriate texts, a discussion method, and a suitable guide. From my own experience in conducting seminars and colloquia for many different age and occupational groups, I can also say that, for the Great Books of the East too, this is a well-tested, workable method.

Two qualifications and some amendments may be called for. The first is that the Great Ideas should be reexamined in the course of incorporating Asian materials into the Great Books program. Reviewing the list now I note some so-called great ideas that would seem strange to the Asian traditions. This is not to deny that they pose valid *questions* for us to ask of any body of literature, since even the failure to mention them can be significant. It is to suggest, rather, that reading the great books of Asia, one would not necessarily come upon some of the ideas so listed as of perennial, universal human concern, or as issues one would inescapably encounter in the traditional discourse. Examples of this type are "Constitution," "Evolution," "Liberty," and "Progress"— fairly recent ideas even in the West.

On the other hand—and this is the second qualification—one does encounter ideas of great prominence or issues of deep concern in more than one of the Asian traditions that fail to appear in the present list. A few of them are: Action, Enlightenment, Emptiness, Heart (as well as Mind), Intuition, Mysticism, Nothingness, Public and Private, Revelation, Ritual, Sacrifice, the Sage, the Self or Person, Spirituality, Structure, and Process. I realize that these are all arguable points. Most of them could be taken up under the heading of one or another of the existing Great Ideas. Revelation or Spirituality, for instance, might well be discussed in connection with either Religion or Theology. I would suggest, however, that in Asian traditions not necessarily theistic or theological in character, the nature of Revelation or Spirituality might prove to be a question of broader significance than, say, Theology. "Prophecy" does appear on the list of Great Ideas, and it is a question which may usefully be raised even in such nontheistic or only quasi-theistic traditions as Confucianism, but it by no means exhausts the possibilities for Revelation. "Mysticism" could also be discussed under the heading of "Experience" (already on the list), but it is a category so important in Oriental religions generally as to warrant separate consideration. Meanwhile "Experience" itself remains a viable subject of discussion, especially in East Asia, even apart from mysticism.

Self or Person is another in the category of ideas that could be discussed under one of the existing headings (in this case the Individual), but the centrality of the question of the Self in South and East Asia—in Hinduism, Buddhism, and Confucianism—and the depth to which it was pursued, go beyond the concept of the Individual, important though that was, in the West. Indeed, from an Oriental perspective, the individual would probably be viewed only as one aspect or subheading of Self.

Authority is still another arguable case. The nature of authority becomes an almost inescapable issue when one is considering alternative traditions, sources of values, and revelation, let alone the specifically political aspects of the matter. It is not included here in my supplementary list because, in formulating the latter, I have tried to keep for the most part to terms for which one can find an equivalent explicitly discussed in the several traditions themselves. This, however, does not seem to have been the case with Authority, which is often simply taken for granted in the East, no less than in the West.

However these may be, my supplementary list of Great Ideas is meant only to be suggestive, not exhaustive or definitive. In proposing it, I have in mind that if the Great Ideas of the West be thought a useful device for focusing discussion of the Western Great Books, then when one comes to the point of expanding that list to include the Great Books of the East, one should consider reviewing and expanding somewhat the list of Great Ideas. The result of such a reconsideration, I am willing to predict, would generally be to confirm the applicability or universality of most of the terms already identified, but the educational benefits of reopening the question and exploring it in new contexts would seem to me to be substantial.

Having come to this point, it may be in order for me to suggest what are the Great Books I would consider essential to a basic reading program—a list that could be defined as what might be appropriate for an introductory, one-year course. A more generous selection is found in *A Guide to Oriental Classics,*[6] which gives the teacher or discussion leader more to choose from in meeting the needs of particular groups or to draw upon for a somewhat more leisurely reading and less pressured learning situation. In this light what I propose here is not necessarily ideal, nor on the other hand does it represent the bare minimum, but rather something more like a "mean." As an introduction to the major Asian traditions, one could hope that it would not misrepresent them but rather provide enough pleasure in the reading and enough stimulus for discussion that most participants would emerge from the experience with an appetite for more, as well as the wherewithal to pursue its satisfaction.

Here then is my list, with a brief comment on each work for the benefit of those to whom the titles alone might be meaningless. (The titles in the original language of those translated here may be found in the corresponding section of the *Guide* referred to in note 6.)

The Islāmic tradition

The Qur'ān: a book of revelation that, because of the unique claims made for it, almost defies reading as a "great book" but is nonetheless indispensable to all reading in the later tradition.

The Assemblies of al-Ḥarīrī (1054–1122): a major work of classical Arabic literature which illustrates in an engaging way some of the tensions between piety and civilization, the desert and the city in Islāmic culture.

The Deliverance from Error of al-Ghazālī (1058–1111): a very personal statement, by perhaps the greatest of the Islāmic theologians, concerning the relation of mystical experience to theology and the rational sciences.

The poems of Jalal al-Din Rumi (1207–1273): chosen as the most representative of the Ṣūfī poets.

The Conference of the Birds by ʿAṭṭār (ca. 1141–1220): a symposium on the stages of religious experience in the contemplative ascent to union with God.

The Prolegomena [*Muqaddimah*] to World History of Ibn Khaldūn (1332–1406): often called the world's first "social scientist" (a subject of useful discussion itself). Ibn Khaldūn's encyclopedic discourses on the historical factors in the rise and fall of civilizations is already a classic among modern world historians.

(Options not selected above but obvious candidates for inclusion in a more ample listing: *The Seven Odes* of pre-Islāmic poetry; *The Thousand and One Nights;* other Arab philosophers like Averroës and Ibn al-ʿArabī; other Ṣūfī poets like Hāfez, etc.)

The Indian tradition

Hymns from the *Rigveda:* bedrock of the Hindu tradition.

The Upanishads: classic discourses which laid the foundation for Hindu religious and philosophical speculation.

The *Bhagavad Gītā* [*see GIT* 1985]: major work of religious and philosophical synthesis and basic scripture of Hindu devotionalism.

The *Rāmāyaṇa* of Vālmīki (ca. 300 B.C.): the earlier of the two great Indian epics and the best known in Indian art and legendry. It exemplifies the fundamental values and tensions in the classical Indian tradition.

Basic texts of Theravāda Buddhism: No one text represents a complete statement of Buddhism, but the *Dhammapada, Mahasatipatthana Sutta, Milinda-pañha,* and *Mahāparinibbana Sutta* come closest perhaps to "basic discourses."

Scriptures of Indian Mahāyāna Buddhism: Again no one work suffices, but the Prajñapāramitā texts (especially the *Heart Sutra*), the works of Nāgārjuna and Shāntideva and the *Vimalakīrti Sūtra* all represent basic statements.

The *Śakuntalā:* major work of Kālidāsa (ca. A.D. 400), the greatest of Indian dramatists and arguably the greatest in Asia.

The *Vedānta-sūtras* with Commentary of Śaṅkara (ca. 700–750): generally regarded as the leading Indian philosopher, representing the dominant nondualistic school of the Vedānta.

The *Gītagovinda* of Jayadeva (ca. A.D. twelfth century): a great religious poem in Sanskrit and the major work of medieval devotionalism.

Rabindranath Tagore and Mohandas Gandhi: two contrasting views of the Indian tradition in its encounter with the West. (These are the only modern writers on our list, but Tagore's poems and plays and Gandhi's so-called *Autobiography,* though admittedly not "classics," have been perennial favorites for the way they juxtapose aspects of Indian tradition in response to the challenges of the West.)

(Major options not availed of above: the epic *Mahābhārata;* the *Yoga-sūtras* of Patañjali; Kauṭilya's *Arthaśāstra,* a guide to politics; the *Little Clay Cart* of King Shudraka [ca. A.D. 400], a most entertaining domestic drama; the famous collection of fables in the *Panchatantra;* Bhartrhari's verses on worldly life, passion, and renunciation; Rāmānuja, a rival to Śaṅkara in religious philosophy, etc., as described in the *Guide,* note 6.)

The Chinese tradition

The *Analects* of Confucius (551–479 B.C.): the best single source for the ideas of Confucius.

Mo-tzu or Mo Ti: a sharp critic of Confucianism in the fifth century B.C. and major alternative voice in politics and religion.

Lao-tzu: a basic text of Taoism which has become a world classic because of its radical challenge to the underlying assumptions of both traditional and modern civilizations.

Chuang-tzu: delightful speculative ramblings and philosophical parodies by a Taoist writer of the late fourth–early third century B.C.

Mencius (372–289 B.C.): a thinker second in importance only to Confucius in that school, who addressed a broad range of practical and philosophical problems.

Hsün-tzu (third century B.C.): the third great statement of the Confucian teaching, with special attention to the basis of learning and rites.

Han-fei-tzu (third century B.C.): the fullest theoretical statement and synthesis of the ancient Legalistic school, a major influence on the Chinese political tradition.

Historical Records by Ssu-ma Ch'ien (ca. 145–85 B.C.): a monumental history of early China, notable for its combination of chronicles, topical treatises, and biographical accounts.

The *Lotus Sūtra:* by far the most important text of Chinese Mahāyāna Buddhism, influential throughout East Asia.

The *Platform Sūtra:* an original Chinese work and early statement of Ch'an (Zen) thought, which assumed the status of both classic and scripture because of its unique claim to religious enlightenment.

T'ang poetry: selections from the great poets of the T'ang dynasty, generally viewed as the classic age of Chinese verse.

Chu Hsi (1130–1200): leading exponent and synthesizer of Neo-Confucianism, which became the dominant teaching in later centuries and spread throughout East Asia.

Wang Yang-ming (1472–1529): principal Neo-Confucian thinker of the Ming period, who modified Chu Hsi's philosophy most particularly in respect to the nature and importance of learning (especially the role of moral intuition *vs.* cognitive learning).

Record of a Journey to the West attributed to Wu-Ch'eng-en (1500–ca. 1582): a fantastic fictional account of the epic pilgrimage to India of the Buddhist monk Hsüan-tsang.

Dream of the Red Chamber by Ts'ao Hsüeh-ch'in (d. 1763): an eighteenth-century realistic-allegorical novel of the decline of a great family and its young heirs' involvement in the world of passion and depravity.

(Other options within the Chinese tradition are such Buddhist texts as *The Awakening of Faith,* the *Surangama Sūtra,* and, if it has not been read as a work of the Indian tradition, the *Vimalakīrti Sūtra;* and other major novels like *The Water Margin [All Men Are Brothers]; The Golden Lotus* and *The Scholars* [Ju-lin wai-shih].)

The Japanese tradition

Here it is worthy of special note that women are prominent as authors of the earlier classic works and as dominant figures in many of the later works of drama and fiction.

Man'yō-shū: the earliest anthology of Japanese poetry (eighth century and before).

The Tale of Genji by Murasaki Shikibu (ca. 978–ca. 1014): the world's

first great novel, about court life in Heian-period Japan and the loves
of Prince Genji.

The *Pillow Book* of Sei Shōnagon (b. 966/67–d. 1013?): observations
on life, religion, aesthetic sensibility, and taste in Heian Japan.

The Ten Foot Square Hut by Kamo Chōmei (1155–1216): a kind of
Japanese Thoreau, meditating on the vicissitudes of the world, the
beauties of nature, and the satisfactions of the simple life—but at the
farthest remove from Thoreau's civil disobedience.

Essays in Idleness (*Tsurezure-gusa*) by Yoshida Kenkō (1283–1350): observations on life, society, nature, and art by a worldly monk and
classic literary stylist, in journal form.

Nō plays: the classic drama, distinctive to Japan, but now much admired
in the West as well, preferably seen and heard as well as read.

The novels of Ihara Saikaku (1642–93): fictional writings in a poetic
style, expressive of the new culture of the townspeople in seventeenth-
century Japan.

The poetry of Matsuo Bashō (1644–94): poetry and prose by the master
of the haiku and one of the greatest of all Japanese poets.

The plays of Chikamatsu Monzaemon (1653–1725): works written for
the puppet theater by Japan's leading dramatist, focusing on conflicts
between love and duty.

(Alternative selections: Religious writings of the eminent Japanese
monks Kūkai, Dōgen, and Hakuin, while important in the history of
Japanese religion, were difficult even for the Japanese to understand
and, though respected, did not have a wide readership. The more widely
read literary and dramatic works were probably also more expressive
of the actual religious sentiments of the Japanese, as well as of their
literary preferences. These might include, in addition to the above, the
major poetry anthologies *Kokinshū* and *Shinkokinshu,* the novel *The Tale
of the Heike,* and the eighteenth-century drama *Chūshingura.*)

The foregoing lists give, I hope, a fair representation of the different
preferences and shared values among the great traditions of Asia. They
include works that have withstood the test of nearly forty years of
reading and discussion with American students of all ages. The optional
or alternative readings have been tried from time to time but, for a
variety of reasons, have not always worked well. It should be pointed
out that not everything on the list has been assigned in its entirety. This
is especially true of the long epics and novels. We make concessions to
what works in practice and accept prudent compromises.

The availability of adequate translations has also been a factor in our
decisions, especially in the early days of the program, but it has become
less of a problem as more good translations have been produced in
recent years of a kind suited to our need, i.e., in a form accessible to
students. If earlier it was said that one test of a great book is how well

it survives translation, now the test might well be restated as the great book's ability not only to survive one translation but also to attract, withstand, and outlast several others.

Today, with more than one translation available of a given work, the layman naturally wants the scholar's recommendation as to which is best. Not only laymen but even some scholars still have a touching faith in the idea that there is one "authoritative" or "definitive" translation of a work. In truth it is possible for scholars of equal technical competence to produce translations of almost equal merit, each bringing out different meanings and nuances of the original. Burton Watson and A. C. Graham have each written excellent translations of the *Chuang-tzu;* neither, I suspect, would claim his own was perfect, but Watson's may appeal more to those whose interests and tastes are literary, and Graham's to the more philosophical. Interpretations like Thomas Merton's of the *Chuang-tzu* also have their place but should be understood for what they are and not regarded as translations. It is also possible for nonprofessionals like Ezra Pound, Witter Bynner, or Lin Yutang sometimes to capture the meaning of certain passages in Chinese works and render them in vivid English that is less literal then the sinologue would like, but more meaningful or moving to the reader.

Our practice is to recommend at least one preferred translation (if only for the sake of having a common basis for discussion), but to urge students, wherever possible, to read more than one rendering and arrive at their own sense of where the common denominator among them may lie. In this process of triangulation—getting a bearing or fix on a text from several translators' different angles of vision—the reader has his own proper judgmental part to play, bringing his or her own learning and experience to bear on the assessment of what the original might mean. If so used, translations need not stand in the way of the reader having some active, personal encounter with the text, which the great thinkers and teachers have so often called for.

Further to assist the reader in knowing what to look for in these books, I have asked colleagues knowledgeable in the several traditions to write brief essays on what they perceive to be the most essential values in the works they know well or most enjoy. Among these guest essayists are several distinguished scholars who have themselves contributed substantially to making the great books available in translation. In responding to this opportunity they have, in several cases, chosen to write about works somewhat less well known in the West than those already highly acclaimed.

In conclusion I should like to make one further point concerning the importance of reading the "Great Books of the East." The basic criterion for recognizing them as classics has been that they were first so admired in their own tradition. In quite a few cases this admiration spread to other countries and these works came to be regarded as either scriptures or great books outside their own homeland. Further, after substantial contact was made by the West with Asia in the sixteenth and seventeenth centuries, many of these works came to be translated and admired in the West as well. Some of the exotic appeal of the unknown and "mysterious" East may still attach to them and they can still be called "Great Books of the East" in the sense of their being "from" the East, but for at least two centuries they have been essential reading for many of the best minds in the West—philosophers, historians, poets, and, indeed, major writers in almost every field of thought and scholarship. Thus, one whose education does not include a reading of the "Great Books of the East" today is a stranger not only to Asia but to much of the best that has been thought and written in the modern West. While not perhaps to be called "Great Books of the West," many of these works and their authors have already entered the mainstream of the conversation that is going on in the West today. As that conversation is broadened to include a fairer representation of the Asian traditions, bringing out the implicit dialogue within and among them, it could indeed become a Great Conversation for all the world.*

Kālidāsa's *Śakuntalā*

Barbara Stoler Miller

> If you want the bloom of youth and fruit of later years,
> If you want what enchants, fulfills, and nourishes,
> If you want heaven and earth contained in one name—
> I say Śakuntalā and all is spoken.
>
> —J. W. von Goethe, "Willst du die Blüte . . . "

Kālidāsa's drama the *Śakuntalā* has had many enthusiastic admirers in the West as well as in India, where from the time of its composition in the early fifth century A.D., it has been considered the masterpiece of classical Indian literature. The *Śakuntalā*, first known to Goethe through the English translation of William Jones that was published in 1789, appealed to him for the beauty of its nature imagery, the complexity of its structure, and the unity of art and religion on which it was based.

With its semidivine characters, rich mythological layers, and vast cosmic landscape drawn from an episode in the epic *Mahābhārata*, the *Śakuntalā* is the model of the most elevated Indian dramatic form,

---

*I wish to express my indebtedness to Jacques Barzun and the late Lionel Trilling for background information contained in the introductory portions of this essay, based on earlier conversations with them. In acknowledgment of this particular debt, and for much else that I have learned from them, I should like to dedicate this essay to these two great scholars and teachers.

which may be classed as "heroic romance." Dramatic romances in Western literature, such as Aeschylus's *Oresteia,* Euripides' *Alcestis,* or Shakespeare's *The Tempest,* are comparable. The *Śakuntalā* can be appreciated today for the ways in which it explores the human spirit's potential for harmony with nature in a chaotic world where desire comes into conflict with duty.

Kālidāsa is the greatest poet of Sanskrit, the classical Indo-European language of India. His literary reputation is based on six surviving works that are generally attributed to him by Indian critics and commentators. The coherent language, poetic technique, style, and sentiment that these works express seem to be the product of a single mind. The poems include a lyric monologue of nature, "Meghadūta" ("The Cloud Messenger"), and two long lyric narratives, *Raghuvaṃśa* ("The Dynasty of Raghu") and *Kumārasambhava* ("The Birth of Śiva's Son"). There are three dramas, all of which begin with prologues that refer to Kālidāsa as the author: *Mālavikāgnimitra* ("Mālavikā and Agnimitra"), *Vikramorvaśī* ("Urvaśī Won by Valor"), and *Abhijñānasākuntala* ("Śakuntalā and the Ring of Recollection"), often referred to in critical literature simply as the *Śakuntalā.*

While we have no way of establishing Kālidāsa's exact dates, an upper limit is provided by an inscription on the shrine of Aihoḷe, dated A.D. 634, in which he is praised as a great poet. The sense of the world that one gets from Kālidāsa's work is consonant with historical, geographic, and linguistic factors supporting the Indian tradition what associates the poet with the Gupta monarch Candra Gupta II, who ruled most of northern India from Pāṭaliputra, the ancient capital of the Gangetic valley, between A.D. 380 and 415. The central role played by the figure of the king in his dramas and in his epic *Raghuvaṃśa* suggests that Kālidāsa enjoyed royal patronage.

That Kālidāsa was a devotee of Śiva and his consort, the goddess Kālī, is evident in his work, as well as in legends that recount his transformation from a fool into a poet through the grace of Kālī. The powerful images of nature that dominate his poetry and drama are ultimately determined by his conception of Śiva's creative mystery. This is implicit in the doctrine of Śiva as the god of eight manifest forms (*aṣṭamūrti*), who is Kālidāsa's poetic icon. The most compressed expression of it is in the benediction of the *Śakuntalā:*

> The water that was first created,
> the sacrifice-bearing fire, the priest,
> the time-setting sun and moon,
> audible space that fills the universe,
> what men call nature, the source of all seeds,
> the air that living creatures breathe—
> through his eight embodied forms,
> may Lord Śiva come to bless you!

The natural world of Kālidāsa's poetry is never a static landscape; it reverberates with Śiva's presence. Nature functions, not as a setting or allegorical landscape, but as a dynamic surface on which the unmanifest cosmic unity plays. This unity is Śiva; his creative nature is expressed through the eight essential constituents of empirical existence: the elements (water, fire, ether, earth, air), the sun, and the moon, and the ritual sacrificer, who is integrated into this cosmic system. In their sustained interplay, creation and destruction of life occur.

The conception of Śiva's eight manifest forms also has inherent in it the identification of Śiva himself with Nature (*prakṛti*), the female half of his cosmic totality. Śiva is also called "The God Who is Half Female" (*ardhanarīśvara*). The male and female aspects of existence (*puruṣa* and *prakṛti*), separately personified as Śiva and his consort, are bound into a single androgynous figure. These ideas are fundamental to the meaning of Kālidāsa's poetry; in the *Śakuntalā,* as in his other dramas, they set the romantic relationship between the hero and heroine in a specific religious context.

The mythic origin of drama was a holy presentation that the gods offered to give ethical instruction through diversion when people were no longer listening to the scriptures. Ancient texts stress the reward a king will gain if he presents dramatic performances as a gift to his subjects and an offering to the gods. For centuries, Indian dramas have been commissioned and presented on the occasion of a seasonal festival, the birth of a son, a marriage, a royal consecration, a political victory, or any other auspicious event.

Indian heroic romances represent human emotions in a theatrical universe of symbolically charged characters and events in order to lead the audience into a state of extraordinary pleasure and insight. The goal of a Sanskrit drama is to establish emotional harmony in the microcosm of the theater by exploring the deeper relations that bind apparent conflicts of experience. The manifestation of these relations produces the intense aesthetic experience called *rasa*.

Kālidāsa's dramas focus on the critical tension between desire (*kāma*) and duty (*dharma*) that is aesthetically manifest in the relation of the erotic sentiment (*śṛṅgāra-rasa*) to the heroic (*vīra-rasa*). His dramas achieve their aesthetic and moral impact not through conflicts of individuals but through the perennial human conflict between desire and duty. His dramatic expositions are rooted in an ancient Indian scheme for reconciling life's multiple possibilities. The scheme is called the "four human pursuits" (*puruṣārtha*) and is divided into a worldly triad of duty, material gain, and pleasure, plus a supermundane concern for liberation from worldly existence. The conflict is transformed into aesthetic experience by the poet's skillful presentation of his characters' emotional reactions to various situations. These characters are not unique individuals with personal destinies, like Shakespeare's Hamlet or Lear, but generic types defined within stylized social contexts that reflect the hierarchical nature of traditional Indian society.

In the *Śakuntalā*, the hero and heroine are the main dramatic vehicles for exposing the states of mind of the poet and his audience. They are supported by clusters of characters who, like them, appear as symbolic personalities defined by social position, gender, and language. Besides the king, the male characters are the buffoon, sages, ministers, priests, students, policemen, and a fisherman. The female characters are nymphs, queens, ascetics, doorkeepers, bow-bearers, and serving maids. With the exception of the buffoon and other comic characters like the policemen, the male characters speak Sanskrit. The female characters speak Prākrit, a stylized version of a "natural" language, in contrast to more artificial Sanskrit. It is as if the high-ranking male characters spoke Latin while the others spoke Italian.

The hero of the play is King Duṣyanta, whose character is expressed according to the norms of classical social and dramatic theory. The high qualities of kingship he possesses qualify him to be called a "royal sage." This epithet signifies that the king's spiritual power is equal to his martial strength and moral superiority. The ideal royal sage is a figure of enormous physical strength who also has the power to control his senses. He is a sage by virtue of his discipline, austerity, and knowledge of sacred law. It is his religious duty to keep order in the cosmos by guarding his kingdom; in this he is like a sage guarding the realm of holy sacrifice. His responsibility to guide and protect those beneath him involves him in acts of austerity that place him in the highest position of the temporal and spiritual hierarchy.

The heroine of the play, Śakuntalā, is the daughter born of a union between the nymph Menakā and the royal sage Viśvāmitra. Menakā, a paradigmatic figure of feminine beauty, is sent to seduce Viśvāmitra when his ascetic powers threaten the gods. She succeeds and becomes pregnant with a daughter whom she bears and abandons to birds of prey near a river. The birds worship and protect the child until another great sage, the ascetic Kaṇva, finds her and brings her to live in his forest hermitage as his daughter. Having found her among the śakunta birds, he names her Śakuntalā.

Śakuntalā is a beautiful nymph whose spontaneous love embraces the hero and leads him beyond the world of everyday experience into the imaginative universe where dichotomies of sensual desire and sacred duty are reintegrated. Her presence reassures the audience that the energy of nature is always available to reintegrate conflicting aspects of life. Her body is an object of worship—poetic ornaments are like the auspicious ornaments placed on an image in religious ritual or on a bride for her marriage ritual. The wearer is put in a sacred state in which she is transformed from a nubile creature—whose sexual power invites violence and threatens to produce chaos—into a fecund vessel for the production of offspring. As the heroine of a drama, she is the vehicle for transforming erotic passion into the aesthetic experience of love, which incorporates the erotic and transcends its limitations.

In the realm of passionate desire, the king's general, minister, and chamberlain are replaced as advisers by a Brahman buffoon who is his "minister of amorous affairs." The buffoon's proverbial gluttony, carelessness, and cowardice give a broad caricature of the normally sacred Brahman priest. His words and actions often remind one of Shakespearean clowns like Touchstone and Feste. He speaks a comic Prākrit, in contrast with the king's heroic Sanskrit, and is as obsessed with satisfying his hunger for sweets as the king is with satisfying his erotic desires. His literal interpretation of *rasa* as a feast of flavors makes the king's passion absurdly concrete. His humor provides the comic sentiment (*hāsya-rasa*) that gives the *Śakuntalā* a special liveliness.

Kālidāsa reshapes the ancient epic story through these characters. The epic story begins with the scene of a tumultuous hunt in which Duṣyanta kills numerous forest animals. The play begins with the benediction to Śiva and a prologue. The prologue is a play-within-a-play that initiates a conventional pattern of structural oppositions. They include contrasts between verse and prose, Sanskrit and Prākrit, authority (in the person of the director) and spontaneity (in the person of the actress).

DIRECTOR (*looking backstage*): If you are in costume now, madam, please come on stage!
ACTRESS: I'm here, sir.
DIRECTOR: Our audience is learned. We shall play Kālidāsa's new drama called *Śakuntalā and the Ring of Recollection*. Let the players take their parts to heart!
ACTRESS: With you directing, sir, nothing will be lost.
DIRECTOR: Madam, the truth is:

> I find no performance perfect
> until the critics are pleased;
> the better trained we are
> the more we doubt ourselves.

ACTRESS: So true . . . now tell me what to do first!
DIRECTOR: What captures an audience better than a song? Sing about the new summer season and its pleasures:

> To plunge in fresh waters
> swept by scented forest winds
> and dream in soft shadows
> of the day's ripened charms.

ACTRESS: (singing):

> Sensuous women
> in summer love
> weave
> flower earrings
> from fragile petals
> of mimosa
> while wild bees
> kiss them gently.

DIRECTOR: Well sung, madam! Your melody enchants the audience. The silent theater is like a painting. What drama should we play to please it?
ACTRESS: But didn't you just direct us to perform a new play called Śakuntalā and the Ring of Recollection?
DIRECTOR: Madam, I'm conscious again! For a moment I forgot.

> The mood of your song's melody
> carried me off by force,
> just as the swift dark antelope
> enchanted King Duṣyanta.

The actress's singing, like the beautiful movements of the magical antelope, or the art of poetry, makes the audience "forget" the everyday world and enter the fantastic realm of imagination that is latent within them. The mind of the poet, the hero, and the audience is symbolized here by the director, who holds together the various strands of the theater so that the aesthetic experience (rasa) of the play can be realized and savored. The end of the prologue marks a transition to the action of the drama itself.

The king enters with his charioteer, armed with a bow and arrow, like "the wild bowman Śiva, hunting the dark antelope." We witness the king hunting a fleeing antelope in the sacred forest where Śakuntalā dwells. The movement of the chase creates a sense of uncertainty and excitement for the mind's eye as it is drawn deeper into a mythical world. The poet's intention to pierce the boundaries of ordinary time and space is explicit in the king's description of his perspective as he enters the forest:

> What is small suddenly looms large,
> split forms seem to reunite,
> bent shapes straighten before my eyes—
> from the chariot's speed
> nothing ever stays distant or near.

The intensity of the hunt is interrupted by two ascetics, who identify the antelope as a creature of sage Kaṇva's hermitage.

The mood of the drama is set with great economy and magical speed by the black buck as he penetrates the forest and charges the atmosphere with danger. Kālidāsa portrays the elegant animal altered by the violence of the hunt:

> The graceful turn of his neck
> as he glances back at our speeding car,
> the haunches folded into his chest
> in fear of my speeding arrow,
> the open mouth dropping
> half-chewed grass on our path—
> watch how he leaps, bounding on air,
> barely touching the earth.

The antelope is Śakuntalā's "son," adopted by her when it was orphaned as a fawn. This scene shows the king captivated by the graceful creature of nature he is bent on killing. His passion threatens the calm of the forest. This is the prelude to Duṣyanta's discovery of Śakuntalā. As the buffoon aptly jests to the king, "you've turned that ascetics' grove into a pleasure garden."

It is summertime. Śakuntalā is a nubile virgin. Kaṇva is away on a pilgrimage to avert some danger that threatens her. The king's presence arouses the world of nature. When he enters the hermitage, he hides behind a tree to watch Śakuntalā and her friends watering the trees of the ascetics' grove. While they are watering the trees and plants, the friends notice that the spring vine Śakuntalā loves like a sister is blossoming unseasonably, clinging to the male mango tree. A bee in the grove lustily attacks Śakuntalā, giving the king a chance to reveal himself as her protector. As her apparent inaccessibility to him vanishes with the revelation that she is not the child of a Brahman hermit but of a warrior sage, he pursues her insistently, controlled only by her weak resistance. Finally passion overwhelms them both and they consummate their love in a secret marriage of mutual consent. Śakuntalā transfers her creative energy from the forest animals and plants she nurtured by her touch to her human lover, she herself becoming pregnant in the process. Soon after their union, the king is recalled to his capital and leaves Śakuntalā behind. He gives her his signet ring as a sign of their marriage and promises to send for her.

Śakuntalā is distracted by her lover's parting and neglects her religious duties in the hermitage. She ignores the approach of the irascible sage Durvāsas, arouses his wrath, and incurs his curse that the king will forget her, until he sees the ring again. Kaṇva learns from the voice of the forest that Śakuntalā is pregnant. He presides over the ceremonies that sanctify her marriage and poignantly arranges for her departure from the hermitage. The ascetic women come to worship her, and two hermit boys who had been sent to gather flowers from the trees in the woods enter with offerings of jewels and garments produced by the forest trees. The scene of her last moments in the hermitage represents a ritual of breaking her bonds with the world of her childhood. Indian critics consider it to be the emotional core of the drama. On the way to the king's capital, Śakuntalā and her escorts stop to worship at the river shrine of the consort of Indra, king of the gods. There Śakuntalā loses the ring and with it the power to make the king remember her.

Despite his forgetfulness, the king experiences vague traces of their love. While he and the buffoon are listening to the singing of a lady whom the king once loved, he muses to himself: "Why did hearing the song's words fill me with such strong desire? I'm not parted from anyone I love. . . . "

> Seeing rare beauty,
> hearing lovely sounds,
> even a happy man
> becomes strangely uneasy . . .
> perhaps he remembers,
> without knowing why,
> loves of another life
> buried deep in his being.

When Śakuntalā is brought before him in his palace, the king's clouded memory struggles to clarify what he feels intuitively, increasing the intensity of the lover's "separation" for the audience. When she is rejected by the king and abandoned by the ascetics, Śakuntalā rises to anger and invokes the earth to open and receive her. Before the eyes of the king's astonished priest, a light in the shape of a woman appears and carries her off. Eventually the ring is retrieved by a fisherman, and when the king sees it, the curse is broken.

But Duṣyanta transgressed his duty in the hermitage and he too has to undergo a trial of separation before he is ready to be reunited with Śakuntalā. When his vivid memory is restored by seeing the ring, the image of the bee in the song becomes visible in the picture he paints of Śakuntalā and her friends as he first saw them in the hermitage. He uses the painting to represent his experience, but love makes him create a picture of such perfection that he rises in anger to chastise the painted bee who attacks Śakuntalā. When the buffoon reminds him that he is raving at a picture, he awakens from tasting the joy of love and returns to the painful reality of separation:

> My heart's affection made me feel
> the joy of seeing her—
> but you reminded me again
> that my love is only a picture.

This episode evokes for the audience the first meeting of the king and Śakuntalā, that unique moment of sensory and emotional awareness in which their mutual passion sowed the seed of separation and reunion. The fire of parted love that the king experiences as he worships her in his memory consecrates him for the sacred work of destroying cosmic demons that threaten the gods. Afterward, he is transported by Indra's charioteer to the hermitage of a divine sage on the celestial mountain called Golden Peak. The scene of their descent in Indra's aerial chariot recalls and parallels the earlier entry of Duṣyanta and his earthly charioteer into the forest near Kaṇva's hermitage, where he first encountered Śakuntalā.

In this enchanted grove of coral trees, the king observes a child. As he analyzes his attraction to the boy, the king's Sanskrit is set in contrast with the Prākrit speeches of two female ascetics and the hermit boy whom Duṣyanta begins to suspect is his own son. The boy is portrayed as a natural warrior despite his birth in a hermitage and his education in religious practice. This scene also recalls the beginning of the play, when Duṣyanta discovered Śakuntalā in the company of her two friends in the hermitage of Kaṇva. Here the dialogue culminates in a Prākrit pun on Śakuntalā's name, followed by her appearance before the contrite king. The fugue-like interplay of fluid Prākrit prose with more formal Sanskrit prose and verse emphasizes the tension between emotional responses and socially ordained behavior, which is Kālidāsa's major theme. He is not advocating unrestrained passion, but desire tempered by duty and duty brought alive by desire. Once the balance of these vital forces is restored, the king can recognize his son and his wife Śakuntalā.

Duṣyanta's victory over the demons, unlike his wanton pursuit of the antelope, is an act of heroism that entitles him to the love of his virtuous wife and the joy of knowing that his son is destined to be a universal emperor endowed with great spiritual and temporal power. The richly developed counterpoint of the final act is built from latent impressions of images and events that accumulate throughout the play. By sharing these with Duṣyanta as he moves through the enchanted celestial grove to find his son and Śakuntalā, the audience participates in the celebration of their reunion.

In terms of Kālidāsa's aesthetics, creativity is regenerated by the power of the goddess, whom Śakuntalā embodies. She is endowed with a magical relation of nature that makes beauty come to life in the dramatic process. Duṣyanta is bound to Śakuntalā by shared experience and by a child who symbolizes the integration of religious discipline and royal power. The play ends with the hero's recitation of a benediction. It marks the resolution of dramatic conflicts and the nature of the play's success:

May the king serve nature's good!
May priests honor the goddess of speech!
And may Śiva's dazzling power
destroy my cycle of rebirths!

There have been many translations of the *Śakuntalā* into European languages since Jones first translated it into English in the late eighteenth century. The most recent is a translation of the so-called Devanagari Recension of the text in *Theater of Memory: The Plays of Kālidāsa,* edited by Barbara Stoler Miller (New York: Columbia University Press, 1984). The slightly different Bengali Recension is best read in a translation by Michael Coulson, *Three Sanskrit Plays* (Hammondsworth: Penguin Books, 1981).

The Teaching of Vimalakīrti

Robert A. F. Thurman

The Teaching of Vimalakīrti has been one of the most popular of Asian classics for about two thousand years. It was originally written in Sanskrit, based on accounts preserved in colloquial Indic languages, probably in the first century before the common era. It nevertheless presents itself as recording events and conversations that took place in the time of Śākyamuni Buddha, over four hundred years earlier. It was first translated into Chinese in 170 C.E., into Korean, Uighur, and Tibetan in the seventh through ninth centuries, and eventually into Mongolian and Manchu, as well as twice more into Chinese. In modern times it has been translated into more than ten languages, including most European languages, and at least five times into English (chapter numbering and references in this essay are to R. Thurman, *The Holy Teaching of Vimalakīrti (HTV),* Penn State University Press, 1976.)

The *Vimalakīrti* is one of a class of texts called "*Ārya Mahāyāna Sūtra*" ("Holy Scripture of the Universal Vehicle") of Buddhism. These texts form the "bibles" of Mahāyāna Buddhists, the Buddhists who flourished in India and in Central and East Asia during the first millennium C.E. These Scriptures include hundreds of major texts and thousands of minor ones, with thousands more reportedly lost over the millennia. They began to emerge in India of the first century B.C.E. Their purported claim is of a new gospel of the Buddha, adding to the monastic Buddhist concern for individual liberation from suffering a teaching of universal love and compassion for all beings. The texts say that this explicitly messianic teaching had been taught by the same Śākyamuni Buddha but had been kept esoteric for four hundred years, while Indian civilization developed the need for such a socially progressive doctrine.

In spite of the fact that many monastic Buddhists did not (and still do not) consider these Mahāyāna Scriptures to be authentic teachings of the Buddha, the texts sparked a messianic movement that reached out from the monastic strongholds the Buddha's earlier teaching had established all over India and inspired lay men and women with the "*bodhisattva* ideal." This ideal was that each person should assume responsibility for the salvation of all others, not accepting personal liberation in Nirvāṇa until becoming a perfect Buddha, defined as an enlightened savior with the actual ability to save all beings.

Whatever the provenance of the text, the *Vimalakīrti* attained its importance and popularity as much for its readability as for its sanctity. It opens with the Buddha and his company living in the pleasure grove of Āmrapālī, a famous *femme fatale* of the great merchant city of Vaiśālī. It is a slightly unconventional situation, since this elegant lady has won the race to invite the Buddha and company as her guests, beating the delegation of the fathers of the city. So the dignified society of the city have taken some offense and are temporarily refraining from visiting the Buddha. As the scene opens, however, a group of five hundred noble youths, the cream of the city's younger generation, comes from the city to the grove, to visit the Buddha and request his teaching.

The youths bring five hundred jeweled parasols as offerings, and the Buddha at once performs a miracle and forges these into a jeweled dome over the audience. In its bright surfaces the youths all behold reflected all the parts of the universe, much like a magical planetarium. After their awe has calmed and they have sung his praises, they ask the Buddha not "How do we attain enlightenment?" or "What is the true nature of reality?" but "How does the *bodhisattva* perfect the Buddha-land?" In more modern terms, "how does the messianic idealist make a perfect world for the benefit of all beings?" The Buddha answers with an elaborate description of the perfections of a Buddha-land, and how they evolved from the perfections of the *bodhisattva* who becomes a Buddha.

At the end of this discourse, the wise and saintly monk Śāriputra, one of the Buddha's closest "apostles," becomes doubtful about this notion of a "perfect world," thinking that it contradicts the "holy truth of suffering," and that the world he sees around him is far from perfect. The Buddha reads his mind, chides him for his lack of faith and insight, and then plants his toe on the ground and miraculously grants the entire audience a second vision, a vision of the universe as a place of utter perfection, with each being exalted in his or her own highest fulfillment and enjoyment. The Buddha then lifts his toe and withdraws the fleeting vision.

These dramatic events at the opening of the text set up the core tension of the *Vimalakīrti,* problematic of the Universal Vehicle itself.

If Buddhahood is the perfection of the world as well as of the self, the saving of all beings as well as the freeing of the individual, why then did not the turbulent history of the planet come to an end with the Buddhahood of Śākyamuni? Why did not the struggle of evolution terminate with the Buddhahood of the first *bodhisattva*? Or, if this world is perfect to enlightened eyes, why does this perfection appear to the so-highly-evolved human beings as a faulty mess, an endless, seemingly futile struggle, filled with needless suffering?

Once this problem has been posed, the scene shifts to downtown Vaiśālī, and Vimalakīrti is introduced as the very embodiment of a Buddha's liberative arts. He is a wealthy householder respected by all the citizens from highest to lowest, a jack-of-all-trades but also a deeply religious man, and an accomplished philosopher known for his inspiring brilliance and matchless eloquence. Indeed, as we soon come to see, he is thought by some to be a little too eloquent. As the plot moves forward, Vimalakīrti becomes sick and uses the occasion to lecture the citizens of Vaiśālī about the inadequacy of the ordinary body, the unlivability of the unenlightened life, contrasting his miserable state with the blissful perfect health of an enlightened Buddha, who possesses a body of diamond. Vimalakīrti also complains that, as he has now become ill, the monks of Buddha's company do not come to call on him, to cheer him and raise his spirits.

The scene then changes back to the Buddha in his grove where, on cue, the Buddha begins to ask his major disciples—monks and lay supporters—if they will be so kind as to go to town and pay a sick call on the good Vimalakīrti. To his surprise, no one wants to go. Each of the major apostles among the saintly and learned monks tells a story about the last time he met with Vimalakīrti, how Vimalakīrti challenged the narrowness of some central idea precious to that saint, how he refuted such partiality and powerfully opened up a whole new vista but in the process overwhelmed the poor fellow and left him speechless. The major lay supporters have similar tales to tell. All are united in their aversion to another encounter with the whirlwind of Vimalakīrti's adamant eloquence. Fortunately, the *bodhisattva* Mañjuśrī, known as the "crown prince of wisdom," finally volunteers to go, to save the community the embarrassment of failing to pay a call on one of their most respected members during his time of sickness, as well as to enjoy a chat with the householder sage.

As soon as Mañjuśrī agrees to go, the entire community decides to follow along, as the conversation between Vimalakīrti and Mañjuśrī promises to be richly entertaining. The scene again shifts to the house of Vimalakīrti, where the central scenes occur. First, the two sages engage in cryptic dialogues, during which the profound side of the Mahāyāna is clearly expounded—the teachings of subjective and objective selflessness, and absolute emptiness.

For example: "Mañjuśrī: 'Householder, why is your house empty? 'Why have you no servants?' Vimalakīrti: 'Mañjuśrī, all Buddha-lands are also empty.' M: 'What makes them empty?' V: 'They are empty because of emptiness.' M: 'What is "empty" about emptiness?' V: 'Constructions are empty, because of emptiness.' M: 'Can emptiness be conceptually constructed?' V: 'Even that concept is itself empty, and emptiness cannot construct emptiness.' M: 'Householder, where should emptiness be sought?' V: Mañjuśrī, emptiness should be sought among the sixty-two false convictions.' M: 'Where should the sixty-two convictions be sought?' V: 'They should be sought in the liberation of the Tathāgatas.' M: 'Where should the liberation of the Tathāgatas be sought?' V: 'It should be sought in the prime mental activity of all beings.' " (*HTV*, pp. 43–44.)

Vimalakīrti here turns an ordinary question into a probe into the ultimate nature of things, declaring it to be total emptiness of all intrinsic reality. Mañjuśrī presses him on this, looking for traces of a nihilistic reification of emptiness into a real nothingness. Vimalakīrti holds his ground and reaffirms the emptiness of emptiness, and this logically necessitates the reality of the world of relativity, which contains both delusions and enlightenment. Enlightenment itself is not something far away from ordinary life but something perhaps so close to the heart of every being that it tends to go unnoticed. This nondualism, based on a critique of the monastic Buddhist reification of Nirvāṇa as a realm of freedom apart from *saṃsāric* life, is the hallmark of the Mahāyāna movement and underlies its ultimate concern for universal compassion.

These dialogues were highly cherished by those Taoist intellectuals devoted to "enlightening conversation" during Buddhism's early years in China, who used wit and earnest conversation to open up the deep experience of reality. This served as the earliest model for the type of master-disciple exchanges eventually recorded in the *ko'an*, or "public cases," of the Ch'an/Zen tradition. But it was a little much for Śāriputra, who found himself quite at a loss, with no place to stand or chair to sit on in the realm of ultimate groundlessness.

Once emptiness is opened up for the audience, Vimalakīrti begins to play with the dimensions of relativity as well. He obtains giant lion thrones from another universe and seats everyone upon one, causing each to feel as tall as a mountain. He then teaches the "inconceivable liberation of the *bodhisattvas*," a teaching of the miraculous reality that anything is possible for the compassionate activity of the *bodhisattva*. Vimalakīrti declares that to understand that teaching, one must understand the mystery of how a *bodhisattva* in the inconceivable liberation can place the axial mountain, Sumeru, into a mustard seed, without shrinking the mountain or rupturing the seed. Based on emptiness, he presents the mutual interpenetration and mutual nonobstruction of all things.

He and Mañjuśrī then discuss the problems of the paradoxical mutual indispensability of wisdom and compassion, insight and liberative art. Overjoyed by the inspiring teachings, the goddess of wisdom, Prajñā-pāramitā herself, becomes manifest to bless the audience with flowers. After some deep conversations, she ends up teasing Śāriputra, the typical "male chauvinist" of those times, teaching him the lack of intrinsic reality of maleness and femaleness in the most charming and graphic way imaginable.

Vimalakīrti and Mañjuśrī then turn to the problem of good and evil, as Vimalakīrti expounds the code of *bodhisattva* deeds called "the reconciliation of dichotomies." The high point of events in the mansion is reached after Vimalakīrti has asked twenty-five of the advanced *bodhisattvas* present to give their views of the truth of nonduality, the highest expression of ultimate Truth. Each teaches deeply and subtly, though Mañjuśrī expresses some dissatisfaction with their teachings before giving his own idea. Then they all ask Vimalakīrti his idea, and he maintains a thunderous silence. This silence of Vimalakīrti is perhaps the most famous silence in all Buddhist literature. It is the equivalent of the "Great Statement" of ultimate Truth in the Upanishads, "That Thou Art!" Perhaps Vimalakīrti feels that all his audience are so much That, he needs absolutely not to say so! It has special impact coming from him, of course, as he usually talks so inexhaustibly.

After this "lion's roar" of silence, Vimalakīrti sends out to another universe for lunch, bringing a few grains of rice from the Buddha Sugandhakūṭa of the Perfume Universe, which he multiplies to feed the great crowd that has magically fit into his empty house by this time. Along with the food comes a group of perfume *bodhisattvas* from that universe, who are curious to see the "Barely Tolerable" (*Sahā*) universe of Buddha Śākyamuni and the amazing *bodhisattva* Vimalakīrti who can beam an emanation out across the galaxies to bring back lunch! They are shocked to see how unheavenly our universe is, compared to theirs, and they and Vimalakīrti have an extended dialogue, during which he presents the "answer" to the problem posed in the beginning of the text.

Vimalakīrti persuades the perfume *bodhisattvas* that Śākyamuni's "Tolerable" universe is ideal for *bodhisattvas*—better than a heavenly perfume world—precisely because there is so much struggle and hardship in it. This difficulty of life is just what is needed for the development of compassion. Wisdom can certainly be cultivated in deep contemplation under a perfume tree, perhaps more conveniently than in our busy world. But without struggle, without nearness to suffering and relationship with earthly beings, it is impossible to develop great compassion, and it is only compassion that creates eventually the Body of Buddhahood, as wisdom creates the Mind. This section presents one of the clearest rationalizations of suffering in any Mahāyāna text, a veritable Buddhist "theodicy."

The scene changes again for the final act of the drama, as Vimalakīrti shows his inconceivable liberation yet again. He miniaturizes the entire assembly, picks it up in his hand, and places it gently down outside of town in the grove of Āmrapālī, in the presence of the Buddha. There is a reunion between the monk Buddha and the layman Buddha, as Vimalakīrti has emerged by this point. Vimalakīrti gives a penetrating discourse to the effect that only one who does not see any Buddha can actually see the Buddha, as the Buddha is not this body of form, not sensation, not ideation, and so forth. The Buddha accepts that he is both there and not there and praises his householder colleague.

It is eventually revealed that Vimalakīrti is an Emanation Body of the Akṣobhya Buddha of the Buddha-land known as "Abhirati" ("Intense Delight"). Vimalakīrti performs a last miracle of bringing the entire Abhirati world in miniature form on the palm of his hand into this world, showing it to all present. Abhirati is described as a paradise, but a paradise much more like our world, much more earthy than the heavenly Buddha-lands of perfume and jewel lotus palaces. The main difference between Abhirati and our world is that the stairways from its earth to its heavens are always visible, and gods and humans mingle equally, all gravitating around the august presence of Akṣobhya Buddha. This is the culminating dramatic symbol of the text, with Vimalakīrti holding out a hope for the future of this planet of ours in the Saha universe.

The *Vimalakīrti* seems to have been designed as a kind of anthology of the major themes of all Mahāyāna Scriptures. The wisdom teachings of chapters five and nine especially are as if drawn from the *Transcendent Wisdom* (*Prajñāpāramitā*) Scriptures. The miraculous glimpses of various "pure" Buddha-lands are cameos of the *Pure Land of Bliss* (*Sukhāvatī*) Scriptures. The third and fourth chapters of dialogues between Vimalakīrti and various monks and laymen could have been drawn from any of the early *Jewel Heap* (*Ratnakūṭa*) Scriptures, which are full of the controversies between those clinging to the strict dualism of the old monastic Buddhism and those inspired with the messianic nonduality of the Mahāyāna. The second chapter on "liberative art" or "technique," as well as the chapters proving to the perfume *bodhisattva*s the greater perfection of this seemingly imperfect Buddha-land of Śākyamuni, give the central message of the *White Lotus of Holy Truth* (*Saddharma Puṇḍarīkā* Scriptures. The sixth chapter on "Inconceivable Liberation" actually refers to the *Avataṃsaka* (*Garland*) Scriptures, presenting the teaching of the chapter as a drop of that ocean, and the first miracle of the jeweled canopy resonates with the famous "Jewel Net of Indra" analogy for the mutually interpenetrative nature of all things that is a central vision of the *Garland*. Then come the ritual and magical nature of the mansion of Vimalakīrti, the enthronement of all members of the audience, the consecration of all by the Goddess, the teachings of the "Family of the Tathāgatas" and the reconciliation of dichotomies, and finally the magical, spiritual feast which cannot be digested until the participant achieves a higher stage of enlightenment, all of which convey an atmosphere of esoteric Buddhism, the apocalyptic vehicle later codified in the Buddhist Tantras.

The *Vimalakīrti* can be read in a sitting. Its drama and visions and humor carry a reader past some of the difficult passages. But it can also be repeatedly browsed in, as its mysterious dialogues and paradoxes stimulate contemplative thinking. For those new to the Buddhist literature, or more generally the wisdom literature of India, it serves as an excellent introduction, and for those who have read widely, studied deeply, and taken time to contemplate, it seems to endure as a quintessential summary.

A Note on the *Mencius*

Irene Bloom

The reader of the *Mencius* is frequently reminded of the deep connection between Mencius, who lived during the fourth century B.C., and Confucius, who lived about a century and a half earlier. The connection is apparent even when, in the closing passage of the text (7B:38), Mencius himself seems to brood over the possibility that the transmission or succession he believed had passed over the course of centuries, from the sage kings Yao, Shun, and Yü to the Shang founder, T'ang, and from him down to the Chou founder, King Wen, and from the early Chou rulers to Confucius, might be broken if there were no one in his own time capable of carrying on the mission of the sage. The unpromising nature of the historical situation as Mencius perceives it seems to make that much more unambiguous the depth of his aspiration to fill the role of the sage and of his devotion to Confucius as an exemplar of sagehood.

But the connection between the two is most clearly evident in Mencius's commitment to *jen*, variously translated as goodness, benevolence, humanity, or humaneness. Confucius often spoke about *jen*, nearly always leaving its significance open for further reflection, as though he preferred his hearers to ponder it rather than to presume they could fully grasp it. Mencius says a good deal more about it, making it almost possible to grasp, though certainly not to exhaust its meaning. *Jen* is perhaps the central conception in the *Mencius,* but, more than that, it can be understood as an informing spirit which animates most of the exchanges recorded in the text. By attending to it in the many contexts in which it is present, we may observe Mencius doing philosophy in the characteristically Confucian manner. We see him building on that primary and powerful vision of human relatedness which is found in the Confucian *Analects,* elaborating, clarifying, and restating it in a variety

Mencius (c. 371 BC–289 BC)

of contexts. Such is the power of his language, and his evocation of the human potential for goodness, that it is not difficult to understand in retrospect how it happened that *jen*, as a virtue and a vision, would come following Mencius to fill a place at the heart of a dynamic Confucian humanism which survives down to the present day.

Like Confucius, Mencius was concerned both with fundamental human questions, such as the nature of human nature and functioning of consciousness, and with the matter of government. Nor did he see these issues as in any way separate or distinct. Apparently the concerns which those grounded in Western thought might see subsumed under the categories of "moral philosophy" and "political philosophy" were so continuous for Mencius that he saw no need to argue for or even to explain their relation. It probably would not have occurred to him to propose that the components of individual personality might serve as an analogy for the constituents of the state, as did Plato in the *Republic*. We see no attempt to consider what human beings might be like prior to society or apart from it or even, as with Aristotle in his *Politics,* what human beings might be like in different kinds of polities.

For Mencius, human nature is to be understood through the behavior human beings display in various social situations. He seems to take as a given that the patriarchal family and the monarchical state are constant features of social life and that people are by nature relatively similar. The problem of ethical and political life is to encourage individuals and rulers alike to fulfill the potential of their natures by playing their allotted roles as well as possible. This always involves affirming their interrelatedness, a tendency which is central to the notion of *jen*.

In a sense the *Mencius* is a more public text than the *Analects*. Mencius may have been as complex and multifaceted a personality as the Confucius we encounter in the *Analects,* but we do not observe him, as we do Confucius, in intimate and personal exchanges with his disciples, nor do we seem to discover him in moments of informality or striking personal candor. Mencius usually appears to us, as in the opening chapters of the work, in direct exchanges with rulers of the contending feudal states of the time or at occasions, apparently rather formal in character, when he is engaged in encounters with memorable antagonists over major philosophical questions. His discussions of *jen* come up first in the context of his conversations with rulers of several of the feudal states of the late Chou period. In these conversations Mencius tries to convey to them what constitutes humane government, how the ruler may recognize in himself the impulse to humaneness, and why a humane government is bound to be effective.

The tone of the entire text is set in the opening exchange (1A:1) in which Mencius responds to the aged and besieged King Hui of Liang, who has suggested hopefully that Mencius must have journeyed to Liang prepared with strategies for profiting his state. Mencius dismisses this question as inappropriate, contending with the utmost conviction that "profit," as a motive, must prove divisive and destructive. Once the ruler begins to think in terms of "profit," he insists, everyone in the state, from the ministers to the common people, will do the same. When everyone thinks in terms of profit, the common good will have been forgotten, and, from Mencius's point of view, there can be no greater loss than this. His conclusion is that "All that matters is that there should be humaneness and rightness. What is the point of mentioning the word 'profit'?"

In advancing such an argument, Mencius articulates a view with as much moral resonance as any in Confucian teaching. Echoing and reechoing in virtually all later Confucius discourse is the idea that what ultimately matters in human interactions is the motivation of the actors and their capacity for mutual respect and regard based on recognition of a common humanity. This common humanity is understood to be variously expressed by individuals performing distinct roles and confronting the different circumstances of life according to the complementary principle of *i,* or rightness, a complex idea of what is right in particular situations, coupled with a sense of the judgment required to ensure appropriate behavior.

The depth of Mencius's interest in human motivation and commitment to the ethical complementarity of *jen* and *i* becomes clear when his central concerns are set over against the most compelling alternative views of the time. One of these was Legalism. Though Mencius lived before the time of Han Fei Tzu, who produced the classic distillation of Legalist thought in the late third century B.C., the hard-bitten approach to the problems of government which came to be labeled "the school of laws" had already been current for several centuries. Mencius, when conversing with various rulers of the time, does not allude to Legalist philosophy per se, but it is clear that he is arguing, at least indirectly, against the kind of tough-minded *Realpolitik* which appealed to many who were dedicated to advancing the interests of their states in an age of bitter contention and brutal warfare. The Legalists, in their pragmatism, their exaltation of military might, their reliance on the coercive force of laws and punishments, their contempt for culture, and their almost exclusive concern with the advantage or "profit" of rulers, show little concern for the capacity for moral responsiveness which, for Mencius, is the very essence of being human.

Many of Mencius's pronouncements about humaneness and rightness are targeted at rulers who seem not only skeptical of what he has to say but steeped in an alternative, and much less generous, set of values. It is no doubt a measure of his absolute confidence in the rightness and cogency of his own moral standpoint that he is direct to the point of acerbity in making his case with several rulers against the squandering of life and resources in warfare and belligerence. Nor has he any compunction about informing King Hsüan of Ch'i, who may well have had some sensitivity on this score, that there is no moral principle which precludes the ousting of a ruler who "mutilates humaneness and cripples rightness." Mencius insists that, historically, it was an extreme of corruption that led to the overthrow of the last ruler of the Hsia dynasty by the Shang founder and, in turn, of the last ruler of the Shang by the Chou founders. These acts, having been morally justified, were not regicide but merely the "punishment" of rulers who had done violence against others and against their own humanity (1B:8). This judgment, often understood as representing a defense by Mencius of a "right of revolution," was no doubt intended to apply to only the most extreme circumstances, though, given the high moral standards proposed by Mencius for any ruler, it is hardly surprising that many throughout the centuries have been made decidedly uneasy by it.

Philosophically speaking, Mencius identifies his primary antagonists as the adherents of the schools of Yang Chu and Mo-tzu (3B:9). Yang Chu, sometimes characterized as an individualist, evidently defended the individual's withdrawal from public life or from official service in the interests of self-preservation. As Mencius understood him, Yang saw the individual as appropriately self-regarding, a view which Confucians would consistently condemn as morally vacant. Mo-tzu, often described as a utilitarian, espoused a morality predicated on the idea that a purely rational calculation of personal advantage should prompt everyone to adopt the imperative of universal love, or love without discrimination. Such love, which was to be extended to everyone equally, and correspondingly to be received from everyone equally, without regard to the primacy of familial bonds, put morality at a remove from the familial context which Confucians believed was its natural source and matrix.

For Mencius, Yang Chu's view involved the denial of one's ruler, Mo-tzu's, denial of one's parents. Because his own morality was based on a conception of the subtlety and richness of the human moral sense, with its roots in the deepest dimensions of biologic and psychic life and its ramifications in the whole of human experience, both of these represented a denial of what he took to be truly human. "If the way of Yang and the way of Mo are not stopped and the Way of Confucius is not made manifest, the people will be deluded by perverse views and humaneness and rightness will be blocked. When humaneness and rightness are blocked, then we lead animals to devour humans, and humans to devour one another. I am alarmed about this and am determined to defend the way of the former sages by opposing Yang and Mo."

Profit, whether it is understood to entail the advantage of an individual, a ruler, or the state as a whole, is rejected by Mencius as an appropriate motive for action. But the fact that profit is rejected as a motive does not mean that any concession is made in regard to the potential efficacy of humane government. It is clear from conversations which Mencius has with King Hui, his successor King Hsiang, King Hsüan of Ch'i, and others that he is convinced that it is the complementarity of humaneness and rightness that finally "works." Any narrower calculation of what might be advantageous to a ruler or even to a state as a whole is bound ultimately to be self-defeating because such calculation fails to encourage mutual regard and fellow feeling, impulses which lead in the direction of *jen* and are conducive to that most enduringly important of all political phenomena, human unity.

Jen, for Mencius, involves more than a disposition of the mind and heart. It is that, but it also necessarily carries over into action and, in the case of a ruler, into policy. High as his moral vision is, Mencius is also highly practical in his awareness that human beings have basic needs for food, clothing, shelter, and education and that these must be met if their very existence as human beings is to be possible. In the provisions he advocates for such matters as landholding, taxation, famine relief, the establishment of schools, hunting, arboriculture, and sericulture (1A:3, 2A:5, 3A:3), he seems more specific than the Mohists in projecting what must be done by a ruler in order to provide on a long-term basis for these needs. And whereas the Mohists are concerned, almost as much as the Legalists, with mobilization and control in order to stave off disorder, always underlying Mencius's philosophy of government there is the concern primarily with motivation and with moral authority. Such authority depends above all on the ruler's ability to empathize with his people and to exercise "the transforming influence of morality" (2A:3).

The ability to exercise a "transforming influence" is the mark of a sage. What makes it possible for a sage to perform such a function is that human beings are highly responsive to one another, and they are responsive because they are both alike by nature and aware of this likeness. They differ, according to Mencius, primarily owing to the environment in which they are nurtured. In one of the many passages in the *Mencius* that employ agricultural analogies of plants and growing things (6A:7), the human condition is likened to that of seeds which grow more or less well depending on the richness of the soil, the regularity of the rain and dew, and the amount of human effort invested in cultivation. "Now things of the same kind are all alike. Why should we have doubts when it comes to man? The sage and I are of the same kind." Not only are human beings similar by nature, they are also capable of growing to the kind of perfection exemplified by the sages Yao and Shun of antiquity.

When we survey the history of Confucian thought, Mencius was unquestionably the single most influential contributor to a view of human nature which ultimately became dominant, not only in China but in the rest of Confucianized East Asia as well, and not only in the thought of an intellectual and social elite but in the value system of an entire culture. It is a view quite different from that of the biblical religions, which share a conception of human beings as inherently flawed and having to struggle to reverse the distance between themselves and God, a defect which entered the definition of humanness almost at the beginning of human history. Mencius, for his part, does not delve into the creation of the universe and of man. By the time he begins his reflections, both are understood to be in place, human history to be well under way, the patterns of human behavior and relationship already set. Mencius begins with the here and now and with the actual lives of his contemporaries, all of whom, he finds, have within themselves the potential for goodness.

The evidence he adduces, in perhaps the most celebrated passage in the work (2A:6), rests on a single powerful example. "All men," he says, "have a mind (or heart) which cannot bear to see the sufferings of others."

> When I say that all men have a mind which cannot bear to see the
> sufferings of others, my meaning may be illustrated thus: even nowadays,
> if men suddenly see a child about to fall into a well, they will without
> exception experience a feeling of alarm and distress. They will feel so,
> not as a ground on which they may gain the favor of the child's parents,
> nor as a ground on which they may seek the praise of their neighbours
> and friends, nor from a dislike of the reputation of having been
> unmoved by such a thing. . . .

As Mencius works through this situation, he does not need to tell us what the person who sees the child teetering on the edge of a well will do. We ourselves fill this in out of our own humanity. We recognize that all human beings can be counted on, insofar as they retain their humanity, to act on the spontaneous impulse to save the child by pulling it from danger. This mind or heart (the distinction is not made in Chinese) which cannot bear to see the sufferings of others is, in a positive sense, compassion. "Whoever is devoid of the mind of compassion is not human," he says. Then he extends the argument considerably by adding, "Whoever is devoid of the mind of shame is not human, whoever is devoid of the mind of courtesy and modesty is not human, and whoever is devoid of the mind of right and wrong is not human." These four—compassion, shame, courtesy and modesty, and the sense of right and wrong—he calls the "four beginnings" or the "four seeds" of virtue. These he believes are present in every human being; they figure crucially in the Mencian definition of the human.

As promptings of the mind or heart, as sentiments, these inclinations are not confirmed or complete at any given point in a person's life. Developing them is a matter of experience, effort, and cultivation, but they are always there as a potential. The sense of compassion Mencius recognizes as the beginning of humaneness; the sense of shame, the beginning of rightness; the sense of modesty, the beginning of propriety; and the sense of right and wrong, the beginning of wisdom.

> Human beings have these four beginnings just as they have their four limbs. When one who has these four beginnings, says of himself that he cannot develop them, he acts as a thief to himself, and one who says of his prince that he cannot develop them, acts as a thief to his prince.
>
> We have these four beginnings within us, and if we know how to develop and complete them, it will be like a fire starting to burn or a spring beginning to come through. By bringing them to completion, we are able to protect all within the four seas. In failing to bring them to completion, we have not even the wherewithal to serve our parents.

One may cultivate the "four beginnings" in oneself, or one may not. If one does not, one injures oneself and one's intimates quite as much as others. By even expressing skepticism about the moral capacity of another, one injures that person—one literally steals from him something that is his and that is precious.

The human moral capacity derives, in this view, not from some still, small voice within us that guides us toward the right and away from the wrong, but from a kind of energy that is built up within ourselves in the course of our entire experience and education. In a particularly memorable passage (2A:2) Mencius speaks about his strengths, which he understands to be insight into words and skill in cultivating his "flood-like *ch'i*," or, as one translator aptly puts it, his "overwhelming energy." This *ch'i*, he says,

> . . . is in the highest degree, vast and unyielding. Nourish it with integrity and place no obstacle in its path and it will fill the space between Heaven and Earth. It is *ch'i* which unites rightness and the Way. Deprive it of these and it will collapse. It is born of accumulated rightness and cannot be appropriated by anyone through a sporadic show of rightness. Whenever one acts in a way that falls below the standard in one's heart, it will collapse.

Mencius is arguing here against his principal antagonist, Kao Tzu, who maintains (6A:4) that, whereas humaneness is internal, rightness is external, something assimilated through learning or conditioning, but not inherently in us as part of our nature. Mencius for his part sees rightness as related to physical energy and to our feelings of vitality and well-being and our positive sense of identity as persons. It bears on our stamina and affects the energy with which we lead our lives. It is closely associated with a sense of human dignity, which prompts us to do certain things and to refrain from doing others, which suggests certain priorities that on grounds of simple self-interest might be unintelligible. This *ch'i*, or psychophysical energy, which Mencius would have us carefully and actively cultivate is powerful and yet fragile, dependent on and sensitive to the quality and rightness of our moral lives.

Later Chinese philosophy owes an enormous debt to Mencius. No small part of this debt is for enlarging and clarifying the very sense of what it means to be human—a sense which is quite definite and particular and yet also consciously open and rich with possibilities. "Humaneness is what it means to be human," he says. "When these two are conjoined, the result is 'the Way' " (7B:16). "Humaneness is the mind of man, and rightness his road" (6A:11). However the concepts of humaneness and rightness were interpreted and reinterpreted following Mencius, they would always imply the primary value of the dignity of persons and, particularly, the connectedness among them and the directedness in their moral lives.

It is as if the work of Confucius—which involved drawing attention to the natural equality of human beings, their fundamental relatedness, and their ability to control their own lives through learning and effort—is confirmed by Mencius. It is also furthered by him through his remarkable psychological insight and his secure sense of the scope of the human enterprise. There is in Mencius a deepened confidence concerning the place of human beings in the universe. As he says toward the end of the work that bears his name, "One who gives full realization to his mind (or heart) understands his own nature and, by knowing his own nature, knows Heaven. Preserving one's mind and nourishing one's nature is the way to serve Heaven" (7A:1). His affirmation of the connectedness among persons, past and present, and between human beings and the universe as a whole, has had a long and fruitful career in East Asia and may have much to say to the modern West as well.

Note on translations: One of the best available translations may be found in James Legge's classic rendering, originally completed in 1861 and published in several editions by the Clarendon Press and Oxford University Press and most recently reprinted by Dover Books (New York, 1970). A more recent translation made by D. C. Lau is published in paperback by Penguin (Harmondsworth, 1970) and in hardcover by the Chinese University Press (Hong Kong, 1984).

T'ang Poetry: A Return to Basics

Burton Watson

The history of Chinese poetry begins around 600 B.C. with the compilation of an anthology, the *Shih-ching*, or *Book of Odes*, containing poems that probably date back several centuries earlier. It continues with barely a break down to the present day. Naturally, such an extended period of development saw the evolution of a number of different poetic forms and styles, and countless ebbs and flows in the tide of artistic inspiration.

It has generally been agreed by Chinese critics—and non-Chinese students of the language have found no reason to dissent—that the highest peak in literary achievement in this long process of growth was reached during the T'ang dynasty, which ruled China from A.D. 618 to 907, particularly the middle years of that period. This was the age of Li Po, Tu Fu, Po Chü-i, and numerous other figures renowned in Chinese literary history, when the art of poetry seemed to reach levels of expressive force and universality of statement it had hardly known in the past and was seldom to rival again. I would like here to try to convey some idea of the nature of this poetry and its appeal for English readers of today. Rather than attempting generalities, I will structure the discussion around specific examples of T'ang poetry, touching upon the qualities that can be effectively brought across in translation and those that must inevitably be lost.

Unlike the peoples of Europe and India, the Chinese did not develop a tradition of epic poetry. Though they had their internecine wars and campaigns against foreign invaders—Ezra Pound's "Song of the Bowmen of Shu" is a translation of an early work from the *Book of Odes* dealing with one such campaign—they seldom made feats of arms a theme of poetry. An overwhelmingly agricultural people, they have preferred in their poetry to focus mainly upon the scenes and events of everyday life, which accounts for the generally low-keyed and un-grandiose tone of so much of Chinese poetry. It is also one reason why many of their works, even those written centuries ago, sound strikingly modern in translation.

The first work to be quoted is by the government official and poet Po Chü-i (772–846). Po was one of the most prolific of the major T'ang poets, and his works are particularly well preserved, in part because he took the trouble to compile and edit them himself and deposit copies in the library of an important Buddhist temple in Lo-yang. The poem was written in 835 and is addressed to Po's friend Liu Yü-hsi (772–842), a fellow poet and bureaucrat who was the same age as Po. The Chinese frequently exchanged poems with friends, often replying to one another's poems as one would reply to a letter, the practice constituting both an expression of friendship and an opportunity to exercise literary abilities and invite critical comment. When responding to a friend's poem, one customarily employed the same poetic form and sometimes the same rhymes or rhyme words as the original poem in order to add an element of challenge to the game.

On Old Age, to Send to Meng-te (Liu Yü-hsi)

> The two of us both in old age now,
> I ask myself what it means to be old.
> Eyes bleary, evenings you're the first to bed;
> hair a bother, mornings you leave it uncombed.

Sometimes you go out, a stick to prop you;
sometimes, gate shut, you stay indoors the whole day.
Neglecting to look into the newly polished mirror,
no longer reading books if the characters are very small,
your thoughts dwelling more and more on old friends,
your activities far removed from those of the young,
only idle chatter rouses your interest . . .
When we meet, we still have lots of that don't we!*

The subject of the poem is so universal an experience and the presentation so straightforward that comment seems almost superfluous. The poet, sixty-three at the time, begins by speaking directly to his friend Liu but then quickly falls into a kind of private reverie on the subject of old age and the changes it brings. In the very last line he abruptly shakes himself out of his musings and addresses his friend once more. Unlike many traditional Chinese poems, this one employs no erudite allusions to early literature, though, as may readily be seen in the translation, it makes considerable use of verbal parallelism, a device common in both Chinese prose and poetry. The poem is in *shih* form, essentially the same form used in the *Shih-ching*, or *Book of Odes*. It employs a line which is five characters or five syllables in length and is in the relatively free "old-style" form, which means there is no limit on the number of lines. A single rhyme is employed throughout, the rhymes occurring at the end of the even-numbered lines.

Po Chü-i is particularly remembered for his relaxed, warmly personal works such as the one just quoted. He himself, however, placed a much higher value on his poems of social criticism. Confucius had emphasized the didactic function of poetry, citing the poems of the *Book of Odes* as examples, and Confucian-minded officials in later centuries often employed poetic forms to voice criticisms of the government or expose the ills of society. Po Chü-i in his youthful years as an official enthusiastically carried on this tradition, writing a number of outspoken works that he hoped would bring about changes in government policy. The following is a famous example.

The poem is entitled "Light Furs, Fat Horses," an allusion to a passage in the Confucian *Analects* (VI, 3) in which Confucius censures luxurious living among public officials. It was written in 810, when the poet held advisory posts in the capital, and the region south of the Yangtze River was plagued by drought. The poet had previously asked that the government take steps to aid the drought victims, but his pleas went unheeded. The poem depicts a banquet at a military encampment in or near the capital. It is in the same form as the poem previously quoted.

---

*Poems marked with an asterisk were translated especially for this article and are published here for the first time. Other poems are taken from the author's *Columbia Book of Chinese Poetry* (New York: Columbia University Press, 1984).

白樂天名居易始生七月能展書指
之無二字示之雖百數不差年十
七登進士第詩云慈恩塔上題名
慶士九人中最少年唐元和中對
策擢左拾遺近主名郎中知制誥
晚年放意詩酒彌醉冷先生稱香
山居士人繪九老圖為刑部尚書

Po Chü-i, portrait by an unknown artist; in the National Palace Museum, Taipei.

Light Furs, Fat Horses

A show of arrogant spirit fills the road;
a glitter of saddles and horses lights up the dust.
I ask who these people are—
trusted servants of the ruler, I'm told.
The vermilion sashes are all high-ranking courtiers;
the purple ribbons are probably generals.
Proudly they repair to the regimental feast,
their galloping horses passing like clouds.
Tankards and wine cups brim with nine kinds of spirits;
from water and land, an array of eight delicacies.
For fruit they break open Tung-t'ing oranges,
for fish salad, carve up scaly bounty from T'ien-chih.
Stuffed with food, they rest content in heart;
livened by wine, their mood grows merrier than ever.
This year there's a drought south of the Yangtze.
In Ch'ü-chou, people are eating people.

T'ang poetry—at least, all that has come down to us—is almost entirely the product of a single group in society, the literati or scholar-bureaucrats, men who had received a firm grounding in the classical texts and had chosen to enter government service, often after passing the civil service examinations. For these men, the writing of poetry was no mere hobby or diversion, but an integral part of their lives as gentlemen and public servants, a means of airing their opinions, fulfilling their responsibilities to society, and furthering their spiritual cultivation.

The greatness of T'ang poetry probably derives first of all from this tone of moral seriousness that pervades so much of it. There were other periods in Chinese literary history when poetry was mainly a pleasant pastime for members of the court or aristocracy, a vehicle for displaying verbal ingenuity or embroidering upon the patterns of the past. The T'ang poets, though certainly not incapable of frivolous verse, generally had far more serious purposes in mind when they employed the medium, as we have seen in the example just quoted. They returned poetry to what they believed to be its original function, the addressing of important social and ethical issues.

At the same time, as evidenced in the first poem quoted above, they were not afraid to be frankly personal in their writing. Though this personal note was shunned in some periods of literary history, the best of the T'ang poets such as Tu Fu or Po Chü-i did not hesitate to record the experiences and emotional crises of their daily lives in their works, employing poetry much as the diary or autobiography forms are used in other cultures. To do so was for them a kind of literary and spiritual discipline.

The poet-official Wang Wei (699–759), much of whose poetry describes the scenes of his daily life, purchased a country estate at a place called Wang River in the mountains south of Ch'ang-an, the T'ang capital. The estate had formerly belonged to another well-known poet-official, Sung Chih-wen (d. 712?). In the following poem, the first in a famous series describing scenic spots on the estate, the poet muses on the passing of time, as graphically exemplified in the dying willows planted by the former owner, his own feelings of pity for Sung Chih-wen, and the pity that owners of the estate in years to come will perhaps feel for him. This ability of the T'ang poets, often within the span of a scant four lines, to open out huge vistas in time or space is one of the qualities that endow their poetry with its characteristic air of grandeur and mythic proportions.

Meng-ch'eng Hollow

A new home at the mouth of Meng-ch'eng;
old trees—last of a stand of dying willows:
years to come, who will be its owner,
vainly pitying the one who had it before?

The T'ang poets did not confine themselves to the autobiographical in their subject matter, however. Following a practice that is very old in Chinese poetry, they frequently adopted a persona from the folk-song tradition in order to enlarge the breadth and social significance of their material, speaking through the voice of a peasant pressed into military service, a neglected wife, or a soldier on frontier duty. Here, for example, is such a work by Li Po (701–762), a poet particularly famed for his lyric gift and his works in folk-song form. It is entitled "Tzu-yeh Song," Tzu-yeh being the name of a courtesan of earlier times who was noted for her brief and poignant songs. The poem is set in autumn, the time when women traditionally fulled cloth to make clothes to send to the soldiers at the border, and pictures a woman in the capital city of Ch'ang-an dreaming of her husband at Jade Pass in Kansu, far to the west.

Tzu-yeh Song

Ch'ang-an—one slip of moon;
in ten thousand houses, the sound of fulling mallets.
Autumn winds keep on blowing,
all things make me think of Jade Pass!
When will they put down the barbarians
and my good man come home from his far campaign?

Before leaving this poem we may note that, according to some commentators, the first line should be interpreted to read, "Ch'ang-an—one swath of moonlight." The question, in effect, is whether one chooses to imagine the women working under the thin crescent of a new moon, or under a full moon that floods the ground with light.

Famous as these poems are and as often as they have been commented upon, the nature of classical Chinese language is such that differences of interpretation of this kind continue to exist.

The poems quoted so far have all dealt with the world of human affairs, but this does not mean that T'ang poets neglected the natural scene around them. In very early times, nature was looked on as rather fearful, the abode of fierce beasts or malevolent spirits. But from around the fifth century on, Chinese painters and poets began to show a much greater appreciation of the beauties of the natural world, particularly the mist-filled mountain and river landscapes of southern China. The period was one of foreign invasion and political turmoil, and these mountain landscapes came to be seen as places of peace and safety, where one might escape from the perils of official life and perhaps even acquire the secrets of longevity.

This interest in natural beauty continued to be an important theme in T'ang poetry, often bound up with religious overtones linking it to Buddhism or Taoism. The following poem, from a group of some three hundred poems attributed to a recluse known as Han-shan, or The Master of Cold Mountain, is an example. Han-shan was said to have lived at a place called Cold Mountain (Han-shan) in the T'ien-t'ai mountains of Chekiang Province, the site of many Buddhist and Taoist temples. It is uncertain when he lived, though the late eighth and early ninth centuries is suggested as the most likely possibility. The poem is untitled.

> I climb the road to Cold Mountain,
> the road to Cold Mountain that never ends.
> The valleys are long and strewn with stones,
> the streams broad and banked with thick grass.
> Moss is slippery, though no rain has fallen;
> pines sigh but it isn't the wind.
> Who can break from the snares of the world
> and sit with me among the white clouds?

On the literal level the poem is a description of the scenery along the kind of mountain trail that I myself have climbed in the T'ien-t'ai range, with its rocky streambeds and pine-clad slopes. At the same time the imagery of the ascent suggests a process of spiritual cultivation and the attainment of higher realms of understanding, while the white clouds of the last line—clouds that the Chinese believed were literally breathed forth by the mountain itself—are a frequently recurring symbol in Chinese literature for purity and detachment.

The next poem to be quoted, by a ninth-century writer named Kao P'ien, also deals with the natural scene. But this is nature carefully cultivated and seen in close conjunction with human habitation. As the title "Mountain Pavilion, Summer Day" tells us, the scene is a pleasant

Tu Fu, stone rubbing, Ch'ing dynasty (1644–1911/12).

country retreat in the hush of a long hot summer's day. We are shown the masses of shade trees surrounding the house, the reflections of the building and terrace as they appear upside down in the pond that fronts them, the trellis of roses whose fragrance is so strong in the courtyard. Beyond the courtyard, a curtain strung with crystal beads stirs gently in the cool breeze, but just who is napping behind the curtains we are not told. The poem is an example of the kind of mood piece at which the T'ang poets excelled, deft sketches made up of a few artfully chosen details that serve to rouse the reader's curiosity and invite him to fill out the remainder of the scene from his own imagination.

Mountain Pavilion, Summer Day

Thick shade of green trees, long summer day,
lodge and terrace casting their reflections upside down in the pond.
Crystal-beaded curtains stir, a faint breeze rising;
one trellis of roses, the courtyard full of its scent.*

This poem, along with a Wang Wei poem quoted earlier, is written in a form known as *chüeh-chü,* or "cut-off lines." The form is limited to four lines in length and usually employs a line of five or seven characters. Chinese is a tonal language, and the *chüeh-chü* form, in addition to employing end rhyme, obeys elaborate rules governing the tonal pattern of the words. We do not know just how the four tones of T'ang period Chinese were pronounced, and even if we did, the effect of such tonal patterns could not be reproduced in a nontonal language such as English. But it is well to keep in mind that, though translations of T'ang poetry may give an impression of relative freedom, the originals are often in highly controlled forms. The fact that the T'ang poets not only complied with the exacting prosodic restrictions placed upon them, but even succeeded in dancing in their chains, is one of the wonders of their poetry.

One writer who seems to have welcomed the challenges presented by such demanding forms and who produced in them works of great power and originality was Tu Fu (712–770), often referred to as China's greatest poet. He is particularly noted for the keen observations of nature recorded in his works, as well as for his tone of passionate sincerity and concern for the welfare of the nation. The following poem, entitled simply *Chüeh-chü,* was written in his late years, when conditions of unrest in the country forced him to live the life of a wanderer in the upper reaches of the Yangtze River, hoping always for an opportunity to return to his home in the northeast.

The poem begins with two lines in strict parallel form recording thoughtfully noted observations on the river scene: the fact that the river gulls appear whiter than ever when seen against the intense blue of the river, and that the buds of spring blossoms—probably peach tree buds—seem like so many flames about to burst into color. In the second couplet, however, the tense objectivity of the opening lines suddenly gives way to a rush of feeling as the poet realizes that yet another spring has come and is about to depart, while he is still far removed from his homeland.

> River cobalt-blue, birds whiter against it;
> mountains green, blossoms about to flame:
> as I watch, this spring too passes by—
> what day will I ever go home?*

The last poem in my selection, like the first one, is addressed to a friend and deals with the theme of friendship and separation. It was the custom of Chinese gentlemen to write poems of commemoration when they gathered for a banquet, outing, or other social occasion, and this was particularly true when the purpose of the gathering was to see one of their number off on a journey. Official assignments kept the scholar-bureaucrats moving constantly about the empire, and there are numerous works by T'ang poets bidding farewell to a friend or thanking friends for such a send-off. This poem is by Li Po and is addressed to his friend Meng Hao-jan (689–740), who was sailing east down the Yangtze to Yang-chou (Kuang-ling) in Kiangsu. The farewell party was held at a place called Yellow Crane Tower overlooking the river at Wu-ch'ang in Hupei. All this information is carefully recorded in the heading of the poem, since the Chinese tend to feel that the circumstances that led to the writing of a poem are an important part of its meaning.

At Yellow Crane Tower Taking Leave of Meng Hao-jan as He Sets off for Kuang-ling

My old friend takes leave of the west at Yellow Crane Tower,
in misty third-month blossoms goes down stream to Yang-chou.
The far-off shape of his lone sail disappears in the blue-green void,
and all I see is the long river flowing to the edge of the sky.

Like Wang Wei's poem quoted above on the successive owners of his country estate, this one opens up vistas, here spatial ones that show us the sweeping mountain ranges and river systems of continental China. And unspoken but underlying it is the aching contrast between these vast, long-enduring features of the landscape and the frailty of human existence, symbolized by the lone sail of Meng's boat fading from view on the horizon.

T'ang poetry, to sum up, stands out in the long history of Chinese poetic development because, eschewing the superficiality of an earlier age—the tendency toward bland impersonality and mannered manipulation of stock themes and images—it restored to Chinese poetry the lost note of personal concern. The T'ang poets were not afraid to employ poetry to record their deepest and most intimate feelings, crying out for the alleviation of social ills, noting with wry candor the waning of their physical powers, longing for absent friends, or dreaming of the last journey home. And because they dealt with the basic impulses of the human being, their works easily survive the transition into another language and milieu. T'ang poetry, as one who reads it will readily perceive, is not just the product of a particularly golden age in China's literary history but a part of the universal human heritage.

A Dream of Red Mansions

C. T. Hsia

The Chinese novel *Hung lou meng* is known in English as *The Dream of the Red Chamber* (with or without the initial particle) because earlier partial translations bear this rather enigmatic title. Today its continuing use is unjustified, since we have a complete translation in three volumes by Yang Hsien-yi and Gladys Yang (Peking: Foreign Languages Press, 1978–80) under the apt title *A Dream of Red Mansions*. Another complete translation in five volumes by David Hawkes and John Minford is called *The Story of the Stone* (New York: Penguin Books, 1973–86), which accurately renders the novel's alternative title *Shih-t'ou chi*. Since the work is best known in Chinese as *Hung lou meng*, however, *A Dream of Red Mansions* should be the preferred English title, though the Hawkes-Minford version is richer in style and more interesting to read.

A Dream of Red Mansions is the greatest novel in the Chinese literary tradition. An eighteenth-century work, it draws fully upon that tradition and can indeed be regarded as its crowning achievement. The tradition is early distinguished by its poetry and philosophy. Thus we find, in *Dream,* numerous poems in a variety of meters, including an elegy in the style of the *Ch'u tz'u* (*Songs of the South,* an ancient anthology), along with philosophical conversations that echo the sages of antiquity (Lao-tzu, Chuang-tzu, Mencius) and utilize the subtle language of Zen Buddhism. The principal author of the book, a late traditional man of letters, is further aware of the encyclopedic scope of Chinese learning and the heritage of earlier fiction and drama. He has made obvious use of the Ming domestic novel *Chin P'ing Mei* and romantic masterpieces of Yuan-Ming drama, such as *The Romance of the Western Chamber* (*Hsi-hsiang chi*) and *The Peony Pavilion* (*Mu-tan t'ing*). But his novel is greater than these in its fuller representation of Chinese culture and thought and its incomparably richer delineation of characters in psychological terms. The latter achievement must be solely credited to this author's genius.

His name was Ts'ao Hsüeh-ch'in, and he lived from about 1715 to 1763. He was an ethnic Chinese from a family that had served the Manchu emperors of the Ch'ing dynasty for generations. Though mere bond servants to the throne in status, Ts'ao's great grandfather, grandfather, and father or uncle all held the highly lucrative post of commissioner of Imperial Textile Mills, first briefly in Soochow and then in Nanking. The grandfather, Ts'ao Yin, played host to the K'ang-hsi emperor during his four southern excursions from Peking. But the Yung-cheng emperor, who succeeded K'ang-hsi in 1723, was far less friendly to the Ts'ao house. In 1728 he dismissed Ts'ao Fu, most probably Hsüeh-ch'in's father, from his post as textile commissioner of Nanking and confiscated much of his property. Then thirteen or fourteen years old, Hsüeh-ch'in moved with his parents to Peking in much reduced circumstances. It is believed that the Ts'ao clan temporarily regained favor after the Ch'ien-lung emperor ascended the throne in 1736. But by 1744, when Hsüeh-ch'in started composing his novel, he had moved to the western suburbs of Peking, again living in poverty: the Ts'ao family must have suffered another disaster from which it never recovered. The novelist lost a young son a few months before his own death in February 1763 and was survived by a second wife, of whom we know nothing further.

By all indications Ts'ao Hsüeh-ch'in should have had ample time to complete *Dream* to his own satisfaction, but it would seem that at the time of his death this novel of autobiographical inspiration—about a great family in decline and its young heir—was not yet in publishable shape, though manuscripts of the first eighty chapters, known by title as *The Story of the Stone,* had been in circulation for some time. Scholars now believe that Ts'ao must have completed at least one draft of the whole novel, but that he went on revising it, partly to please the commentators among his kinsmen, prominently a cousin known by his studio name of Red Inkstone (Chih-yen Chai), and partly to remove any grounds for suspicion that his work was critical of the government in devoting space to the tribulations of a family justly deserving of imperial punishment. If Ts'ao had indeed completed the last portion of the novel, but didn't allow it to circulate, it could have been from fear of a literary inquisition.

A corrected second edition of the entire work—120 chapters in all—came out in 1792, only a few months after the first edition of 1791. The second edition contains, in addition to the original preface by Ch'eng Wei-yuan, a new preface by Kao Eh, and a joint foreword by the two. Earlier scholars have arbitrarily taken Ch'eng to be a bookseller who had acquired manuscripts of the later chapters and asked the scholar Kao Eh to put them into shape and edit the work as a whole. Some would even regard Kao Eh as a forger. Now we know that Ch'eng Wei-yuan was a staff member of the gigantic imperial project to assemble a

"Complete Library in Four Branches of Learning and Literature" (*Ssu-k'u ch'üan-shu*). Ho-shen, a Manchu minister enjoying the complete trust of Emperor Ch'ien-lung, was made a director general of the project, and according to a new theory advanced by Chou Ju-ch'ang, a leading authority on the novel, it was Ho-shen himself who had ordered Ch'eng and Kao to prepare a politically harmless version for the perusal of the emperor. This should be taken seriously, for Ch'eng and Kao could not have dreamed of putting out a movable type edition of a massive novel without the backing of a powerful minister like Ho-shen, and without the printing facilities of the imperial court.

Whatever its faults, the Ch'eng-Kao edition has remained the standard text for Chinese readers for almost two hundred years. Scholars, of course, will continue to regret that Ts'ao Hsüeh-ch'in did not live long enough to complete or oversee the publication of his own novel and belittle or give grudging praise to Kao Eh's contributions as an editor and continuator of the first eighty chapters. But if the last forty chapters are not what they should be, the first eighty are also by no means a coherent narrative of seamless unity. In addition to minor inconsistencies in the story line, Ts'ao's inveterate habit for revision would seem to be responsible for more serious instances of narrative ineptitude as well. One plausible theory (endorsed by David Hawkes) proposes that even before starting on his great project, Ts'ao Hsüeh-ch'in had acquired or himself written a manuscript called *A Mirror for the Romantic* (*Feng-yueh pao-chien*), about unhappy youths and maidens belatedly awakened to the illusory nature of love. He was apparently very fond of this manuscript and inserted some of its cautionary tales into his novel. He did so, however, at the cost of upsetting its temporal scheme. The autobiographical hero and his female cousins lead quite unhurried lives, while the trials of the deluded Chia Jui in chapter 12, and of the hapless Yu sisters in chapters 64–67, consume weeks in a few pages. Try as he might, Ts'ao could not have got himself out of this narrative impasse if he was determined to save these somewhat extraneous tales.

The story of the novel's composition and publication thus remains a very complicated affair, demanding further research by the specialists. The novel itself, however, should pose few difficulties for the Western reader unless he is intimidated right away by its sheer size. But the undaunted reader will be amply rewarded and will cherish the experience of having spent days and weeks with many memorable characters in a Chinese setting.

A Dream of Red Mansions is about the aristocratic Chia clan which, like the Ts'ao family, has enjoyed imperial favor for generations. Its two main branches dwell in adjoining compounds in the capital, styled Ningkuofu and Jungkuofu. The nominal head of the Ningkuofu is a selfish student of Taoist alchemy who eventually dies its victim; his son

Chia Chen and grandson Chia Yung are both sensualists. Grandmother Chia, also known as the Lady Dowager in the Yang translation, presides over the Jungkuofu. She has two sons, Chia She and Chia Cheng. Chia Lien, Chia She's pleasure-seeking son, is married to an extremely capable woman, Wang Hsi-feng. Despite her early triumphs in managing the household finances and driving her love rivals to suicide, this handsome and vivacious lady eventually languishes in ill health and dies. Her nefarious dealings are in large part responsible for the raiding of the Chia compounds by imperial guards and the confiscation of their property.

The Dowager's other son, Chia Cheng, is the only conscientious Confucian member of the family in active government service. A lonely man of narrow vision but undeniable rectitude, he has lost a promising son before the novel opens. Naturally, he expects his younger son by his legitimate wife, Lady Wang, to study hard and prepare for the civil service examinations. But Pao-yü, early spoiled by his grandmother, mother, and other female relatives, detests conventional learning and prefers the company of his girl cousins and the maidservants. Since late childhood, he has had as playmate a cousin of delicate beauty beloved by the Dowager, Lin Tai-yü. Some years later, another beautiful cousin, Hsüeh Pao-ch'ai, also moves into the Jungkuofu. In spite of Pao-yü's repeated assurances of his love, Tai-yü regards Pao-ch'ai as her rival and feels very insecure. As she progressively ruins her health by wallowing in self-pity, Pao-ch'ai replaces her as the family's preferred candidate for Pao-yü's wife. But the marriage, when it does take place, brings no joy to Pao-ch'ai, for by that time Pao-yü has turned into an idiot. Broken-hearted and unforgiving, Tai-yü dies on their wedding night.

Pao-yü eventually recovers his mind and obtains the degree of *chü-jen*. But instead of returning home after taking the examination, he renounces the world and becomes a monk. The desolate Pao-ch'ai takes comfort in her pregnancy. A faithful maid, Hsi-jen (called "Aroma" in Hawkes and Minford), is eventually happily married to an actor friend of Pao-yü's. Another maid, Ch'ing-wen ("Skybright" in Hawkes and Minford), to whom Pao-yü was also much attached, had died of calumny and sickness long before his marriage.

Chinese novels before *Dream* are mostly about characters in history and legend. Though a type of short novel about talented and good-looking young lovers had become popular before his time, Ts'ao Hsüeh-ch'in quite properly dismisses these stereotyped romances in his novel for their palpable unreality. But his use of what we may call diurnal realism, the technique of advancing the novel with seemingly inconsequential accounts of day-to-day events, and of lingering over days of family significance, clearly shows his indebtedness to the aforementioned *Chin P'ing Mei*, the only one of the four major Ming novels devoted to tracing the fortunes of a discordant large family. (The other three, all available in English translation, are: *Romance of the Three Kingdoms [San-kuo-chih* yen-i], *Outlaws of the Marsh* [*Shui-hu chuan*], and *The Journey to the West* [*Hsi-yu chi*].) *Chin P'ing Mei* is notorious for its graphic descriptions of Hsi-men Ch'ing's sexual life with his concubines and paramours, but *Dream* is never pornographic, despite its larger cast of male sensualists. The novel maintains instead a note of high culture, focusing attention on the hero and several gifted young ladies whose poetic parties and conversations with him invariably touch upon intellectual and aesthetic matters. The life story of Chia Pao-yü, especially, is tested against all the major ideals of Chinese culture.

At the very beginning of the first chapter, Ts'ao places his hero in a creation myth that mocks his Faustian desire for experience, knowledge, and pleasure. When the goddess Nü-kua is repairing the Dome of Heaven, she rejects as unfit for use a huge rock of considerable intelligence, which consequently bemoans its fate and develops a longing for the pleasures of the mundane world. It can now reduce itself to the size of a stone and, with the help of a Buddhist monk and Taoist priest, it is eventually born with a piece of jade in his mouth as our hero (Pao-yü means "precious jade").

As a supramundane allegory, then, *Dream* is the transcription of a record inscribed on the Stone itself, after it has returned to its original site in the Green Fable Mountains. The Stone has found human life wanting, its pleasures and pains all illusory. Its detailed record—our novel—is by allegorical design a massive substantiation of that truth. Throughout the novel, the celestial agents of that allegory, the mangy Buddhist and lame Taoist, while watching over the spiritual welfare of Pao-yü, periodically mock or enlighten other deluded earthlings as well.

Chia Pao-yü is next characterized, in chapter 2, by two knowledgeable outsiders as an unconventional individualist of the romantic tradition firmly opposed to the Confucian ideal of morality and service as represented by his father. To illustrate his propensity for love, our hero, while taking a nap in the bedchamber of Ch'in K'o-ch'ing (Chia Yung's wife) in chapter 5, is transported to the Land of Illusion presided over by the fairy Disenchantment. After warning him of the dangers of the kind of crazy love (*ch'ih ch'ing*) prized by the romantics, she introduces her own sister to him for the purpose of sexual initiation so that he may see through the vanity of passion and return to the path of Confucian service. The fairy Ko-ch'ing, who combines in her person the charms of both Tai-yü and Pao-ch'ai, of course enraptures Pao-yü, but he soon wakes up screaming, after being chased by demons and wild beasts.

When lecturing Pao-yü, the fairy Disenchantment allows a distinction between lust (*yin*) and love (*ch'ing*), and as someone truly committed to *ch'ing* (also meaning "feeling"), our hero is in no danger of being confused with several of his kinsmen who are often driven by lust to trample upon human feelings. Indeed Pao-yü is so free of lust that the dream allegory confuses matters by presenting him as someone desperate for salvation after only a brief interlude of sexual bliss. And, contrary to popular belief among Chinese readers, he is not a great lover, nor does he function principally as a lover in the novel. It is true that remembrance of the sweeter portion of the dream leads him to make love to the maid Aroma the same evening, and for all we know they may continue to share sexual intimacy thereafter. But his enjoyment of her body, explicitly referred to only once and rarely emphasized again, alters not a whit his high regard for her as a person and a friend. Pao-yü is actually more drawn to his other maid, Skybright, because of her entrancing beauty and fiery temperament, but she dies complaining of being a virgin, untouched by her young master.

Pao-yü is every girl's true friend. When the Takuanyuan, a spacious garden built in honor of his elder sister, an imperial concubine, becomes the residential quarters of Pao-yü and his girl cousins, he sees them and their maids all the time and gives daily proof of his unfeigned friendship and solicitude for their welfare. He admires each and every one of these girls as an embodiment of celestial beauty and understanding, but worries about the time when they will leave the garden to get married. He knows only too well that with marriage their celestial essence will be obscured and that, if they survive their unhappiness, they will become as mean-spirited as the older women in the Chia mansions.

As the sole young master in the Takuanyuan, Pao-yü therefore does his best to keep the young ladies and maids amused and lull their awareness of the misery of approaching adulthood. But for all their lively parties and conversations, the young ladies have to leave, one by one—by marriage, death, or abduction (in the case of the resident nun Miao-yü). It is these tragedies that reduce our helpless hero to a state of idiocy and prepare him for his eventual acceptance of his fate as an insensible Stone, regardless of suffering humanity. In that allegorical dream, the fairy Disenchantment has warned him only of his romantic propensity. Grievously hurt when his elders rob him of his intended bride and marry him to Pao-ch'ai, he is yet ordinarily much more occupied by the tragic fate of Tai-yü, and of all other girls deprived of life or happiness. In accordance with the author's allegorical scheme, we should perhaps feel happy that he has finally gained wisdom and leaves this world of suffering for the life of a monk. But we cannot help feeling that his spiritual wisdom is gained at the expense of his most endearing trait—his active love and compassion for fellow human beings. Despite his irrepressible charm and gaiety, Chia Pao-yü must be regarded as the most tragic hero in all Chinese literature, for he ultimately chooses the path of self-liberation because his sympathy and compassion have failed him.

Pao-yü has a few like-minded male friends whom he sees occasionally, but inside the Chia mansions there are no men to whom he can unburden his soul. Even if he is not partial to girls, he has only these to turn to for genuine companionship. And it is a tribute to Ts'ao's extraordinary genius that he is able to provide his protagonist with so many sharply individualized companions to talk and joke with, to compete with as poets, and to care for and love. Among these, Lin Tai-yü naturally takes pride of place as the principal heroine, with whose fate Pao-yü is most concerned. Alone of the major heroines, she is assigned a role in the supramundane allegory complementary to the hero's. She is supposed to be a plant that blossoms into a fairy after the Stone, then serving as a page at the court of Disenchantment, has daily sprinkled it with dew. The fairy has vowed to repay his kindness with tears if she may join him on earth, and judging by the occasions Tai-yü has to cry while living as an orphan among relatives, never sure of her status in the Jungkuofu nor of her marital future, she has certainly more than repaid her debt to her former benefactor.

Yet, as with Pao-yü's allegorical dreams, Ts'ao Hsüeh-ch'in almost deliberately misleads with his fairy tale about Tai-yü as a grateful plant. The reality of the two cousins in love is far more complex and fascinating than any allegory can suggest. Long before Tai-yü is in danger of being rejected by her elders, she seethes with discontent. Her every meeting with Pao-yü ends in a misunderstanding or quarrel, and these quarrels are, for her, fraught with bitter and lacerated feelings. This is so because the two are diametrically opposed in temperament, despite the similarity of their tastes. Pao-yü is a person of active sympathy capable of ultimate self-transcendence; Tai-yü is a self-centered neurotic who courts self-destruction. Her attraction for Pao-yü lies not merely in her fragile beauty and poetic sensibility but in her very contrariness—a jealous self-obsession so unlike his expansive gaiety that his love for her is always tinged with infinite sadness.

Tai-yü, on her part, can never be sure of Pao-yü's love and yet maintains a fierce pride in her studied indifference to her marital prospects. One could almost say that her tragedy lies in her stubborn impracticality, in the perverse contradiction between her very natural desire to get married to the man of her choice and her fear of compromising herself in the eyes of the world by doing anything to bring about that result. In time her temper gets worse, and so does her health. Ts'ao Hsüeh-ch'in never flinches from physiological details as he traces her growing emotional sickness in terms of her bodily deterioration. Her dream scene in chapter 82, where Pao-yü slashes open his chest in order to show her his heart and finds it missing, and her ghastly death scene in chapter 98 are among the most powerful in the novel. Kao Eh must be given high praise if he had indeed a substantial hand in the writing of these chapters.

Chinese readers partial to Tai-yü are less sympathetic toward Pao-ch'ai, because she gets her man, and find personal satisfaction in seeing her as a hypocritical schemer. This misreading is, of course, unwarranted. It is true that, as a sensible girl docilely accepting her place in a Confucian society, she may have less appeal for Pao-yü and for the modern reader than Tai-yü with her neurotic sensibility and volatile temper. Yet both are strictly comparable in talent and beauty, and both are fatherless children living more or less as dependents among relatives. Though Tai-yü is initially jealous, they become the best of friends after chapter 45, two helpless pawns in the hands of their elders with no control over their marital fate. If the elders prefer Pao-ch'ai as Pao-yü's bride, at the same time they show little regard for her welfare. Though Pao-yü was once a desirable match, by the time the wedding is proposed he is a very sick person with no immediate prospect for recovery. Even more than Tai-yü, Pao-ch'ai is the victim of a cruel hoax: there can be no doubt that the hastily arranged wedding is regarded by the elder Chia ladies as medicine for Pao-yü's health. For Pao-ch'ai's martyrdom, their brutal and desperate self-interest is alone responsible.

As the wife of Pao-yü, Pao-ch'ai remains to the end a Confucian trying to dissuade him from the path of self-liberation. She is in that respect not unlike his parents in wishing to see him entering government service and getting settled as a family man. But in the end she uses the Mencian argument to counter his Taoist resolve to leave the world. Even if the world is full of evil and suffering, or especially because it is so, how can he bear to sever human ties, to leave those who need his love most? How can one remain human by denying the most instinctive promptings of his heart? Pao-ch'ai cannot figure this out, and Pao-yü cannot answer her on the rational level of human discourse. It is only by placing human life in the cosmological scheme of craving and suffering that one can see the need to liberate oneself. It would be too cruel even for the enlightened Pao-yü to tell Pao-ch'ai that to cling to love and compassion is to persist in delusion; in the primordial antiquity of Taoism there was no need to love or commiserate.

As a tragedy, *A Dream of Red Mansions* has thus the overtones of a bitter and sardonic comedy. The Buddhist-Taoist view of the world prevails in the end, and yet the reader cannot but feel that the reality of love and suffering as depicted in the novel stirs far deeper layers of his being than the reality of Buddhist-Taoist wisdom. This Chinese masterpiece is therefore like all the greatest novels of the world in that no philosophical or religious message we extract from it can do justice to its unfolding panorama of wondrous but perverse humanity. And for any reader who would like a panoramic view of traditional Chinese life through the portrayal of unforgettable characters in an authentic social and cultural setting, there can be no richer and more fascinating work.

Murasaki Shikibu, woodblock print by an unknown artist.

The Tale of Genji

Edward Seidensticker

The Tale of Genji is a long tale, romance, or novel about life in the Kyōto court of the Heian period. What is known about it with some certainty, aside from what it tells us about itself, can be summarized easily and briefly. There is not much.

It was written early in the eleventh century by a lady of the Fujiwara clan known as Murasaki Shikibu. This is not her real name, which is unknown, but a traditional epithet or sobriquet. Among the scant known facts about her life, which extended from the late tenth century into the early eleventh, is that she saw court service, beginning in the first decade of the eleventh century and ending we do not know when. The *Genji* was probably begun during that same decade. We do not know when it was finished, and indeed we cannot be sure that it is in fact finished.

Nor can we be sure how closely the earliest surviving texts resemble what she wrote. Nothing survives in her hand. The earliest fragments are from perhaps a century and a half after the probable date of composition, and the earliest complete texts from later still. The best evidence is that what we read today contains dubious details—additions, deletions, miscopyings—but that in its main outlines it is an extraordinary work of fiction written almost a thousand years ago by the most extraordinary woman of her time.

The title comes from the family name of the hero, Genji, or Minamoto. He is the son of the emperor regnant at the beginning of the story. His death is not described, but it occurs between the forty-first and forty-second of the fifty-four chapters into which the story is divided. The remaining chapters have to do largely with the affairs of Kaoru, a young man who is thought by the world to be Genji's son but is in fact the illegitimate son of one of his wives. (Polygamy prevailed on the upper levels of Heian society.)

The action covers upwards of seventy years. There are hundreds of characters, perhaps fifty of them important, yet the plot is essentially simple. The *Genji* is a love story, of a sort dissimilar to that commonly found in European literature. The latter, when it is about love, tends to be about courtship, with marriage either occurring or being frustrated at the very end. The *Genji* is about the maturing of love after marriage. In the fifth chapter Genji finds the young girl who is to be the great love of his life. Their marriage takes place in the ninth chapter. The lady, who, like the author, is known as Murasaki (we are never told her real name), dies in the fortieth chapter, a third of a century later. One more chapter sees Genji through the first full year of his bereavement, and he too is gone from the scene.

Most of the story, then, centers upon a relationship that is deepened by tribulations and the passage of time. The concluding chapters have to do with the altogether less successful and satisfying affairs, largely amorous, of Kaoru. Love, then, is what the *Genji* is chiefly about.

The standard English translation of the title includes the word "tale." It renders a common but ambiguous Japanese word, *monogatari*, which carries strong connotations of the old-fashioned and premodern. "Romance" might do as well. Both terms stand in contrast to "novel," which covers most important European and American fiction since the eighteenth century and most Japanese fiction of the last hundred years. The tale and the romance are not modern, as these terms strongly suggest, but the novel is.

To many Western readers, the most striking thing about the *Genji* is that it does in fact seem so modern. For the past fifty years or so the idea that it should be called a novel, the first great novel in the literature of the world, has had considerable currency. Objections to this idea have also become fairly commonplace, and they have to do largely with the possibility that Murasaki's aims were not those of the modern novelist and the fact that "novel" is so European a term and concept. In effect they argue that Western cultural imperialism has found a non-Western work interesting and is trying to make it over into something Western.

If, however, the narrative and the tale are understood to be forms of narrative fiction in which the chief interest is in plot, and the novel the narrative form in which the chief interest is in character, then the grounds for considering the *Genji* a novel are not at all weak. It seems modern and holds the attention of the modern reader because the characterization is so subtle and skillful. If it were a tale or a romance and the characterization were as flat as it usually is in such a work, then remarkable incident would have to be relied upon to hold the attention of the reader through the very great length (more than a thousand closely printed pages in English translation) of the work. It belongs to a world remote from all of us in time and distant from most of us in place—the world of monarchs and their families.

Yet the *Genji* contains no violence and few really dramatic events. Genji himself may seem a bit too good and talented, at least at the outset, but saints and villains do not abound, as they tend to in romances. The events, though of his world so far above most of us, tend to be ordinary, not beyond the common experience. The *Genji* holds the interest of many a reader all the same, and the explanation must be in its characterization. The fifty or so important characters are kept apart from one another with remarkable skill. The achievement is all the more remarkable in that it has no precedents in the literature of the Orient and probably none in the literature of the world. So, if we know what we mean by the term, we may indeed call the *Genji* a novel.

Like any great work of fiction, it lends itself to many readings. It "means" many things. It is about love, and it is about other things as well. It is also a profoundly pessimistic work in religious, philosophical, and social or historical senses. So it can be read as a grand parable of decline.

In this century evidence has accumulated in such quantities that it seems unanswerable to establish that the *Genji* is a sort of historical novel. If it were a carefully planned and executed historical novel, such as Scott and Thackeray wrote, then of course the action would have to begin at least three-quarters of a century before the narrative present and proceed methodically through the years. The *Genji* is not an elaborately contrived historical novel of this sort. Yet the first readers or hearers of the early chapters (probably the original manuscript was sent out to its earliest audience chapter by chapter) must immediately have been aware that Murasaki Shikibu was writing of a time perhaps a century before her own.

This immediate awareness was soon lost, and evidence has been painstakingly assembled to bring it back to us. In it must surely be one of the "meanings" Murasaki wished to convey. The first sentence of the forty-second chapter announces Genji's death and continues with the sad statement that no one now alive is his equal. The implication is that no one ever again will be. The principal characters of the last chapters, after Genji's death, are but fractions of the man he was. The great ones and the great day are in the past. Social decline is irreversible.

Social decline may be seen as concrete manifestation of absolute, existential decline. A popular idea of the day held that the Buddhist creed itself must decline, passing through three stages, in the last of which form would remain but substance be lost. One chronology had the final stage beginning in the eleventh century. So the *Genji* seems to tell us that even the tenets of "the Good Law" are not immutable. All that is immutable is decline.

There is another sense in which the *Genji* may be seen as a grand Buddhist parable. The great sin of Genji's life is an act of adultery with his father's best-loved wife. Shadows gather over his late years even as his public career moves from triumph to triumph, and among them is the knowledge that a young wife of his late years has had the adulterous affair that results in the birth of Kaoru. So the workings of karma, the Buddhist concept of cause and effect, are apparent. The effects of our deeds, good and bad, will work themselves out, in this life or in future lives. What Genji did, he now has done to him.

Many who see the *Genji* as a novel also see it as a psychological novel, a novel of states of mind, and compare it in this regard to Proust's *Remembrance of Things Past*. Whether or not the comparison is apt, a psychological theme runs through it that also runs through some masterpieces of modern fiction: the quest for a parent.

Genji is still an infant when his mother dies. Mothers are very important in a polygamous society, in which fathers are shared with so many others. The pursuit of his mother's image leads Genji first to the stepmother with whom he has the guilty love affair and then to Murasaki. The stepmother came to court and gained the emperor's love because of a close resemblance to an earlier and much-loved wife, Genji's mother. Murasaki is her niece, and again the resemblance is close. The theme, in attentuated form—life itself seems attenuated after Genji's disappearance from the scene—persists through the concluding chapters. Kaoru sets forth uncertainly on an uncertain love affair because he is looking not for a mother figure but a father figure. He senses that there is something peculiar about his paternity, though he does not know what it is.

If the awareness of karma is fairly explicit in the sequence of events, another Buddhist awareness, of the transience and the illusory nature of the world and all its material surfaces, is implicit throughout the story. Time as the great ravager and destroyer is a constant presence. The knowledge that time moves relentlessly on and levels everything before it does not, however, lead to nihilism and despair. Quite the opposite: the very fact that beauty and pleasure must vanish asks that the whole of the sensible being concentrate upon them. The *Genji* is a work of exquisite sensibility, and it is a strongly lyrical work.

A consciousness of nature and its beauties might suffuse certain masterpieces of European lyric poetry, especially since the early nineteenth century, but one would be hard put to find a major work of fiction in which nature is the continuing presence it is in the *Genji*. On virtually every page we are aware of the seasons and their trees and flowers, and even the phases of the moon; and when, rarely, we are not informed of them, the omission is so conspicuous as to take on a significance it could not have in a Western novel. Natural imagery and the passage of the seasons are tightly interwoven with the characterization and even offer hints by way of solving one of the great mysteries, whether or not the *Genji* is finished. It begins and ends in high summer, an unlikely season; and so two summer scenes form parentheses around a work that is predominantly vernal and autumnal.

It is not improper to find these meanings even though Murasaki Shikibu may not have been aware of or attached great significance to all of them. The nearest she comes to a statement of purpose is a celebrated passage in the twenty-fifth chapter. It seems to say that her chief concern is not character but incident.

Genji speaks in defense of fiction. We may assume that he speaks for Murasaki Shikibu herself: "We are not told of things that happened to specific people exactly as they happened; but the beginning is when there are good things and bad things, things that happen in this life which one never tires of seeing and hearing about, things which one cannot bear not to tell of and must pass on for all generations."

The ladies' apartments of the Heian court must have been very quiet, and their occupants may have found the story exciting. It is not so in our more hurried and crowded day. Interesting people, not exciting events, entice us into following the story and make possible the multiplicity of readings and meanings described above.

The characterization becomes more subtle and successful as the long narrative progresses. In fact this is the best argument that it is essentially by a single author, even though the text we read may not in all its details be the text that emerged from that one author's hand. There have long been theories of dual or multiple authorship, having to do in large measure with the clear break that occurs with Genji's death. It is impossible to believe, however, that one writer could have brought the story and the characterization to so high a level and another writer, without preparation or warning, could have taken over and brought it to yet higher levels.

If it were possible to read the *Genji* as a series of related but independent novels, like the Barchester novels of Trollope, then it might be recommended that the reader begin with one of the stronger pieces and return to the first and weakest after the sense of the pleasures that lie ahead is secure. The *Genji* is a single, continuing story, however, and so a beginning must be made at the beginning, where Murasaki Shikibu's powers are least apparent. One may quickly add, however, that even these earliest chapters are better than anything the Japanese or their mentors, the Chinese, had produced earlier, and better, too, than most Japanese fiction of the millennium since.

The earliest chapters have about them more of the romance or the tale than any other part of the work. Although Murasaki Shikibu already outdoes her predecessors, the romancers of the tenth century, she is still under their influence. The hero is too gifted a man to be quite true, and the story is of his brilliantly successful public career. There is a setback, a time when he must live in exile, but that may be seen as a conventional initiation rite, and one does not for a moment doubt that he will emerge from it prepared for yet greater successes. This first or romantic stage goes through the exile and return, or the first score or so of chapters.

There follows what may be called the comic stage, through the thirty-third chapter, a stage concerned largely with the generation of Genji's children. The characterization is more realistic. Genji, so nearly perfect in the early chapters that one almost comes to dislike him, is an altogether more believable and sympathetic human being.

The thirty-fourth and thirty-fifth chapters are the longest in the book, accounting for about a sixth of the text. Through them and the half-dozen following chapters darkness gathers over Genji's private life as his public career reaches a glorious climax. This third section may be called the tragic phase. Genji's great love, Murasaki, falls ill and dies, and the little princess whom he marries late in life is caught in adultery.

Then, suddenly, comes the announcement that Genji is dead. Three uncertain chapters follow, one of them quite possibly spurious, and the remarkable last section begins. The main action departs the court and the capital, character and incident are on a smaller scale, society falls away layer by layer, and in the end one last sad heroine is left in the solitude of a nunnery. It may be called the abstract or meditative phase of the story, and Kaoru may be called the first nonhero or antihero in the literature of the world. Only a very sure and skillful writer could have undertaken anything so daring. The last stages of the *Genji* are fiction of the highest order.

The *Genji* stands in isolation. Only in the twentieth century has characterization emerged once more as a principal concern for Japanese fiction writers. The new concern is a result of Western influence. With it has come recognition of the fact that a Japanese writer was very good at characterization almost ten centuries ago. The *Genji* did not cease to be read through those centuries. Not all generations have attached the same significance to it, and doubtless our modern reading will presently give way to others. This remarkable writer and her large and complex work lend themselves to modern concerns and will lend themselves to postmodern ones as well.

There are two English translations, complete or nearly so. That by Arthur Waley appeared in installments more than a half century ago and is available in Modern Library. That by Edward Seidensticker was published by Alfred Knopf in 1976. A selection from the latter translation, about a fifth of the whole, was published by Vintage in 1985.

Tsurezure-gusa

Donald Keene

*T*surezure-gusa ("Essays in Idleness") is a collection of essays and observations that range in length from a sentence or two to several pages. The title is derived from a phrase in the preface where the author reveals that he has spent whole days "with nothing better to do" (*tsurezure naru mama ni*), jotting down whatever thoughts happened to enter his head. The work belongs to a tradition known in Japan (following Chinese examples) as *zuihitsu*, or "following the brush," meaning that the author allowed his writing brush free rein to scribble down anything it chose.

The author of *Tsurezure-gusa* is most commonly known by his Buddhist name, Kenkō. His name before he took Buddhist orders is usually given as Urabe Kaneyoshi, but also sometimes as Yoshida Kaneyoshi, presumably because he at one time resided in the Yoshida district of Kyōto. The Urabe family were hereditary Shintō diviners, but this background did not keep Kenkō from pursuing Buddhist studies. The dates of his birth and death have yet to be determined, but it is generally agreed that he was born in 1283 and died in 1352 or somewhat later. As a young man he served at first in a nobleman's household. Later, after his talents were recognized, he was granted official rank, enabling him to serve at the court, where his skill at composing poetry was prized. The knowledge of court precedents and distaste for novelty characteristic of *Tsurezure-gusa* may reflect the years he spent in the conservative milieu of the court. At some time before 1313 Kenkō took orders as a Buddhist monk. It is not known why he took this step, but there are strong suggestions in the poetry he composed about this time of increasing disenchantment with the world.

Even after he took orders, however, Kenkō did not reside in a temple but lived by himself at various places around the capital, occasionally traveling elsewhere. During his lifetime he enjoyed a considerable reputation as a poet and was even known as one of the "four heavenly kings" of the poetry of his time. Some of his poems were included in imperially sponsored anthologies, but they are no longer so highly esteemed. The poems, in the conservative traditions of the Nijō school of poetry, are apt to strike modern readers as being tepid if not downright boring.

Tsurezure-gusa was by far Kenkō's most important literary achievement. We do not know just when he wrote the preface and 243 essays that make up the work. Some scholars have suggested that many years elapsed between the composition of the first and last of the essays, but it is more common to date the work between the years 1330 and 1332. This was not a propitious time for a work of reflection. In 1331 the Emperor Go-Daigo staged a revolt against the Hōjō family, who had ruled the country as surrogates of the shoguns in Kamakura, but he was defeated and exiled the following year to the lonely Oki Islands in the Sea of Japan. The Hōjō family subsequently set up another imperial prince as the emperor. In 1333 Go-Daigo returned from exile and this time he and his supporters succeeded in overthrowing the Hōjōs. These events often divided families because of conflicting allegiances, but they hardly ruffle the surface of *Tsurezure-gusa;* it neither grieves over the turbulent times nor rejoices over the victories of one side or the other but presents instead the reflections of a strikingly civilized man.

At first glance there seems to be no apparent order to the 243 sections. According to one old tradition, Kenkō wrote down his thoughts as they came to him on scraps of paper which he pasted to the walls of his cottage. Years later, the distinguished poet Imagawa Ryōshun, learning of this unusual wallpaper, had the various scraps of paper removed and arranged them in their present order. This account was long accepted, but modern critics tend to reject it, because they can detect subtle connections linking one section to the next that suggest associations in the writer's mind that would probably not have occurred to another person. At least four clusters of essays were unmistakably composed in sequence, and other links have been found. The oldest surviving text, dated 1431, bears the title *Tsurezure-gusa,* but we cannot be sure that this title was given by Kenkō himself. The present arrangement of a preface and 243 numbered sections goes back only to the seventeenth century.

Tsurezure-gusa seems to have been unknown to anyone but the author during Kenkō's lifetime. It was first given attention by the poet and critic Shōtetsu (1381–1475), to whom we owe the 1431 text, but the popularity of the work dates only from the seventeenth century. In 1603 the haiku poet Matsunaga Teitoku (1571–1654), who had previously been instructed in *Tsurezure-gusa* by a scholar of the old school, offered lectures to the general public on the work, breaking the tradition of secret transmission of the traditions surrounding the classics. *Tsurezure-gusa* subsequently became one of the books that every educated Japanese was expected to have read, and Kenkō's thoughts affected many people. The influence of *Tsurezure-gusa,* especially on the formation of Japanese aesthetic preferences, can hardly be exaggerated.

Buddhist thought naturally supplied the background for much of what Kenkō wrote. Specifically Buddhist doctrine is sometimes expressed, but more typical of the work are the general Buddhist beliefs that colored Kenkō's thinking—that the world is no more than a temporary abode and that all things in it are impermanent. Kenkō also described the full cycle of birth, growth, sickness, and death, followed by rebirth: "With the falling of the leaves, too, it is not that first the leaves fall and then young shoots form; the leaves fall because the budding from underneath is too powerful to resist." But the predominant tone is provided by Kenkō's conviction that worldly achievements and possessions are without lasting significance in a world that is itself no more than transitory. Many passages in *Tsurezure-gusa* convey this belief, including,

> The intelligent man, when he dies, leaves no possessions.
>
> If you have power, do not trust in it; powerful men are the first to fall. You may have possessions, but they are not to be depended on; they are easily lost in a moment.
>
> When I see the things people do in their struggle to get ahead, it reminds me of someone building a snowman on a spring day, making ornaments of precious metals and stones to decorate it, and then erecting a hall.

Kenkō again and again reproaches the man who delays taking the Great Step of entering the Buddhist priesthood until he has achieved desired success:

My observation of people leads me to conclude, generally speaking, that
even people with some degree of intelligence are likely to go through life
supposing they have ample time before them. But would a man fleeing
because a fire has broken out in his neighborhood say to the fire, "Wait
a moment, please!"? To save his life, a man will run away, indifferent to
shame, abandoning his possessions. Is a man's life any more likely to wait
for him? Death attacks faster than fire or water, and is harder to escape.
When its hour comes, can you refuse to give up your aged parents,
your little children, your duty to your master, your affection for others,
because they are hard to abandon?

Again,

You must not wait until you are old before you begin practicing the
Way. Most of the gravestones from the past belong to men who died
young.

Such passages are testimony to the depth of Kenkō's religious convictions. Sometimes he also finds unusual implications in Buddhist doctrine,
as when he traces the close relationship between impermanence and
beauty, a particularly Japanese aesthetic principle. He writes, "If man
were never to fade away like the dews of Adashino, never to vanish
like the smoke over Toribeno, but lingered forever in this world, how
things would lose their power to move us! The most precious thing in
life is its uncertainty." Other Buddhists rarely suggested that impermanence itself was valuable; like the ancient Greeks who declined to call a
man happy until he was dead, these Buddhists regarded the uncertainty
of life as a source of grief. But unless (like Kenkō) the Japanese had
appreciated impermanence, they surely would not have displayed such
love for cherry blossoms, which hardly bloom before they fall; and the
preference for building houses of perishable materials like wood and
paper, rather than of brick or stone, was surely not due only to a fear
of earthquakes.

The falling of the cherry blossoms is regretted in innumerable poems,
but the very brevity of their blossoming imparts a special beauty and
makes them more precious than hardier flowers. Thus it is surprising
that while wooden statues and temples erected in Japan a thousand years
ago survive, despite the perishable nature of the materials, the Japanese
made no conscious effort to achieve the permanence of marble. Whatever has survived has also aged, and this faded quality, the reminder
of impermanence, has been prized. Kenkō quotes with approbation the
priest Ton'a who said, "It is only after the silk wrapper has frayed at
top and bottom and the mother-of-pearl has fallen from the roller, that
a scroll looks beautiful." Kenkō constantly warned of the shortness of
life and the close presence of death and urged people to hasten in the
path of Buddha, but he also found in the shortness of human life the

source of its poignance. His delight in the worn, the obviously used, contrasts with the Western craving for objects in mint condition and the desire to annihilate time by restoring works of art to so pristine a state as to make people exclaim, "It might have been painted yesterday!" The Japanese craftsman who repairs a broken or chipped bowl fills in the cracks with gold, as if to emphasize the ravages of time.

Kenkō's preference for objects that reveal the effects of impermanence is accompanied by a similar preference for the irregular and the incomplete. "In everything, no matter what it may be, uniformity is undesirable. Leaving something incomplete makes it interesting, and gives one the feeling there is room for growth," he writes. Again, "It is typical of the unintelligent man to insist on assembling complete sets of everything. Imperfect sets are better."

No doubt most people in Kenkō's time preferred to own complete sets rather than odd volumes, but as anyone knows who has ever confronted the grim volumes of a set of the Harvard Classics or the Complete Works of Sir Walter Scott, they do not tempt one to browse. Asymmetry and irregularity not only allow the possibility of growth but the participation of the outsider; perfection tends to choke the imagination.

Kenkō's love of the imperfect leads him to stress also the importance of beginnings and ends:

> Are we to look at cherry blossoms only in full bloom, the moon only
> when it is cloudless? To long for the moon while looking on the rain, to
> lower the blinds and be unaware of the passing of the spring—these are
> even more deeply moving. Branches about to blossom or gardens strewn
> with faded flowers are worthier of our admiration.

Even in Japan a fondness for the imperfect has usually not caused people to rush to see cherry blossoms before they open, or to wait until they are scattered before paying a visit; and in the West the climactic moments—when Laocoön and his sons are caught in the serpent's embrace or the soprano hits the much-awaited high C—have been given greatest attention. But for Kenkō the climax, whether the full moon or the full flowering of the cherry trees, is less suggestive than the beginnings and ends: the full moon and the cherry blossoms at their peak do not suggest the crescent moon or buds, but the crescent and the buds (or the waning moon and strewn flowers) can evoke with poignance the full cycle. In Japanese poetry hoped-for love affairs and regretted affairs that have ended are often treated, but hardly a poem expresses the pleasure of requited love.

Irregularity and incompleteness accord with another element of Japanese aesthetics emphasized by Kenkō: simplicity, the art of suggesting more than is stated. "A house which multitudes of workmen have polished with every care, where strange and rare Chinese and Japanese furnishings are displayed, and even the grasses and trees of the garden have been trained unnaturally, is ugly to look at and most depressing," he says. It is easier for us to assent to this opinion than it would have been for Western readers of a century ago. In the West the house "which multitudes of workmen have polished with every care" was for long considered beautiful, as we know from photographs showing the profusion of treasures with which the drawing rooms of the rich were adorned. Gardens where even the trees and plants have been trained unnaturally still attract visitors to the great houses of Europe.

"People agree that a house which has plenty of spare room is attractive to look at and may be put to many different uses," Kenkō says in another passage. By a curious coincidence, this preference is now a commonplace of decorators in the West, for whom "less is more" has replaced richness of effect as an ideal. No doubt Kenkō's tastes were formed by earlier traditions, but he was probably the first to define these tastes, and when *Tsurezure-gusa* came to be generally circulated it surely influenced the tastes of later Japanese.

Kenkō exercised even greater influence with his descriptions of the proper behavior of the well-bred man. Indeed, *Tsurezure-gusa* is a kind of manual of gentlemanly conduct.

> A man should avoid displaying deep familiarity with any subject. Can one imagine a well-bred man talking with the airs of a know-it-all, even about a matter with which he is in fact familiar? . . . It is impressive when a man is always slow to speak even on subjects he knows thoroughly, and does not speak at all unless questioned.

Kenkō often contrasts his gentleman with the insensitive, boorish people who make up most of society:

> The man of breeding never appears to abandon himself completely to his pleasures; even his manner of enjoyment is detached. . . . When the well-bred man tells a story he addresses himself to one person, even if many people are present, though the others too listen, naturally. . . .
> You can judge a person's breeding by whether he is quite impassive even when he tells an amusing story or laughs a great deal even when relating a matter of no interest.
> The well-bred man does not tell stories about prodigies.
> When a person who has always been extremely close appears on a particular occasion reserved and formal towards you . . . some people will undoubtedly say, "Why act that way now, after all these years?" But I feel that such behavior shows sincerity and breeding.

Early in the work Kenkō lists the cultural qualifications of a gentleman:

> A familiarity with orthodox scholarship, the ability to compose poetry and prose in Chinese, a knowledge of Japanese poetry and music are

all desirable, and if a man can serve as a model to others in matters
of precedent and court ceremony, he is truly impressive. The mark of
an excellent man is that he writes easily in an acceptable hand, sings
agreeably and in tune, and, appearing reluctant to accept when wine is
pressed on him, is not a teetotaler.

These abilities continued until recent times to be the marks of a gentleman in Japan.

Kenkō's insistence on the importance of knowing precedent and
court ceremony accounts for his inclusion of the least interesting parts
of the text of *Tsurezure-gusa*. He clings to each usage sanctified by
tradition, though some were surely meaningless even in his day. "It is
best not to change something if changing it will not do any good," he
writes, but gives no instances of desirable changes. Instead, he laments
each violation of precedent and praises each act of fidelity to the old
ways. He describes, for example, how an official, deciding that the file
chest in his office was unsightly, ordered it to be rebuilt in a more
elegant style. Other officials, familiar with court precedents, voiced the
opinion that the chest was not to be altered without due consideration:
"This article of government property, dating back many reigns, had by
its very dilapidation become a model." Kenkō enthusiastically approves
the final decision not to remodel the chest.

His nostalgia is eloquently described in various sections, notably:
"When I sit down in quiet meditation, the one emotion hardest to
fight against is a longing in all things for the past." Such feelings make
him treasure even the least important tradition. He is impressed by the
Abbess Genki who remembered from childhood that the "bell-shaped
windows in the Kan'in Palace were rounder and without frames." For
Kenkō even a window whose shape is slightly at variance with tradition
is indicative of the degeneracy of the age. He is dismayed that no one
knows any longer the proper shape of a torture rack nor the manner of
attaching a criminal.

Various essays devoted to precedents and correct usage were omitted from eighteenth- and nineteenth-century editions of the work—
evidence that they had lost their interest—but they are no less typical
of Kenkō than the more celebrated essays. He so startles us again and
again with his insights into the characters of people, the nature of
beauty, the passage of time and other eternally moving subjects that we
are likely to forget that he was acutely aware of belonging to a particular age. He feared that people of his time might be so involved in the
turbulent changes that affected everyone as to destroy by ignorance or
indifference the civilization that had been created in Japan. It probably
seemed just as important to him to preserve the correct nomenclature
for palace ceremonies as to preserve the old texts or the works of art
that survived from the past. His work is not systematic, and its pages

even contain contradictions, but it is central to an understanding of Japanese taste. Kenkō was not the first to be aware of the principles he enunciates, but he gave them permanence by his eloquent and affecting presentation.

[1]The Islāmic tradition is no less of a great tradition in much of Asia for also sharing this common ground with major religious traditions of the West. Since in practice the major works of the Islāmic tradition are rarely included among the "great books" of the West, it is appropriate to recognize them here.

[2]*See* Richard Payne (ed.), *Classics of Western Spirituality,* 60 vols. (New York: Paulist Press, 1978–); and Ewart Cousins (gen. ed.), *World Spirituality: An Encyclopedic History of the Religious Quest,* 25 vols. (New York: Crossroads Publishing Co., 1985–).

[3]J. Bartlet Brebner, et al., *Classics of the Western World* (Chicago: American Library Association, 1934), pp. 11–12.

[4]Ibid., pp. 12–13.

[5]Ibid., pp. 13–14.

[6]W. T. de Bary and A. T. Embree (eds.), *A Guide to Oriental Classics* (New York: Columbia University Press, 1975), rev. ed. A second revision is now in the process of publication.

PART FOUR

Additions
to the
Great Books Library

The Rights of Man

Thomas Paine

Editor's Introduction

Thomas Paine, whose polemical writings made him first a household name and then a despised figure in his day, was the advocate of three great causes which arose in that time: the American War of Independence, the French Revolution, and the triumph, or at least the beginnings of the triumph, of the secular state, without an established religion. Two of these events cannot now be imagined without the words he contributed to them, and the first one would arguably never have been realized, in the way it was, had those words not been said. But the man himself died obscure, his very bones mislaid—as should have been the case, perhaps, with one who spoke always for freedom.

For all this, the man was nothing if not true to the words. Till he found them, or found any occasion to use them, he had no direction. English by birth, self-taught, without fortune or prospects, he appears first in 1774, aged thirty-seven, having made himself known to Benjamin Franklin, who was in London on colonial business. Franklin saw something in him and sent him off to America with letters of introduction. His first job in the colonies was with the *Pennsylvania Magazine,* for which he wrote a passionate attack on the slave trade. Then, having adopted the colonial cause, he wrote the pamphlet called "Common Sense," which argued that the colonial issue was not taxation but tyranny and said that the cure for it was independence. With one stroke, he was on everybody's tongue. "Common Sense," published in January 1776, sold 500,000 copies—nearly the entire reading population of the country—and did much to articulate, if it did not wholly create, the spirit that led, six months later, to the Declaration of Independence. Six months after that, in December 1776, came "The Crisis," a series of papers the first of which, saying that "tyranny, like Hell, is not easily conquered," was read by order of General Washington to the Continental Army, freezing just then at Valley Forge. Paine, now the General's aide-de-camp, had written it on a drumhead by candlelight the night before.

These works, having made him known in what was now his country, led to modest clerical positions first with the Continental Congress and, after the war, with the General Assembly of Pennsylvania. There he served for a time before retiring, as he thought, to a farm in New York which had been granted to him for his public services. In 1787, however, he left for England again, with the object of promoting certain engineering ideas he had conceived, only to become involved almost at once in European politics, in particular with what was to become the French Revolution. Sympathetic with this, and angered by Edmund Burke's attack on it in *Reflections on the Revolution in France,* he characteristically put aside his own business to write a reply, called *The Rights of Man,* thus creating the greatest polemical exchange of the age, or perhaps any age. Part One of that work appeared in 1791, Part Two, the year after.

By that time, Paine was up to his neck, which he nearly lost along with his head, in French politics. Elected to a seat in the National Convention (for which, with some help by Condorcet, he had written the celebrated *Declaration of the Rights of Man and of Citizens*), he left England in time to avoid arrest by the authorities, who tried and convicted him in absentia for seditious libel, declaring him an outlaw and ordering his book suppressed. In France he praised the abolition of the monarchy but protested the terror against the royalists and sought vainly to save the king's life, urging banishment instead of execution. For this he was arrested himself in 1793 when the radicals under Robespierre came to power, and he spent the next year in prison. Indeed, he escaped the guillotine only because on the appointed day his cell was improperly marked.

In prison he wrote the first part of *The Age of Reason* (1794), which was followed, after his release, by a second part (1796). It was this work, though it professed his belief in a Supreme Being and opposed only organized religion (Paine was a Deist), that led to his being regarded thereafter as an unbeliever—a reputation reflected in Theodore Roosevelt's dismissal of him as "a filthy little atheist." Roosevelt had never actually read *The Age of Reason,* and neither, apparently, had Paine's American countrymen, who were not so tolerant in religious matters as their Constitution implied, and who turned their backs to him when in 1802 he returned to the United States. There, forgotten and impoverished (he had never accepted any pay for his writings, which would have made him rich, wanting them to have the widest possible circulation), he lived the remainder of his life. At his death in 1809, he was buried on his New York farm. Ten years later, his bones were exhumed by William Cobbett, a journalist like himself, and transported to England for better disposition, but the project never came off, and the remains were permanently lost.

The text of *The Rights of Man* is complete except for the "Miscellaneous Chapter" in Part One, which has been omitted.

The Rights of Man

BEING AN ANSWER TO MR. BURKE'S ATTACK ON THE FRENCH REVOLUTION

Part the First

To George Washington

President of the United States of America

SIR,

I present you a small treatise in defense of those principles of freedom which your exemplary virtue hath so eminently contributed to establish. That the rights of man may become as universal as your benevolence can wish, and that you may enjoy the happiness of seeing the New World regenerate the Old, is the prayer of

Sir

Your much obliged, and

Obedient humble servant,

THOMAS PAINE

Prefaces

1. Preface to the French edition

The astonishment which the French Revolution has caused throughout Europe should be considered from two different points of view; first as it affects foreign people, second as it affects their governments.

The cause of the French people is that of all Europe, or rather of the whole world; but the governments of all those countries are by no means favourable to it. It is important that we should never lose sight of this distinction. We must not confuse the peoples with their governments; especially not the English people with its government.

The government of England is no friend to the revolution of France. Of this we have sufficient proofs in the thanks given by that weak and witless person, the Elector of Hanover, sometimes called the King of England, to Mr. Burke for the insults heaped on it in his book, and in the malevolent comments of the English minister, Mr. Pitt, in his speeches in Parliament.

In spite of the professions of sincerest friendship found in the official correspondence of the English government with that of France, its conduct gives the lie to all its declarations and shows us clearly that it is not a court to be trusted, but an insane court, plunging in all the quarrels and intrigues of Europe in quest of a war to satisfy its folly and countenance its extravagance.

The English nation, on the contrary, is very favourably disposed toward the French Revolution and to the progress of liberty in the whole world; and this feeling will become more general in England as the intrigues and artifices of its government are better known, and the principles of the revolution better understood. The French should know that most English newspapers are directly in the pay of government or, if indirectly connected with it, always under its orders; and that these papers constantly distort and attack the revolution in France in order to deceive the nation. But, as it is impossible long to prevent the prevalence of truth, the daily falsehoods of those papers no longer have the desired effect.

To be convinced that the voice of truth has been stifled in England, the world needs only to be told that the government regards and prosecutes as a libel that which it should protect.* This outrage on morality is called *law,* and judges are found wicked enough to inflict penalties on truth.

The English government presents just now a curious phenomenon. Seeing that the French and English nations are getting rid of the prejudices and false notions formerly entertained against each other, and which have cost them so much money, that government seems to be placarding its need of a foe; for unless it finds one somewhere, no pretext exists for the enormous revenue and taxation now deemed necessary.

Therefore it seeks in Russia the enemy it has lost in France, and appears to say to the universe, or to say to itself: "If nobody will be so kind as to become my foe, I shall need no more fleets or armies, and shall be forced to reduce my taxes. The American war enabled me to double the taxes; the Dutch business to add more; the Nootka humbug gave me a pretext for raising three millions sterling more; but unless I can make an enemy of Russia the harvest from wars will end. I was the first to incite Turk against Russian, and now I hope to reap a fresh crop of taxes."

If the miseries of war and the flood of evils it spreads over a country did not check all inclination to mirth and turn laughter into grief, the frantic conduct of the government of England would only excite ridicule. But it is impossible to banish from one's mind the images of suffering which the contemplation of such vicious policy presents. To reason with governments, as they have existed for ages, is to argue with brutes. It is only from the nations themselves that reforms can be expected. There ought not now to exist any doubt that the peoples of France, England, and America, enlightened and enlightening each other, shall henceforth be able, not merely to give the world an example of good government, but by their united influence enforce its practice.

2. Preface to the English edition

From the part Mr. Burke took in the American Revolution it was natural that I should consider him a friend to mankind; and as our acquaintance commenced on that ground, it would have been more agreeable to me to have had cause to continue in that opinion than to change it.

At the time Mr. Burke made his violent speech last winter in the English Parliament against the French Revolution and the National Assembly, I was in Paris, and had written to him but a short time before to inform him how prosperously matters were going on. Soon after this I saw his advertisement of the pamphlet he intended to publish: As the attack was to be made in a language but little studied and less understood in France, and as everything suffers by translation, I promised some of the friends of the Revolution in that country that whenever Mr. Burke's pamphlet came forth, I would answer it. This appeared to me the more necessary to be done when I saw the flagrant misrepresentations which Mr. Burke's pamphlet contains; and that while it is an outrageous abuse on the French Revolution and the principles of liberty, it is an imposition on the rest of the world.

I am the more astonished and disappointed at this conduct in Mr. Burke, as (from the circumstances I am going to mention) I had formed other expectations.

I had seen enough of the miseries of war to wish it might nevermore have existence in the world, and that some other mode might be found out to settle the differences that should occasionally arise in the neighbourhood of nations. This certainly might be done if courts were disposed to set honestly about it, or if countries were enlightened enough not to be made the dupes of courts. The people of America had been bred up in the same prejudices

---

*The main and uniform maxim of the judges is, the greater the truth the greater the libel.

Edmund Burke. *"I promised . . . that whenever Mr. Burke's pamphlet came forth, I would answer it."*

against France which at that time characterized the people of England; but experience and an acquaintance with the French nation have most effectually shown to the Americans the falsehood of those prejudices; and I do not believe that a more cordial and confidential intercourse exists between any two countries than between America and France.

When I came to France in the spring of 1787, the Archbishop of Toulouse was then minister, and at that time highly esteemed. I became much acquainted with the private secretary of that minister, a man of an enlarged benevolent heart, and found that his sentiments and my own perfectly agreed with respect to the madness of war and the wretched impolicy of two nations, like England and France, continually worrying each other to no other end than that of a mutual increase of burdens and taxes. That I might be assured I had not misunderstood him, nor he me, I put the substance of our opinions into writing and sent it to him, subjoining a request, that if I should see among the people of England any disposition to cultivate a better understanding between the two nations than had hitherto prevailed, how far I might be authorized to say that

the same disposition prevailed on the part of France? He answered me by letter in the most unreserved manner, and that not for himself only, but for the minister with whose knowledge the letter was declared to be written.

I put this letter into the hands of Mr. Burke almost three years ago, and left it with him, where it still remains, hoping, and at the same time naturally expecting, from the opinion I had conceived of him, that he would find some opportunity of making good use of it for the purpose of removing those errors and prejudices which two neighbouring nations, from the want of knowing each other, had entertained to the injury of both.

When the French Revolution broke out it certainly afforded to Mr. Burke an opportunity of doing some good had he been disposed to it; instead of which, no sooner did he see the old prejudices wearing away, than he immediately began sowing the seeds of a new inveteracy, as if he were afraid that England and France would cease to be enemies. That there are men in all countries who get their living by war, and by keeping up the quarrels of nations, is as shocking as it is true; but when those who are concerned in the government of a

305

country make it their study to sow discord and cultivate prejudices between nations, it becomes more unpardonable.

With respect to a paragraph in this work alluding to Mr. Burke's having a pension, the report has been some time in circula-tion, at least two months; and as a person is often the last to hear what concerns him the most to know, I have mentioned it, that Mr. Burke may have an opportunity of contradicting the rumour, if he thinks proper.

The Rights of Man

Among the incivilities by which nations or individuals provoke and irritate each other, Mr. Burke's pamphlet on the French Revolution is an extraordinary instance. Neither the people of France, nor the National Assembly, were troubling them-selves about the affairs of England, or the English Parliament; and why Mr. Burke should commence an unprovoked attack upon them, both in Parliament and in pub-lic, is a conduct that cannot be pardoned on the score of manners, nor justified on that of policy.

There is scarcely an epithet of abuse to be found in the English language with which Mr. Burke has not loaded the French nation and the National Assembly. Every-thing which rancour, prejudice, ignorance, or knowledge could suggest is poured forth in the copious fury of near four hundred pages. In the strain and on the plan Mr. Burke was writing, he might have writ-ten on to as many thousands. When the tongue or the pen is let loose in a frenzy of passion, it is the man, and not the subject, that becomes exhausted.

Hitherto Mr. Burke has been mistaken and disappointed in the opinions he had formed of the affairs of France; but such is the ingenuity of his hope, or the malig-nancy of his despair, that it furnishes him with new pretenses to go on. There was a time when it was impossible to make Mr. Burke believe there would be any revolu-tion in France. His opinion then was, that the French had neither spirit to undertake it nor fortitude to support it; and now that there is one, he seeks an escape by con-demning it.

Not sufficiently content with abusing the National Assembly, a great part of his work is taken up with abusing Dr. Price (one of the best-hearted men that lives) and the two societies in England known by the name of the Revolution Society and the Society for Constitutional Information.

Dr. Price had preached a sermon on the 4th of November, 1789, being the an-niversary of what is called in England the Revolution, which took place 1688. Mr. Burke, speaking of this sermon, says, "The political Divine proceeds dogmatically to assert, that by the principles of the Revolu-tion, the people of England have acquired three fundamental rights:

1. To choose their own governors.

2. To cashier them for misconduct.

3. To frame a government for our-selves."

Dr. Price does not say that the right to do these things exists in this or in that person, or in this or in that descrip-tion of persons, but that it exists in the *whole;* that it is a right resident in the na-tion. Mr. Burke, on the contrary, denies that such a right exists in the nation, ei-ther in whole or in part, or that it exists anywhere; and, what is still more strange and marvelous, he says, "that the people of England utterly disclaim such a right, and that they will resist the practical asser-tion of it with their lives and fortunes." That men should take up arms and spend their lives and fortunes, *not* to maintain their rights, but to maintain they have *not* rights, is an entirely new species of discov-ery, and suited to the paradoxical genius of Mr. Burke.

The method which Mr. Burke takes to prove that the people of England have no such rights, and that such rights do not now exist in the nation, either in whole or in part, or anywhere at all, is of the same marvelous and monstrous kind with what he has already said; for his arguments are that the persons, or the generation of persons, in whom they did exist, are dead, and with them the right is dead also. To prove this, he quotes a declaration made by parliament about a hundred years ago, to William and Mary, in these words: "The Lords Spiritual and Temporal, and Commons, do, in the name of the people aforesaid [meaning the people of England then living], most humbly and faithfully *submit* themselves, their *heirs* and *posterities,* for EVER." He also quotes a clause of another act of Parliament made in the same reign, the terms of which, he says, "bind us, our *heirs* and our *posterity,* to *them,* their *heirs* and *posterity,* to the end of time."

Mr. Burke conceives his point sufficiently established by producing those clauses, which he enforces by saying that they exclude the right of the nation for *ever.* And not yet content with making such declarations, repeated over and over again, he farther says, "that if the people of England possessed such a right before the Revolution [which he acknowledges to have been the case, not only in England, but throughout Europe, at an early period], yet that the *English nation* did, at the time of the Revolution, most solemnly renounce and abdicate it, for themselves, and for *all their posterity, for ever.*"

As Mr. Burke occasionally applies the poison drawn from his horrid principles (if it is not profanation to call them by the name of principles) not only to the English nation, but to the French Revolution and the National Assembly, and charges that august, illuminated and illuminating body of men with the epithet of *usurpers,* I shall, *sans cérémonie,* place another system of principles in opposition to his.

The English Parliament of 1688 did a certain thing, which, for themselves and their constituents, they had a right to do, and which it appeared right should be done; but, in addition to this right, which they possessed by delegation, *they set up another right by assumption,* that of binding and controlling posterity to the end of time. The case, therefore, divides itself into two parts; the right which they possessed by delegation, and the right which they set up by assumption. The first is admitted; but with respect to the second, I reply—

There never did, there never will, and there never can, exist a Parliament, or any description of men, or any generation of men, in any country, possessed of the right or the power of binding and controlling posterity to the *"end of time,"* or of commanding for ever how the world shall be governed, or who shall govern it; and therefore all such clauses, acts, or declarations by which the makers of them attempt to do what they have neither the right nor the power to do, nor the power to execute, are in themselves null and void. Every age and generation must be as free to act for itself *in all cases* as the ages and generations which preceded it. The vanity and presumption of governing beyond the grave is the most ridiculous and insolent of all tyrannies. Man has no property in man; neither has any generation a property in the generations which are to follow. The Parliament or the people of 1688, or of any other period, had no more right to dispose of the people of the present day, or to bind or to control them *in any shape whatever,* than the Parliament or the people of the present day have to dispose of, bind or control those who are to live a hundred or a thousand years hence. Every generation is, and must be, competent to all the purposes which its occasions require. It is the living, and not the dead, that are to be accommodated. When man ceases to be, his power and his wants cease with him; and having no longer any participation in the concerns of this world, he has no longer any authority in directing who shall be its governors, or how its government shall be organized, or how administered.

I am not contending for nor against any form of government, nor for nor against any party, here or elsewhere. That which a whole nation chooses to do, it has a right to do. Mr. Burke says, No. Where, then, does the right exist? I am contending for the rights of the *living,* and against their being willed away, and controlled and contracted for, by the manuscript assumed authority of the dead; and Mr. Burke is contending for the authority of the dead over the rights and freedom of the living. There was a time when kings disposed of their crowns by will upon their deathbeds, and consigned the people, like beasts of the field, to whatever successor they appointed. This is now so exploded as scarcely to be remembered, and so monstrous as hardly to be believed; but the Parliamentary clauses upon which Mr. Burke builds his political church are of the same nature.

The laws of every country must be analogous to some common principle. In England no parent or master, nor all the authority of Parliament, omnipotent as it has called itself, can bind or control the personal freedom even of an individual beyond the age of twenty-one years. On what ground of right, then, could the Parliament of 1688, or any other Parliament, bind all posterity for ever?

Those who have quitted the world, and those who are not yet arrived at it, are as remote from each other as the utmost stretch of mortal imagination can conceive. What possible obligation, then, can exist between them; what rule or principle can be laid down that of two nonentities, the one out of existence and the other not in, and who never can meet in this world, the one should control the other to the end of time?

In England it is said that money cannot be taken out of the pockets of the people without their consent. But who authorized, or who could authorize, the Parliament of 1688 to control and take away the freedom of posterity (who were not in existence to give or to withhold their consent), and limit and confine their right of acting in certain cases for ever?

A greater absurdity cannot present itself to the understanding of man than what Mr. Burke offers to his readers. He tells them, and he tells the world to come, that a certain body of men who existed a hundred years ago, made a law, and that there does not now exist in the nation, nor ever will, nor ever can, a power to alter it. Under how many subtleties or absurdities has the divine right to govern been imposed on the credulity of mankind! Mr. Burke has discovered a new one, and he has shortened his journey to Rome by appealing to the power of this infallible Parliament of former days; and he produces what it has done as of divine authority, for that power must certainly be more than human which no human power to the end of time can alter.

But Mr. Burke has done some service, not to his cause, but to his country, by bringing those clauses into public view. They serve to demonstrate how necessary it is at all times to watch against the attempted encroachment of power, and to prevent its running to excess. It is somewhat extraordinary that the offense for which James II was expelled, that of setting up power by *assumption,* should be reacted, under another shape and form, by the Parliament that expelled him. It shows that the rights of man were but imperfectly understood at the Revolution; for certain it is that the right which that Parliament set up by *assumption* (for by delegation it had it not, and could not have it, because none could give it) over the persons and freedom of posterity for ever, was of the same tyrannical unfounded kind which James attempted to set up over the Parliament and the nation, and for which he was expelled. The only difference is (for in principle they differ not) that the one was a usurper over the living, and the other over the unborn; and as the one has no better authority to stand upon than the other, both of them must be equally null and void, and of no effect.

From what, or from whence, does Mr. Burke prove the right of any human power to bind posterity for ever? He has produced his clauses, but he must produce also his proofs that such a right existed, and show how it existed. If it ever existed it must now exist, for whatever appertains to the nature of man cannot be annihilated by man. It is the nature of man to die, and he will continue to die as long as he continues to be born. But Mr. Burke has set up a sort of political Adam, in whom all posterity are bound for ever; he must, therefore, prove that his Adam possessed such a power, or such a right.

The weaker any cord is the less will it bear to be stretched, and the worse is the policy to stretch it, unless it is intended to break it. Had anyone proposed the overthrow of Mr. Burke's positions, he would have proceeded as Mr. Burke has done. He would have magnified the authorities, on purpose to have called the *right* of them into question; and the instant the question of right was started, the authorities must have been given up.

It requires but a very small glance of thought to perceive that although laws made in one generation often continue in force through succeeding generations, yet that they continue to derive their force from the consent of the living. A law not repealed continues in force, not because it *cannot* be repealed, but because it *is not* repealed; and the non-repealing passes for consent.

But Mr. Burke's clauses have not even this qualification in their favour. They become null, by attempting to become immortal. The nature of them precludes consent. They destroy the right which they *might* have, by grounding it on a right which they *cannot* have. Immortal power is not a human right, and therefore cannot be a right of Parliament. The Parliament of 1688 might as well have passed an act

to have authorized themselves to live for ever, as to make their authority live for ever. All, therefore, that can be said of those clauses is that they are a formality of words, of as much import as if those who used them had addressed a congratulation to themselves, and in the oriental style of antiquity had said: O Parliament, live for ever!

The circumstances of the world are continually changing, and the opinions of men change also; and as government is for the living, and not for the dead, it is the living only that has any right in it. That which may be thought right and found convenient in one age may be thought wrong and found inconvenient in another. In such cases, Who is to decide, the living, or the dead?

As almost one hundred pages of Mr. Burke's book are employed upon these clauses, it will consequently follow that if the clauses themselves, so far as they set up an *assumed usurped* dominion over posterity for ever, are unauthoritative, and in their nature null and void; that all his voluminous inferences, and declamation drawn therefrom, or founded thereon, are null and void also; and on this ground I rest the matter.

We now come more particularly to the affairs of France. Mr. Burke's book has the appearance of being written as instruction to the French nation; but if I may permit myself the use of an extravagant metaphor, suited to the extravagance of the case, It is darkness attempting to illuminate light.

While I am writing this there are accidentally before me some proposals for a declaration of rights by the Marquis de Lafayette (I ask his pardon for using his former address, and do it only for distinction's sake) to the National Assembly, on the 11th of July, 1789, three days before the taking of the Bastille; and I cannot but remark with astonishment how opposite the sources are from which that gentleman and Mr. Burke draw their principles. Instead of referring to musty records and mouldy parchments to prove that the rights of the living are lost, "renounced and abdicated for ever," by those who are now no more, as Mr. Burke has done, M. de Lafayette applies to the living world, and emphatically says, "Call to mind the sentiments which Nature has engraved in the heart of every citizen, and which take a new force when they are solemnly recognised by all: For a nation to love liberty, it is sufficient that she knows it; and to be free, it is sufficient that she wills it." How dry, barren, and obscure is the source from which Mr. Burke labours; and how ineffectual, though gay with flowers, are all his declamation and his arguments compared with these clear, concise, and soul-animating sentiments! Few and short as they are, they lead to a vast field of generous and manly thinking, and do not finish, like Mr. Burke's periods, with music in the ear, and nothing in the heart.

As I have introduced M. de Lafayette, I will take the liberty of adding an anecdote respecting his farewell address to the Congress of America in 1783, which occurred fresh to my mind when I saw Mr. Burke's thundering attack on the French Revolution. M. de Lafayette went to America at an early period of the war and continued a volunteer in her service to the end. His conduct through the whole of that enterprise is one of the most extraordinary that is to be found in the history of a young man, scarcely then twenty years of age. Situated in a country that was like the lap of sensual pleasure, and with the means of enjoying it, how few are there to be found who would exchange such a scene for the woods and wildernesses of America, and pass the flowery years of youth in unprofitable danger and hardship! But such is the fact. When the war ended, and he was on the point of taking his final departure, he presented himself to Congress, and contemplating, in his affectionate farewell, the Revolution he had seen, expressed himself in these words: "May this great monument raised to liberty, serve as a lesson to

the oppressor, and an example to the oppressed!" When this address came to the hands of Dr. Franklin, who was then in France, he applied to Count Vergennes to have it inserted in the French Gazette, but never could obtain his consent. The fact was that Count Vergennes was an aristocratical despot at home and dreaded the example of the American Revolution in France, as certain other persons now dread the example of the French Revolution in England; and Mr. Burke's tribute of fear (for in this light his book must be considered) runs parallel with Count Vergennes' refusal. But to return more particularly to his work—

"We have seen," says Mr. Burke, "the French rebel against a mild and lawful monarch, with more fury, outrage, and insult, than any people has been known to rise against the most illegal usurper, or the most sanguinary tyrant." This is one among a thousand other instances, in which Mr. Burke shows that he is ignorant of the springs and principles of the French Revolution.

It was not against Louis XVI, but against the despotic principles of the government, that the nation revolted. These principles had not their origin in him, but in the original establishment, many centuries back; and they were become too deeply rooted to be removed, and the Augean stable of parasites and plunderers too abominably filthy to be cleansed, by anything short of a complete and universal revolution. When it becomes necessary to do a thing, the whole heart and soul should go into the measure, or not attempt it. That crisis was then arrived, and there remained no choice but to act with determined vigour, or not to act at all. The King was known to be the friend of the nation, and this circumstance was favourable to the enterprise. Perhaps no man bred up in the style of an absolute king ever possessed a heart so little disposed to the exercise of that species of power as the present King of France. But the principles of the government itself still remained the same. The monarch and the monarchy were distinct and separate things; and it was against the established despotism of the latter, and not against the person or principles of the former, that the revolt commenced, and the Revolution has been carried.

Mr. Burke does not attend to the distinction between *men* and *principles;* and, therefore, he does not see that a revolt may take place against the despotism of the latter, while there lies no charge of despotism against the former.

The natural moderation of Louis XVI contributed nothing to alter the hereditary despotism of the monarchy. All the tyrannies of former reigns, acted under that hereditary despotism, were still liable to be revived in the hands of a successor. It was not the respite of a reign that would satisfy France, enlightened as she then was become. A casual discontinuance of the *practice* of despotism is not a discontinuance of its *principles;* the former depends on the virtue of the individual who is in immediate possession of the power; the latter, on the virtue and fortitude of the nation. In the case of Charles I and James II of England, the revolt was against the personal despotism of the men; whereas in France, it was against the hereditary despotism of the established government. But men who can consign over the rights of posterity for ever on the authority of a mouldy parchment, like Mr. Burke, are not qualified to judge of this Revolution. It takes in a field too vast for their views to explore and proceeds with a mightiness of reason they cannot keep pace with.

But there are many points of view in which this Revolution may be considered. When despotism has established itself for ages in a country, as in France, it is not in the person of the king only that it resides. It has the appearance of being so in show, and in nominal authority; but it is not so in practice and in fact. It has its standard everywhere. Every office and department has its despotism, founded upon custom and

usage. Every place has its Bastille, and every Bastille its despot. The original hereditary despotism resident in the person of the king, divides and subdivides itself into a thousand shapes and forms, till at last the whole of it is acted by deputation. This was the case in France; and against this species of despotism, proceeding on through an endless labyrinth of office till the source of it is scarcely perceptible, there is no mode of redress. It strengthens itself by assuming the appearance of duty, and tyrannizes under the pretense of obeying.

When a man reflects on the condition which France was in from the nature of her government, he will see other causes for revolt than those which immediately connect themselves with the person or character of Louis XVI. There were, if I may so express it, a thousand despotisms to be reformed in France, which had grown up under the hereditary despotism of the monarchy and became so rooted as to be in great measure independent of it. Between the monarchy, the Parliament, and the church, there was a *rivalship* of despotism; besides the feudal despotism operating locally, and the ministerial despotism operating everywhere. But Mr. Burke, by considering the king as the only possible object of a revolt, speaks as if France was a village, in which everything that passed must be known to its commanding officer, and no oppression could be acted but what he could immediately control. Mr. Burke might have been in the Bastille his whole life, as well under Louis XVI as Louis XIV, and neither the one nor the other have known that such a man as Mr. Burke existed. The despotic principles of the government were the same in both reigns, though the dispositions of the men were as remote as tyranny and benevolence.

What Mr. Burke considers as a reproach to the French Revolution (that of bringing it forward under a reign more mild than the preceding ones) is one of its highest honours. The revolutions that have taken place in other European countries have been excited by personal hatred. The rage was against the man, and he became the victim. But in the instance of France we see a revolution generated in the rational contemplation of the rights of man, and distinguishing from the beginning between persons and principles.

But Mr. Burke appears to have no idea of principles when he is contemplating governments. "Ten years ago," says he, "I could have felicitated France on her having a government, without inquiring what the nature of that government was, or how it was administered." Is this the language of a rational man? Is it the language of a heart feeling as it ought to feel for the rights and happiness of the human race? On this ground, Mr. Burke must compliment all the governments in the world, while the victims who suffer under them, whether sold into slavery, or tortured out of existence, are wholly forgotten. It is power, and not principles, that Mr. Burke venerates; and under this abominable depravity he is disqualified to judge between them. Thus much for his opinion as to the occasions of the French Revolution. I now proceed to other considerations.

I know a place in America called Point-no-Point, because as you proceed along the shore, gay and flowery as Mr. Burke's language, it continually recedes and presents itself at a distance before you; but when you have got as far as you can go, there is no point at all. Just thus it is with Mr. Burke's three hundred and fifty-six pages. It is therefore difficult to reply to him. But as the points he wishes to establish may be inferred from what he abuses, it is in his paradoxes that we must look for his arguments.

As to the tragic paintings by which Mr. Burke has outraged his own imagination, and seeks to work upon that of his readers, they are very well calculated for theatrical representation, where facts are manufactured for the sake of show, and accommodated to produce, through the weakness of sympathy, a weeping effect. But Mr. Burke should recollect that he is writing history, and not *plays,* and that his readers will expect truth, and not the spouting rant of high-toned exclamation.

When we see a man dramatically lamenting in a publication intended to be believed that *"The age of chivalry is gone!"* that *"The glory of Europe is extinguished for ever!"* that *"The unbought grace of life* [if anyone knows what it is], *the cheap defence of nations, the nurse of manly sentiment and heroic enterprise is gone!"* and all this because the Quixote age of chivalry nonsense is gone, what opinion can we form of his judgment, or what regard can we pay to his facts? In the rhapsody of his imagination he has discovered a world of windmills, and his sorrows are that there are no Quixotes to attack them. But if the age of aristocracy, like that of chivalry, should fall (and they had originally some connection), Mr. Burke, the trumpeter of the order, may continue his parody to the end, and finish with exclaiming: *"Othello's occupation's gone!"*

Notwithstanding Mr. Burke's horrid paintings, when the French Revolution is compared with the revolutions of other countries, the astonishment will be that it is marked with so few sacrifices; but this astonishment will cease when we reflect that *principles,* and not *persons,* were the meditated objects of destruction. The mind of the nation was acted upon by a higher stimulus than what the consideration of persons could inspire, and sought a higher conquest than could be produced by the downfall of an enemy. Among the few who fell there do not appear to be any that were intentionally singled out. They all of them had their fate in the circumstances of the moment and were not pursued with that long, cold-blooded, unabated revenge which pursued the unfortunate Scotch in the affair of 1745.

Through the whole of Mr. Burke's book I do not observe that the Bastille is mentioned more than once, and that with a kind of implication as if he were sorry it was pulled down, and wished it were built up again. "We have rebuilt Newgate," says he, "and tenanted the mansion; and we have prisons almost as strong as the Bastille for those who dare to libel the queens of France." As to what a madman like the person called Lord G—— G—— might say, to whom Newgate is rather a bedlam than a prison, it is unworthy a rational consideration. It was a madman that libeled, and that is sufficient apology; and it afforded an opportunity for confining him, which was the thing that was wished for. But certain it is that Mr. Burke, who does not call himself a madman (whatever other people may do), has libeled in the most unprovoked manner, and in the grossest style of the most vulgar abuse, the whole representative authority of France, and yet Mr. Burke takes his seat in the British House of Commons! From his violence and his grief, his silence on some points and his excess on others, it is difficult not to believe that Mr. Burke is sorry, extremely sorry, that arbitrary power, the power of the Pope and the Bastille, are pulled down.

Not one glance of compassion, not one commiserating reflection that I can find throughout his book, has he bestowed on those who lingered out the most wretched of lives, a life without hope in the most miserable of prisons. It is painful to behold a man employing his talents to corrupt himself. Nature has been kinder to Mr. Burke than he is to her. He is not affected by the reality of distress touching his heart, but by the showy resemblance of it striking his imagination. He pities the plumage, but forgets the dying bird. Accustomed to kiss the aristocratical hand that hath purloined him from himself, he degenerates into a composition of art, and the genuine soul of nature forsakes him. His hero or his heroine must be a tragedy-victim expiring in show, and not the real prisoner of misery, sliding into death in the silence of a dungeon.

As Mr. Burke has passed over the whole transaction of the Bastille (and his silence is nothing in his favour), and has entertained his readers with reflections on supposed facts distorted into real falsehoods, I will give, since he has not, some account of the circumstances which preceded that transaction. They will serve to show that less mischief could scarcely have accompanied such an event when considered with the treacherous and hostile aggravations of the enemies of the Revolution.

The mind can hardly picture to itself a more tremendous scene than what the city of Paris exhibited at the time of taking the Bastille, and for two days before and after, not conceive the possibility of its quieting so soon. At a distance this transaction has appeared only as an act of heroism standing on itself, and the close political connection it had with the Revolution is lost in the brilliancy of the achievement. But we are to consider it as the strength of the parties brought man to man, and contending for the issue. The Bastille was to be either the prize or the prison of the assailants. The downfall of it included the idea of the downfall of despotism, and this compounded image was become as figuratively united as Bunyan's Doubting Castle and Giant Despair.

The National Assembly, before and at the time of taking the Bastille, was sitting at Versailles, twelve miles distance from Paris. About a week before the rising of the Parisians, and their taking the Bastille, it was discovered that a plot was forming, at the head of which was the Count d'Artois, the King's youngest brother, for demolishing the National Assembly, seizing its members, and thereby crushing, by a *coup de main,* all hopes and prospects of forming a free government. For the sake of humanity, as well as of freedom, it is well this plan did not succeed. Examples are not wanting to show how dreadfully vindictive and cruel are all old governments, when they are successful against what they call a revolt.

This plan must have been some time in contemplation; because, in order to carry it into execution, it was necessary to collect a large military force round Paris and cut off the communication between that city and the National Assembly at Versailles. The troops destined for this service were chiefly the foreign troops in the pay of France, and who, for this particular purpose, were drawn from the distant provinces where they were then stationed. When they were collected to the amount of about twenty-five and thirty thousand, it was judged time to put the plan in execution. The ministry who were then in office, and who were friendly to the Revolution, were instantly dismissed and a new ministry formed of those who had concerted the project, among whom was Count de Broglio, and to his share was given the command of those troops. The character of this man as described to me in a letter which I communicated to Mr. Burke before he began to write his book, and from an authority which Mr. Burke well knows was good, was that of "a high-flying aristocrat, cool, and capable of every mischief."

While these matters were agitating, the National Assembly stood in the most perilous and critical situation that a body of men can be supposed to act in. They were the devoted victims, and they knew it. They had the hearts and wishes of their country on their side, but military authority they had none. The guards of Broglio surrounded the hall where the assembly sat, ready, at the word of command, to seize their persons, as had been done the year before to the Parliament of Paris. Had the National Assembly deserted their trust, or had they exhibited signs of weakness or fear, their enemies had been encouraged and the country depressed. When the situation they stood in, the cause they were engaged in, and the crisis then ready to burst, which was to determine their personal and political fate and that of their country, and probably of Europe, are taken into one view, none but a heart callous with prejudice or corrupted by dependence can avoid interesting itself in their success.

The Archbishop of Vienne was at this time president of the National Assembly—a person too old to undergo the scene that a few days or a few hours might bring forth. A man of more activity and greater fortitude was necessary, and the National Assembly chose (under the form of a vice-president, for the presidency still resided in the Archbishop) M. de Lafayette; and this is the only instance of a vice-president being chosen. It was at the moment that this storm was pending (July 11th) that a declaration of rights was brought forward by M. de Lafayette; and is the same which is alluded to in page 309. It was hastily drawn up and makes only a part of the more extensive declaration of rights agreed upon and adopted afterward by the National Assembly. The particular reason for bringing it forward at this moment (M. de Lafayette has since informed me) was that if the National Assembly should fail in the threatened destruction that then surrounded it, some traces of its principles might have the chance of surviving the wreck.

Everything now was drawing to a crisis. The event was to be freedom or slavery. On one side, an army of nearly thirty thousand men; on the other, an unarmed body of citizens; for the citizens of Paris, on whom the National Assembly must then immediately depend, were as unarmed and as undisciplined as the citizens of London are now. The French guards had given strong symptoms of their being attached to the national cause; but their numbers were small, not a tenth part of the force that Broglio commanded, and their officers were in the interest of Broglio.

Matters being now ripe for execution, the new ministry made their appearance in office. The reader will carry in his mind that the Bastille was taken the 14th of July; the point of time I am now speaking to is the 12th. Immediately on the news of the change of ministry reaching Paris, in the afternoon, all the playhouses and places of entertainment, shops and houses, were shut up. The change of ministry was considered as the prelude of hostilities, and the opinion was rightly founded.

The foreign troops began to advance toward the city. The Prince de Lambesc, who commanded a body of German cavalry, approached by the Palace of Louis XV, which connects itself with some of the streets. In his march, he insulted and struck an old man with his sword. The French are remarkable for their respect to old age; and the insolence with which it appeared to be done, uniting with the general fermentation they were in, produced a powerful effect, and a cry of *"To arms! To arms!"* spread itself in a moment over the city.

Arms they had none, nor scarcely any who knew the use of them; but desperate resolution, when every hope is at stake, supplies, for a while, the want of arms. Near where the Prince de Lambesc was drawn up were large piles of stones collected for building the new bridge, and with these the people attacked the cavalry. A party of the French guards, upon hearing the firing, rushed from their quarters and joined the people; and night coming on, the cavalry retreated.

The streets of Paris, being narrow, are favourable for defense, and the loftiness of the houses, consisting of many stories, from which great annoyance might be given, secured them against nocturnal enterprises; and the night was spent in providing themselves with every sort of weapon they could make or procure: guns, swords, blacksmiths' hammers, carpenters' axes, iron crows, pikes, halberts, pitchforks, spits, clubs, etc., etc. The incredible numbers in which they assembled the next morning, and the still more incredible resolution they exhibited, embarrassed and astonished their enemies. Little did the new ministry expect such a salute. Accustomed to slavery themselves, they had no idea that liberty was capable of such inspiration, or that a body of unarmed citizens would

dare to face the military force of thirty thousand men. Every moment of this day was employed in collecting arms, concerting plans, and arranging themselves into the best order which such an instantaneous movement could afford. Broglio continued lying round the city, but made no farther advances this day, and the succeeding night passed with as much tranquillity as such a scene could possibly admit.

But defense only was not the object of the citizens. They had a cause at stake, on which depended their freedom or their slavery. They every moment expected an attack, or to hear of one made on the National Assembly; and in such a situation, the most prompt measures are sometimes the best. The object that now presented itself was the Bastille; and the *éclat* of carrying such a fortress in the face of such an army could not fail to strike a terror into the new ministry, who had scarcely yet had time to meet. By some intercepted correspondence, it was discovered that the mayor of Paris, M. Defflesselles, who appeared to be in the interest of the citizens, was betraying them; from this discovery, there remained no doubt that Broglio would reinforce the Bastille the ensuing evening. It was therefore necessary to attack it that day; but before this could be done, it was first necessary to procure a better supply of arms than they were then possessed of.

There was, adjoining to the city, a large magazine of arms deposited at the Hospital of the Invalids, which the citizens summoned to surrender; and as the place was not defensible, nor attempted much defense, they soon succeeded. Thus supplied, they marched to attack the Bastille; a vast mixed multitude of all ages, and of all degrees, armed with all sorts of weapons. Imagination would fail in describing to itself the appearance of such a procession, and of the anxiety for the events which a few hours or few minutes might produce. What plans the ministry was forming were as unknown to the people within the

The taking of the Bastille, July 14, 1789. *"That the Bastille was attacked with an enthusiasm of heroism, such only as the highest animation of liberty could inspire, and carried in the space of a few hours, is an event which the world is fully possessed of."*

city as what the citizens were doing was unknown to the ministry; and what movements Broglio might make for the support or relief of the place were to the citizens equally as unknown. All was mystery and hazard.

That the Bastille was attacked with an enthusiasm of heroism, such only as the highest animation of liberty could inspire, and carried in the space of a few hours, is an event which the world is fully possessed of. I am not undertaking a detail of the attack, but bringing into view the conspiracy against the nation which provoked it, and which fell with the Bastille. The prison to which the new ministry were dooming the National Assembly, in addition to its being the high altar and castle of despotism, became the proper object to begin with. This enterprise broke up the new ministry, who began now to fly from the ruin they had prepared for others. The troops of Broglio dispersed, and himself fled also.

Mr. Burke has spoken a great deal about plots, but he has never once spoken of this plot against the National Assembly, and the liberties of the nation; and that he might not, he has passed over all the circumstances that might throw it in his way. The exiles who have fled from France, whose case he so much interests himself in, and from whom he has had his lesson, fled in consequence of the miscarriage of this plot. No plot was formed against them; they were plotting against others; and those who fell, met, not unjustly, the punishment they were preparing to execute. But will Mr. Burke say, that if this plot, contrived with the subtlety of an ambuscade, had succeeded, the successful party would have restrained their wrath so soon? Let the history of all old governments answer the question.

Whom has the National Assembly brought to the scaffold? None. They were themselves the devoted victims of this plot, and they have not retaliated; why, then, are they charged with revenge they have not acted? In the tremendous breaking forth of a whole people, in which all degrees, tempers, and characters are confounded, delivering themselves by a miracle of exertion from the destruction meditated against them, is it to be expected that nothing will happen? When men are sore with the sense of oppressions, and menaced with the prospect of new ones, is the calmness of philosophy or the palsy of insensibility to be looked for? Mr. Burke exclaims against outrage; yet the greatest is that which himself has committed. His book is a volume of outrage, not apologized for by the impulse of a moment, but cherished through a space of ten months; yet Mr. Burke had no provocation, no life, no interest at stake.

More of the citizens fell in this struggle than of their opponents; but four or five persons were seized by the populace and instantly put to death; the governor of the Bastille, and the mayor of Paris, who was detected in the act of betraying them; and afterwards Foulon, one of the new ministry, and Berthier, his son-in-law, who had accepted the office of intendant of Paris. Their heads were stuck upon spikes and carried about the city; and it is upon this mode of punishment that Mr. Burke builds a great part of his tragic scenes. Let us therefore examine how men came by the idea of punishing in this manner.

They learn it from the governments they live under and retaliate the punishments they have been accustomed to behold. The heads stuck upon spikes, which remained for years upon Temple Bar, differed nothing in the horror of the scene from those carried about upon spikes at Paris; yet this was done by the English government. It may perhaps be said that it signifies nothing to a man what is done to him after he is dead; but it signifies much to the living; it either tortures their feelings or hardens their hearts, and in either case it instructs them how to punish when power falls into their hands.

Lay then the axe to the root and teach governments humanity. It is their sanguinary punishments which corrupt mankind. In England the punishment in certain cases is by *hanging, drawing* and *quartering;* the heart of the sufferer is cut out and held up to the view of the populace. In France, under the former government, the punishments were not less barbarous. Who does not remember the execution of Damiens, torn to pieces by horses? The effect of those cruel spectacles exhibited to the populace is to destroy tenderness or excite revenge; and by the base and false idea of governing men by terror, instead of reason, they become precedents. It is over the lowest class of mankind that government by terror is intended to operate, and it is on them that it operates to the worst effect. They have sense enough to feel they are the objects aimed at; and they inflict in their turn the examples of terror they have been instructed to practice.

There is in all European countries a large class of people of that description, which in England is called the *Mob*. Of this class were those who committed the burnings and devastations in London in 1780, and of this class were those who carried the heads upon spikes in Paris. Foulon and Berthier were taken up in the country, and sent to Paris, to undergo their examination at the Hotel de Ville; for the National Assembly, immediately on the new ministry coming into office, passed a decree, which they communicated to the King and Cabinet, that they (the National Assembly) would hold the ministry, of which Foulon was one, responsible for the measures they were advising and pursuing; but the mob, incensed at the appearance of Foulon and Berthier, tore them from their conductors before they were carried to the Hotel de Ville and executed them on the spot. Why then does Mr. Burke charge outrages of this kind on a whole people? As well may he charge the riots and outrages of 1780 on all the people of London, or those in Ireland on all his countrymen.

But everything we see or hear offensive to our feelings and derogatory to the human character should lead to other reflections than those of reproach. Even the beings who commit them have some claim to our consideration. How then is it that such vast classes of mankind as are distinguished by the appellation of the vulgar, or the ignorant mob, are so numerous in all old countries? The instant we ask ourselves this question, reflection feels an answer. They arise, as an unavoidable consequence, out of the ill construction of all old governments in Europe, England included with the rest. It is by distortedly exalting some

men, that others are distortedly debased, till the whole is out of nature. A vast mass of mankind are degradedly thrown into the background of the human picture, to bring forward, with greater glare, the puppet show of state and aristocracy. In the commencement of a revolution, those men are rather the followers of the *camp* than of the *standard* of liberty, and have yet to be instructed how to reverence it.

I give to Mr. Burke all his theatrical exaggerations for facts, and I then ask him if they do not establish the certainty of what I here lay down? Admitting them to be true, they show the necessity of the French Revolution, as much as any one thing he could have asserted. These outrages were not the effect of the principles of the Revolution, but of the degraded mind that existed before the Revolution, and which the Revolution is calculated to reform. Place them then to their proper cause, and take the reproach of them to your own side.

It is to the honour of the National Assembly and the city of Paris that, during such a tremendous scene of arms and confusion, beyond the control of all authority, they have been able, by the influence of example and exhortation, to restrain so much. Never were more pains taken to instruct and enlighten mankind, and to make them see that their interest consisted in their virtue, and not in their revenge, than have been displayed in the Revolution of France. I now proceed to make some remarks on Mr. Burke's account of the expedition to Versailles, October the 5th and 6th.

I cannot consider Mr. Burke's book in any other light than a dramatic performance; and he must, I think, have considered it in the same light himself, by the poetical liberties he has taken of omitting some facts, distorting others, and making the whole machinery bend to produce a stage effect. Of this kind is his account of the expedition to Versailles. He begins this account by omitting the only facts which as causes are known to be true; everything beyond these is conjecture even in Paris; and he then works up a tale accommodated to his own passions and prejudices.

It is to be observed throughout Mr. Burke's book that he never speaks of plots *against* the Revolution; and it is from those plots that all the mischiefs have arisen. It suits his purpose to exhibit the consequences without their causes. It is one of the arts of the drama to do so. If the crimes of men were exhibited with their sufferings, the stage effect would sometimes be lost, and the audience would be inclined to approve where it was intended they should commiserate.

After all the investigations that have been made into this intricate affair (the expedition to Versailles), it still remains enveloped in all that kind of mystery which ever accompanies events produced more from a concurrence of awkward circumstances than from fixed design. While the characters of men are forming, as is always the case in revolutions, there is a reciprocal suspicion, and a disposition to misinterpret each other; and even parties directly opposite in principle will sometimes concur in pushing forward the same movement with very different views, and with the hopes of its producing very different consequences. A great deal of this may be discovered in this embarrassed affair, and yet the issue of the whole was what nobody had in view.

The only things certainly known are that considerable uneasiness was at this time excited at Paris by the delay of the King in not sanctioning and forwarding the decrees of the National Assembly, particularly that of the *Declaration of the Rights of Man,* and the decrees of the *fourth of August,* which contained the foundation principles on which the constitution was to be erected. The kindest, and perhaps the fairest, conjecture upon this matter is that some of the ministers intended to make remarks and observations upon certain parts of them before they were finally sanctioned and sent to the provinces; but be this as it may, the enemies of the Revolution derived hope from the delay, and the friends of the Revolution uneasiness.

During this state of suspense, the *Garde du Corps,* which was composed, as such regiments generally are, of persons much connected with the court, gave an entertainment at Versailles (October 1) to some foreign regiments then arrived; and when the entertainment was at the height, on a signal given the *Garde du Corps* tore the national cockade from their hats, trampled it under foot, and replaced it with a counter-cockade prepared for the purpose. An indignity of this kind amounted to defiance. It was like declaring war; and if men will give challenges they must expect consequences. But all this Mr. Burke has carefully kept out of sight. He begins his account by saying: "History will record that on the morning of the 6th of October, 1789, the King and Queen of France, after a day of confusion, alarm, dismay, and slaughter, lay down under the pledged security of public faith to indulge nature in a few hours of respite, and troubled melancholy repose." This is neither the sober style of history nor the intention of it. It leaves everything to be guessed at and mistaken. One would at least think there had been a battle; and a battle there probably would have been had it not been for the moderating prudence of those whom Mr. Burke involves in his censures. By his keeping the *Garde du Corps* out of sight Mr. Burke has afforded himself the dramatic license of putting the King and Queen in their places, as if the object of the expedition was against them. But to return to my account—

This conduct of the *Garde du Corps,* as might well be expected, alarmed and enraged the Parisians. The colours of the cause, and the cause itself, were become too united to mistake the intention of the insult, and the Parisians were determined to call the *Garde du Corps* to an account. There was certainly nothing of the cowardice of assassination in marching in the face of day to demand satisfaction, if such a phrase may be used, of a body of armed men who had voluntarily given defiance. But the circumstance which serves to throw this affair into embarrassment is, that the enemies of the Revolution appear to have encouraged it as well as its friends. The one hoped to prevent a civil war by checking it in time, and the other to make one. The hopes of those opposed to the Revolution rested in making the King of their party, and getting him from Versailles to Metz, where they expected to collect a force and set up a standard. We have, therefore, two different objects presenting themselves at the same time, and to be accomplished by the same means; the one to chastise the *Garde du Corps*, which was the object of the Parisians; the other to render the confusion of such a scene an inducement to the King to set off for Metz.

On the 5th of October a very numerous body of women, and men in the disguise of women, collected round the Hotel de Ville or town hall at Paris and set off for Versailles. Their professed object was the *Garde du Corps*; but prudent men readily recollect that mischief is more easily begun than ended; and this impressed itself with the more force from the suspicions already stated, and the irregularity of such a cavalcade. As soon, therefore, as a sufficient force could be collected, M. de Lafayette, by orders from the civil authority of Paris, set off after them at the head of twenty thousand of the Paris militia. The Revolution could derive no benefit from confusion, and its opposers might. By an amiable and spirited manner of address he had hitherto been fortunate in calming disquietudes, and in this he was extraordinarily successful; to frustrate, therefore, the hopes of those who might seek to improve this scene into a sort of justifiable necessity for the King's quitting Versailles and withdrawing to Metz, and to prevent at the same time the consequences that might ensue between the *Garde du Corps* and this phalanx of men and women, he forwarded expresses to the King, that he

was on his march to Versailles, by the orders of the civil authority of Paris, for the purpose of peace and protection, expressing at the same time the necessity of restraining the *Garde du Corps* from firing upon the people.

He arrived at Versailles between ten and eleven at night. The *Garde du Corps* was drawn up, and the people had arrived some time before, but everything had remained suspended. Wisdom and policy now consisted in changing a scene of danger into a happy event. M. de Lafayette became the mediator between the enraged parties; and the King, to remove the uneasiness which had arisen from the delay already stated, sent for the President of the National Assembly, and signed the Declaration of the Rights of Man, and such other parts of the Constitution as were in readiness.

It was now about one in the morning. Everything appeared to be composed, and a general congratulation took place. By the beat of drum a proclamation was made that the citizens of Versailles would give the hospitality of their houses to their fellow citizens of Paris. Those who could not be accommodated in this manner remained in the streets, or took up their quarters in the churches; and at two o'clock the King and Queen retired.

In this state matters passed till the break of day, when a fresh disturbance arose from the censurable conduct of some of both parties, for such characters there will be in all such senses. One of the *Garde du Corps* appeared at one of the windows of the palace, and the people who had remained during the night in the streets accosted him with reviling and provocative language. Instead of retiring, as in such a case prudence would have dictated, he presented his musket, fired, and killed one of the Paris militia. The peace being thus broken, the people rushed into the palace in quest of the offender. They attacked the quarters of the *Garde du Corps* within the palace, and pursued them throughout the avenues of it, and to the apartments of the

King. On this tumult, not the Queen only, as Mr. Burke has represented it, but every person in the palace was awakened and alarmed; and M. de Lafayette had a second time to interpose between the parties, the event of which was that the *Garde du Corps* put on the national cockade, and the matter ended as by oblivion, after the loss of two or three lives.

During the latter part of the time in which this confusion was acting, the King and Queen were in public at the balcony, and neither of them concealed for safety's sake, as Mr. Burke insinuates. Matters being thus appeased, and tranquillity restored, a general acclamation broke forth of *Le Roi à Paris—Le Roi à Paris*—The King of Paris. It was the shout of peace, and immediately accepted on the part of the King. By this measure all future projects of trepanning the King to Metz, and setting up the standard of opposition to the Constitution, were prevented, and the suspicions extinguished. The King and his family reached Paris in the evening, and were congratulated on their arrival by M. Bailley, the mayor of Paris, in the name of the citizens. Mr. Burke, who throughout his book confounds things, persons, and principles, as in his remarks on M. Bailley's address, confounded time also. He censures M. Bailley for calling it *"un bon jour,"* a good day. Mr. Burke should have informed himself that this scene took up the space of two days, the day on which it began with every appearance of danger and mischief, and the day on which it terminated without the mischiefs that threatened; and that it is to this peaceful termination that M. Bailley alludes, and to the arrival of the King at Paris. Not less than three hundred thousand persons arranged themselves in the procession from Versailles to Paris, and not an act of molestation was committed during the whole march.

Mr. Burke, on the authority of M. Lally Tollendal, a deserter from the National Assembly, says that on entering Paris, the people shouted *"Tous les évèques à la lanterne."* ("All bishops to be hanged at the lantern or lampposts.") It is surprising that nobody could hear this but Lally Tollendal, and that nobody should believe it but Mr. Burke. It has not the least connection with any part of the transaction and is totally foreign to every circumstance of it. The bishops had never been introduced before into any scene of Mr. Burke's drama: why then are they, all at once, and altogether, *tout à coup, et tous ensemble,* introduced now? Mr. Burke brings forward his bishops and his lantern-like figures in a magic lantern and raises his scenes by contrast instead of connection. But it serves to show, with the rest of his book, what little credit ought to be given where even probability is set at defiance, for the purpose of defaming; and with this reflection, instead of a soliloquy in praise of chivalry, as Mr. Burke has done, I close the account of the expedition to Versailles.

I have now to follow Mr. Burke through a pathless wilderness of rhapsodies, and a sort of descant upon governments, in which he asserts whatever he pleases, on the presumption of its being believed, without offering either evidence or reasons for so doing.

Before anything can be reasoned upon to a conclusion, certain facts, principles, or data, to reason from, must be established, admitted, or denied. Mr. Burke, with his usual outrage, abuses the *Declaration of the Rights of Man,* published by the National Assembly of France as the basis on which the Constitution of France is built. This he calls "paltry and blurred sheets of paper about the rights of man." Does Mr. Burke mean to deny that *man* has any rights? If he does, then he must mean that there are no such things as rights anywhere, and that he has none himself; for who is there in the world but man? But if Mr. Burke means to admit that man has rights, the question then will be: What are those rights, and how came man by them originally?

The error of those who reason by precedents drawn from antiquity, respecting the rights of man, is that they do not go far enough into antiquity. They do not go the whole way. They stop in some of the intermediate stages of a hundred or a thousand years and produce what was then done, as a rule for the present day. This is not authority at all. If we travel still farther into antiquity, we shall find a direct contrary opinion and practice prevailing; and if antiquity is to be authority, a thousand such authorities may be produced, successively contradicting each other; but if we proceed on, we shall at last come out right; we shall come to the time when man came from the hand of his Maker. What was he then? Man. Man was his high and only title, and a higher cannot be given him. But of titles I shall speak hereafter.

We are now got at the origin of man, and at the origin of his rights. As to the manner in which the world has been governed from that day to this, it is no farther any concern of ours than to make a proper use of the errors or the improvements which the history of it presents. Those who lived a hundred or a thousand years ago were then moderns, as we are now. They had *their* ancients, and those ancients had others, and we also shall be ancients in our turn. If the mere name of antiquity is to govern in the affairs of life, the people who are to live a hundred or a thousand years hence may as well take us for a precedent, as we make a precedent of those who lived a hundred or a thousand years ago. The fact is, that portions of antiquity, by proving everything, establish nothing. It is authority against authority all the way, till we come to the divine origin of the rights of man at the creation. Here our inquiries find a resting place, and our reason finds a home. If a dispute about the rights of man had arisen at the distance of a hundred years from the creation, it is to this source of authority they must have referred, and it is to this same source of authority that we must now refer.

Though I mean not to touch upon any sectarian principle of religion, yet it may be worth observing, that the genealogy of Christ is traced to Adam. Why then not trace the rights of man to the creation of man? I will answer the question. Because there have been upstart governments, thrusting themselves between and presumptuously working to *un-make* man.

If any generation of men ever possessed the right of dictating the mode by which the world should be governed for ever, it was the first generation that existed; and if that generation did it not, no succeeding generation can show any authority for doing it, nor can set any up. The illuminating and divine principle of the equal rights of man (for it has its origin from the Maker of man) relates, not only to the living individuals, but to generations of men succeeding each other. Every generation is equal in rights to the generations which preceded it, by the same rule that every individual is born equal in rights with his contemporary.

Every history of the creation, and every traditionary account, whether from the lettered or unlettered world, however they may vary in their opinion or belief of certain particulars, all agree in establishing one point, *the unity of man;* by which I mean that men are all of *one degree,* and consequently that all men are born equal, and with equal natural rights, in the same manner as if posterity had been continued by *creation* instead of *generation,* the latter being only the mode by which the former is carried forward; and consequently every child born into the world must be considered as deriving its existence from God. The world is as new to him as it was to the first man that existed, and his natural right in it is of the same kind.

The Mosaic account of the creation, whether taken as divine authority or merely historical, is fully up to this point, *the unity or equality of man.* The expressions admit of no controversy. "And God said, Let us make man in our own image. In the image of God created he him; male and female created he them." The distinction of sexes is pointed out, but no other distinction is even implied. If this be not divine authority, it is at least historical authority, and shows that the equality of man, so far from being a modern doctrine, is the oldest upon record.

It is also to be observed that all the religions known in the world are founded, so far as they relate to man, on the *unity of man,* as being all of one degree. Whether in heaven or in hell, or in whatever state man may be supposed to exist hereafter, the good and the bad are the only distinctions. Nay, even the laws of governments are obliged to slide into this principle, by making degrees to consist in crimes and not in persons.

It is one of the greatest of all truths, and of the highest advantage to cultivate. By considering man in this light, and by instructing him to consider himself in this light, it places him in a close connection with all his duties, whether to his Creator or to the creation, of which he is part; and it is only when he forgets his origin, or, to use a more fashionable phrase, his *birth and family,* that he becomes dissolute. It is not among the least of the evils of the present existing governments in all parts of Europe that man, considered as man, is thrown back to a vast distance from his Maker, and the artificial chasm filled up by a succession of barriers, or sort of turnpike gates, through which he has to pass. I will quote Mr. Burke's catalogue of barriers that he has set up between man and his Maker. Putting himself in the character of a herald, he says: *We fear God—we look with* AWE *to kings—with affection to Parliaments—with duty to magistrates—with reverence to priests, and with respect to nobility.* Mr. Burke has forgotten to put in *"chivalry."* He has also forgotten to put in Peter.

The duty of man is not a wilderness of turnpike gates, through which he is to pass by tickets from one to the other. It is plain and simple and consists but of two points. His duty to God, which every man must feel; and with respect to his neighbour, to do as he would be done by. If those to whom power is delegated do well, they will be respected; if not, they will be despised; and with regard to those to whom no power is delegated, but who assume it, the rational world can know nothing of them.

Hitherto we have spoken only (and that but in part) of the natural rights of man. We have now to consider the civil rights of man, and to show how the one originates from the other. Man did not enter into society to become *worse* than he was before, not to have fewer rights than he had before, but to have those rights better secured. His natural rights are the foundation of all his civil rights. But in order to pursue this distinction with more precision, it will be necessary to mark the different qualities of natural and civil rights.

A few words will explain this. Natural rights are those which appertain to man in right of his existence. Of this kind are all the intellectual rights, or rights of the mind, and also all those rights of acting as an individual for his own comfort and happiness, which are not injurious to the natural rights of others. Civil rights are those which appertain to man in right of his being a member of society. Every civil right has for its foundation some natural right preexisting in the individual, but to the enjoyment of which his individual power is not, in all cases, sufficiently competent. Of this kind are all those which relate to security and protection.

From this short view it will be easy to distinguish between that class of natural rights which man retains after entering into society and those which he throws into the common stock as a member of society.

The natural rights which he retains are all those in which the *power* to execute it is as perfect in the individual as the right itself. Among this class, as is before mentioned, are all the intellectual rights, or rights of the mind; consequently religion is one of those rights. The natural rights which are not retained are all those in which, though the right is perfect in the individual, the power to execute them is defective. They answer not his purpose. A man, by natural right, has a right to judge in his own cause; and so far as the right of the mind is concerned, he never surrenders it. But what availeth it him to judge, if he has not power to redress? He therefore deposits this right in the common stock of society and takes the arm of society, of which he is a part, in preference and in addition to his own. Society *grants* him nothing. Every man is a proprietor in society and draws on the capital as a matter of right.

From these premises two or three certain conclusions will follow:

First, *That every civil right grows out of a natural right; or, in other words, is a natural right exchanged.*

Second, *That civil power properly considered as such is made up of the aggregate of that class of the natural rights of man, which becomes defective in the individual in point of power, and answers not his purpose, but when collected to a focus becomes competent to the purpose of every one.*

Third, *That the power produced from the aggregate of natural rights, imperfect in power in the individual, cannot be applied to invade the natural rights which are retained in the individual, and in which the power to execute is as perfect as the right itself.*

We have now, in a few words, traced man from a natural individual to a member of society, and shown, or endeavoured to show, the quality of the natural rights retained, and of those which are exchanged for civil rights. Let us now apply these principles to governments.

In casting our eyes over the world, it is extremely easy to distinguish the governments which have arisen out of society, or out of the social compact, from those which have not; but to place this in a clearer light than what a single glance may afford, it will be proper to take a review of the several sources from which governments have arisen and on which they have been founded.

They may be all comprehended under three heads.

First, *Superstition.*

Second, *Power.*

Third, *The common interest of society and the common rights of man.*

The first was a government of priestcraft, the second of conquerors, and the third of reason.

When a set of artful men pretended, through the medium of oracles, to hold intercourse with the Deity, as familiarly as they now march up the back stairs in European courts, the world was completely under the government of superstition. The oracles were consulted, and whatever they were made to say became the law; and this sort of government lasted as long as this sort of superstition lasted.

After these a race of conquerors arose, whose government, like that of William the Conqueror, was founded in power, and the sword assumed the name of a sceptre. Governments thus established last as long as the power to support them lasts; but that they might avail themselves of every engine in their favour, they united fraud to force, and set up an idol which they called *Divine Right,* and which, in imitation of the Pope, who affects to be spiritual and temporal, and in contradiction to the founder of the Christian religion, twisted itself afterward into an idol of another shape, called *Church and State.* The key of St. Peter and the key of the Treasury became quartered on one another, and the wondering cheated multitude worshipped the invention.

When I contemplate the natural dignity of man, when I feel (for Nature has not been kind enough to me to blunt my feelings) for the honour and happiness of its character, I become irritated at the attempt to govern mankind by force and fraud, as if they were all knaves and fools and can scarcely avoid disgust at those who are thus imposed upon.

We have now to review the governments which arise out of the society, in contradistinction to those which arose out of superstition and conquest.

It has been thought a considerable advance toward establishing the principles of freedom to say that government is a compact between those who govern and those who are governed; but this cannot be true, because it is putting the effect before the cause; for as man must have existed before governments existed, there necessarily was a time when governments did not exist, and consequently there could originally exist no governors to form such a compact with. The fact therefore must be that the *individuals themselves,* each in his own personal and sovereign right, *entered into a compact with each other* to produce a government; and this is the only mode in which governments have a right to arise, and the only principle on which they have a right to exist.

To possess ourselves of a clear idea of what government is, or ought to be, we must trace it to its origin. In doing this we shall easily discover that governments must have arisen either *out* of the people or *over* the people. Mr. Burke has made no distinction. He investigates nothing to its source, and therefore he confounds everything; but he has signified his intention of undertaking, at some future opportunity, a comparison between the constitutions of England and France. As he thus renders it a subject of controversy by throwing the gauntlet, I take him up on his own ground. It is in high challenges that high truths have the right of appearing; and I accept it with the more readiness because it affords me, at the same time, an opportunity of pursuing the subject with respect to governments arising out of society.

But it will be first necessary to define what is meant by a *constitution.* It is not sufficient that we adopt the word; we must fix also a standard signification to it.

A constitution is not a thing in name only but in fact. It has not an ideal, but a real existence; and wherever it cannot be produced in a visible form, there is none.

A constitution is a thing *antecedent* to a government, and a government is only the creature of a constitution. The constitution of a country is not the act of its government, but of the people constituting a government. It is the body of elements, to which you can refer, and quote article by article; and which contains the principles on which the government shall be established, the manner in which it shall be organized, the powers it shall have, the mode of elections, the duration of Parliaments, or by what other name such bodies may be called; the powers which the executive part of the government shall have; and in fine, everything that relates to the complete organization of a civil government, and the principles on which it shall act, and by which it shall be bound. A constitution, therefore, is to a government what the laws made afterward by that government are to a court of judicature. The court of judicature does not make the laws, neither can it alter them; it only acts in conformity to the laws made: and the government is in like manner governed by the constitution.

Can, then, Mr. Burke produce the English Constitution? If he cannot, we may fairly conclude that though it has been so much talked about, no such thing as a constitution exists, or ever did exist, and consequently that the people have yet a constitution to form.

Mr. Burke will not, I presume, deny the position I have already advanced—namely, that governments arise either *out* of the people or *over* the people. The English government is one of those which arose out of a conquest, and not out of society, and consequently it arose over the people; and though it has been much modified from the opportunity of circumstances since the time of William the Conqueror, the country has never yet regenerated itself, and is therefore without a constitution.

I readily perceive the reason why Mr. Burke declined going into the comparison between the English and French constitutions, because he could not but perceive, when he sat down to the task, that no such thing as a constitution existed on his side of the question. His book is certainly bulky enough to have contained all he could say on this subject, and it would have been the best manner in which people could have judged of their separate merits. Why then has he declined the only thing that was worthwhile to write upon? It was the strongest ground he could take, if the advantages were on his side, but the weakest if they were not; and his declining to take it is either a sign that he could not possess it or could not maintain it.

Mr. Burke said, in a speech last winter in Parliament, that *when the National Assembly first met in three Orders* (the Tiers Etats, the Clergy, and the Noblesse), *France had then a good constitution.* This shows, among numerous other instances, that Mr. Burke does not understand what a constitution is. The persons so met were not a *constitution,* but a *convention,* to make a constitution.

The present National Assembly of France is, strictly speaking, the *personal social compact.* The members of it are the delegates of the nation in its *original* character; future assemblies will be the delegates of the nation in its *organized* character. The authority of the present assembly is different to what the authority of future assemblies will be. The authority of the present one is to form a constitution; the authority of future assemblies will be to legislate according to the principles and forms prescribed in that constitution; and if experience should hereafter show that alterations, amendments, or additions are necessary, the constitution will point out the mode by which such things shall be done, and not leave it to the discretionary power of the future government.

A government on the principles on which constitutional governments arising out of society are established cannot have the right of altering itself. If it had, it would be arbitrary. It might make itself what it pleased; and wherever such a right is set up, it shows there is no constitu-tion. The act by which the English Parliament empowered itself to sit seven years shows there is no constitution in England. It might, by the same self-authority, have sat any greater number of years, or for life. The bill which the present Mr. Pitt brought into Parliament some years ago, to reform Parliament, was on the same erroneous principle. The right of reform is in the nation in its original character, and the constitutional method would be by a general convention elected for the purpose. There is, moreover, a paradox in the idea of vitiated bodies reforming themselves.

From these preliminaries I proceed to draw some comparisons. I have already spoken of the declaration of rights; and as I mean to be as concise as possible, I shall proceed to other parts of the French Constitution.

The Constitution of France says *that every man who pays a tax of sixty sous per annum* (2s. 6d. English) *is an elector.* What article will Mr. Burke place against this? Can anything be more limited, and at the same time more capricious, than the qualifications of electors are in England? Limited—because not one man in a hundred (I speak much within compass) is admitted to vote. Capricious—because the lowest character that can be supposed to exist, and who has not so much as the visible means of an honest livelihood, is an elector in some places; while in other places, the man who pays very large taxes, and has a known fair character, and the farmer who rents to the amount of three or four hundred pounds a year, with a property on that farm to three or four times that amount, is not admitted to be an elector.

Everything is out of nature, as Mr. Burke says on another occasion, in this strange chaos, and all sorts of follies are blended with all sorts of crimes.

William the Conqueror and his descendants parceled out the country in this manner and bribed some parts of it by what they called charters to hold the other parts of it the better subjected to their will.

This is the reason why so many of those charters abound in Cornwall; the people were averse to the government established at the conquest, and the towns were garrisoned and bribed to enslave the country. All the old charters are the badges of this conquest, and it is from this source that the capriciousness of elections arises.

The French Constitution says *that the number of representatives for any place shall be in a ratio to the number of taxable inhabitants or electors.*

What article will Mr. Burke place against this? The county of Yorkshire, which contains nearly a million of souls, sends two county members; and so does the county of Rutland, which contains not a hundredth part of that number. The town of Old Sarum, which contains not three houses, sends two members; and the town of Manchester, which contains upwards of sixty thousand souls, is not admitted to send any. Is there any principle in these things? Is there anything by which you can trace the marks of freedom or discover those of wisdom? No wonder then Mr. Burke has declined the comparison and endeavoured to lead his readers from the point by a wild, unsystematical, display of paradoxical rhapsodies.

The French Constitution says *that the National Assembly shall be elected every two years.*

What article will Mr. Burke place against this? Why, that the nation has no right at all in the case; that the government is perfectly arbitrary with respect to this point; and he can quote for his authority the precedent of a former Parliament.

The French Constitution says *there shall be no game laws, that the farmer on whose lands wild game shall be found (for it is by the produce of his lands they are fed) shall have a right to what he can take; that there shall be no monopolies of any kind—that all trade shall be free and every man free to follow any occupation by which he can procure an honest livelihood, and in any place, town, or city throughout the nation.*

What will Mr. Burke say to this? In England, game is made the property of those at whose expense it is not fed; and with respect to monopolies, the country is cut up into monopolies. Every chartered town is an aristocratical monopoly in itself, and the qualification of electors proceeds out of those chartered monopolies. Is this freedom? Is this what Mr. Burke means by a constitution?

In these chartered monopolies, a man coming from another part of the country is hunted from them as if he were a foreign enemy. An Englishman is not free of his own country; every one of those places presents a barrier in his way and tells him he is not a freeman—that he has no rights. Within these monopolies are other monopolies. In a city, such for instance as Bath, which contains between twenty and thirty thousand inhabitants, the right of electing representatives to Parliament is monopolized by about thirty-one persons. And within these monopolies are still others. A man even of the same town, whose parents were not in circumstances to give him an occupation, is debarred, in many cases, from the natural right of acquiring one, be his genius or industry what it may.

Are these things examples to hold out to a country regenerating itself from slavery, like France? Certainly they are not, and certain am I, that when the people of England come to reflect upon them they will, like France, annihilate those badges of ancient oppression, those traces of a conquered nation. Had Mr. Burke possessed talents similar to the author of "On the Wealth of Nations," he would have comprehended all the parts which enter into, and, by assemblage, form a constitution. He would have reasoned from minutiæ to magnitude. It is not from his prejudices only, but from the disorderly cast of his genius, that he is unfitted for the subject he writes upon. Even his genius is without a constitution. It is a genius at random, and not a genius constituted. But he must say something. He has therefore mounted in the air like a balloon, to draw the eyes of the multitude from the ground they stand upon.

Much is to be learned from the French Constitution. Conquest and tyranny transplanted themselves with William the Conqueror from Normandy into England, and the country is yet disfigured with the marks. May, then, the example of all France contribute to regenerate the freedom which a province of it destroyed!

The French Constitution says *that to preserve the national representation from being corrupt no member of the National Assembly shall be an officer of the government, a placeman or a pensioner.*

What will Mr. Burke place against this? I will whisper his answer—loaves and fishes. Ah! this government of loaves and fishes has more mischief in it than people have yet reflected on. The National Assembly has made the discovery, and it holds out the example to the world. Had governments agreed to quarrel on purpose to fleece their countries by taxes, they could not have succeeded better than they have done.

Many things in the English government appear to me the reverse of what they ought to be and what they are said to be. The Parliament, imperfectly and capriciously elected as it is, is nevertheless *supposed* to hold the national purse in *trust* for the nation; but in the manner in which an English Parliament is constructed it is like a man being both mortgager and mortgagee, and in the case of misapplication of trust it is the criminal sitting in judgment upon himself. If those who vote the supplies are the same persons who receive the supplies when voted, and are to account for the expenditure of those supplies to those who voted them, it is *themselves accountable to themselves,* and the Comedy of Errors concludes with the Pantomime of Hush. Neither the ministerial party nor the Opposition will touch upon this case. The national purse is the common hack which each mounts upon. It is like what the country people call "Ride and tie— You ride a little way, and then I." They order these things better in France.

The French Constitution says *that the right of war and peace is in the nation.*

Where else should it reside but in those who are to pay the expense?

In England this right is said to reside in a *metaphor* shown at the Tower for sixpence or a shilling a piece: so are the lions; and it would be a step nearer to reason to say it resided in them, for any inanimate metaphor is no more than a hat or a cap. We can all see the absurdity of worshipping Aaron's molten calf, or Nebuchadnezzar's golden image; but why do men continue to practice themselves the absurdities they despise in others?

It may with reason be said that in the manner the English nation is represented it signifies not where this right resides, whether in the Crown or in the Parliament. War is the common harvest of all those who participate in the division and expenditure of public money, in all countries. It is the art of *conquering at home;* the object of it is an increase of revenue; and as revenue cannot be increased without taxes, a pretense must be made for expenditures. In reviewing the history of the English government, its wars and its taxes, a bystander, not blinded by prejudice nor warped by interest, would declare that taxes were not raised to carry on wars, but that wars were raised to carry on taxes.

Mr. Burke, as a member of the House of Commons, is a part of the English government; and though he professes himself an enemy of war, he abuses the French Constitution, which seeks to explode it. He holds up the English government as a model, in all its parts, to France; but he should first know the remarks which the French make upon it. They contend in favour of their own, that the portion of liberty enjoyed in England is just enough to enslave a country by more productively than by despotism, and that as the real object of all despotism is revenue, a government so formed obtains more than it could do either by direct despotism, or in a full state of freedom, and is, therefore, on the ground of interest, opposed to both. They account also for the readiness which always appears in such governments for engaging in wars by remarking on the different motives which produce them. In despotic governments wars are the effect of pride; but in those governments in which they become the means of taxation, they acquire thereby a more permanent promptitude.

The French Constitution, therefore, to provide against both these evils, has taken away the power of declaring war from kings and ministers and placed the right where the expense must fall.

When the question of the right of war and peace was agitating in the National Assembly, the people of England appeared to be much interested in the event, and highly to applaud the decision. As a principle it applies as much to one country as another. William the Conqueror, *as a conqueror,* held this power of war and peace in himself, and his descendants have ever since claimed it under him as a right.

Although Mr. Burke has asserted the right of the Parliament at the Revolution to bind and control the nation and posterity *for ever,* he denies at the same time that the Parliament or the nation had any right to alter what he calls the succession of the Crown in anything but in part, or by a sort of modification. By his taking this ground he throws the case back to the *Norman Conquest,* and by thus running a line of succession springing from William the Conqueror to the present day, he makes it necessary to inquire who and what William the Conqueror was, and where he came from, and into the origin, history, and nature of what are called prerogatives. Everything must have had a beginning, and the fog of time and antiquity should be penetrated to discover it. Let, then, Mr. Burke bring forward his William of Normandy, for it is to this origin that his argument goes. It also unfortunately happens, in running this line of succession, that another line parallel thereto presents itself, which is, that if the succession runs in the line of the conquest, the nation runs in the line of being conquered, and it ought to rescue itself from this reproach.

But it will perhaps be said that though the power of declaring war descends in the heritage of the conquest, it is held in check by the right of the Parliament to withhold the supplies. It will always happen when a thing is originally wrong that amendments do not make it right, and it often happens that they do as much mischief one way as good the other, and such is the case here, for if the one rashly declares war as a matter of right, and the other peremptorily withholds the supplies as a matter of right, the remedy becomes as bad, or worse, than the disease. The one forces the nation to a combat, and the other ties its hands; but the more probable issue is that the contest will end in a collusion between the parties, and be made a screen to both.

On this question of war, three things are to be considered. First, the right of declaring it; second, the expense of supporting it; third, the mode of conducting it after it is declared. The French Constitution places the *right* where the *expense* must fall, and this union can be only in the nation. The mode of conducting it after it is declared, it consigns to the executive department. Were this the case in all countries, we should hear but little more of wars.

Before I proceed to consider other parts of the French Constitution, and by way of relieving the fatigue of argument, I will introduce an anecdote which I had from Dr. Franklin.

While the Doctor resided in France as Minister from America during the war, he had numerous proposals made to him by projectors of every country and of every kind, who wished to go to the land that floweth with milk and honey, America; and among the rest, there was one who offered himself to be king. He introduced his proposal to the Doctor by letter, which is now in the hands of M. Beaumarchais, of Paris—stating first, that as the Americans had dismissed or sent away their king, that they would want another. Second, that himself was a Norman. Third, that he was of a more ancient family than the dukes of Normandy, and of a more honourable descent, his line having never been bastardized. Fourth, that there was already a precedent in England of kings coming out of Normandy, and on these grounds he rested his offer, *enjoining* that the Doctor would forward it to America. But as the Doctor neither did this, nor yet sent him an answer, the projector wrote a second letter in which he did not, it is true, threaten to go over and conquer America, but only with great dignity proposed that if his offer was not accepted, an acknowledgment of about £30,000 might be made to him for his generosity! Now, as all arguments respecting succession must necessarily connect that succession with some beginning, Mr. Burke's arguments on this subject go to show that there is no English origin of kings, and that they are descendants of the Norman line in right of the Conquest. It may, therefore, be of service to his doctrine to make this story known and to inform him, that in case of that natural extinction to which all mortality is subject, kings may again be had from Normandy, on more reasonable terms than William the Conqueror; and consequently that the good people of England at the Revolution of 1688 *might have done much better*, had such a generous Norman as *this* known *their* wants, and they had known *his!* The chivalry character which Mr. Burke so much admires is certainly much easier to make a bargain with than a *hard dealing Dutchman.* But to return to the matters of the Constitution.

The French Constitution says *there shall be no titles;* and, of consequence, all that class of equivocal generation which in some countries is called "*aristocracy*" and in others "*nobility,*" is done away, and the *peer* is exalted into MAN.

Titles are but nicknames, and every nickname is a title. The thing is perfectly harmless in itself, but it marks a sort of foppery in the human character, which degrades it. It reduces man into the diminutive of man in things which are great, and the counterfeit of woman in things which are little. It talks about its fine *blue ribbon* like a girl, and shows its new *garter* like a child. A certain writer, of some antiquity, says: "*When I was a child, I thought as a child; but when I became a man, I put away childish things.*"

It is, properly, from the elevated mind of France that the folly of titles has fallen. It has outgrown the baby clothes of *count* and *duke,* and breeched itself in manhood. France has not leveled, it has exalted. It has put down the dwarf, to set up the man. The punyism of a senseless word like *duke* or *count* or *earl* has ceased to please. Even those who possessed them have disowned the gibberish, and as they outgrew the rickets, have despised the rattle. The genuine mind of man, thirsting for its native home, society, contemns the gewgaws that separate him from it. Titles are like circles drawn by the magician's wand, to contract the sphere of man's felicity. He lives immured within the Bastille of a word and surveys at a distance the envied life of man.

Is it, then, any wonder that titles should fall in France? Is it not a greater wonder they should be kept up anywhere? What are they? What is their worth, and "what is their amount"?

When we think or speak of a *judge* or a *general,* we associate with it the ideas of office and character; we think of gravity in the one and bravery in the other; but when we use a word *merely as a title,* no ideas associate with it. Through all the vocabulary of Adam there is not such an animal as a duke or a count; neither can we connect any certain idea with the words. Whether they mean strength or weakness, wisdom or folly, a child or a man, or the rider or the horse, is all equivocal. What respect then can be paid to that which describes

French aristocrats surrender their badges (symbols of title) to revolutionary authorities. *"The French Constitution says there shall be no titles; . . . "nobility" is done away, and the peer is exalted into MAN. Titles are but nicknames, and every nickname is a title."*

nothing, and which means nothing? Imagination has given figure and character to centaurs, satyrs, and down to all the fairy tribe; but titles baffle even the powers of fancy and are a chimerical nondescript.

But this is not all. If a whole country is disposed to hold them in contempt, all their value is gone, and none will own them. It is common opinion only that makes them anything or nothing, or worse than nothing. There is no occasion to take titles away, for they take themselves away when society concurs to ridicule them. This species of imaginary consequence has visibly declined in every part of Europe, and it hastens to its exit as the world of reason continues to rise. There was a time when the lowest class of what are called *nobility* was more thought of than the highest is now, and when a man in armour riding through Christendom in quest of adven-

tures was more stared at than a modern duke. The world has seen this folly fall, and it has fallen by being laughed at, and the farce of titles will follow its fate. The patriots of France have discovered in good time that rank and dignity in society must take a new ground. The old one has fallen through. It must now take the substantial ground of character, instead of chimerical ground of titles; and they have brought their titles to the altar, and made of them a burnt offering to Reason.

If no mischief had annexed itself to the folly of titles they would not have been worth a serious and formal destruction, such as the National Assembly have decreed them; and this makes it necessary to inquire farther into the nature and character of aristocracy.

That, then, which is called aristocracy in some countries and nobility in others arose out of the governments founded upon conquest. It was originally a military order for the purpose of supporting military government (for such were all governments founded in conquest); and to keep up a succession of this order for the purpose for which it was established, all the younger branches of those families were disinherited and the law of *primogenitureship* set up.

The nature and character of aristocracy shows itself to us in this law. It is a law against every law of nature, and Nature herself calls for its destruction. Establish family justice and aristocracy falls. By the aristocratical law of primogenitureship, in a family of six children five are exposed. Aristocracy has never more than one child. The rest are begotten to be devoured. They are thrown to the cannibal for prey, and the natural parent prepares the unnatural repast.

As everything which is out of nature in man affects, more or less, the interest of society, so does this. All the children which the aristocracy disowns (which are all except the eldest) are, in general, cast like orphans on a parish, to be provided for by the public, but at a greater charge. Unnecessary offices and places in governments and courts are created at the expense of the public to maintain them.

With what kind of parental reflections can the father or mother contemplate their younger offspring? By nature they are children, and by marriage they are heirs; but by aristocracy they are bastards and orphans. They are the flesh and blood of their parents in one line, and nothing akin to them in the other. To restore, therefore, parents to their children, and children to their parents—relations to each other, and man to society—and to exterminate the monster aristocracy, root and branch—the French Constitution has destroyed the law of PRIMOGENITURESHIP. Here then lies the monster; and Mr. Burke, if he pleases, may write its epitaph.

Hitherto we have considered aristocracy chiefly in one point of view. We have now to consider it in another. But whether we view it before or behind, or sideways, or any way else, domestically or publicly, it is still a monster.

In France aristocracy had one feature less in its countenance than what it has in some other countries. It did not compose a body of hereditary legislators. It was not a *"Corporation of Aristocracy,"* for such I have heard M. de Lafayette describe an English House of Peers. Let us then examine the grounds upon which the French Constitution has resolved against having such a House in France.

Because, in the first place, as is already mentioned, aristocracy is kept up by family tyranny and injustice.

Second, because there is an unnatural unfitness in an aristocracy to be legislators for a nation. Their ideas of *distributive justice* are corrupted at the very source. They begin life by trampling on all their younger brothers and sisters, and relations of every kind, and are taught and educated so to do. With what ideas of justice or honour can that man enter a house of legislation, who absorbs in his own person the inheritance of a whole family of children or doles out to them some pitiful portion with the insolence of a gift?

Third, because the idea of hereditary legislators is as inconsistent as that of hereditary judges, or hereditary juries; and as absurd as a hereditary mathematician, or a hereditary wise man; and as ridiculous as a hereditary poet laureate.

Fourth, because a body of men, holding themselves accountable to nobody, ought not to be trusted by anybody.

Fifth, because it is continuing the uncivilized principle of governments founded in conquest, and the base idea of man having property in man, and governing him by personal right.

Sixth, because aristocracy has a tendency to degenerate the human species. By the universal economy of nature it is known, and by the instance of the Jews it is proved, that the human species has a tendency to degenerate, in any small number of persons, when separated from the general stock of society, and intermarrying constantly with each other. It defeats even its pretended end, and becomes in time the opposite of what is noble in man. Mr. Burke talks of nobility; let him show what it is. The greatest characters the world have known have risen on the democratic floor. Aristocracy has not been able to keep a proportionate pace with democracy. The artificial NOBLE shrinks into a dwarf before the noble of nature; and in the few instances of those (for there are some in all countries) in whom nature, as by a miracle, has survived in aristocracy, THOSE MEN DESPISE IT. But it is time to proceed to a new subject.

The French Constitution has reformed the condition of the clergy. It has raised the income of the lower and middle classes and taken from the higher. None is now less than twelve hundred livres (fifty pounds sterling) nor any higher than about two or three thousand pounds. What will Mr. Burke place against this? Hear what he says. He says—

That the people of England can see without pain or grudging, an archbishop precede a duke; they can see a Bishop of Durham, or a Bishop of Winchester in possession of £10,000 a year; and cannot see why it is in worse hands than estates to the like amount, in the hands of this earl or that 'squire.

And Mr. Burke offers this as an example to France.

As to the first part, whether the archbishop precedes the duke, or the duke the bishop, it is, I believe, to the people in general, somewhat like *Sternhold* and *Hopkins,* or *Hopkins* and *Sternhold;* you may put which you please first; and as I confess that I do not understand the merits of this case, I will not contend it with Mr. Burke.

But with respect to the latter, I have something to say—Mr. Burke has not put the case right. The comparison is out of

order, by being put between the bishop and the earl or the 'squire. It ought to be put between the bishop and the curate, and then it will stand thus—

The people of England can see without pain or grudging, a Bishop of Durham, or a Bishop of Winchester, in possession of ten thousand pounds a year, and a curate on thirty or forty pounds a year, or less.

No, sir, they certainly do not see those things without great pain or grudging. It is a case that applies itself to every man's sense of justice, and is one among many that calls aloud for a constitution.

In France the cry of *"the Church! the Church!"* was repeated as often as in Mr. Burke's book, and as loudly as when the Dissenters' Bill was before the English Parliament; but the generality of the French clergy were not to be deceived by this cry any longer. They knew that whatever the pretense might be it was themselves who were one of the principal objects of it. It was the cry of the high beneficed clergy, to prevent any regulation of income taking place between those of ten thousand pounds a year and the parish priest. They therefore joined their case to those of every other oppressed class of men and by this union obtained redress.

The French Constitution *has abolished tithes,* that source of perpetual discontent between the tithe-holder and the parishioner. When land is held on tithe, it is in the condition of an estate held between two parties; the one receiving one-tenth, and the other nine-tenths of the produce: and consequently, on principles of equity, if the estate can be improved, and made to produce by that improvement double or treble what it did before, or in any other ratio, the expense of such improvement ought to be borne in like proportion between the parties who are to share the produce. But this is not the case in tithes; the farmer bears the whole expense, and the tithe-holder takes a tenth of the improvement, in addition to the original tenth, and by this means gets the value of two-tenths instead of one. This is another case that calls for a constitution.

The French Constitution hath abolished or renounced *toleration* and *intoleration* also, and hath established UNIVERSAL RIGHT OF CONSCIENCE.

Toleration is not the *opposite* of intolerance, but is the *counterfeit* of it. Both are despotisms. The one assumes to itself the right of withholding liberty of conscience, and the other of granting it. The one is the Pope armed with fire and faggot, and the other is the Pope selling or granting indulgences. The former is church and state, and the latter is church and traffic.

But toleration may be viewed in a much stronger light. Man worships not himself, but his Maker; and the liberty of conscience which he claims is not for the service of himself, but of his God. In this case, therefore, we must necessarily have the associated idea of two beings: the *mortal* who renders the worship, and the IMMORTAL BEING who is worshipped. Toleration, therefore, places itself, not between man and man, nor between church and church, nor between one denomination of religion and another, but between God and man; between the being who worships, and the BEING who is worshipped; and by the same act of assumed authority by which it tolerates man to pay his worship, it presumptuously and blasphemously sets itself up to tolerate the Almighty to receive it.

Were a bill brought into any Parliament, entitled, "*An Act to tolerate or grant liberty to the Almighty to receive the worship of a Jew or a Turk,*" or "to prohibit the Almighty from receiving it," all men would startle and call it blasphemy. There would be an uproar. The presumption of toleration in religious matters would then present itself unmasked; but the presumption is not the less because the name of "man" only appears to those laws, for the associated idea of the *worshipped* and the *worshipper* cannot be separated. Who then art thou, vain

dust and ashes! by whatever name thou art called, whether a king, a bishop, a church, or a state, a parliament, or anything else, that obtrudest thine insignificance between the soul of man and its maker? Mind thine own concerns. If he believes not as thou believest, it is a proof that thou believest not as he believeth, and there is no earthly power can determine between you.

With respect to what are called denominations of religion, if everyone is left to judge of his own religion, there is no such thing as a religion that is wrong; but if they are to judge of each other's religion, there is no such thing as a religion that is right; and therefore all the world is right, or all the world is wrong. But with respect to religion itself, without regard to names, and as directing itself from the universal family of mankind to the divine object of all adoration, *it is man bringing to his Maker the fruits of his heart;* and though those fruits may differ from each other like the fruits of the earth, the grateful tribute of every one is accepted.

A bishop of Durham, or a bishop of Winchester, or the archbishop who heads the dukes, will not refuse a tithe-sheaf of wheat because it is not a cock of hay, nor a cock of hay because it is not a sheaf of wheat; nor a pig, because it is neither one nor the other; but these same persons, under the figure of an established church, will not permit their Maker to receive the varied tithes of man's devotion.

One of the continual choruses of Mr. Burke's book is "church and state." He does not mean some one particular church, or some one particular state, but any church and state; and he uses the term as a general figure to hold forth the political doctrine of always uniting the church with the state in every country, and he censures the National Assembly for not having done this in France. Let us bestow a few thoughts on this subject.

All religions are in their nature kind and benign, and united with principles of morality. They could not have made proselytes at first by professing anything that was vicious, cruel, persecuting, or immoral. Like everything else, they had their beginning; and they proceeded by persuasion, exhortation, and example. How then is it that they lose their native mildness and become morose and intolerant?

It proceeds from the connection which Mr. Burke recommends. By engendering the church with the state, a sort of mule-animal, capable only of destroying, and not of breeding up, is produced, called *The Church established by Law*. It is a stranger, even from its birth, to any parent mother, on whom it is begotten, and whom in time it kicks out and destroys.

The Inquisition in Spain does not proceed from the religion originally professed but from this mule-animal engendered between the church and the state. The burnings in Smithfield proceeded from the same heterogeneous production; and it was the regeneration of this strange animal in England afterward that renewed rancour and irreligion among the inhabitants, and that drove the people called Quakers and Dissenters to America. Persecution is not an original feature in *any* religion; but it is always the strongly marked feature of all law-religions, or religions established by law. Take away the law-establishment and every religion reassumes its original benignity. In America a Catholic priest is a good citizen, a good character, and a good neighbour; an Episcopalian minister is of the same description; and this proceeds, independently of the men, from there being no law establishment in America.

If also we view this matter in a temporal sense we shall see the ill effects it has had on the prosperity of nations. The union of church and state has impoverished Spain. The revoking the Edict of Nantes drove the silk manufacture from France into England; and church and state are driving the cotton manufacture from England to America and France. Let then Mr. Burke continue to preach his antipolitical doctrine of church and state. It will do some

good. The National Assembly will not follow his advice, but will benefit by his folly. It was by observing the ill effects of it in England, that America has been warned against it; and it is by experiencing them in France, that the National Assembly have abolished it, and, like America, have established UNIVERSAL RIGHT OF CONSCIENCE AND UNIVERSAL RIGHT OF CITIZENSHIP.

I will here cease the comparison with respect to the principles of the French Constitution and conclude this part of the subject with a few observations on the organization of the formal parts of the French and English governments.

The executive power in each country is in the hands of a person styled the king; but the French Constitution distinguishes between the king and the sovereign. It considers the station of king as official and places sovereignty in the nation.

The representatives of the nation who compose the National Assembly, and who are the legislative power, originate in and from the people by election, as an inherent right in the people. In England it is otherwise; and this arises from the original establishment of what is called its monarchy; for as by the Conquest all the rights of the people or the nation were absorbed into the hands of the conqueror, and who added the title of king to that of conqueror, those same matters which in France are now held as rights in the people, or in the nation, are held in England as grants from what is called the Crown. The Parliament in England, in both its branches, was erected by patents from the descendants of the conqueror. The House of Commons did not originate as a matter of right in the people to delegate or elect, but as a grant or boon.

By the French Constitution the nation is always named before the king. The third article of the Declaration of Rights says: *"The nation is essentially the source (or fountain) of all sovereignty."* Mr. Burke argues that in England a king is the fountain— that he is the fountain of all honour. But

335

as this idea is evidently descended from the Conquest I shall make no other remark upon it, than that it is the nature of conquest to turn everything upside down; and as Mr. Burke will not be refused the privilege of speaking twice, and as there are but two parts in the figure, the *fountain* and the *spout,* he will be right the second time.

The French Constitution puts the legislative before the executive, the law before the king; *la Loi, le Roi.* This also is in the natural order of things, because laws must have existence before they can have execution.

A king in France does not, in addressing himself to the National Assembly, say "My Assembly," similar to the phrase used in England of "*my* Parliament"; neither can he use it consistently with the Constitution, nor could it be admitted. There may be propriety in the use of it in England, because as is before mentioned, both Houses of Parliament originated from what is called the Crown by patent or boon—and not from the inherent rights of the people, as the National Assembly does in France, and whose name designates its origin.

The president of the National Assembly does not ask the king *to grant to the Assembly liberty of speech,* as is the case with the English House of Commons. The constitutional dignity of the National Assembly cannot debase itself. Speech is, in the first place, one of the natural rights of man always retained; and with respect to the National Assembly the use of it is their *duty,* and the nation is their *authority.* They were elected by the greatest body of men exercising the right of election the European world ever saw. They sprung not from the filth of rotten boroughs, nor are they the vassal representatives of aristocratical ones. Feeling the proper dignity of their character, they support it. Their parliamentary language, whether for or against the question, is free, bold, and manly and extends to all the parts and circumstances of the case. If any matter or subject respecting the executive department or the person

who presides in it (the king) comes before them it is debated on with the spirit of men, and the language of gentlemen; and their answer or their address is returned in the same style. They stand not aloof with the gaping vacuity of vulgar ignorance, nor bend with the cringe of sycophantic insignificance. The graceful pride of truth knows no extremes and preserves, in every latitude of life, the right-angled character of man.

Let us now look to the other side of the question. In the addresses of the English Parliaments to their kings we see neither the intrepid spirit of the old Parliaments of France, nor the serene dignity of the present National Assembly; neither do we see in them anything of the style of English manners, which borders somewhat on bluntness. Since then they are neither of foreign extraction, nor naturally of English production, their origin must be sought for elsewhere, and that origin is the Norman Conquest. They are evidently of the vassalage class of manners and emphatically mark the prostrate distance that exists in no other condition of men than between the conqueror and the conquered. That this vassalage idea and style of speaking was not got rid of even at the Revolution of 1688 is evident from the declaration of Parliament to William and Mary in these words: "We do most humbly and faithfully *submit* ourselves, our heirs and posterities, for ever." Submission is wholly a vassalage term, repugnant to the dignity of freedom, and an echo of the language used at the Conquest.

As the estimation of all things is by comparison, the Revolution of 1688, however from circumstances it may have been exalted beyond its value, will find its level. It is already on the wane, eclipsed by the enlarging orb of reason, and the luminous revolutions of America and France. In less than another century it will go, as well as Mr. Burke's labours, "to the family vault of all the Capulets." Mankind will then scarcely believe that a country calling itself free would send to Holland for a man, and clothe him with power on purpose to put themselves in fear of him, and give him almost a million sterling a year for leave to *submit* themselves and their posterity, like bondmen and bondwomen, for ever.

But there is a truth that ought to be made known: I have had the opportunity of seeing it; which is, *that notwithstanding appearances, there is not any description of men that despise monarchy so much as courtiers.* But they well know that if it were seen by others, as it is seen by them, the juggle could not be kept up. They are in the condition of men who get their living by a show, and to whom the folly of that show is so familiar that they ridicule it; but were the audience to be made as wise in this respect as themselves, there would be an end to the show and the profits with it. The difference between a republican and a courtier with respect to monarchy, is that the one opposes monarchy, believing it to be something; and the other laughs at it, knowing it to be nothing.

As I used sometimes to correspond with Mr. Burke believing him then to be a man of sounder principles than his book shows him to be, I wrote to him last winter from Paris and gave him an account how prosperously matters were going on. Among other subjects in that letter, I referred to the happy situation the National Assembly were placed in; that they had taken a ground on which their moral duty and their political interest were united. They have not to hold out a language which they do not themselves believe, for the fraudulent purpose of making others believe it. Their station requires no artifice to support it and can only be maintained by enlightening mankind. It is not their interest to cherish ignorance, but to dispel it. They are not in the case of a ministerial or an opposition party in England, who, though they are opposed, are still united to keep up the common mystery. The National Assembly must throw open a magazine of light. It must show man the proper

character of man; and the nearer it can bring him to that standard, the stronger the National Assembly becomes.

In contemplating the French Constitution, we see in it a rational order of things. The principles harmonize with the forms, and both with their origin. It may perhaps be said as an excuse for bad forms, that they are nothing more than forms; but this is a mistake. Forms grow out of principles and operate to continue the principles they grow from. It is impossible to practice a bad form on anything but a bad principle. It cannot be ingrafted on a good one; and wherever the forms in any government are bad, it is a certain indication that the principles are bad also.

I will here finally close this subject. I began it by remarking that Mr. Burke had *voluntarily* declined going into a comparison of the English and French constitutions. He apologizes for not doing it, by saying that he had not time. Mr. Burke's book was upwards of eight months in hand, and is extended to a volume of three hundred and sixty-six pages. As his omission does injury to his cause, his apology makes it worse; and men on the English side of the water will begin to consider whether there is not some radical defect in what is called the English Constitution that made it necessary for Mr. Burke to suppress the comparison, to avoid bringing it into view.

As Mr. Burke has not written on constitutions so neither has he written on the French Revolution. He gives no account of its commencement or its progress. He only expresses his wonder. "It looks," says he, "to me, as if I were in a great crisis, not of the affairs of France alone, but of all Europe, perhaps of more than Europe. All circumstances taken together, the French Revolution is the most astonishing that has hitherto happened in the world."

As wise men are astonished at foolish things, and other people at wise ones, I know not on which ground to account for Mr. Burke's astonishment; but certain it is, that he does not understand the French

Revolution. It has apparently burst forth like a creation from a chaos, but it is no more the consequence of a mental revolution priorily existing in France. The mind of the nation had changed beforehand, and the new order of things has naturally followed the new order of thoughts. I will here, as concisely as I can, trace out the growth of the French Revolution and mark the circumstances that have contributed to produce it.

The despotism of Louis XIV, united with the gaiety of his court, and the gaudy ostentation of his character had so humbled, and at the same time so fascinated the mind of France, that the people appear to have lost all sense of their own dignity, in contemplating that of their Grand Monarch; and the whole reign of Louis XV, remarkable only for weakness and effeminacy, made no other alteration than that of spreading a sort of lethargy over the nation, from which it showed no disposition to rise.

The only signs which appeared of the spirit of liberty during those periods are to be found in the writings of the French philosophers. Montesquieu, president of the Parliament of Bordeaux, went as far as a writer under a despotic government could well proceed; and being obliged to divide himself between principle and prudence, his mind often appears under a veil, and we ought to give him credit for more than he has expressed.

Voltaire, who was both the flatterer and the satirist of despotism, took another line. His forte lay in exposing and ridiculing the superstitions which priestcraft, united with statecraft, had interwoven with governments. It was not from the purity of his principles, or his love of mankind (for satire and philanthropy are not naturally concordant), but from his strong capacity of seeing folly in its true shape, and his irresistible propensity to expose it, that he made those attacks. They were, however, as formidable as if the motives had been virtuous; and he merits the thanks rather than the esteem of mankind.

On the contrary, we find in the writings of Rousseau, and the Abbé Raynal, a loveliness of sentiment in favour of liberty, that excites respect and elevates the human faculties; but having raised this animation, they do not direct its operations, and leave the mind in love with an object, without describing the means of possessing it.

The writings of Quesnay, Turgot, and the friends of those authors, are of the serious kind; but they laboured under the same disadvantage with Montesquieu; their writings abound with moral maxims of government, but are rather directed to economize and reform the administration of the government, than the government itself.

But all those writings and many others had their weight; and by the different manner in which they treated the subject of government, Montesquieu by his judgment and knowledge of laws, Voltaire by his wit, Rousseau and Raynal by their animation, and Quesnay and Turgot by their moral maxims and systems of economy, readers of every class met with something to their taste, and a spirit of political inquiry began to diffuse itself through the nation at the time the dispute between England and the then colonies of America broke out.

In the war which France afterward engaged in, it is very well known that the nation appeared to be beforehand with the French ministry. Each of them had its view: but those views were directed to different objects; the one sought liberty, and the other retaliation on England. The French officers and soldiers, who after this went to America, were eventually placed in the school of freedom and learned the practice as well as the principles of it by heart.

As it was impossible to separate the military events which took place in America from the principles of the American Revolution, the publication of those events in France necessarily connected themselves with the principles which produced them.

Many of the facts were in themselves principles; such as the Declaration of American Independence, and the treaty of alliance between France and America, which recognized the natural right of man and justified resistance to oppression. The then Minister of France, Count Vergennes, was not the friend of America; and it is both justice and gratitude to say, that it was the Queen of France who gave the cause of America a fashion at the French court. Count Vergennes was the personal and social friend of Dr. Franklin; and the Doctor had obtained, by his sensible gracefulness, a sort of influence over him; but with respect to principles Count Vergennes was a despot.

The situation of Dr. Franklin, as Minister from America to France, should be taken into the chain of circumstances. The diplomatic character is of itself the narrowest sphere of society that man can act in. It forbids intercourse by the reciprocity of suspicion; and a diplomatic is a sort of unconnected atom, continually repelling and repelled. But this was not the case with Dr. Franklin. He was not the diplomatic of a Court, but of MAN. His character as a philosopher had been long established, and his circle of society in France was universal. Count Vergennes resisted for a considerable time the publication in France of the American Constitutions, translated into the French language: but even in this he was obliged to give way to public opinion, and a sort of propriety in admitting to appear what he had undertaken to defend. The American Constitutions were to liberty what a grammar is to language: they define its parts of speech and practically construct them into syntax. The peculiar situation of the then Marquis de Lafayette is another link in the great chain. He served in America as an American officer under a commission of Congress, and by the universality of his acquaintance was in close friendship with the civil government of America, as well as with the military line. He spoke the language of the country, entered into the discussions on the principles of government, and was always a welcome friend at any election.

When the war closed, a vast reinforcement to the cause of liberty spread itself over France, by the return of the French officers and soldiers. A knowledge of the practice was then joined to the theory; and all that was wanting to give it real existence was opportunity. Man cannot, properly speaking, make circumstances for his purpose, but he always has it in his power to improve them when they occur, and this was the case in France.

M. Neckar was displaced in May 1781; and by the ill-management of the finances afterward, and particularly during the extravagant administration of M. Calonne, the revenue of France, which was nearly twenty-four millions sterling per year, was become unequal to the expenditure, not because the revenue had decreased, but because the expenses had increased; and this was a circumstance which the nation laid hold of to bring forward a revolution. The English Minister, Mr. Pitt, has frequently alluded to the state of the French finances in his budgets, without understanding the subject. Had the French Parliaments been as ready to register edicts for new taxes as an English Parliament is to grant them, there had been no derangement in the finances, nor yet any revolution; but this will better explain itself as I proceed. It will be necessary here to show how taxes were formerly raised in France. The king, or rather the court or ministry acting under the use of that name, framed the edicts for taxes at their own discretion, and sent them to the Parliaments to be registered; for until they were registered by the Parliaments they were not operative. Disputes had long existed between the court and the Parliaments with respect to the extent of the Parliaments' authority on this head. The court insisted that the authority of Parliaments went no farther than to remonstrate or show reasons against the tax, reserving to itself the right of determining whether the reasons were well or ill-founded; and in consequence thereof, either to withdraw the edict as a matter of choice, or to *order* it to be enregistered as a matter of authority. The Parliaments on their part insisted that they had not only a right to remonstrate, but to reject; and on this ground they were always supported by the nation. But to return to the order of my narrative M. Calonne wanted money: and as he knew the sturdy disposition of the Parliaments with respect to new taxes, he ingeniously sought either to approach them by a more gentle means than that of direct authority, or to get over their heads by a maneuver; and for this purpose he revived the project of assembling a body of men from the several provinces, under the style of an "Assembly of the Notables," or men of note, who met in 1787, and who were either to recommend taxes to the Parliaments, or to act as a Parliament themselves. An assembly under this name had been called in 1617.

As we are to view this as the first practical step toward the Revolution, it will be proper to enter into some particulars respecting it. The Assembly of the Notables has in some places been mistaken for the States-General, but was wholly a different body, the States-General being always by election. The persons who composed the Assembly of the Notables were all nominated by the King, and consisted of one hundred and forty members. But as M. Calonne could not depend upon a majority of this Assembly in his favour, he very ingeniously arranged them in such a manner as to make forty-four a majority of one hundred and forty; to effect this he disposed of them into seven separate committees, of twenty members each. Every general question was to be decided, not by a majority of persons, but by a majority of committees; and as eleven votes would make a majority in a committee, and four committees a majority of seven, M.

Calonne had good reason to conclude that as forty-four would determine any general question he could not be outvoted. The then Marquis de Lafayette was placed in the second committee, of which the Count D'Artois was president, and as money matters were the object, it naturally brought into view every circumstance connected with it. M. de Lafayette made a verbal charge against Calonne for selling crown lands to the amount of two millions of livres, in a manner that appeared to be unknown to the King. The Count D'Artois (as if to intimidate, for the Bastille was then in being) asked the Marquis if he would render the charge in writing? He replied that he would. The Count D'Artois did not demand it, but brought a message from the King to that purport. M. de Lafayette then delivered in his charge in writing, to be given to the King, undertaking to support it. No farther proceedings were had upon this affair, but M. Calonne was soon after dismissed by the King and sent off to England.

As M. de Lafayette, from the experience of what he had seen in America, was better acquainted with the science of civil government than the generality of the members who composed the Assembly of the Notables could then be, the brunt of the business fell considerably to his share. The plan of those who had a constitution in view was to contend with the court on the ground of taxes, and some of them openly professed their object. Disputes frequently arose between Count D'Artois and M. de Lafayette upon various subjects. With respect to the arrears already incurred the latter proposed to remedy them by accommodating the expenses to the revenue instead of the revenue to the expenses; and as objects of reform he proposed to abolish the Bastille and all the state prisons throughout the nation (the keeping of which was attended with great expense), and to suppress *lettres de cachet;* but those matters were not then much attended to, and with respect to *lettres de cachet,* a majority of the nobles appeared to be in favour of them.

On the subject of supplying the Treasury by new taxes the Assembly declined taking the matter on themselves, concurring in the opinion that they had not authority. In a debate on this subject M. de Lafayette said that raising money by taxes could only be done by a National Assembly, freely elected by the people, and acting as their representatives. Do you mean, said the Count D'Artois, the *States-General?* M. de Lafayette replied that he did. Will you, said the Count D'Artois, sign what you say to be given to the King? The other replied that he would not only do this but that he would go farther, and say that the effectual mode would be for the King to agree to the establishment of a constitution.

As one of the plans had thus failed, that of getting the Assembly to act as a Parliament, the other came into view, that of recommending. On this subject the Assembly agreed to recommend two new taxes to be enregistered by the Parliament: the one a stamp tax and the other a territorial or sort of land tax. The two have been estimated at about five millions sterling per annum. We have now to turn our attention to the Parliaments, on whom the business was again devolving.

The Archbishop of Toulouse (since Archbishop of Sens, and now a Cardinal) was appointed to the administration of the finances soon after the dismission of Calonne. He was also made Prime Minister, an office that did not always exist in France. When this office did not exist, the chiefs of the principal departments transacted business immediately with the King, but when a prime minister was appointed they did business only with him. The Archbishop arrived to more state-authority than any minister since the Duke de Choiseul, and the nation was strongly disposed in his favour; but by a line of conduct scarcely to be accounted for he perverted every opportunity, turned out a despot, and sunk into disgrace, and a Cardinal.

The Assembly of the Notables having broken up, the new Minister sent the edicts for the two taxes recommended by the Assembly to the Parliaments to be enregistered. They of course came first before the Parliament of Paris, who returned for answer, *that with such a revenue as the nation then supported the name of taxes ought not to be mentioned but for the purpose of reducing them,* and threw both the edicts out.

On this refusal the Parliament was ordered to Versailles, where, in the usual form, the King held what under the old government was called a Bed of Justice; and the two edicts were enregistered in presence of the Parliament by an order of state.

On this the Parliament immediately returned to Paris, renewed their session in form, and ordered the enregistering to be struck out, declaring that everything done at Versailles was illegal. All the members of the Parliament were then served with *lettres de cachet,* and exiled to Trois; but as they continued as inflexible in exile as before, and as vengeance did not supply the place of taxes, they were after a short time recalled to Paris.

The edicts were again tendered to them, and the Count D'Artois undertook to act as representative of the King. For this purpose he came from Versailles to Paris, in a train of procession; and the Parliament were assembled to receive him. But show and parade had lost their influence in France; and whatever ideas of importance he might set off with, he had to return with those of mortification and disappointment. On alighting from his carriage to ascend the steps of the Parliament House, the crowd (which was numerously collected) threw out trite expressions saying: "This is Monsieur D'Artois, who wants more of our money to spend." The marked disapprobation which he saw impressed him with apprehensions, and the word *Aux armes!* (To arms!) was given out by the officer of the guard who attended him. It was so loudly vociferated, that it echoed through the avenues of the House and produced a temporary confusion. I was then standing in one of the apartments through which he had to pass and could not avoid reflecting how wretched was the condition of a disrespected man.

He endeavoured to impress the Parliament by great words and opened his authority by saying, "The King, our Lord and Master." The Parliament received him very coolly and with their usual determination not to register the taxes; and in this manner the interview ended.

After this a new subject took place: In the various debates and contests which arose between the court and the Parliaments on the subject of taxes, the Parliament of Paris at last declared that although it had been customary for Parliaments to enregister edicts for taxes as a matter of convenience, the right belonged only to the States-General; and that, therefore, the Parliament could no longer with propriety continue to debate on what it had not authority to act. The King after this came to Paris and held a meeting with the Parliament, in which he continued from ten in the morning till about six in the evening, and, in a manner that appeared to proceed from him as if unconsulted upon with the Cabinet or ministry, gave his word to the Parliament that the States-General should be convened.

But after this another scene arose, on a ground different from all the former. The Minister and the Cabinet were averse to calling the States-General. They well knew that if the States-General were assembled, themselves must fall; and as the King had not mentioned *any time,* they hit on a project calculated to elude, without appearing to oppose.

For this purpose, the court set about making a sort of constitution itself. It was principally the work of M. Lamoignon, Keeper of the Seals, who afterward shot himself. This new arrangement consisted in establishing a body under the name of a *Cour Plénière,* or full court, in which were

invested all the powers that the government might have occasion to make use of. The persons composing this court were to be nominated by the King. The contended right of taxation was given up on the part of the King, and a new criminal code of laws and law proceedings was substituted in the room of the former. The thing, in many points, contained better principles than those upon which the government had hitherto been administered; but with respect to the *Cour Plénière,* it was no other than a medium through which despotism was to pass, without appearing to act directly from itself.

The Cabinet had high expectations from their new contrivance. The persons who were to compose the *Cour Plénière* were already nominated; and as it was necessary to carry a fair appearance, many of the best characters in the nation were appointed among the number. It was to commence on the 8th of May, 1788; but an opposition arose to it on two grounds—the one as to principle, the other as to form.

On the ground of principle it was contended that government had not a right to alter itself, and that if the practice was once admitted it would grow into a principle and be made a precedent for any future alterations the government might wish to establish; that the right of altering the government was a national right, and not a right of government. And on the ground of form it was contended that the *Cour Plénière* was nothing more than a larger Cabinet.

The then Duke de la Rouchefoucault, Luxembourg, De Noailles, and many others, refused to accept the nomination and strenuously opposed the whole plan. When the edict for establishing this new court was sent to the Parliaments to be enregistered and put into execution, they resisted also. The Parliament of Paris not only refused, but denied the authority; and the contest renewed itself between the Parliament and the Cabinet more strongly than ever. While the Parliament were sitting in debate on this subject, the ministry ordered a regiment of soldiers to surround the House and form a blockade. The members sent out for beds and provisions and lived as in a besieged citadel; and as this had no effect, the commanding officer was ordered to enter the Parliament House and seize them, which he did, and some of the principal members were shut up in different prisons. About the same time a deputation of persons arrived from the province of Brittany to remonstrate against the establishment of the *Cour Plénière,* and those the Archbishop sent to the Bastille. But the spirit of the nation was not to be overcome, and it was so fully sensible of the strong ground it had taken, that of withholding taxes, that it contested itself with keeping up a sort of quiet resistance, which effectually overthrew all the plans at that time formed against it. The project of the *Cour Plénière* was at last obliged to be given up, and the Prime Minister not long afterward followed its fate, and M. Neckar was recalled into office.

The attempt to establish the *Cour Plénière* had an effect upon the nation which itself did not perceive. It was a sort of new form of government that insensibly served to put the old one out of sight and to unhinge it from the superstitious authority of antiquity. It was government dethroning government; and the old one, by attempting to make a new one, made a chasm.

The failure of this scheme renewed the subject of convening the States-General; and this gave rise to a new series of politics.

There was no settled form for convening the States-General; all that it positively meant was a deputation from what was then called the Clergy, the Noblesse, and the Commons; but their numbers or their proportions had not been always the same. They had been convened only on extraordinary occasions, the last of which was in 1614; their numbers were then in equal proportions, and they voted by orders.

It could not well escape the sagacity of M. Neckar that the mode of 1614 would answer neither the purpose of the then government nor of the nation. As matters were at that time circumstanced it would have been too contentious to agree upon anything. The debates would have been endless upon privileges and exemptions, in which neither the wants of the government nor the wishes of the nation for a constitution would have been attended to. But as he did not choose to take the decision upon himself, he summoned again the *Assembly of the Notables* and referred it to them. This body was in general interested in the decision, being chiefly of the aristocracy and the high-paid clergy, and they decided in favour of the mode of 1614. This decision was against the sense of the nation, and also against the wishes of the court; for the aristocracy opposed itself to both and contended for privileges independent of either. The subject was then taken up by the Parliament, who recommended that the number of the Commons should be equal to the other two: and they should all sit in one house and vote in one body. The number finally determined on was 1,200; 600 to be chosen by the Commons (and this was less than their proportion ought to have been when their worth and consequence is considered on a national scale), 300 by the clergy, and 300 by the aristocracy; but with respect to the mode of assembling themselves, whether together or apart, or the manner in which they should vote, these matters were referred.

The election that followed was not a contested election, but an animated one. The candidates were not men, but principles. Societies were formed in Paris, and committees of correspondence and communication established throughout the nation, for the purpose of enlightening the people, and explaining to them the principles of civil government; and so orderly was the election conducted, that it did not give rise even to the rumour of tumult.

The States-General were to meet at Versailles in April 1789, but did not assemble till May. They situated themselves in three separate chambers, or rather the clergy and the aristocracy withdrew each into a separate chamber.

The majority of the aristocracy claimed what they called the privilege of voting as a separate body, and of giving their consent or their negative in that manner; and many of the bishops and the high-beneficed clergy claimed the same privilege on the part of their order.

The *Tiers État* (as they were then called) disowned any knowledge of artificial orders and artificial privileges; and they were not only resolute on this point, but somewhat disdainful. They began to consider aristocracy as a kind of fungus growing out of the corruption of society, that could not be admitted even as a branch of it; and from the disposition the aristocracy had shown by upholding *lettres de cachet* and in sundry other instances, it was manifest that no constitution could be formed by admitting men in any other character than as National Men.

After various altercations on this head, the *Tiers État* or Commons (as they were then called) declared themselves (on a motion made for that purpose by the Abbé Sieyès) "THE REPRESENTATIVES OF THE NATION; and that the two orders could be considered but as deputies of corporations, and could only have a deliberate voice when they assembled in a national character with the national representatives."

This proceeding extinguished the style of *États Généraux,* or States-General, and erected it into the style it now bears, that of *L'Assemblée Nationale,* or National Assembly.

This motion was not made in a precipitate manner. It was the result of cool deliberation and concerted between the national representatives and the patriotic members of the two chambers, who saw into the folly, mischief, and injustice of artificial privileged distinctions.

It was become evident that no constitution, worthy of being called by that name, could be established on anything less than a national ground. The aristocracy had hitherto opposed the despotism of the court and affected the language of patriotism; but it opposed it as its rival (as the English barons opposed King John), and it now opposed the nation from the same motives.

On carrying this motion, the national representatives, as had been concerted, sent an invitation to the two chambers, to unite with them in a national character and proceed to business.

A majority of the clergy, chiefly of the parish priests, withdrew from the clerical chamber and joined the nation; and forty-five from the other chamber joined in like manner.

There is a sort of secret history belonging to this last circumstance, which is necessary to its explanation; it was not judged prudent that all the patriotic members of the chamber styling itself the Nobles, should quit it at once; and in consequence of this arrangement, they drew off by degrees, always leaving some, as well to reason the case as to watch the suspected.

In a little time the numbers increased from forty-five to eighty, and soon after to a greater number; which, with the majority of the clergy, and the whole of the national representatives, put the malcontents in a very diminutive condition.

The King, who, very different from the general class called by that name, is a man of a good heart, showed himself disposed to recommend a union of the three chambers, on the ground the National Assembly had taken; but the malcontents exerted themselves to prevent it, and began now to have another project in view.

Their numbers consisted of a majority of the aristocratical chamber and a minority of the clerical chamber, chiefly of bishops and high-beneficed clergy; and these men were determined to put everything to issue, as well by strength as by stratagem.

They had no objection to a constitution; but it must be such a one as themselves should dictate, and suited to their own views and particular situations.

Opening of the States-General at Versailles in May 1789. *"This proceeding extinguished the style of* États Généraux, *or States-General, and erected it into the style . . . of* L'Assemblée Nationale, *or National Assembly."*

On the other hand, the nation disowned knowing anything of them but as citizens and was determined to shut out all such upstart pretensions. The more aristocracy appeared, the more it was despised; there was a visible imbecility and want of intellects in the majority—a sort of *je ne sais quoi*, that while it affected to be more than citizen, was less than man. It lost ground from contempt more than from hatred; and was rather jeered at as an ass than dreaded as a lion. This is the general character of aristocracy, or what are called nobles or nobility, or rather no-ability, in all countries.

The plan of the malcontents consisted now of two things; either to deliberate and vote by chambers (or orders), more especially on all questions respecting a constitution (by which the aristocratical chamber would have had a negative on any article of the constitution); or, in case they could not accomplish this object, to overthrow the National Assembly entirely.

To effect one or other of these objects they began now to cultivate a friendship with the despotism they had hitherto attempted to rival, and the Count D'Artois became their chief.

The King (who has since declared himself deceived into their measures) held, according to the old form, a *Bed of Justice*, in which he accorded to the deliberation and vote *par tête* (by head) upon several subjects; but reserved the deliberation and vote upon all questions respecting a constitution to the three chambers separately.

This declaration of the King was made against the advice of M. Neckar, who now began to perceive that he was growing out of fashion at court, and that another minister was in contemplation.

As the form of sitting in separate chambers was yet apparently kept up, though essentially destroyed, the national representatives immediately after this declaration of the King resorted to their own chambers to consult on a protest against it; and the minority of the chamber (calling itself the Nobles), who had joined the national cause, retired to a private house to consult in like manner.

The malcontents had by this time concerted their measures with the court, which Count D'Artois undertook to conduct; and as they saw from the discontent which the declaration excited, and the opposition making against it, that they could not obtain a control over the intended constitution by a separate vote, they prepared themselves for their final object—that of conspiring against the National Assembly, and overthrowing it.

The next morning the door of the chamber of the National Assembly was shut against them, and guarded by troops; and the members were refused admittance. On this they withdrew to a tennis-ground in the neighbourhood of Versailles, as the most convenient place they could find, and, after renewing their session, took an oath never to separate from each other, under any circumstance whatever, death excepted, until they had established a constitution. As the experiment of shutting up the House had no other effect than that of producing a closer connection in the members, it was opened again the next day, and the public business recommenced in the usual place.

We now are to have in view the forming of the new ministry, which was to accomplish the overthrow of the National Assembly. But as force would be necessary, orders were issued to assemble thirty thousand troops, the command of which was given to Broglio, one of the new-intended ministry, who was recalled from the country for this purpose. But as some management was necessary to keep this plan concealed till the moment it should be ready for execution, it is to this policy that a declaration made by Count D'Artois must be attributed, and which is here proper to be introduced.

It could not but occur, while the malcontents continued to resort to their chambers separate from the National Assembly, that more jealousy would be excited than

The Tennis Court Oath, sworn by the Third Estate on June 20, 1789. *"They withdrew to a tennis-ground in the neighbourhood of Versailles . . . and . . . took an oath never to separate . . . until they had established a constitution."*

if they were mixed with it, and that the plot might be suspected. But as they had taken their ground, and wanted a pretense for quitting it, it was necessary that one should be devised. This was effectually accomplished by a declaration made by the Count D'Artois: "That if they took not a part in the National Assembly, the life of the King would be endangered"; on which they quitted their chambers and mixed with the Assembly, in one body.

At the time this declaration was made, it was generally treated as a piece of absurdity in Count D'Artois and calculated merely to relieve the outstanding members of the two chambers from the diminutive situation they were put in; and if nothing more had followed, this conclusion would have been good. But as things best explain themselves by their events, this apparent union was only a cover to the machinations which were secretly going on; and the declaration accommodated itself to answer that purpose. In a little time the National Assembly found itself surrounded by troops, and thousands more were daily arriving. On this a very strong declaration was made by the National Assembly to the King, remonstrating on the impropriety of the measure, and demanding the reason. The King, who was not in the secret of this business, as himself afterward declared, gave substantially for answer, that he had no other object in view than to preserve the public tranquillity, which appeared to be much disturbed.

But in a few days from this time the plot unraveled itself. M. Neckar and the ministry were displaced, and a new one formed of the enemies of the Revolution; and Broglio, with between twenty-five and thirty thousand foreign troops, was arrived to support them. The mask was now thrown off, and matters were come to a crisis. The event was that in a space of three days the new ministry and their abettors found it prudent to fly the nation; the Bastille was taken, and Broglio and his foreign troops dispersed, as is already related in the former part of this work.

There are some curious circumstances in the history of this short-lived ministry, and this short-lived attempt at a counterrevolution. The Palace of Versailles, where the court was sitting, was not more than four hundred yards distant from the hall where the National Assembly was sitting. The two places were at this moment like the separate headquarters of two combatant armies; yet the court was as perfectly ignorant of the information which had arrived from Paris to the National Assembly, as if it had resided at a hundred miles distance. The then Marquis de Lafayette, who (as has been already mentioned) was chosen to preside in the National Assembly on this particular occasion, named by order of the Assembly three successive deputations to the King, on the day and up to the evening on which the Bastille was taken, to inform and confer with him on the state of affairs; but the ministry, who knew not so much as that it was attacked, precluded all communication, and were solacing themselves how dexterously they had succeeded; but in a few hours the accounts arrived so thick and fast that they had to start from their desks and run. Some set off in one disguise, and some in another, and none in their own character. Their anxiety now was to outride the news, lest they should be stopped, which, though it flew fast, flew not so fast as themselves.

It is worth relating that the National Assembly neither pursued those fugitive conspirators, nor took any notice of them, nor sought to retaliate in any shape whatever.

Occupied with establishing a constitution founded on the rights of man and the authority of the people, the only authority on which government has a right to exist in any country, the National Assembly felt none of those mean passions which mark the character of impertinent governments, founding themselves on their own authority, or on the absurdity of hereditary succession. It is the faculty of the human mind to become what it contemplates, and to act in unison with its object.

The conspiracy being thus dispersed, one of the first works of the National Assembly, instead of vindictive proclamations, as has been the case with other governments, published a Declaration of the Rights of Man, as the basis on which the new constitution was to be built, and which is here subjoined.

Declaration of the Rights of Man and of Citizens by the National Assembly of France

The representatives of the people of France, formed into a National Assembly, considering that ignorance, neglect, or contempt of human rights, are the sole causes of public misfortunes and corruptions of government, have resolved to set forth in a solemn declaration, these natural, imprescriptible, and inalienable rights; that this declaration being constantly present to the minds of the members of the body social, they may be ever kept attentive to their rights and their duties; that the acts of the legislative and executive powers of government, being capable of being every moment compared with the end of political institutions, may be more respected; and also, that the future claims of the citizens, being directed by simple and incontestable principles, may always tend to the maintenance of the Constitution, and the general happiness.

For these reasons the National Assembly doth recognize and declare, in the pres-

DÉCLARATION

DES DROITS DE L'HOMME

ET DU CITOYEN,

Décrétés par l'Assemblée Nationale dans les Séances des 20, 21, 23, 24 et 26 août 1789, acceptés par le Roi.

PRÉAMBULE.

Les représentans du peuple François, constitués en assemblée nationale, considérant que l'ignorance, l'oubli ou le mépris des droits de l'homme sont les seules causes des malheurs publics et de la corruption des gouvernemens, ont résolu d'exposer, dans une déclaration solennelle, les droits naturels, inaliénables et sacrés de l'homme; afin que cette déclaration, constamment Présente à tous les membres du corps social, leur rappelle sans cesse leurs droits et leurs devoirs; afin que les actes du pouvoir législatif et ceux du pouvoir exécutif, pouvant être à chaque instant comparés avec le but de toute institution politique, en soient plus respectés; afin que les réclamations des citoyens, fondées desormais sur des principes simples et incontestables, tournent toujours au maintien de la constitution et du bonheur de tous.

En conséquence, l'assemblée nationale reconnoît et déclare, en présence et sous les auspices de l'Être suprême, les droits suivans de l'homme et du citoyen.

ARTICLE PREMIER.

LES hommes naissent et demeurent libres et égaux en droits: les distinctions socciales ne peuvent être fondées que sur l'utilité commune.

ART. II.

LE but de toute association politique est la conservation des droits naturels et imprescriptibles de l'homme; ces droits sont la liberté, la propriété, la sûreté, et la résistance à l'oppression.

ART. III.

LE principe de toute souveraineté réside essentiellement dans la nation: nul corps, nul individu ne peut exercer d'autorité qui n'en émane expressément.

ART. IV.

LA liberté consiste à pouvoir faire tout ce qui ne nuit pas à autrui. Ainsi, l'exercice des droits naturels de chaque homme, n'a de bornes que celles qui assurent aux autres membres de la société la jouissance de ces mêmes droits; ces bornes ne peuvent être déterminées que par la loi.

ART. V.

LA loi n'a le droit de défendre que les actions nuisibles à la société. Tout ce qui n'est pas défendu par la loi ne peut être empêché, et nul ne peut être contraint à faire ce qu'elle n'ordonne pas.

ART. VI.

LA loi est l'expression de la volonté générale; tous les citoyens ont droit de concourir personnellement, ou par leurs représentans, à sa formation; elle doit être la même pour tous, soit qu'elle protege, soit qu'elle punisse. Tous les citoyens étant égaux à ses yeux, sont également admissibles à toutes dignités, places et emplois publics, selon leur capacité et sans autres distinctions que celles de leurs vertus et de leurs talens.

ART. VII.

NUL homme ne peut être accusé, arrêté, ni détenu que dans les cas déterminés par la loi, et selon les formes qu'elle a prescrites. Ceux qui sollicitent, expédient, exécutent ou font exécuter des ordres arbitraires, doivent être punis; mais tout citoyen appelé ou saisi en vertu de la loi, doit obéir à l'instant; il se rend coupable par la résistance.

ART. VIII.

LA loi ne doit établir que des peines strictement et évidemment nécessaires, et nul ne peut être puni qu'en vertu d'une loi établie et promulguée antérieurement au délit, et légalement appliquée.

ART. IX.

TOUT homme étant présumé innocent jusqu'à ce qu'il ait été déclaré coupable, s'il est jugé indispensable de l'arrêter, toute rigueur qui ne seroit pas nécessaire pour s'assurer de sa personne doit être sévèrement réprimée par la loi.

ART. X.

NUL ne doit être inquiété pour ses opinions, mêmes religieuses, pourvu que leur manifestation ne trouble pas l'ordre public établi par la loi.

ART. XI.

LA libre communication des pensées et des opinions est un des droits les plus précieux de l'homme: tout citoyen peut donc parler, écrire, imprimer librement: sauf à répondre de l'abus de cette liberté dans les cas déterminés par la loi.

ART. XII.

LA garantie des droits de l'homme et du citoyen nécessite une force publique: cette force est donc instituée pour l'avantage de tous, et non pour l'utilité particulière de ceux à qui elle est confiée.

ART. XIII.

POUR l'entretien de la force publique, et pour les dépenses d'administration, une contribution commune est indispensable: elle doit être également répartie entre tous les citoyens, en raison de leurs facultés.

ART. XIV.

LES citoyens ont le droit de constater par eux-mêmes ou par leurs représentans, la nécessité de la contribution publique, de la consentir librement, d'en suivre l'emploi, et d'en déterminer la quotité, l'assiette, le recouvrement et la durée.

ART. XV.

LA société a le droit de demander compte à tout agent public de son administration.

ART. XVI.

TOUTE société, dans laquelle la garantie des droits n'est pas assurée, ni la séparation des pouvoirs déterminée, n'a point de constitution.

ART. XVII.

LES propriétés étant un droit inviolable et sacré, nul ne peut en être privé, si ce n'est lorsque la nécessité publique, légalement constatée, l'exige évidemment, et sous la condition d'une juste et préalable indemnité.

Se vend à Paris, chez Gouion, marchand de musique, grand'cour du Palais-royal où se trouve le Tableau de la Constitution faisant pendant à celui-ci.

An early printing of the *Declaration of the Rights of Man and of Citizens* (Paine's own translation of the French title) adopted by the National Assembly of France on August 26, 1789.

ence of the Supreme Being, and with the hope of his blessing and favour, the following *sacred* rights of men and of citizens:

I.   Men are born, and always continue, free and equal in respect of their rights. Civil distinctions, therefore, can be founded only on public utility.

II.   The end of all political associations is the preservation of the natural and imprescriptible rights of man; and these rights are liberty, property, security, and resistance of oppression.

III.   The nation is essentially the source of all sovereignty; nor can any individual, or any body of men, be entitled to any authority which is not expressly derived from it.

IV.   Political liberty consists in the power of doing whatever does not injure another. The exercise of the natural rights of every man has no other limits than those which are necessary to secure to every *other* man the free exercise of the same rights; and these limits are determinable only by the law.

V.   The law ought to prohibit only actions hurtful to society. What is not prohibited by the law should not be hindered; nor should any one be compelled to that which the law does not require.

VI.   The law is an expression of the will of the community. All citizens have a right to concur, either personally or by their representatives, in its formation. It should be the same to all, whether it protects or punishes; and all being equal in its sight, are equally eligible to all honours, places, and employments, according to their different abilities, without any other distinction than that created by their virtues and talents.

VII.   No man should be accused, arrested, or held in confinement, except in cases determined by the law, and according to the forms which it has prescribed. All who promote, solicit, execute, or cause to be executed, arbitrary orders, ought to be punished, and every citizen called upon, or apprehended by virtue of the law, ought

immediately to obey and renders himself culpable by resistance.

VIII.   The law ought to impose no other penalties but such as are absolutely and evidently necessary; and no one ought to be punished, but in virtue of a law promulgated before the offense, and legally applied.

IX.   Every man being presumed innocent till he has been convicted, whenever his detention becomes indispensable, all rigour to him, more than is necessary to secure his person, ought to be provided against by the law.

X.   No man ought to be molested on account of his opinions, not even on account of his religious opinions, provided his avowal of them does not disturb the public order established by the law.

XI.   The unrestrained communication of thoughts and opinions being one of the most precious rights of man, every citizen may speak, write, and publish freely, provided he is responsible for the abuse of this liberty, in cases determined by the law.

XII.   A public force being necessary to give security to the rights of men and of citizens, that force is instituted for the benefit of the community and not for the particular benefit of the persons with whom it is intrusted.

XIII.   A common contribution being necessary for the support of the public force, and for defraying the other expenses of government, it ought to be divided equally among the members of the community, according to their abilities.

XIV.   Every citizen has a right, either by himself or his representative, to a free voice in determining the necessity of public contributions, the appropriation of them, and their amount, mode of assessment, and duration.

XV.   Every community has a right to demand of all its agents an account of their conduct.

XVI.   Every community in which a separation of powers and a security of rights is not provided for, wants a constitution.

XVII. The right of property being inviolable and sacred, no one ought to be deprived of it, except in cases of evident public necessity, legally ascertained, and on condition of a previous just indemnity.

Observations on the Declaration of Rights

The first three articles comprehend in general terms the whole of a Declaration of Rights; all the succeeding articles either originate from them or follow as elucidations. The 4th, 5th, and 6th define more particularly what is only generally expressed in the 1st, 2nd, and 3rd.

The 7th, 8th, 9th, 10th, and 11th articles are declaratory of principles upon which laws shall be constructed, comformable to rights already declared.

But it is questioned by some very good people in France, as well as in other countries, whether the 10th article sufficiently guarantees the right it is intended to accord with; besides which it takes off from the divine dignity of religion and weakens its operative force upon the mind, to make it a subject of human laws. It then presents itself to man like light intercepted by a cloudy medium, in which the source of it is obscured from his sight, and he sees nothing to reverence in the dusky ray.

The remaining articles, beginning with the 12th, are substantially contained in the principles of the preceding articles; but in the particular situation which France then was, having to undo what was wrong, as well as to set up what was right, it was proper to be more particular than what in another condition of things would be necessary.

While the Declaration of Rights was before the National Assembly some of its members remarked that if a Declaration of Rights was published it should be accompanied by a declaration of duties. The observation discovered a mind that re-flected, and it only erred by not reflecting far enough. A Declaration of Rights is, by reciprocity, a declaration of duties also. Whatever is my right as a man is also the right of another; and it becomes my duty to guarantee as well as to possess.

The first three articles are the basis of liberty, as well individual as national; nor can any country be called free whose government does not take its beginning from the principles they contain, and continue to preserve them pure; and the whole of the Declaration of Rights is of more value to the world, and will do more good, than all the laws and statutes that have yet been promulgated.

In the declaratory exordium which prefaces the Declaration of Rights we see the solemn and majestic spectacle of a nation opening its commission, under the auspices of its Creator, to establish a government, a scene so new, and so transcendently unequaled by anything in the European world, that the name of a revolution is diminutive of its character, and it rises into a REGENERATION OF MAN. What are the present governments of Europe but a scene of iniquity and oppression? What is that of England? Do not its own inhabitants say it is a market where every man has his price, and where corruption is common traffic at the expense of a deluded people? No wonder, then, that the French Revolution is traduced. Had it confined itself merely to the destruction of flagrant despotism perhaps Mr. Burke and some others had been silent. Their cry now is, "It has gone too far"—that is, it has gone too far for them. It stares corruption in the face, and the venal tribe are all alarmed. Their fear discovers itself in their outrage, and they are but publishing the groans of a wounded vice. But from such opposition the French Revolution, instead of suffering, receives an homage. The more it is struck the more sparks it will emit; and the fear is it will not be struck enough. It has nothing to dread from attacks: Truth has given it an establishment, and Time will record it with a name as lasting as his own.

Having now traced the progress of the French Revolution through most of its principal stages, from its commencement to the taking of the Bastille, and its establishment by the Declaration of Rights, I will close the subject with the energetic apostrophe of M. de Lafayette—MAY THIS GREAT MONUMENT, RAISED TO LIBERTY, SERVE AS A LESSON TO THE OPPRESSOR, AND AN EXAMPLE TO THE OPPRESSED!

Conclusion

Reason and Ignorance, the opposite of each other, influence the great bulk of mankind. If either of these can be rendered sufficiently extensive in a country, the machinery of government goes easily on. Reason obeys itself; and Ignorance submits to whatever is dictated to it.

The two modes of government which prevail in the world, are—

First, government by election and representation.

Second, government by hereditary succession.

The former is generally known by the name of republic; the latter by that of monarchy and aristocracy.

Those two distinct and opposite forms erect themselves on the two distinct and opposite bases of Reason and Ignorance.

As the exercise of government requires talents and abilities, and as talents and abilities cannot have hereditary descent, it is evident that hereditary succession requires a belief from man to which his reason cannot subscribe, and which can only be established upon his ignorance; and the more ignorant any country is, the better it is fitted for this species of government.

On the contrary, government, in a well-constituted republic, requires no belief from man beyond what his reason can give. He sees the *rationale* of the whole system, its origin and its operation; and as

it is best supported when best understood, the human faculties act with boldness, and acquire under this form of government a gigantic manliness.

As, therefore, each of those forms acts on a different base, the one moving freely by the aid of reason, the other by ignorance, we have next to consider what it is that gives motion to the species of government which is called mixed government, or, as it is sometimes ludicrously styled, a *government of this, that, and t'other.*

The moving power in this species of government is of necessity corruption. However imperfect election and representation may be in mixed governments, they still give exercise to a greater portion of reason than is convenient to the hereditary part; and therefore it becomes necessary to buy the reason up.

A mixed government is an imperfect everything, cementing and soldering the discordant parts together by corruption, to act as a whole. Mr. Burke appears highly disgusted that France, since she had resolved on a revolution, did not adopt what he calls "*A British Constitution*"; and the regretful manner in which he expresses himself on this occasion implies a suspicion that the British Constitution needed something to keep its defects in countenance.

In mixed governments there is no responsibility: the parts cover each other till responsibility is lost; and the corruption which moves the machine, contrives at the same time its own escape. When it is laid down as a maxim, that *a king can do no wrong,* it places him in a state of similar security with that of idiots and persons insane, and responsibility is out of the question with respect to himself.

It then descends upon the minister, who shelters himself under a majority in Parliament, which by places, pensions, and corruption, he can always command; and that majority justifies itself by the same authority with which it protects the minister. In this rotary motion, responsibility is thrown off from the parts, and from the whole.

When there is part in a government which can do no wrong, it implies that it does nothing; and is only the machine of another power, by whose advice and direction it acts.

What is supposed to be the king in a mixed government is the Cabinet; and as the Cabinet is always a part of the Parliament, and the members justifying in one character what they advise and act in another, a mixed government becomes a continual enigma; entailing upon a country, by the quantity of corruption necessary to solder the parts, the expense of supporting all the forms of government at once, and finally resolving them into a government by committee; in which the advisers, the actors, the approvers, the justifiers, the persons responsible, and the persons not responsible, are the same persons.

By this pantomimical contrivance, and change of scene and character, the parts help each other out in matters which neither of them singly would assume to act.

When money is to be obtained, the mass of variety apparently dissolves, and a profusion of parliamentary praises passes between the parts. Each admires with astonishment the wisdom, the liberality, and disinterestedness of the other; and all of them breathe a pitying sigh at the burdens of the nation.

But in a well-constituted republic, nothing of this soldering, praising, and pitying can take place; the representation being equal throughout the country, and complete in itself, however it may be arranged into legislative and executive, they have all one and the same natural source. The parts are not foreigners to each other, like democracy, aristocracy, and monarchy. As there are no discordant distinctions, there is nothing to corrupt by compromise, nor confound by contrivance. Public measures appeal of themselves to the understanding of the nation, and resting on their own merits, disown any flattering applications to vanity. The continual whine of lamenting the burden of taxes, however successfully

it may be practiced in mixed governments, is inconsistent with the sense and spirit of a republic. If taxes are necessary, they are of course advantageous, but if they require an apology, the apology itself implies an impeachment. Why, then, is man imposed upon, or why does he impose upon himself?

When men are spoken of as kings and subjects, or when government is mentioned under the distinct or combined heads of monarchy, aristocracy, and democracy, what is it that *reasoning* man is to understand by the terms? If there really existed in the world two or more distinct and separate *elements* of human power, we should then see the several origins to which those terms would descriptively apply; but as there is but one species of man, there can be but one element of human power, and that element is man himself. Monarchy, aristocracy, and democracy are but creatures of imagination; and a thousand such may be contrived as well as three.

From the revolutions of America and France, and the symptoms that have appeared in other countries, it is evident that the opinion of the world is changed with respect to systems of government, and that revolutions are not within the compass of political calculations.

The progress of time and circumstances, which men assign to the accomplishment of great changes, is too mechanical to measure the force of the mind, and the rapidity of reflection, by which revolutions are generated: All the old governments have received a shock from those that already appear, and which were once more improbable, and are a greater subject of wonder, than a general revolution in Europe would be now.

When we survey the wretched condition of man, under the monarchical and hereditary systems of government, dragged from his home by one power, or driven by another, and impoverished by taxes more than by enemies, it becomes evident that those systems are bad, and that a general revolution in the principle and construction of governments is necessary.

What is government more than the management of the affairs of a nation? It is not, and from its nature cannot be, the property of any particular man or family, but of the whole community, at whose expense it is supported; and though by force and contrivance it has been usurped into an inheritance, the usurpation cannot alter the right of things. Sovereignty, as a matter of right, appertains to the nation only, and not to any individual; and a nation has at all times an inherent, indefeasible right to abolish any form of government it finds inconvenient, and to establish such as accords with its interest, disposition, and happiness. The romantic and barbarous distinction of men into kings and subjects, though it may suit the conditions of courtiers, cannot that of citizens; and is exploded by the principle upon which governments are now founded. Every citizen is a member of the sovereignty; and, as such, can acknowledge no personal subjection: and his obedience can be only to the laws.

When men think of what government is, they must necessarily suppose it to possess a knowledge of all the objects and matters upon which its authority is to be exercised. In this view of government, the republican system, as established by America and France, operates to embrace the whole of a nation; and the knowledge necessary to the interest of all the parts is to be found in the centre, which the parts by representation form; but the old governments are on a construction that excludes knowledge as well as happiness; government by monks, who know nothing of the world beyond the walls of a convent, is as inconsistent as government by kings.

What we formerly called revolutions were little more than a change of persons, or an alteration of local circumstances. They rose and fell like things of course, and had nothing in their existence or their fate that could influence beyond the spot that produced them. But what we now see in the world, from the revolutions of America and France, are a renovation of the natural order of things, a system of principles as universal as truth and the existence of man, and combining moral with political happiness and national prosperity.

I. Men are born, and always continue, free and equal in respect of their rights. Civil distinctions, therefore, can be founded only on public utility.

II. The end of all political associations is the preservation of the natural and imprescriptible rights of man; and these rights are liberty, property, security, and resistance of oppression.

III. The nation is essentially the source of all sovereignty; nor can ANY INDIVIDUAL, *or* ANY BODY OF MEN, *be entitled to any authority which is not expressly derived from it.*

In these principles there is nothing to throw a nation into confusion by inflaming ambition. They are calculated to call forth wisdom and abilities, and to exercise them for the public good, and not for the emolument or aggrandizement of particular descriptions of men or families. Monarchical sovereignty, the enemy of mankind, and the source of misery, is abolished; and sovereignty itself is restored to its natural and original place, the nation. Were this the case throughout Europe, the cause of wars would be taken away.

It is attributed to Henry the Fourth of France, a man of enlarged and benevolent heart, that he proposed, about the year 1610, a plan for abolishing war in Europe: the plan consisted in constituting a European Congress, or as the French authors style it, a Pacific Republic, by appointing delegates from the several nations who were to act as a Court of Arbitration in any disputes that might arise between nation and nation.

Had such a plan been adopted at the time it was proposed, the taxes of England and France, as two of the parties, would have been at least ten millions sterling annually to each nation less than they were at the commencement of the French Revolution.

To conceive a cause why such a plan has not been adopted (and that instead of a congress for the purpose of *preventing* war, it has been called only to *terminate* a war, after a fruitless expense of several years), it will be necessary to consider the interest of governments as a distinct interest to that of nations.

Whatever is the cause of taxes to a nation becomes also the means of revenue to a government. Every war terminates with an addition of taxes, and consequently with an addition of revenue; and in any event of war, in the manner they are now commenced and concluded, the power and interest of governments are increased. War, therefore, from its productiveness, as it easily furnishes the pretense of necessity for taxes and appointments to places and offices, becomes a principal part of the system of old governments; and to establish any mode to abolish war, however advantageous it might be to nations, would be to take from such government the most lucrative of its branches. The frivolous matters upon which war is made show the disposition and avidity of governments to uphold the system of war, and betray the motives upon which they act.

Why are not republics plunged into war, but because the nature of their government does not admit of an interest distinct from that of the nation? Even Holland, though an ill-constructed republic, and with a commerce extending over the world, existed nearly a century without war; and the instant the form of government was changed in France the republican principles of peace and domestic prosperity and economy arose with the new government; and the same consequences would follow the same causes in other nations.

As war is the system of government on the old construction, the animosity which nations reciprocally entertain is nothing more than what the policy of their governments excites to keep up the spirit of the system. Each government accuses the other of perfidy, intrigue, and ambition, as a means of heating the imagination of their respective nations, and incensing them to hostilities. Man is not the enemy of man, but through the medium of a false system of government. Instead, therefore, of exclaiming against the ambition of kings, the exclamation should be directed against the principle of such governments; and instead of seeking to reform the individual, the wisdom of a nation should apply itself to reform the system.

Whether the forms and maxims of governments which are still in practice were adapted to the condition of the world at the period they were established is not in this case the question. The older they are the less correspondence can they have with the present state of things.

Time, and change of circumstances and opinions, have the same progressive effect in rendering modes of government obsolete as they have upon customs and manners. Agriculture, commerce, manufactures, and the tranquil arts, by which the prosperity of nations is best promoted, require a different system of government, and a different species of knowledge to direct its operations, than what might have been required in the former condition of the world.

As it is not difficult to perceive, from the enlightened state of mankind, that hereditary governments are verging to their decline, and that revolutions on the broad basis of national sovereignty and government by representation are making their way in Europe, it would be an act of wisdom to anticipate their approach, and produce revolutions by reason and accommodation, rather than commit them to the issue of convulsions.

From what we now see, nothing of reform in the political world ought to be held improbable. It is an age of revolutions, in which everything may be looked for.

The intrigue of courts, by which the

system of war is kept up, may provoke a confederation of nations to abolish it; and a European Congress to patronize the progress of free government, and promote the civilization of nations with each other, is an event nearer in probability than once were the revolutions and alliance of France and America.

Part the Second
Combining Principles and Practice

To M. de Lafayette

After an acquaintance of nearly fifteen years in difficult situations in America, and various consultations in Europe, I feel a pleasure in presenting to you this small treatise in gratitude for your services to my beloved America, and as a testimony of my esteem for the virtues, public and private, which I know you to possess.

The only point upon which I could ever discover that we differed was not as to principles of government, but as to time. For my own part I think it equally as injurious to good principles to permit them to linger, as to push them on too fast. That which you suppose accomplishable in fourteen or fifteen years I may believe practicable in a much shorter period. Mankind, as it appears to me, are always ripe enough to understand their true interest, provided it be presented clearly to their understanding, and that in a manner not to create suspicion by anything like self-design, nor offend by assuming too much. Where we would wish to reform we must not reproach.

When the American Revolution was established I felt a disposition to sit serenely down and enjoy the calm. It did not appear to me that any object could afterward arise great enough to make me quit tranquillity and feel as I had felt before. But when principle, and not place, is the energetic cause of action, a man, I find, is everywhere the same.

I am now once more in the public world; and as I have not a right to contemplate on so many years of remaining life as you have, I am resolved to labour as fast as I can; and as I am anxious for your aid and your company, I wish you to hasten your principles and overtake me.

If you make a campaign the ensuing spring, which it is most probable there will be no occasion for, I will come and join you. Should the campaign commence, I hope it will terminate in the extinction of German despotism, and in establishing the freedom of all Germany. When France shall be surrounded with revolutions she will be in peace and safety, and her taxes, as well as those of Germany, will consequently become less.

Your sincere,
Affectionate friend,
THOMAS PAINE

LONDON, *February* 9, 1792.

Preface

When I began the chapter entitled the *Conclusion* in the former part of RIGHTS OF MAN, published last year, it was my intention to have extended it to a greater length; but in casting the whole matter in my mind which I wish to add, I found that it must either make the work too bulky, or contract my plan too much. I therefore brought it to a close as soon as the subject would admit and reserved what I had further to say to another opportunity.

Several other reasons contributed to produce this determination. I wished to know the manner in which a work, written in a style of thinking and expression different to what had been customary in England, would be received before I proceeded farther. A great field was opening to the view of mankind by means of the French Revolution. Mr. Burke's outrageous opposition thereto brought the controversy into England. He attacked principles which he knew (from information) I would contest with him, because they are principles I believe to be good, and which I have contributed to establish, and conceive myself bound to defend. Had he not urged the controversy, I had most probably been a silent man.

Another reason for deferring the remainder of the work was that Mr. Burke promised in his first publication to renew the subject at another opportunity, and to make a comparison of which he called the English and French constitutions. I therefore held myself in reserve for him. He has published two works since, without doing this; which he certainly would not have omitted, had the comparison been in his favour.

In his last work, his *"Appeal from the new to the old Whigs,"* he has quoted about ten pages from the *Rights of Man,* and having given himself the trouble of doing this, says he shall "not attempt in the smallest degree to refute them," meaning the principles therein contained. I am enough acquainted with Mr. Burke to know that he would if he could. But instead of contesting them, he immediately after consoles himself with saying that "he has done his part." He has not done his part. He has not performed his promise of a comparison of constitutions. He started the controversy, he gave the challenge, and has fled from it; and he is now a *case in point* with his own opinion that *"the age of chivalry is gone!"*

The title as well as the substance of his last work, his *"Appeal,"* is his condemnation. Principles must stand on their own merits, and if they are good they certainly will. To put them under the shelter of other men's authority, as Mr. Burke has done, serves to bring them into suspicion. Mr. Burke is not very fond of dividing his honours, but in this case he is artfully dividing the disgrace.

But who are those to whom Mr. Burke has made his appeal? A set of childish thinkers, and halfway politicians born in the last century, men who went no farther with any principle than as it suited their purpose as a party; the nation was always left out of the question; and this has been the character of every party from that day to this. The nation sees nothing in such works, or such politics, worthy its attention. A little matter will move a party, but it must be something great that moves a nation.

Though I see nothing in Mr. Burke's *Appeal* worth taking much notice of, there is, however, one expression upon which I shall offer a few remarks. After quoting largely from the *Rights of Man,* and declining to contest the principles contained in that work, he says: "This will most probably be done (*if such writings shall be thought to deserve any other refutation than that of criminal justice*) by others, who may think with Mr. Burke and with the same zeal."

In the first place, it has not yet been done by anybody. Not less, I believe, than eight or ten pamphlets intended as answers to the former part of the *Rights of Man* have been published by different persons, and not one of them to my knowledge has extended to a second edition, nor are even the titles of them so much as generally remembered. As I am averse to unnecessarily multiplying publications, I have answered none of them. And as I believe that a man may write himself out of reputation when nobody else can do it, I am careful to avoid that rock.

But as I would decline unnecessary publications on the one hand, so would I avoid everything that might appear like sullen pride on the other. If Mr. Burke, or any person on his side of the question, will produce an answer to the *Rights of Man* that shall extend to a half, or even to a fourth part of the number of copies to which the *Rights of Man* extended, I will reply to his work. But until this be done, I shall so far take the sense of the public

Lafayette takes an oath on the first anniversary of the French Revolution, July 14, 1790. In presenting the second part of his *Rights of Man* to Lafayette, Paine wrote: *"I feel a pleasure in presenting to you this small treatise . . . as a testimony of my esteem for the virtues, public and private, which I know you to possess."*

for my guide (and the world knows I am not a flatterer) that what they do not think worthwhile to read, is not worth mine to answer. I suppose the number of copies to which the first part of the *Rights of Man* extended, taking England, Scotland, and Ireland, is not less than between forty and fifty thousand.

I now come to remark on the remaining part of the quotation I have made from Mr. Burke.

"If," says he, "such writing shall be thought to deserve any other refutation than that of *criminal* justice."

Pardoning the pun, it must be *criminal* justice indeed that should condemn a work as a substitute for not being able to refute it. The greatest condemnation that could be passed upon it would be a refutation. But in proceeding by the method Mr. Burke alludes to, the condemnation would, in the final event, pass upon the criminality of the process and not upon the work, and in this case, I had rather be the author, than be either the judge or the jury that should condemn it.

But to come at once to the point. I have differed from some professional gentlemen on the subject of prosecutions, and I since find they are falling into my opinion, which I will here state as fully but as concisely as I can.

I will first put a case with respect to any law, and then compare it with a government, or with what in England is, or has been, called a Constitution.

It would be an act of despotism, or what in England is called arbitrary power, to make a law to prohibit investigating the principles, good or bad, on which such a law, or any other, is founded.

If a law be bad it is one thing to oppose the practice of it, but it is quite a different thing to expose its errors, to reason on its defects, and to show cause how it should be repealed, or why another ought to be substituted in its place. I have always held it an opinion (making it also my practice) that it is better to obey a bad law, making use at the same time of every argument to show its errors and procure its repeal, than forcibly to violate it; because the precedent of breaking a bad law might weaken the force and lead to a discretionary violation of those which are good.

The case is the same with respect to principles and forms of government, or to what are called constitutions and the parts of which they are composed.

It is for the good of nations and not for the emolument or aggrandizement of particular individuals, that government ought to be established, and that mankind are at the expense of supporting it. The defects of every government and constitution, both as to principle and form, must on a parity of reasoning, be as open to discussion as the defects of a law, and it is a duty which every man owes to society to point them out. When those defects, and the means of remedying them, are generally seen by a nation, that nation will reform its government or its constitution in the one case, as the government repealed or reformed the law in the other. The operation of government is restricted to the making and the administering of laws; but it is to a nation that the right of forming or reforming, generating or regenerating, constitutions and governments belong; and consequently those subjects, as subjects of investigation, are always before a country *as a matter of right* and cannot, without invading the general rights of that country, be made subjects for prosecution. On this ground I will meet Mr. Burke whenever he pleases. It is better that the whole argument should come out than to seek to stifle it. It was himself that opened the controversy, and he ought not to desert it.

I do not believe that monarchy and aristocracy will continue seven years longer in any of the enlightened countries in Europe. If better reasons can be shown for them than against them, they will stand; if the contrary, they will not. Mankind are not now to be told they shall not think or they shall not read; and publications that go no further than to investigate principles of government, to invite men to reason and to reflect and to show the errors and excellencies of different systems, have a right to appear. If they do not excite attention, they are not worth the trouble of a prosecution, and if they do the prosecution will amount to nothing, since it cannot amount to a prohibition of reading. This would be a sentence on the public instead of the author and would also be the most effectual mode of making or hastening revolutions.

On all cases that apply universally to a nation with respect to systems of government, a jury of *twelve* men is not competent to decide. Where there are no witnesses to be examined, no facts to be proved, and where the whole matter is before the whole public, and the merits or demerits of it resting on their opinion; and where there is nothing to be known in a court, but what everybody knows out of it, any twelve men is equally as good a jury as the other and would most probably reverse another's verdict; or, from the variety of their opinions, not be able to form one. It is one case whether a nation approve a work or a plan; but it is quite another case whether it will commit to any such jury the power of determining whether that nation have a right to or shall reform its government or not. I mention those cases that Mr. Burke may see I have not written on government without reflecting on what is law, as well as on what are rights. The only effectual jury in such cases would be a convention of the whole nation fairly elected; for in all such cases the whole nation is the vicinage. If Mr. Burke will propose such a jury I will waive all privileges of being the citizen of another country and, defending its principles, abide the issue, provided he will do the same; for my opinion is that his work and his principles would be condemned instead of mine.

As to the prejudices which men have from education and habit, in favour of any particular form or system of government, those prejudices have yet to stand the test of reason and reflection. In fact, such prejudices are nothing. No man is prejudiced in favour of a thing knowing it to be wrong. He is attached to it on the belief of its being right, and when he sees it is not so, the prejudice will be gone. We have but a defective idea of what prejudice is. It might be said that until men think for themselves the whole is prejudice, and *not opinion:* for that only is opinion which is the result of reason and reflection. I offer this remark that Mr. Burke may not confide too much in what have been the customary prejudices of the country.

I do not believe that the people of England have ever been fairly and candidly dealt by. They have been imposed on by parties and by men assuming the character of leaders. It is time that the nation should rise above those trifles. It is time to dismiss that inattention which has so long been the encouraging cause of stretching taxation to excess. It is time to dismiss all those songs and toasts which are calculated to enslave and operate to suffocate reflection. On all such subjects men have but to think and they will neither act wrong nor be misled. To say that any people are not fit for freedom is to make poverty their choice, and to say that they had rather be loaded with taxes than not. If such a case could be proved it would equally prove that those who govern are not fit to govern them, for they are a part of the same national mass.

But admitting governments to be changed all over Europe; it certainly may be done without convulsion or revenge. It is not worth making changes or revolutions, unless it be for some great national benefit: and when this shall appear to a nation the danger will be as in America and France, to those who oppose; and with this reflection I close my preface.

THOMAS PAINE

LONDON, *February* 9, 1792.

Introduction

What Archimedes said of the mechanical powers may be applied to reason and liberty. *"Had we,"* said he *"a place to stand upon, we might raise the world."*

The Revolution of America presented in politics what was only theory in mechanics. So deeply rooted were all the governments of the old world, and so effectually had the tyranny and the antiquity of habit established itself over the mind, that no beginning could be made in Asia, Africa, or Europe to reform the political condition of man. Freedom had been hunted round the globe; reason was considered as rebellion; and the slavery of fear had made men afraid to think.

But such is the irresistible nature of truth that all it asks, and all it wants, is the liberty of appearing. The sun needs no inscription to distinguish him from darkness; and no sooner did the American governments display themselves to the world than despotism felt a shock and man began to contemplate redress.

The independence of America, considered merely as a separation from England, would have been a matter of but little importance, had it not been accompanied by a revolution in the principles and practice of governments. She made a stand, not for herself only, but for the world, and looked beyond the advantages herself could receive. Even the Hessian, though hired to fight against her, may live to bless his defeat; and England, condemning the viciousness of its government, rejoice in its miscarriage.

As America was the only spot in the political world where the principles of universal reformation could begin, so also was it the best in the natural world. An assemblage of circumstances conspired not only to give birth, but to add gigantic maturity to its principles. The scene which that country presents to the eye of a spectator has something in it which generates and encourages great ideas. Nature appears to him in magnitude. The mighty objects he beholds act upon his mind by enlarging it, and he partakes of the greatness he contemplates. Its first settlers were emigrants from different European nations, and of diversified professions of religion, retiring from the governmental persecutions of the old world, and meeting in the new, not as enemies, but as brothers. The wants which necessarily accompany the cultivation of a wilderness produced among them a state of society which countries long harassed by the quarrels and intrigues of governments had neglected to cherish. In such a situation man becomes what he ought. He sees his species, not with the inhuman idea of a natural enemy, but as kindred; and the example shows to the artificial world that man must go back to nature for information.

From the rapid progress which America makes in every species of improvement, it is rational to conclude that, if the governments of Asia, Africa, and Europe had begun on a principle similar to that of America, or had not been very early corrupted therefrom, those countries must by this time have been in a far superior condition to what they are. Age after age has passed away, for no other purpose than to behold their wretchedness. Could we suppose a spectator who knew nothing of the world, and who was put into it merely to make his observations, he would take a great part of the old world to be new, just struggling with the difficulties and hardships of an infant settlement. He could not suppose that the hordes of miserable poor with which old countries abound could be any other than those who had not yet had time to provide for themselves. Little would he think they were the consequence of what in such countries is called government.

If, from the more wretched parts of the old world, we look at those which are in an advanced stage of improvement, we still find the greedy hand of government thrusting itself into every corner and crevice of industry, and grasping the spoil of the multitude. Invention is continually exercised to furnish new pretenses for revenue and taxation. It watches prosperity as its prey and permits none to escape without a tribute.

As revolutions have begun (and as the probability is always greater against a thing beginning than of proceeding after it has begun), it is natural to expect that other revolutions will follow. The amazing and still increasing expenses with which old governments are conducted, the numerous wars they engage in or provoke, the embarrassments they throw in the way of universal civilization and commerce, and the oppression and usurpation they practice at home, have wearied out the patience and exhausted the property of the world. In such a situation and with the examples already existing, revolutions are to be looked for. They are become subjects of universal conversation and may be considered as the *Order of the Day.*

If systems of government can be introduced less expensive and more productive of general happiness than those which have existed, all attempts to oppose their progress will in the end be fruitless. Reason, like time, will make its own way, and prejudice will fall in a combat with interest. If universal peace, civilization, and commerce are ever to be the happy lot of man, it cannot be accomplished but by a revolution in the system of governments. All the monarchical governments are military. War is their trade, plunder and revenue their objects. While such governments continue, peace has not the absolute security of a day. What is the history of all monarchical governments but a disgustful picture of human wretchedness, and the accidental respite of a few years' repose? Wearied with war, and tired with human butchery, they sat down to rest and called it peace. This certainly is not the condition that heaven intended for man; and if *this*

be monarchy, well might monarchy be reckoned among the sins of the Jews.

The revolutions which formerly took place in the world had nothing in them that interested the bulk of mankind. They extended only to a change of persons and measures, but not of principles, and rose or fell among the common transactions of the moment. What we now behold may not improperly be called a *"counterrevolution."* Conquest and tyranny, at some early period, dispossessed man of his rights, and he is now recovering them. And as the tide of all human affairs has its ebb and flow in directions contrary to each other, so also is it in this. Government founded on a *moral theory, on a system of universal peace, on the indefeasible hereditary Rights of Man,* is now revolving from west to east by a stronger impulse than the government of the sword revolved from east to west. It interests not particular individuals, but nations in its progress, and promises a new era to the human race.

The danger to which the success of revolutions is most exposed is that of attempting them before the principles on which they proceed, and the advantages to result from them, are sufficiently seen and understood. Almost everything appertaining to the circumstances of a nation has been absorbed and confounded under the general and mysterious word *government.* Though it avoids taking to its account the errors it commits, and the mischiefs it occasions, it fails not to arrogate to itself whatever has the appearance of prosperity. It robs industry of its honours, by pedantically making itself the cause of its effects; and purloins from the general character of man the merits that appertain to him as a social being.

It may therefore be of use in this day of revolutions to discriminate between those things which are the effect of government, and those which are not. This will best be done by taking a review of society and civilization, and the consequences resulting therefrom, as things distinct from what are called governments. By beginning with this investigation, we shall be able to assign effects to their proper cause and analyze the mass of common errors.

Chapter I: Of society and civilization

Great part of that order which reigns among mankind is not the effect of government. It has its origin in the principles of society and the natural constitution of man. It existed prior to government and would exist if the formality of government was abolished. The mutual dependence and reciprocal interest which man has upon man, and all the parts of a civilized community upon each other, create that great chain of connection which holds it together. The landholder, the farmer, the manufacturer, the merchant, the tradesman, and every occupation, prospers by the aid which each receives from the other, and from the whole. Common interest regulates their concerns and forms their law; and the laws which common usage ordains have a greater influence than the laws of government. In fine, society performs for itself almost everything which is ascribed to government.

To understand the nature and quantity of government proper for man, it is necessary to attend to his character. As Nature created him for social life, she fitted him for the station she intended. In all cases she made his natural wants greater than his individual powers. No one man is capable, without the aid of society, of supplying his own wants; and those wants, acting upon every individual, impel the whole of them into society, as naturally as gravitation acts to a centre.

But she has gone further. She has not only forced man into society by a diversity of wants which the reciprocal aid of each other can supply, but she has implanted in him a system of social affections, which,

though not necessary to his existence, are essential to his happiness. There is no period in life when this love for society ceases to act. It begins and ends with our being.

If we examine with attention the composition and constitution of man, the diversity of his wants and talents in different men for reciprocally accommodating the wants of each other, his propensity to society, and consequently to preserve the advantages resulting from it, we shall easily discover that a great part of what is called government is mere imposition.

Government is no farther necessary than to supply the few cases to which society and civilization are not conveniently competent; and instances are not wanting to show that everything which government can usefully add thereto has been performed by the common consent of society, without government.

For upwards of two years from the commencement of the American War, and to a longer period in several of the American states, there were no established forms of government. The old governments had been abolished, and the country was too much occupied in defense to employ its attention in establishing new governments; yet during this interval order and harmony were preserved as inviolate as in any country in Europe. There is a natural aptness in man, and more so in society, because it embraces a greater variety of abilities and resources, to accommodate itself to whatever situation it is in. The instant formal government is abolished, society begins to act: a general association takes place, and common interest produces common security.

So far is it from being true, as has been pretended, that the abolition of any formal government is the dissolution of society, that it acts by a contrary impulse, and brings the latter the closer together. All that part of its organization which it had committed to its government devolves again upon itself and acts through its medium. When men, as well from natural instinct as from reciprocal benefits, have habituated themselves to social and civilized life, there is always enough of its principles in practice to carry them through any changes they may find necessary or convenient to make in their government. In short, man is so naturally a creature of society that it is almost impossible to put him out of it.

Formal government makes but a small part of civilized life; and when even the best that human wisdom can devise is established, it is a thing more in name and idea than in fact. It is to the great and fundamental principles of society and civilization—to the common usage universally consented to, and mutually and reciprocally maintained—to the unceasing circulation of interest, which passing through its million channels, invigorates the whole mass of civilized man—it is to these things, infinitely more than to anything which even the best instituted government can perform, that the safety and prosperity of the individual and of the whole depends.

The more perfect civilization is, the less occasion has it for government, because the more it does regulate its own affairs and govern itself; but so contrary is the practice of old governments to the reason of the case, that the expenses of them increase in the proportion they ought to diminish. It is but few general laws that civilized life requires, and those of such common usefulness, that whether they are enforced by the forms of government or not, the effect will be nearly the same. If we consider what the principles are that first condense men into society, and what the motives that regulate their mutual intercourse afterward, we shall find, by the time we arrive at what is called government, that nearly the whole of the business is performed by the natural operation of the parts upon each other.

Man, with respect to all those matters, is more a creature of consistency than he is aware, or that governments would wish him to believe. All the great laws of society are laws of nature. Those of trade and commerce, whether with respect to the intercourse of individuals or of nations, are laws of mutual and reciprocal interests. They are followed and obeyed, because it is the interest of the parties so to do, and not on account of any formal laws their governments may impose or interpose.

But how often is the natural propensity to society disturbed or destroyed by the operations of government! When the latter, instead of being ingrafted on the principles of the former, assumes to exist for itself, and acts by partialities of favour and oppression, it becomes the cause of the mischiefs it ought to prevent.

If we look back to the riots and tumults which at various times have happened in England, we shall find that they did not proceed from the want of a government, but that government was itself the generating cause: instead of consolidating society it divided it; it deprived it of its natural cohesion and engendered discontents and disorders which otherwise would not have existed. In those associations, which men promiscuously form for the purpose of trade, or of any concern in which government is totally out of the question, and in which they act merely on the principles of society, we see how naturally the various parties unite; and this shows, by comparison, that governments, so far from being always the cause or means of order, are often the destruction of it. The riots of 1780 had no other source than the remains of those prejudices which the government of itself had encouraged. But with respect to England there are also other causes.

Excess and inequality of taxation, however disguised in the means, never fail to appear in their effects. As a great mass of the community are thrown thereby into poverty and discontent, they are constantly on the brink of commotion; and deprived, as they unfortunately are, of the means of information, are easily heated to outrage. Whatever the apparent cause of any riots may be, the real one is always want of happiness. It shows that something is wrong in

An 18th-century Frenchman reads to his forlorn family from the Bible. *"But how often is the natural propensity to society disturbed or destroyed by the operations of government! When the latter . . . assumes to exist for itself . . . it becomes the cause of the mischiefs it ought to prevent."*

the system of government that injures the felicity by which society is to be preserved.

But as fact is superior to reasoning, the instance of America presents itself to confirm these observations. If there is a country in the world where concord, according to common calculation, would be least expected, it is America. Made up as it is of people from different nations, accustomed to different forms and habits of government, speaking different languages, and more different in their modes of worship, it would appear that the union of such a people was impracticable; but by the simple operation of constructing government on the principles of society and the rights of man, every difficulty retires, and all the parts are brought into cordial unison. There the poor are not oppressed, the rich are not privileged. Industry is not mortified by the splendid extravagance of a court rioting at its expense. Their taxes are few, because their government is just: and as there is nothing to render them wretched, there is nothing to engender riots and tumults.

A metaphysical man, like Mr. Burke, would have tortured his invention to discover how such a people could be governed. He would have supposed that some must be managed by fraud, others by force, and all by some contrivance; that genius must be hired to impose upon ignorance, and show and parade to fascinate the vulgar. Lost in the abundance of his researches, he would have resolved and re-resolved, and finally overlooked the plain and easy road that lay directly before him.

One of the great adventures of the American Revolution has been that it led to a discovery of the principles, and laid open the imposition of governments. All the revolutions till then had been worked within the small sphere of a court, and never on the great floor of a nation. The parties were always of the class of courtiers; and whatever was their rage for reformation, they carefully preserved the fraud of the profession.

In all cases they took care to represent government as a thing made up of mysteries, which only themselves understood; and they hid from the understanding of the nation the only thing that was beneficial to know, namely, *that government is nothing more than a national association acting on the principles of society.*

Having thus endeavoured to show that the social and civilized state of man is capable of performing within itself almost everything necessary to its protection and government, it will be proper, on the other hand, to take a review of the present old governments and examine whether their principles and practice are correspondent thereto.

Chapter II: Of the origin of the present old governments

It is impossible that such governments as have hitherto existed in the world would have commenced by any other means than a total violation of every principle, sacred and moral. The obscurity in which the origin of all the present old governments is buried implies the iniquity and disgrace with which they began. The origin of the present government of America and France will ever be remembered, because it is honourable to record it; but with respect to the rest, even flattery has consigned them to the tomb of time, without an inscription.

It could have been no difficult thing in the early and solitary ages of the world, while the chief employment of men was that of attending flocks and herds, for a banditti of ruffians to overrun a country and lay it under contributions. Their power being thus established, the chief of the band contrived to lose the name of robber in that of monarch; and hence the origin of monarchy and kings.

The origin of the government of England, so far as relates to what is called its line of monarchy, being one of the latest, is perhaps the best recorded. The hatred which the Norman invasion and tyranny begat must have been deeply rooted in the nation, to have outlived the contrivance to obliterate it. Though not a courtier will talk of the curfew-bell, not a village in England has forgotten it.

Those bands of robbers having parceled out the world, and divided it into dominions, began, as is naturally the case, to quarrel with each other. What at first was obtained by violence was considered by others as lawful to be taken, and a second plunderer succeeded the first. They alternately invaded the dominions which each had assigned to himself, and the brutality with which they treated each other explains the original character of monarchy. It was ruffian torturing ruffian. The conqueror considered the conquered, not as his prisoner, but his property. He led him in triumph rattling in chains and doomed him, at pleasure, to slavery or death. As time obliterated the history of their beginning, their successors assumed new appearances, to cut off the entail of their disgrace, but their principles and objects remained the same. What at first was plunder assumed the softer name of revenue; and the power originally usurped, they affected to inherit.

From such beginning of governments, what could be expected but a continual system of war and extortion? It has established itself into a trade. The vice is not peculiar to one more than to another, but is the common principle of all. There does not exist within such governments sufficient stamina whereon to engraft reformation; and the shortest, easiest, and most effectual remedy is to begin anew on the ground of the oration.

What scenes of horror, what perfection in iniquity, present themselves in contemplating the character and reviewing the history of such governments! If we would delineate human nature with a baseness of heart and hypocrisy of countenance that reflection would shudder at and humanity disown, it is kings, courts, and cabinets that must sit for the portrait. Man, naturally as he is, with all his faults about him, is not up to the character.

Can we possibly suppose that if governments had originated in a right principle, and had not an interest in pursuing a wrong one, the world could have been in the wretched and quarrelsome condition we have seen it? What inducement has the farmer, while following the plow, to lay aside his peaceful pursuits and go to war with the farmer of another country? Or what inducement has the manufacturer? What is dominion to them, or to any class of men in a nation? Does it add an acre to any man's estate or raise its value? Are not conquest and defeat each of the same price, and taxes the never-failing consequence? Though this reasoning may be good to a nation, it is not so to a government. War is the Pharo table of governments, and nations the dupes of the games.

If there is anything to wonder at in this miserable scene of governments more than might be expected, it is the progress which the peaceful arts of agriculture, manufacture, and commerce have made beneath such a long accumulating load of discouragement and oppression. It serves to show that instinct in animals does not act with stronger impulse than the principles of society and civilization operate in man. Under all discouragements, he pursues his object, and yields to nothing but impossibilities.

Chapter III: Of the old and new systems of government

Nothing can appear more contradictory than the principles on which the old governments began, and the condition to which society, civilization, and commerce are capable of carrying mankind. Government, on the old system, is an assumption of power, for the aggrandizement of itself; on the new a delegation of power for the common benefit of society. The former supports itself by keeping up a system of war; the latter promotes a system of peace, as the true means of enriching a nation. The one encourages national prejudices; the other promotes universal society, as the means of universal commerce. The one measures its prosperity by the quantity of revenue it extorts; the other proves its excellence by the small quantity of taxes it requires.

Mr. Burke has talked of old and new whigs. If he can amuse himself with childish names and distinctions, I shall not interrupt his pleasure. It is not to him, but to the Abbé Sieyès, that I address this chapter. I am already engaged to the latter gentleman to discuss the subject of monarchical government; and as it naturally occurs in comparing the old and new systems, I make this the opportunity of presenting to him my observations. I shall occasionally take Mr. Burke in my way.

Though it might be proved that the system of government now called the NEW is the most ancient in principle of all that have existed, being founded on the original inherent Rights of Man; yet, as tyranny and the sword have suspended the exercise of those rights for many centuries past, it serves better the purpose of distinction to call it the *new* than to claim the right of calling it the old.

The first general distinction between those two systems is that the one now called the old is *hereditary,* either in whole or in part; and the new is entirely *representative.* It rejects all hereditary government:

First, as being an imposition on mankind.

Second, as inadequate to the purposes for which government is necessary.

With respect to the first of these heads— It cannot be proved by what right hereditary government could begin; neither does there exist within the compass of mortal power a right to establish it. Man has no authority over posterity in matters of personal right; and, therefore, no man or body of men had, or can have, a right to set up hereditary government. Were even ourselves to come again into existence, instead of being succeeded by posterity, we have not now the right of taking from ourselves the rights which would then be ours. On what ground, then, do we pretend to take them from others?

All hereditary government is in its nature tyranny. A heritable crown, or a heritable throne, or by what other fanciful name such things may be called, have no other significant explanation than that mankind are heritable property. To inherit a government is to inherit the people, as if they were flocks and herds.

With respect to the second head, that of being inadequate to the purposes for which government is necessary, we have only to consider what government essentially is and compare it with the circumstances to which hereditary succession is subject.

Government ought to be a thing always in full maturity. It ought to be so constructed as to be superior to all the accidents to which individual man is subject; and, therefore, hereditary succession, by being *subject to them all,* is the most irregular and imperfect of all the systems of government.

We have heard the *Rights of Man* called a leveling system; but the only system to which the word *leveling* is truly applicable is the hereditary monarchical system. It is a system of *mental leveling.* It indiscriminately admits every species of character to the same authority. Vice and virtue, ignorance and wisdom, in short, every quality, good or bad, is put on the same level. Kings succeed each other, not as rationals, but as animals. It signifies not what their mental or moral characters are. Can we then be surprised at the abject state of the human mind in monarchical countries, when the government itself is formed on such an abject leveling system? It has no fixed character. Today it is one thing; tomorrow it is something else. It changes with the temper of every succeeding individual, and is subject to all the varieties of each. It is government through the medium of passions and accidents. It appears under all the various characters of childhood, decrepitude, dotage; a thing at nurse, in leading-strings, or in crutches. It reverses the wholesome order of nature. It occasionally puts children over men, and the conceits of nonage over wisdom and experience. In short, we cannot conceive a more ridiculous figure of government than hereditary succession, in all its cases, presents.

Could it be made a decree in nature, or an edict registered in heaven, and man could know it, that virtue and wisdom should invariably appertain to hereditary succession, the objections to it would be removed; but when we see that Nature acts as if she disowned and sported with the hereditary system; that the mental characters of successors, in all countries, are below the average of human understanding; that one is a tyrant, another an idiot, a third insane, and some all three together, it is impossible to attach confidence to it, when reason in man has power to act.

It is not to the Abbé Sieyès that I need apply this reasoning; he has already saved me that trouble by giving his own opinion upon the case. "If it be asked," says he, "what is my opinion with respect to hereditary right, I answer, without hesitation, that, in good theory, a hereditary transmission of any power or office, can never accord with the laws of a true representation. Hereditaryship is, in this sense, as much an attaint upon principle, as an outrage upon society. But let us," continues he, "refer to the history of all elective

Louis XV, who reigned as King of France from the age of five, goes for a ride in his garden. "*The hereditary monarchical system . . . occasionally puts children over men, and the conceits of nonage over wisdom and experience.*"

monarchies and principalities: is there one in which the elective mode is not worse than the hereditary succession?"

As to debating on which is the worse of the two, it is admitting both to be bad: and herein we are agreed. The preference which the Abbé has given is a condemnation of the thing that he prefers. Such a mode of reasoning on such a subject is inadmissible, because it finally amounts to an accusation upon Providence, as if she had left to man no other choice with respect to government than between two evils, the best of which he admits to be "an attaint upon principle, and an outrage upon society."

Passing over for the present all the evils and mischiefs which monarchy has occasioned in the world, nothing can more effectually prove its uselessness in a state of *civil government* than making it hereditary. Would we make any office hereditary that required wisdom and abilities to fill it? And where wisdom and abilities are not necessary, such an office, whatever it may be, is superfluous or insignificant.

Hereditary succession is a burlesque upon monarchy. It puts it in the most ridiculous light, by presenting it as an office which any child or idiot may fill. It requires some talents to be a common mechanic; but to be a king requires only the animal figure of man—a sort of breathing automaton. This sort of superstition may last a few years more, but it cannot long resist the awakened reason and interest of man.

As to Mr. Burke, he is a stickler for monarchy, not altogether as a pensioner, if he is one, which I believe, but as a political man. He has taken up a contemptible opinion of mankind, who, in their turn, are taking up the same of him. He considers them as a herd of beings that must be governed by fraud, effigy, and show; and an idol would be as good a figure of monarchy with him as a man. I will, however, do him the justice to say that, with respect to

America, he has been very complimentary. He always contended, at least in my hearing, that the people of America were more enlightened than those of England, or of any country in Europe; and that therefore the imposition of show was not necessary in their governments.

Though the comparison between hereditary and elective monarchy, which the Abbé has made, is unnecessary to the case, because the representative system rejects both; yet, were I to make the comparison, I should decide contrary to what he has done.

The civil wars which have originated from contested hereditary claims are more numerous, and have been more dreadful, and of longer continuance, than those which have been occasioned by election. All the civil wars in France arose from the hereditary system; they were either produced by hereditary claims, or by the imperfection of the hereditary form, which admits of regencies, or monarchy at nurse. With respect to England, its history is full of the same misfortunes. The contests for succession between the houses of York and Lancaster lasted a whole century; and others of a similar nature have renewed themselves since that period. Those of 1715 and 1745 were of the same kind. The succession war for the crown of Spain embroiled almost half Europe. The disturbances in Holland are generated from the hereditaryship of the stadtholder. A government calling itself free, with a hereditary office, is like a thorn in the flesh that produces a fermentation which endeavours to discharge it.

But I might go further and place also foreign wars, of whatever kind, to the same cause. It is by adding the evil of hereditary succession to that of monarchy that a permanent family interest is created, whose constant objects are dominion and revenue. Poland, though an elective monarchy, has had fewer wars than those which are hereditary; and it is the only government that has made a voluntary essay, though but a small one, to reform the condition of the country.

Having thus glanced at a few of the defects of the old, or hereditary systems of government, let us compare it with the new, or representative system.

The representative system takes society and civilization for its basis; nature, reason, and experience for its guide.

Experience, in all ages and in all countries, has demonstrated that it is impossible to control nature in her distribution of mental powers. She gives them as she pleases. Whatever is the rule by which she, apparently to us, scatters them among mankind, that role remains a secret to man. It would be as ridiculous to attempt to fix the hereditaryship of human beauty as of wisdom. Whatever wisdom constituently is, it is like a seedless plant; it may be reared when it appears, but it cannot be voluntarily produced. There is always a sufficiency somewhere in the general mass of society for all purposes; but with respect to the parts of society, it is continually changing its place. It rises in one today, in another tomorrow, and has most probably visited in rotation every family of the earth and again withdrawn.

As this is in the order of nature, the order of government must necessarily follow it, or government will, as we see it does, degenerate into ignorance. The hereditary system, therefore, is as repugnant to human wisdom as to human rights; and is as absurd as it is unjust.

As the republic of letters brings forward the best literary productions, by giving to genius a fair and universal chance; so the representative system of government is calculated to produce the wisest laws, by collecting wisdom from where it can be found. I smile to myself when I contemplate the ridiculous insignificance into which literature and all the sciences would sink, were they made hereditary; and I carry the same idea into governments. A hereditary

governor is as inconsistent as a hereditary author. I know not whether Homer or Euclid had sons; but I will venture an opinion that if they had, and had left their works unfinished, those sons could not have completed them.

Do we need a stronger evidence of the absurdity of hereditary government than is seen in the descendants of those men, in any line of life, who once were famous? Is there scarcely an instance in which there is not a total reverse of the character? It appears as if the tide of mental faculties flowed as far as it could in certain channels and then forsook its course and arose in others. How irrational then is the hereditary system, which establishes channels of power, in company with which wisdom refuses to flow! By continuing this absurdity, man is perpetually in contradiction with himself; he accepts, for a king, or a chief magistrate, or a legislator, a person whom he would not elect for a constable.

It appears to general observation that revolutions create genius and talents; but those events do no more than bring them forward. There is existing in man a mass of sense lying in a dormant state, and which, unless something excites to action, will descend with him, in that condition, to the grave. As it is to the advantage of society that the whole of the faculties should be employed, the construction of government ought to be such as to bring forward by a quiet and regular operation all that extent of capacity which never fails to appear in revolutions.

This cannot take place in the insipid state of hereditary government, not only because it prevents, but because it operates to benumb. When the mind of a nation is bowed down by any political superstition in its government, such as hereditary succession is, it loses a considerable portion of its powers on all other subjects and objects. Hereditary succession requires the same obedience to ignorance as to wisdom; and when once the mind can bring itself to pay this indiscriminate reverence, it descends below the stature of mental manhood. It is fit to be great only in little things. It acts a treachery upon itself and suffocates the sensations that urge to detection.

Though the ancient governments present to us a miserable picture of the condition of man, there is one which above all others exempts itself from the general description. I mean the democracy of Athenians. We see more to admire, and less to condemn, in that great, extraordinary people than in anything which history affords.

Mr. Burke is so little acquainted with constituent principles of government that he confounds democracy and representation together. Representation was a thing unknown in the ancient democracies. In those the mass of the people met and enacted laws (grammatically speaking) in the first person. Simple democracy was no other than the common hall of the ancients. It signifies the *form* as well as the public principle of the government. As those democracies increased in population, and the territory extended, the simple democratical form became unwieldy and impracticable; and as the system of representation was not known, the consequence was they either degenerated convulsively into monarchies or became absorbed into such as then existed. Had the system of representation been then understood, as it now is, there is no reason to believe that those forms of government now called monarchical or aristocratical would ever have taken place. It was the want of some method to consolidate the parts of society after it became too populous and too expensive for the simple democratical form, and also the lax and solitary condition of shepherds and herdsmen in other parts of the world, that afforded opportunities to those unnatural modes of government to begin.

As it is necessary to clear away the rubbish of errors into which the subject of government has been thrown, I shall proceed to remark on some others.

It has always been the political craft of courtiers and court governments to abuse something which they called republicanism; but what republicanism was or is they never attempt to explain. Let us examine a little into this case.

The only forms of government are the democratical, the aristocratical, the monarchical, and what is now called the representative.

What is called a *republic* is not any *particular form* of government. It is wholly characteristical of the purport, matter, or object for which government ought to be instituted, and on which it is to be employed: RES-PUBLICA, the public affairs, or the public good; or, literally translated, the *public thing*. It is a word of a good original, referring to what ought to be the character and business of government; and in this sense it is naturally opposed to the word *monarchy,* which has a base original signification. It means arbitrary power in an individual person; in the exercise of which, *himself,* and not the *res-publica,* is the object.

Every government that does not act on the principle of a *republic,* or, in other words, that does not make the *res-publica* its whole and sole object, is not a good government. Republican government is no other than government established and conducted for the interest of the public, as well individually as collectively. It is not necessarily connected with any particular form, but it most naturally associates with the representative form, as being best calculated to secure the end for which a nation is at the expense of supporting it.

Various forms of government have affected to style themselves a republic. Poland calls itself a republic which is an hereditary aristocracy, with what is called an elective monarchy. Holland calls itself a republic which is chiefly aristocratical, with a hereditary stadtholdership. But the government of America, which is wholly on the system of representation, is the only real republic, in character and in practice, that now

Demosthenes speaks before the Greek Assembly. Paine wrote: "*Though the ancient governments present to us a miserable picture of the condition of man, there is one which above all others exempts itself from the general description. I mean the democracy of Athenians.*"

exists. Its government has no other object than the public business of the nation, and therefore it is properly a republic; and the Americans have taken care that THIS, and no other, shall always be the object of their government, by their rejecting everything hereditary, and establishing government on the system of representation only.

Those who have said that a republic is not a *form* of government calculated for countries of great extent, mistook, in the first place, the *business* of a government, for a *form* of government; for the *res-publica* equally appertains to every extent of territory and population. And, in the second place, if they meant anything with respect to *form,* it was the simple democratical form, such as was the mode of government in the ancient democracies, in which there was no representation. The case, therefore, is not that a republic cannot be extensive, but that it cannot be extensive on the simple democratical form; and the question naturally presents itself, *what is the best form of government for conducting the* RES-PUBLICA, *or the* PUBLIC BUSINESS *of a nation, after it becomes too extensive and populous for the simple democratical form?*

It cannot be monarchy, because monarchy is subject to an objection of the same amount to which the simple democratical form was subject.

It is possible that an individual may lay down a system of principles, on which government shall be constitutionally established to any extent of territory. This is no more than an operation of the mind, acting by its own powers. But the practice upon those principles, as applying to the various and numerous circumstances of a nation, its agriculture, manufacture, trade, commerce, etc., etc., requires a knowledge of a different kind, and which can be had only from the various parts of society. It is an assemblage of practical knowledge, which no one individual can possess; and therefore the monarchical form is as much limited, in useful practice, from the incompetency of knowledge, as was the democratical

form from the multiplicity of population. The one degenerates, by extension, into confusion; the other into ignorance and incapacity, of which all the great monarchies are an evidence. The monarchical form, therefore, could not be a substitute for the democratical, because it has equal inconveniences.

Much less could it when made hereditary. This is the most effectual of all forms to preclude knowledge. Neither could the high democratical mind have voluntarily yielded itself to be governed by children and idiots, and all the motley insignificance of character which attends such a mere animal system, the disgrace and the reproach of reason and of man.

As to the aristocratical form, it has the same vices and defects with the monarchical, except that the chance of abilities is better from the proportion of numbers, but there is still no security for the right use and application of them.

Referring then to the original simple democracy, it affords the true data from which government on a large scale can begin. It is incapable of extension, not from its principle, but from the inconvenience of its form; and monarchy and aristocracy, from their incapacity. Retaining, then, democracy as the ground, and rejecting the corrupt systems of monarchy and aristocracy, the representative system naturally presents itself; remedying at once the defects of the simple democracy as to form, and the incapacity of the other two with respect to knowledge.

Simple democracy was society governing itself without the aid of secondary means. By ingrafting representation upon democracy, we arrive at a system of government capable of embracing and confederating all the various interests and every extent of territory and population; and that also with advantages as much superior to hereditary government as the republic of letters is to hereditary literature.

It is on this system that the American government is founded. It is representation ingrafted upon democracy. It has fixed the form by a scale parallel in all cases to the extent of the principle. What Athens was in miniature, America will be in magnitude. The one was the wonder of the ancient world; the other is becoming the admiration, the model of the present. It is the easiest of all the forms of government to be understood and the most eligible in practice, and excludes at once the ignorance and insecurity of the hereditary mode, and the inconvenience of the simple democracy.

It is impossible to conceive a system of government capable of acting over such an extent of territory, and such a circle of interests, as is immediately produced by the operation of representation. France, great and populous as it is, is but a spot in the capaciousness of the system. It is preferable to simple democracy even in small territories. Athens, by representation, would have outrivaled her own democracy.

That which is called government, or rather that which we ought to conceive government to be, is no more than some common centre, in which all the parts of society unite. This cannot be accomplished by any method so conducive to the various interests of the community as by the representative system. It concentrates the knowledge necessary to the interest of the parts, and of the whole. It places government in a state of constant maturity. It is, as has already been observed, never young, never old. It is subject neither to nonage nor dotage. It is never in the cradle nor on crutches. It admits not of a separation between knowledge and power, and is superior, as government always ought to be, to all the accidents of individual man, and is therefore superior to what is called monarchy.

A nation is not a body, the figure of which is to be represented by the human body, but is like a body contained within a circle, having a common centre in which every radius meets; and that centre is formed by representation. To connect representation with what is called monarchy is eccentric government. Representation is of itself the delegated monarchy of a nation and cannot debase itself by dividing it with another.

Mr. Burke has two or three times, in his parliamentary speeches, and in his publication, made use of a jingle of words that convey no ideas. Speaking of government, he says: "It is better to have monarchy for its basis, and republicanism for its corrective, than republicanism for its basis, and monarchy for its corrective." If he means that it is better to correct folly with wisdom than wisdom with folly, I will not otherwise contend with him, than that it would be much better to reject the folly entirely.

But what is this thing which Mr. Burke calls monarchy? Will he explain it? All men can understand what representation is; and that it must necessarily include a variety of knowledge and talents. But what security is there for the same qualities on the part of monarchy? Or, when this monarchy is a child, where then is the wisdom? What does it know about government? Who then is the monarch, or where is the monarchy? If it is to be performed by regency, it proves to be a farce. A regency is a mock species of republic, and the whole of monarchy deserves no better description. It is a thing as various as imagination can paint. It has none of the stable character that government ought to possess. Every succession is a revolution, and every regency a counterrevolution. The whole of it is a scene of perpetual court cabal and intrigue, of which Mr. Burke is himself an instance. To render monarchy consistent with government, the next in succession should not be born a child, but a man at once, and that man a Solomon. It is ridiculous that nations are to wait and government be interrupted till boys grow to be men.

Whether I have too little sense to see, or too much to be imposed upon; whether I have too much or too little pride, or of anything else, I leave out of the question; but certain it is that what is called

375

monarchy always appears to me a silly contemptible thing. I compare it to something kept behind a curtain, about which there is a great deal of bustle and fuss, and a wonderful air of seeming solemnity; but when, by an accident, the curtain happens to be opened, and the company see what it is, they burst into laughter.

In the representative system of government, nothing of this can happen. Like the nation itself, it possesses a perpetual stamina, as well of body as of mind, and presents itself on the open theatre of the world in a fair and manly manner. Whatever are its excellencies or defects, they are visible to all. It exists not by fraud and mystery; it deals not in cant and sophistry but inspires a language that, passing from heart to heart, is felt and understood.

We must shut our eyes against reason, we must basely degrade our understanding, not to see the folly of what is called monarchy. Nature is orderly in all her works; but this is a mode of government that counteracts nature. It turns the progress of the human faculties upside down. It subjects age to be governed by children, and wisdom by folly.

On the contrary, the representative system is always parallel with the order and immutable laws of nature, and meets the reason of man in every part. For example—

In the American federal government, more power is delegated to the President of the United States than to any other individual member of Congress. He cannot, therefore, be elected to this office under the age of thirty-five years. By this time the judgment of man becomes matured, and he has lived long enough to be acquainted with man and things, and the country with him. But on the monarchical plan (exclusive of the numerous chances there are against every man born into the world, of drawing a prize in the lottery of human faculties), the next in succession, whatever he may be, is put at the head of a nation, and of a government, at the age of eighteen years. Does this appear like an act of

wisdom? Is it consistent with the proper dignity and manly character of a nation? Where is the propriety of calling such a lad the father of the people? In all other cases, a person is a minor until the age of twenty-one years. Before this period, he is not entrusted with the management of an acre of land, or with the heritable property of a flock of sheep or a herd of swine; but wonderful to tell! he may at the age of eighteen years be trusted with a nation.

That monarchy is all a bubble, a mere court artifice to procure money, is evident (at least to me) in every character in which it can be viewed. It would be impossible, on the rational system of representative government, to make out a bill of expenses to such an enormous amount as this deception admits. Government is not of itself a very chargeable institution. The whole expense of the federal government of America, founded, as I have already said, on the system of representation, and extending over a country nearly ten times as large as England, is but six hundred thousand dollars, or one hundred and thirty-five thousand pounds sterling.

I presume that no man in his sober sense will compare the character of the kings of Europe with that of General Washington. Yet in France, and also in England, the expense of the civil list only, for the support of one man, is eight times greater than the whole expense of the federal government in America. To assign a reason for this appears almost impossible. The generality of the people of America, especially the poor, are more able to pay taxes than the generality of people either in France or England.

But the case is that the representative system diffuses such a body of knowledge throughout a nation, on the subject of government, as to explode ignorance and preclude imposition. The craft of courts cannot be acted on that ground. There is no place for mystery; nowhere for it to begin. Those who are not in the representation know as much of the nature of business as those who are. An affectation of mysterious importance would there be scouted. Nations can have no secrets; and the secrets of courts, like those of individuals, are always their defects.

In the representative system, the reason for everything must publicly appear. Every man is a proprietor in government and considers it a necessary part of his business to understand. It concerns his interest, because it affects his property. He examines the cost and compares it with the advantages; and above all, he does not adopt the slavish custom of following what in other governments are called LEADERS.

It can only be by blinding the understanding of man, and making him believe that government is some wonderful mysterious thing, that excessive revenues are obtained. Monarchy is well calculated to ensure this end. It is the popery of government, a thing kept up to amuse the ignorant and quiet them into taxes.

The government of a free country, properly speaking, is not in the persons, but in the laws. The enacting of those requires no great expense; and when they are administered the whole of civil government is performed—the rest is all court contrivance.

Chapter IV: Of constitutions

That men mean distinct and separate things when they speak of constitutions and of governments is evident; or why are those terms distinctly and separately used? A constitution is not the act of a government, but of a people constituting a government; and government without a constitution is power without a right.

All power exercised over a nation must have some beginning. It must either be delegated or assumed. There are no other sources. All delegated power is trust, and all assumed power is usurpation. Time does not alter the nature and quality of either.

In viewing this subject, the case and circumstances of America present themselves as in the beginning of a world; and our enquiry into the origin of government is shortened by referring to the facts that have arisen in our own day. We have no occasion to roam for information into the obscure field of antiquity nor hazard ourselves upon conjecture. We are brought at once to the point of seeing government begin, as if we had lived in the beginning of time. The real volume, not of history, but of fact, is directly before us, unmutilated by contrivance or the errors of tradition.

I will here concisely state the commencement of the American constitutions: by which the difference between constitutions and governments will sufficiently appear.

It may not be improper to remind the reader that the United States of America consist of thirteen separate states, each of which established a government for itself, after the Declaration of Independence, done the 4th of July, 1776. Each state acted independently of the rest, in forming its government; but the same general principle pervades the whole. When the several state governments were formed, they proceeded to form the federal government that acts over the whole in all matters which concern the interest of the whole, or which relate to the intercourse of the several states with each other, or with foreign nations. I will begin with giving an instance from one of the state governments (that of Pennsylvania) and then proceed to the federal government.

The state of Pennsylvania, though nearly of the same extent of territory as England, was then divided into only twelve counties. Each of these counties had elected a committee at the commencement of the dispute with the English government; and as the city of Philadelphia, which also had its committee, was the most central for intelligence, it became the centre of communication to the several county committees. When it became necessary to proceed to the formation of a government, the committee of Philadelphia proposed a conference of all the committees, to be held in that city, and which met the latter end of July 1776.

Though these committees had been elected by the people, they were not elected expressly for the purpose, nor invested with the authority, of forming a constitution; and as they could not, consistently with the American ideas of right, assume such a power, they could only confer upon the matter and put it into a train of operation. The conferees, therefore, did no more than state the case and recommend to the several counties to elect six representatives for each county, to meet in convention at Philadelphia, with powers to form a constitution and propose it for public consideration.

This convention, of which Benjamin Franklin was president, having met and deliberated, and agreed upon a constitution, they next ordered it to be published, not as a thing established, but for the consideration of the whole people, their approbation or rejection, and then adjourned to a stated time. When the time of adjournment was expired, the convention reassembled, and as the general opinion of the people in approbation of it was then known, the Constitution was signed, sealed, and proclaimed, on the *authority of the people,* and the original instrument deposited as a public record. The convention then appointed a day for the general election of the representatives who were to compose the government, and the time it should commence; and having done this they dissolved and returned to their several homes and occupations.

In this Constitution were laid down, first, a declaration of rights; then followed the form which the government should have, and the powers which it should possess— the authority of the courts of judicature and of juries—the manner in which elections should be conducted, and the proportion of representatives to the number of electors—the time which each succeeding assembly should continue, which was one year—the mode of levying, and the accounting for the expenditure, of public money—of appointing public officers, etc., etc.

No article of this Constitution could be altered or infringed at the discretion of the government that was to ensue. It was to the government a law. But as it would have been unwise to preclude the benefit of experience, and in order also to prevent the accumulation of errors, if any should be found, and to preserve a unison of government with the circumstances of the state to all times, the Constitution provided that at the expiration of every seven years, a convention should be elected for the express purpose of revising the Constitution and making alterations, additions, or abolitions therein, if any such should be found necessary.

Here we see a regular process—a government issuing out of a Constitution, formed by the people in their original character; and that Constitution serving not only as an authority, but as a law of control to the government. It was the political Bible of the state. Scarcely a family was without it. Every member of the government had a copy; and nothing was more common when any debate arose on the principle of a bill, or on the extent of any species of authority, than for the members to take the printed Constitution out of their pocket and read the chapter with which such matter in debate was connected.

Having thus given an instance from one of the states, I will show the proceedings by which the federal Constitution of the United States arose and was formed.

Congress, at its first two meetings, in September 1774, and May 1775, was nothing more than a deputation from the legislatures of the several provinces, afterward states; and had no other authority than what arose from common consent, and the necessity of its acting as a public body. In everything which related to the internal affairs of America, Congress went no further than to issue recommendations to

From left to right: Benjamin Franklin, Thomas Jefferson, William Livingston, Samuel Adams, and Roger Sherman drafting the Declaration of Independence. *"After the Declaration of Independence . . . each state acted independently of the rest, in forming its government; but the same general principle pervades the whole."*

the several provincial assemblies, who at discretion adopted them or not. Nothing on the part of Congress was compulsive; yet in this situation, it was more faithfully and affectionately obeyed than was any government in Europe. This instance, like that of the National Assembly of France, sufficiently shows that the strength of government does not consist of anything *within* itself, but in the attachment of a nation, and the interest which the people feel in supporting it. When this is lost government is but a child in power, and though like the old government of France it may harass individuals for a while, it but facilitates its own fall.

After the Declaration of Independence it became consistent with the principle on which representative government is founded that the authority of Congress should be defined and established. Whether that authority should be more or less than Congress then discretionarily exercised, was not the question. It was merely the rectitude of the measure.

For this purpose, the act called the Act of Confederation (which was a sort of imperfect federal constitution) was proposed, and after long deliberation was concluded in the year 1781. It was not the Act of Congress, because it is repugnant to the principles of representative government that a body should give power to itself. Congress first informed the several states of the powers which it conceived were necessary to be invested in the union, to enable it to perform the duties and services required from it; and the states severally agreed with each other and concentrated in Congress those powers.

It may not be improper to observe that in both those instances (the one of Pennsylvania, and the other of the United States) there is no such thing as an idea of a compact between the people on one side and the government on the other. The compact was that of the people with each other to produce and constitute a government. To suppose that any government can be a party in a compact with the whole people is to suppose it to have existence before it can have a right to exist. The only instance in which a compact can take place between the people and those who exercise the government is that the people shall pay them while they choose to employ them.

Government is not a trade which any man, or any body of men, has a right to set up and exercise for his own emolument but is altogether a trust in right of those by whom the trust is delegated, and by whom it is always resumable. It has of itself no rights; they are altogether duties.

Having thus given two instances of the original formation of a constitution, I will show the manner in which both have been changed since their first establishment.

The powers vested in the governments of the several states, by the state Constitutions, were found upon experience to be too great, and those vested in the federal government by the Act of Confederation, too little. The defect was not in the principle but in the distribution of power.

Numerous publications, in pamphlets and in newspapers, appeared on the propriety and necessity of new modeling the federal government. After some time of public discussion, carried on through the channel of the press, and in conversations, the state of Virginia, experiencing some inconvenience with respect to commerce, proposed holding a continental conference; in consequence of which, a deputation from five or six of the state assemblies met at Annapolis, Maryland, in 1786. This meeting, not conceiving itself sufficiently authorized to go into business of a reform, did no more than state their general opinions of the propriety of the measure and recommend that a convention of all the states should be held the year following.

The convention met at Philadelphia in May 1787, of which General Washington was elected President. He was not at that time connected with any of the state governments, or with Congress. He delivered up his commission when the war ended and since then had lived a private citizen.

The convention went deeply into all the subjects; and having, after a variety of debate and investigation, agreed among themselves upon the several parts of a federal constitution, the next question was, the manner of giving it authority and practice.

For this purpose they did not, like a cabal of courtiers, send for a Dutch stadtholder, or a German elector; but they referred the whole matter to the sense and interests of the country.

They first directed that the proposed Constitution should be published. Second, that each state should elect a convention expressly for the purpose of taking it into consideration, and of ratifying or rejecting it; and that as soon as the approbation and ratification of any nine states should be given, that those states should proceed to the election of their proportion of members to the new federal government; and that the operation of it should then begin, and the federal government cease.

The several states proceeded accordingly to elect their conventions. Some of those conventions ratified the Constitution by very large majorities, and two or three unanimously. In others there were much debate and division of opinion. In the Massachusetts convention, which met at Boston, the majority was not above nineteen or twenty in about three hundred members; but such is the nature of representative government, that it quietly decides all matters by majority. After the debate in the Massachusetts convention was closed, and the vote taken, the objecting members rose and declared: *"That though they had argued and voted against it because certain parts appeared to them in a different light to what they appeared to other members; yet, as the vote had decided in favour of the Constitution as proposed, they should give it the same practical support as if they had voted for it."*

As soon as nine states had concurred (and the rest followed in the order their conventions were elected), the old fabric of the federal government was taken down, and the new erected, of which General Washington is President. In this place I cannot help remarking that the character and services of this gentleman are sufficient to put all those men called kings to shame. While they are receiving from the sweat and labours of mankind a prodigality of pay, to which neither their abilities nor their services can entitle them, he is rendering every service in his power and refusing every pecuniary reward. He accepted no pay as commander-in-chief; he accepts none as President of the United States.

After the new federal Constitution was established, the state of Pennsylvania, conceiving that some parts of its own Constitution required to be altered, elected a convention for that purpose. The proposed alterations were published, and the people concurring therein, they were established.

In forming those constitutions, or in altering them, little or no inconvenience took place. The ordinary course of things was not interrupted, and the advantages have been much. It is always the interest of a far greater number of people in a nation to have things right than to let them remain wrong; and when public matters are open to debate, and the public judgment free, it will not decide wrong, unless it decides too hastily.

In the two instances of changing the constitutions, the governments then in being were not actors either way. Government has no right to make itself a party in any debate respecting the principles or modes of forming, or of changing, constitutions. It is not for the benefit of those who exercise the powers of government that constitutions, and the governments issuing from them, are established. In all those matters the right of judging and acting are in those who pay, and not in those who receive.

A constitution is the property of a nation, and not of those who exercise the government. All the constitutions of America are declared to be established on the authority of the people. In France, the word *nation* is used instead of *the people;* but in both cases a constitution is a thing antecedent to the government and always distinct therefrom.

In England it is not difficult to perceive that everything has a constitution, except the nation. Every society and association that is established first agreed upon a number of original articles, digested into form, which are its constitution. It then appointed its officers, whose powers and authorities are described in that constitution, and the government of that society then commenced. Those officers, by whatever name they are called, have no authority to add to, alter, or abridge the original articles. It is only to the constituting power that this right belongs.

From the want of understanding the difference between a constitution and a government, Dr. Johnson and all writers of his description have always bewildered themselves. They could not but perceive that there must necessarily be a *controlling* power existing somewhere, and they placed this in the discretion of the persons exercising the government, instead of placing it in a constitution formed by the nation. When it is in a constitution it has the nation for its support, and the natural and the political controlling powers are together. The laws which are enacted by governments control men only as individuals, but the nation, through its constitution, controls the whole government and has a natural ability so to do. The final controlling power, therefore, and the original constituting power are one and the same power.

Dr. Johnson could not have advanced such a position in any country where there was a constitution; and he is himself an evidence that no such thing as a constitution exists in England. But it may be put as a question, not improper to be investigated, that if a constitution does not exist how came the idea of its existence so generally established.

In order to decide this question, it is necessary to consider a constitution in both its cases: First, as creating a government and giving it powers. Second, as regulating and restraining the powers so given.

If we begin with William of Normandy, we find that the government of England was originally a tyranny, founded on an invasion and conquest of the country. This being admitted, it will then appear that the exertion of the nation at different periods to abate that tyranny and render it less intolerable has been credited for a constitution.

Magna Carta, as it was called (it is now like an almanac of the same date), was no more than compelling the government to renounce a part of its assumptions. It did not create and give powers to government in the manner a constitution does; but was, as far as it went, of the nature of a re-conquest, and not a constitution; for could the nation have totally expelled the usurpation as France has done its despotism, it would then have had a constitution to form.

The history of the Edwards and the Henries, and up to the commencement of the Stuarts, exhibits as many instances of tyranny as could be acted within the limits to which the nation had restricted it. The Stuarts endeavoured to pass those limits, and their fate is well known. In all those instances we see nothing of a constitution, but only of restrictions on assumed power.

After this, another William, descended from the same stock, and claiming from the same origin, gained possession; and of the two evils, *James* and *William,* the nation preferred what it thought the least; since, from circumstances, it must take one. The act, called the Bill of Rights, comes here into view. What is it but a bargain which the parts of the government made with each other, to divide powers, profits, and privileges? You shall have so much, and I will have the rest; and with respect to the nation, it said, for *your share* YOU *shall have the right of petitioning.* This being the case, the Bill of Rights is more properly the bill of wrongs and of insult. As to what is called the convention Parliament, it was a thing that made itself and then made the authority by which it acted. A few persons got together and called themselves by that name. Several of them had never been elected, and none of them for the purpose.

From the time of William a species of government arose, issuing out of this coalition Bill of Rights; and more so since the corruption introduced at the Hanover succession, by the agency of Walpole, that can be described by no other name than a despotic legislation. Though the parts may embarrass each other, the whole has no bounds; and the only right it acknowledges out of itself is the right of petitioning. Where then is the constitution that either gives or restrains power?

It is not because a part of the government is elective, that makes it less a despotism, if the persons so elected possess afterward, as a Parliament, unlimited powers. Election in this case becomes separated from representation, and the candidates are candidates for despotism.

I cannot believe that any nation, reasoning on its own right, would have thought of calling those things a *constitution,* if the cry of constitution had not been set up by the government. It has got into circulation like the words *bore* and *quiz,* by being chalked up in the speeches of Parliament, as those words were on window shutters and doorposts; but whatever the constitution may be in other respects, it has undoubtedly been *the most productive machine of taxation that was ever invented.* The taxes in France, under the new Constitution, are not quite thirteen shillings per head, and the taxes in England, under what is called its present Constitution, are forty-eight shillings and sixpence per head—men, women, and children—amounting to nearly seventeen millions sterling, besides the expense of collecting, which is upwards of a million more.

In a country like England, where the whole of the civil government is executed by the people of every town and county by means of parish officers, magistrates, quarterly sessions, juries, and assize, without any trouble to what is called the government or any other expense to the revenue than the salary of the judges, it is astonishing how such a mass of taxes can be employed. Not even the internal defense of the country is paid out of the revenue. On all occasions, whether real or contrived, recourse is continually had to new loans and new taxes. No wonder, then, that a machine of government so advantageous to the advocates of a court should be so triumphantly extolled. No wonder, that St. James's or St. Stephen's should echo with the continual cry of Constitution! No wonder that the French Revolution should be reprobated, and the *res-publica* treated with reproach! The *red book* of England, like the red book of France, will explain the reason.

I will now, by way of relaxation, turn a thought or two to Mr. Burke. I ask his pardon for neglecting him so long.

"America," says he (in his speech on the Canada Constitution Bill), "never dreamed of such absurd doctrine as the *Rights of Man.*"

Mr. Burke is such a bold presumer, and advances his assertions and his premises with such a deficiency of judgment, that without troubling ourselves about the principles of philosophy or politics, the mere logical conclusions they produce are ridiculous. For instance:

If governments, as Mr. Burke asserts, are not founded on the Rights of MAN, and are founded on *any rights* at all, they consequently must be founded on the right of *something* that is *not man.* What then is that something?

Generally speaking, we know of no other creatures that inhabit the earth than man and beast; and in all cases where only two things offer themselves, and one must be admitted, a negation proved on any one amounts to an affirmative on the other;

and therefore, Mr. Burke, by proving against the Rights of *Man* proves in behalf of the *beast;* and consequently, proves that government is a beast; and as difficult things sometimes explain each other, we now see the origin of keeping wild beasts in the Tower; for they certainly can be of no other use than to show the origin of the government. They are in the place of a constitution. O, John Bull, what honours thou has lost by not being a wild beast. Thou mightest, on Mr. Burke's system, have been in the Tower for life.

If Mr. Burke's arguments have not weight enough to keep one serious, the fault is less mine than his; and as I am willing to make an apology to the reader for the liberty I have taken, I hope Mr. Burke will also make his for giving the cause.

Having thus paid Mr. Burke the compliment of remembering him, I return to the subject.

From the want of a constitution in England to restrain and regulate the wild impulse of power, many of the laws are irrational and tyrannical, and the administration of them vague and problematical.

The attention of the government of England (for I rather choose to call it by this name than the English government) appears since its political connection with Germany to have been so completely engrossed and absorbed by foreign affairs, and the means of raising taxes, that it seems to exist for no other purposes. Domestic concerns are neglected; and with respect to regular law there is scarcely such a thing.

Almost every case now must be determined by some precedent, be that precedent good or bad, or whether it properly applies or not; and the practice is become so general as to suggest a suspicion that it proceeds from a deeper policy than at first sight appears.

Since the Revolution of America, and more so since that of France, this preaching up the doctrines of precedents, drawn from times and circumstances antecedent to those events, has been the studied practice of the English government. The generality of those precedents are founded on principles and opinions, the reverse of what they ought; and the greater distance of time they are drawn from the more they are to be suspected. But by associating those precedents with a superstitious reverence for ancient things, as monks show relics and call them holy, the generality of mankind are deceived into the design. Governments now act as if they were afraid to awaken a single reflection in man. They are softly leading him to the sepulchre of precedents to deaden his faculties and call attention from the scene of revolutions. They feel that he is arriving at knowledge faster than they wish, and their policy of precedent is the barometer of their fears. This political popery, like the ecclesiastical popery of old, has had its day and is hastening to its exit. The ragged relic and the antiquated precedent, the monk and the monarch, will moulder together.

Government by precedent, without any regard to the principle of the precedent, is one of the vilest systems that can be set up. In numerous instances the precedent ought to operate as a warning, and not as an example, and requires to be shunned instead of imitated; but instead of this, precedents are taken in the lump, and put at once for constitution and for law.

Either the doctrine of precedents is policy to keep man in a state of ignorance, or it is a practical confession that wisdom degenerates in governments as governments increase in age and can only hobble along by the stilts and crutches of precedents. How is it that the same persons who would proudly be thought wiser than their predecessors appear at the same time only as the ghosts of departed wisdom? How strangely is antiquity treated! To answer some purposes it is spoken of as the times of darkness and ignorance, and to answer others, it is put for the light of the world.

If the doctrine of precedents is to be followed, the expenses of government need not continue the same. Why pay men extravagantly who have but little to do? If everything that can happen is already in precedent, legislation is at an end, and precedent, like a dictionary, determines every case. Either, therefore, government has arrived at its dotage, and requires to be renovated, or all the occasions for exercising its wisdom have already occurred.

We now see all over Europe, and particularly in England, the curious phenomenon of a nation looking one way, and the government the other—the one forward and the other backward. If governments are to go on by precedent, while nations go on by improvement, they must at last come to a final separation; and the sooner, and the more civilly they determine this point, the better.

Having thus spoken of constitutions generally, as things distinct from actual governments, let us proceed to consider the parts of which a constitution is composed.

Opinions differ more on this subject than with respect to the whole. That a nation ought to have a constitution, as a rule, for the conduct of its government is a simple question in which all men not directly courtiers will agree. It is only on the component parts that questions and opinions multiply.

But this difficulty, like every other, will diminish when put into a train of being rightly understood.

The first thing is that a nation has a right to establish a constitution.

Whether it exercises this right in the most judicious manner at first is quite another case. It exercises it agreeably to the judgment it possesses; and by continuing to do so, all errors will at last be exploded.

When this right is established in a nation, there is no fear that it will be employed to its own injury. A nation can have no interest in being wrong.

Though all the constitutions of America are on one general principle, yet no two of them are exactly alike in their component parts or in the distribution of the powers which they give to the actual governments. Some are more, and others less complex.

In forming a constitution, it is first necessary to consider what are the ends for which government is necessary? Second, what are the best means, and the least expensive, for accomplishing those ends?

Government is nothing more than a national association; and the object of this association is the good of all, as well individually as collectively. Every man wishes to pursue his occupation, and to enjoy the fruits of his labours and the produce of his property in peace and safety, and with the least possible expense. When these things are accomplished, all the objects for which government ought to be established are answered.

It has been customary to consider government under three distinct general heads: the legislative, the executive, and the judicial.

But if we permit our judgment to act unencumbered by the habit of multiplied terms, we can perceive no more than two divisions of power, of which civil government is composed, namely that of legislating or enacting laws, and that of executing or administering them. Everything, therefore, appertaining to civil government, classes itself under one or other of these two divisions.

So far as regards the execution of the laws, that which is called the judicial power is strictly and properly the executive power of every country. It is that power to which every individual has to appeal, and which causes the law to be executed; neither have we any other clear idea with respect to the official execution of the laws. In England, and also in America and France, this power begins with the magistrate and proceeds up through all the courts of judicature.

I leave to courtiers to explain what is meant by calling monarchy the executive power. It is merely a name in which acts of government are done; and any other, or none at all, would answer the same purpose. Laws have neither more or less authority on this account. It must be from the justness of their principles, and the interest which a nation feels therein, that they derive support; if they require any other than this, it is a sign that something in the system of government is imperfect. Laws difficult to be executed cannot be generally good.

With respect to the organization of the *legislative power,* different modes have been adopted in different countries. In America it is generally composed of two houses. In France it consists but of one, but in both countries it is wholly by representation.

The case is that mankind (from the long tyranny of assumed power) have had so few opportunities of making the necessary trials on modes and principles of government, in order to discover the best, *that government is but now beginning to be known,* and experience is yet wanting to determine many particulars.

The objections against two houses are, first, that there is an inconsistency in any part of a whole legislature, coming to a final determination by vote on any matter, while *that matter,* with respect to *that whole,* is yet only in a train of deliberation, and consequently open to new illustrations.

Second. That by taking a vote on each, as a separate body, it always admits of the possibility, and is often the case in practice, that the minority governs the majority, and that in some instances to a degree of great inconsistency.

Third. That two houses arbitrarily checking or controlling each other is inconsistent; because it cannot be proved on the principles of just representation that either should be wiser or better than the other. They may check in the wrong as well as in the right—and therefore to give the power where we cannot give the wisdom to use it, nor be assured of its being rightly used, renders the hazard at least equal to the precaution.

The objection against a single house is that it is always in a condition of committing itself too soon. But it should at the same time be remembered that when there is a constitution which defines the power, and establishes the principles within which a legislature shall act, there is already a more effectual check provided, and more powerfully operating, than any other check can be. For example:

Were a bill to be brought into any of the American legislatures similar to that which was passed into an act by the English Parliament, at the commencement of George the First, to extend the duration of the assemblies to a longer period than they now sit, the check is in the Constitution, which in effect says, *Thus far shalt thou go and no further.*

But in order to remove the objection against a single house, that of acting with too quick an impulse, and at the same time to avoid the inconsistencies, in some cases absurdities, arising from two houses, the following method has been proposed as an improvement upon both.

First, to have but one representation.

Second, to divide that representation, by lot, into two or three parts.

Third, that every proposed bill shall be first debated in those parts by succession, that they may become the hearers of each other, but without taking any vote. After which the whole representation to assemble for a general debate and determination by vote.

To this proposed improvement has been added another, for the purpose of keeping the representation in the state of constant renovation; which is that one-third of the representation of each country shall go out at the expiration of one year, and the number be replaced by new elections. Another third at the expiration of the second year replaced in like manner, and every third year to be a general election.

But in whatever manner the separate parts of a constitution may be arranged, there is *one* general principle that distinguishes freedom from slavery, which is, *that all hereditary* government over a people is to them a species of slavery, and representative government is freedom.

Considering government in the only light in which it should be considered, that of a NATIONAL ASSOCIATION, it ought to be so constructed as not to be disordered by any accident happening among the parts; and, therefore, no extraordinary power, capable of producing such an effect, should be lodged in the hands of any individual. The death, sickness, absence, or defection of any one individual in a government ought to be a matter of no more consequence, with respect to the nation, than if the same circumstances had taken place in a member of the English Parliament, or the French National Assembly.

Scarcely anything presents a more degrading character of national greatness than its being thrown into confusion, by anything happening to or acted by any individual; and the ridiculousness of the scene is often increased by the natural insignificance of the person by whom it is occasioned. Were a government so constructed that it could not go on unless a goose or a gander were present in the senate, the difficulties would be just as great and as real, on the flight or sickness of the goose, or the gander, as if it were called a king. We laugh at individuals for the silly difficulties they make to themselves, without perceiving that the greatest of all ridiculous things are acted in governments.

All the constitutions of America are on a plan that excludes the childish embarrassments which occur in monarchical countries. No suspension of government can there take place for a moment, from any circumstances whatever. The system of representation provides for everything and is the only system in which nations and governments can always appear in their proper character.

As extraordinary power ought not to be lodged in the hands of any individual, so ought there to be no appropriations of public money to any person, beyond what his services in a state may be worth. It signifies not whether a man be called a president, a king, an emperor, a senator, or by any other name which propriety or folly may devise or arrogance assume, it is only a certain service he can perform in the state; and the service of any such individual in the routine of office, whether such office be called monarchical, presidential, senatorial, or by any other name or title, can never exceed the value of ten thousand pounds a year. All the great services that are done in the world are performed by volunteer characters, who accept nothing for them; but the routine of office is always regulated to such a general standard of abilities as to be within the compass of numbers in every country to perform, and therefore cannot merit very extraordinary recompence. *Government*, says Swift, *is a plain thing, and fitted to the capacity of many heads.*

It is inhuman to talk of a million sterling a year, paid out of the public taxes of any country, for the support of an individual, while thousands who are forced to contribute thereto are pining with want and struggling with misery. Government does not consist in a contrast between prisons and palaces, between poverty and pomp; it is not instituted to rob the needy of his mite and increase the wretchedness of the wretched. But of this part of the subject I shall speak hereafter and confine myself at present to political observations.

When extraordinary power and extraordinary pay are allotted to any individual in a government, he becomes the centre, round which every kind of corruption generates and forms. Give to any man a million a year, and add thereto the power of creating and disposing of places, at the expense of a country, and the liberties of that country are no longer secure. What is called the splendour of a throne is no other than the corruption of the state. It is made up of a band of parasites living in luxurious indolence out of the public taxes.

When once such a vicious system is established it becomes the guard and protection of all inferior abuses. The man who is in the receipt of a million a year is the last person to promote a spirit of reform, lest, in the event, it should reach to himself. It is always his interest to defend inferior abuses, as do many outworks to protect the citadel; and on this species of political fortification, all the parts have such a common dependence that it is never to be expected that they will attack each other.

Monarchy would not have continued so many ages in the world had it not been for the abuses it protects. It is the master fraud, which shelters all others. By admitting a participation of the spoil, it makes itself friends; and when it ceases to do this it will cease to be the idol of courtiers.

As the principle on which constitutions are now formed rejects all hereditary pretensions to government, it also rejects all that catalogue of assumptions known by the name of prerogatives.

If there is any government where prerogatives might with apparent safety be entrusted to any individual, it is in the federal government of America. The President of the United States of America is elected only for four years. He is not only responsible in the general sense of the word, but a particular mode is laid down in the Constitution for trying him. He cannot be elected under thirty-five years of age; and he must be a native of the country.

In a comparison of these cases with the government of England, the difference when applied to the latter amounts to an absurdity. In England the person who exercises prerogative is often a foreigner; always half a foreigner, and always married to a foreigner. He is never in full natural or political connection with the country, is not responsible for anything, and becomes of age at eighteen years; yet such a person is permitted to form foreign alliances, without even the knowledge of the nation, and

to make war and peace without its consent.

But this is not all. Though such a person cannot dispose of the government in the manner of a testator, he dictates the marriage connections, which, in effect, accomplish a great part of the same end. He cannot directly bequeath half the government to Prussia, but he can form a marriage partnership that will produce the same thing. Under such circumstances, it is happy for England that she is not situated on the Continent, or she might, like Holland, fall under the dictatorship of Prussia. Holland, by marriage, is as effectually governed by Prussia as if the whole tyranny of bequeathing the government had been the means.

The presidency in America (or, as it is sometimes called, the executive) is the only office from which a foreigner is excluded, and in England it is the only one to which he is admitted. A foreigner cannot be a member of Parliament, but he may be what is called a king. If there is any reason for excluding foreigners, it ought to be from those offices where mischief can be most acted, and where, by uniting every bias of interest and attachment, the trust is best secured. But as nations proceed in the great business of forming constitutions, they will examine with more precision into the nature and business of that department which is called executive. What the legislative and judicial departments are everyone can see; but with respect to what, in Europe, is called the executive, as distinct from these two, it is either a political superfluity or a chaos of unknown things.

Some kind of official department, to which reports shall be made from the different parts of a nation, or from abroad, to be laid before the national representatives, is all that is necessary; but there is no consistency in calling this the executive; neither can it be considered in any other light than as inferior to the legislative. The sovereign authority in any country is the power of making laws, and everything else is an official department.

Next to the arrangement of the principles and the organization of the several parts of a constitution is the provision to be made for the support of the persons to whom the nation shall confide the administration of the constitutional powers.

A nation can have no right to the time and services of any person at his own expense, whom it may choose to employ or entrust in any department whatever; neither can any reason be given for making provision for the support of any one part of a government and not for the other.

But admitting that the honour of being entrusted with any part of a government is to be considered a sufficient reward, it ought to be so to every person alike. If the members of the legislature of any country are to serve at their own expense, that which is called the executive, whether monarchical or by any other name, ought to serve in like manner. It is inconsistent to pay the one and accept the service of the other gratis.

In America, every department in the government is decently provided for; but no one is extravagantly paid. Every member of Congress, and of the assemblies, is allowed a sufficiency for his expenses. Whereas in England, a most prodigal provision is made for the support of one part of the government and none for the other, the consequence of which is that the one is furnished with the means of corruption and the other is put into the condition of being corrupted. Less than a fourth part of such expense, applied as it is in America, would remedy a great part of the corruption.

Another reform in the American constitutions is the exploding of all oaths of personality. The oath of allegiance in America is to the nation only. The putting any individual as a figure for a nation is improper. The happiness of a nation is the superior object, and therefore the intention of an oath of allegiance ought not to be obscured by being figuratively taken to, or in the name of, any person. The oath, called the civic oath, in France, viz., the *"Nation, the Law, and the King,"* is improper. If taken at all, it ought to be as in America, to the nation only. The law may or may not be good; but in this place it can have no other meaning than as being conducive to the happiness of the nation and therefore is included in it. The remainder of the oath is improper on the ground that all personal oaths ought to be abolished. They are the remains of tyranny on one part and slavery on the other; and the name of the CREATOR ought not to be introduced to witness the degradation of his creation; or if taken, as is already mentioned, as figurative of the nation, it is in this place redundant. But whatever apology may be made for oaths at the first establishment of a government, they ought not to be permitted afterward. If a government requires the support of oaths, it is a sign that it is not worth supporting and ought not to be supported. Make government what it ought to be, and it will support itself.

To conclude this part of the subject— One of the greatest improvements that has been made for the perpetual security and progress of constitutional liberty is the provision which the new constitutions make for occasionally revising, altering, and amending them.

The principle upon which Mr. Burke formed his political creed, that of *binding and controlling posterity to the end of time, and of renouncing and abdicating the rights of all posterity for ever,* is now become too detestable to be made a subject of debate; and therefore I pass it over with no other notice than exposing it.

Government is but now beginning to be known. Hitherto it has been the mere exercise of power which forbade all effectual enquiry into rights and grounded itself wholly on possession. While the enemy of liberty was its judge, the progress of its principles must have been small indeed.

The constitutions of America, and also that of France, have either affixed a period for their revision or laid down the mode by which improvement shall be made. It is perhaps impossible to establish anything that combines principles with opinions and practice, which the progress of circumstances, through a length of years, will not in some measure derange, or render inconsistent; and, therefore, to prevent inconveniences accumulating, till they discourage reformations or provoke revolutions, it is best to provide the means of regulating them as they occur. The Rights of Man are the rights of all generations of men and cannot be monopolized by any. That which is worth following will be followed for the sake of its worth, and it is in this that its security lies, and not in any conditions with which it may be encumbered. When a man leaves property to his heirs, he does not connect it with an obligation that they shall accept it. Why, then, should we do otherwise with respect to constitutions?

The best constitution that could now be devised, consistent with the condition of the present moment, may be far short of that excellence which a few years may afford. There is a morning of reason rising upon man on the subject of government that has not appeared before. As the barbarism of the present old governments expires, the moral condition of nations with respect to each other will be changed. Man will not be brought up with the savage idea of considering his species as his enemy, because the accident of birth gave the individuals existence in countries distinguished by different names; and as constitutions have always some relation to external as well as to domestic circumstances, the means of benefiting by every change, foreign or domestic, should be a part of every constitution.

We already see an alteration in the national disposition of England and France toward each other, which, when we look back to only a few years, is itself a revolution. Who could have foreseen, or who would have believed, that a French National Assembly would ever have been a popular toast in England, or that a friendly alliance of the two nations should become

the wish of either? It shows that man, were he not corrupted by governments, is naturally the friend of man, and that human nature is not of itself vicious. That spirit of jealousy and ferocity, which the governments of the two countries inspired, and which they rendered subservient to the purpose of taxation, is now yielding to the dictates of reason, interest, and humanity. The trade of courts is beginning to be understood, and the affectation of mystery, with all the artificial sorcery by which they imposed upon mankind, is on the decline. It has received its death wound; and though it may linger, it will expire.

Government ought to be as much open to improvement as anything which appertains to man, instead of which it has been monopolized from age to age, by the most ignorant and vicious of the human race. Need we any other proof of their wretched management than the excess of debts and taxes with which every nation groans, and the quarrels into which they have precipitated the world?

Just emerging from such a barbarous condition, it is too soon to determine to what extent of improvement government may yet be carried. For what we can foresee, all Europe may form but one great republic, and man be free of the whole.

Chapter V: Ways and means of improving the condition of Europe, interspersed with miscellaneous observations

In contemplating a subject that embraces with equatorial magnitude the whole region of humanity it is impossible to confine the pursuit in one single direction. It takes ground on every character and condition that appertains to man and blends the individual, the nation, and the world.

From a small spark, kindled in America, a flame has arisen not to be extinguished. Without consuming, like the *ultima ratio regum,* it winds its progress from nation to nation and conquers by a silent operation.

Man finds himself changed, he scarcely perceives how. He acquires a knowledge of his rights by attending justly to his interest and discovers in the event that the strength and powers of despotism consist wholly in the fear of resisting it, and that in order *"to be free it is sufficient that he wills it."*

Having in all the preceding parts of this work endeavoured to establish a system of principles as a basis on which governments ought to be erected, I shall proceed in this to the ways and means of rendering them into practice. But in order to introduce this part of the subject with more propriety and stronger effect, some preliminary observations, deducible from, or connected with those principles, are necessary.

Whatever the form or constitution of government may be, it ought to have no other object than the *general* happiness. When instead of this it operates to create and increase wretchedness, in any of the parts of society, it is on a wrong system and reformation is necessary.

Customary language has classed the condition of man under the two descriptions of civilized and uncivilized life. To the one it has ascribed felicity and affluence: to the other hardship and want. But, however our imagination may be impressed by painting and comparison, it is nevertheless true that a great portion of mankind, in what are called civilized countries, are in a state of poverty and wretchedness, far below the condition of an Indian. I speak not of one country, but of all. It is so in England, it is so all over Europe. Let us enquire into the cause.

It lies not in any natural defect in the principles of civilization, but in preventing those principles having a universal operation; the consequence of which is a perpetual system of war and expense, that drains the country and defeats the general felicity of which civilization is capable.

All the European governments (France now excepted) are constructed not on the principle of universal civilization, but on the reverse of it. So far as those governments relate to each other they are in the same condition as we conceive of savage uncivilized life, they put themselves beyond the law as well of GOD as of man and are with respect to principle and reciprocal conduct like so many individuals in a state of nature.

The inhabitants of every country, under the civilization of laws, easily civilize together, but governments being yet in an uncivilized state, and almost continually at war, they pervert the abundance which civilized life produces to carry on the uncivilized part to a greater extent. By thus engrafting the barbarism of government upon the internal civilization of a country, it draws from the latter, and more especially from the poor, a great portion of those earnings which should be applied to their own subsistence and comfort. Apart from all reflections of morality and philosophy, it is a melancholy fact that more than one-fourth of the labour of mankind is annually consumed by this barbarous system.

What has served to continue this evil is the pecuniary advantage which all the governments of Europe have found in keeping up this state of uncivilization. It affords to them pretenses for power and revenue, for which there would be neither occasion nor apology if the circle of civilization were rendered complete. Civil government alone, or the government of laws, is not productive of pretenses for many taxes; it operates at home, directly under the eye of the country, and precludes the possibility of much imposition. But when the scene is laid in the uncivilized contention of governments, the field of pretenses is enlarged, and the country, being no longer a judge, is open to every imposition which governments please to act.

Not a thirtieth, scarcely a fortieth, part of the taxes which are raised in England are either occasioned by, or applied to, the purposes of civil government. It is not difficult to see that the whole which the actual government does in this respect is to enact laws, and that the country administers

391

and executes them, at its own expense, by means of magistrates, juries, sessions, and assize, over and above the taxes which it pays.

In this view of the case, we have two distinct characters of government; the one the civil government, or the government of laws, which operates at home, the other the court or Cabinet government, which operates abroad, on the rude plan of uncivilized life; the one attended with little charge, the other with boundless extravagance; and so distinct are the two, that if the latter were to sink, as it were, by a sudden opening of the earth, and totally disappear, the former would not be deranged. It would still proceed, because it is the common interest of the nation that it should, and all the means are in practice.

Revolutions, then, have for their object a change in the moral condition of governments, and with this change the burden of public taxes will lessen, and civilization will be left to the enjoyment of that abundance of which it is now deprived.

In contemplating the whole of this subject, I extend my views into the department of commerce. In all my publications, where the matter would admit, I have been an advocate for commerce, because I am a friend to its effects. It is a pacific system, operating to cordialize mankind, by rendering nations, as well as individuals, useful to each other. As to the mere theoretical reformation, I have never preached it up. The most effectual process is that of improving the condition of man by means of his interest; and it is on this ground that I take my stand.

If commerce were permitted to act to the universal extent it is capable, it would extirpate the system of war and produce a revolution in the uncivilized state of governments. The invention of commerce has arisen since those governments began, and it is the greatest approach toward universal civilization that has yet been made by any means not immediately flowing from moral principles.

Whatever has a tendency to promote the civil intercourse of nations by an exchange of benefits is a subject as worthy of philosophy as of politics. Commerce is no other than the traffic of two individuals, multiplied on a scale of number; and the same rule that Nature intended the intercourse of two, she intended for all. For this purpose she has distributed the materials of manufactures and commerce in various and distant parts of a nation and of the world; and as they cannot be procured by war so cheaply or so commodiously as by commerce, she has rendered the latter the means of extirpating the former.

As the two are nearly the opposites of each other, consequently, the uncivilized state of the European governments is injurious to commerce. Every kind of destruction or embarrassment serves to lessen the quantity, and it matters but little in what part of the commercial world the reduction begins. Like blood, it cannot be taken from any of the parts, without being taken from the whole mass in circulation, and all partake of the loss. When the ability in any nation to buy is destroyed, it equally involves the seller. Could the government of England destroy the commerce of all other nations, she would most effectually ruin her own.

It is possible that a nation may be the carrier for the world, but she cannot be the merchant. She cannot be the seller and buyer of her own merchandise. The ability to buy must reside out of herself; and, therefore, the prosperity of any commercial nation is regulated by the prosperity of the rest. If they are poor she cannot be rich, and her condition, be it what it may, is an index of the height of the commercial tide in other nations.

That the principles of commerce, and its universal operation, may be understood, without understanding the practice, is a position that reason will not deny; and it is on this ground only that I argue the subject. It is one thing in the countinghouse, in the world it is another. With respect to its operation it must necessarily be contemplated as a reciprocal thing; that only one-half of its power resides within the nation, and that the whole is as effectually destroyed by destroying the half that resides without, as if the destruction had been committed on that which is within; for neither can act without the other.

When in the last, as well as in the former wars, the commerce of England sunk, it was because the general quantity was lessened everywhere; and it now rises, because commerce is in a rising state in every nation. If England, at this day, imports and exports more than at any former period, the nation with which she trades must necessarily do the same; her imports are their exports, and *vice versa.*

There can be no such thing as a nation flourishing alone in commerce; she can only participate; and the destruction of it in any part must necessarily affect all. When, therefore, governments are at war, the attack is made upon the common stock of commerce, and the consequence is the same as if each had attacked his own.

The present increase of commerce is not to be attributed to ministers, or to any political contrivances, but to its own natural operations in consequence of peace. The regular markets had been destroyed, the channels of trade broken up, the high road of the seas infested with robbers of every nation, and the attention of the world called to other objects. Those interruptions have ceased, and peace has restored the deranged condition of things to their proper order.

It is worth remarking that every nation reckons the balance of trade in its own favour; and therefore something must be irregular in the common ideas upon this subject.

The fact, however, is true, according to what is called a balance; and it is from this case that commerce is universally supported. Every nation feels the advantage, or it would abandon the practice; but the deception lies in the mode of making up

the accounts, and in attributing what are called profits to a wrong cause.

Mr. Pitt has sometimes amused himself, by showing what he called a balance of trade from the customhouse books. This mode of calculation not only affords no rule that is true, but one that is false.

In the first place, every cargo that departs from the customhouse appears on the books as an export; and according to the customhouse balance, the losses at sea, and by foreign failures, are all reckoned on the side of profit because they appear as exports.

Second, because the importation by the smuggling trade does not appear on the customhouse books, to arrange against the exports.

No balance, therefore, as applying to superior advantages, can be drawn from those documents: and if we examine the natural operation of commerce, the idea is fallacious, and if true, would soon be injurious. The great support of commerce consists in the balance being a level of benefits among all nations.

Two merchants of different nations trading together will both become rich, and each makes the balance in his own favour; consequently they do not get rich out of each other; and it is the same with respect to the nations in which they reside. The case must be that each nation must get rich out of its own means and increase that riches by something which it procures from another in exchange.

If a merchant in England sends an article of English manufacture abroad which costs him a shilling at home and imports something which sells for two, he makes a balance of one shilling in his own favour; but this is not gained out of the foreign nation or the foreign merchant, for he also does the same by the articles he receives, and neither has a balance of advantage upon the other. The original value of the two articles in their proper countries was but two shillings, but by changing their places, they acquire a new idea of value equal to double what they had at first, and that increased value is equally divided.

There is no otherwise a balance on foreign than on domestic commerce. The merchants of London and Newcastle trade on the same principles, as if they resided in different nations, and make their balances in the same manner; yet London does not get rich out of Newcastle, any more than Newcastle out of London; but coals, the merchandise of Newcastle, have an additional value at London, and London merchandise has the same at Newcastle.

Though the principle of all commerce is the same, the domestic, in a national view, is the part the most beneficial; because the whole of the advantages, on both sides, rests within the nation; whereas, in foreign commerce, it is only participation of one-half.

The most unprofitable of all commerce is that connected with foreign dominion. To a few individuals it may be beneficial, merely because it is commerce; but to the nation it is a loss. The expense of maintaining dominion more than absorbs the profits of any trade. It does not increase the general quantity in the world, but operates to lessen it, and as a greater mass would be afloat by relinquishing dominion, the participation without the expense would be more valuable than a greater quantity with it.

But it is impossible to engross commerce by dominion; and therefore it is still more fallacious. It cannot exist in confined channels and necessarily breaks out by regular or irregular means that defeat the attempt; and to succeed would be still worse. France, since the Revolution, has been more than indifferent as to foreign possessions, and other nations will become the same when they investigate the subject with respect to commerce.

To the expense of dominion is to be added that of navies, and when the amount of the two are subtracted from the profits of commerce, it will appear that what is called the balance of trade, even admitting it to exist, is not enjoyed by the nation but absorbed by the government.

The idea of having navies for the protection of commerce is delusive. It is putting the means of destruction for the means of protection. Commerce needs no other protection than the reciprocal interest which every nation feels in supporting it—it is common stock—it exists by a balance of advantages to all; and the only interruption it meets is from the present uncivilized state of governments, and which it is common interest to reform.

Quitting this subject, I now proceed to other matters. As it is necessary to include England in the prospect of a general reformation, it is proper to enquire into the defects of its government. It is only by each nation reforming its own that the whole can be improved, and the full benefit of reformation enjoyed. Only partial advantages can flow from partial reforms.

France and England are the only two countries in Europe where a reformation in government could have successfully begun. The one secure by the ocean, and the other by the immensity of its internal strength, could defy the malignancy of foreign despotism. But it is with revolutions as with commerce, the advantages increase by their becoming general, and double to either what each would receive alone.

As a new system is now opening to the view of the world, the European courts are plotting to counteract it. Alliances, contrary to all former systems, are agitating, and a common interest of courts is forming against the common interest of man. This combination draws a line that runs throughout Europe and presents a cause so entirely new as to exclude all calculations from former circumstances. While despotism warred with despotism, man had no interest in the contest; but in a cause that unites the soldier with the citizen, and nation with nation, the despotism of courts, though it feels the danger, and meditates revenge, is afraid to strike.

No question has arisen within the records of history that pressed with the importance of the present. It is not whether this or that party shall be in or not, or Whig or Tory, or high or low shall prevail; but whether man shall inherit his rights, and universal civilization take place? Whether the fruits of his labours shall be enjoyed by himself or consumed by the profligacy of governments? Whether robbery shall be banished from courts, and wretchedness from countries?

When, in countries that are called civilized, we see age going to the workhouse and youth to the gallows, something must be wrong in the system of government. It would seem, by the exterior appearances of such countries, that all was happiness; but there lies hidden from the eye of common observation a mass of wretchedness that has scarcely any other chance than to expire in poverty or infamy. Its entrance into life is marked with the presage of its fate; and until this is remedied, it is in vain to punish.

Civil government does not consist in executions; but in making that provision for the instruction of youth and the support of age, as to exclude, as much as possible, profligacy from the one and despair from the other. Instead of this, the resources of a country are lavished upon kings, upon courts, upon hirelings, imposters, and prostitutes; and even the poor themselves, with all their wants upon them, are compelled to support the fraud that oppresses them.

Why is it that scarcely any are executed but the poor? The fact is a proof, among other things, of a wretchedness in their condition. Bred up without morals, and cast upon the world without a prospect, they are the exposed sacrifice of vice and legal barbarity. The millions that are superfluously wasted upon governments are more than sufficient to reform those evils, and to benefit the condition of every man in a nation, not included within the purlieus of a court. This I hope to make appear in the progress of this work.

It is the nature of compassion to associate with misfortune. In taking up this subject I seek no recompense—I fear no consequence. Fortified with that proud integrity that disdains to triumph or to yield, I will advocate the Rights of Man.

It is to my advantage that I have served an apprenticeship to life. I know the value of moral instruction, and I have seen the danger of the contrary.

At an early period, little more than sixteen years of age, raw and adventurous, and heated with the false heroism of a master who had served in a man-of-war, I began the carver of my own fortune, and entered on board the terrible privateer, *Captain Death.* From this adventure I was happily prevented by the affectionate and moral remonstrance of a good father, who, from his own habits of life, being of the Quaker profession, must begin to look upon me as lost. But the impression, much as it affected at the time, began to wear away, and I entered afterward in the King of Prussia privateer, *Captain Mendez,* and went with her to sea. Yet from such a beginning, and with all the inconvenience of early life against me, I am proud to say that with a perseverance undismayed by difficulties, a disinterestedness that compelled respect, I have not only contributed to raise a new empire in the world, founded on a new system of government, but I have arrived at an eminence in political literature, the most difficult of all lines to succeed and excel in, which aristocracy with all its aids has not been able to reach or to rival.

Knowing my own heart and feeling myself as I now do, superior to all the skirmish of party, the inveteracy of interested or mistaken opponents, I answer not to falsehood or abuse, but proceed to the defects of the English government.

I begin with charters and corporations.

It is a perversion of terms to say that a charter gives rights. It operates by a contrary effect—that of taking rights away. Rights are inherently in all the inhabitants; but charters, by annulling those rights in the majority, leave the right, by exclusion, in the hands of a few. If charters were constructed so as to express in direct terms, *"that every inhabitant, who is not a member of a corporation, shall not exercise the right of voting,"* such charters would, in the face, be charters not of rights, but of exclusion. The effect is the same under the form they now stand; and the only persons on whom they operate are the persons whom they exclude. Those whose rights are guaranteed, by not being taken away, exercise no other rights than as members of the community they are entitled to without a charter; and, therefore, all charters have no other than an indirect negative operation. They do not give rights to A, but they make a difference in favour of A by taking away the right of B and consequently are instruments of injustice.

But charters and corporations have a more extensive evil effect than what relates merely to elections. They are sources of endless contentions in the places where they exist, and they lessen the common rights of national society. A native of England, under the operation of these charters and corporations, cannot be said to be an Englishman in the full sense of the word. He is not free of the nation in the same manner that a Frenchman is free of France, and an American of America. His rights are circumscribed to the town, and in some cases to the parish of his birth; and all other parts, though in his native land, are to him as a foreign country. To acquire a residence in these he must undergo a local naturalization by purchase, or he is forbidden or expelled the place. This species of feudality is kept up to aggrandize the corporations at the ruin of towns; and the effect is visible.

The generality of corporation towns are in a state of solitary decay and prevented from further ruin only by some circumstance in their situation, such as a navigable river, or a plentiful surrounding country. As population is one of the chief sources of wealth (for without it land itself has no value), everything which operates to prevent it must lessen the value of property; and as corporations have not only this tendency, but directly this effect, they cannot be but injurious. If any policy were to be followed, instead of that of general freedom to every person to settle where he choose (as in France or America) it would be more consistent to give encouragement to newcomers than to preclude their admission by exacting premiums from them.

The persons most immediately interested in the abolition of corporations are the inhabitants of the towns where corporations are established. The instances of Manchester, Birmingham, and Sheffield show, by contrast, the injury which those Gothic institutions are to property and commerce. A few examples may be found, such as that of London, whose natural and commercial advantages, owing to its situation on the Thames, is capable of bearing up against the political evils of a corporation; but in almost all other cases the fatality is too visible to be doubted or denied.

Though the whole nation is not so directly affected by the depression of property in corporation towns as the inhabitants themselves, it partakes of the consequence. By lessening the value of property, the quantity of national commerce is curtailed. Every man is a customer in proportion to his ability; and as all parts of the nation trade with each other, whatever affects any of the parts must necessarily communicate to the whole.

As one of the houses of the English Parliament is, in a great measure, made up of elections from these corporations; and as it is unnatural that a pure stream should flow from a foul fountain, its vices are but a continuation of the vices of its origin. A man of moral honour and good political principles cannot submit to the mean drudgery and disgraceful arts by which such elections are carried. To be a successful candidate he must be destitute of the qualities that constitute a just legislator; and being thus disciplined to corruption by the mode of entering into Parliament, it is not to be expected that the representative should be better than the man.

Mr. Burke, in speaking of the English representation, has advanced as bold a challenge as ever was given in the days of chivalry. "Our representation," says he, "has been found *perfectly adequate to all the purposes* for which a representation of the people can be desired or devised. I defy," continues he, "the enemies of our Constitution to show the contrary." This declaration from a man who has been in constant opposition to all the measures of Parliament the whole of his political life, a year or two excepted, is most extraordinary; and, comparing him with himself, admits of no other alternative than that he acted against his judgment as a member, or has declared contrary to it as an author.

But it is not in the representation only that the defects lie, and therefore I proceed in the next place to the aristocracy.

What is called the House of Peers is constituted on a ground very similar to that against which there is a law in other cases. It amounts to a combination of persons in one common interest. No reason can be given why a house of legislation should be composed entirely of men whose occupation consists in letting landed property, than why it should be composed of those who hire, or of brewers, or bakers, or any other separate class of men.

Mr. Burke calls this house *"the great ground and pillar of security to the landed interest."* Let us examine this idea.

What pillar of security does the landed interest require more than any other interest in the state, or what right has it to a distinct and separate representation from the general interest of a nation? The only use to be made of this power (and which it has always made) is to ward off taxes from itself and throw the burden upon such articles of consumption by which itself would be least affected.

That this has been the consequence (and will always be the consequence) of constructing governments on combinations is evident with respect to England from the history of its taxes.

Notwithstanding taxes have increased and multiplied upon every article of common consumption, the land tax, which more particularly affects this "pillar," has diminished. In 1788 the amount of the land tax was £1,950,000, which is half-a-million less than it produced almost a hundred years ago, notwithstanding the rentals are in many instances doubled since that period.

Before the coming of the Hanoverians, the taxes were divided in nearly equal proportions between the land and articles of consumption, the land bearing rather the largest share; but since that era nearly thirteen millions annually of new taxes have been thrown upon consumption; the consequence of which has been a constant increase in the number and wretchedness of the poor, and in the amount of the poor rates. Yet here again the burden does not fall in equal proportions on the aristocracy with the rest of the community. Their residences, whether in town or country, are not mixed with the habitations of the poor. They live apart from distress and the expense of relieving it. It is in manufacturing towns and labouring villages that those burdens press the heaviest, in many of which it is one class of poor supporting another.

Several of the most heavy and productive taxes are so contrived as to give an exemption to this pillar, thus standing in its own defense. The tax upon beer brewed for sale does not affect the aristocracy, who brew their own beer free of this duty. It falls only on those who have not conveniency or ability to brew, and who must purchase it in small quantities. But what will mankind think of the justice of taxation when they know that this tax alone, from which the aristocracy are from circumstances exempt, is nearly equal to the whole of the land tax, being in the year 1788, and it is not less now, £1,666,152, and with its proportion of the taxes on malt and hops, it exceeds it. That a single article, thus partially consumed, and that chiefly by the working part, should be subject to a tax, equal to that on the whole rental of a nation, is, perhaps, a fact not to be paralleled in the histories of revenues.

This is one of the consequences resulting from a house of legislation composed on the ground of a combination of common interest; for whatever their separate politics as to parties may be, in this they are united. Whether a combination acts to raise the price of any article for sale, or the rate of wages, or whether it acts to throw taxes from itself upon another class of the community, the principle and the effect are the same; and if the one be illegal, it will be difficult to show that the other ought to exist.

It is to no use to say that taxes are first proposed in the House of Commons; for as the other House has always a negative it can always defend itself; and it would be ridiculous to suppose that its acquiescence in the measures to be proposed were not understood beforehand. Besides which it has obtained so much influence by borough traffic, and so many of its relations and connections are distributed on both sides of the Commons, as to give it, besides an absolute negative in one House, a preponderancy in the other in all matters of common concern.

It is difficult to discover what is meant by the *landed interest,* if it does not mean a combination of aristocratical landholders opposing their own pecuniary interest to that of the farmer, and every branch of trade, commerce, and manufacture. In all other respects it is the only interest that needs no partial protection. It enjoys the general protection of the world. Every individual, high or low, is interested in the fruits of the earth; men, women, and children, of all ages and degrees, will turn out to assist the farmer, rather than a harvest should not be got in; and they will not act thus by any other property. It is the

only one for which the common prayer of mankind is put up, and the only one that can never fail from the want of means. It is the interest, not of the policy, but of the existence of man, and when it ceases he must cease to be.

No other interest in a nation stands on the same united support. Commerce, manufactures, arts, sciences, and everything else, compared with this, are supported but in parts. Their prosperity or their decay has not the same universal influence. When the valleys laugh and sing it is not the farmer only but all creation that rejoices. It is a prosperity that excludes all envy; and this cannot be said of anything else.

Why, then, does Mr. Burke talk of his House of Peers as the pillar of the landed interest? Were that pillar to sink into the earth, the same landed property would continue, and the same plowing, sowing, and reaping would go on. The aristocracy are not the farmers who work the land and raise the produce but are the mere consumers of the rent; and when compared with the active world, are the drones, a seraglio of males, who neither collect the honey nor form the hive, but exist only for lazy employment.

Mr. Burke, in his first essay, called aristocracy "*the Corinthian capital of polished society.*" Toward completing the figure he has now added the *pillar;* but still the base is wanting: and whenever a nation choose to act a Samson, not blind, but bold, down go the temple of Dagon, the Lords and the Philistines.

If a house of legislation is to be composed of men of one class for the purpose of protecting a distinct interest, all the other interests should have the same. The inequality as well as the burden of taxation arises from admitting it in one case and not in all. Had there been a house of farmers, there had been no game laws; or a house of merchants and manufacturers, the taxes had neither been so unequal nor so excessive. It is from the power of taxation being in the hands of those who can throw so great a part of it from their own shoulders that it has raged without a check.

Men of small or moderate estates are more injured by the taxes being thrown on articles of consumption than they are eased by warding it from landed property for the following reasons:

First, they consume more of the productive taxable articles, in proportion to their property, than those of large estates.

Second, their residence is chiefly in towns, and their property in houses; and the increase of the poor rates, occasioned by taxes on consumption, is in much greater proportion than the land tax has been favoured. In Birmingham, the poor rates are not less than seven shillings in the pound. From this, as already observed, the aristocracy are in a great measure exempt.

These are but a part of the mischiefs flowing from the wretched scheme of a House of Peers.

As a combination, it can always throw a considerable portion of taxes from itself; and as an hereditary house, accountable to nobody, it resembles a rotten borough, whose consent is to be courted by interest. There are but a few of its members who are not in some mode or other participators, or disposers of the public money. One turns a candleholder, or a lord in waiting; another a lord of the bedchamber, a groom of the stole, or any insignificant nominal office to which a salary is annexed, paid out of the public taxes, and which avoids the direct appearance of corruption. Such situations are derogatory to the character of man; and where they can be submitted to, honour cannot reside.

To all these are to be added the numerous dependents, the long list of younger branches and distant relations, who are to be provided for at the public expense; in short, were an estimation to be made of the charge of aristocracy to a nation, it will be found nearly equal to that of supporting the poor. The Duke of Richmond alone (and there are cases similar to his) takes away as much for himself as would maintain two thousand poor and aged persons. Is it, then, any wonder that under such a system of government, taxes and rates have multiplied to their present extent?

In stating these matters, I speak an open and disengaged language dictated by no passion but that of humanity. To me, who have not only refused offers because I thought them improper; but have declined rewards I might with reputation have accepted; it is no wonder that meanness and imposition appear disgustful. Independence is my happiness, and I view things as they are, without regard to place or person; my country is the world, and my religion is to do good.

Mr. Burke, in speaking of the aristocratical law of primogeniture, says: "It is the standing law of our land inheritance; and which, without question, has a tendency, and I think," continues he, "a happy tendency, to preserve a character of weight and consequence."

Mr. Burke may call this law what he pleases, but humanity and impartial reflection will denounce it a law of brutal injustice. Were he not accustomed to the daily practice, and did we only hear of that as the law of some distant part of the world, we should conclude that the legislators of such countries had not yet arrived at a state of civilization.

As to its preserving a character of *weight and consequence,* the case appears to me directly the reverse. It is an attaint upon character; a sort of privateering on family property. It may have weight among dependent tenants, but it gives none on a scale of national, and much less of universal, character. Speaking for myself, my parents were not able to give me a shilling beyond what they gave me in education; and to do this they distressed themselves; yet I possess more of what is called consequence in the world than anyone in Mr. Burke's catalogue of aristocrats.

Having thus glanced at some of the defects of the two Houses of Parliament, I proceed to what is called the Crown, upon which I shall be very concise.

It signifies a nominal office of a million sterling a year, the business of which consists in receiving the money. Whether the person be wise or foolish, sane or insane, a native or a foreigner, matters not. Every ministry acts upon the same idea that Mr. Burke writes, namely, that the people must be hoodwinked, and held in superstitious ignorance by some bugbear or other; and what is called the Crown answers this purpose, and therefore it answers all the purposes to be expected from it. This is more than can be said of the other two branches.

The hazard to which this office is exposed in all countries is not from anything that can happen to the man, but from what may happen to the nation—the danger of its coming to its senses.

It has been customary to call the Crown the executive power, and the custom is continued, though the reason has ceased.

It was called the *executive,* because the person whom it signified used formerly to sit in the character of a judge, in administering or executing the laws. The tribunals were then a part of the Court. The power, therefore, which is now called the judicial, is what was called the executive; and, consequently, one or other of the terms is redundant, and one of the offices useless. We speak of the Crown now, it means nothing; it signifies neither a judge nor a general; besides which it is the laws that govern, and not the man. The old terms are kept up, to give an appearance of consequence to empty forms; and the only effect they have is that of increasing expenses.

. . . The fraud, hypocrisy, and imposition of governments are now beginning to be too well understood to promise them any long career. The farce of monarchy and aristocracy in all countries is following that of chivalry, and Mr. Burke is dressing for the funeral. Let it then pass quietly to the tomb of all other follies, and the mourners be comforted.

The time is not very distant when England will laugh at itself for sending to Holland, Hanover, Zell, or Brunswick, for men, at the expense of a million a year, who understood neither her laws, her language, nor her interest, and whose capacities would scarcely have fitted them for the office of a parish constable. If government could be trusted to such hands, it must be some easy and simple thing indeed, and materials fit for all the purposes may be found in every town and village in England.

When it shall be said in any country in the world my poor are happy; neither ignorance nor distress is to be found among them; my jails are empty of prisoners, my streets of beggars; the aged are not in want; the taxes are not oppressive; the rational world is my friend, because I am the friend of its happiness: When these things can be said, then may that country boast its constitution and its government.

Within the space of a few years we have seen two revolutions, those of America and France. In the former the contest was long, and the conflict severe; in the latter the nation acted with such a consolidated impulse that, having no foreign enemy to contend with, the Revolution was complete in power the moment it appeared. From both those instances it is evident that the greatest forces that can be brought into the field of revolutions are reason and common interest. Where these can have the opportunity of acting, opposition dies with fear or crumbles away by conviction. It is a great standing which they have now universally obtained; and we may hereafter hope to see revolutions, or changes in governments, produced with the same quiet operation, by which any measure, determinable by reason and discussion, is accomplished.

When a nation changes its opinion and habits of thinking it is no longer to be governed as before; but it would not only be wrong, but bad policy, to attempt by force what ought to be accomplished by reason.

Rebellion consists in forcibly opposing the general will of a nation, whether by a party or by a government. There ought, therefore, to be in every nation a method of occasionally ascertaining the state of public opinion with respect to government. On this point the old government of France was superior to the present government of England, because, on extraordinary occasions, recourse could be had to what was then called the States-General. But in England there are no such occasional bodies; and as to those who are now called representatives, a great part of them are mere machines of the court, placemen, and dependents.

I presume that though all the people of England pay taxes, not a hundredth part of them are electors, and the members of one of the Houses of Parliament represent nobody but themselves. There is, therefore, no power but the voluntary will of the people that has a right to act in any matter respecting a general reform; and by the same right that two persons can confer on such a subject, a thousand may. The object in all such preliminary proceedings is to find out what the general sense of a nation is and to be governed by it. If it prefer a bad or defective government to a reform, or choose to pay ten times more taxes than there is occasion for, it has a right so to do: and so long as the majority do not impose conditions on the minority, different from what they impose on themselves, though there may be much error, there is no injustice. Neither will the error continue long. Reason and discussion will soon bring things right, however wrong they may begin. By such a process no tumult is to be apprehended. The poor in all countries are naturally both peaceable and grateful in all reforms in which their interest and happiness is included. It is only by neglecting and rejecting them that they become tumultuous.

The objects that now press on the public attention are the French Revolution, and the prospect of a general revolution in governments. Of all nations in Europe there is none so much interested in the French Revolution as England. Enemies for ages, and that at a vast expense, and without any rational object, the opportunity now presents itself of amicably closing the scene, and joining their efforts to reform the rest of Europe. By doing this they will not only prevent the further effusion of blood and increase of taxes but be in a condition of getting rid of a considerable part of their present burdens, as has been already stated. Long experience, however, has shown that reforms of this kind are not those which old governments wish to promote; and therefore it is to nations, and not to such governments, that these matters present themselves.

In the preceding part of this work I have spoken of an alliance between England, France, and America, for purposes that were to be afterward mentioned. Though I have no direct authority on the part of America, I have good reason to conclude that she is disposed to enter into a consideration of such a measure, provided that the governments with which she might ally acted as national governments, and not as courts enveloped in intrigue and mystery. That France as a nation, and a national government, would prefer an alliance with England, is a matter of certainty. Nations, like individuals, who have long been enemies without knowing each other, or knowing why, become the better friends when they discover the errors and impositions under which they had acted.

Admitting, therefore, the probability of such a connection, I will state some matters by which such an alliance, together with that of Holland, might render service, not only to the parties immediately concerned, but to all Europe.

It is, I think, certain, that if the fleets of England, France, and Holland were confederated they could propose, with effect, a limitation to, and a general dismantling of, all the navies of Europe, to a certain proportion to be agreed upon.

First, that no new ship of war shall be built by any power in Europe, themselves included.

Second, that all the navies now in existence shall be put back, suppose to one-tenth of their present force. This will save to France and England at least two millions sterling annually to each, and their relative force be in the same proportion as it is now. If men will permit themselves to think, as rational beings ought to think, nothing can appear more ridiculous and absurd, exclusive of all moral reflections, than to be at the expense of building navies, filling them with men, and then hauling them into the ocean, to try which can sink each other fastest. Peace, which costs nothing, is attended with infinitely more advantage than any victory with all its expense. But this, though it best answers the purpose of nations, does not that of court governments, whose habited policy is pretense for taxation, places, and offices.

It is, I think, also certain, that the above confederated powers, together with that of the United States of America, can propose with effect, to Spain, the independence of South America, and the opening those countries of immense extent and wealth to the general commerce of the world, as North America now is.

With how much more glory and advantage to itself does a nation act when it exerts its powers to rescue the world from bondage and to create itself friends, than when it employs those powers to increase ruin, desolation, and misery. The horrid scene that is now acting by the English government in the East Indies is fit only to be told of Goths and Vandals, who, destitute of principle, robbed and tortured the world they were incapable of enjoying.

The opening of South America would produce an immense field of commerce, and a ready money market for manufactures, which the eastern world does not. The east is already a country full of manufactures, the importation of which is not only an injury to the manufactures of England, but a drain upon its specie. The balance against England by this trade is regularly upwards of half a million annually sent out in the East India ships in silver; and this is the reason, together with German intrigue and German subsidies, there is so little silver in England.

But any war is harvest to such governments, however ruinous it may be to a nation. It serves to keep up deceitful expectations, which prevent a people looking into the defects and abuses of government. It is the *lo here!* and the *lo there!* that amuses and cheats the multitude.

Never did so great an opportunity offer itself to England, and to all Europe, as is produced by the two revolutions of America and France. By the former, freedom has a national champion in the western world; and by the latter, in Europe. When another nation shall join France, despotism and bad government will scarcely dare to appear. To use a trite expression, the iron is becoming hot all over Europe. The insulted German and the enslaved Spaniard, the Russ and the Pole, are beginning to think. The present age will hereafter merit to be called the Age of Reason, and the present generation will appear to the future as the Adam of a new world.

When all the governments of Europe shall be established on the representative system, nations will become acquainted, and the animosities and the prejudices fomented by the intrigue and artifice of courts will cease. The oppressed soldier will become a freeman; and the tortured sailor, no longer dragged along the streets like a felon, will pursue his mercantile voyage in safety. It would be better that nations should continue the pay of their soldiers during their lives, and give them their discharge, and restore them to freedom and their friends, and cease recruiting, than retain such multitudes at the same expense in a condition useless to society and themselves. As soldiers have hitherto been treated in most countries they might be said to be without a friend. Shunned by the citizens on an apprehension of being enemies to liberty, and too often insulted by those who commanded them, their condition was a double oppression. But where general principles of liberty pervade a people everything is restored to order; and the soldier, civilly treated, returns the civility.

In contemplating revolutions, it is easy to perceive that they may arise from two distinct causes; the one, to avoid or get rid of some great calamity; the other, to obtain some great and positive good; and the two may be distinguished by the names of active and passive revolutions. In those which proceed from the former cause, the temper becomes incensed and soured; and the redress, obtained by danger, is too often sullied by revenge. But in those which proceed from the latter, the heart, rather animated than agitated, enters serenely upon the subject. Reason and discussion, persuasion and conviction, become the weapons in the contest, and it is only when those are attempted to be suppressed that recourse is had to violence. When men unite in agreeing that a *thing is good,* could it be obtained, such as relief from a burden of taxes and the extinction of corruption, the object is more than half accomplished. What they approve as the end they will promote in the means.

Will any man say, in the present excess of taxation, falling so heavily on the poor, that a remission of five pounds annually of taxes to one hundred and four thousand poor families is not a *good thing?* Will he say that a remission of seven pounds annually to one hundred thousand other poor families, of eight pounds annually to another hundred thousand poor families, and of ten pounds annually to fifty thousand poor and widowed families, are not *good things?* And to proceed a step farther in this climax, will he say that to provide against the misfortunes to which all human life is subject, by securing six pounds an-

nually for all poor, distressed, and reduced persons of the age of fifty and until sixty, and of ten pounds annually after sixty, is not a *good thing?*

Will he say that an abolition of two million of poor rates to the housekeepers, and of the whole of the house and window light tax, and of the commutation tax, is not a *good thing?* Or will he say that to abolish corruption is a *bad thing?*

If, therefore, the good to be obtained be worthy of a passive, rational, and costless revolution, it would be bad policy to prefer waiting for a calamity that should force a violent one. I have no idea, considering the reforms which are now passing and spreading throughout Europe, that England will permit herself to be the last; and where the occasion and the opportunity quietly offer, it is better than to wait for a turbulent necessity. It may be considered as an honour to the animal faculties of man to obtain redress by courage and danger, but it is far greater honour to the rational faculties to accomplish the same object by reason, accommodation, and general consent.

As reforms, or revolutions, call them which you please, extend themselves among nations, those nations will form connections and conventions, and when a few are thus confederated, the progress will be rapid, till despotism and corrupt government be totally expelled, at least out of two quarters of the world, Europe and America. The Algerine piracy may then be commanded to cease, for it is only by the malicious policy of old governments, against each other, that it exists.

Throughout this work, various and numerous as the subjects are, which I have taken up and investigated, there is only a single paragraph upon religion, viz., *"that every religion is good that teaches man to be good."*

I have carefully avoided to enlarge upon the subject, because I am inclined to believe that what is called the present ministry wish to see contentions about religion kept up, to prevent the nation turning its attention to subjects of government. It is as if they were to say, "*Look that way, or any way, but this.*"

But as religion is very improperly made a political machine, and the reality of it is thereby destroyed, I will conclude this work with stating in what light religion appears to me.

If we suppose a large family of children, who, on any particular day, or particular circumstance, made it a custom to present to their parent some token of their affection and gratitude, each of them would make a different offering, and most probably in a different manner. Some would pay their congratulations in themes of verse or prose; some by little devices, as their genius dictated, or according to what they thought would please; and, perhaps the least of all, not able to do any of those things, would ramble into the garden, or the field, and gather what it thought the prettiest flower it could find, though perhaps it might be but a simple weed. The parent would be more gratified by such variety than if the whole of them had acted on a concerted plan, and each had made exactly the same offering. This would have the cold appearance of contrivance, or the harsh one of control. But of all unwelcome things nothing could more afflict the parent than to know that the whole of them had afterward gotten together by the ears, boys and girls fighting, scratching, reviling, and abusing each other about which was the best or the worst present.

Why may we not suppose that the great Father of all is pleased with variety of devotion? and that the greatest offense we can act is that by which we seek to torment and render each other miserable? For my own part I am fully satisfied that what I am now doing, with an endeavour to conciliate mankind, to render their condition happy, to unite nations that have hitherto been enemies, and to extirpate the horrid practice of war, and break the chains of slavery and oppression, is acceptable in his sight; and being the best service I can perform I act it cheerfully.

I do not believe that any two men, on what are called doctrinal points, think alike, who think at all. It is only those who have not thought that appear to agree. It is in this case as with what is called the British Constitution. It has been taken for granted to be good, and encomiums have supplied the place of proof. But when the nation comes to examine into its principles and the abuses it admits, it will be found to have more defects than I have pointed out in this work and the former.

As to what are called national religions, we may with as much propriety talk of national Gods. It is either political craft or the remains of the pagan system, when every nation had its separate and particular deity. Among all the writers of the English Church clergy, who have treated on the general subject of religion, the present Bishop of Llandaff has not been excelled: and it is with much pleasure that I take the opportunity of expressing this token of respect.

I have now gone through the whole of the subject, at least as far as it appears to me at present. It has been my intention for the five years I have been in Europe to offer an address to the people of England on the subject of government; if the opportunity presented itself, before I returned to America. Mr. Burke has thrown it in my way and I thank him. On a certain occasion, three years ago, I pressed him to propose a national convention, to be fairly elected, for the purpose of taking the state of the nation into consideration; but I found that however strongly the parliamentary current was then setting against the party he acted with, their policy was to keep everything within that field of corruption, and trust to accidents. Long experience had shown that Parliaments would follow any change of ministers, and on this they rested their hopes and expectations.

Formerly, when divisions arose respecting governments, recourse was had to the sword, and a civil war ensued. That savage custom is exploded by the new system; and reference is had to national conventions. Discussion and the general will arbitrate the question, and to this private opinion yields with a good grace, and order is preserved uninterrupted.

Some gentlemen have affected to call the principles upon which this work and the former part of the *Rights of Man* are founded "a new fangled doctrine." The question is not whether those principles are new or old, but whether they are right or wrong. Suppose the former, I will show their effect by a figure easily understood.

It is now towards the middle of February. Were I to take a turn into the country the trees would present a leafless winterly appearance. As people are apt to pluck twigs as they walk along, I perhaps might do the same, and by chance might observe that a *single bud* on that twig had begun to swell. I should reason very unnaturally, or rather not reason at all, to suppose *this* was the *only* bud in England which had this appearance. Instead of deciding thus, I should instantly conclude that the same appearance was beginning, or about to begin, everywhere; and though the vegetable sleep will continue longer on some trees and plants than on others, and though some of them may not *blossom* for two or three years, all will be in leaf in the summer, except those which are *rotten*. What pace the political summer may keep with the natural, no human foresight can determine. It is, however, not difficult to perceive that the spring is begun. Thus wishing, as I sincerely do, freedom and happiness to all nations, I close the SECOND PART.

Śakuntalā and the Ring of Recollection

Kālidāsa

Translated by Barbara Stoler Miller

The Indian goddess Kālī

Editor's Introduction

It is unnecessary to say anything about the *Śakuntalā,* a play by Kālidāsa which is discussed elsewhere in this issue of *The Great Ideas Today* by Barbara Stoler Miller, and impossible to give an account of the playwright himself, as to whom the difficulty is, as Dr. Miller has said, that "we lack any historical evidence of his life." He is nevertheless widely regarded, on the basis of some half a dozen works—including three plays—which are generally attributed to him, as the greatest Sanskrit poet, and from the evidence of these, as well as from legend and what may be inferred from other records, we may form some conception of who and what he was.

He lived some time between the third and the seventh centuries— most probably during the fifth—in northern India, most likely during the reign of Candra Gupta II (380–415), who himself was of the so-called Gupta dynasty, which ruled in that region between the years 300 and 700, approximately. This dynasty is noted for having inspired or encouraged many great Sanskrit writings and Hindu works both of art and of science, while we owe to it as well the invention of the decimal system of notation. Its sophistication seems to be reflected in Kālidāsa's work, which is looked upon as the perfection of Gupta culture.

Presumably Kālidāsa was a Brahman, i.e., a priest, devoted to the deity called Śiva (as indicated in the benediction to the *Śakuntalā* and other of his writings) and to Śiva's hideous consort, Kālī, whose name is part of his own. Śiva is the god of creativity, distinct, for example, from Vishnu, who governs the moral order (*dharma*). As such, he is androgynous, his female half being Nature, and the reconciliation of these elements is the religious aspect of Hindu drama that depicts their earthly counterparts—the king, especially, being always seen as the god's vicar on earth. But equally (and lest one suppose that Hindu theology can be wholly rendered in such simple terms), there are elements of desire and duty, or the erotic and the heroic, that must be reconciled, too, in the king's own character—such a king, for example, as we find in the *Śakuntalā.* The inference from the celebration of kingship in his works is that Kālidāsa enjoyed royal patronage, and if so, it was perhaps the more generous for the indication he gives that kings possessed spiritual powers, by virtue of which they could be regarded as royal sages.

Of Kālidāsa's other plays, one, called *Vikramorvaśī* (or, the *Vikramor-vashiya*), is the story of the love between a mortal king and a divine maiden who is banished from heaven as a result, though eventually she returns. It is famous for a scene in which the king wanders grief-stricken through a forest where he addresses trees and flowers as if they were the embodiment of the one he has lost. But the decisive event in it, as in the *Śakuntalā,* is the king's recognition of his son—born in this case of the union between himself and the goddess.

The third play, known as the *Mālavikāgnimitra,* is less elevated—indeed a harem intrigue, comic in tone—whose heroine, Mālavikā, is a student of the palace dancing master, in a setting where all the king's wives and other courtiers study dance and drama. This allows for discussion of dramatic theory among the courtiers themselves, one of whom praises a performance of a love song in dance with the following words:

> The meaning was set forth
> with gesture and interwoven words,
> dance steps followed time,
> truth was in every mood,
> the portrayal was gentle,
> and seemed natural to her limbs;
> emotion wrought emotion from the matter—
> it was a very work of passion.

Such a judgment, recognizing as it does the passionate element in theatrical representation, reminds us of Aristotle in its indication of the emotional satisfaction which an audience may be imagined to have from dramatic performances. This also was Kālidāsa's object, apparently, in the kind of heroic romance he produced in the *Śakuntalā.* His story does not require him to effect the purgation of pity and fear—their transformation into the pleasure of recognition and insight—which is the business, Aristotle suggests, of tragedy. But the aim of his plays, as of Hindu drama generally, was to create an equally pleasurable experience, called *rasa,* which also involved recognition, in this case of the harmony that was held to underlie the apparently disparate elements of human existence. *Rasa,* usually translated as "mood" or "sentiment," literally means rather "taste" or "flavor," and signifies what may be distilled from the emotional situation by the poet in order to make it available for aesthetic appreciation. Such, we gather, was the intended effect of the love song rendered in dance as described by the courtier of the *Mālavikāgnimitra,* as well as of the story of the *Śakuntalā.*

The play, which has been translated many times into English, is reprinted here in the version provided by Dr. Miller herself, to whose introductory notes we are indebted for some of these remarks.

Śakuntalā and the Ring of Recollection

Characters

Players in the prologue:
DIRECTOR: Director of the players and manager of the theater (*sūtradhāra*).
ACTRESS: The lead actress (*naṭī*).

Principal roles:
KING: Duṣyanta, the hero (*nāyaka*); ruler of Hastināpura; a royal sage of the lunar dynasty of Puru.
ŚAKUNTALĀ: The heroine (*nāyikā*); daughter of the royal sage Viśvāmitra and the celestial nymph Menakā; adoptive daughter of the ascetic Kaṇva.
BUFFOON: Māḍhavya, the king's comical brahman companion (*vidūṣaka*).

Members of Kaṇva's hermitage:
ANASŪYĀ and PRIYAMVADĀ: Two young female ascetics; friends of Śakuntalā.
KAṆVA: Foster father of Śakuntalā and master of the hermitage; a sage belonging to the lineage of the divine creator Marīci, and thus related to Mārīca.
GAUTAMĪ: The senior female ascetic.
ŚĀRṄGARAVA and ŚĀRADVATA: Kaṇva's disciples.

Various inhabitants of the hermitage: a monk with his two pupils, two boy ascetics (named Gautama and Nārada), a young disciple of Kaṇva, a trio of female ascetics.

Members of the king's forest retinue:
CHARIOTEER: Driver of the king's chariot (*sūta*).
GUARD: Raivataka, guardian of the entrance to the king's quarters (*dauvārika*).
GENERAL: Commander of the king's army (*senāpati*).
KARABHAKA: Royal messenger.

Various attendants, including Greco-Bactrian bow-bearers (*yavanyaḥ*).

Members of the king's palace retinue:
CHAMBERLAIN: Vātāyana, chief officer of the king's household (*kañcukī*).
PRIEST: Somarāta, the king's religious preceptor and household priest (*purohita*).
DOORKEEPER: Vetravatī, the female attendant who ushers in visitors and presents messages (*pratīhārī*).
PARABHṚTIKĀ and MADHUKARIKĀ: Two maids assigned to the king's garden.
CATURIKĀ: A maidservant.

City dwellers:
MAGISTRATE: The king's low-caste brother-in-law (*śyāla*); chief of the city's policemen.
POLICEMEN: Sūcaka and Jānuka.
FISHERMAN: An outcaste.

Celestials:
MĀRĪCA: A divine sage; master of the celestial hermitage in which Śakuntalā gives birth to her son; father of Indra, king of the gods, whose armies Duṣyanta leads.
ADITI: Wife of Mārīca.
MĀTALI: Indra's charioteer.
SĀNUMATĪ: A nymph; friend of Śakuntalā's mother Menakā.

Various members of Mārīca's hermitage: two female ascetics, Mārīca's disciple Gālava.

BOY: Sarvadamana, son of Śakuntalā and Duṣyanta; later known as Bharata.

Offstage voices:
VOICE OFFSTAGE: From the backstage area or dressing room (*nepathye*); behind the curtain, out of view of the audience. The voice belongs to various players before they enter the stage, such as the monk, Śakuntalā's friends, the buffoon, Mātali; also to figures who never enter the stage, such as the angry sage Durvāsas, the two bards who chant royal panegyrics (*vaitālikau*).
VOICE IN THE AIR: A voice chanting in the air (*ākāśe*) from somewhere offstage: the bodiless voice of Speech quoted in Sanskrit by Priyaṁvadā (4.4); the voice of a cuckoo who represents the trees of the forest blessing Śakuntalā in Sanskrit (4.11); the voice of Haṁsapadikā singing a Prakrit love song (5.1).

Aside from Duṣyanta, Śakuntalā, and the buffoon, most of the characters represent types that reappear in different contexts within the play itself, an aspect of the circular structure of the play in which complementary relations are repeated. In terms of their appearance, the following roles might be played by the same actor or actress:

Kaṇva—Mārīca
Gautamī—Aditi
Anasūyā and Priyaṁvadā—
    Sānumatī and Caturikā—
    Two Ascetic Women in the hermitage of Mārīca
Charioteer—Mātali
Monk—Sārṅgarava
General—Chamberlain
Karabhaka—Priest

The setting of the play shifts from the forest hermitage (Acts 1–4) to the palace (Acts 5–6) to the celestial hermitage (Act 7). The season is early summer when the play begins and spring during the sixth act; the passage of time is otherwise indicated by the birth and boyhood of Śakuntalā's son.

ACT ONE

The water that was first created,
the sacrifice-bearing fire, the priest,
the time-setting sun and moon,
audible space that fills the universe,
what men call nature, the source of all seeds,
the air that living creatures breathe—
through his eight embodied forms,
may Lord Śiva come to bless you! (1)

Prologue

DIRECTOR (*looking backstage*): If you are in costume now, madam, please come on stage!
ACTRESS: I'm here, sir.
DIRECTOR: Our audience is learned. We shall play Kālidāsa's new drama called *Śakuntalā and the Ring of Recollection*. Let the players take their parts to heart!
ACTRESS: With you directing, sir, nothing will be lost.
DIRECTOR: Madam, the truth is:

I find no performance perfect
until the critics are pleased;
the better trained we are
the more we doubt ourselves. (2)

ACTRESS: So true . . . now tell me what to do first!
DIRECTOR: What captures an audience better than a song? Sing about the new summer season and its pleasures:

To plunge in fresh waters
swept by scented forest winds
and dream in soft shadows
of the day's ripened charms. (3)

ACTRESS (*singing*):

Sensuous women
in summer love
weave
flower earrings
from fragile petals
of mimosa
while wild bees
kiss them gently. (4)

DIRECTOR: Well sung, madam! Your melody enchants the audience. The silent theater is like a painting. What drama should we play to please it?
ACTRESS: But didn't you just direct us to perform a new play called *Śakuntalā and the Ring of Recollection?*

411

DIRECTOR: Madam, I'm conscious again! For a moment I forgot.

> The mood of your song's melody
> carried me off by force,
> just as the swift dark antelope
> enchanted King Duṣyanta. (5)

(They both exit; the prologue ends. Then the king enters with his charioteer, in a chariot, a bow and arrow in his hand, hunting an antelope.)

CHARIOTEER *(watching the king and the antelope)*:

> I see this black buck move
> as you draw your bow
> and I see the wild bowman Śiva,
> hunting the dark antelope. (6)

KING: Driver, this antelope has drawn us far into the forest. There he is again:

> The graceful turn of his neck
> as he glances back at our speeding car,
> the haunches folded into his chest
> in fear of my speeding arrow,
> the open mouth dropping
> half-chewed grass on our path—
> watch how he leaps, bounding on air,
> barely touching the earth. (7)

(He shows surprise.)
Why is it so hard to keep him in sight?
CHARIOTEER: Sir, the ground was rough. I tightened the reins to slow the chariot and the buck raced ahead. Now that the path is smooth, he won't be hard to catch.
KING: Slacken the reins!
CHARIOTEER: As you command, sir.
(He mimes the speeding chariot.)
Look!

> Their legs extend as I slacken the reins,
> plumes and manes set in the wind, ears angle back;
> our horses outrun their own clouds of dust,
> straining to match the antelope's speed. (8)

KING: These horses would outrace the steeds of the sun.

> What is small suddenly looms large,
> split forms seem to reunite,
> bent shapes straighten before my eyes—
> from the chariot's speed
> nothing ever stays distant or near. (9)

CHARIOTEER: The antelope is an easy target now.
(He mimes the fixing of an arrow.)

VOICE OFFSTAGE: Stop! Stop, king! This antelope belongs to our hermitage! Don't kill him!

CHARIOTEER (*listening and watching*): Sir, two ascetics are protecting the black buck from your arrow's deadly aim.

KING (*showing confusion*): Rein in the horses!

CHARIOTEER: It is done!

(*He mimes the chariot's halt. Then a monk enters with two pupils, his hand raised.*)

MONK: King, this antelope belongs to our hermitage.

> Withdraw your well-aimed arrow! Your weapon
> should rescue victims, not destroy the innocent! (10)

KING: I withdraw it.

(*He does as he says.*)

MONK: An act worthy of the Puru dynasty's shining light!

> Your birth honors
> the dynasty of the moon!
> May you beget a son
> to turn the wheel of your empire! (11)

THE TWO PUPILS (*raising their arms*): May you beget a son to turn the wheel of your empire!

KING (*bowing*): I welcome your blessing.

MONK: King, we were going to gather firewood. From here you can see the hermitage of our master Kaṇva on the bank of the Mālinī river. If your work permits, enter and accept our hospitality.

> When you see the peaceful rites of devoted ascetics,
> you will know how well your scarred arm protects us. (12)

KING: Is the master of the community there now?

MONK: He went to Somatīrtha, the holy shrine of the moon, and put his daughter Śakuntalā in charge of receiving guests. Some evil threatens her, it seems.

KING: Then I shall see her. She will know my devotion and commend me to the great sage.

MONK: We shall leave you now.

(*He exits with his pupils.*)

KING: Driver, urge the horses on! The sight of this holy hermitage will purify us.

CHARIOTEER: As you command, sir.

(*He mimes the chariot's speed.*)

KING (*looking around*): Without being told one can see that this is a grove where ascetics live.

CHARIOTEER: How?

KING: Don't you see—

> Wild rice grains under trees
> where parrots nest in hollow trunks,
> stones stained by the dark oil
> of crushed iṅgudī nuts,
> trusting deer who hear human voices
> yet don't break their gait,

and paths from ponds streaked
by water from wet bark cloth. (13)

CHARIOTEER: It is perfect.

KING (*having gone a little inside*): We should not disturb the grove! Stop the chariot and let me get down!

CHARIOTEER: I'm holding the reins. You can dismount now, sir.

KING (*dismounting*): One should not enter an ascetics' grove in hunting gear. Take these!

(*He gives up his ornaments and his bow.*)

Driver, rub down the horses while I pay my respects to the residents of the hermitage!

CHARIOTEER: Yes, sir!

(*He exits.*)

KING: This gateway marks the sacred ground. I will enter.

(*He enters, indicating he feels an omen.*)

The hermitage is a tranquil place,
yet my arm is quivering . . .
do I feel a false omen of love
or does fate have doors everywhere? (14)

VOICE OFFSTAGE: This way, friends!

KING (*straining to listen*): I think I hear voices to the right of the grove. I'll find out.

(*Walking around and looking.*)

Young female ascetics with watering pots cradled on their hips are coming to water the saplings.

(*He mimes it in precise detail.*)

This view of them is sweet.

These forest women have beauty
rarely seen inside royal palaces—
the wild forest vines far surpass
creepers in my pleasure garden. (15)

I'll hide in the shadows and wait.

(*Śakuntalā and her two friends enter, acting as described.*)

ŚAKUNTALĀ: This way, friends!

ANASŪYĀ: I think Father Kaṇva cares more about the trees in the hermitage than he cares about you. You're as delicate as a jasmine, yet he orders you to water the trees.

ŚAKUNTALĀ: Anasūyā, it's more than Father Kaṇva's order. I feel a sister's love for them.

(*She mimes the watering of trees.*)

KING (*to himself*): Is this Kaṇva's daughter? The sage does show poor judgment in imposing the rules of the hermitage on her.

The sage who hopes to subdue
her sensuous body by penances

is trying to cut firewood
with a blade of blue-lotus leaf.   (16)

Let it be! I can watch her closely from here in the trees.
(*He does so.*)
ŚAKUNTALĀ: Anasūyā, I can't breathe! Our friend Priyaṁvadā tied my bark
dress too tightly! Loosen it a bit!
ANASŪYĀ: As you say.
(*She loosens it.*)
PRIYAṀVADĀ (*laughing*): Blame your youth for swelling your breasts. Why
blame me?
KING: This bark dress fits her body badly, but it ornaments her beauty . . .

A tangle of duckweed adorns a lotus,
a dark spot heightens the moon's glow,
the bark dress increases her charm—
beauty finds its ornaments anywhere.   (17)

ŚAKUNTALĀ (*looking in front of her*): The new branches on this mimosa tree are
like fingers moving in the wind, calling to me. I must go to it!
(*Saying this, she walks around.*)
PRIYAṀVADĀ: Wait, Śakuntalā! Stay there a minute! When you stand by this
mimosa tree, it seems to be guarding a creeper.
ŚAKUNTALĀ: That's why your name means "Sweet-talk."
KING: "Sweet-talk" yes, but Priyaṁvadā speaks the truth about Śakuntalā:

Her lips are fresh red buds,
her arms are tendrils,
impatient youth is poised
to blossom in her limbs.   (18)

ANASŪYĀ: Śakuntalā, this is the jasmine creeper who chose the mango tree in
marriage, the one you named "Forestlight." Have you forgotten her?
ŚAKUNTALĀ: I would be forgetting myself!
(*She approaches the creeper and examines it.*)
The creeper and the tree are twined together in perfect harmony. Forestlight
has just flowered and the new mango shoots are made for her pleasure.
PRIYAṀVADĀ (*smiling*): Anasūyā, don't you know why Śakuntalā looks so lov-
ingly at Forestlight?
ANASŪYĀ: I can't guess.
PRIYAṀVADĀ: The marriage of Forestlight to her tree makes her long to have a
husband too.
ŚAKUNTALĀ: You're just speaking your own secret wish.
(*Saying this, she pours water from the jar.*)
KING: Could her social class be different from her father's? There's no doubt!

She was born to be a warrior's bride,
for my noble heart desires her—
when good men face doubt,
inner feelings are truth's only measure.   (19)

Still, I must learn everything about her.

415

ŚAKUNTALĀ (*flustered*): The splashing water has alarmed a bee. He is flying from the jasmine to my face.
(*She dances to show the bee's attack.*)
KING (*looking longingly*):

Bee, you touch the quivering
corners of her frightened eyes,
you hover softly near
to whisper secrets in her ear;
a hand brushes you away,
but you drink her lips' treasure—
while the truth we seek defeats us,
you are truly blessed. (20)

ŚAKUNTALĀ: This dreadful bee won't stop. I must escape.
(*She steps to one side, looking about.*)
Oh! He's pursuing me . . . Save me! Please save me! This mad bee is chasing me!
BOTH FRIENDS (*laughing*): How can we save you? Call King Duṣyanta. The grove is under his protection.
KING: Here's my chance. Have no fear . . .
(*With this half-spoken, he stops and speaks to himself.*)
Then she will know that I am the king . . . Still, I shall speak.
ŚAKUNTALĀ (*stopping after a few steps*): Why is he still following me?
KING (*approaching quickly*):

While a Puru king rules the earth
to punish evildoers,
who dares to molest
these innocent young ascetics? (21)

(*Seeing the king, all act flustered.*)
ANASŪYĀ: Sir, there's no real danger. Our friend was frightened when a bee attacked her.
(*She points to Śakuntalā.*)
KING (*approaching Śakuntalā*): Does your ascetic practice go well?
(*Śakuntalā stands speechless.*)
ANASŪYĀ: It does now that we have a special guest. Śakuntalā, go to our hut and bring the ripe fruits. We'll use this water to bathe his feet.
KING: Your kind speech is hospitality enough.
PRIYAṀVADĀ: Please sit in the cool shadows of this shade tree and rest, sir.
KING: You must also be tired from your work.
ANASŪYĀ: Śakuntalā, we should respect our guest. Let's sit down.
(*All sit.*)
ŚAKUNTALĀ (*to herself*): When I see him, why do I feel an emotion that the forest seems to forbid?
KING (*looking at each of the girls*): Youth and beauty complement your friendship.
PRIYAṀVADĀ (*in a stage whisper*): Anasūyā, who is he? He's so polite, fine looking, and pleasing to hear. He has the marks of royalty.
ANASŪYĀ: I'm curious too, friend. I'll just ask him.
(*Aloud.*)
Sir, your kind speech inspires trust. What family of royal sages do you adorn?

What country mourns your absence? Why does a man of refinement subject himself to the discomfort of visiting an ascetics' grove?

ŚAKUNTALĀ (*to herself*): Heart, don't faint! Anasūyā speaks your thoughts.

KING (*to himself*): Should I reveal myself now or conceal who I am? I'll say it this way:

(*Aloud.*)

Lady, I have been appointed by the Puru king as the officer in charge of religious matters. I have come to this sacred forest to assure that your holy rites proceed unhindered.

ANASŪYĀ: Our religious life has a guardian now.

(*Śakuntalā mimes the embarrassment of erotic emotion.*)

BOTH FRIENDS (*observing the behavior of Śakuntalā and the king; in a stage whisper*): Śakuntalā, if only your father were here now!

ŚAKUNTALĀ (*angrily*): What if he were?

BOTH FRIENDS: He would honor this distinguished guest with what he values most in life.

ŚAKUNTALĀ: Quiet! Such words hint at your hearts' conspiracy. I won't listen.

KING: Ladies, I want to ask about your friend.

BOTH FRIENDS: Your request honors us, sir.

KING: Sage Kaṇva has always been celibate, but you call your friend his daughter. How can this be?

ANASŪYĀ: Please listen, sir. There was a powerful royal sage of the Kauśika clan . . .

KING: I am listening.

ANASŪYĀ: He begot our friend, but Kaṇva is her father because he cared for her when she was abandoned.

KING: "Abandoned"? The word makes me curious. I want to hear her story from the beginning.

ANASŪYĀ: Please listen, sir. Once when this great sage was practicing terrible austerities on the bank of the Gautamī river, he became so powerful that the jealous gods sent a nymph named Menakā to break his self-control.

KING: The gods dread men who meditate.

ANASŪYĀ: When springtime came to the forest with all its charm, the sage saw her intoxicating beauty . . .

KING: I understand what happened then. She is the nymph's daughter.

ANASŪYĀ: Yes.

KING: It had to be!

No mortal woman could give birth to such beauty—
lightning does not flash out of the earth.   (22)

(*Śakuntalā stands with her face bowed. The king continues speaking to himself.*)

My desire is not hopeless. Yet, when I hear her friends teasing her about a bridegroom, a new fear divides my heart.

PRIYAṀVADĀ (*smiling, looking at Śakuntalā, then turning to the king*): Sir, you seem to want to say more.

(*Śakuntalā makes a threatening gesture with her finger.*)

KING: You judge correctly. In my eagerness to learn more about your pious lives, I have another question.

PRIYAṀVADĀ: Don't hesitate! Ascetics can be questioned frankly.

KING: I want to know this about your friend:

> Will she keep the vow of hermit life
> only until she marries . . .
> or will she always exchange
> loving looks with deer in the forest? (23)

PRIYAṀVADĀ: Sir, even in her religious life, she is subject to her father, but he does intend to give her to a suitable husband.

KING (*to himself*): His wish is not hard to fulfill.

> Heart, indulge your desire—
> now that doubt is dispelled,
> the fire you feared to touch
> is a jewel in your hands. (24)

ŚAKUNTALĀ (*showing anger*): Anasūyā, I'm leaving!

ANASŪYĀ: Why?

ŚAKUNTALĀ: I'm going to tell Mother Gautamī that Priyaṁvadā is talking nonsense.

ANASŪYĀ: Friend, it's wrong to neglect a distinguished guest and leave as you like.

(*Śakuntalā starts to go without answering.*)

KING (*wanting to seize her, but holding back, he speaks to himself*): A lover dare not act on his impulsive thoughts!

> I wanted to follow the sage's daughter,
> but decorum abruptly pulled me back;
> I set out and returned again
> without moving my feet from this spot. (25)

PRIYAṀVADĀ (*stopping Śakuntalā*): It's wrong of you to go!

ŚAKUNTALĀ (*bending her brow into a frown*): Give me a reason why!

PRIYAṀVADĀ: You promised to water two trees for me. Come here and pay your debt before you go!

(*She stops her by force.*)

KING: But she seems exhausted from watering the trees:

> Her shoulders droop, her palms
> are red from the watering pot—
> even now, breathless sighs
> make her breasts shake;
> beads of sweat on her face
> wilt the flower at her ear;
> her hand holds back
> disheveled locks of hair. (26)

Here, I'll pay her debt!

(*He offers his ring. Both friends recite the syllables of the name on the seal and stare at each other.*)

Don't mistake me for what I am not! This is a gift from the king to identify me as his royal official.

PRIYAṀVADĀ: Then the ring should never leave your finger. Your word has

already paid her debt.
(*She laughs a little.*)
Śakuntalā, you are freed by this kind man . . . or perhaps by the king. Go now!
ŚAKUNTALĀ (*to herself*): If I am able to . . .
(*Aloud.*)
Who are you to keep me or release me?
KING (*watching Śakuntalā*): Can she feel toward me what I feel toward her? Or is my desire fulfilled?

> She won't respond directly to my words,
> but she listens when I speak;
> she won't turn to look at me,
> but her eyes can't rest anywhere else. (27)

VOICE OFFSTAGE: Ascetics, be prepared to protect the creatures of our forest grove! King Duṣyanta is hunting nearby!

> Dust raised by his horses' hooves
> falls like a cloud of locusts swarming
> at sunset over branches of trees
> where wet bark garments hang. (28)

> In terror of the chariots, an elephant
> charged into the hermitage
> and scattered the herd of black antelope,
> like a demon foe of our penances—
> his tusks garlanded with branches
> from a tree crushed by his weight,
> his feet tangled in vines
> that tether him like chains. (29)

(*Hearing this, all the girls are agitated.*)
KING (*to himself*): Oh! My palace men are searching for me and wrecking the grove. I'll have to go back.
BOTH FRIENDS: Sir, we're all upset by this news. Please let us go to our hut.
KING (*showing confusion*): Go, please. We will try to protect the hermitage.
(*They all stand to go.*)
BOTH FRIENDS: Sir, we're ashamed that our bad hospitality is our only excuse to invite you back.
KING: Not at all. I am honored to have seen you.
(*Śakuntalā exits with her two friends, looking back at the king, lingering artfully.*)
I have little desire to return to the city. I'll join my men and have them camp near the grove. I can't control my feelings for Śakuntalā.

> My body turns to go,
> my heart pulls me back,
> like a silk banner
> buffeted by the wind. (30)

(*All exit.*)

END OF ACT ONE

ACT TWO

(The buffoon enters, despondent.)

BUFFOON *(sighing)*: My bad luck! I'm tired of playing sidekick to a king who's hooked on hunting. "There's a deer!" "There's a boar!" "There's a tiger!" Even in the summer midday heat we chase from jungle to jungle on paths where trees give barely any shade. We drink stinking water from mountain streams foul with rusty leaves. At odd hours we eat nasty meals of spit-roasted meat. Even at night I can't sleep. My joints ache from galloping on that horse. Then at the crack of dawn, I'm woken rudely by a noise piercing the forest. Those sons of bitches hunt their birds then. The torture doesn't end—now I have sores on top of my bruises. Yesterday, we lagged behind. The king chased a buck into the hermitage. As luck would have it, an ascetic's daughter called Śakuntalā caught his eye. Now he isn't even thinking of going back to the city. This very dawn I found him wide-eyed, mooning about her. What a fate! I must see him after his bath.

(He walks around, looking.)

Here comes my friend now, wearing garlands of wild flowers. Greek women carry his bow in their hands. Good! I'll stand here pretending my arms and legs are broken. Maybe then I'll get some rest.

(He stands leaning on his staff. The king enters with his retinue, as described.)

KING *(to himself)*:

My beloved will not be easy to win,
but signs of emotion revealed her heart—
even when love seems hopeless,
mutual longing keeps passion alive. (1)

(He smiles.)

A suitor who measures his beloved's state of mind by his own desire is a fool.

She threw tender glances
though her eyes were cast down,
her heavy hips swayed
in slow seductive movements,
she answered in anger
when her friend said, "Don't go!"
and I felt it was all for my sake . . .
but a lover sees in his own way. (2)

BUFFOON *(still in the same position)*: Dear friend, since my hands can't move to greet you, I have to salute you with my voice.

KING: How did you cripple your limbs?

BUFFOON: Why do you ask why I cry after throwing dust in my eyes yourself?

KING: I don't understand.

BUFFOON: Dear friend, when a straight reed is twisted into a crooked reed, is it by its own power, or is it the river current?

KING: The river current is the cause.

BUFFOON: And so it is with me.

KING: How so?

BUFFOON: You neglect the business of being a king and live like a woodsman in this awful camp. Chasing after wild beasts every day jolts my joints and muscles till I can't control my own limbs anymore. I beg you to let me rest for just one day!

KING (*to himself*): He says what I also feel. When I remember Kaṇva's daughter, the thought of hunting disgusts me.

> I can't draw my bowstring
> to shoot arrows at deer
> who live with my love
> and teach her tender glances. (3)

BUFFOON: Sir, you have something on your mind. I'm crying in a wilderness.

KING (*smiling*): Yes, it is wrong to ignore my friend's plea.

BUFFOON: Live long!

(*He starts to go.*)

KING: Dear friend, stay! Hear what I have to say!

BUFFOON: At your command, sir!

KING: When you have rested, I need your help in some work that you will enjoy.

BUFFOON: Is it eating sweets? I'm game!

KING: I shall tell you. Who stands guard?

GUARD (*entering*): At your command, sir!

KING: Raivataka! Summon the general!

(*The guard exits and reenters with the general.*)

GUARD: The king is looking this way, waiting to give you his orders. Approach him, sir!

GENERAL (*looking at the king*): Hunting is said to be a vice, but our king prospers:

> Drawing the bow only hardens his chest,
> he suffers the sun's scorching rays unburned,
> hard muscles mask his body's lean state—
> like a wild elephant, his energy sustains him. (4)

(*He approaches the king.*)

Victory, my lord! We've already tracked some wild beasts. Why the delay?

KING: Mādhavya's censure of hunting has dampened my spirit.

GENERAL (*in a stage whisper, to the buffoon*): Friend, you stick to your opposition! I'll try to restore our king's good sense.

(*Aloud.*)

This fool is talking nonsense. Here is the king as proof:

> A hunter's belly is taut and lean,
> his slender body craves exertion;
> he penetrates the spirit of creatures
> overcome by fear and rage;
> his bowmanship is proved
> by arrows striking a moving target—
> hunting is falsely called a vice.
> What sport can rival it? (5)

BUFFOON (*angrily*): The king has come to his senses. If you keep chasing from forest to forest, you'll fall into the jaws of an old bear hungry for a human nose . . .

KING: My noble general, we are near a hermitage; your words cannot please me now.

> Let horned buffaloes plunge into muddy pools!
> Let herds of deer huddle in the shade to eat grass!
> Let fearless wild boars crush fragrant swamp grass!
> Let my bowstring lie slack and my bow at rest! (6)

GENERAL: Whatever gives the king pleasure.

KING: Withdraw the men who are in the forest now and forbid my soldiers to disturb the grove!

> Ascetics devoted to peace
> possess a fiery hidden power,
> like smooth crystal sunstones
> that reflect the sun's scorching rays. (7)

GENERAL: Whatever you command, sir!

BUFFOON: Your arguments for keeping up the hunt fall on deaf ears!

(*The general exits.*)

KING (*looking at his retinue*): You women, take away my hunting gear! Raivataka, don't neglect your duty!

RETINUE: As the king commands!

(*They exit.*)

BUFFOON: Sir, now that the flies are cleared out, sit on a stone bench under this shady canopy. Then I'll find a comfortable seat too.

KING: Go ahead!

BUFFOON: You first, Sir!

(*Both walk about, then sit down.*)

KING: Māḍhavya, you haven't really used your eyes because you haven't seen true beauty.

BUFFOON: But you're right in front of me, sir!

KING: Everyone is partial to what he knows well, but I'm speaking about Śakuntalā, the jewel of the hermitage.

BUFFOON (*to himself*): I won't give him a chance!

(*Aloud.*)

Dear friend, it seems that you're pursuing an ascetic's daughter.

KING: Friend, the heart of a Puru king wouldn't crave a forbidden fruit . . .

> The sage's child is a nymph's daughter,
> rescued by him after she was abandoned,
> like a fragile jasmine blossom
> broken and caught on a sunflower pod. (8)

BUFFOON (*laughing*): You're like the man who loses his taste for dates and prefers sour tamarind! How can you abandon the gorgeous gems of your palace?

KING: You speak this way because you haven't seen her.

BUFFOON: She must be delectable if you're so enticed!

KING: Friend, what is the use of all this talk?

The divine creator imagined perfection
and shaped her ideal form in his mind—
when I recall the beauty his power wrought,
she shines like a gemstone among my jewels. (9)

BUFFOON: So she's the reason you reject the other beauties!
KING: She stays in my mind:

A flower no one has smelled,
a bud no fingers have plucked,
an uncut jewel, honey untasted,
unbroken fruit of holy deeds—
I don't know who is destined
to enjoy her flawless beauty. (10)

BUFFOON: Then you should rescue her quickly! Don't let her fall into the arms
of some ascetic who greases his head with ingudī oil!
KING: She is someone else's ward and her guardian is away.
BUFFOON: What kind of passion did her eyes betray?
KING: Ascetics are timid by nature:

Her eyes were cast down in my presence,
but she found an excuse to smile—
modesty barely contained the love
she could neither reveal nor conceal. (11)

BUFFOON: Did you expect her to climb into your lap when she'd barely seen you?
KING: When we parted her feelings for me showed despite her modesty.

"A blade of kuśa grass
pricked my foot,"
the girl said for no reason
after walking a few steps away;
then she pretended to free
her bark dress from branches
where it was not caught
and shyly glanced at me. (12)

BUFFOON: Stock up on food for a long trip! I can see you've turned that ascetics'
grove into a pleasure garden.
KING: Friend, some of the ascetics recognize me. What excuse can we find to
return to the hermitage?
BUFFOON: What excuse? Aren't you the king? Collect a sixth of their wild rice
as tax!
KING: Fool! These ascetics pay tribute that pleases me more than mounds of
jewels.

Tribute that kings collect
from members of society decays,
but the share of austerity
that ascetics give lasts forever. (13)

423

VOICE OFFSTAGE: Good, we have succeeded!

KING (*listening*): These are the steady, calm voices of ascetics.

GUARD (*entering*): Victory, sir! Two boy ascetics are waiting near the gate.

KING: Let them enter without delay!

GUARD: I'll show them in.

(*He exits; reenters with the boys.*)

Here you are!

FIRST BOY: His majestic body inspires trust. It is natural when a king is virtually a sage.

> His palace is a hermitage
> with its infinite pleasures,
> the discipline of protecting men
> imposes austerities every day—
> pairs of celestial bards praise
> his perfect self-control,
> adding the royal word "king"
> to "sage," his sacred title. (14)

SECOND BOY: Gautama, is this Duṣyanta, the friend of Indra?

FIRST BOY: Of course!

SECOND BOY:

> It is no surprise that this arm of iron
> rules the whole earth bounded by dark seas—
> when demons harass the gods, victory's hope
> rests on his bow and Indra's thunderbolt. (15)

BOTH BOYS (*coming near*): Victory to you, king!

KING (*rising from his seat*): I salute you both!

BOTH BOYS: To your success, sir!

(*They offer fruits.*)

KING (*accepting their offering*): I am ready to listen.

BOTH BOYS: The ascetics know that you are camped nearby and send a petition to you.

KING: What do they request?

BOTH BOYS: Demons are taking advantage of Sage Kaṇva's absence to harass us. You must come with your charioteer to protect the hermitage for a few days!

KING: I am honored to oblige.

BUFFOON (*in a stage whisper*): Your wish is fulfilled!

KING (*smiling*): Raivataka, call my charioteer! Tell him to bring the chariot and my bow!

GUARD: As the king commands!

(*He exits.*)

BOTH BOYS (*showing delight*):

> Following your ancestral duties
> suits your noble form—

the Puru kings are ordained
to dispel their subjects' fear. (16)

KING (*bowing*): You two return! I shall follow.

BOTH BOYS: Be victorious!

(*They exit.*)

KING: Mādhavya, are you curious to see Śakuntalā?

BUFFOON: At first there was a flood, but now with this news of demons, not a drop is left.

KING: Don't be afraid! Won't you be with me?

BUFFOON: Then I'll be safe from any demon . . .

GUARD (*entering*): The chariot is ready to take you to victory . . . but Karabhaka has just come from the city with a message from the queen.

KING: Did my mother send him?

GUARD: She did.

KING: Have him enter then.

GUARD: Yes.

(*He exits; reenters with Karabhaka.*)

Here is the king. Approach!

KARABHAKA: Victory, sir! Victory! The queen has ordered a ceremony four days from now to mark the end of her fast. Your Majesty will surely give us the honor of his presence.

KING: The ascetics' business keeps me here and my mother's command calls me there. I must find a way to avoid neglecting either!

BUFFOON: Hang yourself between them the way Triśaṅku hung between heaven and earth.

KING: I'm really confused . . .

My mind is split in two
by these conflicting duties,
like a river current split
by boulders in its course. (17)

(*Thinking.*)

Friend, my mother has treated you like a son. You must go back and report that I've set my heart on fulfilling my duty to the ascetics. You fulfill my filial duty to the queen.

BUFFOON: You don't really think I'm afraid of demons?

KING (*smiling*): My brave brahman, how could you be?

BUFFOON: Then I can travel like the king's younger brother.

KING: We really should not disturb the grove! Take my whole entourage with you!

BUFFOON: Now I've turned into the crown prince!

KING (*to himself*): This fellow is absent-minded. At any time he may tell the palace women about my passion. I'll tell him this:

(*Taking the buffoon by the hand, he speaks aloud.*)

Dear friend, I'm going to the hermitage out of reverence for the sages. I really feel no desire for the young ascetic Śakuntalā.

What do I share with a rustic girl
reared among fawns, unskilled in love?
Don't mistake what I muttered
in jest for the real truth, friend!   (18)

(*All exit.*)

END OF ACT TWO

ACT THREE

(*A disciple of Kaṇva enters, carrying kuśa grass for a sacrificial rite.*)

DISCIPLE: King Duṣyanta is certainly powerful. Since he entered the hermitage, our rites have not been hindered.

Why talk of fixing arrows?
The mere twang of his bowstring
clears away menacing demons
as if his bow roared with death.   (1)

I'll gather some more grass for the priests to spread on the sacrificial altar.
(*Walking around and looking, he calls aloud.*)
Priyaṁvadā, for whom are you bringing the ointment of fragrant lotus root fibers and leaves?
(*Listening.*)
What are you saying? Śakuntalā is suffering from heat exhaustion? They're for rubbing on her body? Priyaṁvadā, take care of her! She is the breath of Father Kaṇva's life. I'll give Gautamī this water from the sacrifice to use for soothing her.
(*He exits; the interlude ends. Then the king enters, suffering from love, deep in thought, sighing.*)
KING:

I know the power ascetics have
and the rules that bind her,
but I cannot abandon my heart
now that she has taken it.   (2)

(*Showing the pain of love.*)
Love, why do you and the moon both contrive to deceive lovers by first gaining our trust?

Arrows of flowers and cool moon rays
are both deadly for men like me—
the moon shoots fire through icy rays
and you hurl thunderbolts of flowers.   (3)

(Walking around.)
Now that the rites are concluded and the priests have dismissed me, where can I rest from the weariness of this work?
(Sighing.)
There is no refuge but the sight of my love. I must find her.
(Looking up at the sun.)
Śakuntalā usually spends the heat of the day with her friends in a bower of vines on the Mālinī riverbank. I shall go there.
(Walking around, miming the touch of breeze.)
This place is enchanted by the wind.

> A breeze fragrant with lotus pollen
> and moist from the Mālinī waves
> can be held in soothing embrace
> by my love-scorched arms. (4)

(Walking around and looking.)

> I see fresh footprints
> on white sand in the clearing,
> deeply pressed at the heel
> by the sway of full hips. (5)

I'll just look through the branches.
(Walking around, looking, he becomes joyous.)
My eyes have found bliss! The girl I desire is lying on a stone couch strewn with flowers, attended by her two friends. I'll eavesdrop as they confide in one another.
(He stands watching. Śakuntalā appears as described, with her two friends.)
BOTH FRIENDS *(fanning her affectionately)*: Śakuntalā, does the breeze from this lotus leaf please you?
ŚAKUNTALĀ: Are you fanning me?
(The friends trade looks, miming dismay.)
KING *(deliberating)*: Śakuntalā seems to be in great physical pain. Is it the heat or is it what is in my own heart?
(Miming ardent desire.)
My doubts are unfounded!

> Her breasts are smeared with lotus balm,
> her lotus-fiber bracelet hangs limp,
> her beautiful body glows in pain—
> love burns young women like summer heat,
> but its guilt makes them more charming. (6)

PRIYAMVADĀ *(in a stage whisper)*: Anasūyā, Śakuntalā has been pining since she first saw the king. Could he be the cause of her sickness?
ANASŪYĀ: She must be suffering from lovesickness. I'll ask her . . .
(Aloud.)
Friend, I have something to ask you. Your pain seems so deep . . .
ŚAKUNTALĀ *(raising herself halfway)*: What do you want to say?
ANASŪYĀ: Śakuntalā, though we don't know what it is to be in love, your

condition reminds us of lovers we have heard about in stories. Can you tell us the cause of your pain? Unless we understand your illness, we can't begin to find a cure.

KING: Anasūyā expresses my own thoughts.

ŚAKUNTALĀ: Even though I want to, suddenly I can't make myself tell you.

PRIYAṂVADĀ: Śakuntalā, my friend Anasūyā means well. Don't you see how sick you are? Your limbs are wasting away. Only the shadow of your beauty remains . . .

KING: What Priyaṃvadā says is true:

> Her cheeks are deeply sunken,
> her breasts' full shape is gone
> her waist is thin, her shoulders bent,
> and the color has left her skin—
> tormented by love,
> she is sad but beautiful to see,
> like a jasmine creeper
> when hot wind shrivels its leaves. (7)

ŚAKUNTALĀ: Friends, who else can I tell? May I burden you?

BOTH FRIENDS: We insist! Sharing sorrow with loving friends makes it bearable.

KING:

> Friends who share her joy and sorrow
> discover the love concealed in her heart—
> though she looked back longingly at me,
> now I am afraid to hear her response. (8)

ŚAKUNTALĀ: Friends, since my eyes first saw the guardian of the hermits' retreat, I've felt such strong desire for him!

KING: I have heard what I want to hear.

> My tormentor, the god of love,
> has soothed my fever himself,
> like the heat of late summer
> allayed by early rain clouds. (9)

ŚAKUNTALĀ: If you two think it's right, then help me to win the king's pity. Otherwise, you'll soon pour sesame oil and water on my corpse . . .

KING: Her words destroy my doubt.

PRIYAṂVADĀ (*in a stage whisper*): She's so dangerously in love that there's no time to lose. Since her heart is set on the ornament of the Puru dynasty, we should rejoice that she desires him.

ANASŪYĀ: What you say is true.

PRIYAṂVADĀ (*aloud*): Friend, by good fortune your desire is in harmony with nature. A great river can only descend to the ocean. A jasmine creeper can only twine around a mango tree.

KING: Why is this surprising when the twin stars of spring serve the crescent moon?

ANASŪYĀ: What means do we have to fulfill our friend's desire secretly and quickly?

PRIYAṂVADĀ: "Secretly" demands some effort. "Quickly" is easy.

ANASŪYĀ: How so?

PRIYAMVADĀ: The king was charmed by her loving look; he seems thin these days from sleepless nights.

KING: It's true . . .

> This golden armlet
> slips to my wrist
> without touching the scars
> my bowstring has made;
> its gemstones are faded
> by tears of secret pain
> that every night wets my arm
> where I bury my face. (10)

PRIYAMVADĀ (*thinking*): Compose a love letter and I'll hide it in a flower. I'll deliver it to his hand on the pretext of bringing an offering to the deity.

ANASŪYĀ: This subtle plan pleases me. What does Śakuntalā say?

ŚAKUNTALĀ: I'll try my friend's plan.

PRIYAMVADĀ: Then compose a poem to declare your love!

ŚAKUNTALĀ: I'm thinking, but my heart trembles with fear that he'll reject me.

KING (*delighted*):

> The man you fear will reject you
> waits longing to love you, timid girl—
> a suitor may lose or be lucky,
> but the goddess always wins. (11)

BOTH FRIENDS: Why do you belittle your own virtues? Who would cover his body with a piece of cloth to keep off cool autumn moonlight?

ŚAKUNTALĀ (*smiling*): I'm trying to follow your advice.

(*She sits thinking.*)

KING: As I gaze at her, my eyes forget to blink.

> She arches an eyebrow,
> struggling to compose the verse—
> the down rises on her cheek,
> showing the passion she feels. (12)

ŚAKUNTALĀ: I've thought of a verse, but I have nothing to write it on.

PRIYAMVADĀ: Engrave the letters with your nail on this lotus leaf! It's as delicate as a parrot's breast.

ŚAKUNTALĀ (*miming what Priyamvadā described*): Listen and tell me if this makes sense!

BOTH FRIENDS: We're both paying attention.

ŚAKUNTALĀ (*singing*):

> I don't know
> your heart,
> but day and night
> for wanting you,
> love violently
> tortures

my limbs,
cruel man. (13)

KING (*suddenly revealing himself*):

Love torments you, slender girl,
but he completely consumes me—
daylight spares the lotus pond
while it destroys the moon. (14)

BOTH FRIENDS (*looking, rising with delight*): Welcome to the swift success of love's desire!
(*Śakuntalā tries to rise.*)
KING: Don't exert yourself!

Limbs lying among crushed petals
like fragile lotus stalks
are too weakened by pain
to perform ceremonious acts. (15)

ANASŪYĀ: Then let the king sit on this stone bench!
(*The king sits; Śakuntalā rises in embarrassment.*)
PRIYAMVADĀ: The passion of two young lovers is clear. My affection for our friend makes me speak out again now.
KING: Noble lady, don't hesitate! It is painful to keep silent when one must speak.
PRIYAMVADĀ: We're told that it is the king's duty to ease the pain of his suffering subjects.
KING: My duty, exactly!
PRIYAMVADĀ: Since she first saw you, our dear friend has been reduced to this sad condition. You must protect her and save her life.
KING: Noble lady, our affection is shared and I am honored by all you say.
ŚAKUNTALĀ (*looking at Priyamvadā*): Why are you keeping the king here? He must be anxious to return to his palace.
KING:

If you think that my lost heart
could love anyone but you,
a fatal blow strikes a man
already wounded by love's arrows! (16)

ANASŪYĀ: We've heard that kings have many loves. Will our dear friend become a sorrow to her family after you've spent time with her?
KING: Noble lady, enough of this!

Despite my many wives
on two the royal line rests—
sea-bound earth
and your friend. (17)

BOTH FRIENDS: You reassure us.
PRIYAMVADĀ (*casting a glance*): Anasūyā, this fawn is looking for its mother. Let's take it to her!
(*They both begin to leave.*)

ŚAKUNTALĀ: Come back! Don't leave me unprotected!
BOTH FRIENDS: The protector of the earth is at your side.
ŚAKUNTALĀ: Why have they gone?
KING: Don't be alarmed! I am your servant.

> Shall I set moist winds in motion
> with lotus-leaf fans to cool your pain,
> or rest your soft red lotus feet
> on my lap to stroke them, my love? (18)

ŚAKUNTALĀ: I cannot sin against those I respect!
(*Standing as if she wants to leave.*)
KING: Beautiful Śakuntalā, the day is still hot.

> Why should your frail limbs
> leave this couch of flowers
> shielded by lotus leaves
> to wander in the heat? (19)

(*Saying this, he forces her to turn around.*)
ŚAKUNTALĀ: Puru king, control yourself! Though I'm burning with love, how can I give myself to you?
KING: Don't fear your elders! The father of your family knows the law. When he finds out, he will not blame you.

> The daughters of royal sages often marry
> in secret and then their fathers bless them. (20)

ŚAKUNTALĀ: Release me! I must ask my friends' advice!
KING: Yes, I shall release you.
ŚAKUNTALĀ: When?
KING:

> Only let my thirsting mouth
> gently drink from your lips,
> the way a bee sips nectar
> from a fragile virgin blossom. (21)

(*Saying this, he tries to raise her face. Śakuntalā evades him with a dance.*)
VOICE OFFSTAGE: Red goose, bid farewell to your gander! Night has arrived!
ŚAKUNTALĀ (*flustered*): Puru king, Mother Gautamī is surely coming to ask about my health. Hide behind this tree!
KING: Yes.
(*He conceals himself and waits. Then Gautamī enters with a vessel in her hand, accompanied by Śakuntalā's two friends.*)
BOTH FRIENDS: This way, Mother Gautamī!
GAUTAMĪ (*approaching Śakuntalā*): Child, does the fever in your limbs burn less?
ŚAKUNTALĀ: Madam, I do feel better.
GAUTAMĪ: Kuśa grass and water will soothe your body.
(*She sprinkles Śakuntalā's head.*)
Child, the day is ended. Come, let's go back to our hut!
(*She starts to go.*)
ŚAKUNTALĀ (*to herself*): My heart, even when your desire was within reach, you

were bound by fear. Now you'll suffer the torment of separation and regret.
(*Stopping after a few steps, she speaks aloud.*)
Bower of creepers, refuge from my torment, I say goodbye until our joy
can be renewed . . .
(*Sorrowfully, Śakuntalā exits with the other women.*)
KING (*coming out of hiding*): Fulfillment of desire is fraught with obstacles.

> Why didn't I kiss her face
> as it bent near my shoulder,
> her fingers shielding lips
> that stammered lovely warning? (22)

Should I go now? Or shall I stay here in this bower of creepers that my love
enjoyed and then left?

> I see the flowers her body pressed
> on this bench of stone,
> the letter her nails inscribed
> on the faded lotus leaf,
> the lotus-fiber bracelet
> that slipped from her wrist—
> my eyes are prisoners
> in this empty house of reeds. (23)

VOICE IN THE AIR: King!

> When the evening rituals begin,
> shadows of flesh-eating demons swarm
> like amber clouds of twilight,
> raising terror at the altar of fire. (24)

KING: I am coming.
(*He exits.*)

END OF ACT THREE

ACT FOUR

(*The two friends enter, miming the gathering of flowers.*)

ANASŪYĀ: Priyaṁvadā, I'm delighted that Śakuntalā chose a suitable husband
for herself, but I still feel anxious.
PRIYAṀVADĀ: Why?
ANASŪYĀ: When the king finished the sacrifice, the sages thanked him and
he left. Now that he has returned to his palace women in the city, will he
remember us here?
PRIYAṀVADĀ: Have faith! He's so handsome, he can't be evil. But I don't know
what Father Kaṇva will think when he hears about what happened.
ANASŪYĀ: I predict that he'll give his approval.

PRIYAṀVADĀ: Why?

ANASŪYĀ: He's always planned to give his daughter to a worthy husband. If fate accomplished it so quickly, Father Kaṇva won't object.

PRIYAṀVADĀ (*looking at the basket of flowers*): We've gathered enough flowers for the offering ceremony.

ANASŪYĀ: Shouldn't we worship the goddess who guards Śakuntalā?

PRIYAṀVADĀ: I have just begun.

(*She begins the rite.*)

VOICE OFFSTAGE: I am here!

ANASŪYĀ (*listening*): Friend, a guest is announcing himself.

PRIYAṀVADĀ: Śakuntalā is in her hut nearby, but her heart is far away.

ANASŪYĀ: You're right! Enough of these flowers!

(*They begin to leave.*)

VOICE OFFSTAGE: So . . . you slight a guest . . .

> Since you blindly ignore
> a great sage like me,
> the lover you worship
> with mindless devotion
> will not remember you,
> even when awakened—
> like a drunkard who forgets
> a story he just composed! (1)

PRIYAṀVADĀ: Oh! What a terrible turn of events! Śakuntalā's distraction has offended someone she should have greeted.

(*Looking ahead.*)

Not just an ordinary person, but the angry sage Durvāsas himself cursed her and went away in a frenzy of quivering, mad gestures. What else but fire has such power to burn?

ANASŪYĀ: Go! Bow at his feet and make him return while I prepare the water for washing his feet!

PRIYAṀVADĀ: As you say.

(*She exits.*)

ANASŪYĀ (*after a few steps, she mimes stumbling*): Oh! The basket of flowers fell from my hand when I stumbled in my haste to go.

(*She mimes the gathering of flowers.*)

PRIYAṀVADĀ (*entering*): He's so terribly cruel! No one could pacify him! But I was able to soften him a little.

ANASŪYĀ: Even that is a great feat with him! Tell me more!

PRIYAṀVADĀ: When he refused to return, I begged him to forgive a daughter's first offense, since she didn't understand the power of his austerity.

ANASŪYĀ: Then? Then?

PRIYAṀVADĀ: He refused to change his word, but he promised that when the king sees the ring of recollection, the curse will end. Then he vanished.

ANASŪYĀ: Now we can breathe again. When he left, the king himself gave her the ring engraved with his name. Śakuntalā will have her own means of ending the curse.

PRIYAṀVADĀ: Come friend! We should finish the holy rite we're performing for her.

(*The two walk around, looking.*)

Anasūyā, look! With her face resting on her hand, our dear friend looks like a picture. She is thinking about her husband's leaving, with no thought for herself, much less for a guest.

ANASŪYĀ: Priyaṁvadā, we two must keep all this a secret between us. Our friend is fragile by nature; she needs our protection.

PRIYAṀVADĀ: Who would sprinkle a jasmine with scalding water?

(*They both exit; the interlude ends. Then a disciple of Kaṇva enters, just awakened from sleep.*)

DISCIPLE: Father Kaṇva has just returned from his pilgrimage and wants to know the exact time. I'll go into a clearing to see what remains of the night.

(*Walking around and looking.*)

It is dawn.

> The moon sets over the western mountain
> as the sun rises in dawn's red trail—
> rising and setting, these two bright powers
> portend the rise and fall of men. (2)

> When the moon disappears, night lotuses
> are but dull souvenirs of its beauty—
> when her lover disappears, the sorrow
> is too painful for a frail girl to bear. (3)

ANASŪYĀ (*throwing aside the curtain and entering*): Even a person withdrawn from worldly life knows that the king has treated Śakuntalā badly.

DISCIPLE: I'll inform Father Kaṇva that it's time for the fire oblation.

(*He exits.*)

ANASŪYĀ: Even when I'm awake, I'm useless. My hands and feet don't do their work. Love must be pleased to have made our innocent friend put her trust in a liar . . . but perhaps it was the curse of Durvāsas that changed him . . . otherwise, how could the king have made such promises and not sent even a message by now? Maybe we should send the ring to remind him. Which of these ascetics who practice austerities can we ask? Father Kaṇva has just returned from his pilgrimage. Since we feel that our friend was also at fault, we haven't told him that Śakuntalā is married to Duṣyanta and is pregnant. The problem is serious. What should we do?

PRIYAṀVADĀ (*entering, with delight*): Friend, hurry! We're to celebrate the festival of Śakuntalā's departure for her husband's house.

ANASŪYĀ: What's happened, friend?

PRIYAṀVADĀ: Listen! I went to ask Śakuntalā how she had slept. Father Kaṇva embraced her and though her face was bowed in shame, he blessed her: "Though his eyes were filled with smoke, the priest's oblation luckily fell on the fire. My child, I shall not mourn for you . . . like knowledge given to a good student I shall send you to your husband today with an escort of sages."

ANASŪYĀ: Who told Father Kaṇva what happened?

PRIYAṀVADĀ: A bodiless voice was chanting when he entered the fire sanctuary.

(*Quoting in Sanskrit.*)

> Priest, know that your daughter
> carries Duṣyanta's potent seed
> for the good of the earth—
> like fire in mimosa wood. (4)

ASŪYĀ: I'm joyful, friend. But I know that Śakuntalā must leave us today and sorrow shadows my happiness.

PRIYAṀVADĀ: Friend, we must chase away sorrow and make this hermit girl happy!

ANASŪYĀ: Friend, I've made a garland of mimosa flowers. It's in the coconut-shell box hanging on a branch of the mango tree. Get it for me! Meanwhile I'll prepare the special ointments of deer musk, sacred earth, and blades of dūrvā grass.

PRIYAṀVADĀ: Here it is!

(*Anasūyā exits; Priyaṁvadā gracefully mimes taking down the box.*)

VOICE OFFSTAGE: Gautamī! Śārṅgarava and some others have been appointed to escort Śakuntalā.

PRIYAṀVADĀ (*listening*): Hurry! Hurry! The sages are being called to go to Hastināpura.

ANASŪYĀ (*reentering with pots of ointments in her hands*): Come, friend! Let's go!

PRIYAṀVADĀ (*looking around*): Śakuntalā stands at sunrise with freshly washed hair while the female ascetics bless her with handfuls of wild rice and auspicious words of farewell. Let's go to her together.

(*The two approach as Śakuntalā enters with Gautamī and other female ascetics, and strikes a posture as described. One after another, the female ascetics address her.*)

FIRST FEMALE ASCETIC: Child, win the title "Chief Queen" as a sign of your husband's high esteem!

SECOND FEMALE ASCETIC: Child, be a mother to heroes!

THIRD FEMALE ASCETIC: Child, be honored by your husband!

BOTH FRIENDS: This happy moment is no time for tears, friend.

(*Wiping away her tears, they calm her with dance gestures.*)

PRIYAṀVADĀ: Your beauty deserves jewels, not these humble things we've gathered in the hermitage.

(*Two boy ascetics enter with offerings in their hands.*)

BOTH BOYS: Here is an ornament for you!

(*Everyone looks amazed.*)

GAUTAMĪ: Nārada, my child, where did this come from?

FIRST BOY: From Father Kaṇva's power.

GAUTAMĪ: Was it his mind's magic?

SECOND BOY: Not at all! Listen! You ordered us to bring flowers from the forest trees for Śakuntalā.

> One tree produced this white silk cloth,
> another poured resinous lac to redden her feet—
> the tree nymphs produced jewels in hands
> that stretched from branches like young shoots. (5)

PRIYAṀVADĀ (*watching Śakuntalā*): This is a sign that royal fortune will come to you in your husband's house.

(*Śakuntalā mimes modesty.*)

FIRST BOY: Gautama, come quickly! Father Kaṇva is back from bathing. We'll tell him how the trees honor her.

SECOND BOY: As you say.

(*The two exit.*)

BOTH FRIENDS: We've never worn them ourselves, but we'll put these jewels on your limbs the way they look in pictures.

ŚAKUNTALĀ: I trust your skill.

(*Both friends mime ornamenting her. Then Kaṇva enters, fresh from his bath.*)

KAṆVA:

> My heart is touched with sadness
> since Śakuntalā must go today,
> my throat is choked with sobs,
> my eyes are dulled by worry—
> if a disciplined ascetic
> suffers so deeply from love,
> how do fathers bear the pain
> of each daughter's parting? (6)

(*He walks around.*)

BOTH FRIENDS: Śakuntalā, your jewels are in place; now put on the pair of silken cloths.

(*Standing, Śakuntalā wraps them.*)

GAUTAMĪ: Child, your father has come. His eyes filled with tears of joy embrace you. Greet him reverently!

ŚAKUNTALĀ (*modestly*): Father, I welcome you.

KAṆVA: Child,

> May your husband honor you
> the way Yayāti honored Śarmiṣṭhā.
> As she bore her son Puru,
> may you bear an imperial prince. (7)

GAUTAMĪ: Sir, this is a blessing, not just a prayer.

KAṆVA: Child, walk around the sacrifical fires!

(*All walk around; Kaṇva intoning a prayer in Vedic meter.*)

> Perfectly placed around the main altar,
> fed with fuel, strewn with holy grass,
> destroying sin by incense from oblations,
> may these sacred fires purify you! (8)

You must leave now!

(*Looking around.*)

Where are Śārṅgarava and the others?

DISCIPLE (*entering*): Here we are, sir!

KAṆVA: You show your sister the way!

ŚĀRṄGARAVA: Come this way!

(*They walk around.*)

KAṆVA: Listen, you trees that grow in our grove!

Until you were well watered
she could not bear to drink;
she loved you too much
to pluck your flowers for her hair;
the first time your buds bloomed,
she blossomed with joy—
may you all bless Śakuntalā
as she leaves for her husband's house.   (9)

(Miming that he hears a cuckoo's cry.)

The trees of her forest family
have blessed Śakuntalā—
the cuckoo's melodious song
announces their response.   (10)

VOICE IN THE AIR:

May lakes colored by lotuses mark her path!
May trees shade her from the sun's burning rays!
May the dust be as soft as lotus pollen!
May fragrant breezes cool her way!   (11)

(All listen astonished.)

GAUTAMĪ: Child, the divinities of our grove love you like your family and bless you. We bow to you all!

ŚAKUNTALĀ *(bowing and walking around; speaking in a stage whisper)*: Priyaṁvadā, though I long to see my husband, my feet move with sorrow as I start to leave the hermitage.

PRIYAṀVADĀ: You are not the only one who grieves. The whole hermitage feels this way as your departure from our grove draws near.

Grazing deer
drop grass,
peacocks
stop dancing,
vines loose
pale leaves
falling
like tears.   (12)

ŚAKUNTALĀ *(remembering)*: Father, before I leave, I must see my sister, the vine Forestlight.

KAṆVA: I know that you feel a sister's love for her. She is right here.

ŚAKUNTALĀ: Forestlight, though you love your mango tree, turn to embrace me with your tendril arms! After today, I'll be so far away . . .

KAṆVA:

Your merits won you the husband
I always hoped you would have

437

and your jasmine has her mango tree—
my worries for you both are over. (13)

Start your journey here!
ŚAKUNTALĀ (*facing her two friends*): I entrust her care to you.
BOTH FRIENDS: But who will care for us?
(*They wipe away their tears.*)
KAṆVA: Anasūyā, enough crying! You should be giving Śakuntalā courage!
(*All walk around.*)
ŚAKUNTALĀ: Father, when the pregnant doe who grazes near my hut gives birth,
please send someone to give me the good news.
KAṆVA: I shall not forget.
ŚAKUNTALĀ (*miming the interrupting of her gait*): Who is clinging to my skirt?
(*She turns around.*)
KAṆVA: Child,

> The buck whose mouth you healed with oil
> when it was pierced by a blade of kuśa grass
> and whom you fed with grains of rice—
> your adopted son will not leave the path. (14)

ŚAKUNTALĀ: Child, don't follow when I'm abandoning those I love! I raised you
when you were orphaned soon after your birth, but now I'm deserting you too.
Father will look after you. Go back!
(*Weeping, she starts to go.*)
KAṆVA: Be strong!

> Hold back the tears that blind
> your long-lashed eyes—
> you will stumble if you cannot see
> the uneven ground on the path. (15)

ŚĀRṄGARAVA: Sir, the scriptures prescribe that loved ones be escorted only to the
water's edge. We are at the shore of the lake. Give us your message and return!
ŚAKUNTALĀ: We shall rest in the shade of this fig tree.
(*All walk around and stop; Kaṇva speaks to himself.*)
What would be the right message to send to King Duṣyanta?
(*He ponders.*)
ŚAKUNTALĀ (*in a stage whisper*): Look! The wild goose cries in anguish when her
mate is hidden by lotus leaves. What I'm suffering is much worse.
ANASŪYĀ: Friend, don't speak this way!

> This goose spends
> every long night
> in sorrow
> without her mate,
> but hope lets her
> survive
> the deep pain
> of loneliness. (16)

KAṆVA: Śārṅgarava, speak my words to the king after you present Śakuntalā!

ŚĀRṄGARAVA: As you command, sir!

KAṆVA:

> Considering our discipline,
> the nobility of your birth
> and that she fell in love with you
> before her kinsmen could act,
> acknowledge her with equal rank
> among your wives—
> what more is destined for her,
> the bride's family will not ask. (17)

ŚĀRṄGARAVA: I grasp your message.

KAṆVA: Child, now I must instruct you. We forest hermits know something about worldly matters.

ŚĀRṄGARAVA: Nothing is beyond the scope of wise men.

KAṆVA: When you enter your husband's family:

> Obey your elders, be a friend to the other wives!
> If your husband seems harsh, don't be impatient!
> Be fair to your servants, humble in your happiness!
> Women who act this way become noble wives;
> sullen girls only bring their families disgrace. (18)

But what does Gautamī think?

GAUTAMĪ: This is good advice for wives, child. Take it all to heart!

KAṆVA: Child, embrace me and your friends!

ŚAKUNTALĀ: Father, why must Priyaṁvadā and my other friends turn back here?

KAṆVA: They will also be given in marriage. It is not proper for them to go there now. Gautamī will go with you.

ŚAKUNTALĀ (*embracing her father*): How can I go on living in a strange place, torn from my father's side, like a vine torn from the side of a sandalwood tree growing on a mountain slope?

KAṆVA: Child, why are you so frightened?

> When you are your husband's honored wife,
> absorbed in royal duties and in your son,
> born like the sun to the eastern dawn,
> the sorrow of separation will fade. (19)

(*Śakuntalā falls at her father's feet.*)

Let my hopes for you be fulfilled!

ŚAKUNTALĀ (*approaching her two friends*): You two must embrace me together!

BOTH FRIENDS (*embracing her*): Friend, if the king seems slow to recognize you, show him the ring engraved with his name!

ŚAKUNTALĀ: Your suspicions make me tremble!

BOTH FRIENDS: Don't be afraid! It's our love that fears evil.

ŚĀRṄGARAVA: The sun is high in the afternoon sky. Hurry, please!

ŚAKUNTALĀ (*facing the sanctuary*): Father, will I ever see the grove again?

KAṆVA:

> When you have lived for many years
> as a queen equal to the earth
> and raised Duṣyanta's son
> to be a matchless warrior,
> your husband will entrust him
> with the burdens of the kingdom
> and will return with you
> to the calm of this hermitage. (20)

GAUTAMĪ: Child, the time for our departure has passed. Let your father turn back! It would be better, sir, if you turn back yourself. She'll keep talking this way forever.

KAṆVA: Child, my ascetic practice has been interrupted.

ŚAKUNTALĀ: My father's body is already tortured by ascetic practices. He must not grieve too much for me!

KAṆVA (*sighing*):

> When I see the grains of rice
> sprout from offerings you made
> at the door of your hut,
> how shall I calm my sorrow! (21)

(*Śakuntalā exits with her escort.*)

BOTH FRIENDS (*watching Śakuntalā*): Śakuntalā is hidden by forest trees now.

KAṆVA: Anasūyā, your companion is following her duty. Restrain yourself and return with me!

BOTH FRIENDS: Father, the ascetics' grove seems empty without Śakuntalā. How can we enter?

KAṆVA: The strength of your love makes it seem so.

(*Walking around in meditation.*)

Good! Now that Śakuntalā is on her way to her husband's family, I feel calm.

> A daughter belongs to another man—
> by sending her to her husband today,
> I feel the satisfaction
> one has on repaying a loan. (22)

(*All exit.*)

END OF ACT FOUR

ACT FIVE

(*The king and the buffoon enter; both sit down.*)

BUFFOON: Pay attention to the music room, friend, and you'll hear the notes of a song strung into a delicious melody . . . the lady Haṁsapadikā is practicing her singing.

KING: Be quiet so I can hear her!

VOICE IN THE AIR (*singing*):

> Craving sweet
> new nectar,
> you kissed
> a mango bud once—
> how could you
> forget her, bee,
> to bury your joy
> in a lotus? (1)

KING: The melody of the song is passionate.

BUFFOON: But did you get the meaning of the words?

KING: I once made love to her. Now she reproaches me for loving Queen Vasumatī. Friend Mādhavya, tell Haṁsapadikā that her words rebuke me soundly.

BUFFOON: As you command!

(*He rises.*)

But if that woman grabs my hair tuft, it will be like a heavenly nymph grabbing some ascetic . . . there go my hopes of liberation!

KING: Go! Use your courtly charm to console her.

BUFFOON: What a fate!

(*He exits.*)

KING (*to himself*): Why did hearing the song's words fill me with such strong desire? I'm not parted from anyone I love . . .

> Seeing rare beauty,
> hearing lovely sounds,
> even a happy man
> becomes strangely uneasy . . .
> perhaps he remembers,
> without knowing why,
> loves of another life
> buried deep in his being. (2)

(*He stands bewildered. Then the king's chamberlain enters.*)

CHAMBERLAIN: At my age, look at me!

> Since I took this ceremonial bamboo staff
> as my badge of office in the king's chambers
> many years have passed; now I use it
> as a crutch to support my faltering steps. (3)

A king cannot neglect his duty. He has just risen from his seat of justice and though I am loath to keep him longer, Sage Kaṇva's pupils have just arrived. Authority to rule the world leaves no time for rest.

> The sun's steeds were yoked before time began,
> the fragrant wind blows night and day,

the cosmic serpent always bears earth's weight,
and a king who levies taxes has his duty. (4)

Therefore, I must perform my office.
(*Walking around and looking.*)

Weary from ruling them like children,
he seeks solitude far from his subjects,
like an elephant bull who seeks cool shade
after gathering his herd at midday. (5)

(*Approaching.*)
Victory to you, king! Some ascetics who dwell in the forest at the foothills of
the Himālayas have come. They have women with them and bring a message
from Sage Kaṇva. Listen, king, and judge!
KING (*respectfully*): Are they Sage Kaṇva's messengers?
CHAMBERLAIN: They are.
KING: Inform the teacher Somarāta that he should welcome the ascetics with the
prescribed rites and then bring them to me himself. I'll wait in a place suitable
for greeting them.
CHAMBERLAIN: As the king commands.
(*He exits.*)
KING (*rising*): Vetravatī, lead the way to the fire sanctuary.
DOORKEEPER: Come this way, king!
KING (*walking around, showing fatigue*): Every other creature is happy when the
object of his desire is won, but for kings success contains a core of suffering.

High office only leads to greater greed;
just perfecting its rewards is wearisome—
a kingdom is more trouble than it's worth,
like a royal umbrella one holds alone. (6)

TWO BARDS OFFSTAGE: Victory to you, king!
FIRST BARD:

You sacrifice your pleasures every day
to labor for your subjects—
as a tree endures burning heat
to give shade from the summer sun. (7)

SECOND BARD:

You punish villains with your rod of justice,
you reconcile disputes, you grant protection—
most relatives are loyal only in hope of gain,
but you treat all your subjects like kinsmen. (8)

KING: My weary mind is revived.
(*He walks around.*)
DOORKEEPER: The terrace of the fire sanctuary is freshly washed and the cow is
waiting to give milk for the oblation. Let the king ascend!
KING: Vetravatī, why has Father Kaṇva sent these sages to me?

Does something hinder their ascetic life?
Or threaten creatures in the sacred forest?
Or do my sins stunt the flowering vines?
My mind is filled with conflicting doubts. (9)

DOORKEEPER: I would guess that these sages rejoice in your virtuous conduct and come to honor you.
(*The ascetics enter; Śakuntalā is in front with Gautamī; the chamberlain and the king's priest are in front of her.*)
CHAMBERLAIN: Come this way, sirs!
ŚĀRṄGARAVA: Śāradvata, my friend:

I know that this renowned king is righteous
and none of the social classes follows evil ways,
but my mind is so accustomed to seclusion
that the palace feels like a house in flames. (10)

ŚĀRADVATA: I've felt the same way ever since we entered the city.

As if I were freshly bathed, seeing a filthy man,
pure while he's defiled, awake while he's asleep,
as if I were a free man watching a prisoner,
I watch this city mired in pleasures. (11)

ŚAKUNTALĀ (*indicating she feels an omen*): Why is my right eye twitching?
GAUTAMĪ: Child, your husband's family gods turn bad fortune into blessings!
(*They walk around.*)
PRIEST (*indicating the king*): Ascetics, the guardian of sacred order has left the seat of justice and awaits you now. Behold him!
ŚĀRṄGARAVA: Great priest, he seems praiseworthy, but we expect no less.

Boughs bend, heavy with ripened fruit,
clouds descend with fresh rain,
noble men are gracious with wealth—
this is the nature of bountiful things. (12)

DOORKEEPER: King, their faces look calm. I'm sure that the sages have confidence in what they're doing.
KING (*seeing Śakuntalā*):

Who is she? Carefully veiled
to barely reveal her body's beauty,
surrounded by the ascetics
like a bud among withered leaves. (13)

DOORKEEPER: King, I feel curious and puzzled too. Surely her form deserves closer inspection.
KING: Let her be! One should not stare at another man's wife!
ŚAKUNTALĀ (*placing her hand on her chest, she speaks to herself*): My heart, why are you quivering? Be quiet while I learn my noble husband's feelings.
PRIEST (*going forward*): These ascetics have been honored with due ceremony. They have a message from their teacher. The king should hear them!
KING: I am paying attention.

SAGES (*raising their hands in a gesture of greeting*): May you be victorious, king!
KING: I salute you all!
SAGES: May your desires be fulfilled!
KING: Do the sages perform austerities unhampered?
SAGES:

> Who would dare obstruct the rites
> of holy men whom you protect—
> how can darkness descend
> when the sun's rays shine? (14)

KING: My title "king" is more meaningful now. Is the world blessed by Father Kanva's health?
SAGES: Saints control their own health. He asks about your welfare and sends this message . . .
KING: What does he command?
ŚĀRṄGARAVA: At the time you secretly met and married my daughter, affection made me pardon you both.

> We remember you to be a prince of honor;
> Śakuntalā is virtue incarnate—
> the creator cannot be condemned
> for mating the perfect bride and groom. (15)

And now that she is pregnant, receive her and perform your sacred duty together.
GAUTAMĪ: Sir, I have something to say, though I wasn't appointed to speak:

> She ignored her elders
> and you failed to ask her kinsmen—
> since you acted on your own,
> what can I say to you now? (16)

ŚAKUNTALĀ: What does my noble husband say?
KING: What has been proposed?
ŚAKUNTALĀ (*to herself*): The proposal is as clear as fire.
ŚĀRṄGARAVA: What's this? Your Majesty certainly knows the ways of the world!

> People suspect a married woman who stays
> with her kinsmen, even if she is chaste—
> a young wife should live with her husband,
> no matter how he despises her. (17)

KING: Did I ever marry you?
ŚAKUNTALĀ (*visibly dejected, speaking to herself*): Now your fears are real, my heart!
ŚĀRṄGARAVA:

> Does one turn away from duty in contempt
> because his own actions repulse him? (18a)

KING: Why ask this insulting question?

ŚĀRṄGARAVA:

Such transformations take shape
when men are drunk with power. (18b)

KING: This censure is clearly directed at me.

GAUTAMĪ: Child, this is no time to be modest. I'll remove your veil. Then your husband will recognize you.

(*She does so.*)

KING: (*staring at Śakuntalā*):

Must I judge whether I ever married
the flawless beauty they offer me now?
I cannot love her or leave her, like a bee
near a jasmine filled with frost at dawn. (19)

(*He shows hesitation.*)

DOORKEEPER: Our king has a strong sense of justice. Who else would hesitate when beauty like this is handed to him?

ŚĀRṄGARAVA: King, why do you remain silent?

KING: Ascetics, even though I'm searching my mind, I don't remember marrying this lady. How can I accept a woman who is visibly pregnant when I doubt that I am the cause?

ŚAKUNTALĀ (*in a stage whisper*): My lord casts doubt on our marriage. Why were my hopes so high?

ŚĀRṄGARAVA: It can't be!

Are you going to insult the sage
who pardons the girl you seduced
and bids you keep his stolen wealth,
treating a thief like you with honor? (20)

ŚĀRADVATA: Śārṅgarava, stop now! Śakuntalā, we have delivered our message and the king has responded. He must be shown some proof.

ŚAKUNTALĀ (*in a stage whisper*): When passion can turn to this, what's the use of reminding him? But, it's up to me to prove my honor now.

(*Aloud.*)

My noble husband . . .

(*She breaks off when this is half-spoken.*)

Since our marriage is in doubt, this is no way to address him. Puru king, you do wrong to reject a simple-hearted person with such words after you deceived her in the hermitage.

KING (*covering his ears*): Stop this shameful talk!

Are you trying to stain my name
and drag me to ruin—
like a river eroding her own banks,
soiling water and uprooting trees? (21)

ŚAKUNTALĀ: Very well! If it's really true that fear of taking another man's wife turns you away, then this ring will revive your memory and remove your doubt.

KING: An excellent idea!

ŚAKUNTALĀ (*touching the place where the ring had been*): I'm lost! The ring is gone from my finger.

(*She looks despairingly at Gautamī.*)

GAUTAMĪ: The ring must have fallen off while you were bathing in the holy waters at the shrine of the goddess near Indra's grove.

KING (*smiling*): And so they say the female sex is cunning.

ŚAKUNTALĀ: Fate has shown its power. Yet, I will tell you something else.

KING: I am still obliged to listen.

ŚAKUNTALĀ: One day, in a jasmine bower, you held a lotus-leaf cup full of water in your hand.

KING: We hear you.

ŚAKUNTALĀ: At that moment the buck I treated as my son approached. You coaxed it with the water, saying that it should drink first. But he didn't trust you and wouldn't drink from your hand. When I took the water, his trust returned. Then you jested, "Every creature trusts what its senses know. You both belong to the forest."

KING: Thus do women further their own ends by attracting eager men with the honey of false words.

GAUTAMĪ: Great king, you are wrong to speak this way. This child raised in an ascetics' grove doesn't know deceit.

KING: Old woman,

> When naive female beasts show cunning,
> what can we expect of women who reason?
> Don't cuckoos let other birds nurture
> their eggs and teach the chicks to fly? (22)

ŚAKUNTALĀ (*angrily*): Evil man! you see everything distorted by your own ignoble heart. Who would want to imitate you now, hiding behind your show of justice, like a well overgrown with weeds?

KING (*to himself*): Her anger does not seem feigned; it makes me doubt myself.

> When the absence of love's memory
> made me deny a secret affair with her,
> this fire-eyed beauty bent her angry brows
> and seemed to break the bow of love. (23)

(*Aloud.*)

Lady, Duṣyanta's conduct is renowned, so what you say is groundless.

ŚAKUNTALĀ: All right! I may be a self-willed wanton woman! But it was faith in the Puru dynasty that brought me into the power of a man with honey in his words and poison in his heart.

(*She covers her face at the end of the speech and weeps.*)

ŚĀRṄGARAVA: A willful act unchecked always causes pain.

> One should be cautious
> in forming a secret union—
> unless a lover's heart is clear,
> affection turns to poison. (24)

KING: But, sir, why do you demean me with such warnings? Do you trust the lady?

ŚĀRṄGARAVA (*scornfully*): You have learned everything backwards.

> If you suspect the word of one
> whose nature knows no guile,
> then you can only trust
> people who practice deception. (25)

KING: I presume you speak the truth. Let us assume so. But what could I gain by deceiving this woman?

ŚĀRṄGARAVA: Ruin.

KING: Ruin? A Puru king has no reason to want his own ruin!

ŚĀRADVATA: Śārṅgarava, this talk is pointless. We have delivered our master's message and should return.

> Since you married her, abandon her or take her—
> absolute is the power a husband has over his wife. (26)

GAUTAMĪ: You go ahead.

(*They start to go.*)

ŚAKUNTALĀ: What? Am I deceived by this cruel man and then abandoned by you?

(*She tries to follow them.*)

GAUTAMĪ (*stopping*): Śārṅgarava my son, Śakuntalā is following us, crying pitifully. What will my child do now that her husband has refused her?

ŚĀRṄGARAVA (*turning back angrily*): Bold woman, do you still insist on having your way?

(*Śakuntalā trembles in fear.*)

> If you are what the king says you are,
> you don't belong in Father Kaṇva's family—
> if you know that your marriage vow is pure,
> you can bear slavery in your husband's house. (27)

Stay! We must go on!

KING: Ascetic, why do you disappoint the lady too?

> The moon only makes lotuses open,
> the sun's light awakens lilies—
> a king's discipline forbids him
> to touch another man's wife. (28)

ŚĀRṄGARAVA: If you forget a past affair because of some present attachment, why do you fear injustice now?

KING (*to the priest*): Sir, I ask you to weigh the alternatives:

> Since it's unclear whether I'm deluded
> or she is speaking falsely—
> should I risk abandoning a wife
> or being tainted by another man's? (29)

PRIEST (*deliberating*): I recommend this . . .

KING: Instruct me! I'll do as you say.

PRIEST: Then let the lady stay in our house until her child is born. If you ask why: the wise men predict that your first son will be born with the marks of a king who turns the wheel of empire. If the child of the sage's daughter bears the marks, congratulate her and welcome her into your palace chambers. Otherwise, send her back to her father.

KING: Whatever the elders desire.

PRIEST: Child, follow me!

ŚAKUNTALĀ: Mother earth, open to receive me!

(*Weeping, Śakuntalā exits with the priest and the hermits. The king, his memory lost through the curse, thinks about her.*)

VOICE OFFSTAGE: Amazing! Amazing!

KING (*listening*): What could this be?

PRIEST (*reentering, amazed*): King, something marvelous has occurred!

KING: What?

PRIEST: When Kaṇva's pupils had departed,

> The girl threw up her arms and wept,
> lamenting her misfortune . . . then . . . (30a)

KING: Then what?

PRIEST:

> Near the nymph's shrine a ray of light
> in the shape of a woman carried her away. (30b)

(*All mime amazement.*)

KING: We've already settled the matter. Why discuss it further?

PRIEST (*observing the king*): May you be victorious!

(*He exits.*)

KING: Vetravatī, I am bewildered. Lead the way to my chamber!

DOORKEEPER: Come this way, my lord!

(*She walks forward.*)

KING:

> I cannot remember marrying
> the sage's abandoned daughter,
> but the pain my heart feels
> makes me suspect that I did. (31)

(*All exit.*)

END OF ACT FIVE

ACT SIX

(*The king's wife's brother, who is city magistrate, enters with two policemen leading a man whose hands are tied behind his back.*)

BOTH POLICEMEN (*beating the man*): Speak, thief! Where'd you steal this handsome ring with the king's name engraved in the jewel?

MAN (*showing fear*): Peace, sirs! I wouldn't do a thing like that.

FIRST POLICEMAN: Don't tell us the king thought you were some famous priest and gave it to you as a gift!

MAN: Listen, I'm a humble fisherman who lives near Indra's grove.

SECOND POLICEMAN: Thief, did we ask you about your caste?

MAGISTRATE: Sūcaka, let him tell it all in order! Don't interrupt him!

BOTH POLICEMEN: Whatever you command, chief!

MAN: I feed my family by catching fish with nets and hooks.

MAGISTRATE (*mocking*): What a pure profession!

MAN:

> The work I do
> may be vile
> but I won't deny
> my birthright—
> a priest
> doing his holy rites
> pities the animals
> he kills.

(1)

MAGISTRATE: Go on!

MAN: One day as I was cutting a red carp, I saw the shining stone of this ring in its belly. When I tried to sell it, you grabbed me. Kill me or let me go! That's how I got it!

MAGISTRATE: Jānuka, I'm sure this ugly butcher's a fisherman by his stinking smell. We must investigate how he got the ring. We'll go straight to the palace.

BOTH POLICEMEN: Okay. Go in front, you pickpocket!

(*All walk around.*)

MAGISTRATE: Sūcaka, guard this villain at the palace gate! I'll report to the king how we found the ring, get his orders, and come back.

BOTH POLICEMEN: Chief, good luck with the king!

(*The magistrate exits.*)

FIRST POLICEMAN: Jānuka, the chief's been gone a long time.

SECOND POLICEMAN: Well, there are fixed times for seeing kings.

FIRST POLICEMAN: Jānuka, my hands are itching to tie on his execution garland.

(*He points to the man.*)

MAN: You shouldn't think about killing a man for no reason.

SECOND POLICEMAN (*looking*): I see our chief coming with a letter in his hand. It's probably an order from the king. You'll be thrown to the vultures or you'll see the face of death's dog again . . .

MAGISTRATE (*entering*): Sūcaka, release this fisherman! I'll tell you how he got the ring.

FIRST POLICEMAN: Whatever you say, chief!

SECOND POLICEMAN: The villain entered the house of death and came out again. (*He unties the prisoner.*)

MAN (*bowing to the magistrate*): Master, how will I make my living now?

MAGISTRATE: The king sends you a sum equal to the ring. (*He gives the money to the man.*)

MAN (*bowing as he grabs it*): The king honors me.

FIRST POLICEMAN: This fellow's certainly honored. He was lowered from the execution stake and raised up on a royal elephant's back.

SECOND POLICEMAN: Chief, the reward tells me this ring was special to the king.

MAGISTRATE: I don't think the king valued the stone, but when he caught sight of the ring, he suddenly seemed to remember someone he loved, and he became deeply disturbed.

FIRST POLICEMAN: You served him well, chief!

SECOND POLICEMAN: I think you better served this king of fish.

(*Looking at the fisherman with jealousy.*)

MAN: My lords, half of this is yours for your good will.

FIRST POLICEMAN: It's only fair!

MAGISTRATE: Fisherman, now that you are my greatest and dearest friend, we should pledge our love over kadamba-blossom wine. Let's go to the wine shop!

(*They all exit together; the interlude ends. Then a nymph named Sānumatī enters by the skyway.*)

SĀNUMATĪ: Now that I've performed my assigned duties at the nymph's shrine, I'll slip away to spy on King Duṣyanta while the worshipers are bathing. My friendship with Menakā makes me feel a bond with Śakuntalā. Besides, Menakā asked me to help her daughter.

(*Looking around.*)

Why don't I see preparations for the spring festival in the king's palace? I can learn everything by using my mental powers, but I must respect my friend's request. So be it! I'll make myself invisible and spy on these two girls who are guarding the pleasure garden.

(*Sānumatī mimes descending and stands waiting. Then a maid servant named Parabhṛtikā, "Little Cuckoo," enters, looking at a mango bud. A second maid, named Madhukarikā, "Little Bee," is following her.*)

FIRST MAID:

> Your pale green stem
> tinged with pink
> is a true sign
> that spring has come—
> I see you,
> mango-blossom bud,
> and I pray
> for a season of joy.

(2)

SECOND MAID: What are you muttering to yourself?

FIRST MAID: A cuckoo goes mad when she sees a mango bud.

SECOND MAID (*joyfully rushing over*): Has the sweet month of spring come?

FIRST MAID: Now's the time to sing your songs of love.

SECOND MAID: Hold me while I pluck a mango bud and worship the god of love.

FIRST MAID: Only if you'll give me half the fruit of your worship.

SECOND MAID: That goes without saying . . . our bodies may be separate, but our lives are one . . .

(*Leaning on her friend, she stands and plucks a mango bud.*)

The mango flower is still closed, but this broken stem is fragrant.

(*She makes the dove gesture with her hands.*)

> Mango-blossom bud,
> I offer you to Love

as he lifts
his bow of passion.
Be the first
of his flower arrows
aimed at lonely girls
with lovers far away! (3)

(*She throws the mango bud.*)
CHAMBERLAIN (*angrily throwing aside the curtain and entering*): Not now, stupid girl! When the king has banned the festival of spring, how dare you pluck a mango bud!
BOTH MAIDS (*frightened*): Please forgive us, sir. We don't know what you mean.
CHAMBERLAIN: Did you not hear that even the spring trees and the nesting birds obey the king's order?

The mango flowers bloom without spreading pollen,
the red amaranth buds, but will not bloom,
cries of cuckoo cocks freeze though frost is past,
and out of fear, Love holds his arrow half-drawn. (4)

BOTH MAIDS: There is no doubt about the king's great power!
FIRST MAID: Sir, several days ago we were sent to wait on the queen by Mitrāvasu, the king's brother-in-law. We were assigned to guard the pleasure garden. Since we're newcomers, we've heard no news.
CHAMBERLAIN: Let it be! But don't do it again!
BOTH MAIDS: Sir, we're curious. May we ask why the spring festival was banned?
SĀNUMATĪ: Mortals are fond of festivals. The reason must be serious.
CHAMBERLAIN: It is public knowledge. Why should I not tell them? Has the scandal of Śakuntalā's rejection not reached your ears?
BOTH MAIDS: We only heard from the king's brother-in-law that the ring was found.
CHAMBERLAIN (*to himself*): There is little more to tell.
(*Aloud.*)
When he saw the ring, the king remembered that he had married Śakuntalā in secret and had rejected her in his delusion. Since then the king has been tortured by remorse.

Despising what he once enjoyed,
he shuns his ministers every day
and spends long sleepless nights
tossing at the edge of his bed—
when courtesy demands that
he converse with palace women,
he stumbles over their names,
and then retreats in shame. (5)

SĀNUMATĪ: This news delights me.
CHAMBERLAIN: The festival is banned because of the king's melancholy.
BOTH MAIDS: It's only right.
VOICE OFFSTAGE: This way, sir!
CHAMBERLAIN (*listening*): The king is coming. Go about your business!

BOTH MAIDS: As you say.

(*Both maids exit. Then the king enters, costumed to show his grief, accompanied by the buffoon and the doorkeeper.*)

CHAMBERLAIN (*observing the king*): Extraordinary beauty is appealing under all conditions. Even in his lovesick state, the king is wonderful to see.

> Rejecting his regal jewels,
> he wears one golden bangle
> above his left wrist;
> his lips are pale with sighs,
> his eyes wan from brooding at night—
> like a gemstone ground in polishing,
> the fiery beauty of his body
> makes his wasted form seem strong. (6)

SĀNUMATĪ (*seeing the king*): I see why Śakuntalā pines for him though he rejected and disgraced her.

KING (*walking around slowly, deep in thought*):

> This cursed heart slept
> when my love came to wake it,
> and now it stays awake
> to suffer the pain of remorse. (7)

SĀNUMATĪ: The girl shares his fate.

BUFFOON (*in a stage whisper*): He's having another attack of his Śakuntalā disease. I doubt if there's any cure for that.

CHAMBERLAIN (*approaching*): Victory to the king! I have inspected the grounds of the pleasure garden. Let the king visit his favorite spots and divert himself.

KING: Vetravatī, deliver a message to my noble minister Piśuna: "After being awake all night, we cannot sit on the seat of justice today. Set in writing what your judgment tells you the citizens require and send it to us!"

DOORKEEPER: Whatever you command!

(*She exits.*)

KING: Vātāyana, attend to the rest of your business!

CHAMBERLAIN: As the king commands!

(*He exits.*)

BUFFOON: You've cleared out the flies. Now you can rest in some pretty spot. The garden is pleasant now in this break between morning cold and noonday heat.

KING: Dear friend, the saying "Misfortunes rush through any crack" is absolutely right:

> Barely freed by the dark force
> that made me forget Kaṇva's daughter,
> my mind is threatened by an arrow
> of mango buds fixed on Love's bow. (8)

BUFFOON: Wait, I'll destroy the love god's arrow with my wooden stick.

(*Raising his staff, he tries to strike a mango bud.*)

KING (*smiling*): Let it be! I see the majesty of brahman bravery. Friend, where may I sit to divert my eyes with vines that remind me of my love?

BUFFOON: Didn't you tell your maid Caturikā, "I'll pass the time in the jasmine bower. Bring me the drawing board on which I painted a picture of Śakuntalā with my own hand!"

KING: Such a place may soothe my heart. Show me the way!

BUFFOON: Come this way!

(*Both walk around; the nymph Sānumatī follows.*)

The marble seat and flower offerings in this jasmine bower are certainly trying to make us feel welcome. Come in and sit down!

(*Both enter the bower and sit.*)

SĀNUMATĪ: I'll hide behind these creepers to see the picture he's drawn of my friend. Then I'll report how great her husband's passion is.

(*She does as she says and stands waiting.*)

KING: Friend, now I remember everything. I told you about my first meeting with Śakuntalā. You weren't with me when I rejected her, but why didn't you say anything about her before? Did you suffer a loss of memory too?

BUFFOON: I didn't forget. You did tell me all about it once, but then you said, "It's all a joke without any truth." My wit is like a lump of clay, so I took you at your word . . . or it could be that fate is powerful . . .

SĀNUMATĪ: It is!

KING: Friend, help me!

BUFFOON: What's this? It doesn't become you! Noblemen never take grief to heart. Even in storms, mountains don't tremble.

KING: Dear friend, I'm defenseless when I remember the pain of my love's bewilderment when I rejected her.

> When I cast her away, she followed her kinsmen,
> but Kaṇva's disciple harshly shouted, "Stay!"
> The tearful look my cruelty provoked
> burns me like an arrow tipped with poison.   (9)

SĀNUMATĪ: The way he rehearses his actions makes me delight in his pain.

BUFFOON: Sir, I guess that the lady was carried off by some celestial creature or other.

KING: Who else would dare to touch a woman who worshiped her husband? I was told that Menakā is her mother. My heart suspects that her mother's companions carried her off.

SĀNUMATĪ: His delusion puzzled me, but not his reawakening.

BUFFOON: If that's the case, you'll meet her again in good time.

KING: How?

BUFFOON: No mother or father can bear to see a daughter parted from her husband.

KING:

> Was it dream or illusion or mental confusion,
> or the last meager fruit of my former good deeds?
> It is gone now, and my heart's desires are
> like riverbanks crumbling of their own weight.   (10)

BUFFOON: Stop this! Isn't the ring evidence that an unexpected meeting is destined to take place?

453

KING (*looking at the ring*): I only pity it for falling from such a place.

Ring, your punishment is proof
that your fate is as flawed as mine—
you were placed in her lovely fingers,
glowing with crimson nails, and you fell. (11)

SĀNUMATĪ: The real pity would have been if it had fallen into some other hand.
BUFFOON: What prompted you to put the signet ring on her hand?
SĀNUMATĪ: I'm curious too.
KING: I did it when I left for the city. My love broke into tears and asked, "How long will it be before my noble husband sends news to me?"
BUFFOON: Then? What then?
KING: Then I placed the ring on her finger with this promise:

One by one, day after day,
count each syllable of my name!
At the end, a messenger will come
to bring you to my palace. (12)

But in my cruel delusion, I never kept my word.
SĀNUMATĪ: Fate broke their charming agreement!
BUFFOON: How did it get into the belly of the carp the fisherman was cutting up?
KING: While she was worshiping at the shrine of Indra's wife, it fell from her hand into the Gaṅgā.
BUFFOON: It's obvious now!
SĀNUMATĪ: And the king, doubtful of his marriage to Śakuntalā, a female ascetic, was afraid to commit an act of injustice. But why should such passionate love need a ring to be remembered?
KING: I must reproach the ring for what it's done.
BUFFOON (*to himself*): He's gone the way of all madmen . . .
KING:

Why did you leave her delicate finger
and sink into the deep river? (13a)

Of course . . .

A mindless ring can't recognize virtue,
but why did I reject my love? (13b)

BUFFOON (*to himself*): Why am I consumed by a craving for food?
KING: Oh ring! Have pity on a man whose heart is tormented because he abandoned his love without cause! Let him see her again!
(*Throwing the curtain aside, the maid Caturikā enters, with the drawing board in her hand.*)
CATURIKĀ: Here's the picture you painted of the lady.
(*She shows the drawing board.*)
BUFFOON: Dear friend, how well you've painted your feelings in this sweet scene! My eyes almost stumble over the hollows and hills.
SĀNUMATĪ: What skill the king has! I feel as if my friend were before me.

KING:

> The picture's imperfections are not hers,
> but this drawing does hint at her beauty. (14)

SĀNUMATĪ: Such words reveal that suffering has increased his modesty as much as his love.

BUFFOON: Sir, I see three ladies now and they're all lovely to look at. Which is your Śakuntalā?

SĀNUMATĪ: Only a dim-witted fool like this wouldn't know such beauty!

KING: You guess which one!

BUFFOON: I guess Śakuntalā is the one you've drawn with flowers falling from her loosened locks of hair, with drops of sweat on her face, with her arms hanging limp and tired as she stands at the side of a mango tree whose tender shoots are gleaming with the fresh water she poured. The other two are her friends.

KING: You are clever! Look at these signs of my passion!

> Smudges from my sweating fingers
> stain the edges of the picture
> and a tear fallen from my cheek
> has raised a wrinkle in the paint. (15)

Caturikā, the scenery is only half-drawn. Go and bring my paints!

CATURIKĀ: Noble Mādhavya, hold the drawing board until I come back!

KING: I'll hold it myself.

(*He takes it, the maid exits.*)

> I rejected my love when she came to me,
> and now I worship her in a painted image—
> having passed by a river full of water,
> I'm longing now for an empty mirage. (16)

BUFFOON (*to himself*): He's too far gone for a river now! He's looking for a mirage!

(*Aloud.*)

Sir, what else do you plan to draw here?

SĀNUMATĪ: He'll want to draw every place my friend loved.

KING:

> I'll draw the river Mālinī
> flowing through Himālaya's foothills
> where pairs of wild geese nest in the sand
> and deer recline on both riverbanks,
> where a doe is rubbing her left eye
> on the horn of a black buck antelope
> under a tree whose branches
> have bark dresses hanging to dry. (17)

BUFFOON (*to himself*): Next he'll fill the drawing board with mobs of ascetics wearing long grassy beards.

KING: Dear friend, I've forgotten to draw an ornament that Śakuntalā wore.

BUFFOON: What is it?

SĀNUMATĪ: It will suit her forest life and her tender beauty.

KING:

> I haven't drawn the mimosa flower on her ear,
> its filaments resting on her cheek,
> or the necklace of tender lotus stalks,
> lying on her breasts like autumn moonbeams.   (18)

BUFFOON: But why does the lady cover her face with her red lotus-bud fingertips and stand trembling in fear?
(*Looking closely.*)
The son-of-a-bee who steals nectar from flowers is attacking her face.
KING: Drive the impudent rogue away!
BUFFOON: You have the power to punish criminals. You drive him off!
KING: All right! Bee, favored guest of the flowering vines, why do you frustrate yourself by flying here?

> A female bee waits on a flower,
> thirsting for your love—
> she refuses to drink
> the sweet nectar without you.   (19)

SĀNUMATĪ: How gallantly he's driving him away!
BUFFOON: When you try to drive it away, this creature becomes vicious.
KING: Why don't you stop when I command you?

> Bee, if you touch the lips of my love
> that lure you like a young tree's virgin buds,
> lips I gently kissed in festivals of love,
> I'll hold you captive in a lotus flower cage.   (20)

BUFFOON: Why isn't he afraid of your harsh punishment?
(*Laughing, he speaks to himself.*)
He's gone crazy and I'll be the same if I go on talking like this.
(*Aloud.*)
But sir, it's just a picture!
KING: A picture? How can that be?
SĀNUMATĪ: When I couldn't tell whether it was painted, how could he realize he was looking at a picture?
KING: Dear friend, are you envious of me?

> My heart's affection made me feel
> the joy of seeing her—
> but you reminded me again
> that my love is only a picture.   (21)

(*He wipes away a tear.*)
SĀNUMATĪ: The effects of her absence make him quarrelsome.
KING: Dear friend, why do I suffer this endless pain?

> Sleepless nights prevent our meeting in dreams;
> her image in a picture is ruined by my tears.   (22)

SĀNUMATĪ: You have clearly atoned for the suffering your rejection caused Śakuntalā.

CATURIKĀ (*entering*): Victory my lord! I found the paint box and started back right away . . . but I met Queen Vasumatī with her maid Taralikā on the path and she grabbed the box from my hand, saying, "I'll bring it to the noble lord myself!"

BUFFOON: You were lucky to get away!

CATURIKĀ: The queen's shawl got caught on a tree. While Taralikā was freeing it, I made my escape.

KING: Dear friend, the queen's pride can quickly turn to anger. Save this picture!

BUFFOON: You should say, "Save yourself!"

(*Taking the picture, he stands up.*)

If you escape the woman's deadly poison, then send word to me in the Palace of the Clouds.

(*He exits hastily.*)

SĀNUMATĪ: Even though another woman has taken his heart and he feels indifferent to the queen, he treats her with respect.

DOORKEEPER (*entering with a letter in her hand*): Victory, king!

KING: Vetravatī, did you meet the queen on the way?

DOORKEEPER: I did, but when she saw the letter in my hand, she turned back.

KING: She knows that this is official and would not interrupt my work.

DOORKEEPER: King, the minister requests that you examine the contents of this letter. He said that the enormous job of reckoning the revenue in this one citizen's case had taken all his time.

KING: Show me the letter!

(*The girl hands it to him and he reads barely aloud.*)

What is this? "A wealthy merchant sea captain named Dhanamitra has been lost in a shipwreck and the laws say that since the brave man was childless, his accumulated wealth all goes to the king." It's terrible to be childless! A man of such wealth probably had several wives. We must find out if any one of his wives is pregnant!

DOORKEEPER: King, it's said that one of his wives, the daughter of a merchant of Ayodhyā, has performed the rite to ensure the birth of a son.

KING: The child in her womb surely deserves his paternal wealth. Go! Report this to my minister!

DOORKEEPER: As the king commands!

(*She starts to go.*)

KING: Come here a moment!

DOORKEEPER: I am here.

KING: Is it his offspring or not?

> When his subjects lose a kinsman,
> Duṣyanta will preserve the estates—
> unless there is some crime.
> Let this be proclaimed. (23)

DOORKEEPER: It shall be proclaimed loudly.

(*She exits; reenters.*)

The king's order will be as welcome as rain in the right season.

KING (*sighing long and deeply*): Families without offspring whose lines of succession are cut off lose their wealth to strangers when the last male heir dies. When I die, this will happen to the wealth of the Puru dynasty.

DOORKEEPER: Heaven forbid such a fate!

KING: I curse myself for despising the treasure I was offered.

SĀNUMATĪ: He surely has my friend in mind when he blames himself.

KING:

> I abandoned my lawful wife, the holy ground
> where I myself planted my family's glory,
> like earth sown with seed at the right time,
> ready to bear rich fruit in season.

(24)

SĀNUMATĪ: But your family's line will not be broken.

CATURIKĀ (*in stage whisper*): The king is upset by the story of the merchant. Go and bring noble Mādhavya from the Palace of the Clouds to console him!

DOORKEEPER: A good idea!

(*She exits.*)

KING: Duṣyanta's ancestors are imperiled.

> Our fathers drink the yearly libation
> mixed with my childless tears,
> knowing that there is no other son
> to offer the sacred funeral waters.

(25)

(*He falls into a faint.*)

CATURIKĀ (*looking at the bewildered king*): Calm yourself, my lord!

SĀNUMATĪ: Though a light shines, his separation from Śakuntalā keeps him in a state of dark depression. I could make him happy now, but I've heard Indra's consort consoling Śakuntalā with the news that the gods are hungry for their share of the ancestral oblations and will soon conspire to have her husband welcome his lawful wife. I'll have to wait for the auspicious time, but meanwhile I'll cheer my friend by reporting his condition.

(*She exits, flying into the air.*)

VOICE OFFSTAGE: Help! Brahman-murder!

KING (*regaining consciousness, listening*): Is it Mādhavya's cry for pain? Who's there?

DOORKEEPER: King, your friend is in danger. Help him!

KING: Who dares to threaten him?

DOORKEEPER: Some invisible spirit seized him and dragged him to the roof of the Palace of the Clouds.

KING (*getting up*): Not this! Even my house is haunted by spirits.

> When I don't even recognize
> the blunders I commit every day,
> how can I keep track
> of where my subjects stray?

(26)

VOICE OFFSTAGE: Dear friend! Help! Help!

KING (*breaking into a run*): Friend, don't be afraid! I'm coming!

VOICE OFFSTAGE (*repeating the call for help*): Why shouldn't I be afraid? Someone is trying to split my neck in three, like a stalk of sugar cane.

KING (*casting a glance*): Quickly, my bow!

BOW-BEARER (*entering with a bow in hand*): Here are your bow and quiver.

(*The king takes his bow and arrows.*)

VOICE OFFSTAGE:

> I'll kill you as a tiger kills a struggling prey!
> I'll drink fresh blood from your tender neck!
> Take refuge now in the bow Duṣyanta lifts
> to calm the fear of the oppressed! (27)

KING (*angrily*): How dare you abuse my name? Stop, carrion-eater! Or you will not live!
(*He strings his bow.*)
Vetravatī, lead the way to the stairs!
DOORKEEPER: This way, king.
(*All move forward in haste.*)
KING (*searching around*): There is no one here!
VOICE OFFSTAGE: Help! Help! I see you. Don't you see me? I'm like a mouse caught by a cat! My life is hopeless!
KING: Don't count on your powers of invisibility! My magical arrows will find you. I aim this arrow:

> It will strike its doomed target
> and spare the brahman it must save—
> a wild goose can extract the milk
> and leave the water untouched. (28)

(*He aims the arrow. Then Indra's charioteer Mātali enters, having released the buffoon.*)
MĀTALI: King!

> Indra sets demons as your targets;
> draw your bow against them!
> Send friends gracious glances
> rather than deadly arrows! (29)

KING (*withdrawing his arrow*): Mātali, welcome to great Indra's charioteer!
BUFFOON (*entering*): He tried to slaughter me like a sacrificial beast and this king is greeting him with honors!
MĀTALI (*smiling*): Your majesty, hear why Indra has sent me to you!
KING: I am all attention.
MĀTALI: There is an army of demons descended from one-hundred-headed Kālanemi, known to be invincible . . .
KING: I have already heard it from Nārada, the gods' messenger.
MĀTALI:

> He is invulnerable to your friend Indra,
> so you are appointed to lead the charge—
> the moon dispels the darkness of night
> since the sun cannot drive it out. (30)

Take your weapon, mount Indra's chariot, and prepare for victory!
KING: Indra favors me with this honor. But why did you attack Mādhavya?
MĀTALI: I'll tell you! From the signs of anguish Your Majesty showed, I knew that you were despondent. I attacked him to arouse your anger.

A fire blazes when fuel is added;
a cobra provoked raises its hood—
men can regain lost courage
if their emotions are roused. (31)

KING (*in a stage whisper*): Dear friend, I cannot disobey a command from the lord of heaven. Inform my minister Piśuna of this and tell him this for me:

Concentrate your mind on guarding my subjects!
My bow is strung to accomplish other work. (32)

BUFFOON: Whatever you command!
(*He exits.*)
MĀTALI: Mount the chariot, Your Majesty!
(*The king mimes mounting the chariot; all exit.*)

END OF ACT SIX

ACT SEVEN

(*The king enters with Mātali by the skyway, mounted on a chariot.*)

KING: Mātali, though I carried out his command, I feel unworthy of the honors Indra gave me.
MĀTALI (*smiling*): Your Majesty, neither of you seems satisfied.

You belittle the aid you gave Indra
in face of the honors he conferred,
and he, amazed by your heroic acts,
deems his hospitality too slight. (1)

KING: No, not so! When I was taking leave, he honored me beyond my heart's desire and shared his throne with me in the presence of the gods:

Indra gave me a garland of coral flowers
tinged with sandalpowder from his chest,
while he smiled at his son Jayanta,
who stood there barely hiding his envy. (2)

MĀTALI: Don't you deserve whatever you want from Indra?

Indra's heaven of pleasures has twice
been saved by rooting out thorny demons—
your smooth-jointed arrows have now done
what Viṣṇu once did with his lion claws. (3)

KING: Here too Indra's might deserves the praise.

When servants succeed in great tasks,
they act in hope of their master's praise—

460

would dawn scatter the darkness
if he were not the sun's own charioteer? (4)

MĀTALI: This attitude suits you well!
(*He moves a little distance.*)
Look over there, Your Majesty! See how your own glorious fame has reached
the vault of heaven!

Celestial artists are drawing your exploits
on leaves of the wish-granting creeper
with colors of the nymphs' cosmetic paints,
and bards are moved to sing of you in ballads. (5)

KING: Mātali, in my desire to do battle with the demons, I did not notice the
path we took to heaven as we climbed through the sky yesterday. Which course
of the winds are we traveling?
MĀTALI:

They call this path of the wind Parivaha—
freed from darkness by Viṣṇu's second stride,
it bears the Gaṅgā's three celestial streams
and turns stars in orbit, dividing their rays. (6)

KING: Mātali, this is why my soul, my senses, and my heart feel calm.
(*He looks at the chariot wheels.*)
We've descended to the level of the clouds.
MĀTALI: How do you know?
KING:

Crested cuckoos fly between the spokes,
lightning flashes glint off the horses' coats,
and a fine mist wets your chariot's wheels—
all signs that we go over rain-filled clouds. (7)

MĀTALI: In a moment you'll be back in your own domain, Your Majesty.
KING (*looking down*): Our speeding chariot makes the mortal world appear fantastic. Look!

Mountain peaks emerge as the earth descends,
branches spread up from a sea of leaves,
fine lines become great rivers to behold—
the world seems to hurtle toward me. (8)

MĀTALI: You observe well! (*He looks with great reverence.*)
The beauty of earth is sublime.
KING: Mātali, what mountain do I see stretching into the eastern and western
seas, rippled with streams of liquid gold, like a gateway of twilight clouds?
MĀTALI: Your Majesty, it is called the "Golden Peak," the mountain of the
demigods, a place where austerities are practiced to perfection.

Mārīca, the descendant of Brahmā,
a father of both demons and gods,

lives the life of an ascetic here
in the company of Aditi, his wife. (9)

KING: One must not ignore good fortune! I shall perform the rite of circumambulating the sage.
MĀTALI: An excellent idea!
(*The two mime descending.*)
KING (*smiling*):

The chariot wheels make no sound,
they raise no clouds of dust,
they touch the ground unhindered—
nothing marks the chariot's descent. (10)

MĀTALI: It is because of the extraordinary power that you and Indra both possess.
KING: Mātali, where is Mārīca's hermitage?
MĀTALI (*pointing with his hand*):

Where the sage stands staring at the sun,
is immobile as the trunk of a tree,
his body half-buried in an ant hill,
with a snake skin on his chest,
his throat pricked by a necklace
of withered thorny vines,
wearing a coil of long matted hair
filled with nests of śakunta birds. (11)

KING: I do homage to the sage for his severe austerity.
MĀTALI (*pulling hard on the chariot reins*): Great king, let us enter Mārīca's hermitage, where Aditi nurtures the celestial coral trees.
KING: This tranquil place surpasses heaven. I feel as if I'm bathing in a lake of nectar.
MĀTALI (*stopping the chariot*): Dismount, Your Majesty!
KING (*dismounting*): Mātali, what about you?
MĀTALI: I have stopped the chariot. I'll dismount too.
(*He does so.*)
This way, Your Majesty!
(*He walks around.*)
You can see the grounds of the ascetics' grove ahead.
KING: I am amazed!

In this forest of wish-fulfilling trees
ascetics live on only the air they breathe
and perform their ritual ablutions
in water colored by golden lotus pollen.
They sit in trance on jeweled marble slabs
and stay chaste among celestial nymphs,
practicing austerities in the place
that others seek to win by penances. (12)

MĀTALI: Great men always aspire to rare heights!

(*He walks around, calling aloud.*)

O venerable Śakalya, what is the sage Mārīca doing now? What do you say? In response to Aditi's question about the duties of a devoted wife, he is talking in a gathering of great sages' wives.

KING (*listening*): We must wait our turn.

MĀTALI (*looking at the king*): Your Majesty, rest at the foot of this aśoka tree. Meanwhile, I'll look for a chance to announce you to Indra's father.

KING: As you advise . . .

(*He stops.*)

MĀTALI: Your Majesty, I'll attend to this.

(*He exits.*)

KING (*indicating he feels an omen*):

> I have no hope for my desire.
> Why does my arm throb in vain?
> Once good fortune is lost,
> it becomes constant pain. (13)

VOICE OFFSTAGE: Don't be so wild! Why is his nature so stubborn?

KING (*listening*): Unruly conduct is out of place here. Whom are they reprimanding?

(*Looking toward the sound, surprised.*)

Who is this child, guarded by two female ascetics? A boy who acts more like a man.

> He has dragged this lion cub
> from its mother's half-full teat
> to play with it, and with his hand
> he violently tugs its mane. (14)

(*The boy enters as described, with two female ascetics.*)

BOY: Open your mouth, lion! I want to count your teeth!

FIRST ASCETIC: Nasty boy, why do you torture creatures we love like our children? You're getting too headstrong! The sages gave you the right name when they called you "Sarvadamana, Tamer-of-everything."

KING: Why is my heart drawn to this child, as if he were my own flesh? I don't have a son. That is why I feel tender toward him . . .

SECOND ASCETIC: The lioness will maul you if you don't let go of her cub!

BOY (*smiling*): Oh, I'm scared to death!

(*Pouting.*)

KING:

> This child appears to be
> the seed of hidden glory,
> like a spark of fire
> awaiting fuel to burn. (15)

FIRST ASCETIC: Child, let go of the lion cub and I'll give you another toy!

BOY: Where is it? Give it to me!

(*He reaches out his hand.*)

KING: Why does he bear the mark of a king who turns the wheel of empire?

> A hand with fine webs connecting the fingers
> opens as he reaches for the object greedily,
> like a single lotus with faint inner petals
> spread open in the red glow of early dawn. (16)

SECOND ASCETIC: Suvratā, you can't stop him with words! The sage Mārkaṇḍeya's son left a brightly painted clay bird in my hut. Get it for him!
FIRST ASCETIC: I will!
(*She exits.*)
BOY: But until it comes I'll play with this cub.
KING: I am attracted to this pampered boy . . .

> Lucky are fathers whose laps give refuge
> to the muddy limbs of adoring little sons
> when childish smiles show budding teeth
> and jumbled sounds make charming words. (17)

SECOND ASCETIC: Well, he ignores me.
(*She looks back.*)
Is one of the sage's sons here?
(*Looking at the king.*)
Sir, please come here! Make him loosen his grip and let go of the lion cub! He's tormenting it in his cruel child's play.
KING (*approaching the boy, smiling*): Stop! You're a great sage's son!

> When self-control is your duty by birth,
> why do you violate the sanctuary laws
> and ruin the animals' peaceful life,
> like a young black snake in a sandal tree? (18)

SECOND ASCETIC: Sir, he's not a sage's son.
KING: His actions and his looks confirm it. I based my false assumption on his presence in this place.
(*He does what she asked; responding to the boy's touch, he speaks to himself.*)

> Even my limbs feel delighted
> from the touch of a stranger's son—
> the father at whose side he grew
> must feel pure joy in his heart. (19)

SECOND ASCETIC (*examining them both*): It's amazing! Amazing!
KING: What is it, madam?
SECOND ASCETIC: This boy looks surprisingly like you. He doesn't even know you, and he's acting naturally.
KING (*fondling the child*): If he's not the son of an ascetic, what lineage does he belong to?
SECOND ASCETIC: The family of Puru.
KING (*to himself*): What? His ancestry is the same as mine . . . so this lady thinks he resembles me. The family vow of Puru's descendants is to spend their last days in the forest.

As world protectors they first choose
palaces filled with sensuous pleasures
but later, their homes are under trees
and one wife shares the ascetic vows.   (20)

(*Aloud.*)
But mortals cannot enter this realm on their own.

SECOND ASCETIC: You're right, sir. His mother is a nymph's child. She gave birth to him here in the hermitage of Marīca.

KING (*in a stage whisper*): Here is a second ground for hope!

(*Aloud.*)
What famed royal sage claims her as his wife?

SECOND ASCETIC: Who would even think of speaking the name of a man who rejected his lawful wife?

KING (*to himself*): Perhaps this story points to me. What if I ask the name of the boy's mother? No, it is wrong to ask about another man's wife.

FIRST ASCETIC (*returning with a clay bird in her hand*): Look, Sarvadamana, a śakunta! Look! Isn't it lovely?

BOY: Where's my mother?

BOTH ASCETICS: He's tricked by the similarity of names. He wants his mother.

SECOND ASCETIC: Child, she told you to look at the lovely clay śakunta bird.

KING (*to himself*): What? Is his mother's name Śakuntalā? But names can be the same. Even a name is a mirage . . . a false hope to herald despair.

BOY: I like this bird!

(*He picks up the toy.*)

FIRST ASCETIC (*looking frantically*): Oh, I don't see the amulet-box on his wrist!

KING: Don't be alarmed! It broke off while he was tussling with the lion cub.

(*He goes to pick it up.*)

BOTH ASCETICS: Don't touch it! Oh, he's already picked it up!

(*With their hands on their chests, they stare at each other in amazement.*)

KING: Why did you warn me against it?

FIRST ASCETIC: It contains the magical herb called Aparājitā, honored sir. Marīca gave it to him at his birth ceremony. He said that if it fell to the ground no one but his parents or himself could pick it up.

KING: And if someone else does pick it up?

FIRST ASCETIC: Then it turns into a snake and strikes.

KING: Have you two seen it so transformed?

BOTH ASCETICS: Many times.

KING (*to himself, joyfully*): Why not rejoice in the fulfillment of my heart's desire?

(*He embraces the child.*)

SECOND ASCETIC: Suvratā, come, let's tell Śakuntalā that her penances are over.

(*Both ascetics exit.*)

BOY: Let me go! I want my mother!

KING: Son, you will greet your mother with me.

BOY: My father is Duṣyanta, not you!

KING: This contradiction confirms the truth.

(*Śakuntalā enters, wearing the single braid of a woman in mourning.*)

ŚAKUNTALĀ: Even though Sarvadamana's amulet kept its natural form instead of changing into a snake, I can't hope that my destiny will be fulfilled. But maybe what my friend Sānumatī reports is right.

KING (*looking at Śakuntalā*): It is Śakuntalā!

> Wearing dusty gray garments,
> her face gaunt from penances,
> her bare braid hanging down—
> she bears with perfect virtue
> the trial of long separation
> my cruelty forced on her. (21)

ŚAKUNTALĀ (*seeing the king pale with suffering*): He doesn't resemble my noble husband. Whose touch defiles my son when the amulet is protecting him?

BOY (*going to his mother*): Mother, who is this stranger who calls me "son"?

KING: My dear, I see that you recognize me now. Even my cruelty to you is transformed by your grace.

ŚAKUNTALĀ (*to herself*): Heart, be consoled! My cruel fate has finally taken pity on me. It is my noble husband!

KING:

> Memory chanced to break my dark delusion
> and you stand before me in beauty,
> like the moon's wife Rohiṇī
> as she rejoins her lord after an eclipse. (22)

ŚAKUNTALĀ: Victory to my noble husband! Vic . . .

(*She stops when the word is half-spoken, her throat choked with tears.*)

KING: Beautiful Śakuntalā,

> Even choked by your tears,
> the word "victory" is my triumph
> on your bare pouting lips,
> pale-red flowers of your face. (23)

BOY: Mother, who is he?

ŚAKUNTALĀ: Child, ask the powers of fate!

KING (*falling at Śakuntalā's feet*):

> May the pain of my rejection
> vanish from your heart;
> delusion clouded my weak mind
> and darkness obscured good fortune—
> a blind man tears off a garland,
> fearing the bite of a snake. (24)

ŚAKUNTALĀ: Noble husband, rise! Some crime I had committed in a former life surely came to fruit and made my kind husband indifferent to me.

(*The king rises.*)

But how did my noble husband come to remember this woman who was doomed to pain?

KING: I shall tell you after I have removed the last barb of sorrow.

In my delusion I once ignored
a teardrop burning your lip—
let me dry the tear on your lash
to end the pain of remorse! (25)

(*He does so.*)

ŚAKUNTALĀ (*seeing the signet ring*): My noble husband, this is the ring!

KING: I regained my memory when the ring was recovered.

ŚAKUNTALĀ: When it was lost, I tried in vain to convince my noble husband who I was.

KING: Let the vine take back this flower as a sign of her union with spring.

ŚAKUNTALĀ: I don't trust it. Let my noble husband wear it!

(*Mātali enters.*)

MĀTALI: Good fortune! This meeting with your lawful wife and the sight of your son's face are reasons to rejoice.

KING: The sweet fruit of my desire! Mātali, didn't Indra know about all this?

MĀTALI: What is unknown to the gods? Come, Your Majesty! The sage Mārīca grants you an audience.

KING: Śakuntalā, hold your son's hand! We shall go to see Mārīca together.

ŚAKUNTALĀ: I feel shy about appearing before my elders in my husband's company.

KING: But it is customary at a joyous time like this. Come! Come!

(*They all walk around. Then Mārīca enters with Aditi; they sit.*)

MĀRĪCA (*looking at the king*):

Aditi, this is king Duṣyanta,
who leads Indra's armies in battle;
his bow lets your son's thunderbolt
lie ready with its tip unblunted. (26)

ADITI: He bears himself with dignity.

MĀTALI: Your Majesty, the parents of the gods look at you with affection reserved for a son. Approach them!

KING: Mātali, the sages so describe this pair:

Source of the sun's twelve potent forms,
parents of Indra, who rules the triple world,
birthplace of Viṣṇu's primordial form,
sired by Brahmā's sons, Marīci and Dakṣa. (27)

MĀTALI: Correct!

KING (*bowing*): Indra's servant, Duṣyanta, bows to you both.

MĀRĪCA: My son, live long and protect the earth!

ADITI: My son, be an invincible warrior!

ŚAKUNTALĀ: I worship at your feet with my son.

MĀRĪCA:

Child, with a husband like Indra
and a son like his son Jayanta,

you need no other blessing.
Be like Indra's wife Paulomī! (28)

ADITI: Child, may your husband honor you and may your child live long to give both families joy! Be seated!
(*All sit near Mārīca.*)
MĀRĪCA (*pointing to each one*):

By the turn of fortune,
virtuous Śakuntalā, her noble son,
and the king are reunited—
faith and wealth with order. (29)

KING: Sir, first came the success of my hopes, then the sight of you. Your kindness is unparalleled.

First flowers appear, then fruits,
first clouds rise, then rain falls,
but here the chain of events is reversed—
first came success, then your blessing. (30)

MĀTALI: This is the way the creator gods give blessings.
KING: Sir, I married your charge by secret marriage rites. When her relatives brought her to me after some time, my memory failed and I sinned against the sage Kaṇva, your kinsman. When I saw the ring, I remembered that I had married his daughter. This is all so strange!

Like one who doubts the existence
of an elephant who walks in front of him
but feels convinced by seeing footprints,
my mind has taken strange turns. (31)

MĀRĪCA: My son, you need not take the blame. Even your delusion has another cause. Listen!
KING: I am attentive.
MĀRĪCA: When Menakā took her bewildered daughter from the steps of the nymphs' shrine and brought her to my wife, I knew through meditation that you had rejected this girl as your lawful wife because of Durvāsas' curse, and that the curse would end when you saw the ring.
KING (*sighing*): So I am freed of blame.
ŚAKUNTALĀ (*to herself*): And I am happy to learn that I wasn't rejected by my husband without cause. But I don't remember being cursed. Maybe the empty heart of love's separation made me deaf to the curse . . . my friends did warn me to show the ring to my husband . . .
MĀRĪCA: My child, I have told you the truth. Don't be angry with your husband!

You were rejected when the curse
that clouded memory made him cruel,
but now darkness is lifted
and your power is restored—
a shadow has no shape

in a badly tarnished mirror,
but when the surface is clean
it can easily be seen.   (32)

KING: Sir, here is the glory of my family!
(*He takes the child by the hand.*)
MĀRĪCA: Know that he is destined to turn the wheel of your empire!

His chariot will smoothly cross
the ocean's rough waves
and as a mighty warrior
he will conquer the seven continents.
Here he is called Sarvadamana,
Tamer-of-everything;
later when his burden is the world,
men will call him Bharata, Sustainer.   (33)

KING: Since you performed his birth ceremonies, we can hope for all this.
ADITI: Sir, let Kaṇva be told that his daughter's hopes have been fulfilled.
Menakā, who loves her daughter, is here in attendance.
ŚAKUNTALĀ (*to herself*): The lady expresses my own desire.
MĀRĪCA: He knows everything already through the power of his austerity.
KING: This is why the sage was not angry at me.
MĀRĪCA: Still, I want to hear his response to this joyful reunion. Who is there?
DISCIPLE (*entering*): Sir, it is I.
MĀRĪCA: Gālava, fly through the sky and report the joyous reunion to Kaṇva in
my own words: "The curse is ended. Śakuntalā and her son are embraced by
Duṣyanta now that his memory is restored."
DISCIPLE: As you command, sir!
(*He exits.*)
MĀRĪCA: My son, mount your friend Indra's chariot with your wife and son and
return to your royal capital!
KING: As you command, sir!
MĀRĪCA: My son, what other joy can I give you?
KING: There is no greater joy, but if you will:

May the king serve nature's good!
May priests honor the goddess of speech!
And may Śiva's dazzling power
destroy my cycle of rebirths!   (34)

(*All exit.*)

END OF ACT SEVEN AND OF THE PLAY

PICTURE CREDITS

N ow there's a way to identify all
your fine books with flair and style.
As part of our continuing service to you,
Britannica Home Library Service, Inc. is
proud to be able to offer you the fine quality
item shown on the next page.

B ooklovers will love the heavy-duty
personalized embosser. Now you can
personalize all your fine books with
the mark of distinction, just the way all the
fine libraries of the world do.

T o order this item,
please type or print your name,
address and zip code on a plain sheet
of paper. (Note special instructions for
ordering the embosser). Please send a check
or money order only (your money will be
refunded in full if you are not delighted) for
the full amount of purchase, including
postage and handling, to:

Britannica Home Library Service, Inc.
Attn: Yearbook Department
Post Office Box 6137
Chicago, Illinois 60680

IN THE BRITANNICA TRADITION OF QUALITY...

PERSONAL EMBOSSER

A mark of distinction for your fine books. A book embosser just like the ones used in libraries. The 1½″ seal imprints "Library of _____" (with the name of your choice) and up to three centered initials. Please type or print clearly BOTH full name (up to 26 letters including spaces between names) and up to three initials.
Please allow six weeks for delivery.

Just $20.00

plus $2.00 shipping and handling

Britannica Home Library Service, Inc.

Authors

in Great Books of the Western World

Homer	Nicomachus
Aeschylus	Ptolemy
Sophocles	Marcus Aurelius
Herodotus	Galen
Euripides	Plotinus
Thucydides	Augustine
Hippocrates	Thomas Aquinas
Aristophanes	Dante
Plato	Chaucer
Aristotle	Machiavelli
Euclid	Copernicus
Archimedes	Rabelais
Apollonius	Montaigne
Lucretius	Gilbert
Virgil	Cervantes
Plutarch	Francis Bacon
Tacitus	Galileo
Epictetus	Shakespeare
	Kepler